Family Law for the Paralegal

CONCEPTS AND APPLICATIONS

Mary E. Wilson
Northern Essex Community College

PEARSON
Prentice
Hall

Upper Saddle River, New Jersey
Columbus, Ohio

Cataloging-in-Publication data is on file at the Library of Congress

Editor in Chief: Vernon Anthony
Acquisitions Editor: Gary Bauer
Development Editor: Linda Cupp
Editorial Assistant: Megan Heintz
Production Coordination: Elm Street Publishing Services
Project Manager: Christina M. Taylor
Senior Operations Supervisor: Pat Tonneman
Art Director: Diane Ernsberger
Cover Designer: Jason Moore
Cover art/image/photo[s]: SuperStock
Director of Marketing: David Gesell
Marketing Manager: Leigh Ann Sims
Marketing Assistant: Thomas Hayward

Photo credits: Chapter 1: Getty Images; Chapter 2: Roger Dixon © Dorling Kindersley; Chapters 3, 4, 5, 7, 10, 12, 14, 15: Richard A. Tauson; Chapter 6: © Joel Gordon 2004; Chapter 8: Estelle Tomson; Chapter 9: Photolibrary.com; Chapter 11: Steve Gorton © Dorling Kindersley

This book was set in Minion by Integra Software Services, Inc. and was printed and bound by Edwards Brothers. The cover was printed by Phoenix Color Corp./Hagerstown.

Pearson Prentice Hall™ is a trademark of Pearson Education, Inc.
Pearson® is a registered trademark of Pearson plc
Prentice Hall® is a registered trademark of Pearson Education, Inc.

Pearson Education Ltd., London
Pearson Education Singapore Pte. Ltd.
Pearson Education Canada, Inc.
Pearson Education—Japan

Pearson Education Australia Pty. Limited
Pearson Education North Asia Ltd., Hong Kong
Pearson Educación de Mexico, S.A. de C.V.
Pearson Education Malaysia Pte. Ltd.

10 9 8 7 6 5 4 3 2 1
ISBN-13: 978-0-13-159368-8
ISBN-10:   0-13-159368-4

Dedication

This book is dedicated to:

My mother, Florence Ruth Purcell Wilson,
who is, at 104, an abiding source of love and inspiration

My father, the late Honorable Robert Gardiner Wilson, Jr.,
who set the bar high

My partner in life and in this work, Richard A. Tauson,
who encourages me to accept uncertainty and embrace adventure

My professors, the Honorable John E. Fenton, Jr. and John G. Schuler,
who made a difference

and

My students, past, present, and future,
who keep me learning and who make it all worthwhile

Brief Contents

Contents

CHAPTER 3   Marriage   60

Preface

Given my professional background as an attorney, a professor, a department chair, and a dean, I appreciate the fact that the best textbooks address the demands of several audiences with related needs:

- **Students** who want an interesting, readable text that presents course content in a manner designed to build their knowledge base, strengthen their skills, and enhance their employment prospects
- **Instructors** who want to employ diverse teaching strategies but who often lack the time or resources to develop course materials that will promote conceptual, critical-thinking, problem-solving, interpersonal, and technical job skills
- **Prospective employers** who want well-trained graduates who can transition easily into the workplace setting
- **Accrediting bodies** that articulate program requirements designed to ensure the quality and integrity of paralegal programs and their graduates
- **Educational institutions and paralegal programs** that are compelled to address the sometimes competing needs of all of the above

This text is designed to effectively meet the needs of each of these groups. To that end, each chapter includes the following features:

Opening scenario. The scenario is designed to pique the reader's interest and place the chapter content in context. Each scenario anticipates one or more of the exercises at the end of the chapter.

In this chapter you will learn. The scenario is accompanied by a series of learning objectives that essentially introduce the basic content and organization of the chapter.

Paralegal Applications. Each chapter includes a number of real-world applications and exercises designed to reinforce substantive content, illustrate applications in the workplace, and promote class discussion.

Paralegal Practice and Drafting Tips. Tips provide nuggets of information that are useful to be aware of in a family law practice and that may enhance job performance and give a paralegal an "edge" in the workplace. Many of them expose students to ideas, concepts, beliefs, and points of view different from their own. They also provide a level of practical detail not usually available in texts or reached in class lectures.

Cases. The text contains a broad selection of excerpts from current and landmark cases, some with accompanying questions designed to promote case analysis, application of legal concepts, critical-thinking skills, and lively class discussion. Full texts of a majority of featured opinions are readily accessible on the companion website for the text.

Exhibits. Each chapter contains a series of exhibits that summarize and visually illustrate a variety of concepts, forms, terms, principles, etc., reinforcing the chapter content in another format. Many of the exhibits highlight multistate variations in approaches to specific family law topics and issues in order to sensitize the reader to the importance of researching and applying the law and procedure applicable to a particular case.

Key Terms.   A list of chapter-specific key terms appears at the end of each chapter. Context specific definitions are provided in chapter margins for emphasis as well as in a Glossary at the end of the text.

Review Questions.   A series of review questions are presented at the end of each chapter to focus content review.

Focus on the Job.   An extensive hypothetical is provided at the end of each chapter that picks up on the opening scenario and calls for students individually, in a pair, or in a small group to complete a work assignment, such as drafting a pleading, preparing a discovery request, or conducting an interview.

Focus on Ethics.   Attention to ethical concerns permeates the text. In particular, each chapter includes an end-of-chapter exercise that requires the student to analyze, discuss, and/or recommend a response to a situation related to the Focus on the Job hypothetical with reference to a specific code of paralegal conduct.

Focus on Case Law.   This focus requires the student to address a particular case in some fashion (e.g., IRAC, brief, respond to a series of questions, etc.).

Focus on State Law and Procedure.   This end-of-chapter activity requires the student to relate chapter content to his or her home state by locating a form, statute, case, etc., and completing a related assignment.

Focus on Technology.   This focus provides a list and brief description of websites related to the chapter content as well one or more online assignments.

Message to Students

Welcome to *Family Law for the Paralegal: Concepts and Applications.* As you embark on your study of family law, I want to share a few thoughts with you about the nature, purpose, and use of this text as a resource.

- One of the primary purposes of the book is to introduce you to basic principles of family law and procedure. Although the focus is on traditional terminology and generic topics, an effort is made to alert you to the considerable variation that exists in both law and procedure from jurisdiction to jurisdiction. Each chapter provides opportunities for you to consider issues through the lens of your own state and the facts of a particular case. You are likely to find that the initial response to almost every question is "It depends." It depends on the facts of the case, the client's needs and goals, where the action is brought, how many and which jurisdictions are involved, which areas of substantive law must be considered (probate, tax, contract, tort, etc.), the source and nature of law governing the matter, and a host of other potential factors. No textbook can address these issues with respect to a particular case. However this text can help you identify the questions that need to be raised, explored, and addressed, and point you in the direction of answers.
- A major purpose of this text is to foster development of your practical skills and self-confidence so that you are better prepared to enter the workforce well equipped to carry out your responsibilities as a valued member of a family law team or as a resource in a general practice that addresses domestic as well as other matters. This text focuses specifically on the role of the family law paralegal afforded the opportunity to be involved in all phases of legal representation including, for example, interviewing clients, maintaining client contact in emotionally charged contexts, preparing discovery requests, drafting documents, conducting research, engaging in creative problem solving, and preparing for and assisting at trial.
- Every effort has been made to ensure that the material contained in this text is current and accurate including URL addresses. However, sources of information and the law continually evolve. The success of a client's case may ultimately turn on a recently decided case or a newly passed statute. Practical applications and exercises throughout the text are designed to emphasize the need to continually update your knowledge base, particularly with respect to the governing law and procedure where you are employed.
- Family law is an exciting and rapidly evolving area of substantive law. It is no longer solely about who is to blame for the breakup of the marriage and who gets the kids and the house. You may well be surprised and challenged by the range of topics considered in this text. Although grounds for divorce, child custody, and property division are still central to family law, it now encompasses many additional emotionally charged and frequently controversial topics: Should same-sex partners be permitted to marry? Should a "father" who has been defrauded by the mother of a child as to his parental status be permitted to disestablish paternity? If couples freeze embryos for later use and then divorce, what should happen to the embryos? Should grandparents be granted visitation rights

over the objection of a biological parent? Should premarital agreements be treated like contracts between strangers rather than between partners who owe each other a special fiduciary duty? Should a mother be deprived of custody of her child if the child witnesses her being abused by an intimate partner? Should visitation provisions include opportunities for "virtual" visitation? Should parties to a divorce action be required to participate in mediation before litigating their case? Should gay individuals or couples be permitted to adopt minor children? There is much to learn about.

Companion Website Students can access a wealth of study aids at www.prenhall.com/wilson. The online Companion Website includes the following for each chapter: learning objectives, test-prep quizzes with immediate feedback, cases, statutes, various state forms, and additional resources including models of motions, charts, statistics, and supplemental terms.

Now take a deep breath and enjoy the adventure!

Message to Instructors

When I began teaching family law more than a decade ago, I initially assumed that if I wasn't lecturing, students weren't learning and I wasn't doing my job. After all, as an adjunct faculty member, I was being paid to bring my real-world knowledge and expertise into the classroom. However, accomplishing that purpose solely through lectures contradicts everything we know about adult learners. It sacrifices the opportunity for discussion and debate, for questions and explanations, and for practical exercises and skill building.

This book is designed to address this tension and the need for balance. It is a more self-contained text than most and requires less outside supplementation. Pedagogical assists woven into the body and at the end of each chapter provide built-in opportunities to, for example, explore an ethical challenge using a hypothetical situation commonly encountered in a family law practice, debate a cutting-edge issue such as disestablishment of paternity, role-play an interview with an abused spouse, or draft documents in class such as a complaint for divorce, parenting plan, or property division proposal based on a comprehensive fact pattern. The text is not designed to teach a family law course for you. Rather, it is designed to provide built-in tools that enable you to actively engage students in the teaching and learning experience. I sincerely hope you enjoy using them as much as I do and will welcome your comments and suggestions regarding any aspect of the text or ancillary materials at rooesq@juno.com.

Resources for Instructors   The Instructor's Manual, Microsoft PowerPoint slides, and additional instructor resources are available for download from our Instructor's Resource Center. To access supplementary materials online, instructors need to request an instructor access code. Go to http://www.pearsonhighered.com/educator, click the "download instructor resources" link, and then click "Register Today" for an instructor access code. Within 48 hours of registering you will receive a confirmation e-mail with an instructor access code. Once you have received your code, go to the site and log on for full instructions on downloading the materials that you wish to use.

Instructor's Manual with Test Item File   The Instructor's Manual contains chapter objectives, lecture outlines and several suggested class activities, answers to discussion questions and case problems, and comments about the exercises.

Prentice Hall Testgenerator

Powerpoint Lecture Presentation Package

Acknowledgments

Primary thanks go to my partner, Richard Tauson. Ric has been my number-one supporter and most constructive critic. His long hours of research, attention to detail, manuscript preparation, and review were invaluable. His patience, and that of friends and family, make many things possible.

Much appreciation is due the Commonwealth of Massachusetts Trial Court Law Library—Lawrence Division (Head Law Librarian Brian J. Archambault, Assistant Law Librarians Kathleen J. MacKinnon, Laurie Paszko, and Rachel A. Diaz); the Massachusetts Trial Court Library—Salem Division (Head Law Librarian Richard Adamo); and the Northern Essex Community College Library (most especially Librarians Gail Stuart and Louise Bevilacqua). I also want to thank my paralegal program colleagues for providing input and encouragement, and my family law students at Northern Essex for their enthusiastic pilot testing of several of the Paralegal Applications, research assignments, ethics exercises, and drafting projects.

Finally, I want to thank personnel at Prentice Hall for their guidance, assistance, and support, especially Gary Bauer, Linda Cupp, Christina Taylor, and Leigh Ann Sims. Thanks also are due the following reviewers for their helpful suggestions:

Richard Q. Barrett, *Simpson College*
Heidi Getchell-Bastien, *Northern Essex Community College*
Erma Hart, *Wharton County Junior College*
Annette R. Heim, *University of North Carolina-Charlotte*
Jennifer Jenkins, *South College*
Tracy Kaiser, *Manor College*
Heidi K. Koeneman, *Ivy Tech Community College, Ft. Wayne*
Genia Lee, *McNeese State University*
Elaine S. Lerner, *Kaplan University*
Beth R. Pless, *Northeast Wisconsin Technical College*
Annalinda Ragazzo, *Bryant and Stratton College*
Joan Stevens, *Loyola University of Chicago*
Laura Tolsma, *Lansing Community College*
Buzz Wheeler, *Highline Community College*
and, most especially,
Julia O. Tryk, *Cuyahoga Community College*

About the Author

Mary E. Wilson is a graduate of Suffolk University Law School in Boston, Massachusetts. In addition to her law degree, she earned a Masters in Education from Boston University and a Bachelor's Degree from Middlebury College in English and Psychology. She presently is a member of the American Bar Association Family Law Section and is admitted to the practice of law in Massachusetts and New Hampshire. She is an adjunct faculty member at Northern Essex Community College in Haverville and Lawrence, MA where she teaches courses in the paralegal and criminal justice programs, having retired as a full professor in 1997. In her more than twenty years of teaching at both public and private institutions, she has designed and taught a variety of behavioral science and education courses. She has also directed a statewide training program for foster parents and social workers through the Massachusetts Community College system and has authored training manuals on child discipline and working with abused and neglected children. A former department chair, she has also served as a director and dean at Northern Essex.

List of Exhibits

chapter **one**
INTRODUCTION

Florence Purcell did well in her paralegal coursework in college, and graduated with honors. This morning she starts work at a law firm that specializes in family law. While driving to the office, she recalls how each chapter of her family law textbook began with a factual scenario related to the content of the chapter and ended with challenging exercises based on that scenario. Now those challenges will involve real people and their well-being, and she will be called upon to use her skills to deal with them. As her feelings of anxiety and excitement build, she recalls her father once telling her that the Chinese expression for "crisis" is made up of two characters. One means danger and the other, opportunity. That's just how she feels today. She has the opportunity to become one of the "experienced and trusted" paralegals about whom she has read, provided she remains mindful of her responsibilities and the strict limitations imposed by professional ethics.

IN THIS CHAPTER YOU WILL LEARN

- How family law has changed over the past fifty years
- What the scope is of a contemporary family law practice
- How technology has impacted the practice of family law
- What a paralegal's role is in a family law practice
- What the objectives are of an initial client interview
- Why fee agreements and time sheets are important
- Which legal research resources are used most often by family law paralegals
- What the various kinds of jurisdiction are
- What kinds of jurisdictional issues commonly arise in family law cases
- What the ethical principles are that guide the professional conduct of paralegals
- What kinds of ethical issues arise in the family law context

INTRODUCTION

When the author's father commenced his thirty-year tenure on a probate and family court bench in the 1940s and when her brother began practicing in the 1960s, the law governing family law matters had been firmly in place for decades. By the 1980s, when the author and her nephew attended law school and were admitted to the Bar, family law had undergone a major transformation. Some of the dimensions of that transformation include the following:

No-fault divorce

divorce based on the irremediable breakdown of the marital relationship rather than on the fault of one or both of the parties

- *No-fault divorce*: In the first half of the twentieth century, divorce occurred far less often and was far more difficult to obtain than it has now become. It required proof of fault aired in public litigation followed by the social stigma of divorce and perpetuated by the ball and chain of alimony paid to the "innocent" spouse by the "blameworthy" spouse (usually presumed to be the husband). In sharp contrast, by the year 2000, approximately half of all marriages across the country were ending in divorces largely obtained on no-fault grounds available in every state and with alimony awards generally limited, temporary, and non-punitive in nature.
- **Division of marital property:** Except in the small number of community property states, prior to the 1970s the only vehicle for providing for an economically disadvantaged spouse was alimony. Beginning in the early 1970s, the majority of states began adopting the present system of dividing marital property on the basis of equitable factors that take into consideration the contributions of each party to the marriage, both economic and noneconomic.
- **Dispute resolution:** Forty years ago, judges were essentially the sole arbiters of disputes between adversarial parties represented by dueling attorneys. Today the courts encourage parties to resolve their differences through mediation and negotiation, resulting in mutual agreements and uncontested final hearings in which many parties proceed **pro se** with the assistance of court personnel. Before and during marriage, on their own or with assistance, couples increasingly privately define and agree upon their rights and obligations with respect to each other and memorialize their agreements in a variety of documents.

Pro se

denotes the condition under which a person represents himself or herself in a legal proceeding without the assistance of an attorney

- **Parental autonomy:** Prior to the 1990s, the right of biological parents to raise their children and to do so as they saw fit enjoyed staunch constitutional protection. Over the past decade, that protection has begun to erode as the courts have chosen, in some circumstances, to tip the balance in favor of the best interests of children and recognize "rights" of third parties. Individuals such as grandparents, "psychological" parents, co-parents, and others are increasingly seeking and being granted an opportunity to play a significant parenting role in children's lives even if against the wishes of the "actual" parents.
- **Public welfare system:** Prior to the 1980s, there was significant growth in the number of children born to unwed mothers, placing increasing pressure on an already overburdened public welfare system. Largely in response to federal mandates, the states have taken steps to address the problem. Although the system is by no means perfect, each state has implemented programs to determine paternity, establish child support awards based on child support guidelines, and enforce them aggressively through a host of far-reaching measures.
- **Federal regulation:** Up until the 1970s, creation and enforcement of substantive family law and policy were primarily left to the states. However, since that time, the federal government has assumed a leadership role in creating national standards, rules, and regulations impacting family law in areas such as taxes, jurisdiction, paternity, child support

enforcement, bankruptcy, adoption, and family violence. In addition to being partially shaped by federal law, family law is also increasingly influenced by model acts promulgated by the National Conference of Commissioners on Uniform State Laws for consideration by the states. These Acts promote uniform legislation and policy in many areas, such as premarital agreements, parentage, assisted conception, marital property, custody, and child support. Among the most significant of these Acts are the Uniform Child Custody Jurisdiction and Enforcement Act (UCCJEA) and the Uniform Interstate Family Support Act (UIFSA), which has now been adopted in all fifty states.

- **Equality of the sexes:**   Over the past forty years, dramatic changes have taken place with respect to recognition and treatment of the legal rights and obligations of men and women in the family law context. Even if not greeted with equal enthusiasm by all or fully realized in actual practice, the trend in domestic relations law is away from rigid, stereotypic views of males and females and toward equality and gender neutrality. This is particularly evident with respect to child custody arrangements and spousal support awards.

- **Access to marital rights:**   The view of marriage that has prevailed in the United States for five centuries defines marriage as the legal union of one man and one woman, and the right to marry has enjoyed sustained constitutional protection. Although it is subject to limited regulation by the states, it cannot be unreasonably restricted, for example, on the basis of race or economics. As the millennium approached, however, so too did the national social, religious, political, and legal debate about the rights of homosexuals generally, and same-sex partners in particular, to equal protection and freedom from discrimination based on sexual orientation. At present, despite the fears of many that the institution of marriage is threatened, several states, municipalities, and private employers are granting status to such relationships in a variety of forms ranging from marriage to civil unions to domestic partnerships.

- **Reproductive technology:**   Four decades ago, babies were produced as a result of a man and a woman engaging in sexual relations. The controversial issues surrounding reproduction focused on whether or not the pregnancy was planned or the parents were married to each other. In the last three decades, the reproductive landscape has altered dramatically, outpacing the capacity of courts and legislatures to respond. Advances in reproductive technology initially led to artificial insemination and surrogate parenting arrangements. Now the horizon appears limitless. Among other options, we have *in vitro* fertilization, cryopreserved embryos subject to disposition upon divorce, postmortem reproduction, cloning, and cytoplasmic egg donation in which genetic material is transferred from one woman's eggs to another's, creating two genetic mothers.

THE NATURE AND SCOPE OF A CONTEMPORARY FAMILY LAW PRACTICE

Family law is the body of law that deals with marriage, divorce, custody, adoption, support, paternity, and other domestic relations issues. It addresses the rights and obligations of individuals in the formation, continuation, and dissolution of marriages and other "family" relationships. A "traditional" pre-1970 family law practice focused primarily on grounds for divorce and alimony. A family law practice today is much more complex. Given that approximately half of all first marriages end in divorce, exposing the parties' assets to risk of loss, many

Family law
the body of law that deals with marriage, divorce, custody, adoption, support, paternity, and other domestic relations issues including matters related to nonmarital family units

couples are electing to execute premarital agreements or, in the alternative, to postpone or forego marriage entirely and negotiate cohabitation or "living-together" agreements. Courts now pay minimal attention to marital infidelity unless the "misconduct" has economic consequences for the marital unit. They also no longer uniformly cast the husband in the role of breadwinner and the wife in the roles of homemaker and primary caretaker of the children. Today, both partners are viewed as contributors to the marriage. Alimony is gender neutral by law, if not in actual practice, and marital assets are divided equally or assigned on the basis of principles of fairness depending on the jurisdiction. In a majority of states, both parents are at least initially perceived as having equal rights to custody of the children of the marriage. Adoptive parents are no longer the sole option for third-party parental status, and unwed dads are increasingly described as "thwarted" fathers and less as "deadbeat" dads.

It is not solely the substantive and procedural aspects of family law that have changed. Technology has dramatically altered the practice of law and the ways in which law firms create, receive, obtain, store, and retrieve information. Wireless laptops, cell phones, personal digital assistants (PDAs), voice mail, and fax machines were just a beginning. The "paperless" office is looming on the horizon. To compete in a digital age and properly serve clients, members of the family law team must be aware of the potential of technology and its advantages and disadvantages. A full discussion of this topic is beyond the scope of this text, but it is appropriate to at least mention some of the implications of technological advances for a family law practice.

- Some jurisdictions now manage dockets electronically and permit electronic filing. This will likely be the standard in the not-too-distant future.
- Under federal and state law, subject to evolving procedural rules, data retained in electronic form by a client is discoverable, just as information contained in a client's or opponent's file cabinet is if not protected by privilege or other consideration.
- Parties have an obligation to preserve evidence and may be sanctioned by the court for willfully destroying relevant electronic files and documents, such as financial records and e-mails.
- **Ex parte** motions may be needed to preserve evidence when there is a strong likelihood that relevant electronic documents may be altered or destroyed prior to production.
- Servers and freestanding storage media (tapes, disks, and memory "sticks," etc.) are gradually replacing cumbersome file cabinets since digitally stored data is far more conveniently organized, accessible, compact, and transportable. Faxes are replacing the U.S. mail, and e-mail is taking the place of the telephone and written letter. This can present problems when, for example, a client exercises the right to request his or her "file." Technically, the "file" is the property of the client, but in the age of digital technology, what constitutes the "file" and where is it located? To answer this question, the paralegal needs to be aware of the firm's records maintenance, retention, and destruction policies as well as any applicable federal or state rules.[1]
- Computer "forensics" experts are becoming as commonplace as traditional private investigators as they "cyber-sleuth" to gather information to support a client's case.
- Software products designed to support law practices now allow them to manage caseloads, client lists, documents, and billing far more efficiently.
- At trial, attorneys are increasingly using PowerPoint presentations (often created by paralegals) to highlight elements of the client's case—for example, to illustrate the dissipation of marital assets over time.

Ex parte
without advance notice to or argument from the opposing party

• The family law team can now perform most research online without necessarily either maintaining expansive in-house libraries or visiting law libraries.

A family law practice presents challenges and opportunities for paralegals. Progressing through this text, the reader will see that family law not only encompasses divorce law and related issues but also touches on many other areas of substantive law, such as tax, corporate, bankruptcy, criminal, evidence, tort, property, contract, intellectual property, juvenile delinquency, child care and protection, probate, immigration, and conflict law. It tests interviewing, research, organizational, computer, and problem-solving skills. It poses challenging, new ethical dilemmas. Last, but not least, it stretches to the maximum the emotional stamina of practitioners.

THE ROLE OF A PARALEGAL IN A FAMILY LAW PRACTICE

The National Association of Legal Assistants' Code of Ethics and Professional Responsibility of Legal Assistants (amended in 1995) defines a paralegal as follows:

Legal assistants, also known as paralegals, are a distinguishable group of persons who assist attorneys in the delivery of legal services. Through formal education, training, and experience, legal assistants have knowledge and expertise regarding the legal system and substantive and procedural law which qualify them to do work of a legal nature under the supervision of an attorney.[2]

The role of a paralegal in a family law practice is shaped by four primary forces:

• **The size of the practice:**   In a small practice, the paralegal may be called upon to function as a legal assistant, a secretary, and a receptionist. In a larger practice, the paralegal is more likely to be utilized as a *true* legal support person.
• **The style and expectations of the supervising attorney:**   Some attorneys have high expectations of paralegals and delegate a wide range of responsibilities. Others provide close supervision and delegate only the most fundamental tasks.
• **The scope of the practice:**   Although the major focus of most family law practices continues to be on divorce, as a member of a family law team, a paralegal may have an opportunity to address a broad range of matters including, for example, enforceability of cohabitation agreements, rights of unwed fathers, grandparent visitation, sealed adoption records, parental "kidnapping," concealed marital assets, termination of parental rights, and issues raised by same-sex relationships. Some family law practitioners specialize in particular aspects of family law such as alternative dispute resolution, appellate law, child support collection and enforcement, international adoption, or matters involving the care and protection of children.
• **The skill of the paralegal:**   Entry-level paralegals are likely to focus initially on completing standard forms, drafting routine correspondence, preparing basic discovery requests, scheduling meetings, and preparing invoices. More experienced paralegals may organize trial notebooks, search for hidden assets, prepare pretrial memoranda, and draft appellate briefs.

The job description of a paralegal in a family law practice is, in many respects, like a generic paralegal job description. The sample description provided

Paralegal Practice Tip
Job descriptions can be deceiving and no single job description applies in all settings. When interviewing for a position, a candidate should try to get a sense of how paralegals actually are treated and utilized in the practice. Do they function as legal assistants or legal secretaries? Knowing in advance can help promote realistic expectations and enhance later job satisfaction.

in Exhibit 1.1 presumes a highly skilled paralegal and a family law attorney willing to delegate responsibilities and provide appropriate supervision. Paralegal Application 1.1 provides a series of practical suggestions designed to supplement the formal job description and improve the paralegal's efficiency, productivity, and job satisfaction.

EXHIBIT 1.1 Paralegal Job Description

The following functions are performed by paralegals under the direction and supervision of a licensed attorney. The terms "draft" or "prepare" refer to a preliminary writing to be approved and signed by the attorney, if required.

- develop office management systems: record keeping, filing, billing, calendaring of meetings and court dates, etc.
- screen potential clients for conflicts of interest
- conduct or participate in initial and follow-up interviews with the client and record notes in a memorandum for the supervising attorney and the file
- prepare letters of engagement (or nonengagement) and fee agreements as directed
- maintain communication with the client throughout the period of representation
- gather preliminary information and documents essential to the case
- prepare release and authorization forms necessary to obtain copies of documents such as employment records, income tax returns, financial records, medical records, police reports, and social service agency records and reports
- research legal issues and assist in drafting briefs and memoranda
- draft initial complaints/petitions and responsive pleadings such as answers and counterclaims, along with accompanying documents such as affidavits for review, approval, signature(s), filing, and service
- draft motions for temporary orders and other forms of relief, along with supporting affidavits and proposed orders, if required
- assist the client in gathering data on income, expenses, assets, and liabilities and in preparing financial statements
- draft and edit successive versions of stipulations/agreements between the parties
- file pleadings and other documents with appropriate transmittal letters and copies as directed and arrange for service, if necessary
- check calendars and schedule hearings as required and then mark all appropriate calendars
- schedule meetings as directed with mediators, clients, opposing counsel, witnesses, experts, etc.
- prepare and draft discovery requests and draft responses to discovery requests received from the opposition
- review and analyze discovery responses received from opposing parties
- monitor deadlines to confirm that all are met by the paralegal, supervising attorney, and the opposition
- review and analyze property inventories and documentation of values and proof of ownership
- facilitate activity and payment of accountants, appraisers, **guardians ad litem,** experts, private investigators, and other agents as needed
- assist with preparation of trial materials such as pretrial memoranda, exhibits, PowerPoint presentations, trial notebooks, etc.

Guardian *ad litem*
a person, usually a lawyer, appointed by the court to conduct an investigation and/or represent a party who is a minor or otherwise unable to represent themselves in a legal proceeding; the guardian's role may be limited to investigation of a particular matter such as custody

- assist with preparation and orientation of witnesses (including clients) as directed
- draft any necessary post-trial materials such as *Qualified Domestic Relations Orders (QDROs),* deeds, and other documents transferring assets as ordered
- draft post-trial pleadings, motions, etc., such as notices of appeal, motions to enforce judgment, requests for modification, etc., as warranted
- draft letters concluding representation, including an opinion as to the tax-deductible portion of fees paid (i.e., the amount attributable to the provision of tax advice and analysis)

Qualified Domestic Relations Order (QDRO)
a court order directing the administrator of a pension plan to pay a specified portion of a current or former employee's pension to an alternate payee to satisfy a support or other marital obligation

PARALEGAL APPLICATION 1.1

TIPS FOR EFFECTIVE JOB PERFORMANCE AND SATISFACTION

There are many tasks effective family law paralegals perform that do not appear on formal job descriptions but that have the potential to significantly improve job performance and satisfaction. Several of these appear below.

- Maintain checklists regarding the tasks commonly performed to guide and double-check your work. Several such lists are provided throughout this text. For example, what are the elements of a separation or marital agreement? What materials need to be filed with a complaint/petition for divorce? What steps should be followed when serving or responding to various types of discovery requests? What kinds of property are subject to division upon divorce? Which statutes and court rules apply to the matters most commonly encountered on a daily basis in a family law practice?

- Maintain lists of key governing case law on a variety of issues, particularly cases that establish standards for the court as it makes decisions. For example, what is the standard in the jurisdiction for assessing a custodial parent's request to relocate to another state or country with his or her child? If not set by statute, under what circumstances will a court "impute" income to a party who is understating income on a financial statement? Such lists are very useful when drafting pretrial memoranda or appellate briefs or when considering the kinds of information to include in motions and supporting affidavits.

- Develop your own "tickler" (reminder) file with respect to various dates (hearings, etc.) and deadlines (discovery, etc.).

- Keep models/templates of various kinds of motions, pleadings, discovery requests, and types of correspondence (transmittal letters, confirmation of hearings and appointments, letters of engagement, etc.). Many forms are now available on disks accompanying practice manuals and online through court-sponsored sites and the like. These resources can save you significant time and avoid reinvention of the wheel, BUT remember to verify which forms and formats are mandatory and/or currently in use and to tailor each document to the specific facts of your client's case.

- Proofread and never solely rely on spell- and grammar-check. Accuracy is essential. Errors reflect poorly on the paralegal and the attorney and can have costly consequences.

continued

- When given an assignment, make a note of the date you receive it and the date by which it is to be completed. Listen and be sure you understand the instructions. Repeat them if necessary. If warranted, ask for feedback as you move forward with the task. It is a strength rather than a weakness to recognize your limitations and when you need guidance and supervision.

- When overwhelmed with a multiplicity of tasks to be performed, prioritize them with your supervisor.

- Be respectful of other members of the family law team and other professional colleagues, both in and out of the office.

- Learn the names of court personnel and others you communicate with in your professional capacity and address them by name.

- Be alert to the unique practices and procedures of various courts and agencies the firm deals with on a regular basis and to any idiosyncrasies of contact personnel in those settings.

- Maintain high standards of professional ethics. If something doesn't feel right, check it out—it probably isn't!

- Keep your skills current and participate in continuing legal education programs (preferably with the encouragement and financial support of the firm).

- Be aware of your own personal biases and remember, everyone is entitled to representation. Personal, moral, or religious beliefs should not compromise competent advocacy. If you perceive a personal conflict, bring it to the attention of your supervisor.

- Be prepared for the often physically and emotionally draining nature of the job. Family law is perhaps the most stressful area of legal practice. Much too often, hearts are broken, dreams are shattered, children are forced to choose between two loving parents and are used as pawns by angry combatants, finances are exhausted, and no one is a "winner." To maintain a healthy perspective in the midst of such emotional chaos, be sure to "have a life" apart from the job!

TOPICS APPLICABLE TO LAW PRACTICES IN GENERAL

Before beginning the adventure into family law, this segment of the chapter provides basic introductory material on five fundamental topics common to virtually all areas of practice. For some it will provide a review, for others, an introduction to:

> Client intake
> Fee agreements and billing
> Legal research
> Jurisdiction
> Ethics

Client Intake

A paralegal is often a prospective client's first contact with a family law practice. This contact typically occurs by telephone when the client calls to schedule a meeting with the attorney. The initial interview (sometimes called an initial consultation or intake interview) is occasionally conducted over the telephone, but most often involves a face-to-face meeting in which the participants essentially screen each other. It is an important meeting, because it sets the tone for a future

PARALEGAL APPLICATION **1.2**

INITIAL CLIENT INTAKE INTERVIEW CHECKLIST

The primary objectives of an initial client intake interview are to:

☐ identify the nature of the client's need for services

☐ establish whether or not any conflict of interest exists that would prohibit or restrict representation

☐ discuss the client's goals and expectations for the representation and indicate what the firm can and cannot do with respect to those goals

☐ determine whether or not the attorney is able *and* willing to represent the client and whether or not the client wants to retain the attorney

☐ discuss the scope of representation and potential fees, costs, and payment terms

☐ introduce the primary members of the family law team and describe their respective roles, emphasizing the paralegal's greater accessibility and the cost efficiency of having the paralegal perform certain tasks and maintain basic communication with the client

☐ describe the nature and scope of attorney-client confidentiality

☐ identify any urgent deadlines or emergency situations needing immediate attention

☐ confirm and/or gather all information called for in an initial Client Intake Form (A sample Client Intake Form is contained in the resource material for Chapter 1 on the companion website for this text at http://www.prenhall.com/wilson.)

☐ agree on a course of action and plan for follow-up, including execution of a fee agreement, completion of a comprehensive client questionnaire tailored to the subject matter of the representation, and identification of materials to be gathered

working relationship. Occasionally the meeting will be taped with the consent of the client, but many attorneys find that taping inhibits the openness and free flow of the interview. Paralegal Application 1.2 provides a checklist identifying the primary objectives of an initial meeting with a prospective client.

Given the purposes of an initial intake interview, it is advisable that an attorney conduct it, at least in part. The kinds of decisions needing to be made, such as whether or not to accept the case, setting the fee, and determining an appropriate course of action, are all decisions that the attorney must make. It is difficult, if not impossible, for a paralegal to accomplish the same purposes without engaging in the ***unauthorized practice of law.*** A common compromise approach is to divide the meeting into two parts: The attorney conducts the first part and makes the legal decisions while the paralegal takes notes, observes the client and records any follow-up activity needed and/or requested by either the client or the attorney. The paralegal should observe the client's demeanor as well as their language, being alert to potential "red flags." For example, are there any signs of deception? Does it appear the client intends to lie in court regarding assets or conduct? Does the client give any indication of being a victim or perpetrator of abuse? Is the client uncertain about the course of action he or she wants to pursue, e.g. divorce or reconciliation? If the client and attorney agree on the terms, purposes, and scope of the representation, the paralegal may then be asked to conduct the second portion of the meeting, which is essentially an information-gathering session.

Interviewing, even if only to collect data, is a skill that usually develops with practice and experience. The paralegal may want to consult some of the many

Unauthorized practice of law (UPL)
engaging in the practice of law without a license

Paralegal Practice Tip
Some attorneys use a comprehensive client questionnaire to guide the initial interview, but such forms may be overwhelming for the client, detract from the spontaneity of the meeting, and force attention on "nitty-gritty" items usually best left to follow-up by the paralegal and the client. An example of a generic comprehensive client questionnaire suitable for use in a divorce case is available on the companion website in the material related to Chapter 6.

resources available on basic interviewing techniques and structuring interviews in the legal context. Research can be helpful, but good interviewing flows primarily from strong interpersonal skills that allow the paralegal to exercise:

- an unconditional positive regard (a nonjudgmental respect and acceptance) for the client
- an ability to focus on, listen to, and hear the client
- a capacity to empathize with the client while maintaining an appropriate professional demeanor

(See Paralegal Application 1.3.)

PARALEGAL APPLICATION **1.3**

BASIC INTERVIEWING TIPS FOR PARALEGALS

- Determine how the client would like to be addressed, e.g., by his or her first name or by a professional title such as Dr.

- Communicate with the client in plain English and avoid the use of "legalese" unless the client has a legal background.

- Adopt a style you are comfortable with and then tailor it as much as possible to the client's communication style. Each client is different. Some will feel free to present a spontaneous, open-ended narrative but will eventually need a degree of structure in the form of focused questions. Others will need to be encouraged, reassured, and drawn out.

- Focus on the client and maintain eye contact as much as possible unless the client is from a cultural background that views eye contact as hostile or threatening (as in certain American Indian cultures). Be sensitive to the fact that for people from some backgrounds, it is especially difficult to discuss "private failures" that bring shame to the family.

- Use a basic interview format as a guide, but be flexible, allowing the client to tell his or her story without interruption. The gaps can always be filled in later.

- Assuming the interview is not taped, strike a balance between focusing on the client and note taking. Note taking can be distracting and convey the message that the client is being ignored. It helps to explain to the client the purpose of note taking and to develop a personal shorthand for abbreviating common terms.

- Be prepared for a variety of emotions to be expressed in the context of the interview, given the emotionally charged nature of issues commonly addressed in a family law practice (and have a supply of tissues readily available!).

- Be empathetic when appropriate, but try to keep focused on the progression of the interview. If it appears the client might benefit from a referral to a mental health professional or other resource, suggest that course of action to the supervising attorney.

- Avoid the temptation to interject your own life story. A certain amount of small talk is appropriate at the outset to establish an initial rapport, but remember, the client may be paying by the hour and will not appreciate the banter when the bill arrives!

- Remember that everyone is entitled to representation and, as a client, to 100 percent of your attention, energy, and skill. If the attorney has decided to accept a client you find offensive or threatening, remain objective in the context of the interview but bring your concerns to the attention of the supervisor. If the client becomes extremely hostile or assaultive, call for assistance and remove yourself to a safe location if possible.

Following the initial interview, the paralegal will customarily perform the following tasks:

- Draft a *letter of engagement,* or a *letter of nonengagement* if the attorney does not accept the case. Attorneys elect to decline cases for one or more reasons that may include:
  - the prospective client's inability to pay
  - the likelihood that the person is raising frivolous or baseless claims
  - the person's unrealistic expectations or stated intent to "do whatever is necessary" to prevail, including concealing assets and lying under oath in court
  - the existence of a conflict of interest
  - a case complexity that calls for a level of skill and expertise far beyond that of the attorney such that accepting the case would violate the attorney's ethical duty to provide competent representation

  (See Paralegal Application 1.4.)

- Prepare an interview summary for the supervising attorney, including highlights, issues, concerns, and follow-up matters
- Prepare a fee agreement based on the attorney's instructions and make arrangements to have it signed by both the client and the attorney
- Open a client file and ensure that the client's name is promptly added to the firm's master client list to facilitate future conflicts checks
- Send the client any documents needing to be completed and/or signed, such as:
  - a client questionnaire
  - a financial statement
  - release forms authorizing the attorney to seek and receive information concerning the client from third parties such as hospitals, doctors, accountants, social service agencies, the Internal Revenue Service, and others

Letter of engagement
a letter from an attorney to a client confirming that the attorney agrees to represent the client in a particular legal matter

Letter of nonengagement
a letter from an attorney to an individual confirming that the attorney will NOT be representing that individual with respect to a particular legal matter

PARALEGAL APPLICATION 1.4

DISCRIMINATION OR DISCRIMINATING: WHAT DO YOU THINK?
THE FACTS

Assume that you were recently hired by an attorney in a private family law practice. After being employed there for about six months, you have noticed that your supervising attorney, Judith, represents male clients in some matters but never in divorce actions. When you casually mention this observation to her at lunch one day, she tells you that she has deliberately chosen not to represent males in divorces because she wants to "promote more equal treatment of women in the judicial system" and does not feel she can advocate zealously for males in that context. A week later, a man whom Judith refused to represent in a divorce files a complaint against her with the state's commission against discrimination. The complaint is for gender discrimination in a public accommodation (an office open to the public and advertising legal services to the general public). Judith argues that compelling her to represent males would violate her constitutional rights to freedom of speech and free association.

SIDEBAR

If you were sitting on the Commission, would you find for the spurned client seeking representation or the attorney advocating for women? To what extent should attorneys be permitted to pick and choose their clients in family law matters, if at all? Technically,
continued

as members of the Bar, attorneys are "officers of the court." Should they be held to higher standards than other businesspersons? For an interesting case that addressed the appeal of the Commission's decision against the attorney in this fact pattern, see *Nathanson v. Commonwealth et al,* 16 Mass. L. Rep. 761 (Mass. Super. 2003).

Fee Agreements and Billing

Fee Agreements. One of the major sources of malpractice actions and tension between attorneys and clients relates to fees and costs. Fee agreements are designed to help prevent such problems. A *fee agreement* is a contract between an attorney and a client, and a failure of either party to comply with its terms may give rise to an action for breach of contract or malpractice. An effective fee agreement:

- is executed at the outset of the representation
- describes the rights and responsibilities of both the attorney and the client
- is written in plain terms and in the language of the client if he or she is non-English speaking
- clearly describes the scope of the legal services to be performed (and the tasks that will not be performed, if appropriate)
- specifies the fees to be charged for professional employees working on the client's case including the lead attorney, associate attorneys, and paralegals
- identifies the kinds of costs the client will be responsible for, including, for example, filing fees and telephone calls, travel, and photocopying charges
- spells out the circumstances under which the attorney may terminate the representation

Exhibit 1.2 identifies the most common types of fee agreements used by attorneys. An example of a fee agreement suitable for use in a family law case is included in the Chapter1 resource material on the companion website.

EXHIBIT 1.2 Fee Agreements—Basic Terminology

Flat fee	A fixed dollar amount is charged to handle a specific legal matter, such as the negotiating and drafting of a cohabitation agreement.
Hourly rate	The attorney charges the client for each hour worked on the case (usually billing in tenths of an hour) plus fees (filing, recording, etc.) and costs (telephone, postage, copying, etc.).
Retainer (1)	This term is sometimes used in general to describe the contract between the attorney and the client, particularly with respect to fees.
Retainer (2)	The client advances a lump-sum payment to an attorney for deposit in a client trust fund account. The attorney withdraws funds from the retainer as the client incurs fees and costs. If the retainer is exhausted and the representation has not yet concluded, the client is asked to provide an additional retainer or to continue payments on some other basis. Any unused portion of a retainer is returned to the client at the conclusion of the representation.
Retainer (3)	Occasionally an attorney is paid a retainer for the purpose of making him- or herself readily available to the client whenever needed. A retainer of this type, in effect, pays the attorney for declining other employment.

continued

Fee agreement
a contract between an attorney and a client regarding payment for the attorney's professional services

---

Paralegal Practice Tip
Attorneys are usually permitted to withdraw, and in some instances must withdraw, from representation of a client if continued representation would result in a violation of the law or an ethical rule or if the attorney's representation is impaired by a conflict of interest or by his or her physical or mental condition. If litigation has already begun, permission of the court may be required to withdraw.

Paralegal Practice Tip
Throughout this text, an effort is made to provide examples of cases, laws, and procedural rules of many states. A major reason for providing these illustrations is to sensitize the reader to the critical importance of knowing and adhering to the applicable law and rules governing a specific matter in a particular jurisdiction. For example, in New York, an attorney representing a client in a domestic relations matter is required to provide the client with a statement of the client's rights and responsibilities with respect to fees.[3]

Contingent fee   The attorney is paid a certain percentage of the amount recovered by the client in a settlement or court judgment (plus fees and costs). Common in personal injury cases, contingent fees based on results obtained usually are not permitted in divorce cases, as they have a tendency to fuel litigation and discourage settlement or reconciliation. Limited exceptions to the general rule may apply when, for example, reconciliation is no longer a possibility or an attorney is retained for the sole purpose of recovering a debt owed to a client in the form of unpaid alimony or delinquent child support payments.

Fee splitting   The dividing of a fee between attorneys is permissible under certain circumstances (e.g., the total fee is in reasonable proportion to the work performed, and the client consents).[4] Dividing a fee for legal services with a nonattorney is not permitted.

A developing trend in legal representation, and particularly with respect to family law matters, is toward "***unbundling***" legal services provided to parties proceeding in part *pro se* (representing themselves). This option affords the client the benefit of legal services when needed at reduced overall expense. When permitted, rather than comprehensive representation, the client retains the attorney to perform certain discrete tasks for a fee. In order to prevent abuse, confusion, and misunderstanding, fee agreements in such cases (***limited scope agreements***) must be carefully drafted to specify the precise tasks to be performed, such as researching a specific issue or drafting a particular document to be filed under the client's signature. (In some states, if the attorney actually drafts the document and the client files it, the document must be marked "prepared by counsel" in order to avoid a lack of candor before the court.) The agreement should also indicate major blocks of services, such as trial preparation, court appearances, or post-divorce services, that the attorney will not perform.

Billing. Billing is viewed by some practitioners as a burden but clearly a necessary one. If not properly managed, it is a potential source of malpractice actions. Keeping accurate track of time spent on a case and for what specific purpose needs to become an automatic function, an integral part of each attorney's and paralegal's *modus operandi*. Because the cost of paralegal services is a recoverable component of overall attorneys' fees,[5] paralegals are required to keep track of the time they spend working on client files. This is customarily accomplished through the use of time sheets that include the client's name, file/docket number, time spent, and nature of services performed. (See Exhibit 1.3.) These sheets provide necessary documentation to support client billing. Attorneys establish paralegal fees, and such fees have been allowed by courts if they are reasonable, for appropriate services, and properly documented. (See Case 1.1.)

Legal Research

One of the most important functions a paralegal performs is legal research. Research is not merely a job requirement, it is an ethical obligation. A failure to conduct adequate research may expose an attorney to liability for malpractice. For example, in a case in which it upheld a lower court's award of $100,000 to an

Unbundling of legal services
an alternative to full representation in which an attorney performs discrete tasks rather than comprehensive representation in a legal matter, usually at a substantial overall savings to the client

Limited scope agreement
an agreement between an attorney and a client that specifically limits the nature and extent of the professional representation to be provided

Paralegal Practice Tip
Attorneys and paralegals often spend far more time on cases than is eventually billed to the client. The decision as to how much of the time spent is ultimately billed to the client is made by the attorney.

attorney's former client, the California Supreme Court held that "Even as to doubtful matters, an attorney is expected to perform sufficient research to enable him to make an informed and intelligent judgment on behalf of his client."[6] Paralegals are often surprised to learn that consistent with an ethical duty of candor before the court, attorneys have an obligation to bring to its attention not only controlling primary authority that supports the client's position but also contradictory primary authority if opposing counsel fails to do so.[7] In the face of unfavorable controlling authority, every effort must be made to distinguish the facts of the client's particular case from the facts of "controlling" case law. In the event that the reader has not yet completed a course in legal research and writing, a list and brief description of major research resources and related terminology used in this text is available on the companion website in the resources for this chapter. Paralegal Application 1.5 provides a description of the components of a paralegal's basic family law library.

Paralegal Practice Tip

Several cases and statutes are referenced throughout the text that are "good law" as of the fall of 2007. However, the law is constantly evolving, and attorneys and paralegals must always verify current law, use up-to-date forms, and apply presently existing rules and procedures. This means continually checking pocket parts, advance sheets, and legal publications, and sheperdizing cases and statutes before using them.

PARALEGAL APPLICATION 1.5

THE PARALEGAL'S BASIC FAMILY LAW LIBRARY

The legal materials most often utilized by a family law paralegal on a day-to-day basis are the following:

- **The state's statutory code**, primarily those sections governing domestic relations matters such as marriage, divorce, custody, child support, spousal support, property division, adoption, and related jurisdictional requirements
- **Court rules** governing domestic relations practice and procedure
- **Case law** contained in state, regional, and Supreme Court reporters with "pocket parts" (Most states and regions also have digests containing brief summaries of court opinions.)
- **Practice manuals** providing a wealth of information about substantive law and procedure as well as forms and useful checklists
- **Form books** containing forms for use in a variety of actions
- **A legal dictionary,** such as the current edition of *Black's Law Dictionary*
- **A citation manual,** such as the *Bluebook*
- **Legal newspapers:** Often published weekly by state bar associations, these newspapers are available in libraries and by subscription. They provide current information on recent cases, legislative developments, legal trends and publications, state and local bar association activities, etc.

Codes, Rules of Procedure, and reporters are available in law and college libraries, many law offices, and online through law libraries and commercial databases such as Lexis-Nexis, WESTLAW, and Loislaw. In some states they may also be available through state-sponsored public sites at no cost, although the commercial databases are generally more likely to be accurate and up-to-date. Throughout this text, various websites are cited in the end-of-chapter activity called Focus on Technology. Several of these sites contain links to laws on a variety of topics on a state-by-state basis. A list of websites of general interest last visited in the spring of 2008 is available in Appendix D.

Paralegal Practice Tip

Although there is much useful material available free on the Internet, the reader is reminded that much of it is anonymous, unregulated, and unmonitored. Caution needs to be exercised. Remember that information located on the Internet that is referenced needs to be cited. Rule 18 of the *Bluebook* provides rules for citing Internet sources.

CASE 1.1 *McMackin v. McMackin,* 651 A.2d 778 (Del. Fam. Ct. 1993)

BACKGROUND INFORMATION

In this case, a Delaware Family Court granted a wife's request for fees in a divorce action, including attorney's fees, paralegal fees, and costs. The wife's total fees and costs came to $12,785.50 and the husband's to $9,768.35. In its opinion, the court provided an overview of the treatment of fees for services provided by paralegals in Delaware.

FROM THE OPINION

. . .

In the past, Family Court Judges have treated paralegal fees in a variety of ways. Some judges have permitted them. Others have steadfastly denied them. In my view, paralegal costs should be uniformly allowed, so long as certain information is specifically addressed by the supervising attorney in the fee affidavit presented to the court.

13 Del.C §1515 is the controlling statute regarding an award of fees following a division of marital assets and debts. That statute reads as follows:

> The Court from time to time after considering the financial resources of both parties may order a party to pay all or part of the cost to the other party of maintaining or defending any proceeding under this title and for attorney's fees, including sums for legal services rendered and costs incurred prior to the commencement of the proceeding or after the entry of judgment. The Court may order that the amount be paid directly to the attorney, who may enforce the order in his name.

The phrase "all or part of the costs of the other party of maintaining or defending" has previously been found broad enough to include fees incurred by a legal assistant or paralegal. *P.J.M v. F.M.,* Del. Fam., File No. 2118–82, Horgan, J. (April 18, 1988, *amended* June 9, 1998).

. . .

The United States Supreme Court has found that the term "attorney's fee" refers not only to the work performed by members of the Bar but also to reasonable fees for the work product of an attorney, which includes the work of paralegals, law clerks and recent law graduates at market rates for their services. *Missouri v. Jenkins,* 491 U.S. 274, 109 S. Ct. 2463, 105 L. Ed.2d 229 (1989).

. . .

Paralegal fees are not part of the overall overhead of a law firm. Paralegal services are billed separately by attorneys, and these legal assistants have the potential for greatly decreasing litigation expenses and, for that matter, greatly increasing the efficiency of many attorneys. By permitting paralegal fees, the danger of charging these fees off as the attorney's work is hopefully extinguished. By the same token, the danger of charging off a secretary's services as those of a paralegal is very real and present, thereby mandating that certain information be provided by the supervising attorney before paralegal fees can be awarded by this Court in the future. Those criteria are as follows:

1. The time spent by the person in question on the task;

2. The hourly rate as charged to clients (will vary based on expertise and years of experience);

continued

3. The education, training or work experience of the person which enabled him or her to acquire sufficient knowledge of legal concepts. The Court recognizes that not all those who work in a paralegal capacity have a paralegal degree or license, but many of these people do possess expertise, which should be recognized in family law matters;

4. The type of work involved in detail. The work must *not* be purely clerical or secretarial in nature. Such work would fall under costs and may not be charged as paralegal fees at the market rate. The task must contain substantive legal work under the direction or supervision of an attorney such that if that assistant were not present, the work would be performed by the attorney and not a secretary. However, the assistant may not do work that only an attorney is allowed to do under the rules of practice and ethics. Substantive legal work which may be performed by legal assistants and billed at the market rate includes, but is not limited to, such activities as:

    a. Factual investigation, including locating and interviewing witnesses;
    b. Assistance with depositions, interrogatories and document preparation;
    c. Compilation of statistical and financial data;
    d. Checking legal citations;
    e. Correspondence with clients/opposing counsel/courts; and
    f. Preparing/reviewing/answering petitions and other pleadings.

· · ·

Applying the above standards to the two Affidavits received in the matters *sub judice*, it is evident that both of these contain the required information. Both affidavits clearly comply with all four criteria previously discussed. For example, they describe the time spent by the paralegal, the hourly rate, and the education, training or work experience of the paralegal. The type of affidavit submitted by Husband's counsel is exactly what this court expects when reviewing fees. The affidavit of Wife's counsel leaves a bit to be desired in that it merely attaches invoices sent to the client. These invoices are very difficult to read and should be consolidated into one document with a separate affidavit attached by the paralegal. Husband's affidavit complies in every respect, but Wife's affidavit is certainly within the guidelines. Both attorneys have described in detail the type of work performed by the paralegal. This work includes such activities as reviewing depositions, preparing subpoenas, reviewing discovery, assisting in preparing Rule 52(d) Submissions, conferences with clients and correspondence. Clearly the type of work involved is that which would normally have been prepared or accomplished by the attorney and not a secretary.

Having made the decision that paralegal fees are and will be henceforth permissible by this Court, and having also decided that the Affidavits presented by counsel in this specific case rise to the required standards, I nevertheless must make a determination of counsel fees in accordance with *13 Del. C.* §1515, supra.

· · ·

Husband has stated in his answer to Wife's Motion for Counsel Fees that he has no cash available to pay her fees. It is my opinion that his substantial income of approximately $82,000.00 per year versus Wife's income of approximately $35,000.00 per year mandates that he pay 60% of her fees or $7,671.30.

continued

This amount is to be added to the lump sum which Husband owes to Wife and is to be paid at the same time.

It is so Ordered.

SIDEBAR

This opinion is available in its entirety on the companion website for this text in the material related to Chapter 1.

EXHIBIT 1.3 Sample Time Sheet

Law Offices of Robert G. Wilson, III

7 Faneuil Marketplace

Boston, Massachusetts 02180

TIME SHEET

Employee:_____

Client's name: _____

Address:_____

Telephone: Home_____Business:_____Cell:_____

E-mail address: _____

In re: _____Docket #_____

Date	In	Out	Hours	Description of Services

TOTAL:

Employee signature: _____

Jurisdiction

Virtually every case involves a consideration of jurisdictional issues. In a majority of cases, jurisdictional issues are relatively straightforward. However, some cases are jurisdictionally complex. They may involve multiple parties in multiple states, and where a document is prepared or an action is brought may determine the outcome of a case. Attorneys often assign paralegals to research jurisdictional issues and gather information necessary for the attorney to make informed recommendations and decisions. Paralegals do not need to understand all the subtle intricacies of jurisdictional issues, but they at least need to be able to ask the right questions, know where to look for possible answers, and recognize the kinds of facts that will be necessary to support a client's position.

There are two primary meanings of ***jurisdiction*** in the legal context:

1. A geographical location, such as a country, circuit, state, or county in which a certain body of law is governing or a particular procedure is required. The potential impact of a jurisdiction on the rights of individuals can be significant. Consider the following:
   - If a same-sex couple is interested in adopting a child, as of June 2008, they would be unable to do so in Florida, definitely could petition to do so in Massachusetts or California, and may or may not be able to do so in other states ("jurisdictions") depending on the governing law in each state.
   - Community property jurisdictions (such as Arizona, California, Idaho, and Texas) provide that a husband and wife hold a one-half interest each in property acquired during a marriage other than by gift or inheritance. In non-community property jurisdictions, husbands and wives are entitled to an equitable (fair) but not necessarily equal division of marital property upon divorce.
   - When considering the enforceability of a premarital agreement, some jurisdictions will treat the document as an agreement between two people who owe a special ***fiduciary duty*** to each other. Others will apply a contract standard and hold people to the bad bargains they make!
   - All states now allow divorce actions based on no-fault grounds. Some have totally eliminated fault grounds, such as adultery and cruel and abusive treatment.
   - All states consider the best interests of a child to some extent in custody actions. In some states, parents are initially presumed to have equal rights to custody. In at least one state (West Virginia), custody usually will be awarded based on the extent to which each parent acted as the child's primary caretaker while the parties were residing together.
2. The authority of a court to issue enforceable orders concerning:
   - A particular type of legal matter = ***subject matter jurisdiction***
   - A particular person = ***personal jurisdiction***
   - A particular property or thing = **in rem** ***jurisdiction***

(See Exhibit 1.4.)

Jurisdictional rules and issues vary by topic and are, therefore, considered in several chapters of this text. Some of the jurisdictional issues discussed include the following:

- Chapter 2, Premarital Agreements: Jurisdictional standards governing the validity and enforceability of premarital agreements
- Chapter 3, Marriage: Existence of same-sex and common law marriage in some states
- Chapter 5, Nonmarital Families: Variations among jurisdictions particularly with respect to treatment of civil unions and domestic partnerships
- Chapter 6, Divorce Process: Variations among jurisdictions in grounds for divorce; circumstances under which a court has jurisdiction to dissolve a

---

Jurisdiction
a geographical area in which a certain law or procedure is governing; the authority of a court to issue enforceable orders concerning a particular type of legal matter, person, or thing

Fiduciary duty
a duty of good faith, loyalty, and trust owed by one person to another based upon the existence of a special relationship

Subject matter jurisdiction
the authority of a court to hear and decide a particular type of claim or controversy

Personal jurisdiction
the authority of a court to issue and enforce orders binding a particular individual

***In rem* jurisdiction**
the authority a court has over a property or thing rather than over a person

marriage or effect a division of property; lack of personal, subject matter, or *in rem* jurisdiction as a defense to a divorce action; residency requirements as a basis for jurisdiction

- Chapter 8, Child Custody: Jurisdictional requirements for establishing and modifying child custody awards, particularly when multiple states are involved
- Chapter 9, Child Support: Circumstances under which a court can issue an enforceable child support order against a parent
- Chapter 11, Property Division: Jurisdictional variations in treatment of marital property
- Chapter 15, Family Violence: Jurisdictional rules governing where actions for protective orders can be brought and resulting orders enforced

---

EXHIBIT 1.4 Types of Jurisdiction

Type of Jurisdiction	How It Is Acquired
Subject Matter Jurisdiction is the authority of a court to hear and decide a particular type of claim or controversy.	Subject matter jurisdiction is conferred by a state statute authorizing the court to hear and decide a particular type of action. It cannot be created by agreement of the parties. • **General jurisdiction**: the court has jurisdiction over more than one type of claim • **Specific jurisdiction**: the court has exclusive jurisdiction over a particular type of legal matter (e.g., the U.S. Bankruptcy Court over bankruptcy actions) • **Concurrent jurisdiction**: the court shares subject matter jurisdiction with other courts (e.g., protective orders usually can be sought in family and criminal courts)
Personal Jurisdiction is the authority of a court to issue and enforce orders binding a particular individual.	In order for a court to exercise personal jurisdiction over a defendant, he or she must have notice of the action and an opportunity to be heard. Personal jurisdiction is customarily acquired over a defendant by personal service of process, consent, substituted service on a resident defendant (e.g., by mail or publication in a newspaper), or under a state's long-arm statute if the defendant is a nonresident who has sufficient minimum contacts with the state. The emphasis is on the fairness of requiring a person to come into court in a particular jurisdiction.
***In Rem* Jurisdiction** is the authority a court has over a thing (in some states includes a status) rather than a person.	A state court can exercise its powers over property located inside of that state's boundaries.

Ethics

Ethics
the standards or rules of conduct
to which members of a profession
are expected to conform

Ethics are standards or rules of conduct to which members of a profession are expected to conform. *Black's Law Dictionary* (8th edition) specifically defines legal ethics as "The minimum standards of appropriate conduct within the legal profession involving the duties that its members owe one another, their clients, and the courts." Across the country, there exist a number of paralegal codes and guidelines for practice, sometimes called canons or rules of professional responsibility. Some are written by attorneys for attorneys such as the American Bar Association's Model Guidelines for the Utilization of Legal Assistants (adopted in several states) and rules promulgated by State Bar Associations. Some are written, at least in part, by paralegals under the auspices of professional paralegal associations at the local, state, or national level, such as the National Federation of Paralegal Associations (NFPA) (see Appendix B) or the National Association of Legal Assistants (NALA).

Codes of conduct for attorneys are backed by sanctions, such as suspension or disbarment. The sanctions may be issued as a result of the attorney's own direct actions or due to the actions of paralegals and others employed by the attorney under the ***doctrine of* respondeat superior.** Under this doctrine, the lawyer is vicariously liable for acts of the paralegal performed within the scope of employment if those acts would violate the attorney's code of conduct if performed by the attorney, provided:

Doctrine of *respondeat superior*
the doctrine under which an attorney is held vicariously liable for the acts of his or her employees performed within the scope of employment

- the lawyer knows of or ratifies the conduct, or
- the lawyer has supervisory authority over the paralegal, knows of the conduct at a time when the consequences of the harm could be avoided, and fails to take remedial action, or
- the lawyer fails to exercise adequate supervision over the paralegal

Codes of conduct for paralegals commonly are not backed by sanctions, although organizations such as the NFPA urge a move in that direction. To that end, in 1997, the NFPA adopted the Model Disciplinary Rules to promote enforcement of the Canons and Ethical Considerations in the NFPA Model Code of Ethics and Professional Responsibility. Paralegals may be sanctioned by the state in some instances, particularly those involving the unauthorized practice of law. (See Case 1.2.) Even if not sanctioned by the state for ethical violations, they may, of course, lose their jobs and their professional reputations or be sued for actions taken outside of the scope of employment that resulted in harm to a client. If they "hold themselves out" as attorneys or as possessing a higher level of legal skills, they may be held to that higher standard in a civil action. In addition, a paralegal is not insulated as an employee from potential criminal liability if he or she knowingly participates in criminal activity such as "borrowing" client funds from a trust account to pay for law school tuition.

Malpractice
intentional or negligent professional misconduct of an attorney that may occur in the form of a failure to properly supervise a paralegal

The vast majority of law firms maintain **malpractice** insurance to cover negligence of attorneys and employees within the scope of their employment. Some states (such as New Hampshire) require attorneys to notify clients in writing if they do not maintain a certain level of malpractice insurance. In New Hampshire in 2005, the largest percentage of professional conduct complaints (42% of the total) were in the area of family law and adoption.[8] In the domestic relations context, malpractice actions typically involve:

- failure to properly advise a client
- failure to investigate the nature and extent of marital assets
- failure to protect pension or retirement rights
- failure to draft appropriate terms for a property settlement agreement or proposed divorce decree
- failure to give proper notice
- failure to timely perfect an appeal
- failure to assure the payment of money or the transfer of property[9]

CASE **1.2** *Columbus Bar Association v. Thomas,* 109 Ohio St. 3d
89, 2006 Ohio 1930, 846 N.E.2d 31 (2006)

BACKGROUND

William Thomas was employed by attorney James Watson for several years as a
legal assistant. In 2002, attorney Watson was recovering at home for several months
after sustaining a serious injury. During that period, he relied on his legal assistant
to perform duties subject to his supervision and approval. Thomas, who was not
licensed to practice law in Ohio, exceeded the authority granted to him and acted
independently on behalf of Richard Zahner in a divorce case. He prepared and filed
an answer and counterclaim as well as a motion for a restraining order and a supporting affidavit. Zahner denied that the signature on the affidavit was his
although Thomas had notarized it by using attorney Watson's notary seal and
signing Watson's name. Without Watson's knowledge, authority, or approval,
Thomas also drafted a letter to Zahner describing the domestic relations process
and giving legal advice on his case. He signed the attorney's name on the letter. In
response to Watson's instructions, he also prepared objections to a magistrate's
order in the case, but did not obtain Watson's approval of the filing or specific
authority to sign it on his behalf.

While working for Watson during 1997, Thomas also assisted a relative, Inez
Faulkes, with preparation of her will, and following her death, prepared legal documents regarding the estate using Watson's signature but without his knowledge or
review.

Based on these facts, the Board on the Unauthorized Practice of Law of the
Ohio Supreme Court found that Thomas had engaged in the unauthorized practice of law and also found that he had not cooperated in the board proceedings.
Based on lack of cooperation, the flagrancy of the violations, and harm to third
parties, the board recommended a $10,000 civil penalty representing $5,000 for
each count (Zahner and Faulkes cases). (No. UPL 05–01)

FROM THE OPINION

We agree that respondent engaged in the unauthorized practice of law.
Section 2(B)(1)(g), Article IV, Ohio Constitution confers on this court original
jurisdiction regarding admission to the practice of law, the discipline of persons so
admitted, and all other matters relating to the practice of law. A person who is not
admitted to the practice of law pursuant to the Supreme Court Rules for the
Government of the Bar engages in the unauthorized practice of law when he or she
provides legal services to another in this state. . . .

The practice of law is not limited to appearances in court. It also embraces
the preparation of papers that are to be filed in court on another's behalf and that
are otherwise incident to a lawsuit. . . .

We have specifically held that a lay employee engages in the unauthorized
practice of law by preparing legal documents for another to be filed in domestic-
relations court without a licensed attorney's oversight. *Cleveland Bar Assn. v. Para-
Legals, Inc.,* 106 Ohio St. 3d 455, 2005 Ohio 5519, 835 N.E.2d 1240. Providing legal
counsel by a layperson in preparing another person's will also constitutes the unauthorized practice of law. . . . Further, unauthorized practice occurs when a layperson renders legal advice in the pursuit of managing another person's legal actions
and proceedings before courts of law. . . .

Rules prohibiting the unauthorized practice of law are "intended to protect
Ohio citizens from the dangers of faulty legal representation rendered by persons
not trained in, examined on, or licensed to practice by the laws of this state."
Disciplinary Counsel v. Pavlik (2000), 89 Ohio St.3d 458, 461, 2000 Ohio 219, 732
N.E.2d 985. Thus, although laypersons may assist lawyers in preparing legal papers

continued

to be filed in court and managing pending claims, those activities must be carefully supervised and approved by a licensed practitioner.... Because respondent lacked this professional oversight, his actions with respect to Zahner and Faulkes violated the prohibitions against the unauthorized practice of law.

To discourage such practices, we agree that a civil penalty is warranted, but we find the recommended $10,000 civil penalty to be excessive. Respondent did not appear before the board; however, he did cooperate during relator's investigation by being deposed twice and candidly admitting many of the facts underlying relator's complaint. From this testimony, we are convinced that respondent did not understand, despite his years of experience as a legal assistant, the extent to which he had overstepped the bounds of that role. We find what the panel and board conceded was possible: that respondent believed, although he was seriously mistaken, that he had Watson's permission to prepare and sign documents on his behalf.

Respondent is enjoined from engaging in acts constituting the unauthorized practice of law, including preparing and filing in court papers to determine the legal rights of others and offering legal advice to others about how to protect those rights. We also order respondent to pay a civil penalty of $5,000 pursuant to Gov.Bar R. VII(8)(B) and VII(19)(D)(1)(c). Costs are taxed to the respondent.

Judgment accordingly.

SIDEBAR

What do you think of the Ohio Supreme Court's decision in this case? Was the court too hard on the legal assistant? Too lenient? The opinion is available in its entirety on the companion website.

Clearly, no matter how hard members of a family law team work, few family law cases can be described as "total victories," and sometimes mistakes are made. Dissatisfied clients often seek redress but are not necessarily successful, absent particularly egregious promises or conduct on the part of the attorney. The "standard of care" to be applied in determining whether or not an attorney has been negligent has been described as follows:

An attorney who acts in good faith and in an honest belief that his advice and acts are well founded and in the best interest of his client is not answerable for a mere error of judgment or for a mistake in a point of law which has not been settled by the court of last resort in his State and on which reasonable doubt may be entertained by well-informed lawyers. Conversely, he is answerable in damages for any loss to his client which proximately results from a want of that degree of knowledge and skill ordinarily possessed by others of his profession similarly situated, or from the omission to use reasonable care and diligence, or from the failure to exercise in good faith his best judgment in attending to the litigation committed to his care.[10]

The topic of paralegal ethics is sometimes covered in a semester-long course with a dedicated text. In this text, an effort is made to weave ethical considerations into all of the chapters, each of which includes a Focus on Ethics exercise. Paralegal Application 1.6 provides an initial introduction to paralegal dos and don'ts.

Conflicts of Interest. An attorney (and by extension the family law team) has a duty of undivided loyalty to the client. Any situation that interferes with that duty and the exercise of independent judgment may place a client at a disadvantage and impair the capacity of team members to competently and zealously advocate for the client.

PARALEGAL APPLICATION **1.6**

PARALEGAL ETHICS IN A NUTSHELL

- The paralegal may participate in an initial interview with a prospective client under an attorney's direction **BUT** may not solicit clients, accept or reject cases on behalf of the firm, or set any fee for representation.

- The paralegal may be paid a reasonable fee for services and receive bonuses and profit sharing plan benefits unrelated to a specific case **BUT** may not split legal fees with an attorney.

- The paralegal can provide to a client factual information that is a matter of public record (such as a court's order or the content of a statute) and may relay advice from the attorney to the client **BUT** may not give legal advice to or counsel a client, as that would constitute an unauthorized practice of law (practice of law without a license). The giving of legal advice to a client involves an exercise of professional judgment based on knowledge of the law. It includes advising a client about their rights and responsibilities, recommending a course of action, or predicting an outcome. For example, if a client asks what a counterclaim for divorce is, the paralegal can provide a definition (based on an established source such as a legal dictionary) but cannot advise the client as to whether or not and why he or she should file a counterclaim.[11]

- The paralegal may communicate with opposing counsel as directed by the supervisor **BUT** may not communicate directly with an opposing party who is represented by counsel unless that party's counsel consents to the contact.

- The paralegal may assist in maintaining a relationship with a client, **BUT** the attorney must maintain control over the relationship.

- The paralegal may complete tasks delegated by an attorney (such as drafting pleadings and discovery requests), **BUT** the tasks must be performed under the supervision of the attorney, be subject to the attorney's review and approval, and merge with the attorney's work product.

- In a majority of states, the paralegal's name may appear in a firm's letterhead or on the paralegal's business card, **BUT** the paralegal's title and nonattorney status must be clearly indicated and the paralegal may not be a partner with a lawyer when any of the activities of the partnership include the practice of law.

- The paralegal should communicate to the supervising attorney confidential information provided by the client **BUT** must not reveal those confidences to anyone else in or outside of the firm—not even a spouse or a parent. Special care needs to be exercised when utilizing cell phones, e-mail, and fax machines or leaving files open on a desk or on a computer screen where passersby may see them. The confidentiality rule extends to all communication relating to representation of a client.

- The paralegal may perform work on a case in which the firm represents multiple parties in a particular matter (sometimes called joint or common representation) if permitted under governing rules of professional conduct **BUT** otherwise must avoid conflicts of interest and bring them to the attention of the attorney.

- The paralegal may prepare and sign basic correspondence as directed by a supervisor (such as transmittal cover letters or letters confirming appointments, etc.) **BUT** may not sign actual ***pleadings*** (informing an adverse party of the nature of a claim or defense) or ***motions*** (applications to the court for an order) filed with the court and requiring the attorney's signature. The attorney's signature is a certification that the attorney has read the pleading and that, to the best of his or her knowledge, it is filed in good faith, that there are grounds to support it, that it is supported by existing law (or by a good-faith argument for extension, modification,

continued

Pleading
a document in which a party to a legal proceeding sets forth or responds to a claim, allegation, defense, or denial

Motion
a written or oral request that a court issue a particular ruling or order

Conflict of interest
a situation or circumstance that interferes with the attorney's duties of zealous advocacy and loyalty to the client

Ethical wall
a screening mechanism designed to protect a client from a conflict of interest by preventing one or more lawyers (or paralegals) within a firm from participating in any legal matter involving that client

or reversal of existing law), and that it is not filed for the purpose of delaying the underlying action or harassing the opposing party.

- The paralegal may assist and "represent" clients at a variety of administrative hearings (such as before the Social Security or Veterans Administration or a workman's compensation board)[12] **BUT** generally may not represent a client in court. The paralegal may assist an attorney in court with the court's permission and provided the paralegal is introduced and his or her role clearly indicated. However, some states allow paralegals to appear in court with clients in uncontested matters or domestic violence cases.

- The paralegal must seek to maintain a high level of competence **BUT** should not perform tasks for which he or she is unqualified. The client is entitled to competent representation.

Situations that constitute *conflicts of interest* arise in a variety of contexts. When a conflict exists disqualifying one attorney or paralegal in a firm from working on a case, the disqualification may be imputed to the entire firm. However, sometimes disqualification may not be necessary if an "*ethical wall*" can be created around the employee who creates the conflict. With respect to paralegals, the NFPA Model Code defines an "Ethical Wall" as a "screening method implemented in order to protect a client from a conflict of interest. An ethical wall generally includes, but is not limited to, the following elements: (1) prohibit the paralegal from having any connection with the matter; (2) ban discussions with or the transfer of documents to or from the paralegal; (3) restrict access to files; and (4) educate all members of the firm, corporation, or entity as to the separation of the paralegal (both organizationally and physically) from the pending matter."[14] Paralegal Application 1.7 presents some examples of ethical dilemmas encountered by paralegals in a family law practice.[15]

PARALEGAL APPLICATION 1.7

PARALEGAL ETHICAL DILEMMAS INVOLVING CONFLICTS OF INTEREST

- At law firm A, Mikayla worked on Charlie Morgan's criminal case. He was charged with statutory rape and was eventually acquitted following a brief trial. During the representation, she was privy to a considerable amount of confidential information about Charlie. Two months after his acquittal, she got a job nearer to her home as a paralegal at firm B. In her first week there, she became aware that her new employer was representing Ava Morgan, Charlie's wife, in her action for divorce. Although not the same matter, the divorce action is substantially related to the criminal case, as Ava is suing her husband for divorce on the grounds of adultery with a series of young women. The paralegal's duty to the earlier client did not end when the relationship or prior employment ended. In such circumstances, the paralegal must promptly bring the conflict to the supervisor's attention, because it would not be apparent in a conflicts check against the firm's master client list. In this set of facts, it is unlikely the conflict can be overcome (even with creation of an "ethical wall" around the paralegal), and the disqualification may extend to other members of the firm as well. However, if the nature of the later action had been totally unrelated to the earlier representation (such as drafting of a bill of sale for an automobile) and the former client consents, the paralegal's new employer may be permitted to represent the former client's adversary.

continued

- Brooke's supervisor has just agreed to represent Jackie Notar, who has a two-year-old daughter named Shayla. Shayla's dad is Jackie's ex-boyfriend, Scott, and he is seeking sole custody of their child. Jackie has told her attorney that she is living alone and never uses drugs despite Scott's claims to the contrary. Brooke's cousin, Martin, is Jackie's present boyfriend, and Brooke knows that he is living with Jackie and that drugs and drug paraphernalia are openly present in the home and frequently used by the couple in front of the child. Brooke believes strongly that Jackie is not a fit mother for Shayla and that Scott appears to be a great dad. Brooke nevertheless has a duty of loyalty to Jackie. If her bias against Jackie is so strong that it interferes with her work performance, Brooke must bring the conflict to the supervising attorney's attention.

- Against his own better judgment, Hank develops an intimate relationship with a client, Liz, after working closely with her for almost a year. Liz initially was heartbroken when her husband sued her for divorce. Hank tried to comfort and reassure her that there is life after divorce. He hopes that her new life will be with him. However, that hope soon may be dashed because Liz's husband is seeking to reconcile with his wife. Hank's interests are now potentially at odds with Liz's in light of their personal relationship. If the personal relationship interferes with his capacity to work on her case, Hank must bring the situation to his supervisor's attention. Paralegals should strive to avoid even the appearance of impropriety in their professional lives. It is therefore generally ill-advised to engage in personal relationships with clients.

- Dennis invests his modest savings in a start-up computer company owned by a client of the firm where he is employed. The client, Bonnie, is in the midst of a bitter divorce and doesn't want her husband to benefit in any way from her company. Bonnie has told both Dennis and his supervisor that she intends to run the company into the ground so that her husband never sees a dime from it. A conflict arises if the business relationship compromises undivided loyalty to the client and creates competing interests, as it appears to do in this instance. Some "business relationships" with clients do not create conflicts of interest. For example, no conflict is created if Bonnie owns the only insurance company in the small town where they both live and work and Dennis insures his automobile through that company.

- Klara is very attentive to ethical conduct. She is concerned that her supervisor, Belle, is violating ethical rules by representing both parties to an uncontested no-fault divorce action. Joint representation (also sometimes called common or multiple representation) is usually considered inappropriate in family law cases. However, the ABA Model Rules of Professional Conduct do not impose a blanket prohibition on common representation. In some circumstances, if the parties are allegedly in agreement, as in a joint action for dissolution of marriage, they consent to joint representation, and the attorney explains the risks and reasonably believes neither client will be disadvantaged, in some states the attorney will be permitted to represent both parties.

Protection of Attorney-Client Communications. The protection of communications between attorney and client arises in two areas of law, each of which is governed by its own rules:

- The ***attorney-client privilege*** (and work product doctrine) in the law of evidence applies in proceedings in which the lawyer is called as a witness or is required to produce evidence relating to a client. The "privilege" belongs to the client and prevents the attorney from disclosing attorney-client communications subject to limited exceptions. It is based on state and federal rules of evidence.
- The ***rule of attorney-client confidentiality*** is established in codes of professional ethics. It refers to the attorney's duty not to reveal *any* information relating to representation of the client, not merely "confidences" or

Attorney-client privilege
the client's right to refuse to disclose and to prevent the attorney from disclosing confidential communications between the client and the attorney unless the communication concerns future commission of a serious crime; the privilege is established by statute

Rule of attorney-client confidentiality
the duty of an attorney not to reveal any information relating to representation of a client; the rule is an ethical rule established in codes of professional conduct

"secrets." Some firms require employees to sign agreements in which they promise not to reveal client information. Violation of the agreement may result in loss of employment and, in some states, criminal sanctions. The duty is triggered even if the individual came in only for a consultation and later retains another attorney.

For the duty and the privilege to apply, the client must have communicated the information to the attorney (or his or her paralegal) in confidence for the purpose of obtaining legal advice from a person acting as a legal professional.

Although members of the family law team are obligated to maintain client confidentiality, there are exceptions to this general rule established by court rules and codes of ethics on a state-by-state basis. The attorney usually may reveal confidential information:

- If the client consents to the release of information, preferably in a writing that sets forth what can be released, when, to whom, and under what circumstances
- If the attorney reasonably believes the client is about to engage in conduct that will result in serious bodily harm or death or the wrongful execution of another (e.g., there is a movement toward including serious financial harm, such as the depletion of a company's retirement fund)
- If a third person is present when the client "confides" in his or her attorney or paralegal, the disclosure is not protected by the attorney/client privilege. This might occur, for example, if the client were to communicate with the attorney in a restaurant or a crowded elevator or in the presence of her best friend, whom she wanted to have present at a meeting with the attorney for moral support
- To the extent necessary to establish a claim or defense on behalf of the lawyer, for example, in litigation between the attorney and the client in a malpractice action or a suit for nonpayment of fees
- If necessary to rectify a client fraud in which the lawyer's services were used without his or her knowledge

PARALEGAL APPLICATION 1.8

ETHICS AND E-MAIL

E-mail has tremendous potential for facilitating communication between counsel and members of the family law team and their clients. Messages are transmitted over a variety of networks in a largely open environment and often include attachments such as financial statements or agreements. As such, they are vulnerable to misuse, alteration, and interception. They may also run afoul of the attorney's duty to protect the confidentiality of client communications. The paralegal needs to be aware of the firm's policy with respect to e-mail communications. The firm may, for example:

- Prohibit e-mail communication with clients.
- Utilize encryption software to help ensure the security of communications.
- Include boilerplate language on every e-mail (and facsimile) providing that the message is private and confidential and intended only for the recipient and that if it is received by another in error, it should be returned to the sender and may not be copied or destroyed.
- Advise clients of the risks and benefits of communication by e-mail and have them sign a waiver consenting to communication by that means if they wish to do so.

Can you think of other ways of protecting e-mail communications?

PARALEGAL APPLICATION **1.9**

ETHICS AND FIRM WEBSITES

The majority of law firms today maintain websites that are designed in part to market their services to prospective clients. They customarily provide a description of the firm including areas of specialization, background information on the attorneys employed by the firm and their respective areas of expertise, and sometimes informational material on legal topics. It is important to be sure that the content that appears on such sites complies with applicable state bar regulations and any laws governing advertising and solicitation. Although the states vary, the U.S. Supreme Court has held that the public has a right to learn about the availability and cost of legal services and that attorneys have a constitutional right to advertise, although that advertising may be subject to reasonable regulation by the states.[16] For example, it is reasonable to require that the advertising not be false or misleading (e.g., it should not guarantee results). Although they may advertise to the general public, attorneys ordinarily are not permitted to solicit business directly from strangers (e.g., persons who are neither relatives nor already clients). The distinction between advertising and solicitation relates to the fact that personal contact tends to subject prospective clients to undue pressure when they are most vulnerable (hence the phrase "ambulance chasing").

Substantive law
laws that relate to rights and obligations/duties rather than to technical procedures

Procedural law
the technical rules for bringing and defending actions before a court or administrative agency

CHAPTER **SUMMARY**

A family law practice can be exhilarating and heartbreaking. It tests the skills and ethical integrity of practitioners and provides opportunities for creative and constructive problem solving in the midst of family chaos and disruption. Family law is also one of the most rapidly evolving areas of legal practice as it tracks many of the social, political, and economic issues of the day. It is also one of the most essential areas, given that approximately half of all first marriages end in divorce[17] and more than half of all children under eighteen are being raised in one-parent households. At the individual level it addresses issues at the core of people's personal and intimate lives, usually in the context of a dispute. Members of a family law team are in a position to help shape the lives and futures of these adults and children. The paralegal is an invaluable member of that team.

This text is designed to introduce paralegals to the body of *substantive* and *procedural law* involved in regulating family-related matters and resolving related disputes. This first chapter touches on fundamental topics such as research and jurisdiction and on basic office management tasks as well as client intake and billing. Because ethical issues and challenges permeate every area of practice, the broad topic of paralegal ethics is introduced in this chapter. Each subsequent chapter addresses at least one ethical dilemma

encountered by paralegals in the family law context. Paralegals rarely receive formal on-the-job training in ethical conduct. They must, therefore, build on what they learn in their coursework. They must internalize basic ethical principles in the interest of their own professional integrity and success. They must also do so because, as agents of an attorney, their misconduct or negligence may expose their supervising attorney and the firm to liability and sanctions. The paralegal should strive to avoid even an appearance of impropriety, and the attorney must make a reasonable effort to ensure that the paralegal's conduct comports with the attorney's own ethical obligations.

Basic training as a paralegal that includes a family law course is simply the beginning. Many underlying principles, concepts, and procedures have their roots in longstanding traditions. However, the application of those fundamentals to emerging cultural and societal challenges yields a constantly changing context for every legal professional. The law is continually evolving, and some of the material in law-related textbooks is outdated as soon as the books go to print. Therefore, a career in law and the fulfillment of the ethical duty to maintain one's competence require ongoing education through attending seminars and workshops, reading legal publications, and utilizing other strategies for updating knowledge and skills.

KEY **TERMS**

Attorney-client privilege
Conflict of interest
Contingent fee
Doctrine of *respondeat superior*
Ethical wall
Ethics
Ex parte
Family law
Fee agreement
Fiduciary duty
Flat fee

Guardian *ad litem*
In rem jurisdiction
Jurisdiction
Letter of engagement
Letter of nonengagement
Limited scope agreement
Malpractice
Motion
No-fault divorce
Personal jurisdiction
Pleading

Procedural law
Pro se
Qualified Domestic Relations Orders
   (QDROs)
Retainer
Rule of attorney-client
   confidentiality
Subject matter jurisdiction
Substantive law
Unauthorized practice of law
Unbundling

REVIEW **QUESTIONS**

1. Describe five of the ways in which the nature of family law practice has changed over the past fifty years.
2. Define family law and identify the kinds of issues that are addressed in a family law practice.
3. Describe the role of a paralegal in a family law practice.
4. Identify the primary purposes of an initial client interview.
5. Describe the characteristics of effective fee agreements, and identify the various types of fee agreements that may be used in divorce cases.
6. Define unbundled legal services.
7. Identify the kinds of resources included in a basic family law library.

8. Define jurisdiction in both of its basic meanings.
9. Define and distinguish among subject matter, personal, and *in rem* jurisdiction.
10. Identify at least ten ethical "dos" that should guide the professional conduct of paralegals.
11. Define and give an example of the unauthorized practice of law.
12. Describe at least three kinds of conflicts of interest that paralegals encounter in the family law setting.
13. Describe the nature and purpose of an "ethical wall."
14. Distinguish between the attorney-client privilege and the ethical rule of attorney-client confidentiality.

FOCUS ON **THE JOB**

THE FACTS

You are a paralegal working in a firm of six attorneys. Each of the six specializes in a particular area: Ben in wills and trusts; Judy in adoption and foster care; Sabrina in real estate; David in contracts and employment; Gardiner in criminal; and your supervisor, Robert Wilson IV, in domestic relations. Each attorney has his or her own support staff consisting of a paralegal, a clerk/receptionist, and a student intern presently attending law school. Maria has contacted Attorney Wilson by telephone and has scheduled an appointment to discuss the possibility of his representing her in a divorce action. You have no additional information about the specific nature of her situation, but you do know that three years ago, Sabrina handled a real estate transaction for Maria and her husband, Mark, and that

Ben drafted their wills when they first married. The firm is in a small community where there are only fourteen other practicing attorneys.

THE ASSIGNMENT

Divide the class into groups of three. One student will play the role of Attorney Wilson, another Maria, and the third will function as the attorney's paralegal. (The group size can be modified to accommodate the number of students in the class, e.g., one or two groups may consist of two students each. One may consist of the paralegal and the client and the other the attorney and the client.) Role-play an initial interview applying the information you have learned thus far about interviewing and the purposes of an initial client intake interview. Refer to Paralegal Application 1.2 in particular for guidance.

FOCUS ON **ETHICS**

Assume that you are a paralegal working for Attorney Wilson on a divorce case involving William and Elizabeth Beauregard. Attorney Wilson represents Elizabeth, who is convinced that William is attempting to conceal marital assets. His attorney, Hiram Hechtl, telephones you to say that he is faxing a copy of his client's financial statement for Attorney Wilson's information. When you go to the fax machine, you discover that Attorney Hechtl apparently accidentally faxed not only the promised statement but also a note from his client that reads: "H—This is the revised statement and the version I want to give her. I took

a few accounts out and upped my expenses! She'll never know the difference. WB"

What ethical concerns arise in this situation? What do you think you should do? Would your response be the same if the wife had found the note at home and brought it in to Attorney Wilson? Do you find any guidance in the ethical canons for paralegals promulgated by the National Federation of Paralegal Associations (NFPA) contained in Appendix B ? Does your state's Bar Association or code of professional responsibility for attorneys address circumstances like this?[18]

FOCUS ON **CASE LAW**

The landmark decision of the U.S. Supreme Court in *Kulko v. Kulko,* 436 U.S. 84, 98 S. Ct. 1690, 56 L. Ed. 132 (1978), addresses the topic of personal jurisdiction in the child support context in a fact pattern involving multiple states. Locate and

read the case and then brief it using the format available on the companion website or one prescribed by your instructor. Both the case and the brief format are on the website in the material related to Chapter1.

FOCUS ON **STATE LAW AND PROCEDURE**

In the Focus on the Job fact pattern above, assume that Maria's husband, Mark, has already contacted the only other family law attorney in town for an initial consultation and has e-mailed Attorney Wilson, indicating an interest in "chatting with him" about a probable divorce action. The nearest town is an hour away, and no attorneys there specialize in domestic relations matters. Attorney Wilson would like to represent Maria but has an uneasy feeling about whether it would be ethical to do so. He has asked you to research the problem he is facing and make a recommendation. Locate the rules governing the ethical conduct of attorneys in your state. Prepare an internal memorandum to Attorney Wilson in which you identify each of the ethical issues raised by this situation and your recommendation with respect to how each can be addressed, if at all. You should conclude with an overall recommendation.

MEMORANDUM

To: Attorney Wilson

From: *Your Name, Paralegal*

Re: *The nature of the assignment (Include client name and case number)*

Date: *Insert date*

Description of the assignment: *What is it that you have been asked to do?*

Statement of the facts: *Relate the basic facts*

Governing Law/Principles: *Describe the applicable rules/ principles*

Discussion: *Apply the rules/principles to the facts of Maria's case*

Conclusion: *What is your recommendation with respect to whether or not Attorney Wilson should represent Maria?*

FOCUS ON **TECHNOLOGY**

COMPANION WEBSITE

http://www.prenhall.com/wilson

The reader is urged to make frequent use of the companion website for this text. It contains full opinions of many of the cases featured in the text; a selection of illustrative forms and statutes; and a variety of resources such as sample forms, motions, discovery requests, and checklists. The website is organized by chapter, and a document will appear in the material for the chapter in which it is mentioned unless otherwise indicated.

WEBSITES OF INTEREST

http://www.abanet.org/legalservices/client development/adrules

This is the ABA website link to state rules on advertising and solicitation.

http://www.aprl.net/statetop.html

This is the site for the Association of Professional Responsibility Lawyers. It provides links to a variety of websites related to professional responsibility.

http://www.lawcrawler.com

This site is a legal search engine provided by findlaw. It links to federal, academic, commercial, and foreign law-related sources and sites.

http://www.legalethics.com

This site abstracts and provides links to recently published articles on a number of topics related to legal ethics. It also provides links to other ethics-related sites.

http://www.nala.org

This is the site of the National Association of Legal Assistants (NALA).

http://www.paralegals.org

This is the site of the National Federation of Paralegal Associations (NFPA).

Note: Both of the above sites contain information regarding News & Events, Positions & Issues, CLE, Legal Resources, Opportunities, Networking, etc., for paralegals as well as links to other law-related sites.

http://www.virtualchase.com/legalresearcher/ index.html

This is a commercial site provided by a law firm as a service to the legal profession. It offers articles, guides, teaching materials, and an alert service, etc., on Internet research strategies and resources. Its intended audience is experienced researchers and legal professionals.

ASSIGNMENTS

1. Find out if your state's statutory code is available on the Internet. If so, what is the address (URL, Uniform Resource Locator) where it can be accessed?

2. Locate online the body of ethical rules governing attorneys in your state. Determine if there are also state or local rules governing the professional conduct of paralegals. If so, locate a copy of the document setting forth those rules.

3. Assume that you are assigned to create the home page for the website of the firm where you are employed. Locate the rules governing legal advertising in your state, if any, to guide your design. Then create a design after having visited at least five websites of other attorneys practicing in your state.

4. Go to the website for the National Association of Legal Assistants (NALA) at www.nala.org to locate that association's criteria for certification as a paralegal. Would you qualify?

5. Locate online the paralegal codes of ethics and professional responsibility of the state paralegal associations in Illinois, Kansas, and Delaware. What, if anything, does each of them provide with respect to the paralegal's duty to maintain a high level of competence? Do they differ in any significant respects from the NFPA code? (See Appendix B.)

6. Locate and review the American Bar Association's Model Guidelines for Utilization of Legal Assistant Services, available for download at http://www.abanet.org/ legalservices/paralegals/.

7. Search online to see if you can locate any resources for conducting conflict checks. If you are unsuccessful online, contact the office of a local attorney, explain that you are a paralegal student completing an assignment for class, and ask if someone can describe for you the procedure used in that office for identifying when a prospective client presents a conflict of interest.

chapter **two**

PREMARITAL AGREEMENTS

Richard, 72, a retired engineer with five adult children, has been married and divorced three times. He believes he has finally met the ONE true love for him, Elaine, 32, a widow and mother of three children. He wants very much to marry her but not without a premarital agreement, given his past experiences with divorce. Elaine has said, "Whatever you want is fine with me."

IN THIS CHAPTER YOU WILL LEARN

- What a premarital agreement is and the primary purpose it serves

- How the treatment of premarital agreements has evolved in society and the law

- How premarital agreements differ from other kinds of agreements made by married and unmarried partners

- In what circumstances premarital agreements may be appropriate

- The legal requirements for a valid premarital agreement

- What a basic premarital agreement covers

- The current trends regarding enforceability of premarital agreements

- The paralegal's potential role with respect to premarital agreements

WHAT IS A PREMARITAL AGREEMENT AND WHAT IS ITS PURPOSE?

Premarital agreement
an agreement made by two persons about to be married defining for themselves their respective rights, duties, and responsibilities in the event their marriage terminates by death, annulment, separation, or divorce

A *premarital agreement* (sometimes called a premarital contract, prenuptial agreement, or antenuptial agreement) is an agreement made by two persons about to be married. The agreement is an effort by the parties to define for themselves rights, duties, and responsibilities that flow from the marital relationship and that otherwise would be regulated and determined by state law upon death, annulment, separation, or divorce. What usually happens in a premarital agreement is that one or both of the parties agree to give up spousal support, an equal or equitable division of property, or other rights they might be entitled to under state law. Despite past fears that premarital agreements encourage divorce, they may actually promote marriage. People may choose to marry who might not do so without the personalized "safety net" or "insurance policy" the premarital agreement provides in the event the marriage does not last.

PREMARITAL AGREEMENTS IN PERSPECTIVE

Public policy
an idea or principle that is considered right and fair and in the best interest of the general public

In an effort to maintain social order and protect the general public interest, state and federal legislatures regulate various dimensions of our lives. For example, we have laws and regulations about education and employment, about finances and business transactions, about children and families, about marriage and death. Statutes and judicial rulings are designed to balance individual freedom and protection of the larger society and are based on *public policies*. Public policies are ideas or principles that are considered right and fair and in the best interest of the general public. They reflect current morals and established customs. For example, mandatory education laws requiring children to attend school until a certain age are based on the broad public policy that children are vulnerable and need to be protected and provided the foundation they need to become healthy, productive adults. In response, the state establishes and manages a public education system to ensure that children receive the education required by law. In addition, however, we have private and "charter" schools, parochial schools, and "home schooling" of children as educational alternatives for parents who want to create their own vehicles for complying with the law, vehicles tailored to their unique goals and needs. The state still monitors these alternatives to an extent but at the same time recognizes the right of parents to raise their children as they see fit as long as they do not break the law or violate an overriding public policy. Public policies that impact various other family law issues are referenced throughout this text.

One of the primary public policies that legislatures and courts in the United States historically have supported is one favoring the marital relationship as the fundamental structural unit of society. In support of that policy they have legislated and decreed regulations designed to protect the institution of marriage and the members of the family in the event of death or divorce. These regulations have been influenced by prevailing societal views about sexual morality, the vulnerability of children, and gender-related issues including the respective roles and relative power of men and women in society. In this context, the states were initially unwilling to permit couples to design their own agreements determining what would happen to their property upon divorce.

Per se invalid
invalid in and of itself, standing alone, without reference to any additional facts or circumstances

Although courts had, for many years, enforced premarital agreements that addressed property distribution upon death,[1] agreements made in contemplation of marriage that anticipated the possibility of divorce were viewed as **per se *invalid*** until the 1970s. The basic concern was that the party who would benefit most from the agreement (usually the male partner) would be motivated to terminate the marriage and the female partner would be left destitute. This perception has gradually changed over the past four decades along with views about men and women, fault-based divorce, and the institution of marriage generally. We now live in a society in which the rate of divorce has risen and few presume that marriage is a permanent union. As a result, we have an increasing number of individuals, both male and female, taking steps to develop their own approaches to distribution of property upon divorce or death. A premarital agreement is one vehicle for accomplishing this end.

The opinion in the landmark *Posner* case (see Case 2.1) describes the shift in public policy from one that presumes the permanence of marriage to one that acknowledges and enforces, under certain conditions, agreements regulating rights upon the dissolution of marriage. In *Posner*, the wife appealed the portion of the divorce decree that awarded the divorce to her husband and alimony to her in the amount of $600 a month pursuant to the terms of a premarital agreement between the parties. The wife's position was that, consistent with prior case law, the agreement should not be enforced. The court held that such agreements should no longer be considered ***void*** as contrary to public policy when the divorce is pursued in good faith on proper grounds.

Void
invalid and of no legal effect

CASE **2.1** *Posner v. Posner,* 233 So.2d 381 (Fla. 1970)

FROM THE OPINION

At the outset, we must recognize that there is a vast difference between a contract made in the market place and one relating to the institution of marriage.

It has long been the rule in a majority of the courts of this country and in this state that contracts intended to facilitate or promote the procurement of a divorce will be declared illegal as contrary to public policy. . . .

The state's interest in the preservation of the marriage is the basis of the rule that . . . an antenuptial agreement by which a prospective wife waives or limits her right to alimony or to the property of her husband in the event of a divorce or separation, regardless of who is at fault, has been in some states held to be invalid. . . .

There can be no doubt that the institution of marriage is the foundation of the familial and social structure of our nation and, as such, continues to be of vital interest to the State; but we cannot blind ourselves to the fact that the concept of the "sanctity" of a marriage—as being practically indissoluble, once entered into—held by our ancestors only a few generations ago, has been greatly eroded in the last several decades. . . .

With divorce such a commonplace fact of life, it is fair to assume that many prospective marriage partners whose property and familial situation is such as to generate a valid antenuptial agreement settling their property rights upon the death of either, might want to consider and discuss also—and agree upon, if possible—the disposition of their property and the alimony rights of the wife in the event their marriage, despite their best efforts, should fail. . . .

We know of no community or society in which the public policy that condemned a husband and wife to a lifetime of misery as an alternative to the opprobrium of divorce still exists. And a tendency to recognize this change in public policy and to give effect to the antenuptial agreements of the parties relating to divorce is clearly discernible. . . .

SIDEBAR

The full opinion in this case is available on the companion website. What are the major reasons for not recognizing premarital agreements? What are the major reasons for enforcing them? If you were presently contemplating getting married, would you want to have such an agreement? Why?

HOW IS A PREMARITAL AGREEMENT DIFFERENT FROM OTHER KINDS OF AGREEMENTS MADE BY MARRIED AND UNMARRIED PARTNERS?

A premarital agreement is one of several kinds of agreements made by adults entering into, presently in, or exiting from a relationship with another adult. Others include, for example, cohabitation agreements, postmarital agreements, and separation agreements.

Cohabitation agreement
an agreement between two unmarried individuals who live or intend to live together, defining their intentions, rights, and obligations with respect to one another while living together and upon termination of their relationship

Postmarital agreement
an agreement made by two people already married to each other who want both to continue their marriage and also to define their respective rights upon separation, divorce, or death of one of the spouses

Separation agreement
an agreement made between spouses in anticipation of divorce or a legal separation concerning the terms of the divorce or separation and any continuing obligations of the parties to each another

- A *cohabitation agreement* is an agreement between two unmarried individuals who live or intend to live together, defining their intentions, rights, and obligations with respect to one another while living together and upon termination of their relationship.
- A *postmarital or postnuptial agreement*[2] is an agreement made by two people already married to each other who want both to continue their marriage and also to define their respective rights upon separation, divorce, or death of one of the spouses. Some states, such as Ohio, prohibit postmarital agreements by statute.
- A *separation agreement* is an agreement made between spouses in anticipation of divorce or a legal separation concerning the terms of the divorce or separation and any continuing obligations of the parties to one another. Customarily the parties ask that the court approve the agreement and make it part of the court's judgment.

WHAT KINDS OF INDIVIDUALS AND COUPLES MIGHT WANT TO EXECUTE A PREMARITAL AGREEMENT?

Once thought of as appropriate only for the rich and famous, premarital agreements are becoming increasingly more common. This is not all that surprising when one considers that about half of first marriages end in divorce. Although premarital agreement statistics are scarce, according to one source, some twenty percent of remarried couples use premarital agreements, and they have quintupled in overall frequency over the past twenty years.[3] The New York-based nonprofit organization the Equality in Marriage Institute reported that over the two-year period between 2003 and 2005, calls about premarital agreements tripled in number.[4]

With shifts in demographics and expanding life spans, the growing senior population has become an audience for whom premarital agreements provide an especially useful vehicle for addressing the challenges and fears this segment of the population faces with respect to marriage and remarriage late in life. "Various deterrents to marriage are of particular concern to seniors, including problems of wealth preservation from the significant other, avoidance of the other's financial obligations related to health care and other debts, protection of pension benefits from previous marriages, protection against intestate succession, and interactions with adult children,"[5] who may not be as enthusiastic about the impending marriage as are the parties! To protect the children's interests, a premarital agreement can work in tandem with a will to achieve desired ends.

Premarital agreements are also particularly appropriate for parties in circumstances such as the following:

- There is a significant age difference between the parties.
- One or both of the parties have substantial property of their own including real estate, investments, businesses, and retirement accounts.

- A party has an interest in a family business that he or she wants to "keep in the family."
- A party is responsible for taking care of third parties such as elderly parents or siblings with disabilities.
- One of the parties is pursuing a degree or license in a potentially lucrative field such as medicine, and the other party will be supporting the couple through an extended education program.
- The parties have been out of high school for several years, remained single, and had an opportunity to accumulate significant property.
- One of the parties is giving up a successful career in order to be a "stay-at-home" parent.
- One or both of the parties have children or grandchildren from a previous marriage.
- One of the parties is involved in a speculative business venture that may result in a significant increase or loss in wealth.
- One or both of the parties want to ensure a new spouse's inheritance, especially if that spouse will lose his or her right to a social security benefit or alimony from a prior spouse upon marriage.
- One or both of the parties suffered through a prior divorce that was emotionally and financially devastating, and they do not want to repeat the experience.

The more common premarital contracts become, the less sensitive a topic they are for couples approaching marriage. The usual approach to creating an agreement is that the parties first discuss the possibility of executing an agreement and their reasons for doing so. Then one of the parties (customarily the one with the greater incentive and the most to gain) selects an attorney to draft an agreement. The other party ideally retains a second attorney to review the agreement, recommend revisions, and advise him or her before signing. Occasionally the parties will utilize traditional **mediation** to resolve their differences concerning the proposed terms of their agreement. A neutral third party, the mediator, helps the parties clarify their differences, consider options for addressing them, and structure an agreement acceptable to both parties.

An additional alternative approach to reaching consensus involves use of the less adversarial **collaborative law** process. It affords an effective method for developing premarital agreements tailored to the unique circumstances of the two people about to be married. When the collaborative law process is used, "the written agreement is prepared last and only after the partners have discussed the issues and concerns important to them and their shared life, and have reached shared agreements about those concerns. The collaborative agreement becomes a mutually developed blueprint for the marriage."[6] Although the parties still have to address challenging questions and require the assistance of specially trained counsel during the process, the "difference is that the collaborative process provides a safe and supportive setting...and...enhances the couple's togetherness rather than emphasizing their separateness."[7]

Mediation
approach to resolving differences in which a neutral third person helps the parties identify their differences, consider their options, and structure an agreement acceptable to both parties

Collaborative law
an approach to reaching agreements and resolving differences that stresses cooperation, joint problem solving, and the avoidance of litigation

WHAT ARE THE LEGAL REQUIREMENTS FOR A VALID PREMARITAL AGREEMENT?

A premarital agreement is both a contract and an agreement between two parties who bear a special relationship to each other. Unlike contracts negotiated in the business world involving strangers who deal at arm's length, a premarital agreement is a contract between two individuals presumably engaged in a relationship of mutual trust and confidence. Given the couple's special relationship, courts

Fiduciary
a person who owes another a duty of good faith, trust, loyalty, and candor

Procedural fairness
fairness in the negotiation and execution of an agreement

Substantive fairness
fairness in the specific terms of an agreement

Consideration
a bargained-for exchange or mutual promise underlying the formation of a contract

often impose additional requirements and a higher standard of care on the parties, whom the courts view as having a *fiduciary* duty to one another, a special duty of fairness in dealing.

Although states vary with respect to specific requirements for validity, generally a premarital agreement must satisfy the following three requirements:

1. the basic requirements applicable to all contracts
2. the requirement of *procedural fairness,* meaning fairness in the negotiation and execution of the agreement
3. the requirement of *substantive fairness,* which means fairness in the actual terms of the agreement

The Basic Requirements Applicable to All Contracts

1. There must be an offer and acceptance (generally evidenced by the parties' signatures on the agreement).
2. The parties must have the capacity to contract in terms of age and mental competence (although a failure to understand the legal effect of the terms of the agreement will not necessarily render it invalid).
3. The subject matter of the contract must not be illegal (i.e., the parties cannot agree to commit an illegal act).
4. The contract must be supported by *consideration,* a bargained-for exchange of something of value (usually the mutual promise to marry in the case of premarital agreements, although courts may look for additional consideration when one party appears to gain everything and give up nothing).

The Requirement of Procedural Fairness

The focus of procedural fairness is on fairness during the negotiation and execution of the agreement. In assessing procedural fairness, the courts usually will look at the surrounding circumstances to answer such questions as the following:

- Was each party represented by independent counsel?
- Was there adequate disclosure by each of the parties of the nature and value of their assets and liabilities?
- Was there sufficient time to discuss, negotiate, and reflect on the agreement prior to execution?
- Was there any fraud, duress, or undue influence in the negotiation or execution of the agreement?

Was each party represented by independent counsel? Even though the parties are generally not antagonistic as they look forward to their forthcoming marriage, they do have "adverse" interests. Each of them is being asked to waive or vary certain rights to which they would otherwise be entitled upon divorce, separation, or death. For example, a husband residing in a community property state such as California, Arizona, Texas, or Idaho has a right to 50% of his spouse's earnings from the date of marriage. If a man is going to enter a premarital agreement in one of those states, he needs to understand how his rights and responsibilities under state law may be altered by that agreement. He should have a reasonable opportunity to consult with independent counsel of his own choosing. This is an especially important consideration when the parties are of unequal bargaining power, such as when one party is much more highly educated and financially sophisticated than the other. (See Paralegal Application 2.1.)

PARALEGAL APPLICATION **2.1**

REPRESENTATION BY INDEPENDENT COUNSEL

It is difficult, if not impossible, for one attorney to represent the interests of both parties to a premarital agreement. The conflict of interest inherent in such a multiple representation leaves the attorney open to allegations of ethical misconduct. In an effort to protect against such a result, the following steps may be taken:

1. If one party declines to seek counsel, it is wise for the attorney representing the other party to confirm in writing to both parties which of them he or she represents and to strongly advise and explain why it is important that the other party seek independent counsel. This should be done in the best interests of the client *and* the attorney. The paralegal may be asked to draft such a letter.

2. Many agreements now contain statements to be signed by counsel and/or by the parties under oath confirming that each has been instructed to seek legal counsel to advise them of their respective statutory rights in the property of the other and the effect that execution of the agreement will have on those rights. The paralegal should keep this option in mind when assisting in the drafting of an agreement, particularly one involving an unrepresented party.

3. In some states, the prohibitions against multiple representation require that the non-represented individual provide a written statement acknowledging the fact that the sole attorney is not protecting his or her interests. This requirement affords additional protection against a later malpractice claim for the attorney representing the other party.

Was there adequate disclosure by each of the parties of the nature and value of their assets and liabilities? Virtually all states require some degree of financial disclosure but vary with respect to how much is necessary. Some states require full disclosure, while others provide that a general picture of one's financial worth is enough. Many states allow a party to waive his or her right to seek or receive disclosure. Ideally financial disclosure should accurately and adequately reveal a party's assets, liabilities, and net worth to protect against later claims of fraud or misrepresentation. The preferred form of disclosure is a separate schedule of income, assets, and liabilities for each of the parties that is referenced in the body of the agreement and appended as an exhibit. Completed financial affidavits, tax returns, and other documents such as deeds and appraisals may also be attached. The paralegal is often involved in the collection, review, and/or preparation of these materials.

In assessing adequacy of disclosure, a court is likely to ask: Given the surrounding circumstances, did each party have, or should they have had, sufficient knowledge of the other's worth such that each of them could make an informed decision with respect to the terms of the agreement? Generally, there is no "*meeting of the minds*" with respect to the contract if one party was provided inadequate information regarding the other's assets and the value of the rights waived.

Meeting of the minds
a shared understanding with respect to the terms and conditions of a contract

Was there sufficient time to discuss, negotiate, and reflect on the agreement prior to execution? Although the time period between execution of the agreement and the marriage ceremony is not necessarily determinative, it is a factor the courts will consider in evaluating the validity of an agreement. The best advice is to allow reasonable time for negotiation and review. Some states automatically invalidate any premarital agreement that is signed on the day of the wedding. In general, the longer the time period (within limits) between when a party was presented with the agreement and when it was executed, the greater the likelihood the execution will be deemed voluntary, but the states go both ways. In a 1991 case in Alabama, a court held that a premarital agreement was valid despite the husband's threat to call off the wedding if the wife did not sign the agreement.[8] An Ohio court took the opposite position in a 1994 case and held "…the presentation of an agreement a very short time before the wedding ceremony will create a presumption of overreaching or coercion…the postponement of the wedding would cause significant hardship, embarrassment or emotional stress."[9]

Generally, timing will be considered in the context of the nature, scope, and complexity of the agreement. A simple agreement the parties discussed for months addressing one bank account of modest value may well be considered valid even if presented for review and signature on the wedding eve. On the other hand, a complex agreement covering millions of dollars of diverse assets between a party with significant bargaining power and an individual with little power, few assets, and much to lose warrants ample time for review and deliberation with the assistance of competent, independent counsel. Although many courts will consider whether each of the parties had the background, experience, and time necessary to evaluate options and the consequences of choices to be made, there is not always a requirement that a party actually understand the legal effect of the terms of the agreement.[10] **Ignorantia legis non excusat**! (See Case 2.2 later in this chapter.)

Ignorantia legis non excusat
Ignorance of the law is not an excuse

Was there any fraud, duress, or undue influence in the negotiation or execution of the agreement? Because the parties to a premarital agreement are involved in a special, confidential relationship with each other, they tend to be more vulnerable making agreements than strangers would be negotiating in the business world. They may be eager to please each other. One partner may dominate and perhaps even abuse the other emotionally or physically. One of the parties may have limited English skills and/or may rely on the other, blindly trusting that individual's superior knowledge and skill. Ideally, the parties should be equals in the process.

One of the ways in which some attorneys try to protect against a later claim that an agreement was executed under undue influence or duress is to have the parties and their respective attorneys all present at the execution and to videotape the event. A paralegal may be asked to schedule this taping and should be certain the necessary equipment is available and in good working order. A series of questions such as the following can be asked of the parties on this occasion:

1. Have you had an opportunity to review the agreement?
2. Have you had an opportunity to consult with counsel of your own choosing regarding the agreement?
3. Do you understand its terms?
4. Are you satisfied with those terms?
5. Have you disclosed all of your assets and liabilities and is a summary of them attached to the agreement?
6. What other documents are attached to the agreement?
7. Have you had an opportunity to review and ask questions about the attached documents?
8. Has anyone made any promises to you other than what is contained in the agreement?
9. Do you understand that this is the whole agreement and that no promises made outside of the agreement will be enforced?
10. Are you presently under the influence of any drug or condition that might impair your ability to understand what you are signing?
11. Do you have any questions?
12. Are you prepared to sign the agreement at this time?

PARALEGAL APPLICATION 2.2

ELDERLY CLIENTS

Agreements involving elderly clients or other clients whose competency may be questioned require special consideration. Many attorneys require elderly clients to obtain an *Affidavit of Competency* from a physician prior to execution of legal documents such as wills, powers of attorney, or premarital agreements to help protect against later claims that the documents were executed under undue influence. Paralegals may be asked to work with clients to facilitate this task.

Affidavit of Competency
an affidavit from a physician that an individual is competent to perform a particular act

The Requirement of Substantive Fairness

Substantive fairness refers to fairness in the actual terms of the agreement. A few states require the agreement to be fair to both parties. Some take the position that people are free to make "bad bargains," but most courts will not enforce an agreement if its terms are so unfair to one of the parties that they "shock the conscience of the court." Generally, the scope of the inquiry with respect to substantive fairness is whether the terms of the agreement are fair and not *unconscionable.* Under normal contract review, (U.C.C. §2–302), unconscionability is determined at the time of execution. States vary with respect to whether the determination of fairness is made only as of the date of execution or also at the time of performance.

Unconscionable
so substantially unfair in terms or result as to shock the conscience

Substantive Fairness at the Time of Execution.   Fairness at the time of execution involves a review of the agreement as written, and the court will consider such matters as the following:

> **Is the division of property** *per se* **unfair or unconscionable at the time of execution?** Given that the purpose of a premarital agreement is to allow the parties to alter the usual division of property at divorce and/or death, it is likely that the agreement will result in an unequal division of property. The court will consider fairness under the parties' circumstances. An agreement that calls for one party to receive everything while the other receives nothing and will end up a public charge on welfare is likely to be scrutinized closely and not enforced.
>
> **Is an agreement to waive alimony or spousal support fair at the time of execution?** An agreement that limits or waives spousal support is likely to be deemed valid if it is entered into freely, with knowledge of the rights waived, after adequate disclosure by both parties, and without undue influence. This is especially likely to be the case if the *waiver* is made by a party with ample assets at the time the agreement is signed. A waiver providing for the allowance of alimony under certain extreme and unforeseen circumstances (serious illness, etc.) or a waiver that is effective only if the marriage lasts less than a certain number of years is likely to be enforceable. Increasingly, agreements provide that the amount of alimony to be received, if any, will be based on the length of the marriage.

Waiver
the giving up of a right or privilege

Substantive Fairness at the Time of Performance.   A consideration of fairness at the time of performance (upon divorce or death) allows a court to consider whether terms that were fair at the time of execution are still fair at the time of enforcement. Generally the focus is on whether, due to unforeseen circumstances, an agreement that was once fair and reasonable has become so unfair that its enforcement would be unconscionable. There is no precise definition of "unconscionable" that binds all courts. Rather the assessment is made on a case-by-case basis. A New Hampshire court has described unconscionability in terms of "circumstances so changed since execution that enforcement would shock the conscience of the court," and "changed circumstances so far beyond the contemplation of the parties at the time of execution that enforcement would work an unconscionable hardship."[11]

PREPARATION FOR DRAFTING A PREMARITAL AGREEMENT

Paralegal Application 2.3 identifies several of the tasks that should be performed prior to the actual drafting of a premarital agreement.

Paralegal Practice Tip
Parties in both common law and community property jurisdictions may execute valid premarital agreements.

Paralegal Practice Tip
Clients often ask paralegals questions concerning the law as it applies to their cases. Even if the paralegal knows the answer, he or she must resist the temptation to engage in the unauthorized practice of law by responding with legal advice or analysis. The safest response is to indicate that he or she will bring the question to the attention of the attorney and get back to the client with a response. Many firms prepare in-house publications covering "most frequently asked questions" on a variety of topics or obtain them from professional organizations, such as the American Bar Association. The availability of such publications allows the paralegal to avoid an ethical problem and yet meet the client's need by giving him or her the handout and saying, "Perhaps this material will be helpful in answering your question."

PARALEGAL APPLICATION **2.3**

IN ANTICIPATION OF AN AGREEMENT—TASKS FOR THE ATTORNEY AND THE PARALEGAL

- The attorney should advise the client of the basic law governing rights and responsibilities upon separation, divorce, annulment, or death.

- The attorney should advise the client of the law regarding premarital agreements and their enforceability.

- The attorney should discuss the importance of independent representation for the prospective spouses.

- The attorney should learn what the client's motivations and goals are so that a decision can be made as to whether or not a premarital agreement is the most appropriate means for accomplishing the client's objectives. This may involve an assessment of any federal income tax, gift tax, and estate tax consequences of various options.

- Necessary background information and copies of documents need to be gathered including the following, a task often accomplished by or at least with the assistance of the paralegal:

  - the names, addresses, ages, and social security numbers of the parties
  - the date of the intended marriage and the flexibility with respect to that date
  - information regarding prior marriages and children/grandchildren of both parties
  - information regarding all forms of income and assets of the parties. A threshold value may be set for assets that should be identified, e.g., any property valued at over $5,000 or $25,000 based on the size of the parties' estates. A paralegal or the attorney will often work with the client to be certain that all kinds of assets of value are included (collections, stock portfolios, antiques, etc.).
  - copies of potentially relevant documents, including, for example, trusts, deeds, retirement plans, insurance policies, and appraisals of real estate, artwork, jewelry, and the like
  - information regarding debts/liabilities of each of the parties
  - information about any unique and/or foreseeable circumstances (such as one party already having been diagnosed with a debilitating or terminal disease or special needs of any children of a party, such as severe physical or mental impairments)

- The paralegal should confirm current requirements for premarital agreements in the state of execution, such as whether the agreement must be witnessed, notarized, and recorded.

WHAT KINDS OF PROVISIONS DOES A PREMARITAL AGREEMENT CONTAIN?

Each premarital agreement is unique because it reflects the intentions of two specific people, each with their own goals and needs. However, there are some provisions that are present in virtually all premarital agreements:

1. A preamble (introductory segment) that identifies the parties and describes their intentions
2. Schedules of each party's assets and liabilities, which may include anticipated gifts and inheritances that are reasonably certain and of known value
3. A definition of "separate property" and a description of how each party's "separate property" and its appreciation and proceeds, if sold, will be treated in the event of death or divorce
4. A definition of marital or "joint property" and a description of how marital property of various kinds (real estate, jewelry, other personal property) will be treated and what role, if any, contribution will play
5. A statement of the rights each party will have to alimony or spousal support if the marriage ends in a legal separation or divorce, or a waiver of those rights
6. A provision relating to death benefits or waivers thereof

The Uniform Premarital Agreement Act (UPAA) provides that the parties may also contract with respect to personal rights and obligations during their marriage, provided the terms do not violate public policy or existing statutes. The parties are generally free to contract, and may want to include provisions relating to several aspects of their life together. One or more of these terms may taint the entire agreement and render it void and unenforceable. An attorney may want to confirm with the client in writing that there is no guarantee that a particular provision will be enforced by the courts. Paralegal Application 2.4 identifies some potentially problematic terms.

PARALEGAL APPLICATION **2.4**

POTENTIAL RED FLAGS

- The parties cannot agree to engage in criminal activity.

- The parties may include provisions relating to child custody and support but they cannot bargain away the rights of third persons (their children). Such provisions will be subject to approval by the court that retains jurisdiction over child-related issues. An agreement that children from a party's prior marriage may not live with the parties may be held unenforceable as a violation of public policy and not in the best interests of the children.

- Terms that tread on constitutional rights may not be enforceable, such as:

  - An agreement to raise children in a particular religion may be viewed as violating a party's (or a child's) right to freedom of religion,[12] although a court may enforce a provision that a party be required to participate cooperatively in obtaining a religious separation or annulment.[13] In some countries where the civil law is based on the teachings of Islam, agreements contain both religious and secular provisions. If a party seeks enforcement of the agree-

continued

ment at the time of a divorce action in the United States, the court may make an effort to separate out provisions that are secular and enforceable and those that are religious in nature and not enforceable.

- An agreement to work or render certain services may be deemed a form of involuntary servitude if enforced by the court.

- Terms that invade a "right to privacy" are unlikely to be enforced, such as:

  - A promise to perform certain sexual acts or to engage in sexual relations according to a particular schedule.[14]

  - A promise to use contraception or to not have an abortion.

  - A promise to not have children.[15]

- Courts may not enforce a promise to prosecute or not prosecute a divorce action.

- Certain "spousal" waivers of retirement benefits may not be valid and enforceable if made prior to marriage under the requirements of the Employee Retirement Income Security Act (ERISA) and the Retirement Equity Act (REA) (See 29 U.S.C. Section 1055.)[16]

EXHIBIT 2.1 Sample Premarital Agreement

PREMARITAL AGREEMENT
PREAMBLE

THIS AGREEMENT, is made this _____ day of _____ , 2008, by and between _____Name of prospective spouse A_____ of _____address,_____, _____("first name")_____ and _____Name of prospective spouse B_____ of _____address_____ , _____("first name"),_____ collectively referred to as "the parties."

Drafting Tip

The preamble establishes the identity of the parties. Some practitioners include social security numbers, a step that can be helpful if a party later needs to be located. Others do not include them in an effort to prevent identity theft as premarital agreements eventually may become public documents if recorded in Registries of Deeds or as part of the pleadings in a divorce action or estate administration.

RECITALS

WHEREAS,

A. The parties plan to be married in _____city, state_____ on or about _____date_____ , 2008. Neither of the parties has been married previously.

Drafting Tip

Reference should be made in this part of the agreement to any prior marriages and existing children or grandchildren of either or both of the parties, if applicable.

B. Each recognizes that the other is gainfully employed and possesses property and assets independently acquired prior to their intended marriage such that each is able to provide for his or her own individual needs. Each desires to enter this agreement realizing that either or both of the parties' financial, health, or other circumstances may change substantially in the future.

continued

Drafting Tip
Paragraph B lays the basis for a determination that the agreement is fair at the time of execution. It also makes clear that the parties intend their agreement to take effect with full knowledge of the uncertainties of life such as early retirement, fluctuations in income, health problems, or pursuit of a new career.

> C. The parties intend by this Agreement to define and fix their respective rights and obligations to each other with regard to spousal support and to any property now owned or hereafter acquired before or after the date of their marriage, in the event of the termination of their marriage by death or legal process.

Drafting Tip
Paragraph C addresses the basic purpose of the agreement.

> D. A owns certain property, both real and personal, as listed on Exhibit 1 attached hereto and incorporated herein, the nature and approximate value of which has been fully disclosed to B prior to execution of this Agreement. Also listed on Exhibit 1 and previously disclosed to B is A's indebtedness exclusive of his personal expenses.

> E. B owns certain property, both real and personal, as listed on Exhibit 2 attached hereto and incorporated herein, the nature and approximate value of which has been fully disclosed to A prior to execution of this Agreement. Also listed on Exhibit 2 and previously disclosed to A is B's indebtedness exclusive of her personal expenses.

Drafting Tip
Paragraphs D and E and the Schedules that will be attached to the agreement as Exhibit 1 and 2 address the requirement of disclosure of assets and liabilities. Some agreements provide that these schedules will be updated on a periodic basis without affecting the nature, validity, or effect of the underlying agreement.

Drafting Tip
Sometimes the agreement will include a paragraph that provides that disclosures of property will be kept confidential absent consent or legal necessity. This is particularly appropriate when a party's business interests are listed and he or she would be disadvantaged if a competitor were aware of the information.

Drafting Tip
Other related exhibits may also be attached such as copies of trusts, tax returns, appraisals, etc.

> F. The parties acknowledge that each has had an adequate opportunity to negotiate, review, and consider the terms of this Agreement prior to execution; that each has been advised by independent counsel of his or her individual choice as to their rights as a spouse under the law and the legal effect of the Agreement on those rights; that each believes the provisions of the Agreement are fair, just, and reasonable; that each understands, assents to, and intends to be bound by its provisions; and that each enters the Agreement freely, voluntarily, and without any duress, undue influence, or illegal consideration.

Drafting Tip
Paragraph F addresses procedural fairness in the negotiation and execution of the agreement including the requirement that it be freely and voluntarily executed. The reference to counsel of individual choice makes clear that each party chose and retained his or her own independent attorney and not one chosen by the other party. The content presumes that counsel has described the state's approach to allocation of property upon divorce and death so each party appreciates what they are gaining and/or giving up in the agreement.

continued

G.   This Agreement shall become effective only upon the marriage of the parties within a period of one (1) year from the date hereof, and, if such marriage is not solemnized within said period, then this Agreement shall be null and void.

Drafting Tip

The one-year time frame is intended to protect against such a long period passing that the nature of the assets and liabilities of the parties may have changed in some significant manner.

NOW THEREFORE, in consideration of the mutual promises and covenants set forth herein, the parties mutually agree as follows:

Drafting Tip

This paragraph identifies the consideration that supports the agreement.

AGREEMENTS

1.   **Definition of Separate Property**

For purposes of this Agreement, "separate property" shall be defined as:

a. all assets in which each presently has an interest exclusive of the other as shown on the Schedules contained in Exhibit 1 and 2;

b. any inheritances, gifts, bequests, or devises received by either of them after the date of the parties' marriage;

c. all appreciation, reinvestments, and proceeds of sale or redemption of any of the above property after the date of the parties' marriage;

d. any property designated as separate property by both parties in writing after the date of their marriage; and

e. any income earned by either party during the marriage including salaries and bonuses.

Drafting Tip

"Separate property" must be carefully defined because each party is giving up an interest he or she might otherwise have in that property. The definition of separate property provided here is broad. For example, some agreements do not designate income earned during the marriage as separate property.

Drafting Tip

This definition does not include as separate property retirement benefits (pension, profit sharing, or deferred compensation, etc.) because potential rights in certain retirement plans cannot be waived by a non-spouse under ERISA. However, the agreement could include a provision that the other party will agree to execute a waiver after an appropriate period post marriage.

Drafting Tip

Sometimes the agreement will specify whether ownership of property will be exclusively determined by title or whether one party's contributions (financial or nonfinancial) to appreciation in the value of the other party's property will be considered in some manner. The agreement may also address the effect of commingling of assets and income or future increases in the value of separate property. For example, what happens if the parties purchase a boat together and each contributes to its purchase and maintenance but not equally?

---

2.   **Separate Property During Marriage**

Each party agrees to keep and retain the sole ownership and control of any property held as his or her separate property as herein defined without interference from the other and in the same manner as if the marriage had not occurred.

continued

Drafting Tip

Given the broad definition of separate property in this agreement, each party may be in a position to transfer significant assets by will, trust, gift, or otherwise to children from a prior marriage, other parties or charities, or the spouse if he or she chooses to do so.

3. **Separate Obligations of the Parties**

Obligations of a party incurred prior to the marriage shall remain the separate obligations of that party. The other party shall not be liable for those obligations, and shall be indemnified and held harmless from them by the responsible party. Such existing obligations shall be paid from the separate property of the responsible party.

Drafting Tip

It is important to address liabilities as well as assets in premarital agreements. This provision could be expanded to address liabilities incurred during marriage by either or both of the parties.

4. **Definition of Marital Property**

For purposes of this Agreement, with the exception of either party's separate property as herein defined, marital property ("Marital Property") shall be defined as all property accumulated by the parties during the marriage until the date of the death of either party or the date on which any legal action for separation, annulment, or divorce is commenced. Marital property shall also include any property designated as marital property by both parties in writing after the date of the marriage.

Drafting Tip

This paragraph sets the date of the filing of an action as a key date. Other options might be the date of separation, the date of divorce, etc.

Drafting Tip

In the case of annulment, if the marriage was *void ab initio* (invalid from the outset), no valid marriage will ever have occurred and the agreement will never have taken effect, absent a provision that addresses that circumstance.

Drafting Tip

Most often agreements address income and asset issues. At this point in the agreement, however, the parties may choose to include provisions regarding various aspects of their life together. Some agreements will address how various responsibilities will be managed during the marriage. How will bank accounts be set up? How will payment of bills be handled? Who will perform various household responsibilities? What are the parties' intentions with respect to childrearing roles and responsibilities? Provisions that pertain to medical, disability, life insurance, and long-term care expenses and insurance are especially appropriate in agreements involving elderly and/or disabled parties. Occasionally an agreement will address a behavioral issue such as excess spending, gambling, drinking, drug abuse, or infidelity during the marriage. Although such provisions may clarify expectations of the parties, some of them may be unenforceable.

5. **Marital Property Upon Termination of the Marriage**

a. In the event of termination of the marriage by legal proceedings, all assets then jointly owned by the parties as joint tenants, tenants by the entirety, or otherwise and not herein defined as separate property shall be divided equally between the parties.

Drafting Tip

This particular agreement provides for an equal rather than an equitable division of marital property regardless of the jurisdiction in which legal process is commenced and whether it is a community property or equitable distribution state. Parties to other agreements may elect different options.

continued

Drafting Tip

This agreement adopts what some call a "three-pot" approach to property: "his," "hers," and "theirs." Some parties will set forth further provisions requiring the transfer of an asset of one party to the other party or creation of an asset for the other party's benefit. This is particularly likely if the agreement contains a waiver of spousal support or estate claim and/or a party is giving up employment or an alimony payment from a prior spouse as a result of the upcoming marriage. Additional provisions might include, for example, a lump sum payment; a health, disability, or life insurance policy for the other's benefit; or transfer of an asset to the other party such as a vacation home. Such provisions are sometimes tied to the length of the marriage.

---

    b. In the event of the termination of the marriage by the death of a party, all assets defined as marital property shall become the sole property of the surviving party to the exclusion of the decedent's estate. The surviving party shall own said property subject to any liens, mortgages, or encumbrances secured by the property.

Drafting Tip

It is important to specify if the marital property will be transferred subject to encumbrances pursuant to the agreement (by contract rather than by inheritance). Otherwise, the decedent's estate would not receive the asset but would be liable for the decedent's share of the encumbrances.

---

    6. **Mutual Waivers**

      a. Waiver of Rights to Property: In the event of termination of the marriage by divorce or annulment, the parties agree not to assert any claim of any kind to the separate property of the other as herein defined. This waiver shall not apply to marital property.

      b. Waiver of Rights to Maintenance and Support: In the event of a legal separation, divorce, or annulment, the parties agree to waive any rights to spousal support or maintenance of any kind to which either might otherwise be entitled. The parties agree that this provision may be entered as a complete defense by either party in response to an action for alimony. The parties further agree that nothing herein shall be deemed a waiver of either party's right to claim child support for support of any minor children born to or legally adopted during their marriage.

Drafting Tip

The parties cannot waive rights or obligations pertaining to child custody and support that remain subject to the jurisdiction of the court.

Drafting Tip

This model sets forth a waiver of spousal support. If, in the alternative, it provided for support, the agreement could spell out a method for determining the appropriate amount. For example, the amount could be tied to a certain event (e.g., disability, reduction in income) or the length of the marriage (i.e., the longer the marriage, the greater the amount of support). Some agreements provide for reductions or elimination of support if there is proof of adultery by the recipient spouse during the marriage.

Drafting Tip

The enforceability of spousal support waivers in premarital agreements varies from state to state and they may not be effective if enforcement would bring about an "unconscionable" result.

---

      c. Waiver of Estate Claims: In the event of the death of one of the parties, each party hereby relinquishes and waives all rights, claims, and interests that he or she may have or acquire as surviving spouse, heir at law, or otherwise in the estate of the other party.

continued

Drafting Tip

Paragraphs a and b are waivers of statutory rights upon divorce, and c is a waiver of rights upon death. It is common to specifically list the scope of the rights being waived upon death of a party (the right to inherit under the state's laws of descent and distribution, the right to claim a distributive or forced share as a surviving spouse, the right to petition to serve as administrator of the deceased spouse's estate, etc.).

7. **Wills/Trusts**

Nothing contained herein shall preclude or prevent either party from freely executing a will or settling a trust that confers benefits on the other party, or from nominating the other party as executor or trustee, or from exercising any power of appointment in favor of the other party.

Drafting Tip

Generally, a premarital agreement is not a replacement for a will, although if the agreement is executed with all the formalities of a will, a party may assert that it serves as a will "substitute." Clients should consider their agreement and wills in tandem. Even though the parties may waive statutory rights in the agreement, they are still free to voluntarily make provisions for each other as is provided in this model.

8. **General Provisions**

a. Entire Agreement

The parties agree that this Agreement contains their entire understanding and that there have been no additional promises, representations, or agreements made to either party by the other, oral or written, except as set forth herein.

Drafting Tip

Under contract law, judges look to "the four corners" of the agreement (the "face" of the written instrument) to determine what the parties intended at the time the agreement was executed. Sometimes, however, if an agreement is ambiguous, the court will go outside the contract and hear testimony ("parol evidence") from witnesses, not to create terms but rather to clarify the parties' intentions with respect to specific existing terms.

Drafting Tip

A paralegal should maintain a complete file including successive drafts, revisions suggested by the other party, and written confirmations of telephone exchanges, etc. Even though an agreement may never be challenged, if it is, the contents of a complete file can be very valuable as forensic evidence for use in court.

b. Modification

This Agreement may be modified, amended, or rescinded at any time after the solemnization of the marriage, only by a subsequent written agreement between and signed by the parties.

Drafting Tip

This paragraph leaves the door open for the parties to alter or rescind their agreement at a later date if their circumstances alter. However, modification provisions should not be included in a jurisdiction where postmarital agreements are prohibited. In such jurisdictions, inclusion of a modification provision may cause rescission of the entire agreement.

c. Waiver of Breach or Default

No waiver of breach or default with respect to a provision of this Agreement shall be deemed a waiver of any subsequent breach or default.

continued

Drafting Tip

This provision means that if a party allows the other party to default on a particular obligation under the agreement, he or she is not waiving the right to object to a subsequent default on that or any other provision.

d. Binding Effect

This Agreement shall be binding on the parties hereto and their respective legal representatives, heirs, successors, and assigns.

Drafting Tip

The agreement binds the parties with respect to each other but is not necessarily binding on third parties such as creditors or bona fide purchasers of property without notice. To ensure that the agreement will be enforceable against a purchaser of a piece of real estate, for example, a copy of the agreement should be recorded in the appropriate Registry of Deeds. Some states have statutes that specifically address this issue.[17]

e. Severability

In the event any provision of this Agreement shall be held illegal, invalid, or otherwise unenforceable, such holding shall not invalidate or render unenforceable any other provisions hereof, and the offending provision shall be severed from this Agreement and be null and void and of no force and effect.

Drafting Tip

Severability clauses are common in most contracts. They are especially important in premarital agreements when a client insists on including a provision that is likely to be unenforceable (such as a term that the parties will have no children or must practice a particular religion).

f. Governing Law

This Agreement shall be governed, controlled, and interpreted under the laws of the state of _____.

Drafting Tip

Given that laws vary from state to state, this provision anticipates a possible "conflict of law" question. For example, the parties may agree that the law of Maryland will govern but they eventually divorce in California. According to basic choice of law principles, the California court will apply Maryland law in construing the agreement unless the result of doing so would violate strong public policy in California. This is a potentially important choice given the degree to which states vary in their approaches to dividing property upon divorce and to determining the validity of premarital agreements.[18]

Drafting Tip

Some agreements include a provision that sets out the steps to be taken in the event of a dispute regarding any terms of the agreement in addition to judicial relief (a party seeking to enforce a surviving agreement can sue for breach of contract and seek specific performance). It may include options such as mediation and arbitration.

Drafting Tip

The provisions in this last section of the sample premarital agreement are "boilerplate" to a considerable extent. **Boilerplate** is standard language commonly used in a particular kind of document. However, as with all documents, care must be taken to tailor even boilerplate to jurisdictional requirements and the facts of a case at hand.

Boilerplate
standard language commonly used in a particular kind of document and that usually does not require negotiation

continued

IN WITNESS WHEREOF, the parties have signed, sealed, and acknowledged this Agreement on the day and year indicated below.

Witness_____

Name of prospective spouse A_____

Date:_____

Witness_____

Name of prospective spouse B_____

Date:_____

Drafting Tip

Certifications by notaries, etc., should be provided in a form appropriate to the jurisdiction. It is important to verify and comply with applicable procedural rules, such as witness requirements and the like. Even if not required, each page of the agreement and any attached exhibits should be signed or initialed to protect against later claims that a particular provision was not included in the original agreement.

EXHIBIT 1

SCHEDULE OF ASSETS FOR <u>Prospective Spouse A.</u>

(abbreviated in length)

Assets	Fair Market Value	Adjustments	Net Value
<u>Real Estate</u>			
<u>(List) Personal Property</u>			
Bank accounts			
Stocks and securities			
Retirement funds			
Life insurance			
Antiques			
Jewelry			
Collections			
Vehicles including boats, etc.			
Other			
Total			

continued

Liabilities

(List)

   Total

   Net Worth

Date: _____

                                                 Signature of prospective spouse A

I hereby acknowledge that I have received and reviewed this schedule of assets and liabilities.

Date: _____

                                                 Signature of prospective spouse B

WHAT ARE THE TRENDS REGARDING ENFORCEABILITY OF PREMARITAL AGREEMENTS?

A premarital agreement may be deemed valid because it meets all of the technical jurisdictional requirements for such documents. If there is never a controversy surrounding the agreement and the parties simply abide by its provisions, enforceability does not become an issue. However, if challenged, the burden of proof of invalidity is on the party challenging enforcement of the agreement.

The Uniform Premarital Agreement Act's Position on Enforceability

Each state sets forth by statute and/or case law its own requirements for what constitutes a valid and enforceable agreement. Some states invest premarital agreements with a presumption of validity as long as certain requirements are satisfied.[19] Approximately half of the states have adopted the Uniform Premarital Agreement Act (UPAA) approved by the National Conference of Commissioners on Uniform State Laws in 1983. The goal of the UPAA is to create uniformity and increased enforceability of premarital agreements through ordinary contract principles. Even in states that have not enacted the UPAA, its provisions frequently reflect trends in the law and are often considered by the courts.

Under §6 of the UPAA, premarital agreements will not be enforced if:

. . . the party against whom enforcement is sought proves that:

a. [he or she] did not execute the agreement voluntarily; or
b. the agreement was unconscionable when it was executed and, before execution of the agreement, that party
    i. was not provided a fair and reasonable disclosure of the property or financial obligations of the other party,
    ii. did not voluntarily and expressly waive, in writing, any right to disclosure of the property or financial obligations of the other party beyond the disclosure provided, and
    iii. did not have, or reasonably could not have had, an adequate knowledge of the property and financial obligations of the other party.

In general, subject to §6, the UPAA favors enforcement of the terms of premarital agreements as long as they do not lead to an unconscionable result. That determination is one to be made by the court as a matter of law. However, the act states a specific position with respect to provisions designed to modify or eliminate spousal support. If enforcement would result in a party becoming eligible for public assistance upon divorce or separation, the act provides that a court may order the other party to provide support to the extent necessary to avoid that result.

Enforceability of Premarital Agreements in States That Have Not Adopted the UPAA

The "Traditional View"—The Fairness Approach.   After years of not enforcing premarital agreements that addressed rights upon divorce, following *Posner*, states have increasingly accepted premarital agreements on a case-by-case basis, focusing attention on whether an agreement at issue constituted a valid contract and was substantively and procedurally fair to the parties. This "traditional view" treats premarital agreements as contracts and as agreements between people who bear a special "fiduciary" relationship to one another and therefore holds them to a higher standard than contracts between strangers. It is essentially a fairness approach.

Some states that apply this approach look only to fairness considerations at the time of execution of the agreement. Other states have adopted a "*second look*" or "second glance" doctrine examining agreements to determine if they remain fair at the time of performance, i.e., divorce.

The Contemporary Approach—A Freedom to Contract Approach.   In more recent years, there has been a trend away from subjecting premarital agreements to a higher standard and toward treating them as basic contracts. Contract law protects both freedom to contract and expectations that the terms of an agreement will be met by each of the contracting parties. Under contract law, absent proof of fraud, misrepresentation, or duress, agreements will be enforced unless enforcement will bring about an "unconscionable" result. Absent such a result, parties are free to make hasty, unfair bargains against their own self-interest. A party cannot avoid performance of a contract simply because it seems unfair, unreasonable, or to his or her disadvantage. However, a court may elect to reform a portion of the agreement to limit the effects of an unforeseen hardship or provide some other equitable remedy such as imposition of a constructive trust over the property of one party for the benefit of a seriously disadvantaged or abused party.

The opinion in the Pennsylvania case of *Simeone v. Simeone* describes how and why this trend has evolved in response to broad societal changes. (See Case 2.2.) In *Simeone*, the wife appealed a lower court's decision upholding the validity of the premarital agreement that she and her husband had executed on the eve of their wedding in 1975. At the time, the wife was an unemployed twenty-three-year-old nurse. Her spouse was a thirty-nine-year-old neurosurgeon earning $90,000 a year with an additional $300,000 in assets. She signed the agreement without the advice of an attorney or knowing which legal rights she was giving up. The terms of the agreement limited her to support payments of $200 per week in the event of separation or divorce, up to a maximum of $25,000. When the premarital agreement was upheld and her petition for further alimony was denied by the Superior Court, she appealed to the Pennsylvania Supreme Court.

Second look doctrine
an approach to determining enforceability of premarital agreements adopted by some courts that involves examining the terms of a premarital agreement for fairness at the time of performance

CASE **2.2** *Simeone v. Simeone*, 525 Pa. 392, 581 A.2d 162 (1990)

FROM THE OPINION:

There is no longer validity in the implicit presumption that supplied the basis for…earlier decisions. Such decisions rested upon a belief that spouses are of unequal status and that women are not knowledgeable enough to understand the nature of contracts that they enter. Society has advanced, however, to the point where women are no longer regarded as the "weaker" party in marriage, or in society generally. Indeed, the stereotype that women serve as homemakers while men work as breadwinners is no longer viable. Quite often today both spouses are income earners. Nor is there validity in the presumption that women are uninformed, uneducated, and readily subjected to unfair advantage in marital agreements. Indeed, women nowadays often have substantial education, financial awareness, income, and assets.

Accordingly, the law has advanced to recognize the equal status of men and women in our society. . . . Paternalistic presumptions and protections that arose to shelter women from the inferiorities and incapacities that they were perceived as having in earlier times have, appropriately, been discarded. . . .

. . . Traditional principles of contract law provide perfectly adequate remedies where contracts are procured through fraud, misrepresentation, or duress. . . . Prenuptial agreements are contracts, and, as such, should be evaluated under the same criteria as are applicable to other types of contracts. . . . Absent fraud, misrepresentation, or duress, spouses should be bound by the terms of their agreements.

Contracting parties are normally bound by their agreements, without regard to whether the terms thereof were read and fully understood and irrespective of whether the agreements embodied reasonable or good bargains. . . . *Ignorant[i]a legis non excusat.*

Accordingly we find no merit in a contention raised by the appellant that the agreement should be declared void on the ground that she did not consult with independent legal counsel. To impose a *per se* requirement that parties entering a premarital agreement must obtain independent legal counsel would be contrary to traditional principles of contract law, and would constitute a paternalistic and unwarranted interference with the parties' freedom to enter contracts.

Further, the reasonableness of a prenuptial bargain is not a proper subject for judicial review. . . .

. . . If parties viewed an agreement as reasonable at the time of its inception, as evidenced by their having signed the agreement, they should be foreclosed from later trying to evade its terms by asserting that it was not in fact reasonable. . . .

Further, everyone who enters a long-term agreement knows that circumstances can change during its term, so that what initially appeared desirable might prove to be an unfavorable bargain. Such are the risks that contracting parties routinely assume. . . .

We are reluctant to interfere with the power of persons contemplating marriage to agree upon, and to act in reliance upon, what *they* regard as an acceptable distribution scheme for their property. A court should not ignore the parties' expressed intent by proceeding to determine whether a prenuptial agreement was, in the court's view, reasonable at the time of inception or at the time of divorce. . . .

. . . we do not depart from the longstanding principle that a full and fair disclosure of the financial positions of the parties is required. . . .

SIDEBAR

Read the full opinion in the *Simeone* case available on the companion website. After reading the opinion, what do you think the requirements should be in order for a premarital agreement to be valid and enforceable?

When working on a case that involves a premarital agreement, it is important to know what the current criteria for enforceability are in the applicable jurisdiction based on both statutes and case law. For example, in a "contract" approach jurisdiction, the party challenging validity of the agreement will have to show that the agreement did not satisfy the basic requirements of a contract, that the contract was the result of fraud or duress, or that a term was unconscionable in some fashion at the time of execution. In a "second look" fairness approach jurisdiction, courts will focus primarily on procedural fairness at the time of execution, and substantive fairness both at the time of execution and at performance. Knowing what has to be proved or defended against should guide the paralegal's information-gathering efforts. Paralegal Application 2.5 describes information-gathering needs in a "second look" jurisdiction.

In addition to the three kinds of requirements indicated earlier in this chapter, most contracts, including premarital agreements, must satisfy a state's ***Statute of Frauds,*** which specifies the kinds of contracts that must be in writing and signed in order to be enforced. A contract in consideration of marriage is one of the traditional Statute of Frauds exceptions to oral contract validity. It is important to determine whether the validity or enforcement of a premarital agreement at issue may be subject to an exception in the particular Statute of Frauds governing the case.[20]

Statute of Frauds
the requirement that certain types of contracts be in writing such as a contract that by its terms cannot be completed within a year or a contract for the sale of land

PARALEGAL APPLICATION 2.5

INFORMATION-GATHERING NEEDS IF A PREMARITAL AGREEMENT IS CHALLENGED IN A "SECOND LOOK" JURISDICTION—TASKS FOR A PARALEGAL

- Obtain a copy of the agreement and the file if available.

- Locate the state statute governing premarital agreements, if any, so it can be determined if its requirements were met.

- Research state case law on point.

- Research circumstances surrounding the drafting and execution of the agreement such as:

  Who suggested the agreement?

  Who drafted it?

  Was each party represented? How was counsel obtained and who paid for the representation?

  What was the timing of the drafting and execution?

  What financial disclosures were made and how complete and accurate were they?

  What were the parties' respective financial circumstances, education levels, and business backgrounds?

  Was there any history of threats or emotional or physical abuse prior to execution of the agreement?

  Was the execution taped?

- Identify potential witnesses with whom either party may have discussed the agreement, including attorneys, financial advisors, friends, family members, etc.

- Find out how circumstances have changed since the execution of the agreement. What are the current financial circumstances of each of the parties? Have children been born to the marriage? Has one of the parties developed a serious health problem?

- Recommend a discovery strategy, if warranted. Discovery methods for premarital agreement controversies are the same as for divorce: Interrogatories, Depositions, Requests for Admissions, Production of Documents, or Mental Examinations, and other informal methods such as interviews, examination of public records, etc.

PARALEGAL APPLICATION **2.6**

AN ENFORCEABLE AGREEMENT? WHAT DO YOU THINK?

THE FACTS

Joseph and Susan were married in March of 1990, when he was forty-seven and she was forty-one. They had known each other in high school, dated occasionally in the 1970s, and renewed their acquaintance in 1987. Joseph proposed marriage in 1989 on condition that Susan sign a premarital agreement, which she agreed to do. At the time of the marriage, she was living with her daughter from her first marriage in a two-bedroom house. She was working as a secretary earning $25,000 a year. She owned no real property and had few assets. On request of Susan's attorney, two weeks before the agreement was signed, Joseph disclosed assets indicating his net worth was between $108 and $133 million. Although she requested a significant share of those assets during negotiations, she eventually settled for an agreement providing that, in the event of divorce, she would receive the marital home free of encumbrances, yearly support of $35,000 until her death or remarriage with an annual cost-of-living increase, an automobile, and medical insurance until her death or remarriage. Both attorneys were present when Susan and Joseph executed the agreement and the signing was recorded. The videotape shows Joseph's attorney reciting the terms and the parties communicating their understanding and consent. They also acknowledged that they each had counsel of their own choice, exchanged financial disclosure, and understood what their rights would be in the absence of an agreement. (The wife testified at the time of the divorce that she did not want to sign and felt ill on that day, but the tape revealed no sign of distress, resistance, or unwillingness to sign.)

In March 1998, the husband filed for divorce. The trial court held that the agreement was invalid because it was not fair and reasonable at the time of execution or enforcement. The husband appealed.

SIDEBAR

How would this appeal most likely be decided under the traditional fairness approach? Why? How would it be decided under the freedom to contract approach applying an unconscionability standard? Why? How do you think it should be decided? What additional information would you like to have? To learn how the Massachusetts Supreme Judicial Court decided the case, go to the companion website and read *DeMatteo v. DeMatteo*, 436 Mass. 18, 762 N.E.2d 797 (2002).

PARALEGAL APPLICATION **2.7**

RELATIONSHIP BETWEEN A PREMARITAL AGREEMENT AND AN ACTION FOR DIVORCE

When a Premarital Agreement exists, the Divorce Complaint should put the court on notice of its existence and indicate whether the party filing for divorce seeks to have it enforced or challenges its validity on one or more grounds. The paralegal should keep this in mind when drafting a complaint.

The case *In re Marriage of Shaban*, 88 Cal. App. 4th 398, 105 Cal. Rptr. 2d 863 (2001), available on the companion website in the material related to Chapter 2, addresses the applicability of the statute of frauds to a premarital agreement executed in Egypt. The opinion also touches on:

- the nature of the document at issue as a premarital agreement
- the recognition of premarital agreements in California

- problems that arise when documents are written in a foreign language
- the admissibility of parol evidence to prove the validity of an agreement
- conflict of law issues between the law of Islam and the law of the State of California. (The court notes that the term "Islamic Law" is relatively uncertain, as there are at least four schools of interpretation of Islamic law.)

THE ROLE OF THE PARALEGAL IN A PREMARITAL AGREEMENT CASE

The role of a paralegal in a premarital agreement case primarily will depend on whether the case involves the negotiation and execution of an agreement, or the enforceability of an already existing agreement. The sample agreement and several of the paralegal applications provided in this chapter address some aspects of the paralegal's role at each of these stages. An experienced paralegal may perform the following tasks:

Tasks Common to Both Stages

- participate in meetings with the client as requested by the supervisor
- research the jurisdictional requirements for valid and enforceable premarital agreements
- help the client and the attorney gather necessary information and documents
- maintain communication with the client
- schedule meetings with the client, the other party and his or her attorney, and any other essential individuals (e.g., mediators, etc.)
- prepare related forms and correspondence (including fee agreements, confirmation of meetings, etc.)
- track/monitor progress on the case and ensure that required timelines are met

Negotiation and Execution of the Agreement

- prepare exhibits for use in negotiations
- draft successive versions of an agreement and related schedules and attachments based on instructions from the supervising attorney (Law offices customarily have a variety of premarital agreement "forms" available for reference in office files, form books, on disks, and/or online.)
- review proposed agreements from the other party for consistency with the client's position and agreed-upon terms based on information provided by the supervisor
- make arrangements for obtaining an affidavit of competency, if appropriate
- arrange for execution of the agreement

Enforcement of an Existing Agreement

- be certain that the client's Complaint for Divorce (or Answer) puts the court on notice as to the existence of the agreement and the client's position with respect to potential enforceability
- prepare related memoranda based on research as requested
- draft discovery materials such as interrogatories, requests for admissions, requests for production of documents, requests for physical or mental examinations, and proposed questions for depositions
- draft responses to discovery requests, working with the client and the supervising attorney
- assist with preparation for hearings or a trial on the merits including drafting pretrial memoranda for review, preparing exhibits, and arranging for service of subpoenas on potential witnesses, if needed
- help identify and prepare prospective witnesses

PARALEGAL APPLICATION 2.8

AN ALERT

This chapter began by noting that premarital agreements providing for rights upon divorce were unenforceable for generations. That has clearly changed and we now have new issues to consider. The highly controversial topic of same-sex marriage will no doubt be debated over the next decade on public policy grounds favoring a traditional definition of marriage as the legal union of one man and one woman. In a state that allows same-sex marriage, a premarital agreement between the parties may well be enforceable in that state at least with respect to matters governed by that state's law. Whether or not it will be enforceable in any other state remains to be seen.

CHAPTER **SUMMARY**

A premarital agreement is a contract executed by two individuals about to marry that takes effect upon their marriage. In it the parties establish for themselves their respective rights in the event the marriage terminates by legal process (divorce, legal separation, or annulment) and/or as a result of the death of one of the parties. Typically, the agreement will address financial issues of spousal support and property division, but it may also address nonfinancial matters related to the parties' expectations during the marriage.

Premarital agreements establishing the rights of spouses upon divorce are a relatively recent development. Their origins, evolution, and current trends are highlighted in pertinent case excerpts. In general, to be valid, a premarital agreement must satisfy the requirements for a valid contract (capacity to contract, offer and acceptance, consideration, and legal subject matter) as well as the requirements of agreements between individuals who bear a fiduciary relationship to one another: procedural fairness (fairness in negotiation and execution) and substantive fairness (fairness in its terms). The agreement must also satisfy the applicable Statute of Frauds.

Although agreements customarily contain some "boilerplate" or standard provisions, considerable care must be taken to tailor each agreement to the unique needs of the parties involved. The sample agreement provided in the chapter is very basic, and suggestions are offered with respect to potential variations based on the wishes of the parties involved. It includes features that one would expect to see in most agreements: recitations regarding representation by counsel, financial disclosure, and voluntariness of execution; definitions and dispositions of separate and marital property; a provision relating to spousal support; and a provision relating to benefits or rights upon death of a party.

Whether or not a particular agreement or specific provision within an otherwise valid agreement will be enforceable depends on the approach applied in a given jurisdiction based on its governing statutes and case law. Just over half of the states have adopted the Uniform Premarital Agreement Act (UPAA). The remaining states apply either a traditional fairness approach or the more contemporary freedom to contract approach. In assessing fairness, some states have adopted the "second look" doctrine, which calls for a consideration of fairness of the terms of an agreement at the time of performance as well as at the time of execution.

Throughout the chapter a number of tasks are identified that a supervisor might assign to a paralegal. Several paralegal applications and tips are also provided, which are designed to alert the paralegal to special issues related to the drafting, execution, and enforcement of premarital agreements.

KEY **TERMS**

Affidavit of Competency
Boilerplate
Cohabitation agreement
Collaborative law

Consideration
Fiduciary
Ignorantia legis non excusat
Mediation

Meeting of the minds
Per se invalid
Postmarital agreement (postmarital contract, postnuptial agreement)

Premarital agreement (premarital
   contract, antenuptial agreement)
Procedural fairness
Public policy

Second look doctrine
Separation agreement
Statute of Frauds
Substantive fairness

Unconscionable
Void
Waiver

REVIEW **QUESTIONS**

1. Describe the nature and purpose of a premarital agreement.

2. Identify reasons why an individual might want to have a premarital agreement.

3. Identify the requirements for a valid contract.

4. Define procedural fairness. What factors will a court consider in determining procedural fairness with respect to premarital agreements?

5. Define substantive fairness. What factors will a court consider in determining the substantive fairness of a premarital agreement?

6. Explain why one attorney should not represent both parties to a premarital agreement.

7. Identify the kinds of information that a client should be given by his or her attorney before entering a premarital agreement.

8. Describe the kinds of information that should be gathered in preparation for the drafting of a premarital agreement.

9. Identify the most commonly included provisions of a premarital agreement.

10. Identify some of the kinds of terms individuals may want to include in a premarital agreement that may not be enforceable and explain why. In this context, explain the importance of a severability clause in an agreement.

11. Describe the historical trend from non-enforceability to enforceability of premarital agreements. In this context, indicate the significance of the *Posner* case.

12. Explain the difference between a freedom to contract and a fairness approach to enforcement. In this context, what is the significance of the *Simeone* case?

13. What is the "second glance" or "second look" doctrine?

14. What is the position of the Uniform Premarital Agreement Act on enforceability of agreements?

FOCUS ON **THE JOB**

THE FACTS

Richard Marshall is 72 years old. He is a retired engineer who had a very successful career in the telecommunications industry. He has been married three times and is paying alimony to two of his three prior wives. The third wife is independently wealthy and is paying him alimony of $2,000 per month, which will cease if and when he marries again. He has a vacation home on the New Jersey shore; a pension from AT&T; a 48-foot world-class cruising yacht valued at approximately $1 million; a 401(K) that since his retirement, has grown to a value of $1.5 million; a collection of antique BMW motorcycles with a book value of approximately $100,000; and an investment portfolio presently valued at $700,000. He calls this account his "toy," and with it he makes aggressive and highly speculative investments. In addition, he has several very valuable paintings he inherited from his grandmother that are on display in a local museum of art. He has never had them appraised but believes they are worth well over a million dollars. He doesn't see any reason to mention them to his bride-to-be because he never intends to retrieve them from the museum. His five much-loved children are now all adults with families of their own. He has seven grandchildren with whom he visits

regularly. His father is deceased but his mother is still alive and in her nineties. She has all her faculties but has some physical limitations. He wants her to live with him and his fiancée, Elaine, when they are married, and expects that the two of them will be his mother's primary caretakers until her death.

Richard's "one true love," Elaine Cannon, is 32 years old. Her only husband died three years ago. They had three children, who are aged 6, 9, and 11. The children are presently living with her in her New York condominium valued at $1.5 million. She also has a vacation home in Bar Harbor, Maine which she inherited from her husband. It had been in his family for years, and she lets several of his relatives continue to use the cabin (assessed at $225,000), as they always had before her husband's death. She has a successful career as a television news broadcaster, but Richard wants her to give up her career and be a stay-at-home mom to her three children. He loves and enjoys her children but wants her to promise not to have any more. She presently earns about $500,000 a year, and the rest of her assets are in a trust fund for the benefit of her children. The fund is substantial, given her contributions and those flowing from her late husband's estate. She has always worked hard and is looking forward to leaving her job and "just being a mom." She is very happy and feels fortunate to have found Richard. She believes he will be a wonderful husband. Given what she is giving up in terms of her career, Richard wants to be responsible for paying all of the expenses related to their life together (housing, food, utilities, vacations, etc.) but expects her to be responsible for expenses relating to her children.

The parties intend to marry in about three months. Richard has asked Elaine to execute a premarital agreement. She says that whatever he wants is fine with her, and she sees no need to go to the expense of hiring an attorney to represent her. She believes that she is sufficiently educated and informed to make her own decisions. She is perfectly willing to share her financial information with Richard and trusts him implicitly. She is very excited about the wedding and looks forward to a large celebration with over 200 family and friends. She is aware that her future husband does not want any more children but suspects she may be one-month pregnant. She is quite sure that when

he finds out, he will be just as excited as she is about their "love child."

THE ASSIGNMENT

Working in teams of three—one person playing the role of Richard, one the role of Elaine, and the third the role of Richard's attorney, Juliana Wilson—draft a premarital agreement with attached schedules that is tailored to the above fact pattern. Assign local addresses within your state to each of the parties and counsel. Your draft should reflect what you have learned from reading this chapter class discussion, and any additional research you may have done or are required by your instructor to do. You should begin by determining the requirements for a valid premarital agreement in your jurisdiction and locating a variety of models in form books and/or online. When doing the latter, you will likely learn whether your state is a community property or an equitable division state and whether or not it has adopted the Uniform Premarital Agreement Act.

FOCUS ON **ETHICS**

As indicated in the above fact pattern, Elaine does not believe she needs to have another attorney advise her with respect to the negotiation and execution of the proposed premarital agreement. She has told both Richard and his attorney, Juliana Wilson, how she feels and that she trusts both of them to be fair with her. Assume that you are the paralegal for Attorney Wilson. Draft a letter to Elaine for your supervisor's review and signature in which you explain why it is strongly advised that she be represented by independent counsel and what the potential risks are of

failing to do so. Indicate, if she insists on not obtaining counsel, what steps, if any, need to be taken in an effort to protect your client against a later allegation that the agreement was unfair in its terms or execution or that it was the product of fraud or duress, etc. The tone of the letter needs to be firm but also reflect sensitivity to the situation—you have two people who care for each other and want to marry and, at the same time, you are talking about an agreement that would govern their rights upon divorce and death!

FOCUS ON **CASE LAW**

Locate the most recently decided case in the state where you live that governs the issue of the enforceability (or non-enforceability) of a premarital agreement in whole or in part and the standard to be applied in making that

determination. Read the case and then brief it using a format prescribed by your instructor or, if none, the format available on the companion website for this text in the material related to Chapter 1.

FOCUS ON **STATE LAW AND PROCEDURE**

Assume that Elaine in the above comprehensive fact pattern does not tell Richard about their "love child" until two months after their marriage. Richard is so upset by this turn of events that he promptly files for divorce and seeks to enforce the parties' premarital agreement, which provides that, if the parties are married for less than two years, Elaine receives only what she brought into the marriage. Elaine does

not want the agreement enforced and wants a substantial spousal support award for a six-year period, until the baby enters elementary school and she returns to work. She says that Richard should not be allowed to benefit from the agreement because he never told her about the paintings, and she only recently found out about them by accident at a museum fundraiser. She retains Attorney Olga Carroll to represent her in this matter. Assume that you are Attorney Carroll's paralegal and that she has asked you to research the enforceability of the agreement at issue in your state. Prepare a memorandum describing the results of your research and your conclusion with respect to Elaine's chances of prevailing. Your report should be in a basic internal memo format such as the following:

MEMORANDUM

To: Olga Carroll, Esq.

From: *Your Name, Paralegal*

File Reference: *Name of client followed by case caption with a docket number (to be provided by your instructor)*

Re: *Enforceability of Premarital Agreement*

Date:

Description of Issue/Assignment: *What is it that you have been asked to do?*

Results of Research: *What did you learn about the enforceability of premarital agreements in your state?*

Application to the Case: *Apply the law (case and statutory) to the facts of the case at issue.*

Conclusion: *What is the likelihood that Elaine will prevail with respect to the enforceability of the premarital agreement?*

FOCUS ON **TECHNOLOGY**

WEBSITES OF INTEREST

http://www.divorcenet.com

This site contains information on a number of family law topics. Search by topic and/or by state.

http://www.divorcesource.com

Click on divorce laws and then search by topic and/or state. Links are provided to both articles and sites for cases. A considerable amount of the material cannot be viewed without a subscription (available at a modest fee).

http://www.findlaw.com

This site contains a wide range of information about premarital agreements.

http://www.jlaw.com

The focus of this site is on Jewish law in a variety of topical areas. An example of a premarital agreement is provided (without any guarantee as to enforceability).

http://www.legalforms.com

This is an example of a site where individuals can purchase premarital agreement packages. There is no guarantee that the material provided satisfies particular states' current requirements, although the packages are promoted as state-by-state products.

ASSIGNMENTS

1. Using online resources, determine whether or not your state has adopted the Uniform Premarital Agreement Act.

2. Assume that the firm where you are employed wants to develop a "common question and answers" information/fact sheet regarding premarital agreements. Search the Web for ideas on what should be included in such a sheet. Start with *http://www.findlaw.com*.

chapter **three**
MARRIAGE

IN THIS CHAPTER YOU WILL LEARN

- How the definition of marriage is evolving

- What the different types of marriage are

- How the marital roles of men and women have changed

- Whether there is any remedy for a broken engagement

- Whether citizens have a constitutionally protected right to marry

- How the states regulate and restrict the right to marry

- What the requirements are for a valid ceremonial marriage

- What the requirements are for a valid common law marriage

- What rights, benefits, and obligations flow from marriage

- How the issue of same-sex marriage is being addressed by the courts and state legislatures

- What principles guide the way the federal government and individual states address differences in laws governing marriage

Mary, a 15-year-old girl who lives in Texas, has fallen madly in love with her first cousin, Marty, a 23-year-old professional bull rider in the rodeo circuit who lives in Massachusetts. She has hatched a plan for them to wed and live happily ever after in Colorado. Marty is not so sure they can "get away with it."

MARRIAGE—DEFINITIONS AND HISTORICAL PERSPECTIVE

Definitions

In 1810, the Massachusetts Supreme Judicial Court described marriage as follows:

> Marriage is . . . a civil contract, founded in the social nature of man, and intended to regulate, chasten, and refine, the intercourse between the sexes; and to multiply, preserve, and improve the species. It is an engagement, by which a single man and a single woman, of sufficient discretion, take each other as husband and wife. From the nature of the contract, it exists during the lives of the two parties, unless dissolved for causes which defeat the object of marriage. . . .[1]

In 2003, the Massachusetts high court, in a sharply divided decision, defined marriage as "the voluntary union of two persons as spouses, to the exclusion of all others."[2] The court held that "Limiting the protections, benefits and obligations of civil marriage to opposite sex couples violates the basic premises of individual liberty and equality under law protected by the Massachusetts Constitution."[3]

    The above definitions reflect the fact that the way we define ***marriage*** depends to a considerable extent on the prevailing social, cultural, and political environments. The first definition mirrors our early marriage laws, which, in a majority of the states, were based on English common law. It is moral in tone and emphasizes the union of a man and a woman and the procreative function of marriage. The second definition falls at the other end of the spectrum, where marriage involves two "persons" who voluntarily enter a "union" with each other. In Chapter 5, we focus on shifting definitions as they relate to unmarried couples and the concept of "family." In this chapter, the focus is on marriage and its variations. (See Exhibits 3.1. and 3.2.)

Marriage
a legal status that two people attain by entering a government-approved and regulated contract with each other

---

EXHIBIT 3.1 Types of Monogamous Marriage

Ceremonial Marriage	Available in all 50 states, a ceremonial marriage customarily requires a license and solemnization in a ceremony performed by a person authorized by statute to perform weddings. The ceremony may be civil (performed by a government official/Justice of the Peace), religious (performed by a religious cleric), or, in the case of Native Americans, conducted according to tribal customs.
Covenant Marriage	A covenant marriage is a form of ceremonial marriage available in a small number of states, and under consideration in others. It developed in response to concerns about high divorce rates and the ease with which no-fault divorces are granted. It emphasizes the seriousness of the decision to marry and the goal of permanence in marital relationships. As a result, covenant marriages are more difficult to enter and exit than traditional ceremonial or common law marriages. (See Exhibit 3.2.)

continued

Paralegal Practice Tip
The content of Exhibit 3.1 focuses on types of marriage common in the United States. However, throughout history, four fundamental forms of marriage have existed across the world: (1) monogamy; (2) polygyny (one man with several wives); (3) polyandry (one woman with several husbands); and (4) group marriage. The term *polygamy* encompasses both polygyny and polyandry. The various forms are rooted deeply in the cultures, religious beliefs, and social mores of the societies in which they appear.

Common Law Marriage

A common law marriage is created by the conduct of the parties rather than in a formal ceremony. As of 2007, common law marriages were recognized in a limited number of states, e.g., Alabama, Colorado, Kansas, Montana, Oklahoma, Rhode Island, Texas, Utah, and the District of Columbia. In New Hampshire, common law marriage is recognized for purposes of inheritance and death benefits only. Common law statutes usually require capacity and intent to marry, cohabitation, and a holding out to the public as husband and wife.[4]

Same-Sex Marriage

As of June 2008, same-sex marriage is permitted only in the Commonwealth of Massachusetts and California. It is, in some respects, comparable to traditional marriage, with the important exceptions that the parties are of the same sex, the marriage is not recognized under federal law, and the extent to which it will be recognized in other jurisdictions is still unclear.

Putative Marriage

The putative marriage doctrine is recognized in a limited number of states. Section 209 of the Uniform Marriage and Divorce Act defines a putative spouse as follows: "Any person who has cohabited with another to whom he is not legally married in the good faith belief that he was married to that person is a putative spouse until knowledge of the fact that he is not legally married terminates his status and prevents acquisition of further rights. A *putative spouse* acquires the rights conferred upon a legal spouse, including the right to maintenance following termination of his status, whether or not the marriage is prohibited (Section 207) or declared invalid (Section 208)." The presumed marriage may be either common law or ceremonial in nature. The doctrine does not make the marriage valid, but it does allow the courts to treat it as a valid marriage for purposes of property division and spousal support. The Illinois statute concerning putative spouses can be accessed on the companion website.

Putative spouse
a person who believes in good faith that his or her invalid marriage is legally valid

---

EXHIBIT 3.2 Louisiana Covenant Marriage Statute La. Rev. Stat. Ann. § 9:272–274

The Louisiana legislature enacted the first covenant marriage legislation in the country in 1997, creating a two-tiered system of marriage in that state. Covenant marriage is defined in that statute as follows:

A covenant marriage is a marriage entered into by one male and one female who understand and agree that the marriage between them is a lifelong relationship. Parties to a covenant marriage have received counseling emphasizing the nature and purpose of marriage and the responsibilities thereto.

continued

Only when there has been a total and complete breach of the marital covenant commitment may the non-breaching party seek a declaration that the marriage is no longer legally recognized.

Divorce is granted on fault grounds only: adultery, sentence of death or imprisonment at hard labor for a felony, physical or sexual abuse, abandonment of the marital home for a year, or living separate and apart continuously without reconciliation for two years.

Historical Perspective

The history of marriage in the United States has its roots in ecclesiastical and English common law. Under common law, upon marriage a husband and wife became one, and that one was embodied in the husband.

> By marriage, the husband and wife are one person in law; that is, the very being or legal existence of the woman is suspended during the marriage, or at least is incorporated and consolidated into that of the husband; under whose wing, protection and cover, she performs everything.... Upon this principle, of a union of person in husband and wife, depend almost all the legal rights, duties, and disabilities, that either one of them acquire by the marriage.[5]

Upon marriage, the wife became entitled to support by her husband and, in exchange, she essentially lost her independent legal status. Although she retained title to any real property she owned in her own name when she wed, her husband acquired an exclusive right to manage, control, and collect all income from that property. She lost her right to own personal property, and any she did own became her husband's. She could not execute a contract or a will, and any executed prior to marriage were automatically revoked. She could not sue or be sued in her own name. She could be employed but any income she received belonged to her husband.

The wife's standing in the eight *civil law* or *community property states* influenced primarily by Spanish civil law (Arizona, California, Idaho, Nevada, New Mexico, Texas, and Washington) or French civil law (Louisiana) rather than English common law appeared less onerous on the surface. Her independent legal identity technically did not merge with her husband's, and property acquired during marriage generally constituted "community property" belonging to both spouses. However, the spouses were not "equals." As under the common law tradition, the husband held complete control over his wife's property and earnings during the marriage.

By the mid-to late nineteenth century, the situation of women began to improve somewhat as the states passed *Married Women's Property Acts*. The acts were passed partly in response to pressure from reformers seeking equality for women in political, social, and domestic arenas. Generally, they eliminated several of the disabilities of married women, enabling them to:

- acquire, own, and transfer property
- sue and be sued in their own right
- enter contracts
- retain their own earnings for services performed outside of the home

The New York Statute concerning the property of married women effective on February 17, 1909 is accessible in the Chapter 3 companion website material.

Civil law
one of the two primary legal systems in the western world originating in the Roman Empire and influential in several parts of the world and a small number of states

Community property states
states in which a husband and wife hold property acquired during the marriage (exclusive of gifts and inheritances) in common, with each spouse entitled to a one-half interest in the property upon divorce

Married Women's Property Acts
statutory reforms that helped improve the legal status of married women primarily by extending rights of property ownership and control denied them at common law

Despite this initial progress, during the first half of the twentieth century, it was not until the 1960s that a variety of forces converged and brought about fundamental change in both society and the law relating to marriage and the family: men and women wanting to escape stereotypic roles; fathers wanting to parent their children and take care of their homes; women seeking economic independence; men wanting to be free of financial burdens upon divorce; gay and lesbian individuals wanting to have their identities and lifestyles acknowledged and respected; and both married and unmarried heterosexual couples wanting to shape the contours of their own relationships.

During the past fifty years, many of the major battles have been, and continue to be, waged on constitutional fronts. Although equality has not yet fully been realized in practice, in principle men and women are gradually being liberated from longstanding stereotypes. The U.S. Supreme Court expressly referenced this evolution when, in 1979, it struck down Alabama's alimony statute because it imposed a support obligation on men only:

> [T]he "old [notion]" that "generally it is the man's primary responsibility to provide a home and its essentials," can no longer justify a statute that discriminates on the basis of gender. "No longer is the female destined solely for the home and the rearing of the family, and only the male for the marketplace and world of ideas." . . .
> Legislative classifications which distribute benefits and burdens on the basis of gender carry the inherent risk of reinforcing stereotypes about the "proper place" of women and their need for special protection.[6]

Other decisions based on the U.S. Constitution and the constitutions of the individual states have further altered long-standing perceptions about the institution of marriage. For example:

- In several states, qualifying same-sex couples are now eligible for legal statuses (such as domestic partnerships and civil unions) that recognize their relationships and accord them access to at least some of the benefits customarily available only to married persons. These couples have accomplished this largely by challenging their treatment under due process and equal protection provisions of state constitutions.[7] In at least one state, Massachusetts, they have successfully sought the right to marry. As of June 2008, they have successfully sought the right to marry in two states.[8]
- Historically, definitions of marriage have been premised on the idea that marriage and procreation are intertwined, that people marry, have children, and raise them in the security of a traditional family environment. The reality is that: a substantial number of unmarried women have children; same-sex couples often have children, making use of a range of reproductive technologies as well as adoption; and many married couples cannot, or choose not to, have children. Consistent with these trends, in 1965, the U.S. Supreme Court struck down a Connecticut statute banning any person's use of contraceptives (including married couples) and preventing anyone (including physicians) from counseling people about contraceptives. The court held that the Fourth and Fifth Amendments protect citizens from governmental invasions of the sanctity of the home and the privacies of life including the decision to have or not have children.[9]
- Until the late twentieth century, a majority of the states codified a marital exemption for the crime of rape. It was a complete defense to a charge of rape if a man could prove he was married to the victim. The exemption was based on the concept that the wife was the husband's property and that when she promised to "love, honor, and obey" him, she had impliedly consented and must acquiesce to all his wishes. In 1984, the

New York statute incorporating the exemption was held unconstitutional in *People v. Liberta.* The court stated:

> Rape is not simply a sexual act to which one party does not consent. Rather, it is a degrading, violent act which violates the bodily integrity of the victim and frequently causes severe, long-lasting physical and psychic harm. To ever imply consent to such an act is irrational and absurd.... a marriage license should not be viewed as a license for a husband to forcibly rape his wife with impunity. A married woman has the same right to control her own body as does an unmarried woman....[10]

THE PROMISE TO MARRY AND BREACH OF THE PROMISE—WHAT IF YOU SAY YOU WILL AND THEN YOU WON'T?

At one time, a mutual promise to marry was recognized as a legally enforceable contract, although the courts fell short of ordering **specific performance** of the contract. The remedy was in the form of an action for **breach of promise**. Much like the institution of marriage itself, the evolution of actions for breach of the contract for marriage has reflected the religious, social, and legal climate of the times. In an era in which marriage was viewed more as a religious event than a legal event, ecclesiastical courts brought pressure to bear on engaged couples to keep their promises to marry, or, in particularly egregious cases, face excommunication from the church.

In a cultural climate in which marriage was considered a life-defining event, particularly for women, courts of law also provided relief to brides "left at the altar." The essence of a breach of promise action was the failure to honor the promise to marry. If a prospective spouse acted in a fraudulent manner toward his or her prospective spouse, the courts sought to place the injured party (usually the woman) in the position he or she would have been in had the marriage taken place. The injured party could seek damages for pain and suffering, **expectation damages** for loss of an anticipated lifestyle, and **reliance damages** to recover for actions taken and expenses incurred as a result of the mutual promise to marry.

Few defenses to a breach of promise action were available, with the exception of proof that the plaintiff was "unchaste" during the period of the engagement. "It is the legal as well as moral duty of persons who have plighted mutual vows to marry to preserve themselves during betrothal pure and blameless; and if a betrothed woman prostitutes her person to another man, it will bar her action for breach of contract."[11]

By the early 1900s, however, it had become apparent that breach of contract actions were often abused, and the courts no longer seemed an appropriate forum for dealing with the emotional trauma of "broken hearts." The romance of engagement also began to give way to the more practical view that it made little sense to penalize people for refusing to enter marriages that were doomed to fail. As a result, by the middle of the century, more than half of the states had passed **Anti-Heartbalm Statutes** abolishing breach of contract actions. (See Exhibit 3.3.)

Today, the emphasis on fault has largely been taken out of the marriage equation, and marriage is now viewed more as an economic than an emotional partnership under the law. It should, thus, come as no surprise that what remains of the earlier breach of contract action in most states is at best an action seeking

Specific performance
a court-ordered remedy requiring that a contract be fulfilled as fully as practicable when money damages are inappropriate or inadequate

Breach of promise
under common law, the breaking of an engagement without justification, entitling the innocent party to damages

Expectation damages
compensation awarded for the loss of what a person reasonably anticipated from a contract or transaction that was not completed

Reliance damages
damages awarded to a plaintiff for losses incurred from having acted in reliance on a contract that was breached by the other party

Anti-Heartbalm Statutes
state laws that abolish the cause of action for breach of promise

Compensatory damages
damages sufficient to compensate an injured person for a loss suffered

Liquidated damages
an amount agreed to in a contract as the measure of damages to be paid by the breaching party to the non-breaching party

Donee
the one to whom a gift is made

Donor
the one who gives a gift

compensatory damages for out-of-pocket costs incurred as a natural result of the engagement. These expenses might include, for example, the cost of a non-returnable wedding dress and non-refundable deposits and other *liquidated damages* paid in connection with cancellation of a reception hall reservation or the booking of a band. The courts are divided with respect to treatment of the "engagement" ring:

- Because the ring is the traditional symbol of the commitment to marry, some courts view it as a gift that is contingent on the marriage taking place. To avoid unjust enrichment, if the engagement is broken, the ring should be returned regardless of which party breaks the engagement. The same rule may be applied to wedding gifts or other large gifts made to a party in contemplation of a forthcoming marriage.
- Some view the giving of the ring as a completed and irrevocable gift and thus non-returnable. For the giving of the ring to be a completed gift, the following elements must be satisfied:
  - The ring must actually be "delivered" to the *donee* by the *donor*
  - The transfer of the ring must have been voluntary
  - At the time of the transfer, the donor must have intended to relinquish title, dominion, and control over the ring
  - There must be no consideration for, or condition on, the giving of the ring and
  - The donee must accept the ring
- Still other courts look to the facts of each case, giving particular attention to which party broke the engagement and why and whether or not it appears from the circumstances that the gift was conditional on the agreement to marry (the engagement itself) or on the occurrence of the actual marriage.

EXHIBIT 3.3 The Illinois "AntiHeartbalm" Statute (enacted in 1947) (Prior to 1/1/93 cited as: Ill. Rev. Stat., Ch. 40, para. 1801)

FROM THE STATUTE

§740 ILCS 15/1. [Legislative Declaration]

Sec. 1. It is hereby declared, as a matter of legislative determination, that the remedy heretofore provided by law for the enforcement of actions based upon breaches of promises or agreements to marry has been subject to grave abuses and has been used as an instrument for blackmail by unscrupulous persons for their unjust enrichment, due to the indefiniteness of damages recoverable in such actions and the consequent fear of persons threatened with such actions that exorbitant damages might be assessed against them. It is also hereby declared that the award of monetary damages in such actions is ineffective as a recompense for genuine mental or emotional distress. Accordingly, it is hereby declared as the public policy of the state that the best interests of the people of the state will be served by limiting the damages recoverable in such actions, and by leaving any punishments of wrongdoers guilty of seduction to proceedings under the criminal laws of the state, rather than to the imposition of punitive, exemplary, vindictive or aggravated damages in actions for breach of promise or agreement to marry. Consequently, in the public interest, the necessity for the enactment of this chapter is hereby declared as a matter of legislative determination.

> **PARALEGAL APPLICATION 3.1**

THE MARRIAGE BROKER BUSINESS

Under common law, marriage broker contracts, in which a person was paid to secure a spouse for another person, were considered void and unenforceable. Consider the extensive network of dating services doing business today in this country, many of which promise to locate lifetime partners for their customers and then feature the couples they introduced who subsequently married. Think also about the reality TV shows that involve contests in which the ultimate prize is a rose, a ring, and a spouse. Do you think such business ventures should be permitted? Should they be licensed or otherwise monitored and regulated? Read the case *Ureneck v. Cui*, 59 Mass. App. Ct. 809, 798 N.E.2d 305 (2003), available on the companion website. Do you agree with the decision in that case? Why?

MARRIAGE—A FUNDAMENTAL RIGHT

In the 1967 landmark decision *Loving v. Virginia*, the U.S. Supreme Court definitively established that marriage is a fundamental right under the due process clause of the Constitution:

> The freedom to marry has long been recognized as one of the vital personal rights essential to the orderly pursuit of happiness by free men. . . . Marriage is one of the "basic civil rights of man," fundamental to our very existence and survival.[12]

However, the right to marry is not absolute and the states are permitted to regulate or restrict it to a reasonable extent. In assessing the constitutionality of a statute that restricts a fundamental right such as the right to marry, and/or that discriminates against a "suspect" class or category of persons, the courts apply what is called a "strict scrutiny" test. The test essentially involves a two-part inquiry:

- First, does the state have a compelling interest that justifies the regulation restricting the fundamental right as it applies to a particular class of persons?
- Second, is the statute sufficiently narrowly drawn so as to avoid unnecessary abridgments of the right?

Examples of cases in which the courts have held that state law impermissibly restricted the right to marry include the *Loving* case referenced above. In that case, the U.S. Supreme Court struck down Virginia's anti-miscegenation law prohibiting marriage between white and "colored" persons. (See Case 3.1.) Examples of other statutes found to have impermissibly restricted the right to marry include the following:

- In *Zablocki v. Redhail*,[13] the U.S. Supreme Court struck down a Wisconsin statute requiring proof that child support payments due from a prior marriage were being met and prohibiting noncustodial parents behind in those payments from marrying. The Court indicated that other collection methods were available to accomplish the intended purpose without encroaching on the fundamental right to marry.
- In *Salisbury v. List*,[14] a federal court struck down a blanket prohibition against allowing prisoners with life sentences to marry except when certain conditions were met. Subsequently in 1987, the U.S. Supreme Court held that a Missouri law denying confined persons the right to marry was unconstitutional. The Court observed that many important elements of

marriage, such as expressions of emotional support, eligibility for receipt of government benefits, property rights, and the legitimation of children, remain after taking into account the limitations of prison life. The Court held that a prisoner should not be deprived of the right to marry unless exercise of the right would be inconsistent with the status of the prisoner or with legitimate penological objectives of the corrections system. The state's general interest in rehabilitation and security were deemed insufficient justifications for denial of the fundamental right to marry.[15]

CASE **3.1** *Loving v. Virginia,* 388 U.S. 1, 87 S. Ct. 1817, 18 L. Ed. 1010 (1967)

BACKGROUND

In this case, a couple, Mildred Jeter (an African-American) and Richard Loving (a white man), challenged Virginia's anti-miscegenation law. Similar statutes were still in effect at the time in sixteen other states as well. In June of 1958, the parties, residents of Virginia, traveled to the District of Columbia, where they married under the law of that jurisdiction. They subsequently returned to Virginia, where they were indicted and found guilty of violating the state's ban on interracial marriage. They were sentenced to one year in jail, a sentence that was suspended provided they left Virginia and did not return for twenty-five years. In his opinion, the trial judge stated:

> Almighty God created the races white, black, yellow, malay and red, and he placed them on separate continents. And but for the interference with his arrangement there would be no cause for such marriages. The fact that he separated the races shows that he did not intend for the races to mix.

The convictions were upheld on appeal. The couple relocated to the District of Columbia and filed a motion in the Virginia trial court to vacate their convictions on the ground that the statutes they violated were unconstitutional. The motion was denied and, on appeal, the Virginia Supreme Court of Appeals upheld the constitutionality of the statutes and the convictions. The appeal to the U.S. Supreme Court followed and the statute was held to violate the equal protection clause of the Fourteenth Amendment by restricting a person's choice of a spouse based on racial classifications. The Court also held that the right to marry is a fundamental right under the due process clause.

FROM THE OPINION

This case presents a constitutional question never addressed by this Court: whether a statutory scheme adopted by the State of Virginia to prevent marriages between persons solely on the basis of racial classifications violates the Equal Protection and Due Process Clauses of the Fourteenth Amendment. . . .

The two statutes under which appellants were convicted and sentenced are . . . . § 20–58 [and § 20–59] of the Virginia Code:

> "*Leaving the state to evade law.*—If any white person and colored person shall go out of this State, for the purpose of being married, and with the intention of returning, and be married out of it, and afterwards return to and reside in it, cohabiting as man and wife, they shall be punished as provided in sect. 20–59. . . ."
> "*Punishment for marriage.*—If any white person intermarry with a colored person, or any colored person intermarry with a white person, he shall be guilty of a felony and shall be punished by confinement in the penitentiary for not less than one nor more than five years."

continued

. . . Penalties for miscegenation arose as an incident to slavery and have been common in Virginia since the colonial period. The present statutory scheme dates from the adoption of the Racial Integrity Act of 1924, passed during the period of extreme nativism which followed the end of the First World War. . . .

I. In upholding the constitutionality of these provisions . . . , the Supreme Court of Appeals of Virginia referred to its 1955 decision in *Naim v. Naim*, 197 Va. 80, 87 S. E. 2d 749. . . . In *Naim*, the state court concluded that the State's legitimate purposes were "to preserve the racial integrity of its citizens," and to prevent "the corruption of blood," "a mongrel breed of citizens," and "the obliteration of racial pride," obviously an endorsement of the doctrine of white supremacy. *Id.*, at 90, 87 S. E. 2d, at 756. The court also reasoned that marriage has traditionally been subject to state regulation without federal intervention, and, consequently, the regulation of marriage should be left to exclusive state control by the Tenth Amendment.

While the state court is no doubt correct in asserting that marriage is a social relation subject to the State's police power, . . . the State does not contend in its argument before this Court that its powers to regulate marriage are unlimited notwithstanding the commands of the Fourteenth Amendment. . . . [T]he State contends that, because its miscegenation statutes punish equally both the white and the Negro participants in an interracial marriage, these statutes, despite their reliance on racial classifications, do not constitute an invidious discrimination based on race. . . .

. . . the Equal Protection Clause requires the consideration of whether the classifications drawn by any statute constitute an arbitrary and invidious discrimination. The clear and central purpose of the Fourteenth Amendment was to eliminate all official state sources of invidious racial discrimination in the States. . . .

There can be no question but that Virginia's miscegenation statutes rest solely upon distinctions drawn according to race. . . . Over the years, this Court has consistently repudiated "distinctions between citizens solely because of their ancestry" as being "odious to a free people whose institutions are founded upon the doctrine of equality." *Hirabayashi v. United States*, 320 U.S. 81, 100 (1943). . . . [I]f they are ever to be upheld, they must be shown to be necessary to the accomplishment of some permissible state objective, independent of the racial discrimination which it was the object of the Fourteenth Amendment to eliminate. . . .

There is patently no legitimate overriding purpose independent of invidious racial discrimination which justifies this classification. The fact that Virginia prohibits only interracial marriages involving white persons demonstrates that the racial classifications must stand on their own justification, as measures designed to maintain White Supremacy. We have consistently denied the constitutionality of measures which restrict the rights of citizens on account of race. There can be no doubt that restricting the freedom to marry solely because of racial classifications violates the central meaning of the Equal Protection Clause.

II. These statutes also deprive the Lovings of liberty without due process of law in violation of the Due Process Clause of the Fourteenth Amendment. The freedom to marry has long been recognized as one of the vital personal rights essential to orderly pursuit of happiness by free men.

Marriage is one of the "basic civil rights of man," fundamental to our very existence and survival. *Skinner v. Oklahoma*, 316 U.S. 535, 541 (1942). . . . To deny this fundamental freedom on so unsupportable a basis as the racial classifications embodied in these statutes, classifications so directly subversive of the principle of equality at the heart of the Fourteenth Amendment, is surely to deprive all the State's citizens of liberty without due process of law. The Fourteenth Amendment requires that the freedom of choice to marry not be restricted by invidious racial discriminations. Under our Constitution, the freedom to marry, or not marry, a person of another race resides with the individual and cannot be infringed by the State.

These convictions must be reversed.

continued

SIDEBAR

Despite this ruling, the remnants of anti-miscegenation statutes were still evident nearly twenty years later when the U.S. Supreme Court held in *Palmore v. Sidoti*[16] that a state cannot impose an indirect penalty on a person who marries another of a different race by depriving him or her of child custody based on race.

PARALEGAL APPLICATION 3.2

IS A CONTRACT ENFORCEABLE IF IT RESTRICTS AN INDIVIDUAL'S RIGHT TO MARRY?

THE FACTS

Rabbi Zaltman does not want his beloved daughter, Alexandra, to marry outside of the Jewish faith in which she has been raised. On the occasion of her graduation from college, he gives her a check for $500,000 on condition that, if she ever marries, she will marry only a Jewish man. She agrees, endorses the check, deposits the funds in her account, and spends the full amount over the next five years. At that time, she marries a Catholic man, Patrick Michael Madden. Outraged, her father seeks to recover the $500,000.

SIDEBAR

Should the court enforce the agreement and require the return of the $500,000 or should it find the contract unenforceable because enforcement of its terms by the court would restrict the daughter's fundamental right to marry? Would it make any difference if the father had sought a promise that the daughter never marry? Not marry for a period of five years? Not marry until she completed medical school?

A total prohibition against marriage is unlikely to be enforced by a court even if both parties initially agreed to the terms of the contract. However, a partial or limited restriction that serves a useful purpose may be enforceable. Is an interest in maintaining a particular cultural or religious tradition a sufficiently useful purpose? Explain your response.

MARRIAGE REQUIREMENTS

Although marriage is a contract between the parties, it is a contract regulated by the government. Having established that marriage is a fundamental right that cannot be restricted unreasonably by the states, what kinds of restrictions can and do the states legitimately impose? We cannot simply marry anyone wherever and whenever we please. Each of the states has established its own requirements that couples must satisfy in order to marry. Although there are variations, the requirements are fairly standard state to state. There are basically two types: requirements relating to legal capacity to marry and technical requirements governing particular kinds of marriages.

Requirements Relating to Legal Capacity to Marry

Restrictions on legal capacity to marry fall into six main categories:

- Sex of the parties
- Age of the parties
- Marital status of the parties

- Degree of relationship between the parties by blood (consanguinity) and marriage (affinity)
- Mental capacity of each party
- Physical capacity of each party

A failure to comply with these restrictions may affect the validity of a marriage and is generally raised in the context of annulment actions.

Sex of the Parties.   As of June 2008, every state, with the exception of Massachusetts and California, requires that the parties to a marriage be of different sexes, male and female. This may seem like a reasonably straightforward requirement, but in this era of advanced medical technology, several courts have had to address (in annulment, custody, adoption, wrongful death, and probate cases) the issue of the sex of a transsexual individual who has successfully undergone sex reassignment surgery. In New Jersey, the state's highest court has held that the "new" sex is the operative sex for determining marital status and legal rights.[17] Courts in other states (such as Florida and Texas) have held that a person's sex at birth is controlling.[18]

Age of the Parties.   At common law, the minimum age of consent for marriage was 12 for a female and 14 for a male. Every state now establishes by statute the minimum age at which parties may marry without parental consent, usually 18. The basic rationale for this restriction is the assumption that individuals need to have attained at least some degree of maturity before they can appreciate the nature of marriage, understand the rights and responsibilities that flow from it, and be capable of bearing and raising children in a healthy and responsible family environment. There are, however, several common exceptions to the general rule:

- Youths within an age range such as 16 and 18 may be permitted to marry if they have the consent of a parent or guardian and/or the court
- Courts may waive the age requirement if the female is pregnant
- If one or both of the parties is emancipated, the court may grant a request for waiver of the age requirement. *Emancipation* may be established in a number of ways and generally includes no longer living with one's parents and being self-supporting.

Even if a party marries while underage, he or she may ratify the marriage by remaining with the spouse in a marital relationship after attaining the age of consent.

Marital Status of the Parties.   Each of the parties must be "free" to marry in the sense that neither is married to another individual still living at the time of the marriage. *Bigamy,* a crime in all states (usually a misdemeanor), is defined as entering a second marriage while a prior marriage is still valid. *Polygamy,* also a crime, refers to a situation in which one individual (usually a male) has multiple spouses at the same time.[19] Most states provide that bigamous and polygamous marriages are *void,* but if at least one party enters the marriage in good faith, the impediment is eventually removed (by death or divorce), and the parties continue to live together in a marital relationship, the marriage may be considered valid from the date the impediment was removed.

Degree of Relationship Between the Parties by Blood (Consanguinity) and Marriage (Affinity).   States establish, by statute, the minimum degrees of relationship that can exist by consanguinity and affinity in order for two persons to marry. Such regulations are based primarily on the state's interests in promoting family harmony, protecting children from sexual exploitation, and limiting the genetic transmission of negative recessive traits (such as hemophilia and congenital deafness). These regulations are designed to be consistent with provisions of state criminal codes regarding crimes such as *incest*.

Emancipation
the point at which a child is considered an adult and granted adult rights; usually occurs at the age of majority or upon the occurrence of certain acts or events such as marriage or entering the armed services

Bigamy
the act of entering a subsequent marriage while a prior marriage of one or both of the parties is still in effect; in most states constitutes a criminal offense if committed knowingly; a ground for annulment and/or divorce in virtually all states

Polygamy
the state of having more than one spouse at the same time

Void
invalid and of no legal effect

Incest
sexual intercourse between two people who are too closely related, usually as defined by civil and criminal statutes

---

Paralegal Practice Tip
Some anti-incest taboos are based
on broad cultural, political, and
social rather than genetic concerns.
For example, one of the author's
colleagues has noted that among
the Navajo, incest has been based
on membership in one of several
major "clans," each potentially
consisting of hundreds of people,
resulting in a rule that a person
must not be intimate with anyone
in either the father's ("born for") clan
or the mother's ("born to") clan.

Affinity
a relationship resulting from marriage (i.e., the relationship a
spouse has to the blood relatives of
the other spouse)

Consanguinity provisions specify impermissible blood relationships in marriage such as parent and child, sister and brother (of the whole or half blood), and uncle and niece. Several states still prohibit the marriage of first cousins based on an assumption that such marriages result in genetic defects in children due to inbreeding. Rather than totally restricting the right of first cousins to marry, it has been suggested that this concern can be effectively addressed by providing genetic counseling for parties to such unions[20] or, as provided in some states, by permitting marriage only after the parties have passed their procreative years (e.g., both are over age 65). The Uniform Marriage and Divorce Act permits first cousins, as well as individuals related to one another through adoption, to marry.

Affinity provisions establish impermissible unions based on relationships created by marriage rather than by blood, such as a wife and her father-in-law or a husband and his sister-in-law. Some states have eliminated restrictions based on affinity. States that have not eliminated them vary with respect to whether or not the prohibitions are lifted when the person who created the prohibited relationship dies. There are also variations among the states with respect to the impact of relationships created by adoption or through step-parents.

Mental Capacity.   Initially, the requirement that the parties have sufficient mental capacity to marry was based to some extent on a fear that mentally deficient individuals would marry, bear similarly limited children, and create financial and social burdens for society at large. Today, mental capacity most often becomes an issue in cases where a party is seriously ill, of advanced age, under guardianship, or under the influence of drugs or alcohol at the time of the marriage ceremony. It should be noted that even if a person lacks mental capacity a majority of the time, courts have held that he or she can contract a valid marriage in a "lucid interval."

Lack of sufficient mental capacity is described in the following excerpt from an opinion of a North Dakota court:

> While there has been a hesitancy on the part of the courts to judicially define the phrase "unsound mind," it is established that such [a] term has reference to the mental capacity of the parties at the very moment of inception of the marriage contract. Ordinarily, lack of mental capacity, which renders a party incapable of entering into a valid marriage contract, must be such that it deprives him of the ability to understand the objects of marriage, its ensuing duties and undertakings, its responsibilities and relationship. There is a general agreement of the authorities that the terms "unsound mind" and "lack of mental capacity" carry greater import than eccentricity or mere weakness of mind or dullness of intellect.[21]

Physical Capacity.   Historically, the presence of "incurable diseases" acted as a bar to marriage in some states. In a small number of states (such as Nebraska[22]), applicants for a marriage license still must be free of syphilis, creating a particular dilemma for a clerk issuing licenses in a state (such as Ohio) where blood tests have been eliminated but the restriction remains in force.

Technical Requirements for a Ceremonial Marriage

In addition to satisfying the legal requirements for capacity to marry, the states also establish fairly consistent technical requirements for ceremonial marriages. These requirements commonly include the following components:

- an application for a license
- a medical certificate or provision of information concerning certain diseases
- a license

- a waiting period
- a ceremony
- recording of the license/certification

When one or more of these "requirements" are not met, the marriage usually still will be upheld, given the strong public policy favoring the validity of marriages. Some states expressly provide by statute that if the marriage is lawful in all other respects and is consummated in the belief of either party that it is lawful, the marriage will be deemed valid notwithstanding any failure to satisfy a technical requirement.[23] The penalty for noncompliance is usually in the form of a modest fine. However, the penalty for falsifying public documents may carry a heavier penalty, including a period of incarceration.

Application for a License. The parties pay a fee and file a written application for a license to marry (sometimes called a notice of intention) usually in the county where they intend to marry. A copy of the Application for a Marriage License for the state of Hawaii is accessible on the companion website. Both parties complete the application and sign it under pain and penalty of perjury. If one of the parties is seriously ill or in the armed services, a parent, guardian, or the other party may be permitted to provide the absent party's information. Customarily, the application requires information such as the following:

- the parties' names and the names they intend to use once married
- their places of residence
- their birthplaces and ages (Documentation may be required, given reasonable doubt as to a party's stated age.)
- their parents' names
- the number of any prior marriages of each party and the means by which they were terminated or dissolved (Some states require documentation such as a death certificate or a divorce decree.)
- Some forms also require the parties to affirm a general statement that there are no legal impediments to the marriage such as a prohibited degree of blood relationship between the applicants.

The parties will also be asked to provide any information required by the state's child support enforcement agency including their respective social security numbers, ideally on a separate form for sending to the agency and not part of the public record, given the present-day emphasis on privacy rights and the potential for identity theft.

Medical Certificate. Historically, the requirement of physical examinations and/or blood tests was designed to determine whether either party had incurable tuberculosis or a sexually transmitted disease such as syphilis, or if the female had been vaccinated for rubella unless she was past her childbearing years. Today, many of the states have eliminated this requirement, largely because of advances in medical technology and an increased emphasis on privacy. However, some still require the filing of a medical certificate indicating that the parties have undergone certain laboratory tests within a specified period prior to filing their application. Others require that information regarding AIDS and other sexually transmitted diseases be provided to marriage applicants. (See Exhibits 3.4 and 3.5.)

License. The license is issued by the statutorily designated authority, usually within a specified period after the application is made.

Waiting Period. Some states establish a waiting period (commonly not more than three days) between application for and issuance of a license, although the period may be waived by statute under certain conditions or by the court on a Motion for a Marriage Without Delay. The general purpose of the waiting period is to promote deliberate consideration of the decision to marry.

Paralegal Practice Tip
Under common law, a wife automatically assumed her husband's surname upon marriage, a practice consistent with the doctrine of marital unity. This tradition has faded somewhat. States may address the topic by statute, case law, or procedural rules or practices. For example, in New York, the parties are given notice that their names will not automatically change upon marriage and are asked to indicate the names they intend to use after marriage on the application for a marriage license.

EXHIBIT 3.4 Selected Marriage Laws—State by State (as of Summer 2007)

State	Minimum Age Requirement Male/Female without Parental Consent	Minimum Age with Parental Consent Male/Female	Physical Examination/ Blood Tests Required	Common Law Marriage State (Most states will recognize common law marriages if valid where entered.)
Alabama	18/18	16/16		X
Alaska	18/18	16/16		Not after 1/1/64
Arizona	18/18	16/16		
Arkansas	18/18	17/16*		
California	18/18	No statutory age limit	Brochure provided re AIDS, genetic defects, and domestic violence	Not after 1895
Colorado	18/18	16/16		X
Connecticut	18/18	16/16	X	
Delaware	18/18	18/16*		
District of Columbia	18/18	16/16	X	X
Florida	18/18	16/16		Not after 1/1/68
Georgia	18/18	16/16	Provided information re AIDS + tests	Not after 1/1/97
Hawaii	18/18	16/16 (15 with parental consent and judicial approval)	Certify rec'd + read AIDS info	
Idaho	18/18	16/16	Certify rec'd + read AIDS info	Not after 1/1/96
Illinois	18/18	16/16	Provided brochure re STDs + certain diseases	Not after 6/30/1905
Indiana	18/18	17/17	Provided information re AIDS + tests	Not after 1/1/58
Iowa	18/18	16/16		
Kansas	18/18	16/16		X
Kentucky	18/18	16/16		

continued

Louisiana	18/18	16/16	X	
Maine	18/18	16/16		
Maryland	18/18	16/16		
Massachusetts	18/18	No minimum age by statute		
Michigan	18/18	16/16		Not after 1/1/57
Minnesota	18/18	16/16		Not after 4/26/41
Mississippi	21/21	17/15*	X	Not after 4/5/56
Missouri	18/18	15/15	Provided brochure re effects of drugs and alcohol on fetus	Not after 3/3/21
Montana	18/18	16/16	X females only	X
Nebraska	17/17	No minimum age by statute	X	Not after 1923
Nevada***	18/18	16/16		Not after 3/29/43
New Hampshire	18/18	14/13*		X
New Jersey	18/18	16/16		Not after 1/12/39
New Mexico	18/18	16/16	X	
New York	18/18	16/16	Sickle cell anemia for certain applicants	Not after 4/29/33
North Carolina	18/18	16/16		
North Dakota***	18/18	16/16		
Ohio	18/18	18/16*		Not after 10/10/91
Oklahoma***	18/18	16/16	X	X
Oregon	18/18	17/17		
Pennsylvania	18/18	16/16		Not after 1/1/2005
Puerto Rico	21/21	18/16*	X	
Rhode Island**	18/18	18/16*		X
South Carolina	18/18	16/16; younger if female pregnant or has borne a child		Not after 1/1/2006
South Dakota	18/18	16/16	Provided information re AIDS + tests	Not after 7/1/59

continued

Tennessee	18/18	16/16	Provided information re AIDS + tests	
Texas	18/18	14/14	Provided information re AIDS + tests	X
Utah	18/18	15/15		X Enacted 1987
Vermont	18/18	16/16	X	
Virginia	18/18	16/16	Provided information re AIDS + tests	
Virgin Islands	18/18	16/14*		
Washington	18/18	17/17	Must file affidavit of no STDs	
West Virginia	18/18	16/16	X	
Wisconsin	18/18	16/16	Provided AIDS info	Not after 1913
Wyoming	18/18	16/16		

*Distinctions based on sex may be unconstitutional absent a compelling state interest.

**By statute, marriages between Jewish people within degrees of consanguinity permitted by their religion are allowed.

***Expressly recognizes marriages celebrated according to Native American customs.

EXHIBIT 3.5 West Virginia Code §16–3C-2

FROM THE STATUTE

§16–3C-2. Testing

(a) Premarital screening:

1. Every person who is empowered to issue a marriage license shall, at the time of issuance thereof, distribute to the applicants for the license information concerning acquired immunodeficiency syndrome (AIDS) and inform them of the availability of HIV-related testing and counseling. The informational brochures shall be furnished by the bureau.

2. A notation that each applicant has received the AIDS informational brochure shall be placed on file with the marriage license on forms provided by the bureau.

Ceremony.   A ceremony is performed, usually by a religious cleric, a Justice of the Peace, or another governmental official authorized by statute to perform such functions.[24] During the ceremony, the parties express their intentions to marry in the presence of witnesses. Some states (such as Colorado and Texas) allow *proxy marriages* in which the marriage ceremony takes place with one of the parties absent. A third-party agent is given authority to act on behalf of the missing person. Situations in which proxy marriages occur include those involving a party serving in the armed services and stationed overseas, a person who is incarcerated, or an American citizen who enters a proxy marriage with someone in another country, thereby qualifying that person for citizenship. Given the potential for abuse, proxy marriages generally are not favored.

Proxy marriage
a marriage ceremony in which a designated agent stands in for and acts on behalf of one of the absent parties (prohibited in most states)

Recording of the License/Certificate.   The individual who performs the ceremony records the license or certificate of marriage in the public office designated by statute within a certain time frame (usually from three to ten days).

REQUIREMENTS FOR A COMMON LAW MARRIAGE

The requirements for a valid common law marriage vary in states that recognize this form of union. They customarily include the following:

- The parties must have the legal capacity to marry.
- They must intend and simultaneously agree to be married. (Some states require that the agreement be expressed; others will infer an agreement from the conduct of the parties.)
- They must cohabit (although consummation may not be required).
- They must hold themselves out to the public as husband and wife.

The popular belief that the parties to a common law marriage must cohabit for a specific length of time is largely a misconception. However, the New Hampshire statute does include such a requirement. (See Exhibit 3.6.) In all states where common law marriage is permitted, with the exception of New Hampshire, once a common law marriage is established, it carries with it the same rights, benefits, and duties as a traditional ceremonial marriage, and children born to the parties are legitimate. It also must be formally dissolved by divorce if the relationship terminates and either or both of the parties wish to marry another.

At the end of the nineteenth century, the U.S. Supreme Court ruled that common law marriages are valid unless prohibited by a state.[25] At that time, they were recognized in most states. However, because of the potential for abuse, especially when the existence of a common law marriage is claimed after the death of a party, and the argument that they promote immoral behavior, such marriages are not always favored even in jurisdictions where they are authorized. However, abuse should not be presumed, given that people opt for common law marriage for a variety of legitimate reasons including, but not limited to, convenience, lack of expense, and a desire to minimize involvement with either the government or religious bodies.

Although common law marriage now has been abolished in a majority of states, there are legal scholars who argue that it should be revived as a vehicle for avoiding inequitable results, particularly for unmarried women and minorities. As one such scholar has phrased it:

> ...the common law marriage doctrine should be revived because it protects the interests of women, especially poor women and women of color,... Most of the original reasons for abolishing common law marriage—fears of fraud, protection of morality and the family, racism, eugenics, and health-related reasons—do not withstand scrutiny; and other arguments, based on administrative convenience, are outweighed by more important values. The impact of nonrecognition is clearly disparate: it hurts most those women who are most vulnerable, and its effect is greatest on issues with a significant impact on their welfare, such as the ability to leave a violent relationship or to obtain a variety of benefits upon the death of a family's breadwinner. The negative impact also differs significantly by class, race, ethnic group, and cultural tradition, falling most harshly on those groups that are already disadvantaged.
>
> The absence of common law marriage leaves a significant gap in the law, causing courts and some legislatures to seek escape routes to avoid inequitable results. None of the alternatives they have embraced, however, provides the comprehensive remedy that common law marriage did.[26]

Paralegal Practice Tip

The New Hampshire Cohabitation Statute is unusual in two respects:

1. It includes a requirement that the parties cohabit for at least three years.
2. It is applicable only in the context of inheritance or death benefit claims.

EXHIBIT 3.6 New Hampshire Statute Concerning Cohabitation New Hampshire Revised Statutes Annotated 457:39

FROM THE STATUTE

457:39 Cohabitation, etc.—Persons cohabiting and acknowledging each other as husband and wife, and generally reputed to be such, for the period of three years, and until the decease of one of them, shall thereafter be deemed to have been legally married.

PARALEGAL APPLICATION 3.3

MARRIAGE BY ACCIDENT?

THE FACTS

Charles and Juanita lived together for sixteen years and had one child together. They resided in Connecticut (not a common law marriage jurisdiction) throughout their relationship. During their years together, they took annual two-week trips to South Carolina and Alabama (in alternate years) to visit relatives. While there, they slept together, had sexual relations, held themselves out to others as married, and were regarded by friends and family members as married. South Carolina and Alabama were both common law marriage jurisdictions at the time. When Charles died as a result of a work-related injury, Juanita sought payment of worker's compensation benefits as his common law wife.

SIDEBAR

Do you think Juanita should be deemed Charles' common law wife? Should she receive the benefits she sought? Read the case *Collier v. Milford*, 537 A.2d 474 (Conn. 1988), available on the companion website. Do you agree with the decision? Why?

PARALEGAL APPLICATION **3.4**

INFORMATION GATHERING IN A COMMON LAW MARRIAGE CASE

In a case in which a client is alleging the existence of a common law marriage, a paralegal may be asked to gather information from the client and other sources regarding the following:

- the date and circumstances under which the parties met
- any children born to or adopted by the parties
- the parties' decision to live together—when and how it was made
- details regarding when, where, and for how long the parties have lived together
- details regarding travel by the parties, if any, to other states that recognize common law marriage
- the nature of the parties' relationship, including whether or not they engaged in sexual relations
- details regarding the parties' financial arrangements, including payment of expenses, maintenance of bank and credit card accounts, etc.
- the parties' history with respect to payment of taxes—were joint returns filed?
- the existence and location of documents pertaining to any property, real or personal, owned by the parties, individually or jointly
- the existence and location of documents executed by the parties, such as wills, health care proxies, powers of attorney, trusts, insurance policies, etc.
- details regarding any oral or written agreement between the parties regarding marriage, including why they did not enter a traditional ceremonial marriage
- details regarding the parties' social life and how they have represented themselves to others
- names and contact information for individuals familiar with the parties as friends, relatives, and business associates who regard and treat them as husband and wife
- the existence and location of other evidence of the parties' intent, such as inscriptions on photographs, engraving on jewelry, inclusion of the parties' names and marital relationship in family trees and bibles, etc.

MARRIAGE AS A SOURCE OF RIGHTS, BENEFITS, AND OBLIGATIONS

According to an audit report of the U.S. General Accounting Office, there are more than one thousand rights and duties that flow from a valid marriage, either ceremonial or common law.[27] Some of the most important of these include the following:

- Each spouse is entitled to receive support from and has a duty to provide support to the other spouse.
- Absent a valid and enforceable premarital agreement to the contrary and subject to the statutory provisions of state law, parties to a valid marriage acquire an interest in all "marital property" acquired by the spouses during their marriage (generally exclusive of property received by a spouse through an inheritance or gift from a third party). A spouse may seek division of the marital property upon divorce.

Intestate
dying without leaving a valid will

Laws of descent and distribution
the laws governing inheritance of property by heirs when a decedent dies without leaving a valid will

- When the marital property is divided, one spouse may receive payment of a portion of the other spouse's pension. Given an exception to the general federal policy prohibiting assignment of retirement interests, a Qualified Domestic Relations Order (QDRO) issued by the court may make a spouse an alternate payee under an employee spouse's pension plan.
- In some states, spouses may hold title to real property as tenants by the entirety, a form of ownership available only to spouses, which grants each spouse a right in the whole property. Generally, if title to the marital residence is held in this form, the property will not be able to be seized by the creditors of a debtor spouse.
- Absent an enforceable premarital agreement, each spouse is entitled to inherit property from his or her spouse. If the spouse dies **intestate** (without a will), the surviving spouse will inherit property to the extent provided in the **laws of descent and distribution** in force in the state where the spouse was domiciled at death. Essentially, these laws specify that the estate of the deceased person will be distributed among his or her closest relatives (spouse, children, parents, siblings, etc). Usually, a surviving spouse will inherit the entire estate or will receive half of it, with the other half being distributed to any surviving children in equal shares. If the spouse dies testate (with a will) and the will largely disinherits or fails to make adequate provisions for the surviving spouse, some states allow him or her to "waive the will" and claim a "forced share" of the estate as set by statute. Such laws may seem harsh, particularly if the testator dies during a divorce proceeding, but they have strong roots in the marital duty of support, which, in effect, continues after death.
- Provided any necessary conditions are satisfied (such as age or a minimum length of marriage), spouses are entitled to receive certain governmental benefits, such as social security administration and veterans' benefits after the death of a wage earner or veteran.
- A divorced, separated, or surviving spouse may be entitled to continued employer-provided health insurance coverage for a specific period, generally up to thirty-six months under the Consolidated Omnibus Budget Reconciliation Act of 1985 (COBRA).

Tort
a civil wrong (other than breach of contract) for which a court provides a remedy, usually in the form of money damages; the wrong must involve harm resulting from breach of a duty owed to another

Consortium
companionship, affection, and, in the case of spouses, sexual relations, that one is entitled to receive from another based on existence of a legal relationship (e.g., husband-wife, parent-child)

- In **tort** law, the existence of a valid marriage still is a threshold requirement in most states to recover for "loss of consortium" resulting from the negligent conduct of another. **Consortium:** commonly includes a loss of services, companionship, support, guidance, comfort, affection, and, in the case of spouses, a loss of sexual relations. For example, if an individual is paralyzed as a result of the negligence of a drunk driver, then his or her spouse may seek to recover for loss of consortium.
- Surviving spouses are also eligible to file claims for the wrongful death of their marital partners. For example, if Harry dies as a result of an explosion caused by the installation of a faulty furnace, his wife may file a wrongful death action against the installer and the manufacturer of the furnace. As callous as it may sound, damages are measured by the monetary value of the decedent to the surviving spouse in terms of loss of reasonably expected income as well as loss of consortium.
- Marriage customarily confers the ability to make medical decisions on behalf of a spouse in times of crisis or incapacity.
- Under federal law, a non-resident alien who marries a U.S. citizen obtains permanent resident status (if no deportation proceeding is pending), although the marriage will be treated as conditional until two years after the marriage takes place.[28]
- A spouse generally cannot be criminally charged as an accessory-after-the-fact for harboring or concealing his or her spouse after the latter has committed a felony.
- The law values the important functions served by confidential communications in a variety of contexts (attorney-client, priest-penitent,

doctor-patient), and the relationship between husband and wife is one of those contexts. The husband-wife or *marital communications privilege* prohibits compelled disclosure of statements made by spouses to each other within the privacy of the marital relationship. It does not apply to actions the spouse may have seen or to written communications. It also does not apply in civil actions for divorce, separation, custody, spousal or child support, or in criminal actions for non-support, incest, or abuse.

SAME-SEX MARRIAGE

A client asks her partner, "Can I, Kelly Sue, take thee, Dorothy Ann, to be my wedded spouse from this day forward?" As is the case with most legal questions, the answer is, "It depends." The first same-sex marriages were performed in April of 2001 in the Netherlands. A small number of other countries have elected to permit them since that time, including Belgium and Canada. And on May 17, 2004, after decades of battling for the right to do so, over one thousand same-sex couples successfully obtained marriage licenses in cities and towns across the Commonwealth of Massachusetts. Some regard that monumental event as just the beginning. Some view it as the beginning of the end of the institution of marriage. Few are without an opinion on the subject.

Once the Supreme Court established marriage as a fundamental right in the *Loving* case in 1967, same-sex couples across the United States began challenging state laws restricting that right to heterosexual couples primarily as discriminatory denials of equal protection and due process. Initially, plaintiffs in states such as Kentucky and Minnesota hit a brick wall. The courts reasoned that the due process clause did not encompass same-sex couples because of the essential nature of marriage as a union between a man and a woman. Statutes restricting marriage to heterosexual couples were held to serve the states' legitimate interests in protecting the traditional family as the fundamental building block of society, promoting procreation within the family environment, and discouraging illegal sexual activity between unmarried and, specifically, same-sex partners.

Cracks in the brick wall began appearing in the 1990s as the question of whether same-sex partners have a right to marry started to become as controversial and hotly debated an issue in the field of family law as is abortion. In its 1993 decision in *Baehr v. Lewin*,[30] the Hawaii Supreme Court declined to find that same-sex couples have a right to marry, but it did hold that denial of the right *might* constitute a denial of equal protection under the Hawaii state constitution. On remand, the trial court ordered the state to stop denying marriage licenses to same-sex couples, holding that the marriage ban was not necessary for the protection of children as had been alleged by the state. The door that appeared to open while that decision was on appeal slammed shut on same-sex marriage in that state when the voters supported a constitutional amendment that gave the legislature the authority to limit marriage to opposite-sex couples. The legislature promptly passed a statute expressly stating that a valid marriage "shall be only between a man and a woman."[31]

Finally in 2003, plaintiffs in the *Goodridge* case in Massachusetts prevailed where others had not when the Massachusetts Supreme Judicial Court held that denying same-sex couples the right to marry constituted a denial of equal protection under the state's constitution.[32] In May 2008, California followed suit when its Supreme Court struck down that state's ban on gay marriage on equal protection grounds in a controversial 4–3 decision. The life span of the legal right of same-sex couples to marry in these two states is uncertain given Constitutional Amendments hoveing in the wings.

Marital communications privilege the privilege that allows a spouse to refuse to testify, and to prevent others from testifying, about confidential communications between spouses during their marriage

---

Paralegal Practice Tip
The husband-wife privilege protects the privacy of spouses against third persons and against the state in some circumstances. It also protects spouses from each other to a degree by placing limitations on the extent to which a spouse may use private surveillance to "spy on" the other spouse while a divorce is pending and the parties are living separate and apart. A client may need to be cautioned by counsel regarding any federal or state prohibition against electronically recording the phone calls of his or her spouse while a divorce action is pending.[29]

Paralegal Practice Tip
Given that same-sex marriages are not recognized under federal law, the rights and obligations conferred on parties to same-sex marriages are limited to those extended under state law. In Chapter 5, we consider legal frameworks, such as domestic partnerships and civil unions, that extend varying degrees of state-created rights, benefits, and obligations of married persons to nonmarital partners.

Paralegal Practice Tip
There is no "same-sex marriage statute" in Massachusetts. The same laws and procedures that govern traditional marriage apply as well to same-sex marriage. On the Notice of Intention to Marry (the application for a license), the parties are now designated Party A and Party B.

Whatever position one holds with respect to same-sex marriage, it is well worth reading the lengthy *Goodridge* opinion. It touches on the vast majority of the questions raised in the cases and public debate surrounding this topic:

- What is the definition of marriage?
- What is the function of marriage?
- Is procreation the primary purpose of marriage?
- Does it make a difference if children are created through "noncoital" rather than "coital" means of reproduction?
- What is the "optimal setting" in which to raise children?
- Are heterosexual parents "better" parents than same-sex parents?
- Is the *sine qua non* of marriage an exclusive commitment between two individuals regardless of gender?
- Does particular statutory language limit marriage to heterosexual couples?
- Does the fundamental right to marry extend to same-sex couples?
- Does equal protection require that the right to marry be granted to same-sex couples?[33]
- Do due process considerations require the right to marry be afforded to same-sex couples?
- Does the state have a legitimate and/or compelling interest in confining marriage to heterosexual couples, and, if so, what is it?
- What standard/test applies to restrictions on the right to marry: Rational basis? Strict scrutiny?
- Is restricting marriage to heterosexual couples cost-effective?
- What are the respective roles of the legislature and the judiciary in addressing the issue of same-sex marriage?
- What role should the electorate play in the decision-making process?
- What influence do anti-gay prejudices have in influencing (clouding) decisions regarding same-sex marriage?
- How do religious, moral, and ethical convictions influence decisions in this area?
- Will permitting same-sex marriage destabilize the social order?
- What are the rights, benefits, and duties that come with legal marital status?
- How does denying same-sex couples the right to marry impact those couples and their children?
- Does denial of the right to marry create a population of second-class citizens?
- Does extending the right to marry to same-sex couples "trivialize" or devalue the institution of marriage?

CASE **3.2** *Goodridge v. Department of Public Health,* 440 Mass. 309, 98 N.E.2d 941 (2003)

BACKGROUND

The plaintiffs in this case were fourteen individuals, seven couples, from five Massachusetts counties. They had been in committed same-sex relationships for periods ranging from four to thirty years. In March and April of 2001, each of the couples had applied for and been denied marriage licenses on the ground that Massachusetts did not recognize same-sex marriage. The couples then filed suit in Superior Court against the Department of Public Health (and the Commissioner), seeking a judgment that the exclusion of the couples, and other qualified same-sex couples, "from access to marriage licenses, and the legal and social status of civil marriage, as well as the protections, benefits, and obligations of marriage" violated state law, including the Massachusetts Constitution. The Superior Court judge

continued

Paralegal Practice Tip

In its 2008 decision, *In re Marriage Cases,* the California Supreme Court held that "In contrast to earlier times, our state now recognizes that an individual's capacity to establish a loving and long-term committed relationship with another person and responsibly to care for and raise children does not depend upon the individual's sexual orientation.

dismissed the plaintiffs' claim. He concluded that the plain wording of the relevant Massachusetts marriage statutes precluded marriage between members of the same sex. With respect to the constitutional claims, the judge held that the marriage exclusion did not offend "the liberty, freedom, equality or due process provisions of the Massachusetts Constitution," and that the Massachusetts Declaration of Rights did not guarantee a fundamental right to same-sex marriage. He concluded that the prohibition rationally furthered the state's legitimate interest in safeguarding the primary purpose of marriage—procreation—because opposite-sex couples are more likely to have children and to do so without relying on "inherently more cumbersome" noncoital means of reproduction. The ruling was successfully appealed to the Massachusetts Supreme Judicial Court, which found that the marriage ban violated both equal protection and due process clauses of the state constitution. The court effectively modified the common law definition of marriage and then stayed implementation of the ruling for 180 days so that the legislature could conform the state's marital laws to the decision.

FROM THE OPINION

. . . Marriage is a vital social institution. The exclusive commitment of two individuals to each other nurtures love and mutual support; it brings stability to our society. For those who choose to marry, and for their children, marriage provides an abundance of legal, financial, and social benefits. The question before us is whether, consistent with the Massachusetts Constitution, the Commonwealth may deny the protections, benefits, and obligations conferred by civil marriage to two individuals of the same sex who wish to marry. We conclude that it may not. The Massachusetts Constitution affirms the dignity and equality of all individuals. It forbids the creation of second-class citizens. . . .

We are mindful that our decision marks a change in the history of our marriage law. Many people hold deep-seated religious, moral and ethical convictions that marriage should be limited to the union of one man and one woman, and that homosexual conduct is immoral. Many hold equally strong religious, moral, and ethical convictions that same-sex couples are entitled to be married. . . . Neither view answers the question before us. Our concern is with the Massachusetts Constitution. . . .

Barred access to the protections, benefits, and obligations of civil marriage, a person who enters into an intimate, exclusive union with another of the same sex is arbitrarily deprived of membership in one of our community's most rewarding and cherished institutions. That exclusion is incompatible with the constitutional principles of respect for individual autonomy and equality under law.

SIDEBAR

An excerpt from the lengthy opinion in this case is available on the companion website.

PARALEGAL APPLICATION **3.5**

WHICH CAMP ARE YOU IN?

"A battle for the hearts and minds of the American people is being waged, and the battleground is the institution of public marriage."[34] The warriors fall into four main camps:

- Those who seek to preserve marriage in its traditional form, viewing it as a crucially important social, cultural, religious, and legal institution. Justice

continued

Scalia articulated the fear driving this camp in his dissent in *Lawrence v. Texas*, the case in which the U.S. Supreme Court held it unconstitutional for a state to prosecute consenting same-sex adults for engaging in private sexual conduct that does not involve prostitution. He expressed his view that the majority in that case "largely signed onto the so-called homosexual agenda" and effectively decreed "the end of all morals legislation" causing "massive disruption of the current social order."[35] This camp does not want to extend any legally recognized status to same-sex couples.

- Those who believe that same-sex marriage is inevitable. This position has recently been described as follows:

  Attempts to amend constitutions so as to make legal marriage impossible for same-sex couples are futile.... Where such amendments have been adopted, they will eventually be repealed or invalidated, because the "incoming tide," i.e., the long-term international trend, will eventually bring full legal equality to our fellow human beings who happen to be lesbian and gay individuals, or members of same-sex couples, with or without children.[36]

- Those who would abolish civil marriage. "The law should not define, regulate, or recognize marriage. Marriage—the structured, publicly-proclaimed, communally-supported relationship of mutual commitment—should become solely a religious and cultural institution with no legal definition or status. . . . Culturally, marriage no longer plays the role in our society it once did."[37] In this option, with a variety of religious models to choose from, the door might open to polygamous marriages.

- Those who believe marriage should continue to be restricted to heterosexual couples but that under the Equal Protection Clause of the Constitution, an alternative legal status according equivalent rights (such as civil unions) should be established for same-sex couples.

SIDEBAR

As responsible citizens and voters, we will each be called upon to consider this issue over the next decade. Which position do you presently espouse? Why? Are you persuaded in any respect by the *Goodridge* decision?

FEDERAL AND INTERSTATE RECOGNITION OF MARRIAGE

The choice of law rule traditionally applied with respect to interstate recognition of marriage provides that the validity of a marriage will be determined according to the law of the state in which it was entered. This common law rule is reinforced by Article IV, Section 1 of the U.S. Constitution, which provides that "Full Faith and Credit shall be given in each State to the public Acts, Records, and judicial Proceedings of every other state." Guided by these principles, the states have historically validated out-of-state marriages, even if a marriage would have been prohibited under local law (for example, a marriage between first cousins valid in Massachusetts is recognized and given effect in a state that does not permit such marriages under its own law). This approach appeared to work satisfactorily, until same-sex marriage and other nonmarital family forms came onto the scene.

Following the *Baehr* case in Hawaii, opponents of same-sex marriage became alarmed that another state might do exactly what Hawaii had almost done—and what Massachusetts eventually did in 2003 and California did in 2008—legalize same-sex marriage. In response, at the federal level, Congress passed (and President Clinton signed into law in 1998) the *Defense of Marriage Act (DOMA)*. The Act does not go so far as to declare same-sex marriages illegal, but it does provide that, for purposes of federal law, "the word 'marriage' means only a legal union between one man and one woman as husband and wife, and the word 'spouse' refers only to a person of the opposite sex who is a husband or wife."[38] The practical effect of this legislation is to deny to same-sex married couples all of the rights and privileges granted under federal law to heterosexual married couples. The Act further provides that no state can be forced to recognize a same-sex marriage, stating:

> No State, territory, or possession of the United States, or Indian tribe, shall be required to give effect to any public act, record, or judicial proceeding of any other State, territory, possession, or tribe respecting a relationship between persons of the same sex that is treated as a marriage under the laws of such other State, territory, possession, or tribe or a right or claim arising from such relationship.[39]

Following the federal lead, many states have enacted legislation in the form of statutes (commonly called mini-DOMAs) banning same-sex marriage and, in some states, civil unions and domestic partnerships as well.

In addition to the federal DOMA, there continues to be considerable public support and legislative commitment to passage of a Federal Marriage Amendment to the U.S. Constitution. The amendment would define marriage as the union of a man and a woman and could be used to overrule state or local protections for same-sex couples and their children. To become part of the Constitution, the amendment would need to be approved by two-thirds of Congress and then be ratified by the legislatures of three-fourths of the states.

Defense of Marriage Act (DOMA)
a federal law restricting the definition of marriage to the union of one man and one woman for purposes of federal law and allowing the states to deny full faith and credit to same-sex marriages valid in a sister state

Paralegal Practice Tip
Some states, for many years, have had Marriage Evasion Statutes, under which a marriage may not be recognized if the parties leave their state of residence and go to another state with more lenient marriage rules for the sole purpose of marrying there and with the intention of returning to their home state following the marriage.

THE PARALEGAL'S ROLE

The paralegal's role with respect to marriage is evolving with the changes that are occurring in our society's culture as well as in the law. Forty years ago, that role was minimal and entailed such tasks as obtaining certified copies of marriage certificates or documenting the incidents of a common law marriage in a small number of cases. Today the ramifications of same-sex marriage are being felt in every area of substantive law. The scope of the paralegal's role with regard to marriage will continue to grow and may well include being active in a case that "pushes the envelope."

CHAPTER **SUMMARY**

In this chapter, we have reviewed:

- the evolution of marriage and the respective rights and roles of husbands and wives within it
- the significance of the right to marry as a "fundamental" right
- the various kinds of marriage and the requirements for establishing them
- the rights, benefits, and obligations that flow from marriage
- the trends and controversy surrounding same-sex marriage

In 1965, this chapter would have been one-third as long and the content would have been cut-and-dried. It was a different era then. In that year, the U.S. Supreme Court described marriage in the following terms in the *Griswold* decision:

> Marriage is a coming together for better or worse, hopefully enduring and intimate to the degree of being sacred. It is an association that promotes a way of life, not causes; a harmony in living, not political faiths; a bilateral loyalty, not commercial or social projects. Yet it is an association for as noble a purpose as any involved in our prior decisions.[40]

Today marriage appears to have become the antithesis of all the things the *Griswold* Court held it to be. Fewer people are choosing to marry (56% of men and 52% of women in the year 2000)[41] and increasing numbers of those who do marry eventually divorce. Marriage has become the focal point for a variety of causes including the gay, gender, religious, and states' rights agendas. It has become a political football at the national and local levels. It is now treated as an economic partnership between alleged equals who are increasingly privately structuring their "marital" rights. It is also decreasingly the environment in which children are born and raised, as new forms of legal relationships are established.

Whatever view an individual espouses, we can be certain that the federal government and the states will continue to take a strong interest in marriage and the family as the fundamental social through which culture, values, and wealth are transmitted from one generation to the next. The Massachusetts Supreme Court's 4–3 decision in the *Goodridge* case has fueled the fire. Its impact is being felt across the nation. As of November 2006, 19 states already had constitutions limiting marriage to one man and one woman, and 26 states had laws enforcing that limitation.[42] It is likely that the current flurry of legislation and challenges will continue with mixed results.[43] The constitutionality of the Defense of Marriage Act itself is likely to be called into question as there are those who strongly contend that Congress does not have the power to limit the effect of the Full Faith and Credit clause of the Constitution.[44] And only time will reveal the extent to which same-sex marriages entered in Massachussetts and California will be recognized by the courts of the other states. The next decade promises to be a dynamic one as zealous citizens, the courts, and legislatures attempt to deal with the challenges that inevitably accompany change.

KEY TERMS

Affinity

Anti-Heartbalm Statutes

Bigamy

Breach of promise

Civil law

Common law marriage

Community property state

Compensatory damages

Consanguinity

Consortium

Covenant marriage

Defense of Marriage Act (DOMA)

Donee

Donor

Emancipation

Expectation damages

Incest

Intestate

Laws of descent and distribution

Liquidated damages

Marital communications privilege

Marriage

Marriage Evasion Statute

Married Women's Property Acts

Polygamy

Proxy marriage

Putative spouse

Reliance damages

Specific performance

Tort

Void

REVIEW QUESTIONS

1. Describe how the definition of marriage has evolved over the past 200 years.

2. Describe covenant marriage.

3. Define "putative spouse" and discuss its significance.

4. Describe a woman's status in marriage under the common law.

5. Describe the purpose of a "married women's property act."

6. Identify the purpose of an action for breach of promise, and describe why such causes of actions were eliminated.

7. Describe the significance of the Supreme Court's decision in *Loving v. Virginia*.

8. Distinguish between prohibitions against marriage based on consanguinity and affinity and give an example of each.

9. Identify the common technical requirements for a ceremonial marriage and indicate what the consequence commonly is for failure to comply with a technical requirement.

10. Identify the common requirements for a valid common law marriage.

11. Identify a minimum of six rights and benefits that flow from a valid ceremonial or common law marriage.

12. Describe the significance of the *Goodridge* case decided by the Massachusetts Supreme Judicial Court in 2003.

13. Distinguish same-sex marriage from other forms of marriage in its effect.

14. Identify the most common objections to same-sex marriage and the most common arguments favoring it.

15. Describe the position of the federal government with respect to same-sex marriage and identify the form in which it is expressed.

FOCUS ON **THE JOB**

THE FACTS

Mary W. is a 15-year-old girl who resides in Texas. She believes she has fallen madly in love with a man, Marty C., who rides bulls in the rodeo circuit. He is a resident of Massachusetts and is 23 years old. Mary says they were bound to find each other because, looking at their family histories, they have discovered they are actually first cousins. Mary says she has done her legal homework and that she and Marty have come up with a plan. Because her mother opposes the marriage, Mary is going to get her step-father to consent to the marriage in writing. Then she will go to Massachusetts and she and Marty will get married there and then move to Colorado, where she is firmly convinced they will live happily ever after. Mary spoke with your supervisor, Attorney Tauson, about this at a recent family party. He is not interested in becoming involved in the case, as he knows Mary's mother personally. However, he says that it would be a good exercise for you, his paralegal, to research the legal issues relating to Mary's circumstances.

THE ASSIGNMENT

Research the law in Texas, Massachusetts, and Colorado to determine whether or not Mary and Marty can enter a valid marriage in any of those states under the circumstances described. You will need, at the least, to look at:

- the minimum age for marrying with and without parental consent in each state
- the circumstances under which a minimum age requirement may be waived in each state
- whether or not first cousins are permitted to marry in any of the states
- whether any of the states has a marriage evasion law that might affect the validity of any purported marriage
- whether any of the states permits common law marriages and, if so, under what circumstances

Summarize your research and conclusions in a memorandum to Attorney Tauson.

FOCUS ON **ETHICS**

Assume that you are Attorney Tauson's paralegal and that he has been retained to advise Mary in the above fact pattern. He has asked you to interview her and prepare a brief report about what you learn and your general impressions of Mary. Assume that the fact pattern reflects the basic content of the interview with one exception: Mary tells you that she plans to forge her mother's signature consenting to the marriage. She is confident she can do it because she has "been doing it for years on report cards and absence slips at school." She directs you not to tell Attorney Tauson about this little scheme, because he knows her mom and would "tell on her." What do you plan to do? Indicate how the ethical canons for paralegals promulgated by the National Federation of Paralegal Associations (NFPA) (contained in Appendix B) apply to this situation.

FOCUS ON **CASE LAW**

The South Carolina case of *Callen v. Callen*, 365 S.C. 618, 620 S.E.2d 59 (2005), is located on the companion website for this text in the material related to Chapter 3. Locate and read the case and then respond to the following questions:

1. What was the legal history of the case: What kind of a case is it? Where was it considered prior to reaching the South Carolina Supreme Court and with what result?

2. What issue(s) are being appealed, and by whom?

3. What was the South Carolina Supreme Court's holding?

4. What is the significance of the fact that the parties lived in several different states during the course of their relationship?

5. According to the South Carolina Supreme Court, what is the proper standard for determining whether the parties entered a common law marriage?

6. What is the appropriate burden of proof?

7. What was the "impediment" to the parties' "marriage"? Could it have been overcome? Was it?

8. According to the South Carolina Supreme Court, what is the nature of the intent a party must have to be married?

9. What did the court say the problem was regarding the admission of testimony by three "surprise" witnesses?

10. Why had the trial court awarded the purported wife more than $100,000 in attorneys' fees? Did the South Carolina Supreme Court agree?

11. What were the main concerns raised in the dissenting opinion of the Chief Justice of the South Carolina Supreme Court?

Note: The decision in this case was handed down shortly after a proposal to eliminate common law marriage was introduced in the South Carolina General Assembly. (See End Note 4.)

FOCUS ON **STATE LAW AND PROCEDURE**

Identify and prepare a report on the relevant statutes in the state where you live regarding the following:

1. relationships prohibited from marrying
2. minimum age for a person to be married
3. exceptions, if any, to the minimum age requirement
4. location where marriage licenses can be obtained
5. types of medical tests required, if any
6. recognition of common law marriage in your state

Information is included in this chapter regarding some of these questions, but you need to research current law in your jurisdiction in case there have been changes.

FOCUS ON **TECHNOLOGY**

WEBSITES OF INTEREST

http://www.findlaw.com

This site provides state-by-state links to a variety of marriage laws. Accuracy and currency of information should be verified prior to use.

http://www.law.cornell.edu

This is an academically based site that is very informative and provides a variety of links including links to federal and state codes.

http://www.polygamy.org

This is the website for the group Tapestry Against Polygamy, an organization that advocates against polygamy and provides assistance to individuals who leave polygamous cults.

http://www.usmarriagelaws.com

This site provides a summary of marriage laws of the states and selected countries. Information should be verified prior to use.

ASSIGNMENTS

1. Using online resources, locate your state's "anti-heartbalm" statute, if any.
2. Using online resources, locate the provisions in your state governing the recognition of same-sex marriage. When were they enacted?
3. Locate the California decision striking down that state's ban on gay marriage. Then search for two law review articles that discuss the decision.

chapter **four**
ANNULMENT

A udrey's husband, John, recently told her that he'd initially married her only because she was pregnant and that he'd never had any intention of consummating the marriage or staying married. She is heartbroken and wants to have their marriage annulled. John says he no longer feels the way he did when they got married. He loves their son and there is no way that he wants the marriage to terminate by annulment or divorce.

IN THIS CHAPTER YOU WILL LEARN

- What an annulment is
- What the differences are between annulment and divorce
- What the difference is between a void and a voidable marriage
- What the procedure is for obtaining an annulment
- What the grounds for annulment are
- What the defenses are to an annulment action
- What the consequences of an annulment are
- What the role of a paralegal is in an annulment action

"…if every misrepresentation made by the wooer or the wooed were to pave the way to a courthouse for a disappointed spouse suddenly made aware of unsuspected and deliberately concealed frailties of the other, society would indeed have reached a pretty pass. Shall the wife be entitled to nullify her solemnly accepted status if, forsooth, in the face of previous protestations to the contrary, her husband reveals himself as the possessor of a bewitching glass eye or a set of pearly false teeth…? Of course not, for such fraud has not the slightest bearing on the objectives of matrimony.…*Caveat emptor* [Let the buyer beware] is the harsh but necessary maxim of the law."[1]

DEFINITION OF ANNULMENT

Marriage
a civil contract between a man and a woman or between two same-sex partners in a state that permits marriage of partners of the same sex

Void *ab initio*
of no legal effect from the outset; a contract is void *ab initio* if it seriously offends law or public policy

Voidable marriage
a marriage capable of being nullified because of a circumstance existing at the time it was established; the marriage remains valid unless and until it is declared invalid by a court of competent jurisdiction

Annulment
the legal procedure for declaring that a marriage is null and void because of an impediment existing at its inception

Ecclesiastical law
the law governing the doctrine and discipline of a particular church

Consanguinity
a blood relationship between individuals

Affinity
the relationship a spouse has to the blood relatives of the other spouse; relationship by marriage

Impotence
lack of capacity to procreate due to inability to have sexual intercourse or to incompetent sperm or ova

Marriage is a civil contract between a man and a woman or between two same-sex partners in a state that permits marriage of partners of the same sex. In order for the marriage to be valid, the parties must satisfy the basic legal requirements for entering a marriage contract. There must be an offer, acceptance, and consideration; the parties must have capacity to contract under applicable state law; the subject matter of the contract must not be illegal; and the contract must be freely entered and not the product of fraud or duress. When one or more of these requirements is not met, the marriage contract may be either **void ab initio**—it never existed because of a legal impediment—or **voidable**—able to be rescinded or revoked in an action by a party to the contract who has been wronged, or in some circumstances, by a third party whose rights are impacted by the contract.

An **annulment** is the legal procedure for declaring that a marriage is null and void. Strictly speaking, an annulment refers to nullification of a voidable marriage, a marriage capable of being nullified because of a circumstance existing at the time it was established (such as undue influence or fraud). If no action is taken to annul a voidable marriage, the marriage will continue to be deemed valid. On the other hand, if a marriage is void *ab initio* because it is prohibited by law (such as when a prior marriage of one of the parties has never been terminated by death, divorce, or annulment), the marriage is automatically null and void, invalid from the outset, although a legal declaration of nullity is customarily necessary to establish that a legal marriage never existed. Many states do not distinguish between void and voidable marriages in their statutes, but courts frequently look to common law distinctions as they interpret statutes.

Historical Perspective

The distinction between void and voidable marriages grew out of early **ecclesiastical (church) law** and English common law. For centuries, the Catholic Church, and subsequently the ecclesiastical courts of England, regarded a marriage, once entered, as indissoluble. Although there technically was no divorce under ecclesiastical law, certain "canonical disabilities" existing at the time of the marriage ceremony were viewed as entitling parties to an annulment, essentially a religious ruling that no marriage ever existed between the parties. These disabilities included, for example, **consanguinity, affinity,** and **impotence.** With the decline of the church's jurisdiction over domestic matters, the courts elected to recognize in case law additional grounds for annulment such as fraud, "lunacy," duress, and other incapacities. This heritage is apparent today in the continuing dichotomy between civil and religious annulments in this country. However, civil annulments are sometimes sought based on the failure of one of the parties to live up to a premarital promise to practice a particular religious faith. Whether or not a court will grant an annulment in such circumstances tends to turn on the extent to which religion is central to the marriage and permeates multiple facets of marital life and culture (diet, dress, language, social life, etc.).

DIVORCE AND ANNULMENT: A COMPARISON

Depending on the circumstances of the case, a party may ask a court to dissolve a marriage, annul it, or issue a declaratory judgment regarding the validity of the marriage. Annulment is a viable option for terminating a marriage when appropriate grounds exist and when it better meets a party's personal and strategic needs than a fault or no-fault divorce. Some states establish time limits within which such actions may be brought.

Exhibit 4.1 summarizes the major differences between an annulment and a divorce. Occasionally the law of a state and the facts of a particular case are such that a party may seek either a divorce or an annulment based on the same ground. For example, in Tennessee, an annulment may be sought on the ground that a previous marriage was still in existence at the time of a subsequent marriage (unless the former spouse has been absent for five years or more and is not known to be living).

> **Paralegal Practice Tip**
>
> Several religions provide for annulment in one form or another. For example, although there are divergent views of Muslim family law, each provides for annulment—in effect, "cancellation" of a marriage—if a serious deficiency arises in either party, such as "chronic madness," serious disease, or an inability to fulfill "conjugal obligations" for an extended period. The civil laws that provide for such an annulment without the necessity of a divorce are solidly grounded in Islamic beliefs, principles set forth in the Koran, and the rulings of Imams (religious leaders). An annulment under the principles of Muslim family law thus represents both a secular and a religious event.

EXHIBIT 4.1 Differences Between Divorce and Annulment

ANNULMENT	**DIVORCE**
In an annulment action, one or both of the parties claim that a purported marriage is not valid and does not exist.	A divorce severs a marriage the parties acknowledge exists.
The ground for annulment exists at the time the marriage relationship is formed.	The cause for divorce arises after the marriage was established.
An annulment declares an alleged marriage to be null and void *ab initio*.	A divorce terminates a legal marriage as of the date of divorce.
If a marriage is annulled, the parties generally regain the legal rights and responsibilities they had before the marriage occurred.	Traditionally, after a divorce, the parties have a continuing legal status as former spouses with respect to division of property, custody of children, and spousal support.
Certain rights or entitlements, such as worker's compensation benefits or occasionally alimony from a previous marriage that terminated upon a recipient's remarriage, may be revived upon annulment of the later marriage.	Worker's compensation or alimony benefits flowing from a prior marriage will generally not be revived upon dissolution of the recipient's later marriage.
In some states, annulment will result in the extinguishing of interests in property acquired during the purported marriage. In other states, the interests	Upon divorce, property acquired during the marriage is divided between the parties based on principles of equitable division or community

> **Paralegal Practice Tip**
>
> An Ecclesiastical Tribunal of the Roman Catholic Church can still issue a "Declaration of Nullity," an annulment of a marriage under church law, if a petitioning party can establish that the marriage was not valid at its inception. Such religious annulments are recognized by the church but not the state. Before marrying again, the prior marriage must also be dissolved under the civil law by divorce or annulment.

continued

Quasi-marital property
property treated as if it was acquired by the parties during the marriage even though the marriage was never valid

may be preserved in whole or part through application of equitable remedies, such as the putative spouse doctrine (in effect, treating the property as "*quasi-marital property*").

property rights absent an enforceable agreement to the contrary.

An annulment establishes that no valid marriage ever existed. Because the right to potentially receive spousal support flows from a valid marriage, there customarily is no right to spousal support following an annulment.

Spousal support may be awarded to one of the parties based on need and the other party's ability to pay.

If the parties obtain an annulment establishing that no valid marriage ever existed between them, they must each file amended returns (as unmarried persons) for all tax years within a three-year period of limitations.[2]

Divorced spouses may file joint tax returns provided they are married for some portion of the taxable year.

Declaratory judgment
a binding adjudication that establishes the rights, status, or other legal relations between the parties

Paralegal Practice Tip
Even if not required to establish rights between the parties with respect to each other, it is often desirable to obtain an annulment declaring the marriage null and void when third parties are impacted, such as lenders who may act with respect to the parties under a belief that they are married. A Declaration of Annulment may also be essential to determining the rights of individuals in the probate context. For example, what are the rights of someone who claims to be a "surviving spouse" when the validity of a marriage is in question? Such issues may be especially problematic in states that recognize common law marriage.

Tennessee law also provides as a ground for divorce that "either party has knowingly entered into a second marriage, in violation of a previous marriage, still subsisting."[3] In the case of marriages that are void due to the continuing existence of a prior marriage, decrees of divorce or annulment have the same practical effect of providing a public record declaring that the purported marriage is invalid, void from its inception, and a legal nullity. Because generally only marital property is subject to division upon divorce and spousal support obligations are based on the existence of a valid marriage, when a marriage is terminated by divorce on the ground of bigamy, no property division or alimony will be awarded by the court as "incidents of divorce." If there was no marriage, there was no marital property.[4]

PROCEDURE FOR OBTAINING AN ANNULMENT

The procedure for obtaining an annulment varies from state to state. For example, in some states, a Complaint or Petition for Annulment is filed; in others the action is called a Petition for Declaration of Invalidity of Marriage. (A copy of a Colorado Petition for Declaration of Invalidity of Marriage is accessible on the companion website.) Sometimes a party who is not able to file for an annulment will seek clarification as to his or her marital status by filing a *declaratory judgment* action. Case 4.1 provides an example of such a situation. Once the court conducts an evidentiary hearing and establishes the legal status of the marriage, it may address any potentially related issues, such as property division, spousal support, child custody, and child support.

Under common law, in the absence of a controlling statute to the contrary, a void marriage was absolutely void from its inception (void *ab initio*) and continued to be so. Technically, no judicial pronouncement was necessary to annul the marriage and restore the parties to their original rights. The states now vary with respect to whether or not a decree is necessary to invalidate a void marriage. In Connecticut, for example, in the *Davis* case, the court determined that a marriage deemed void *ab initio* should be declared so by the court rather than by the parties simply asserting its invalidity.

CASE **4.1** *McCombs v. Haley,* 13 Neb. App. 729, 700 N.W.2d 659 (2005)

BACKGROUND

In this case, Dianne McCombs filed a declaratory judgment action seeking a declaration that the purported marriage between herself and Dale Ray Haley was null and void. A question arose as to whether or not the trial court had subject matter jurisdiction to entertain such an action under the facts of the case.

FROM THE OPINION

…Dianne testified that she met Dale in 1969 while she was living in Nebraska. In September 1975, Dale was serving time in prison in Leavenworth, Kansas. At that time, Dale and Dianne entered into an arrangement in which Dianne agreed to be Dale's wife "on paper" so that the parole board would believe he had a wife and son to come home to when he was released. Dianne and an individual named David Harpster obtained a marriage license in Dianne's and Dale's names.…In obtaining the license, Harpster represented to the clerk's office that he was Dale. Dale never… authorized Harpster to act on his behalf. On September 29, 1975, Dianne and Harpster, again representing himself as Dale, participated in a marriage ceremony in Lancaster County. At the time the ceremony took place, Dale was still in prison.…

Dianne testified that when she and Harpster obtained the marriage license and went through the marriage ceremony, she did not intend to actually be Dale's wife. Dianne testified that she never expected she and Dale would live together as husband and wife and that they never did. She further testified that she and Dale never consummated the purported marriage and that she saw Dale only one time between 1977, when Dale was released from prison, and 1978, when she moved out of Nebraska. She had no contact with him after moving out of Nebraska until she contacted him about the declaratory judgment action.

Dale entered a voluntary appearance and did not appear at the trial. Dale's testimony was presented in the form of an affidavit and was consistent with Dianne's testimony.…

At the conclusion of the trial, the trial court found that Dianne's petition should be granted because Dianne and Dale never actually entered into their purported marriage. The court declared that the purported marriage was "null and void ab initio, from the beginning."…

… A declaratory judgment action is to declare the rights, status, or other legal relations between the parties.…

We further recognize that Dianne did not have a remedy, other than a declaratory judgment action, available to her. An action for declaratory judgment does not lie where another equally serviceable remedy is available.…Dianne did not have an equally serviceable remedy available to her, as she could not file an action for an annulment. Dianne could not satisfy the residency requirement for an annulment.…Further, none of the grounds for an annulment listed in Neb. Rev. Stat. §42–374 (Reissue 2004) apply to Dianne's purported marriage to Dale.

continued

> The grounds under that statute include the following: (1) The marriage between the parties is prohibited by law, (2) either party is impotent at the time of the marriage, (3) either party had a spouse living at the time of the marriage, (4) either party was mentally ill or a person with mental retardation at the time of the marriage, or (5) force or fraud. An annulment action can be granted only when one or more of the grounds enumerated in §42–374 exist.... Therefore, based on the above analysis and the circumstances of the present case, we determine that the trial court did not abuse its discretion in entertaining jurisdiction over Dianne's declaratory judgment action.
>
> ### SIDEBAR
>
> This opinion is available in its entirety on the companion website.

The case involved two nineteen-year-old residents of Connecticut who went on an automobile ride with some friends. In the context of the fun-filled occasion, the "wife" dared the "husband" to marry her. He accepted the dare, a license for the marriage was obtained in New York State, and the ceremony was performed there by a Justice of the Peace. Neither party intended at the time to assume a marital status and the parties never cohabited after the ceremony.[5]

Burden of Proof

Burden of proof
a party's duty to prove a disputed assertion or charge

In order to obtain an annulment, proper grounds must exist and the party seeking the annulment must act within any applicable time limitations. Because there is a presumption that a marriage is valid, the burden of proving that one is not rests with the party challenging its validity. The general standard of proof in a civil action is ***preponderance of the evidence.*** However, the standard of proof in an annulment action is commonly the higher burden of ***clear and convincing evidence*** as in a traditional tort action for fraud. Nevada, for example, established this standard in the *Irving* case in 2006. In annulment cases involving allegations of fraud, "Nevada courts will now require a party seeking to annul a marriage on the grounds of fraud to prove the fraud with clear and convincing evidence. Nevada law favors this higher burden of proof because of a strong public policy in favor of marriage and against annulment."[6]

Preponderance of the evidence
standard of proof requiring that the evidence show that it is more likely than not that an alleged fact is true or false as claimed

Clear and convincing evidence
a standard of proof that requires that the evidence show that it is highly probable or reasonably certain that an alleged fact is true or false as claimed; a greater burden than preponderance of the evidence, but less than evidence beyond a reasonable doubt, the standard for criminal trials

Standing to Petition for Annulment

Generally either party to a purported marriage may seek an annulment absent authority to the contrary. However, in some states, only an "innocent" party may be able to seek relief in the form of annulment. In most states, a parent or guardian of a child may petition for an annulment when parental consent was required for marriage and was not provided or the age of the child was misrepresented.

Standing
an individual's right to bring a matter before the court and seek relief based on a claim that he or she has a stake in the outcome of the case

A Conservator or Guardian of an adult may file a Complaint for Annulment on behalf of a ward. In a 2005 case, for example, a Conservator filed a Complaint alleging that his ward lacked the mental capacity to enter into a contract of marriage and that the defendant exerted undue influence on her. The ward's treating neurologist testified that the ward was unable "to understand and appreciate the benefits, obligations and responsibilities of marriage" well before the time of the marriage ceremony, that her condition was steadily deteriorating, and that she had no lucid intervals. Since she also had already been declared incompetent by a court, her ability to enter into contracts or other legally significant acts had been terminated. An appellate court affirmed a trial court's annulment of the marriage.[7]

Courts in several states have addressed the question of whether or not an administrator or executor of a decedent's estate may seek an annulment on behalf of the deceased "spouse" after he or she has died. The prevailing rule is that a void marriage may be annulled after the death of one of the parties, absent a statute or case law to the contrary. The validity of such "marriages" may be challenged by someone who claims to be a surviving spouse as well as by third parties, such as children of the decedent. With a voidable marriage, such as one in which a man marries a woman solely to obtain "**green card**" status, third parties (such as beneficiaries under the will of a decedent) are generally not permitted to seek an annulment of the decedent's marriage post death.[8] Although some courts have held that annulment actions may be commenced after the death of a person entitled to an annulment by a person or persons whose legal rights depend on whether the marriage was valid or void, some place restrictions on such actions if, for example, the marriage was followed by cohabitation and the birth of children.[9]

GROUNDS FOR ANNULMENT

Particularly with the advent of no-fault divorce, courts are more likely than ever to hold to strict standards for granting annulments and to apply the doctrine of *caveat emptor* (let the buyer beware) when it comes to marriages that fail to meet the parties' expectations. Generally, a party may not "question the validity of the marriage upon the ground of reliance upon the express or implied representations of the other with respect to such matters as character, habits, chastity, business or social standing, financial worth or prospects, or matters of similar nature. It is conclusively presumed that each of the parties made his or her own independent investigation and was satisfied with the result. . . ."[10] However, annulment still is an option for parties to an alleged "marriage" in some situations.

Specific grounds for annulment vary considerably from state to state. Commonly, grounds are of two types:

1. Grounds relating to legal capacity to marry, customarily rendering the marriage void *ab initio*:
   - nonage/underage
   - consanguinity
   - affinity
   - bigamy/polygamy
   - physical incapacity or disease (in a limited number of jurisdictions)
2. Grounds relating to intent to marry, customarily rendering the marriage voidable:
   - fraud
   - lack of **consent**
   - duress
   - undue influence
   - impotence

Based on prevailing public policies, all states establish the "marriages" that are prohibited and therefore void. For example, the majority of states expressly prohibit marriage when a prior marriage of either or both parties is still in existence (bigamy/polygamy), when the parties are too closely related by consanguinity (blood), when the parties are of the same sex, or when one or both of the parties is "too young" to marry according to state law. A decreasing number prohibit marriage when the parties are too closely related by affinity (marriage) or when one or both have an incurable, sexually transmitted disease.

Most states also identify by statute the grounds for annulment of a voidable marriage, based on some circumstance existing at the time a marriage was established, such as a lack of free consent or consent based upon a fraudulent representation by one of the parties to the other. Some states, such as Delaware and Arizona, grant annulments only on grounds enumerated by statute.

Green card
a document (registration card) evidencing a resident alien's status as a permanent resident of the United States; a "green card marriage" is a sham marriage in which a U.S. citizen marries a foreign citizen for the sole purpose of allowing the foreign citizen to become a permanent U.S. resident

Consent
the approval, permission, or assent to some act or purpose, given voluntarily by a competent person

Paralegal Practice Tip
The term incest is used in some state statutes to describe prohibited degrees of consanguinity and affinity.

Other states (such as Kansas and Tennessee) have statutes setting forth some grounds but do not consider those to be the exclusive potential grounds for annulment. A small number of states (such as Florida and Rhode Island) have no specific statutory provisions laying out grounds for annulment of voidable marriages.

PARALEGAL APPLICATION 4.1

KNOW THE LAW IN YOUR JURISDICTION

Because there is considerable variation state to state, it is important to know the law governing grounds for annulment and prohibited marriages as well as the procedural rules applicable to a particular annulment action. Examples of some of the unique provisions in certain jurisdictions include the following:

- In Hawaii, a statute expressly provides as a ground for annulment that one of the parties was afflicted by a "loathsome disease" at the time of the marriage that was unknown to the party seeking an annulment. (HRS §580–21 (6))

- A small number of states list "joke," "jest," or "dare" as a ground for annulment. Among these states are Colorado (CRS §14–10–111 (1)(f)) and Delaware (13 Del. C. §1506 (a)(6)).

- Rhode Island provides special exceptions to the prohibited marriages statute with respect to consanguinity and affinity for marriages allowed by Jewish religious law. (R.I. General Laws §15–1–4)

- In Delaware, a marriage between paupers is voidable. (13 Del. C. §101 (c))

- Virginia will grant an annulment "where, prior to the marriage, either party had been, without the knowledge of the other, a prostitute." (Va. Code Ann. §20–89.1(b))

- In Mississippi, a cause for annulment is the "Pregnancy of the wife by another person, if the husband did not know of such pregnancy." (Miss. Code Ann. §93–7–3 (e))

- Being under the influence of alcohol or drugs at the time of the marriage is a ground for annulment in several states such as Texas (§6.105) and Illinois (750 ILCS 5/301 (1)).

- Wisconsin prohibits marriages between persons closer in kin than second cousins unless the parties are first cousins and the woman is 55 or one party is sterile (Wis. Stat. §765.03 (1)). Utah has a similar provision (Utah Code Ann. §30–1–1 (2)(b)).

- Several states provide by statute or case law that a marriage voidable due to fraud or lack of mental capacity may not be annulled if the parties freely cohabit after knowledge of the fraud or restoration of mental capacity.

- Several states require that annulment actions be brought within limited time frames after the impediment is known such as sixty or ninety days or one or two years. In Wisconsin, with the exception of cases involving bigamy, annulments of marriages prohibited by law must be sought within ten years. (Wis. Stat. §767.313 (1)(d))

Bigamy

It is a requirement in every state that in order for a marriage to be valid, all prior marriages, if any, must have been terminated by death, annulment, or dissolution prior to entering the subsequent marriage. If terminated by divorce, the divorce must be final under the law of the jurisdiction where it was granted and any waiting period must have expired before a subsequent marriage takes place. Applications for marriage licenses customarily require that information regarding the termination of any prior marriages be provided (for example, the date of death of the last prior spouse or the date and jurisdiction in which the last decree of dissolution was entered).[11] When a party is seeking to annul a marriage based on the contention that the other party was still married to another individual in another state or another country, proof will need to be presented to the court documenting the prior marriage and the fact that the earlier spouse is still alive.[12] If the other party claims the earlier marriage has been dissolved, proof of dissolution needs to be presented to the court as a defense.

Bigamy
entering a subsequent marriage while a prior marriage of one or both of the parties is still in effect

Impotence

In general, parties to a marriage reasonably anticipate having a sexual relationship with their spouse after marriage. Impotence, or lack of a party's capacity to have sexual intercourse, may be a ground for annulment when the other party did not know of the condition at the time of the marriage. It may make the marriage voidable at the election of the unknowing party. However, that party may *ratify* the marriage by continuing to live with the other party and claiming a marital status under the law and before the general public. Unlike grounds such as bigamy and consanguinity, impotence is usually viewed as a ground available only to a party to the marriage and not to third persons, given the nature of proof required.

Ratification
acceptance or confirmation of a previous act, thereby making it valid from the moment it was done

Failure to *consummate* a marriage (or a concealed intent not to do so) is not necessarily a ground for annulment, but a willful refusal to consummate a marriage and/or cohabit without good cause may be. Even if the ground for annulment is not specifically impotence or lack of consummation, as a practical matter, it is often easier to obtain an annulment when the marriage has not been consummated. Concealment of prior homosexuality may not be a sufficient ground for annulment, but concealment of one's sexual preferences and/or limitations at the time of marriage may be sufficient. A unique challenge arises when courts are called on to consider the validity of a marriage in which one of the partners is a transsexual. (See Paralegal Application 4.3.)

Consummation
to make a marriage complete by engaging in sexual intercourse

PARALEGAL APPLICATION 4.2

ISSUES OF PROOF AND CONFLICT OF LAW WHEN MULTIPLE NATIONS ARE INVOLVED

An interesting question arises when the parties were married in a country where a husband is permitted under that nation's law to have more than one wife. Should a court in the United States view a later marriage as void or voidable? Should an annulment or a divorce be granted?

Foreign laws or judgments are entitled to a degree of deference under the *doctrine of comity,* but comity is a flexible doctrine and a court, in its discretion, may deny recognition of foreign laws or judgments that are inconsistent with public policies of the forum state in this country.[13] A court may also refuse to recognize an annulment obtained in another country if the individual who obtained it perpetrated a fraud in order to do so.[14]

Doctrine of comity
the practice of giving effect to the laws and judicial decisions of another jurisdiction (e.g., nation or state) even if not legally obligated to do so

PARALEGAL APPLICATION 4.3

TO BE A HE OR NOT TO BE A HE—SHOULD IT MATTER?

Courts in Florida, Kansas, New Jersey, New York, Ohio, and Texas have addressed issues related to marriages involving postoperative transsexual persons. In *M.T. v. J.T.*, a New Jersey court not only upheld the validity of a marriage involving a transsexual but also denied an annulment to a husband on the ground that his wife was a male-to-female transsexual. In explaining its rationale, the court stated:

> In sum, it has been established that an individual suffering from the condition of transexualism is one with a disparity between his or her genitalia or anatomical sex and his or her gender, that is, the individual's strong and consistent emotional and psychological sense of sexual being. A transsexual in a proper case can be treated medically by certain supportive measures and through surgery to remove and replace existing genitalia with sex organs which will coincide with the person's gender. If such sex reassignment surgery is successful and the postoperative transsexual is, by virtue of medical treatment, thereby possessed of the full capacity to function sexually as a male or female, as the case may be, we perceive no legal barrier, cognizable social taboo, or reason grounded in public policy to prevent that person's identification at least for purposes of marriage to the sex finally indicated.[15]

States other than New Jersey have tended to apply the narrow traditional meaning of male and female, basing sexual identity on the individual's chromosomal makeup as the true test rather than on concepts of "gender identity" or "self-identity." In a case decided in 2004, for example, a Florida Court of Appeals reversed and remanded a trial court ruling granting a divorce and custody of his adopted child to a female-to-male transsexual husband. The court held that Florida law "does not provide for or allow such marriages" and essentially agreed with the wife's position that the parties' marriage was void *ab initio*.[16]

SIDEBAR

The New Jersey and Florida cases referenced above are both provided in their entirety on the companion website for this text in the material related to Chapter 4 (see *M.T. v. J.T.*, 140 N.J. Super. 77, 355 A.2d 204 (1976) and *Kantaras v. Kantaras*, 884 So.2d 155 (Fla. App. 2004)). Which position do you think the courts should take on this issue? Should it make a difference if the parties are both aware of the sex change at the time the marriage is established?

Fraud

In order for a state to permit a marriage to be annulled on the basis of fraud, the fraud generally must be more than the type of fraud that would be sufficient to rescind an ordinary business contract. The fraud must directly affect the marital relationship in some manner. It must go to "the essentials of marriage." The elements of fraud are described in Paralegal Application 4.4.

Courts are reluctant to annul a marriage for fraud unless the defrauded party would not have entered the marriage except for the fraud. Decisions are made on a case-by-case basis, because what is considered essential to a marriage by one party may be of considerably less significance to another. Fraud related to personal characteristics or habits is generally not considered sufficient to justify annulment

PARALEGAL APPLICATION 4.4

THE ELEMENTS OF FRAUD

If a husband seeks an annulment on fraud grounds based on the fact that his wife lied to him about being pregnant so that he would marry her, he needs to plead and prove all of the elements of fraud:

a. a false representation by the wife—she told him she was pregnant when she was not

b. the wife's knowledge of the falsity or ignorance of its truth—she knew she was not pregnant

c. the misrepresentation concerns an essential of the marital relationship—childbearing and rearing is an essential of the marital relationship

d. the wife's intention that the husband act on the representation—she told him she was pregnant so that he would marry her

e. his reliance on the truth of the representation—he believed her and married her as a result of the misrepresentation

f. he sustained injury as a result of the misrepresentation—he entered a marriage he would otherwise not have entered

of a marriage. Annulments are also rarely, if ever, granted solely based on fraud or misrepresentation of a purely financial nature (business interests, financial worth or prospects, etc.) even when a perpetrator of the fraud admits to misrepresenting financial circumstances or deceiving the other party with respect to allegedly joint-business ventures.[17]

Examples of fraud that some courts have deemed go to the essentials of marriage have included fraud related to undisclosed intentions to not consummate a marriage, sexual orientation, the desire or ability to have children, a woman's concealment of her pregnancy by another man, prior marital status, chastity, promises about religion, and matters of health or drug abuse.[18] The Superior Court of New Jersey granted an annulment to a wife because the husband told her after they had married that he wanted to have children despite the fact that he had signed a premarital agreement in which he stated that he did not wish to have children. The court held that this situation constituted fraud relating to an essential element of the marriage contract.[19]

The Minnesota Supreme Court declined to grant an annulment to a husband who discovered after marriage that his wife had been committed to a mental institution prior to their marriage. After the marriage, she had a relapse and was again committed. In denying the annulment, the court reasoned that the wife had not actively concealed her prior commitment and that her husband had never inquired about it.[20] However, there are some physical conditions that do present a sufficient ground to warrant an annulment under certain circumstances, such as when a party to a marriage conceals from his or her spouse the existence of an incurable sexually transmitted disease (e.g., syphilis or HIV/AIDS). For example, in an unpublished California appellate decision in 2004, a court found that substantial evidence supported a trial court's finding that a wife's concealment of her incurable and highly transmittable syphilitic condition was a fraud going to the essence of the marriage, which warranted granting a judgment of annulment to the husband (who following the marriage had applied to INS for a green card for his wife).

The court concluded that "a spouse's concealment of a medical condition or sexually transmittable disease that does not absolutely foreclose intercourse or childbearing, but nevertheless endangers the life and health of the other spouse or their offspring, is so destructive of marital intimacy and the potential for procreation that it goes to 'the very essence of the marital relation.'..."[21]

Lack of Consent, Duress, and Undue Influence

Marriage is a contract and, like other contracts, may be voided by a lack of mental capacity of one or both of the parties. For a marriage to be valid there needs to be a shared intent to assume the rights and duties of marriage. Each party to a marriage must be capable of consenting at the time of the marriage and must be able to understand and appreciate the benefits, obligations, and responsibilities of marriage. A person who is mentally limited or incompetent for some purposes may still legally consent to marriage in a lucid moment. The standard is generally lower than it would be for a contract under the Uniform Commercial Code for a business transaction. Absent evidence to the contrary, it is generally assumed that an individual who is getting married basically understands what marriage is and wants to be married to his or her partner.

Several states set out by statute grounds for annulment that are related to lack of consent at the time the marriage was solemnized. For example, a party may be incapable of consenting due to a mental condition, duress, undue influence, or the effects of intoxicants of some kind. The lack of consent may also be expressed in statutes as a "lack of mutual assent" to the marriage relationship. If the marriage has been followed by cohabitation or otherwise ratified, consent grounds are usually unavailable.

Undue influence is generally said to occur where there has been a fraudulent influence over the mind and will of another to the extent that an action of that person is not freely done, but rather is the act of the one who procures the result. *Duress* is an extreme form of undue influence. Annulment actions on these grounds may be able to be brought by third parties as well as by a "spouse" and may, in some circumstances, be brought after the death of a party. (See Case 4.2.)

Undue influence
the improper use of power or trust in a way that deprives a person of his or her free will and substitutes another's purposes in its place

Duress
a threat of harm made to compel a person to do something contrary to his or her free will or judgment

CASE **4.2** *Estate of Goodwin v. Foust-Graham,* 171 N.C. App. 707, 615 S.E.2nd 398 (2005)

BACKGROUND

Under North Carolina law, the marriage of a person who is incapable of contracting from want of will is voidable. It will remain valid until it is declared void in a legal action. Prior to this case, North Carolina courts had annulled marriages on the basis of duress, but neither the North Carolina Supreme Court nor an appellate court in the state had addressed "undue influence" as a ground for annulment.

FROM THE OPINION

In the instant case, there was evidence pertaining to each of the factors that our Supreme Court has identified as relevant in analyzing undue influence.... Specifically, Goodwin was elderly at the time of the marriage, and there was testimony tending to establish that he was suffering from dementia and/or Alzheimer's disease. It is not disputed that he was subject to constant association with, and supervision by, Foust-Graham and that he had little association with his family or friends in the months immediately preceding the marriage.

continued

The marriage left Goodwin's previously existing estate plan in doubt and placed Foust-Graham in a position to take action that would substantially reduce the amount that Goodwin's daughter would inherit. Further, there was evidence that Foust-Graham procured the marriage, including Goodwin's apparent confusion as to why he was at the magistrate's office, the fact that Foust-Graham had driven Goodwin to the magistrate's office, and the fact that the marriage was undertaken suddenly. Accordingly, the jury could find that Goodwin was subject to undue influence, that Foust-Graham had the opportunity and disposition to exert undue influence, and that the marriage occurred as a result of undue influence.... a finding of undue influence is tantamount to a finding that Goodwin was incapable of contracting from want of will,...

SIDEBAR

This opinion is available in its entirety on the companion website.

Nonage/Underage

A marriage entered by an underage party in violation of state law may be deemed void or voidable if not ratified. Marriage laws in every state establish the minimum age under which a party may not marry. (See Exhibit 3.4 in Chapter 3.) With the exception of a few states (California, Kansas, Massachusetts, and Nebraska), they also provide a minimum age under which a party may not marry without the consent of a parent or guardian or the permission of the court. If an underage party goes to another state where he or she is of legal age, marries, and soon after returns to the state where he or she resides, some states will consider the marriage invalid (under so-called marriage evasion laws), while others will take the position that the marriage cannot be annulled, as it is valid where it was performed.

Nonage
below the minimum age established by law to perform a particular act

DEFENSES TO AN ANNULMENT ACTION

The most commonly raised defenses to an annulment action are:

- Compliance with state statutes governing marriage
- Ratification of the marriage by subsequent conduct
- Consummation of the marriage
- Laches
- Equitable estoppel
- Judicial estoppel
- Unclean hands

Compliance with State Statutes Governing Marriage

Each state lays out by statute a series of "requirements" for marriage. Those requirements generally include an application for and issuance of a license to marry signed under pain and penalty of perjury by persons eligible to marry (with parental consent or court approval if necessary), a marriage certificate, a ceremony performed by someone licensed in the state to perform marriages, and the return of an executed marriage certificate to the appropriate keeper of public records. Although a party may claim that failure to comply with such requirements should render a marriage void, states generally do not treat as void or voidable marriages contracted in violation of technical or procedural statutory requirements.[22]

Although misstatements on applications for marriage licenses usually do not provide a sufficient basis for an annulment, in some cases they will. For example, a North Carolina Court of Appeals applying Georgia law held that an annulment was appropriate when a wife indicated under oath on a Georgia application for a marriage license that she had been married twice before, when in fact she had been married seven times.[23]

Ratification of the Marriage by Subsequent Conduct

When a marriage is voidable, such as the marriage of a minor without parental consent, it can be ratified by the minor once he or she reaches the age of majority. Ratification is normally accomplished by the parties voluntarily continuing to live together as husband and wife after the minor attains the age of majority. Because of the strong public policy favoring marriage, most states establish, by statute or case law, a time frame within which the injured party (the minor) must disaffirm the marriage. The *Medlin* case decided in 1999 by an Arizona Court of Appeals provides an interesting instance in which a husband (in an apparent effort to avoid paying spousal support) attempted to have his nine-year marriage annulled on the grounds that he was a minor when he married his wife and that he did not have the consent of his custodial parent at the time of the marriage. The case involves ratification, conflict of law issues, a marriage evasion policy, the distinction between void and voidable marriages, and the validity of a step-parent's consent to a minor's marriage. (See Case 4.3.)

CASE **4.3** *Medlin v. Medlin,* 194 Ariz. 306, 981 P. 2d 1087 (Ariz. App. 1999)

In this case, the parties, who were both residents of Arizona, were married in Nevada in 1987 at a time when the wife was twenty-two years old and the husband was sixteen. At the time of the marriage, the husband was in the legal custody of his mother, who refused to consent to the marriage. Arizona law did not provide for stepparent consent but Nevada law did, so the husband obtained a note from his stepfather that described the boy as his son and gave consent to the marriage.

The parties lived together until 1996 at which time the husband sought a divorce. They divided their property by mutual agreement but did not address the issue of spousal maintenance. Following a trial, the trial court awarded the wife spousal maintenance of $300.00 per month for six years or until she remarried or either party died (whichever occurred first). The husband then claimed that the trial court erred in awarding spousal support and amended his petition for dissolution to request an annulment alleging the marriage was void under the laws of Arizona, because he never had consent to marry from his custodial parent. The trial judge denied the motion finding that the laws of Nevada, where the marriage took place, allowed a stepparent to consent to the marriage of a minor and that under Arizona law, out-of-state marriages valid under the law of the state of solemnization are valid under Arizona law.

The appeals court also held that the request to annul the marriage had no merit and it resolved the validity of the marriage by applying Arizona law. It reaffirmed the Arizona marriage evasion statute that provides that an Arizona resident cannot evade the laws of the state by going to another state to get married. By marrying in Nevada without proper consent, the parties evaded the laws of

continued

Arizona and therefore under basic conflict of law principles, the appeals court applied the law of Arizona to determine the validity of the marriage.

In looking at the applicable Arizona statutes, the appeals court stated that certain marriages, like those between close relatives, are prohibited and void. Although minors are required by statute to have the consent of a parent or guardian in order to obtain a license to marry in Arizona, there is no provision that such marriages are void. The court found that a marriage without proper consent is voidable unless ratified by the minor upon reaching the age of majority by continuing to live together as husband and wife. Since the parties in this case cohabited for approximately seven years after the husband reached the age of majority the marriage was deemed valid and the trial court's decree of dissolution and award of spousal maintenance were affirmed.

SIDEBAR

This opinion is available in its entirety on the companion website.

Consummation of the Marriage

In considering a complaint for annulment, courts may consider whether or not there has been cohabitation following a marriage. Cohabitation is evidence that the parties have been validly married, but it is not dispositive, nor is it essential to establish a marriage, particularly when there has been sexual intercourse prior to marriage.

Generally, if a voidable marriage is consummated with knowledge of an impediment, it will be considered to have been ratified. A Florida court, for example, has held that a marriage that has been consummated cannot be annulled on the basis of fraud alone.[24] There are also circumstances in which the parties may marry with full understanding that the marriage will never be consummated, as when one of the parties is incarcerated for life without possibility of parole or conjugal visitation.

Laches

The defense of **laches** is an equitable doctrine that precludes a litigant from asserting a claim if his or her unreasonable delay in raising the claim has prejudiced the opposing party. It is based on the notion that courts should not come to the aid of a party who has knowingly "slept on his rights" to the detriment of the other party.[25]

Laches
unreasonable delay in pursuing a right or claim that prejudices the other party's rights

Equitable Estoppel

A party may raise **equitable estoppel** as a defense when a person, by conduct, induces a second person to rely, to his or her detriment, on the statements or conduct of the first person. The person who asserts a claim of estoppel must have reasonably relied on the acts or representations of the other and have had no knowledge or means of knowing the facts. In exceptional circumstances, some jurisdictions permit a marriage to be created by equitable estoppel to mitigate the effects of fraud and protect the rights of innocent persons who otherwise would be adversely affected. In marriage by estoppel, a marriage is presumed to be valid even though technically it is not. This defense is generally available only with

Equitable estoppel
preventing a party from asserting a claim or a defense because it would be unfair to an opposing party to do otherwise

respect to voidable but not void marriages. For example, courts are highly unlikely to apply the doctrine when parties enter a bigamous marriage, even if neither party was aware of the impediment.[26]

Judicial Estoppel

Judicial estoppel
an equitable doctrine designed to prevent a party from gaining an unfair advantage over another party by making inconsistent statements on the same issue in different lawsuits

A variation on equitable estoppel is ***judicial estoppel***, a doctrine designed to protect the courts (as well as good-faith litigants). Judicial estoppel is an equitable doctrine designed to prevent a party from gaining an unfair advantage over another party by making inconsistent statements on the same issue in different lawsuits. As a North Carolina court phrased it, "…our courts do not permit the submission of new theories, not previously argued, because 'the law does not permit parties to swap horses between courts in order to get a better mount…"[27] In the *Pickard* case decided by a North Carolina Court of Appeals in 2006, the court applied this doctrine and upheld a district court's denial of an annulment to a petitioner. (See Case 4.4.)

Unclean Hands

Unclean hands
the principle that a party should not be granted relief if he or she has acted unfairly, wrongfully, or illegally

The doctrine of ***unclean hands*** provides that "he who comes into Equity must come with clean hands."[28] If a plaintiff in an equity action has, through his or her own misconduct, injured or damaged the defendant, the court should not allow that plaintiff to benefit as a result of his or her own misdeeds. The application of the doctrine is limited to misconduct connected with the matter in litigation. Case 4.5 involves a situation in which a trial court applied both equitable estoppel and the unclean hands doctrine and denied the annulment sought. The appellate court appears to have wanted to affirm that decision but was unable to do so after applying the law to the facts of the case.

CASE **4.4** *Pickard v. Pickard,* 625 S.E.2d 869 (N.C. App. 2006)

Res judicata
an issue that has been definitively settled by judicial decision; the three essential elements are: (1) an earlier decision on the issue, (2) a final judgment on the merits, and (3) the involvement of the original parties

Carl Pickard and his wife, Jane, had been married by a Cherokee Indian in the Native American tradition in June of 1991. The parties had received a North Carolina license and certificate of marriage and filed it with the appropriate Register of Deeds. Both of the parties believed the ceremony was legally sufficient to bind them in marriage and they lived together and conducted themselves as husband and wife for the next eleven years. In 1998, the husband petitioned the court to adopt his wife's adult biological daughter. He provided the court with a sworn statement that he was "the stepfather of the adoptee, having married her natural mother." He also listed his marital status as "married." The clerk of the county superior court subsequently filed a decree of adoption based on his assertions. When the husband subsequently sought an annulment in 2002, he alleged that the marriage ceremony was not properly solemnized because the Cherokee Indian who performed it was not qualified to conduct a marriage ceremony. Because the husband had earlier represented himself to the court as married, the court in effect held that the issue of his marital status was **res judicata** and he was judicially estopped from later claiming his marriage was not valid. The appellate court noted that it also would impose an unfair detriment on the wife if it were to undo an eleven-year marriage by allowing the husband to proceed with his inconsistent position.

SIDEBAR

This opinion is accessible on the companion website.

CASE **4.5** *Emmit v. Emmit,* 174 S.W.3d 248 (Tenn. App. 2005)

BACKGROUND

The plaintiff in this case was seeking to have her second marriage to a Mr. Emmit (who was at all times during this matter incarcerated) annulled on the grounds that when it took place she was still married to her first husband (Mr. Medley). She was living with a third man at the time of her petition. Her primary motivation for seeking the annulment appears to have been a desire to benefit financially from a wrongful death action filed when the first husband died.

FROM THE OPINION

Glenda Emmit ("the plaintiff") brought a petition seeking to annul her marriage to Richard Emmit. She alleged that, unbeknownst to her, her prior marriage to James Randall Medley had not been dissolved at the time of her attempted marriage to Mr. Emmit. She claims that this prior marriage prevented her from contracting a valid marriage with Mr. Emmit. The trial court held that the co-administrators of Mr. Medley's estate . . . were indispensable parties and ordered the plaintiff to amend her complaint to add them. Following a bench trial, the court below entered a judgment denying the plaintiff's petition for annulment on the ground that she had "unclean hands" and was therefore estopped from averring that either her marriage to Mr. Emmit was invalid or that her marriage to Mr. Medley was not dissolved. . . .

. . . The trial court rendered its opinion from the bench and declined to grant the annulment . . . holding that the plaintiff was estopped, (1) from denying the existence and validity of the marriage between herself and Mr. Emmit, and (2) from denying the lack of a valid prior marriage with Mr. Medley or the dissolution of the prior marriage. . . .

The plaintiff appeals the judgment of the trial court on the ground that Tennessee does not recognize a second marriage contracted at a time when one of the parties has a prior subsisting marriage. The plaintiff further argues that the trial court incorrectly applied the doctrine of unclean hands. The co-administrators retort that the trial court properly declined to grant the plaintiff an annulment. . . .

The issue before us is whether there were grounds for an annulment, and, if so, whether the doctrine of unclean hands constitutes a defense to granting an annulment. As we hold that proper grounds exist for granting an annulment, and that the doctrine of unclean hands does not constitute a defense to the plaintiff's request, we reverse the judgment of the trial court.

Tenn. Code Ann. § 36–3–102 (2001) unambiguously provides that "[a] second marriage cannot be contracted before the dissolution of the first." The public policy of Tennessee dictates that bigamous marriages are void. . . . Such marriages are void *ab initio* because, until the first marriage is dissolved, the parties lack the capacity to marry. . . . Consequently, such marriages are neither recognized by the courts nor capable of ratification by the parties. . . . There is a presumption of the validity of marriage such that when there is a second marriage, it is presumed that the first marriage ended in divorce. . . . Such a presumption is strong. . . . However, this presumption may be overcome by evidence that a general search of the court records of divorce produced no record of a divorce.

continued

. . . The trial court seems to have found the plaintiff's conduct during her marriage to Mr. Emmit and beyond to be deplorable and concluded that, because of this conduct, she should not be able to profit financially by annulling the second marriage and gaining from Mr. Medley's wrongful death action. However, the plaintiff's conduct is irrelevant to whether she is legally entitled to an annulment. The sole issue before us is whether the plaintiff is entitled to an annulment on the ground that she was not legally capable of entering into a new marriage when she married Mr. Emmit. As the evidence proffered at trial demonstrates that the plaintiff's marriage to Mr. Medley was never dissolved, we find that the petition for annulment should be granted.

The doctrine of unclean hands enables a court to prevent a party from profiting from her own misconduct . . . namely marrying Mr. Emmit without documentation of her divorce, acting as if she was not married to Mr. Emmit when she was residing with Mr. Harris, and failing to express concern about the status of her marriage until the potential financial gain arose—is relevant to her attempts to annul her marriage to Mr. Emmit. However, where the issue before us is simply whether or not the plaintiff's marriage to Mr. Emmit is void, the plaintiff's alleged misconduct has no bearing on that determination. The plaintiff testified that she believed she was divorced, and learned only two weeks prior to Mr. Medley's death that she was, in fact, not divorced. The fact that she was living with someone else or the timing of this petition is irrelevant to the question of whether the marriage to Mr. Emmit was void. We hold that the doctrine of unclean hands is not a defense in this case to the plaintiff's petition for annulment and, therefore, the plaintiff's petition should be granted.

SIDEBAR

This case is available in its entirety on the companion website. Read the case. Do you agree with the outcome? Do you think the court had any alternative? Do you think the outcome would have been any different if the defense of unclean hands were raised by Mr. Emmit rather than by the co-administrators of Mr. Medley's estate? Assuming the marriage to Mr. Emmit is void, do you think a court would grant the plaintiff any rights to property accumulated during the period she held herself out as married to Mr. Emmit? Explain your response.

CONSEQUENCES OF AN ANNULMENT DECREE
For the Parties

The general rule is that if a marriage ends in an annulment, property division and spousal support provisions technically do not apply as they would in divorce. However, some states with annulment statutes specifically provide that the court may grant alimony and custody and support orders for any minor child, as in the case of divorce.[29] Other states provide for the parties by applying equitable principles on a case-by-case basis. For example, courts in some states (particularly community property states such as California, Texas, and Washington) may declare a marriage void and yet grant a putative spouse, who innocently believed the marriage was valid, a share of the couple's quasi-marital property. Such states use a good-faith analysis to determine whether either of the parties had reason to believe the marriage was invalid. For example, in a 2004 case, the Nevada Supreme Court applied the putative spouse doctrine as a basis for dividing the parties' property. (See Case 4.6.) Even though the putative spouse may be deemed entitled to a share of the quasi-marital property, the marriage itself is considered void.

CASE **4.6** *Williams v. Williams*, 97 P.3d 1124 (Nev. 2004)

FROM THE OPINION

This is a case of first impression involving the application of the putative spouse doctrine in an annulment proceeding. Under the doctrine, an individual whose marriage is void due to a prior legal impediment is treated as a spouse so long as the party seeking equitable relief participated in the marriage ceremony with the good-faith belief that the ceremony was legally valid. A majority of the states recognize the doctrine when dividing property acquired during the marriage, applying equitable principles, based on community property law, to the division. However, absent fraud, the doctrine does not apply to awards of spousal support. While some states have extended the doctrine to permit spousal support awards, they have done so under the authority of state statutes.

We agree with the majority view. Consequently, we adopt the putative spouse doctrine in annulment proceedings for the purposes of property division and affirm the district court's division of property. However, we reject the doctrine as a basis for awarding equitable spousal support. Because Nevada's annulment statutes do not provide for an award of support upon annulment, we reverse the district court's award of spousal support.

On August 26, 1973, appellant Richard E. Williams underwent a marriage ceremony with respondent Marcie C. Williams. At that time, Marcie believed she was divorced from John Allmaras. However, neither Marcie nor Allmaras had obtained a divorce. Richard and Marcie believed they were legally married and lived together, as husband and wife, for 27 years. In March 2000, Richard discovered that Marcie was not divorced from Allmaras at the time of their marriage ceremony.

In August 2000, Richard and Marcie permanently separated. In February 2001, Richard filed a complaint for an annulment. Marcie answered and counterclaimed for one-half of the property and spousal support as a putative spouse. In April 2002, the parties engaged in a one-day bench trial to resolve the matter.

At trial, Richard testified that had he known Marcie was still married, he would not have married her. He claimed that Marcie knew she was not divorced when she married him or had knowledge that would put a reasonable person on notice to check if the prior marriage had been dissolved. . . .

The district court found that Marcie had limited ability to support herself. The district court also concluded that both parties believed they were legally married, acted as husband and wife, and conceived and raised two children. Marcie stayed at home to care for and raise their children. Based on these facts, the district court granted the annulment and awarded Marcie one-half of all the jointly-held property and spousal support. The district court did not indicate whether its award was based on the putative spouse doctrine or an implied contract and quantum meruit theory. . . .

A marriage is void if either of the parties to the marriage has a former husband or wife then living. Richard and Marcie's marriage was void because Marcie was still married to another man when she married Richard. Although their marriage was

continued

void, an annulment proceeding was necessary to legally sever their relationship. An annulment proceeding is the proper manner to dissolve a void marriage and resolve other issues arising from the dissolution of the relationship.

Under the putative spouse doctrine, when a marriage is legally void, the civil effects of a legal marriage flow to the parties who contracted to marry in good faith. That is, a putative spouse is entitled to many of the rights of an actual spouse. A majority of the states have recognized some form of the doctrine. . . .

The doctrine has two elements: (1) a proper marriage ceremony was performed, and (2) one or both of the parties had a good-faith belief that there was no impediment to the marriage and the marriage was valid and proper. "Good faith" has been defined as an "honest and reasonable belief that the marriage was valid at the time of the ceremony." Good faith is presumed. The party asserting lack of good faith has the burden of proving bad faith. Whether the party acted in good faith is a question of fact. Unconfirmed rumors or mere suspicions of a legal impediment do not vitiate good faith "so long as no certain or authoritative knowledge of some legal impediment comes to him or her." However, when a person receives reliable information that an impediment exists, the individual cannot ignore the information, but instead has a duty to investigate further. Persons cannot act "blindly or without reasonable precaution." Finally, once a spouse learns of the impediment, the putative marriage ends.

We have not previously considered the putative spouse doctrine, but we are persuaded by the rationale of our sister states that public policy supports adopting the doctrine in Nevada. Fairness and equity favor recognizing putative spouses when parties enter into a marriage ceremony in good faith and without knowledge there is a factual or legal impediment to their marriage. Nor does the doctrine conflict with Nevada's policy in refusing to recognize common-law marriages or palimony suits. . . . As a majority of our sister states have recognized, the sanctity of marriage is not undermined, but rather enhanced, by the recognition of the putative spouse doctrine. We therefore adopt the doctrine in Nevada.

We now apply the doctrine to the instant case. The district court found that the parties obtained a license and participated in a marriage ceremony on August 26, 1973, in Verdi, Nevada. The district court also found that Marcie erroneously believed that her prior husband, Allmaras, had terminated their marriage by divorce and that she was legally able to marry Richard. In so finding, the district court also necessarily rejected Richard's argument that Marcie acted unreasonably in relying on Allmaras' statements because she had never been served with divorce papers and that she had a duty to inquire about the validity of her former marriage before marrying Richard.

. . . The district court was free to disregard Richard's testimony, and substantial evidence supports the district court's finding that Marcie did not act unreasonably in relying on Allmaras' representations. The record reflects no reason for Marcie to have disbelieved him and, thus, no reason to have investigated the truth of his representations. . . .

Community property states that recognize the putative spouse doctrine apply community property principles to the division of property, including determinations of what constitutes community and separate property. Since putative spouses believe

continued

themselves to be married, they are already under the assumption that community property statutes would apply to a termination of their relationship. There is no point, therefore in devising a completely separate set of rules for dividing property in a putative spouse scenario. . . .

States are divided on whether spousal support is a benefit or civil effect that may be awarded under the putative spouse doctrine. Although some states permit the award of alimony, they do so because their annulment statutes permit an award of rehabilitative or permanent alimony. At least one state, however, has found alimony to be a civil effect under the putative spouse doctrine even in the absence of a specific statute permitting an award of alimony.

Nevada statutes do not provide for an award of alimony after annulment. . . .

. . . We adopt the putative spouse doctrine and conclude that common-law community property principles apply by analogy to the division of property acquired during a putative marriage. However, the putative spouse doctrine does not permit an award of spousal support in the absence of bad faith, fraud or statutory authority. Therefore, we affirm that portion of the district court's order equally dividing the parties' property and reverse that portion of the order awarding spousal support.

SIDEBAR

This case is available in its entirety on the companion website. Do you agree with the outcome? How reasonable is it for a spouse to rely on the oral and undocumented representations of a former spouse that their marriage is dissolved? What would you do in the same circumstances? What do you think the result should be if one of the parties entered the marriage with knowledge of the impediment and does not qualify as a putative spouse?

Alimony commonly terminates upon the recipient's remarriage. If that "remarriage" is subsequently annulled, the recipient may claim that the payor should have to resume paying alimony, as there was no valid subsequent marriage. Courts use a variety of approaches to address this question and generally hold that the annulment does not revive the alimony obligation. (See Case 4.7.)

CASE **4.7** *Fredo v. Fredo,* 49 Conn. Supp. 489, 894 A.2d 399 (Conn. Super. 2005)

BACKGROUND

The issue in this case is whether an order for periodic alimony contained in a dissolution decree pursuant to the parties' agreement is revivable in the event of an annulment of the recipient's subsequent marriage. The parties had married in 1993 and divorced in 2004. The dissolution decree incorporated the parties' agreement that the husband would pay alimony in the amount of $250 a week to the wife terminable upon the earliest of three events: December 31, 2009, the death of either party or the remarriage of the wife. In 2005, the former wife married a man in Nevada, whom she acknowledged she had been seeing on and off.

continued

The husband initially sought to terminate alimony payments based on his former wife's cohabitation with her new companion. When he learned she had remarried, he sought termination based on that circumstance as provided in the decree and agreement.

After a very brief marriage, the wife sought to have her remarriage annulled on the basis that she and her new husband had failed to discuss a number of issues prior to marrying and that the marriage "was a mistake." In contemplation and by reason of the alleged pending annulment, she claimed that her remarriage should not terminate the previously agreed upon and decreed alimony payments. The Connecticut Superior Court at Hartford held that alimony terminates upon remarriage and is not resurrected by subsequent events.

Although this issue had not previously been addressed in Connecticut, the court noted it had frequently been addressed in other states using three different approaches:

1. The first approach provides that "an existing alimony obligation is revived following the annulment of a void marriage and generally, extinguished following the annulment of a voidable marriage. . . . The courts distinguish between void and voidable marriages on the basis that voidable marriages are valid until the annulment is granted . . . whereas a void marriage is void *ab initio*." (Alabama, Florida, Nebraska, Ohio, and Tennessee)

2. Courts applying the second approach "conclude that the remarriage of the alimony recipient automatically terminates the alimony obligation irrespective of subsequent events. . . ." (Arizona, California, Delaware, Kentucky, Massachusetts, Missouri, Nevada, New Jersey, New Mexico, and New York)

3. In the third approach, which has been used by a small minority of courts, the decision is made on a case-by-case basis. (Colorado, Iowa, Montana, South Carolina, and Utah) The Connecticut court deemed this the least desirable approach believing it provides the least certainty and guidance and vests too much discretion in the courts on an issue the parties have decided for themselves.

FROM THE OPINION

This court joins with those courts that have adopted the automatic termination approach, to wit: that alimony automatically terminates upon the recipient's remarriage. This approach accords with the clear and unambiguous language used by the parties [in their agreement]. . . . The approach also accords with the intent of the parties. By entering into another marriage, the alimony recipient has made an election to look to another for support. That election in no way hinged on how the later marriage worked out. . . .

Interests of finality and certainty are furthered only by the automatic termination approach. Upon the recipient's remarriage, the obligor has every right to reorder their life and commit to things which theretofore might not have been practical or possible, . . . If "remarriage" referred only to a valid second marriage, the alimony obligor would be placed in the untenable position of never being certain that the financial responsibility for his former wife would not shift back to him. . . .

Other practical considerations warrant adoption of the automatic termination approach. The obligor may not, indeed likely would not, have access to the facts

continued

which form the basis for the claimed annulment and, moreover, would certainly lack standing in an annulment proceeding to be heard on the issue of the validity of the subsequent marriage.... Finally, resurrection of an extinguished alimony obligation in the context of a self-executing termination provision would contravene the well-established rule in this state that a party who relinquishes their claim to alimony is forever barred from obtaining such relief in the future....

For all of the reasons previously indicated, this court finds that the occurrence of the defendant's ceremonial marriage to her new spouse constituted a remarriage within the meaning of the agreement and decree. By virtue of her election to proceed with that marriage, the plaintiff's alimony obligation to the defendant terminated at that time.

SIDEBAR

In the case *Joye v. Yon*, 355 S.C. 452, 586 S.E.2d 131 (S.C. 2003), the Supreme Court of South Carolina addressed this same issue in a case of first impression in that state and adopted the case-by-case approach as the most appropriate option. Which approach do you think courts should adopt? Explain your response. Both cases are accessible on the companion website.

An annulment decree may revive a party's previous legal status in some circumstances. For example, in Arizona, annulment of a surviving spouse's second marriage entitles that spouse to reinstatement of worker's compensation death benefits by statute. The rationale behind reinstatement is that the burden of death and injury should be carried by industry.

For the Children

Most states now provide by statute that children born to marriages that are subsequently annulled will be deemed "legitimate" for legal purposes under state law. However, there are isolated exceptions. For example, in Mississippi, children born to incestuous marriages are not considered to be legitimate. Nebraska and Iowa provide by statute that children born to annulled marriages are legitimate unless a court decrees otherwise.

Although alimony obligations of a prior spouse are usually not revived by annulment of a recipient's subsequent marriage, annulment of a child's marriage during his or her minority usually will revive the child's unemancipated status and also revive a parent's child support obligation. "Public policy directs that parents financially support their minor children, even if those children make unwise decisions. Moreover, assuming the parent with the support obligation might rely on the validity of the child's marriage in making financial plans, that period of reliance would not last indefinitely but only until the child would otherwise become emancipated."[30]

THE PARALEGAL'S ROLE IN AN ANNULMENT CASE

The tasks most commonly performed by a paralegal in an annulment case are:

- Researching the law governing annulment in the applicable jurisdiction and in other jurisdictions as well, if appropriate
- Preparing related memoranda based on research as requested

- Gathering information and documentation essential to preparation of necessary documents, discovery requests, pleadings, and correspondence
- Scheduling and participating in interviews as assigned
- Drafting complaints/petitions, motions, supporting affidavits, and proposed orders or responses to complaints/petitions
- Drafting discovery requests, if necessary, such as proposed interrogatories, deposition questions, requests for admissions, requests for production of documents, and requests for physical or mental examinations
- Assisting in preparation for hearings or trial, including drafting pretrial memoranda for review, organizing documents and exhibits, etc.
- Preparing subpoenas for witnesses, if necessary
- Helping to prepare the client as well as witnesses appearing for the client
- Tracking progress on the case and being certain that any timelines are met
- Making sure the client is kept informed of progress and upcoming deadlines, hearings, discovery matters, etc.
- Acting as a conduit for providing information such as brochures, prepared charts, instructions, and Frequently Asked Questions (FAQs) sheets

CHAPTER SUMMARY

Prior to the emergence of no-fault divorce in the 1970s, divorce actions all were based on grounds such as cruel and abusive treatment, adultery, abandonment, imprisonment, and chronic alcohol abuse. The process was especially painful and antagonistic and often presented difficult problems of proof. Annulment actions provided an alternative but not necessarily an emotionally and financially less costly one. Although not everyone would agree, divorce today has become somewhat more streamlined and humane. No longer does one spouse have to demonize the other spouse if irreconcilable differences have developed that have caused the breakdown of the marriage. As a result, although annulment is still an appropriate option in some cases, no-fault divorce now may present some couples with a more desirable route to terminating their marriage.

After reviewing the religious origins of annulment and the differences between divorce and annulment, this chapter moves to a discussion of the distinction between an alleged marriage that is void *ab initio* (a marriage that never came into being because of a legal impediment that existed at the time of the marriage) and a voidable marriage (one that remains valid until declared invalid by a court of competent jurisdiction). The basic procedural requirements for obtaining an annulment are briefly described. Various grounds for annulment are reviewed and illustrated, such as bigamy, impotence, fraud, nonage, duress, and undue influence. Also referenced are some of the more common defenses to an annulment action, such as compliance with state law, laches, ratification, consummation, estoppel (equitable and judicial), and unclean hands. The paralegal's role in an annulment action is referenced throughout the chapter with emphasis on the particular importance of being aware of local law and procedure and jurisdictional variations.

KEY TERMS

Affinity	Duress	Preponderance of the evidence
Annulment	Ecclesiastical law	Quasi-marital property
Bigamy	Equitable estoppel	Ratification
Burden of proof	Green card	*Res judicata*
Clear and convincing evidence	Impotence	Standing
Consanguinity	Incest	Unclean hands
Consent	Judicial estoppel	Undue influence
Consummation	Laches	Void *ab initio*
Declaratory judgment	Marriage	Voidable marriage
Doctrine of comity	Nonage	

REVIEW **QUESTIONS**

1. Define annulment.
2. Describe the origins of annulment actions.
3. Define and distinguish between a marriage that is void *ab initio* and a voidable marriage, and give an example of each.
4. Identify the differences between an annulment and a divorce.
5. Describe the nature and purpose of a declaratory judgment in the context of annulment.
6. Identify the kinds of individuals who have standing to bring annulment actions.
7. Identify five grounds for annulment and give an example of each.
8. Identify five defenses to an annulment action.
9. What are the consequences of an annulment for the parties? For their children?
10. Describe the role of a paralegal in an annulment action.

FOCUS ON **THE JOB**

The Facts

John and Audrey Morrison had a nonmarital relationship that began in 2001. John is an attorney and a partner in a law firm. Audrey is a certified public accountant. In the spring of 2005, Audrey became pregnant. John claimed that the pregnancy was Audrey's fault and her responsibility and told her she should get an abortion as soon as possible. He said the pregnancy should be terminated because he was not prepared to be a father at that point in his life. A devout Catholic for her entire life, Audrey was determined not to have an abortion. She and John had a series of arguments on the subject, and Audrey became so upset by the situation that she went to a therapist and was put on strong medication that calmed her down but clouded her thinking. John believed she was suicidal and in an effort to prevent that outcome, agreed to marry her prior to the birth of their child. He felt very pressured and, although he didn't tell her at the time of the marriage, he did not plan to live together as husband and wife after the child was born, nor did he intend to consummate the marriage or remain married. He just wanted to stop her tirades and nagging and thought that if she felt their child was "legitimate," she would accept whatever happened between the two of them. He was quite wrong on several fronts. After the baby was born, a healthy boy named John Morrison, Jr., John decided he wanted to remain married and raise the boy as a couple. He told Audrey that he was very happy as a family man and that he couldn't believe what he had initially intended to do. When she questioned him further and he told her about his earlier plan, she immediately went wild, took the baby, and ran out of the house calling him all sorts of names, and went to live with her sister. The following week she went to meet with an attorney, your supervisor, in order to file for an annulment of their marriage based on her husband's conduct and intentions at the time the parties were married.

The Assignment

Locate the proper form for bringing an annulment action in the state where you are, or you expect to be, employed. Then complete the form for review assuming that you are a paralegal in the firm representing Audrey in the above fact pattern. The firm is Wilson and Tauson, LLP, located at 390 Main Street, your city or town, state, and zip code, and the attorney handling the case is Juliana Wilson, Esq. Audrey is living with her sister at 2 Woodbine Road in your city or town, and John continues to reside at 3 River Road in your city or town. They were married on October 28, 2005, in a Catholic Church in your state (choose a location, if necessary).

FOCUS ON **ETHICS**

Assume the facts in the above hypothetical. Assume further that you have been asked to interview the client, Audrey Morrison, in order to gather background information about the facts of the case so that Attorney Wilson can determine whether or not an annulment is a viable option. During the interview with the client, she tells you, among other things, that she is heartbroken. She had believed that she and her husband were a happy couple, totally compatible, and committed to each other. She further reveals that they had been having sexual relations during the entire period of their relationship and relatively brief marriage. You recall something from your paralegal training about how an annulment cannot be obtained if the parties cohabit and engage in sexual relations after their marriage. You tell Audrey what you recall but reassure her that she doesn't have to worry, as she can still get out of her relationship with John by filing for a divorce instead of an annulment. Audrey tells you that you don't understand. She is a devout Catholic and divorce is simply not an option for her. She leaves the office sobbing hysterically. You try to go after her but the office phone rings and you have to answer it, as you are the only one in the office at the time. When Attorney Wilson returns, she asks how the interview went and when you tell her what happened, she is not pleased to say the least. She asks you if you have any idea what you have done and tells you to leave the office and not return until you figure it out and spell out in writing the ethical errors you made. She also directs you to suggest an appropriate course of action. Do as she has requested, applying the ethical canons for paralegals promulgated by the National Federation of Paralegal Associations (NFPA), which are contained in Appendix B of this text. Your response should be in the form of a memorandum to Attorney Wilson.

FOCUS ON **CASE LAW**

Read the case *In re Marriage of Liu,* 197 Cal. App. 3d 143 (1987), which is available on the companion website for this text in the material related to Chapter 4, and then describe the case using an IRAC format:

Identify the ISSUE.

Identify the RULE of law.

ANALYZE the case in terms of how the rule of law applies to the facts of the case.

Draw a CONCLUSION.

FOCUS ON **STATE LAW AND PROCEDURE**

Identify the grounds for annulment in the state where you are studying family law.

Are they located in one or more statutes and/or in case law? Remember to consider both statutes restricting marriage (underage without parental consent, prior marriage still in existence, etc.) and statutes or cases setting forth grounds for annulment.

FOCUS ON **TECHNOLOGY**

ASSIGNMENTS

1. Learn more about annulment in the Catholic Church at *http://www.rcab.org/marriage.html.*

2. Locate online the forms for bringing an action for annulment in three states other than your own.

3. Go to the following websites to see what you can locate in the way of information about annulment.

   http://alllaw.com

   http://www.findlaw.com

chapter **five**

NONMARITAL FAMILIES

ichard and Mary are both in their sixties. They have been seeing each other for six months and enjoy their relationship tremendously. They have decided to live together and intend to remain intimate partners for the rest of their lives. Each of them is semi-retired after a successful career and is able to provide for his or her own needs. Neither of them has any desire to marry. "Why spoil a good thing?" they laugh and say.

IN THIS CHAPTER YOU WILL LEARN

- How and why the concept of family has evolved over the past fifty years

- What cohabitation is and how it differs from marriage

- What kinds of documents cohabiting partners can use to create and protect their rights

- What a cohabitation agreement is and what kinds of provisions it commonly contains

- What forms of relief are available to cohabiting partners when their relationship dissolves and they have no written agreement

- What some of the new forms of alternative family relationships are, including domestic partnerships and civil unions

- How changes in the concept of family and intimate partnerships have affected other areas of substantive law and what the implications are for the future

- What the role of a paralegal is in a case involving nonmarital families

INTRODUCTION

Once upon a time, there was a nation whose prime-time television shows included *I Remember Mama* and *Father Knows Best*. These programs featured storybook perfect intact traditional families; characters playing highly gendered roles; and classic moral themes. Cohabitation was viewed as "living in sin" and constituted a crime in virtually all states. "Gay" meant cheerful and lighthearted, and "domestic agreements" referred to contracts with hired help to perform household chores. Five decades and two generations ago, cohabitation was a blip in a family law practice.

The above description is clearly a white, middle-class, "idealized" portrait of the nuclear family projected by the media of the day. Although a reality for some, it failed to capture the fact that throughout this country's history, the nature of the nuclear family has adapted to societal conditions such as war, racism, and economic depression, and it continues to do so today. Although the majority of adults in the United States still marry at least once in their lifetimes, significant changes in our society have resulted in expanded, publicly acknowledged, and legally recognized concepts of the family unit that encompass a wide range of lifestyles and diverse living arrangements. A number of forces have converged to promote this broader and more flexible view of both the family and intimate relationships: the women's rights, fathers' rights, and gay rights movements; a decreased emphasis on marriage as a defining event in life (particularly for women); an increased social acceptance of alternative lifestyles; and a greater protection of the right to privacy in sexual conduct between consenting adults.

In the United States, we have no uniform definition of cohabitation nor any national legal registration system that encompasses two people living together in an intimate relationship as a nonmarital "family unit." The U.S. Census Bureau defines family as "two or more persons related by birth, marriage, or adoption who reside in the same household." Thus far, the best measure demographers have developed to gauge the living arrangements of U.S. residents is the Census Bureau's data on household types and relationships. The Bureau defines an "unmarried partner" as "A person age 15 years and over, who is not related to the householder, who shares living quarters, and who has a close personal relationship with the householder."[1] A variety of data sources tell us the following:

- From 1990 to 2000, married-couple households (as a percentage of all households) declined from 55.2% to 51.7%.[2] The decline continued, and in 2005 a Census Bureau survey estimated married-couple households at 49.7%—a new minority.[3] By contrast, 27.1% were singles living alone.[4]
- In 2005, fewer than 22% of all households were "traditional" households (a married couple with one or more minor children).[5]
- In 2004, 36.8% of all births were to unmarried women.[6]
- In 2005, there were about 1.5 million same-sex "unmarried partners" and about 10.5 million opposite-sex "unmarried partners."[7]
- Approximately 75% of cohabiters say they plan to marry their partners, and 55% get married within five years of moving in together; 40% break up within five years; and about 10% remain in an unmarried relationship for five years or longer.[8]

Issues related to intimate relationships between different- and same-sex partners are now at the heart of heated political, religious, social, and cultural controversies, and pose cutting-edge legal questions that are likely to intensify in the next decade.

Paralegal Practice Tip

Religious considerations are usually raised in the context of moral opposition to cohabitation and same-sex relationships, and, to be sure, the voice of the "moral majority" is still a profound social and political force in the United States. However, over history, various religions have addressed cohabitation in differing ways. For example, *pilegesh* is a Hebrew term used to describe a "concubine" who has comparable social and legal standing with a recognized wife. Although she has rights similar to those of a wife, she does not have a formal marriage contract. However, any children born to a pilegesh stand on equal footing with children of a husband and wife.[9]

The differences are deep and complex. For example, those vehemently opposed to civil unions include fundamentalist Christians, who view the unions as sinful, as well as zealous advocates for gay rights, who believe that settling for civil unions' "separate but equal" status is a compromise that falls far too short of full equality. A *Washington Post*-ABC news survey found that 51% of respondents were opposed to gay marriage, and yet 53% also opposed President Bush's call for an amendment to the U.S. Constitution outlawing marriage of same-sex couples and favored leaving the issue to the states to resolve.[10] As of June 2008, same-sex marriage is permitted only in Massachusetts and California, and yet local officials in multiple states such as Oregon, New Jersey, and New York have issued marriage licenses in defiance of state laws banning such unions.

A broad objective of this chapter is to alert the reader to the dramatic evolution that is taking place in society today around the legal recognition of nonmarital families and intimate relationships. Although it is difficult to isolate particular dimensions of this evolution, our primary focus is on:

- Cohabitation in general, the purpose and nature of cohabitation or living-together agreements, and the remedies potentially available (when their relationship ends) to partners who have not executed agreements
- The most common alternative legal frameworks and/or statuses created by states, municipalities, and employers to give unmarried partners a variety of benefits that are customarily available only to spouses
- Some of the potential implications of developments in this area for the family law practitioner and the legal profession in general

COHABITATION

With the changes that have taken place in the landscape of family and social life in this country, cohabitation has become a mainstream behavior for many American couples. *Cohabitation* is broadly defined as two unmarried persons living together in an intimate relationship. Although the term traditionally has been used to refer to heterosexual couples, it technically encompasses both different- and same-sex relationships.

Cohabitation
two unmarried people living together, commonly in an intimate relationship

There are distinct differences between marriage and cohabitation. (See Exhibit 5.1.) The legal effect of these differences is not always fully appreciated by unmarried couples who choose to live together for a host of personal reasons:

- The parties may view a period of cohabitation as a trial marriage.
- One or both of them may not want the social and personal commitment or responsibilities implicit in the marital relationship.
- Many female partners have increased their level of economic independence and become "liberated" from the constraints of rigid gender roles and societal pressure to marry.
- Parties who were previously married and experienced the emotional and financial costs of messy divorces may want to be in a relationship that is easier and less expensive to terminate should it fail.
- The parties may view cohabitation as a convenient way to reduce taxes, housing costs, and other living expenses.
- One or both of the parties may have considerable assets they want to protect in the event the relationship ends.
- The parties may be unable to marry legally—e.g., polygamists, same-sex couples outside of Massachusetts and California, and first cousins in a state that does not permit first cousins to marry.

EXHIBIT 5.1 Marriage and Cohabitation—A Comparison

MARRIAGE	COHABITATION
To enter a marriage, the parties must satisfy certain requirements that vary state to state but customarily include a minimum age for marrying without parental consent, a license, and a ceremony.	Parties may freely elect to cohabit without satisfying any formal requirements. *Note*: Cohabitation is still a misdemeanor in criminal statutes of some states, although such laws are rarely enforced.
Children born during a marriage are presumed to be offspring of the husband and wife, and each spouse owes them a duty of support. *Note*: In most states, the presumption of paternity may be overcome by genetic evidence.	There is no presumption of parentage when a child is born to a female partner in a cohabiting couple and therefore no parallel duty of support.
A marriage is terminated by formal legal process.	A period of cohabitation can be terminated without legal process.
Division of property upon termination of marriage is governed by state law (statutory and case) absent an enforceable premarital agreement.	Division of property may be based on an agreement of the parties, sometimes embodied in the provisions of a cohabitation agreement. In the event of a disagreement absent evidence of "true" ownership of property or an enforceable express agreement, a party may seek equitable relief through the courts in most states.
Spousal support may be awarded to one of the parties based on need and the other party's ability to pay.	Absent a contractual agreement to the contrary, a cohabiting partner will not be ordered to pay support to the other party.
After termination of the marriage, a noncustodial parent generally has a duty to provide child support to the custodial parent.	Absent establishment of paternity/parentage, there is no right to custody and visitation or duty of child support following termination of a period of cohabitation.

Since the social pressure against living together has significantly lessened and cohabitation is no longer a crime in most states, why don't couples simply live together and not worry about formalizing their relationships through contractual agreements and/or establishing a legally recognized status? Consider the following hypothetical situation.

Imagine having lived with a man for five years in a committed, monogamous relationship that you both intend to "last forever." Imagine going to pick him up at an airport and being greeted by airline personnel who advise you that he experienced a heart attack midair and is being rushed to a hospital emergency room. You race to the hospital and the first question you are asked is "Are you a family member?" And that is only the beginning of a series of painful events with devastating consequences. You cannot be admitted to see him in intensive care. You cannot be advised of his condition due to federal privacy regulations, and you cannot consent to his medical treatment, although you know his wishes. You cannot write checks on his bank account to pay his obligations. If he dies, you have no say in the funeral and burial arrangements, and yet only you know what he would want. You cannot enter the home where you lived together, because when it was purchased by the two of you, it was put in his name only. You cannot access his safety deposit box, even though you have valuable personal property in it. You cannot inherit through him if he dies without a will, because you have no legally recognized interest in his estate. The two of you are, in effect, legal strangers.

What could you have done to protect each other in the event of such a tragedy? Lawyers have utilized a wide range of devices in an effort to establish rights and responsibilities between cohabiting parties. These devices are designed primarily to control the legal consequences for the parties in the event of disability or termination of the relationship by death or separation. Cohabitants are commonly advised to do the following:

- Execute *health care proxies* in which each of you designates the other as the person entitled to obtain information regarding your condition and consent to the specifics of your care if you are unable to make medical decisions for yourself.
- Execute *durable powers of attorney* in which each of you designates your partner as the person authorized to act on your behalf with respect to a wide range of matters including, but by no means limited to, banking and business affairs in the event of disability or incapacitation.
- Execute wills in which you each designate the other your personal representative and make appropriate provisions for him or her.
- Purchase property as *joint tenants with a right of survivorship* in case one of you dies while you still own the property.
- Purchase life insurance policies designating each other as primary beneficiaries.
- Execute and fund trusts that provide for each other under a variety of circumstances, such as the death or disability of a party.
- Designate your partner as a primary beneficiary on 401(k)s, IRAs, and/or other retirement accounts not otherwise restricted.
- Execute a joint-partnership agreement if you intend to invest in property jointly and/or operate a business together.
- Execute a Cohabitation/Partnership Agreement.

Health care proxy
a document granting another person the authority to make health care decisions for the grantor in the event of his or her incapacity

Durable power of attorney
a document that grants someone authority to act in the grantor's stead for convenience or in the event of incapacity; the authority survives incapacity but terminates on the death of the grantor

Joint tenant with right of survivorship
a form of ownership of property by two or more persons in which each tenant owns an identical interest in the property, and each joint tenant has a right of survivorship in the other's shares

Paralegal Practice Tip
These documents need to be carefully drafted, particularly in situations involving same-sex couples. Family members who did not know about or who refuse to accept the couple's relationship may challenge the validity of the documents on grounds such as fraud or undue influence.

Cohabitation Agreements

Historically, because of a strong public policy favoring marriage, the legal system has not provided cohabiting couples with a procedure for dissolving their relationships and resolving their disputes. Unlike marriage, absent a legally conferred status such as a domestic partnership or civil union, cohabiting partners do not automatically become entitled to particular rights and benefits when they decide to live together. If they want to establish rules and principles to govern particular aspects of their relationship and/or if they want to secure certain rights or assume specific responsibilities, then they need to do so by executing a contract, a cohabitation agreement (in addition to whatever other documents they may elect to create).

Cohabitation Agreement
an agreement between two unmarried individuals who live or intend to live together, defining their intentions, rights, and obligations with respect to one another while living together and upon termination of their relationship

Paralegal Practice Tip
Although our focus in this segment of the chapter is on cohabitation agreements between intimate partners, living-together agreements may also be executed by roommates residing together primarily for convenience and financial reasons and without any sexual involvement. The parties may be friends or strangers who connect with each other through, for example, postings on bulletin boards, newspaper ads, or Internet resources such as Craig's List. The focus of such agreements is primarily on household responsibilities, financial obligations (e.g., for rent, utilities, phone, and food), and "rules" with respect to such topics as smoking, drinking, overnight guests, and pets.

Paralegal Practice Tip
Even if the parties have expectations with respect to their sexual relationship, caution should be exercised when including language on this topic. A court may not enforce an agreement if it appears that financial support is being provided solely in exchange for sexual services, thereby resembling a contract for prostitution. The courts will not enforce an agreement to commit a crime. The courts often use the phrase *"meretricious sex"* to refer to unlawful or illicit sexual relations.

Meretricious sex
unlawful or illicit sexual relations, such as prostitution or sex outside of marriage

A *Cohabitation Agreement* (sometimes called a Cohabitation Contract, a Living Together Agreement, or a Nonmarital Agreement) is a private contract between two parties living together in a nonmarital relationship, which establishes mutually agreed-upon rights and responsibilities, many of which married persons obtain by statute, agreement, and custom. They are similar to, but usually do not contain all the provisions of, a premarital agreement.

A cohabitation agreement is not a replacement for a will, a health care proxy, a durable power of attorney, or a deed to property protecting a surviving partner in the event the other dies. It also does not necessarily have the same force and effect after marriage as a premarital agreement. It does, however, provide the parties with an opportunity to identify, negotiate, and reach agreement with respect to their expectations of the relationship, both financial and personal. Such agreements reflect the general trend toward couples' private ordering of their legal rights and responsibilities. They are designed, in part, to avoid unanticipated and sometimes disastrous results when children are born, a party develops a long-term illness or dies, the relationship terminates, or a common law marriage is claimed by one of the parties.

A majority of states now permit, and in many instances encourage, unmarried cohabiting couples to contract legally with each other, although sometimes the parties may need to seek the assistance of the courts to enforce those agreements. An individual provision of a cohabitation agreement may be held unenforceable because it violates a law, constitutional right, or strong public policy (such as an agreement to have children, to abort a pregnancy should one occur, or to pay a partner each time the parties engage in a particular sexual act). If the provision is so offensive that it taints the entire agreement, the whole agreement may be ruled unenforceable. Even if not enforceable, the document may be presented as evidence of the parties' intentions with respect to certain issues, such as how they agreed to treat the property accumulated during the term of their cohabitation. Paralegal Application 5.1 contains a description of some of the provisions most commonly included in cohabitation agreements.

PARALEGAL APPLICATION 5.1
COHABITATION AGREEMENTS—COMMON PROVISIONS

Models of cohabitation agreements may be located online, in form and practice books, and very likely in office files (paper and/or electronic). However, it is important to adapt the contents of a particular agreement to the unique needs and intentions of the parties. Because there is little statutory or case law governing the contents of cohabitation agreements beyond the requirements of basic contract law, they tend to be more varied than premarital or separation agreements. They may include provisions such as the following:

- identification of the parties, including their full names and addresses
- statement of the purpose of the agreement and an intention that it be legally binding
- identification of the consideration for the agreement (usually mutual promises contained within it)
- agreement regarding representations to the public with respect to the nature of the relationship
- statement regarding the parties' intentions with respect to the relationship potentially ripening into a common law marriage

continued

- statement regarding the effect that marriage will have on the agreement (Will it be rendered null and void upon marriage, or will it become the parties' premarital agreement?)
- statement that the parties have made mutually satisfactory disclosure of their respective assets and liabilities
- identification of the "rights" or claims that each party may be waiving, such as:
  - the right to claim a common law marriage
  - any claim on the other's separate property including any appreciation of that property during the period of cohabitation
  - a claim to any form of maintenance or support should the relationship terminate
  - any claim of a right to share in the pension or any other retirement accounts of the other party
  - any claim on the other's estate in the event of death other than expressly provided
- statement of understanding with respect to division of household and other joint expenses during the period of cohabitation
- agreement regarding treatment of income and property acquired during the period of cohabitation and/or upon termination
- agreement with respect to treatment of debts and obligations acquired prior to and during the cohabitation period
- statement regarding health insurance coverage
- statement of intentions with respect to having or not having and raising children
- acknowledgment that the parties have been represented by separate counsel during negotiation and execution of the agreement
- statement that the document represents the parties' entire agreement
- identification of the state's law that will govern interpretation and validity of the agreement
- statement regarding the parties' intentions with respect to the effect of future changes in the law that may impact on their respective rights
- description of the means by which the agreement may be modified
- agreement with respect to how disputes will be resolved
- severability clause providing that, if any provision of the agreement is held to be invalid, the remainder of the agreement will be deemed valid and enforceable
- statement of the effective dates of the agreement, including when it will become effective; whether it will be affected by temporary separations (as when one party is away on business for extensive periods); the timing of periodic reviews, if any; and the circumstances under which it will become null and void
- signatures (witnessed and notarized)

Paralegal Practice Tip

If the parties want their cohabitation agreement to serve as their premarital agreement should they eventually marry, the agreement must expressly state that intention, satisfy any jurisdictional requirements for a valid premarital agreement, and be executed with all the appropriate formalities.

Paralegal Practice Tip

Counsel should advise the parties that terms such as whether or not smoking will be permitted in their residence, who will perform household or childcare responsibilities, or whether they will have pets may be helpful in establishing the contours of their personal relationship, but that they may not be enforceable.

Paralegal Practice Tip

The parties to a cohabitation agreement may approach a single attorney to have their agreement drafted. Even though the parties' interests may not presently be antagonistic, they may be at a later date. A law firm may not ethically represent parties with adverse interests. Therefore, each party should retain his or her own counsel in connection with drafting and/or review of the agreement. If only one party is represented, the agreement should indicate that both knew which party was represented, and that the other party was aware of his or her right to representation. Occasionally, the parties may use a collaborative law approach to developing their agreement or have one attorney mediate creation of the document and then each consult separate counsel to review it.

Forms of Relief Absent a Cohabitation Agreement

Prior to the 1970s, the law essentially denied any rights to unmarried cohabitants following a period of cohabitation. The contention was that granting financial and property rights to unmarried couples would demean the institution of marriage and condone "meretricious" or illicit sex. Although legislatures have been compelled to assume a more active role in regulating nonmarital relationships over the past decade, for more than thirty years the courts have carried the primary responsibility for establishing rules governing the rights of cohabitants when their relationships dissolve in the absence of an agreement. The seminal decision in this area is the high-profile case *Marvin v. Marvin*, decided by the California Supreme Court in 1976. (See Case 5.1.) Viewing the case as an alimony action between two unmarried cohabitants, the media coined the term ***palimony*** to describe it.

Without abandoning the strong public policy favoring marriage, the *Marvin* court strongly endorsed the now widely held principle that when the facts warrant it, the courts should fashion appropriate equitable remedies to avoid hardship or injustice.

Palimony

a term that originated in the press, palimony refers to a court-ordered allowance paid by one cohabitant to the other after their relationship terminates; such allowances are recognized in some case law, but generally not by statute

CASE **5.1** *Marvin v. Marvin,* 18 Cal.3d 660, 557 P.2d 106, 134 Cal. Rptr. 815 (1976)

FROM THE OPINION

During the past 15 years, there has been a substantial increase in the number of couples living together without marrying. Such nonmarital relationships lead to legal controversy when one partner dies or the couple separates....

Plaintiff avers that in October of 1964 she and defendant "entered into an oral agreement" that while "the parties lived together they would combine their efforts and earnings and would share equally any and all property accumulated as a result of their efforts whether individual or combined." Furthermore, they agreed to "hold themselves out to the general public as husband and wife" and that "plaintiff would further render her services as a companion, homemaker, housekeeper and cook";... in return defendant agreed to "provide for all of plaintiff's financial needs and support for the rest of her life."

Plaintiff alleges that she lived with defendant from October of 1964 through May of 1970 and fulfilled her obligations under the agreement. During this period the parties as a result of their efforts and earnings acquired in defendant's name substantial real and personal property, including motion picture rights worth over $1 million. In May of 1970, however, defendant compelled plaintiff to leave his household. He continued to support plaintiff until November of 1971, but thereafter refused to provide further support.

On the basis of these allegations plaintiff asserts two causes of action. The first, for declaratory relief, asks the court to determine her contract and property rights; the second seeks to impose a constructive trust upon one half of the property acquired during the course of the relationship.

In the case before us plaintiff,... maintains that the trial court erred in denying her a trial on the merits of her contention. Although the trial court did not specify the ground for its conclusion that plaintiff's contractual allegations stated no cause of action, defendant offers some... theories to support the ruling....

Defendant first and principally relies on the contention that the alleged contract is so closely related to the supposed "immoral" character of the relationship between plaintiff and himself that the enforcement of the contract would violate public policy. He points to cases asserting that a contract between nonmarital partners is unenforceable if it is "involved in" an illicit relationship....

continued

Numerous other cases have upheld enforcement of agreements between nonmarital partners in factual settings essentially indistinguishable from the present case....

...The fact that a man and a woman live together without marriage, and engage in a sexual relationship, does not in itself invalidate agreements between them relating to their earnings, property or expenses....Agreements between nonmarital partners fail only to the extent that they rest upon consideration of meretricious sexual services....

The principle that a contract between nonmarital partners will be enforced unless expressly and inseparably based upon an illicit consideration of sexual services not only represents the distillation of the decisional law, but also offers a far more precise and workable standard than that advocated by defendant....

In summary, we base our opinion on the principle that adults who voluntarily live together and engage in sexual relations are nonetheless as competent as any other persons to contract regarding their earnings and property rights. Of course, they cannot lawfully contract to pay for the performance of sexual services, for such a contract is, in essence, an agreement for prostitution and unlawful for that reason. But they may agree to pool their earnings and to hold all property acquired during the relationship in accord with the law governing community property; conversely they may agree that each partner's earnings and property acquired from those earnings remains the separate property of the earning partner. So long as the agreement does not rest upon illicit meretricious consideration, the parties may order their economic affairs as they choose, and no policy precludes the courts from enforcing such agreements.

Both plaintiff and defendant stand in broad agreement that the law should be fashioned to carry out the reasonable expectations of the parties....

...the cases denying relief do not rest their refusal upon any theory of "punishing" a "guilty" partner. Indeed, to the extent that denial of relief "punishes" one partner, it necessarily rewards the other by permitting him to retain a disproportionate amount of the property. Concepts of "guilt" thus cannot justify an unequal division of property between two equally "guilty" persons.

Other reasons advanced in the decisions fare no better. The principal argument seems to be that "[equitable] considerations arising from the reasonable expectation of... benefits attending the status of marriage...are not present [in a nonmarital relationship]" (*Vallera v. Vallera*...). But, although parties to a nonmarital relationship obviously cannot have based any expectations upon the belief that they were married, other expectations and equitable considerations remain. The parties may well expect that property will be divided in accord with the parties' own tacit understanding and that in the absence of such understanding the courts will freely apportion property accumulated through mutual effort. We need not treat nonmarital partners as putatively married persons in order to apply principles of implied contract, or extend equitable remedies; we need to treat them only as we do any other unmarried persons.

The argument that granting remedies to the nonmarital partners would discourage marriage must fail;...Although we recognize the well-established public policy to foster and promote the institution of marriage,...perpetuation of judicial rules which result in an inequitable distribution of property accumulated during a nonmarital relationship is neither a just nor an effective way of carrying out that policy.

continued

The mores of society have indeed changed so radically in regard to cohabitation that we cannot impose a standard based on alleged moral considerations that have apparently been so widely abandoned by so many. Lest we be misunderstood, however, we take this occasion to point out that the structure of society itself largely depends on the institution of marriage and nothing we have said in this opinion should be taken to derogate from that institution. The joining of the man and woman in marriage is at once the most socially productive and individually fulfilling relationship that one can enjoy in the course of a lifetime.

We conclude that the judicial barriers that may stand in the way of a policy based upon the fulfillment of the reasonable expectations of the parties to a nonmarital relationship should be removed. As we have explained, the courts now hold that express agreements will be enforced unless they rest on an unlawful meretricious consideration. We add that in the absence of an express agreement, the courts may look to a variety of other remedies in order to protect the parties' lawful expectations.

The courts may inquire into the conduct of the parties to determine whether that conduct demonstrates an implied contract or implied agreement of partnership or joint venture... or some other tacit understanding between the parties. The courts may, when appropriate, employ principles of constructive trust... or resulting trust.... Finally, a nonmarital partner may recover in quantum meruit for the reasonable value of household services rendered less the reasonable value of support received if he can show that he rendered services with the expectation of monetary reward.

Since we have determined that plaintiff's complaint states a cause of action for breach of an express contract, and, as we have explained, can be amended to state a cause of action independent of allegations of express contract, we must conclude that the trial court erred in granting defendant a judgment on the pleadings.

The judgment is reversed and the cause remanded for further proceedings consistent with the views expressed herein.

SIDEBAR

In its opinion, the California Supreme Court also discussed California decisions addressing the impact of the state's Family Law Act establishing no-fault divorce in California. It noted that in the *Cary* case (34 Cal. App.3d 345, 109 Cal. Rptr. 862 (1973)), the Court of Appeals reasoned that the Act was designed to eliminate fault as a basis for dividing marital property. It further opined that once fault is excluded, nothing distinguishes the property rights of a nonmarital "spouse" from those of a "***putative spouse***" who is entitled to half the "***quasi-marital property***". The California Supreme Court determined that this reasoning applies by analogy to cohabiting couples who believe they are in a spouse-like relationship. The *Marvin* case is available in its entirety on the companion website.

Putative spouse
a person who believes in good faith that his or her invalid marriage is legally valid

Quasi-marital property
property treated as if it was acquired by the parties during the marriage even though the marriage was never valid; property acquired during a marriage in a non-community property state that would be marital property if acquired in a community property state

When a marriage dissolves, the spouses have property rights that are identified by statute and applied by the courts. Cohabitants lack such rights (unless contained in an enforceable agreement or afforded under a civil union or comparable statute). Absent a guiding legal framework, the courts must consider each cohabitant's petition for relief on a fact-intensive case-by-case basis. Paralegal Application 5.2 describes the kinds of information a paralegal may be required to gather in a cohabitation case. A summary of the primary legal theories various courts have relied on to provide relief to cohabitants is provided in Exhibit 5.2.

PARALEGAL APPLICATION 5.2

GATHERING INFORMATION IN A COHABITATION CASE

In a palimony case, the paralegal may be asked to gather information in an effort to shape and develop support for the client's case and anticipate opposing arguments and defenses that may be raised. The information may be obtained directly from the client and/or other individuals through interviews and also from documents.

- When, where, and why did the parties decide to live together?

- Did either party relocate, change employment, or make any other major changes in order to cohabit?

- What were the dates during which the parties lived together?

- What was the understanding with respect to the sexual relationship between the parties, if any? What specifically was said? To what extent, if at all, was sexual activity a consideration for the agreement between the parties? What was the nature of the parties' sexual relationship before and during the period of cohabitation? Was it monogamous?

- Did the parties discuss their intentions with respect to marriage, and, if so, to what did they agree?

- What, if any, commitments were made regarding:
  - housing: rental or purchase and payment of related costs?
  - payment of household expenses: food, utilities, etc.?
  - homemaking responsibilities: cooking, cleaning, etc.?
  - medical insurance and expenses?

- How did the parties describe their relationship to their families, employers, friends, and the general public? Did they call each other spouses, companions, partners, roommates, significant others, etc.?

- How did the parties manage their finances? Did they have joint and/or separate bank accounts?

- What was said and agreed to with respect to the parties' separate property and property accumulated during the period of cohabitation?

- Were there any discussions and/or agreements concerning: children, the making of wills or other legal documents (such as powers of attorney and health care proxies), or the giving of gifts to each other during the cohabitation period?

- Were any other commitments made and, if so, what were they?

- How, and to what extent, were the parties involved in each other's business activities, and what was the agreement, if any, with respect to that involvement?

- Did either party ever compensate the other for services rendered during the cohabitation and, if so, for what and in what manner and amount?

- Were any of the parties' agreements written down? Were any notes taken?

- Were there witnesses to any of the agreements made?

- What are the names and addresses of witnesses who may be able to testify regarding the parties' relationship and express or implied agreements?

- What documents exist to support any of the above, e.g., lease agreements, deeds to property, checking and savings account statements, tax returns, loan applications, etc.?

- Are there any *defenses* available to either party, such as fraud, undue influence, *unclean hands*, lack of capacity, etc.?

Defense
a defendant's stated reason why a plaintiff has no valid claim or why the court should not grant the relief requested

Unclean hands
the principle that a party should not be granted relief if he or she has acted unfairly, wrongfully, or illegally

---

EXHIBIT 5.2 Legal Bases for Granting Relief to Cohabitants Upon Dissolution of their Relationship

Express contract a contract that is created by an actual articulated agreement of the parties as to certain terms of their relationship expressed orally or in writing	***Express contract***	This is a contract that is created by an actual articulated agreement of the parties as to certain terms of their relationship. The parties negotiate and "express" the terms to each other. As with other contracts, an express contract requires an offer, acceptance, and consideration (other than sexual services). Absent a cohabitation agreement evidencing the parties' intentions, express contracts can be difficult to prove and usually turn on the relative credibility of the parties.
	Example	Marlene and Walter decide to live together. They agree that during the period of their cohabitation (however long it may last), they will equally contribute to expenses, jointly perform household chores, and share equally in whatever assets they accumulate. Although they do not actually commit them to writing, they openly discuss these terms and agree that they are fair. Following the "Marvin Doctrine," many courts are likely to enforce this agreement.
Implied-in-fact contract a judicially created contract, the existence of which is inferred from the conduct of the parties	***Implied-in-fact contract***	This is a judicially created contract. The intentions of the parties are inferred from their conduct given the facts and surrounding circumstances. Even though its terms may not have been actually discussed or "expressed," a court may reasonably conclude there was an agreement based on the parties' actions.
	Example	Marlene and Walter agree to cohabit and they live together for seven years. They open joint checking and savings accounts into which they both make contributions. Marlene gives up her job as an accountant in order to perform the couples' household chores and to take care of Walter's three-year-old son. The couple shares most expenses, and household furnishings, etc. are purchased with commingled funds. Many of their friends assume that they are married. Based on these facts, a court could reasonably find an implied agreement to share assets accumulated during the relationship.
Quasi-contract/implied-in-law contract a contract imposed by a court to prevent unjust enrichment of one party at the expense of the other	***Quasi-contract/ Implied-in-law contract***	Express or implied-in-fact contracts are based on the actual language or conduct of the parties. In a quasi-contract, the court imposes contractual obligations on the parties to avoid unjust enrichment of one party at the expense of the other.

continued

It is a "legal fiction" created by the court in the absence of an express agreement.

Example

Marlene has provided seven years of household and childcare services at a considerable benefit to Walter. A court may now require him to make some payment to her for having done so. Based on a *quantum meruit* (as much as is deserved) approach, the court may award Marlene the reasonable value of services she rendered less any payments actually received. Courts have begun to recognize that such services may be part of a bargained-for exchange and not intended as a gift. An economist may testify as to the estimated economic value of the services in the open marketplace.

quantum meruit
a basis for establishing damages or providing relief based on the reasonable value of services one person has provided to another

Resulting trust/Purchase money resulting trust/ Implied trust

A *resulting trust* is created by the court when one party contributes funds or services toward the acquisition of property and the title to that property is in the name of the other party. It is imposed by the court on an asset for the benefit of a contributing party when it is demonstrated that he or she did not intend for the other party to have all or any ownership rights. The trustee (the one who "owns" the property) is deemed by the court to hold the property for the benefit of the beneficiary (the one who provided the funds).

Resulting trust
a trust created by the court when one party contributes funds or services toward the acquisition of property and the title to that property is in the name of the other party

Example

Marlene and Walter purchase a small condo titled and mortgaged in Walter's name because of his better credit history, but Marlene pays the entire deposit of $25,000 and also pays the monthly mortgage payments out of her inheritance from her brother's estate. A court may reasonably find that Marlene did not intend for Walter to have ownership of the property, but rather that he should hold title to the condo for her benefit.

Constructive trust

A *constructive trust* is imposed by the court on an asset of a party who improperly or wrongfully acquired the property. It is not based on the parties' intentions, but rather is designed to prevent unjust enrichment. The trustee (the holder of the property) is ordered by the court to convey the property to the beneficiary (the wronged party) in order to prevent unjust enrichment.

Constructive trust
a trust imposed by the court on an asset of a party who improperly or wrongfully acquired the property

Example

Shortly before Marlene and Walter stopped living together, without Walter's knowledge or consent, Marlene took all of the funds out of the joint checking and savings accounts to

continued

which they each had contributed. The total amount taken was $24,000. A court may find that she holds at least 50% of that amount in a constructive trust for Walter's benefit and order her to pay him that amount.

Implied partnership
a judicially created partnership, the existence of which is inferred from the conduct of the parties

Implied partnership/Joint venture

Similar to an implied-in-fact contract, when the cohabiting partners work together in a business venture that is owned by one of the parties, the court creates an ***implied partnership*** or joint venture (more limited than a partnership) and then distributes the assets and liabilities of the business based on principles of fairness.

Example

When Marlene and Walter began living together, Walter had a small sailboat chartering business. While she was at home, Marlene learned all she could about operating and marketing such a business. She spent about six hours a day for several years working to build the business. When the couple ceased living together, the business had grown to nearly forty times its value when they moved in together due primarily to her labors. Although she and Walter had no formal employment or partnership agreement, a court may hold that the chartering business represents a joint venture of the parties and that Marlene is entitled to a portion of its value.

Putative spouse doctrine

A putative spouse is a person who reasonably believes he or she entered a valid marriage, until some impediment to the marriage is discovered that renders the marriage invalid. Some courts will provide relief to an innocent "spouse" in such situations. This doctrine is sometimes extended to provide for other "innocent" unmarried partners.

Example

Walter and Marlene initially met when he was forty years old and she was fifteen and they began living together when Marlene was seventeen. To celebrate, they went on a vacation to an Indian Reservation in South Dakota. While there, they participated in a traditional celebration that Walter convinced Marlene was a wedding ceremony. Marlene, albeit naively, continued to believe they were married until they eventually ceased living together several years later. A court may apply the putative spouse doctrine to afford Marlene some degree of relief.

PARALEGAL APPLICATION 5.3

WOULD YOU GRANT RELIEF?

FACT PATTERN:

Roberta and Erwin met in 1986, when Roberta responded to a personal ad in the paper. For the first several years of their relationship, they maintained their separate residences but enjoyed a relationship that included such activities as dining, travel, and visiting with family and friends. In 1993, they agreed to build a home together. The couple purchased a lot for $49,000, shared the cost equally, and titled the property in both their names. Erwin, a professional designer and drafter, designed the new home. He initially estimated it would cost about $370,000 to build, but it eventually cost over $500,000. Erwin paid about a third of the cost and Roberta two-thirds.

In 1995, Erwin deeded his interest in the property to Roberta so she could realize a favorable mortgage and certain tax advantages. The change was also made in response to notice from Roberta's ex-husband that he intended to discontinue alimony payments to her because of her cohabitation and joint ownership of the home. At the time, Erwin advised the former husband in writing that he and Roberta lived together solely for convenience and companionship, that they maintained separate financial accounts, and that his contribution was in exchange for an indefinite period of free rent, thereby disavowing any interest in the home, legal or equitable.

During the cohabitation in the new home, Roberta paid the mortgage payments and Erwin contributed occasionally to the utilities but paid no rent. After a while, they began sleeping in separate bedrooms, and in 1996, Roberta asked Erwin to move out. He initially refused, but after she changed the locks and posted a no trespassing sign, he left. Erwin has filed suit seeking a partition (division) of the property. He argues she should reimburse him for his $170,000 contribution, and his design and construction management services. Roberta claims he negligently designed the home, poorly managed construction, and misrepresented himself as an architect.

SIDEBAR

Would you grant relief to Erwin in this case? Why or why not? If granted, what legal bases do you think a court would use to justify relief? What defenses might Roberta raise? Read the case, *Salzman v. Bachrach*, 996 P.2d 1263 (Colo. 2000), available on the companion website for this text in the material related to Chapter 5. What did the court decide and why? Do you agree or disagree with the decision?

Even though laws relating to cohabitation and consensual sexual behavior are rarely enforced,[11] the paralegal should find out if they are still "on the books" in his or her jurisdiction. Some states still have laws prohibiting male-female cohabitation as lewd and lascivious behavior.[12] The offense is typically a misdemeanor punishable by a short prison term and/or a fine. For example, the relevant Michigan statute appears in a section of the state criminal code with other "Indecency and Immorality" offenses. It provides that "Any man or woman, not being married to each other, who lewdly and lasciviously associates and cohabits together, and any man or woman, married or unmarried, who is guilty of open and gross lewdness and lascivious behavior, is guilty of a misdemeanor…."[13]

If a state enforces a prohibition against unlawful cohabitation, the parties may not be able to execute a Cohabitation Agreement in that state, as the subject matter of a contract must be legal in order for it to be enforceable. (See Exhibit 5.3.)

Paralegal Practice Tip
Courts in some states have refused to provide relief to cohabitants when their relationship terminates or do so only under certain circumstances. (See Exhibit 5.3.)

EXHIBIT 5.3 Minnesota Cohabitation and Necessity of Contract Statutes

FROM THE STATUTES:

513.075 COHABITATION; PROPERTY AND FINANCIAL AGREEMENTS

If sexual relations between the parties are contemplated, a contract between a man and a woman who are living in this state out of wedlock, or who are about to commence living together in this state out of wedlock, is enforceable as to terms concerning the property and financial relations of the parties only if:

1. the contract is written and signed by the parties; and
2. enforcement is sought after termination of the relationship.

513.076 NECESSITY OF CONTRACT

Unless the individuals have executed a contract complying with the provisions of section 513.075, the courts of this state are without jurisdiction to hear and shall dismiss as contrary to public policy any claim by an individual to the earnings or property of another individual if the claim is based on the fact that the individuals lived together in contemplation of sexual relations and out of wedlock within or without this state.

Although most states have repealed their criminal cohabitation statutes, a taxpayer who resides with a dependent cohabiting partner in a state that continues to criminalize cohabitation may not be permitted to claim a federal tax exemption for the partner as a dependant, although he or she may have been entitled to do so if residing in another state where cohabitation is not against the law.[14]

ALTERNATIVE NONMARITAL FAMILY STRUCTURES

Recognition of nonmarital relationships in the United States, thus far, has assumed a number of formats running along a continuum from cohabitation to same-sex marriage. Approaches range from situations in which cohabitants have virtually no rights to ones in which they are treated by a state as though they are married. (See Exhibit 5.4.) Labels abound, definitions overlap, and each model has its own advantages and limitations.[15] The most common models include the following:

- **Cohabitation:** Cohabitation is sometimes referred to as the umbrella under which the other nonmarital relationships are covered. Standing alone, it creates no legal status and affords little legal protection unless formalized in an enforceable cohabitation agreement or recognized by the courts as a suitable candidate for relief.
- **Domestic Partnerships:** Hawaii was the first state to offer a form of domestic partnership status to its employees in 1997. Hawaii grants "reciprocal beneficiary" status to any two unmarried people prohibited from marrying under state law (for example, close relatives and same-sex couples).[16] By the spring of 2008, California,[17] Maine,[18] and the District of Columbia[19] also had enacted domestic partnership legislation, with California's being the most comprehensive model.[20] Several cities and counties confer domestic partnership benefits on employees but not a

comprehensive legal status. Many private companies also afford employee benefits to cohabitants under certain conditions. (See Exhibit 5.5.)

- **Civil Unions:** As of the spring of 2008, five states, including Connecticut,[21] New Hampshire,[22] New Jersey,[23] Oregon,[24] and Vermont,[25] granted civil union status to qualifying couples. Generally speaking, civil unions afford more significant rights than do domestic partnerships. For example, the Connecticut civil union legislation, which became effective October 1, 2005, provides that "parties to a civil union shall have the same benefits, protection and responsibilities under law as granted to spouses in a marriage, which is defined as the union of one man and one woman." The legislation further provides that the terms "spouse," "family," "immediate family," "dependent," and "next of kin" as well as any other term denoting spousal relationship is construed to include a party to a civil union.

- **Same-Sex Marriage:** As of June 2008, Massachusetts and California are the only states to allow same-sex marriage.[26] Although it is labeled "marriage," this form of union is not, in fact, fully equivalent to "traditional" marriage. The most significant difference is that only the latter receives federal benefits and protections.

- **Functional Family Status:** Some courts extend at least limited rights to nonmarital partners in certain circumstances by applying a functional family approach that focuses on the "reality of family life"[27] rather than on definitions of family limited to persons related by blood, marriage, or adoption. Concentrating on the intimacy and strength of the bond between the parties, courts consider factors such as the following:
  - how long the couple has lived together
  - whether or not the relationship is exclusive
  - the degree of the couple's emotional commitment
  - the extent to which their finances are commingled
  - how committed each of the partners is to supporting the other economically
  - the manner in which the parties have conducted themselves in their daily lives (roles, sharing of household responsibilities, etc.)
  - how they have represented themselves to the outside world

(See Paralegal Application 5.4.)

- **Adult Adoption:** Adult adoption is another means of achieving a recognizable family status for same-sex couples. However, it is rarely used and is permitted in only a small number of states. From the parties' perspective, it is a desirable option in that it creates a relationship that brings with it a full array of family benefits. However, it is limited in that it generally cannot be dissolved if the parties' relationship later terminates. From the perspective of the courts, it is often viewed as distorting the intended purpose of adoption, the creation of a parent-child relationship.[28]

- **Meretricious Relationship:** The state of Washington has looked beyond the traditional meaning of the word "meretricious" and uses the phrase "meretricious relationship" to refer to a "stable, marital-like relationship, where both parties cohabit with knowledge that a lawful marriage between them does not exist." Factors the court considers in determining whether or not a meretricious relationship exists "include, but are not limited to: continuous cohabitation, duration of the relationship, purpose of the relationship, pooling of resources and services for joint projects, and the intent of the parties." Once a meretricious relationship is established, a trial court can evaluate the interest each party has in the property acquired during the relationship and make an equitable distribution of that property. Although a meretricious relationship is not considered the same as a marriage, the court focuses on property that would have been community property had the parties been married.[29]

Paralegal Practice Tip

It is important to be aware of the fact that the same term may mean different things in different jurisdictions, at different times, or in different contexts. For example, traditionally the adjective "meretricious" has had a negative connotation and has been associated primarily with illicit sexual conduct. To some degree this is still the case. For example, the Pennsylvania worker's compensation law provides that worker's compensation benefits may be terminated upon proof that the claimant has entered into a "meretricious relationship."[30]

PARALEGAL APPLICATION 5.4

WOULD YOU EVICT?

FACT PATTERN:

Miguel and Leslie were same-sex partners who lived together in a rent-controlled apartment for more than a decade until Leslie died. Leslie was the tenant of record and after his death, the landlord tried to evict Miguel, claiming that he had no right to occupy the apartment, given the applicable rent-control statute. The statute provided that a landlord could not evict a "surviving spouse of the deceased tenant or some other member of the deceased tenant's family who has been living with the tenant of record." The landlord claimed Miguel was neither Leslie's spouse nor a member of his family. Miguel claimed that the interpretation and application of the statute should not be restricted by rigid legal distinctions based solely on a definition of family as individuals related by blood, marriage, or adoption. Rather, the definition should be extended to include two lifetime partners whose relationship is long term and characterized by an emotional and financial commitment and interdependence. Miguel and Leslie had lived together for more than ten years and were regarded by each other and their friends as spouses. They had attended family and other functions as a couple. Miguel considered the apartment his home, used the address on his license and passport, and received his mail there. They had shared all household obligations and maintained joint bank and credit card accounts. Leslie had also granted Miguel Power of Attorney so that he could make necessary medical, financial, and personal decisions for him during his illness.

SIDEBAR

How do you think this case should be decided and why? What is the purpose of such laws? Spouses would automatically have qualified to remain in the apartment. Is it fair to require nonmarital partners to prove the nature and quality of their relationship in order to be protected by the rent-control law? To see how New York's highest court decided this case, read the opinion in *Braschi v. Stahl Associates Co.*, 74 N.Y.2d 201, 543 N.E.2d 49, 544 N.Y.S.2d 784 (1989), available on the companion website for this text in the material related to Chapter 5.

The mixture of approaches to family status and nonmarital relationships described thus far has sent shock waves into the social fabric of this country and into its legal system as well. In describing the evolving and unstable nature of this situation, one writer has commented:

> The result of all this activity is a rather confusing legal situation, in which cohabitants' rights are based on a mixture of remedies that not only vary from state to state, but also result in intrastate legal regimes based on different legal theories and offering a patchwork of remedies from a variety of sources. An additional result is that same-sex couples are better protected in many areas than are heterosexual cohabitants.[31]

A state-by-state summary of these approaches as of June 2008 is provided in Exhibit 5.4. Because developments in this area are so fluid, a copy of this exhibit will be updated annually and made available on the companion website.

EXHIBIT 5.4 Summary of State Approaches to Status of Same-Sex Marital and Nonmarital Couples (as of June 2008)

	Same-Sex Marriage Permitted	Civil Unions Permitted	Domestic Partnerships Permitted	Prohibitions by Statute and/or Constitution	Same-Sex Marriage Undefined or not Prohibited by Statute
Alabama				X	
Alaska				X	
Arizona				X	
Arkansas				X	
California	X		X		
Colorado				X	
Connecticut		X		X	
Delaware				X	
District of Columbia			X		
Florida				X	
Georgia				X	
Hawaii			X*	X	
Idaho				X	
Illinois				X	
Indiana				X	
Iowa				X	
Kansas				X	
Kentucky				X	
Louisiana				X	
Maine			X	X	
Maryland				X**	
Massachusetts	X				
Michigan				X	
Minnesota				X	
Mississippi				X	
Missouri				X	
Montana				X	
Nebraska				X	
Nevada				X	
New Hampshire		X		X	
New Jersey		X	***	X	X
New Mexico				X	X
New York				X	X

continued

continued

Paralegal Practice Tip

It is worth noting that a state may have adopted a defense of marriage provision in the form of a constitutional amendment or a legislative statute (a mini-DOMA, as in Vermont) and yet still provides for domestic partnerships or civil unions. California's statutory provision against same-sex marriage[32] was declared unconstitutional by that state's Supreme Court in June 2008.

Paralegal Practice Tip

Domestic partnerships and civil unions are important vehicles for recognition of nonmarital relationships on the international scene as well as in the United States, with the trend being most apparent in Europe. Beginning with Denmark in 1989, civil unions, under one name or another, have been established in many other countries including, but not limited to, Israel, Norway, Sweden, France, Germany, Portugal, Finland, New Zealand, Switzerland, and the United Kingdom. As of January 2007, Belgium, Canada, the Netherlands, Spain, and South Africa also permit same-sex marriage.[33] The extent to which relationships formed in these nations will be recognized by courts in this country remains to be seen.

North Carolina		X	
North Dakota		X	
Ohio		X	
Oklahoma		X	
Oregon	X	X	
Pennsylvania		X	
Puerto Rico		X	
Rhode Island			X
South Carolina		X	
South Dakota		X	
Tennessee		X	
Texas		X	
Utah		X	
Vermont	X	X	
Virginia		X	
Washington	****	X	
West Virginia		X	
Wisconsin		X	
Wyoming		X	

*Hawaii recognizes "reciprocal beneficiary" relationships

**In January 2006, a state judge held the Maryland statute unconstitutional, but it remained effective pending appeal.

***Prior to enacting its civil union law, New Jersey had permitted domestic partnerships. (See end notes 23 and 41.)

****Washington provides remedies for parties to "meretricious relationships."

Domestic Partnerships

The American Law Institute (ALI) has defined domestic partners as "two persons of the same or opposite sex, not married to one another, who for a significant period of time share a primary residence and a life together...."[34] According to the ALI, factors indicating the existence of a domestic partnership include, among others, oral statements, commingled finances, economic dependency, specialized roles, naming beneficiaries, emotional and sexual intimacy, community reputation, commitment or attempted marriage ceremony, common household, and joint procreation, childrearing, or adoption.

Under the law, a ***domestic partnership*** is a status granted to an unmarried couple who live together and receive a variety of economic and non-economic benefits customarily granted to spouses. The status may be available to heterosexual couples but in most instances is limited to same-sex couples. In a few states, domestic partnership status is granted and regulated by the state. Domestic partnerships are also offered by smaller governmental units, such as counties and municipalities, although the scope of benefits available is more restricted.[35] A number of businesses and educational institutions also afford some form of benefits to domestic partners. (See Exhibit 5.5.)

Domestic partnership
a status granted to an unmarried couple who live together and receive a variety of economic and non-economic benefits customarily granted to spouses

EXHIBIT 5.5 Employers that Lead the Way—Is the Client Missing
Anything?

BUSINESSES

In response to changes in company policy and/or pressure from unions, over the past two decades a significant number of employers have broadened their eligibility requirements for receiving benefits, most to both opposite- and same-sex partners and some only to the latter. The Village Voice union was the first in the nation to fight successfully for benefits for domestic partners and has had them since 1982. Companies providing benefits only to same-sex couples usually premise the decision on cost considerations, and the fact that same-sex partners generally do not have the choice to legalize their relationships through marriage. The primary benefits most commonly extended include medical insurance, life insurance, relocation, and bereavement leave. Some of the major employers extending benefits include Levi Strauss & Company, Ben and Jerry's Ice Cream, Disney Corporation, Lotus, and Apple Computer. Several businesses also offer benefits to their customers. For example, many insurance companies (such as USAA and AAA) offer family rates on health and auto policies to unmarried couples who demonstrate a long-term, financially interdependent relationship even though they are not technically "domestic partners."

COLLEGES AND UNIVERSITIES

A number of academic institutions have extended benefits to domestic partners (primarily same sex) as well. Among the earliest to do so were Harvard University, Princeton University, Stanford University, the University of Chicago, and the University of Iowa. The primary benefits extended are health and dental insurance and bereavement and parental leave. Some institutions also extend housing benefits, recreational facilities privileges, and eligibility for tuition remission and scholarship opportunities.

Paralegal Practice Tip
The future of public sector employer benefits is at risk in some states. In May of 2008, for example, the Michigan Supreme Court ruled that the state's 2004 ban against gay marriage also blocks domestic-partner benefits for gay employees extended by the University of Michigan and other public sector employers.

To become domestic partners, the couple usually must qualify for and register their relationship with the appropriate state agency. Typical requirements for qualification include the following:

- The parties are at least age 18.
- Each partner is unmarried and is not a party to another domestic partnership.
- Their relationship is exclusive.
- They share a residence.
- They agree to be jointly responsible for each other's basic living expenses.
- They are not related in a way that would prevent them from legally marrying under applicable state law.
- They agree that if their relationship ends, they will file a certificate of dissolution.

Domestic partnership status granted under state law generally is less extensive than civil union status in terms of the nature and extent of benefits provided. It also falls far short of marital status, which carries with it more than 1,000 rights under federal law for opposite-sex spouses.[37] However, the benefits obtained through a domestic partnership vary by state and may be extensive.

Paralegal Practice Tip
It is important to be aware that the content of domestic partnership statutes is not uniform. For example, California recognizes domestic partnerships for same-sex partners and also for opposite-sex couples when at least one of the partners is age 62 or older. The state of Maine extends domestic partnership eligibility to both heterosexual and homosexual partners and defines domestic partners as "2 unmarried adults who are domiciled together under long-term arrangements that evidence a commitment to remain responsible indefinitely for each other's welfare."[36]

Paralegal Practice Tip
The future of the California Domestic Partnership Statute is uncertain in light of the legalization of the same-sex marriage in that state as of June 15, 2008.

For example, the rights and benefits granted under the California statute are particularly expansive. The applicable California statute states in part: "(a) Registered domestic partners shall have the same rights, protections, and benefits, and shall be subject to the same responsibilities, obligations and duties under law, ... as are granted to and imposed upon spouses."[38]

Each state that authorizes the creation of domestic partnerships establishes the means by which they can be terminated. Typically, termination is accomplished either by filing a form with the appropriate governmental office or by filing a termination action in the appropriate court. In California, for example, domestic partners who satisfy certain requirements can file with the Secretary of State's Office a Notice of Termination of Domestic Partnership, which will be effective six months after filing without a trial or a hearing if not revoked in the interim. As of January 2008, the requirements for proceeding in this manner include:

- Both parties want to terminate the partnership.
- The partnership has been in existence for less than five years.
- No children were born to or adopted by the parties and neither party is pregnant at the time of filing the Notice.
- Neither owns land or buildings.
- The value of the parties' community property, if any, is less than $33,000.
- The parties' have less than $5,000 in community obligations.
- The parties have prepared and executed a property settlement agreement (or have no community property).
- Neither party is requesting money or support from the other.
- Neither party has separate property valued in excess of $33,000.

PARALEGAL APPLICATION 5.5

WHAT DO YOU THINK?

FACT PATTERN:

Birgit and Kendall are a lesbian couple and domestic partners in a state that legally recognizes such relationships. Birgit belongs to a country club where she and her partner, who is not a member, frequently play golf. The club extends membership benefits to a member's legal spouse and unmarried children under the age of twenty-two without charging additional membership or usage fees. All other non-member golfing partners are "guests," who may play no more than six times a year and who must pay a greens fee each time they play. Birgit has tried to get the club to recognize Kendall as her "significant other" and grant her privileges, but they have refused. She has now sued the club, claiming that she is being discriminated against based on her marital status under the state's civil rights act, which requires businesses to treat customers equally.

SIDEBAR

What do you think the result should be in this case? Why? Should it make a difference if the state in which the country club is located recognizes domestic partnerships? What if the couple were a heterosexual couple? Should the result be the same? Read the case of *Koebke v. Bernardo Heights Country Club*, 36 Cal. 4th 824, 115 P.3d 1212, 31 Cal. Rptr. 3d 565 (2005), which is available on the companion website, to see how the California court resolved this case. Do you agree with the decision? Why? Should the outcome be different now that California has legalized same-sex marriage?

If these conditions are not satisfied, an action for termination can be filed in Superior Court, and the parties are entitled to a hearing and trial before a judge. A copy of the California Petition for Dissolution, Legal Separation, or Nullification of Domestic Partnership can be accessed on the companion website for this text in the material related to Chapter 5.

Civil Unions

In contrast with most domestic partnership laws, *civil unions* are essentially designed to afford same-sex partners the same benefits, protections, and responsibilities that married spouses have under state law. The dissolution of a civil union also parallels dissolution of a marriage. However, although some believe civil unions represent a significant advance for same-sex couples, they fall short of full equality, as the parties are still denied the vast array of rights available to opposite-sex married partners under federal law.

> **Civil union**
> a formal legal status that provides a same-sex couple with the rights, benefits, protections, and responsibilities that a married heterosexual couple has under state but not federal law

Oregon's bill enacting civil unions includes the following rationale for granting legal recognition to relationships between same-sex partners:

> Many gay and lesbian Oregonians have formed lasting, committed, caring and faithful relationships with individuals of the same sex, despite long-standing social and economic discrimination. These couples live together, participate in their communities together and often raise children and care for family members together, just as do couples who are married under Oregon law. Without the ability to obtain some form of legal status for their relationships, same-sex couples face numerous obstacles and hardships in attempting to secure rights, benefits and responsibilities for themselves and their children. Many of the rights, benefits and responsibilities that the families of married couples take for granted cannot be obtained in any way other than through state recognition of committed same-sex relationships. This state has a strong interest in promoting stable and lasting families, including the families of same-sex couples and their children. All Oregon families should be provided with the opportunity to obtain necessary legal protections and status and the ability to achieve their fullest potential.[39]

Vermont was the first state to enact civil unions in 2000, and it has been followed by Connecticut, New Hampshire, New Jersey,[40] and Oregon as of June 2008. In 1999, the Vermont Supreme Court ruled in *Baker v. State*[41] that same-sex couples were entitled under Chapter 1, Article 7 of the Vermont State Constitution to the same benefits and protections afforded under Vermont law to heterosexual married couples. The ruling did not require the issuance of marriage licenses but rather ordered the legislature to create an "equivalent statutory alternative" that would afford essentially the same benefits to same-sex couples as are extended to married couples under Vermont law. After extensive and heated debate (including opposition from the Vermont Bar Association, which had endorsed same-sex marriage), the legislature finally passed H.B. 847, which went into effect on July 1, 2000. Similar to the Hawaii "reciprocal beneficiaries" legislation, Vermont's civil union law also contains a "reciprocal beneficiaries" provision, which provides benefits to non-gay or lesbian couples, who also are not eligible to marry. By December of 2006, Vermont had issued over 8,000 licenses for civil unions, and more than 80% of them involved couples from out of state.[42]

In order to be united in a civil union under Vermont law, the partners must meet the following requirements:

- Neither may be a party to another civil union, marriage, or reciprocal beneficiary relationship.
- Both parties must be of the same sex.
- The parties may not be close family members.
- Both must be at least 18 years of age.
- Both must be mentally competent.
- Neither party may be under a guardianship, unless the guardian consents in writing.

There is no residency requirement for entering a civil union in Vermont, but there is a six-month residency requirement for dissolving one. The dissolution procedure is the same as for divorce. A copy of the Application for Vermont Civil Union is accessible on the companion website for this text in the material related to Chapter 5.

IMPLICATIONS FOR THE FUTURE
The Role of Family Law Practitioners

The creation of new legal frameworks for nonmarital families raises significant legal issues and challenges that must be addressed in the foreseeable future by the courts, legal professionals, legislatures, social and religious institutions, employers, and the voting public. The reverberations from the emergence of alternative family structures are being felt in virtually every area of substantive law. The role of family law practitioners and their paralegals will depend largely on the depth and breadth of each attorney's expertise in various areas. For example:

Probate Law. Partners in nonmarital relationships need to develop multifaceted estate plans if they want to protect and provide for themselves and their partners in the event of death or disability. Documents needed may include, but not necessarily be limited to, wills, trusts, and durable powers of attorney.

Health Care Law. Given the constraints imposed by federal privacy regulations, health care proxies and advanced directives are essential for individuals who want their partners to have access to their medical records and the power to make medical decisions should they be unable to act on their own behalf.

Corporate Law. Even if not required to, many companies that have not already done so are reexamining their personnel policies with an eye to extending a variety of rights to nonmarital partners. Companies customarily require legal advice regarding the drafting of domestic partner benefit policies and the procedures they should put in place to ensure efficient identification of legitimate domestic partner claims and avoid fraud (as when friends move in together for the sole purpose of obtaining medical benefits). Companies also need to be aware of state laws that ban extension of rights to nonmarital partners or that ban discrimination based on marital status.

Tort Law. Courts in several states have afforded cohabitants standing in tort actions. For example, several have provided relief to nonmarital partners for the tort of intentional infliction of emotional distress.[43] However, many remain reluctant to extend standing to nonmarital partners, particularly for loss of *consortium* (although the Supreme Court of New Mexico did so in a 2003 case of first impression in that state).[44]

Consortium
companionship, affection, and, in the case of spouses, sexual relations that one is entitled to receive from another based on existence of a legal relationship (e.g., husband-wife, parent-child)

Constitutional Law. Given the current political climate, the states are likely to continue to pass constitutional amendments addressing various kinds of nonmarital relationships. It is not yet clear whether the amendments will withstand constitutional challenges on equal protection and due process grounds or what effect such amendments will have on domestic partnerships and civil unions.

> The biggest textual difference among constitutional marriage amendments is the extent to which they apply to domestic partnerships, civil unions, or other same-sex legal relationships. Some amendments appear to ban same-sex couples only from the institution of marriage;...Other amendments, however, employ a variety of textual prohibitions designed to prevent both courts and legislators from creating any legal status similar to marriage. For example, Nebraska's constitution states, "the uniting of two persons of the same sex in a civil union, domestic partnership, or other similar same-sex relationship shall not be valid or recognized in Nebraska." Other state amendments prohibit....receipt of the "incidents," "benefits," or "rights" of marriage by same sex couples.... [I]n Ohio the state may not "create or recognize a legal status for [same-sex] relationships...that intends to approximate the design, qualities, significance or effect of marriage." (Citations omitted.)[45]

Other kinds of constitutional challenges may be raised as well. For example, in *Irizarry v. Chicago Board of Education,* a heterosexual woman who had been living with her opposite-sex partner for over twenty years raised an unsuccessful equal protection challenge to the Chicago Board of Education's policy of extending "spousal health benefits" to domestic partners, but only if the domestic partner was of the same sex as the employee.[46]

Conflict/Choice of Law. For over two hundred years, the states have recognized a marital relationship as valid if it were valid in the state where it was entered. They have done so by applying rules based on choice of law provisions and the full faith and credit doctrine. However, there is no similar history of recognizing quasi-marital statuses created to provide the legal rights of marriage to same-sex couples under different names, such as domestic partnerships or civil unions.[47] Thus far, civil unions, domestic partnerships, and reciprocal beneficiary relationships are generally not recognized by states other than those in which they have been adopted. However, there are exceptions,[48] and it is apparent that there will be considerable state-to-state variations as the numbers of petitions for relief increase in future years.

Criminal Law. In 2004, the U.S. Supreme Court overturned a sodomy law in the state of Texas in *Lawrence v. Texas,* holding that a state statute that made "consensual deviate sexual intercourse" with another adult illegal was unconstitutional.[49] Old beliefs are slow to change, but, in light of this decision, states will be driven to reexamine statutes criminalizing various forms of conduct (cohabitation, sodomy, fornication, etc.) between consenting adults in order to withstand inevitable constitutional challenges.

Tax Law. States that have recognized same-sex marriage, domestic partnerships, and civil unions may afford state tax benefits to parties to such relationships. However, as of January 2008, federal tax law does not afford the same benefits to nonmarital families as it does to married persons.

Parties to such relationships must be aware of how they will be treated under federal tax law. For example, under current federal tax law, the amount an employer contributes for a domestic partner's health insurance coverage is includable in the employee's taxable income unless the partner qualifies as a dependent of the employee under the federal tax code.

Family Law. Even if states do not recognize cohabiting couples by affording them specific legal status or rights, it is impossible to ignore the increasing numbers of individuals living in nontraditional family structures (including both same-sex and heterosexual couples). These relationships challenge traditional family law principles and procedures. They generate complex disputes, not only about property, but also about such novel legal issues as surrogacy agreements and other nontraditional reproductive methods. As this trend persists, lawmakers and the courts will be pressured to develop basic family law policies and procedures to address the needs of couples who either cannot or do not wish to marry.

THE PARALEGAL'S ROLE

The paralegal's role in this area will be determined by two major factors:

- The prevailing law in the jurisdiction where the paralegal is employed. For example, is it a domestic partnership, civil union, or same-sex marriage state? A state that vigorously opposes all quasi-marital statuses? A state in transition? and
- The degree to which the firm in which the paralegal is employed extends its expertise into areas of substantive law implicated by developments described in this chapter. For example, will the firm handle probate and tort law as well as family law? Will it take on constitutional challenges?

In a "traditional" family law practice, the paralegal is most likely to focus on the following:

- researching the law governing nonmarital relationships in any relevant jurisdiction
- gathering information in preparation for drafting cohabitation agreements
- drafting cohabitation agreements
- gathering information related to dissolution of nonmarital relationships
- drafting discovery materials, such as interrogatories, proposed deposition questions, and requests for production of documents
- preparing affidavits, exhibits, correspondence, etc., as assigned
- drafting petitions/complaints for relief based on the facts and circumstances of specific cases. The request for relief may come in a variety of forms including, but not limited to, the following:
  - action for breach of contract
  - action seeking specific performance of a contract
  - action in equity for unjust enrichment
  - petition for partition to recover an interest in land
  - petition for an accounting to recover property, money, or other items entrusted to a former cohabitant and not returned
  - an action for deceit and misrepresentation
  - an action for declaratory relief to determine contract and property rights
- assisting with preparation for hearings and/or trial
- making sure the client is kept informed of progress and upcoming deadlines, hearings, discovery matters, etc.

CHAPTER **SUMMARY**

The past five decades have been a time of steady evolution in the structure of family life and intimate relationships in the United States, a trend that promises to continue for the foreseeable future. Although the national political climate may not yet be ready to embrace same-sex marriage, that does not tell the whole story. Marriage is not the only vehicle available for recognizing same-sex couples and affording them legal protections and benefits even in states that have constitutionally banned same-sex marriage. Both same-sex and heterosexual couples increasingly choose to privately order their own relationships through cohabitation agreements. In the near future, other states are likely to join California, Maine, and the District of Columbia by recognizing domestic partnerships, or Vermont, Connecticut, New Jersey, New Hampshire, and Oregon by enacting civil union statutes.[50] Still others may follow Hawaii's reciprocal beneficiaries model or adopt an approach similar to Washington State's recognition of "meretricious relationships."

However, the options discussed in this chapter do not constitute "marriages," and they do not provide the full panoply of rights available to spouses under state and federal law. Some who advocate for same-sex marriage view domestic partnerships and civil unions as interim strategies moving toward a long-term goal, but for many they constitute a "separate but equal" approach that compromises the campaign for full marriage equality. As one writer commenting on the Vermont civil union law has put it:

> No opposite-sex couple would ever imagine it was denied federal recognition, given the huge influence that the federal government has over the day-to-day lives of its citizens. Only same-sex couples are expected to be grateful and accepting of this "pale shadow" of the full range of rights and protections granted to opposite-sex couples who have the freedom to marry.[51]

The general trend in reordering nonmarital relationships has impacted virtually every area of substantive law, as each alternative model raises compelling challenges for judges, legislators, lawyers, employers, and the general public. The challenges are intensified by the fact that some states outpace others in accepting novel arrangements. Conflict between the laws of different jurisdictions is inevitable and promises to shape the future of a family law practice and the role of the paralegal in that practice.[52]

KEY **TERMS**

Civil union
Cohabitation
Cohabitation Agreement
Consortium
Constructive trust
Defense
Domestic partnership
Durable power of attorney

Express contract
Health care proxy
Implied-in-fact contract
Implied partnership/Joint venture
Joint tenant with right of
  survivorship
Meretricious sex
Palimony

Putative spouse
Quantum meruit
Quasi-contract/implied-in-law
  contract
Quasi-marital property
Resulting trust/Purchase money
  resulting trust/Implied trust
Unclean hands

REVIEW **QUESTIONS**

1. Describe how society's view of cohabitation has changed over the past three decades.
2. Identify some of the most common reasons why unmarried couples choose to live together.
3. Identify the primary differences between marriage and cohabitation.
4. Identify five documents cohabitants might execute in order to protect and provide for each other and define their respective rights and responsibilities.
5. Define cohabitation.
6. Identify the main provisions of a cohabitation agreement.
7. Describe the significance of the *Marvin* decision.
8. Distinguish between an express and an implied contract. Give an example of each.
9. Distinguish between a constructive trust and a resulting trust. Give an example of each.
10. Respond to the following regarding domestic partnerships.
    a. Describe the common requirements for establishing a domestic partnership.
    b. Describe the most common benefits of a domestic partnership.
    c. Identify three states that have domestic partnership statutes.

11. Respond to the following regarding civil unions.
    a. Describe the common requirements for entering a civil union.
    b. Describe the nature of the benefits of a civil union.
    c. Identify five states that have enacted civil union legislation.
12. Identify the biggest drawback of domestic partnerships and civil unions in comparison with traditional marriage.
13. Describe the functional family approach as it would apply to resolution of a dispute between two former cohabitants.
14. Describe how the development of alternative models of nonmarital relationships has impacted many areas of substantive law.

FOCUS ON **THE JOB**

THE FACTS

Richard Bauer and Mary Newton have been going out for six months. Although they are very happy and plan to spend the rest of their lives together, for a number of reasons, they have decided to live together but not get married.

Both parties are semi-retired after long and successful careers, he as an engineer, she as a college dean. He is 65 years old, was married once before for 22 years, and has three adult children and four grandchildren. She is 63 years old, a widow (receiving social security benefits through her deceased husband), and has no children or grandchildren.

His Primary Assets	Her Primary Assets
Vacation home on the New Jersey shore (assessed at $350,000)	Vacation cottage in Beverly Farms, Massachusetts (assessed at $200,000)
Bell Laboratories pension	State pension
30-foot trawler valued at $125,000	36-foot sailboat valued at $50,000
401(K) valued at $350,000	Condominium in North Conway, New Hampshire (assessed at $250,000)
Artworks valued at about $40,000	
Investment portfolio (current value $325,000)	Investment portfolio (current value $225,000)
	Jewelry valued at $27,000

Richard and Mary plan to purchase a new home in Florida. Richard will pay a $300,000 down payment, and Mary will get a mortgage for $300,000 and make the associated payments. The deed and mortgage will be in Mary's name only, but they intend that the property will belong to them equally. They will share all home maintenance, utility, and daily living expenses equally and will pay those expenses from a joint account to which they will both contribute. Mary intends to do a significant amount of landscaping to improve and maintain the Florida property.

Richard plans to add a music/art room to the house for his enjoyment and at his expense. Richard is concerned about Mary's housekeeping and has decided he wants to pay for daily maid services. The couple will share grocery shopping and cooking chores. Each party will maintain an individual bank account in addition to their joint account. Each party intends to work part time. Richard will work in a marine supply store two days a week and both parties will teach one or two courses at a local college. Each will be entitled to his or her own earnings. Mary anticipates no inheritance through her family. Richard anticipates a substantial inheritance when his mother dies.

It does not bother them if other people think of or treat them as if they are married, but they have no intention of entering a marriage, common law or otherwise. They do share an intimate and sexual relationship and anticipate that will continue, but that is not the reason why they are moving in together. The couple expects to continue their current lifestyle and do considerable traveling together, particularly by boat. Mary has a beagle, "Spike," and, because Richard is allergic to dogs, she has agreed to not have the dog inside the house or on the boat and to be totally responsible for all expenses related to the dog.

The parties intend their agreement to take effect upon signing and to be unaffected by any periodic, temporary separations. It will terminate only when the parties sign a written declaration of termination or have lived separate and apart for a continuous six-month period. Neither party expects to benefit under the will of the other, but each is free to make whatever provisions he or she wishes. Neither party intends to make a claim for any kind of support if their relationship should terminate even if permitted under current or future legislation. However, each does agree to do the following within thirty days of executing the agreement:

- Establish a $500,000 life insurance policy for the benefit of the other.
- Designate the other as his or her health care proxy.
- Execute a Durable Power of Attorney naming the other as his or her attorney-in-fact in the event of incapacitating disability, etc.

The agreement will be executed in your state. (If such agreements are contrary to law or public policy in your state, assume you live in a nearby state where they are permitted.) The parties intend the agreement to be governed by the law of Florida but have heard that such agreements are prohibited in that state. If they are, the governing law should be the law of the state where the agreement is executed. If either party breaches the agreement, attorney's costs will be paid by the non-prevailing party. Richard's attorney will draft the agreement for review and input from Mary's attorney.

THE ASSIGNMENT

Working either in pairs or individually (depending on the professor's preference), draft an appropriate cohabitation agreement tailored to the above fact pattern. You may find it helpful to refer to Paralegal Application 5.1 for guidance.

FOCUS ON **ETHICS**

Assume that Richard and Mary in the above comprehensive hypothetical have not yet retained separate attorneys. Assume also that they will both be teaching part time at a college that has a strict policy of not hiring spouses or "significant others." Seeking assistance, they come to the family law office where you are employed, and tell you their story. Your supervisor, Attorney Graciela E. Howell, is not in the office when the parties come in. You know the office could really use the business and it is quite evident that this pair is in a position to pay their bill. You explain to them that you are sure that Attorney Howell will be able to draft a cohabitation agreement that will meet their needs. You commend them for their wisdom in executing a written agreement regarding their financial and property rights along with any other agreements they may have reached. You urge them to say nothing about their relationship at work and not to acknowledge it on any employment forms. The less they have to say to anyone, the better. You tell them that, since they have different last names, no one is likely to detect their little fib. You schedule a meeting for them with Attorney Howell for the following week and accept a check from them for a retainer in the amount of $5,000, which you tell them should cover everything with a bit to spare. They leave the office well satisfied with the advice and encouragement they have been given and look forward to meeting with Attorney Howell. When she returns to the office and you hurriedly report on your meeting with Richard and Mary, much to your surprise, Attorney Howell is not pleased. She tells you to: (1) review the ethical canons for paralegals promulgated by the National Federation of Paralegal Associations (NFPA) (contained in Appendix B of this text); and (2) make a list of the canons that you have violated and describe how you have violated them.

FOCUS ON **CASE LAW**

Using whatever format your professor requires, brief the case *Wilcox v. Trautz,* 427 Mass. 326, 693 N.E.2d 141 (1998), which addresses the enforceability of a cohabitation agreement. If no particular format is used in your course, a suggested one is available on the companion website for this text in the material related to Chapter 1. A copy of the case is also available on the website in the material related to Chapter 5.

FOCUS ON **STATE LAW AND PROCEDURE**

Research the law of your state (constitutional, statutory, and case law) to determine the following:

a. whether any law in the state where you live makes any provision for domestic partnerships or civil unions. If so, identify the requirements and benefits of the provision(s);

b. whether your state has enacted any constitutional or statutory provision banning or otherwise restricting legal recognition of same-sex relationships in your state or established in other states;

c. whether courts in your state enforce cohabitation agreements.

FOCUS ON **TECHNOLOGY**

WEBSITES OF INTEREST

http://www.aclu.org

Available on this site are models for domestic partnership policies for governmental bodies (cities, counties, and states) and businesses under the heading Model Domestic Partnerships (12/31/1997).

http://www.dcop.dc.gov

This is the site for the District of Columbia. Go to the link to the Vital Records Division of the Department of Health to find comprehensive information about Domestic Partnerships in the District of Columbia. The content is based on a helpful "Frequently Asked Questions" format.

http://www.findlaw.com

This site contains useful information on family law, marriage, and living together, and other topics related to the content of this chapter.

http://www.hrc.org/worknet

This website, of the Human Rights Campaign WorkNet, contains information about domestic partnerships.

http://www.infoplease.com

This site is sponsored by Pearson Education Publishing. It provides a wide range of information on a variety of topics. Search for material pertaining to domestic partnerships and civil unions.

http://www.lambdalegal.org

This site provides extensive information regarding states, municipalities, and other entities offering domestic partnership and civil union benefits.

http://www.Pilegesh.org

This site is a blog that accepts and publishes information re Pilegesh relationships, personal ads, and links to related websites.

http://www.sos.ca.gov/dpregistry/

This site is maintained by the office of the California Secretary of State. It contains a wealth of information about domestic partnerships in California. Links are provided to information about registration, forms and fees, related legislation, and a "Frequently Asked Questions" resource with further links.

http://www.unmarried.org

This is the website for the Alternatives to Marriage Project. This site contains information and statistics on cohabitation, living single, domestic partner benefits, common law marriage, etc.

http://www.vermontcivilunion.com and

http://www.sec.state.vt.us/otherprg/civilunions

These sites contain information about civil unions in the state of Vermont.

ASSIGNMENTS

1. Use the Internet to determine whether the state of New York provides for domestic partnerships, civil unions, or same-sex marriage. If so, what are the requirements and benefits of the law? If the state does not have any such provisions, does the City of New York? If so, what are the requirements and benefits?

2. Use the Internet to locate information regarding domestic partnerships and civil unions in New Jersey.

a. Domestic Partnerships: Locate the initial domestic partnership statute:

What is its cite?

Who was initially eligible for domestic partnership status?

What impact did the subsequent civil union legislation in New Jersey have on the effect of this statute?

b. Civil Unions: Locate the statutes pertaining to civil unions in New Jersey that will allow you to respond to the following questions:

What is the cite of the initial declaration concerning civil unions in New Jersey?

What was the impetus for passage of the New Jersey civil union legislation?

How is a civil union defined under New Jersey law?

What are the requirements for establishing a civil union in New Jersey?

What are the legal benefits, protections, and responsibilities of civil union couples in New Jersey?

3. Locate three models of formats for cohabitation agreements online. In your opinion, which of the three would be most useful as a model for developing a cohabitation agreement for Richard and Mary, the parties in the Focus on the Job assignment in this chapter?

4. Go to *http://www.sos.ca.gov/dpregistry/* and locate the applicable procedures and form for establishing a domestic partnership in the state of California. If the statute has been repealed or amended since California legalized same-sex marriage, determine the status of domestic partnerships entered when it was in effect. Does the site provide any information regarding same-sex marriage in California?

chapter **six**

THE DIVORCE PROCESS

A
ll is not well with David and Marie's fifteen-year marriage. He is convinced she has twice disrupted his educational goals by getting pregnant. Now, he says, she has begun drinking and not taking proper care of the children and the marital home. She claims he has abused her emotionally and physically, is obsessed with neatness, and is involved with another woman at work. He has decided to move out of their home and file for divorce.

IN THIS CHAPTER YOU WILL LEARN

- How the "culture of divorce" has evolved over the past four decades

- What the four primary methods are for separating or dissolving a marriage

- How civil and religious divorces are related in some faiths

- What the basic stages of the divorce process are

- What the primary purposes of an initial client interview are in divorce cases

- What the major dispute resolution options are in the divorce context

- What the major jurisdictional issues are in divorce cases

- What the major fault and no-fault grounds for divorce are

- What defenses are available to a defendant in a divorce action

- What the role of the paralegal is at each major stage of the divorce process

HISTORICAL PERSPECTIVE

Historically, the states have exercised considerable control over the marital relationship: its creation, its maintenance, and its termination. Until the early 1970s, a family law practice that focused on divorce law was largely a litigation practice, because in order to get a divorce under state law, one of the parties had to prove that there was serious wrongdoing by the other party. Even when both parties wanted to end the marriage, as was often the case, the focus still was on fault and blame. Frequently, the system either trapped people in painfully unhappy and shallow marriages or forced them to deceive the court about their true circumstances in order to fit into the fault mold and obtain a divorce.

The "culture of divorce" has changed dramatically since the 1970s. The emergence of *no-fault divorce* in all fifty states was the most dramatic catalyst in this evolution, and it has been buttressed by:

- an emphasis on divorce as an economic event in which spouses are viewed as equal partners in the marriage
- the institution of child support guidelines
- the codification of criteria to guide decisions pertaining to custody, alimony, and property division
- the introduction of parenting plans and programs
- the creation of support systems and user-friendly court procedures for parties proceeding **pro se**
- a reduction in litigation due to an increased use of alternative approaches to dispute resolution and the collaborative efforts of attorneys to make the divorce process more civil
- a judicial and societal movement toward respect for autonomy and privacy in family relationships.

METHODS OF ALTERING A MARITAL RELATIONSHIP

There are four primary court proceedings used by parties seeking to separate and/or dissolve their marriage:

- Divorce
- Legal separation
- Separate maintenance
- Annulment

Each of these requires that there be grounds for altering the marital status. The grounds for the first three can be traditional *fault grounds* (such as adultery and cruel and abusive treatment) or *no-fault grounds* (irreconcilable differences, living separate and apart, etc.). The grounds for annulment differ in that it is the validity of the marriage itself, rather than the relationship between the parties, that is faulty.

Divorce

In some states a divorce is called an absolute divorce, a dissolution of marriage, or a *divorce* **a vinculo matrimonii** (from the chains or bonds of marriage). A *divorce* is a judicial determination that a marriage is legally terminated. Both ceremonial and common law marriages require judicial intervention to effect a termination and permit the parties to remarry. A divorce may be obtained on the basis of

---

No-fault divorce
divorce based on an irremediable breakdown of the marital relationship rather than on the fault of one or both of the parties

Pro se
denotes the condition under which a person represents himself or herself in a legal proceeding without the assistance of an attorney

Fault grounds
grounds for divorce based on the fault of one of the parties

No-fault grounds
grounds for divorce based on an irremediable breakdown of the marital relationship rather than on the fault of one or both of the parties

Divorce *a vinculo matrimonii*
literally, a divorce from the chains or bonds of matrimony; an absolute divorce that frees the parties to remarry

Divorce
a judicial determination that a marriage is legally terminated

no-fault grounds in all fifty states and also on fault grounds in a majority of states. Termination of the marital status does not necessarily terminate duties arising upon marriage, such as spousal maintenance, nor does it eliminate responsibility for the custody and support of children of the marriage. It also does not automatically provide for the division of marital property. In a bifurcated or divisible divorce, the dissolution of marriage is resolved in one proceeding, and all other issues such as property division and child custody are resolved in one or more later separate proceedings in the same or another state. Bifurcated divorces are not favored and usually occur only when there is some urgency for dissolution of the marriage (such as advanced age or illness) and/or there is no personal jurisdiction over the defendant in the state where the action is filed. A list of terms used to describe or refer to divorce and a summary of selected statistics on divorce are provided on the companion website for this text in the resource material related to chapter 6.

Legal Separation

Legal separations are most often sought by parties who are not yet ready to divorce for a variety of personal reasons or who are opposed to divorce on religious grounds. A decree of *legal separation* establishes the rights and obligations of two spouses who wish to live separate and apart but remain married. The obligations can then be enforced by the court. In some states, it is called a judicial separation, a limited divorce, or a ***divorce* a mensa et thoro** (divorce from bed and board). Grounds must exist to support an action for a legal separation and are essentially the same as would be used in the divorce context. The end result is not the same, however, because the marriage is not actually terminated and the parties are not free to remarry. The court can make alimony and child custody and support awards, grant a party freedom from interference by the other party, and incorporate a separation agreement executed by the parties that addresses these issues as well as division of property in some states. The agreement should state clearly whether or not various terms of the agreement will continue to be binding on the parties if they eventually divorce or reconcile. If the parties do subsequently reconcile, the court's order of legal separation is still in force until it is vacated, one of the parties dies, or the marriage is formally terminated by annulment or a full divorce. Several states permit the conversion of a legal separation into a divorce after a period of time set by statute.

Separate Maintenance

An action for *separate maintenance* or separate support is usually an option in jurisdictions that do not grant legal separations. It, too, may require the existence of grounds that are essentially the same as the grounds for divorce. It serves the same purpose of allowing the parties to live apart under a court order that defines the terms of the separation, including spousal support, insurance coverage, occupancy and maintenance of the former marital home, etc. In most states, child custody is determined in a separate action. A decree granting separate maintenance does not terminate the marriage, permanently divide the parties' property, or permit either of the parties to remarry. Separate maintenance decrees can be enforced in the same manner as support awards in the context of a divorce or a legal separation. They also remain in effect as do legal separations, even if the parties reconcile, until such time as vacated by the court, one of the parties dies, or the marriage is terminated by judicial process.

Legal separation
a judicial decree that allows the parties to live separate and apart without dissolving their legal relationship as husband and wife; sometimes called a limited divorce

Divorce *a mensa et thoro*
a divorce from bed and board only; a legal separation

Separate maintenance
court-ordered spousal support while the parties are living separate and apart but not divorced

Paralegal Practice Tip
An action for separate support may also be brought by a guardian of a minor child. If the family is receiving public assistance and the state's Title IV-D agency believes that one of the spouses/parents has the ability to pay support and is not doing so, then that agency may also bring an action for separate support.

Annulment

Annulment
the legal procedure for declaring that a marriage is null and void because of an impediment existing at its inception

An **annulment** is a judicial determination that a marriage never existed. The marriage may be either **void** *ab initio* or **voidable** because of the existence of a defect at the inception of the marriage, such as a prior existing marriage of one of the parties or inability of a party to enter a valid marriage due to nonage, lack of mental capacity, duress, etc.

Void *ab initio*
of no legal effect from the outset; a contract may be void *ab initio* if it seriously offends law or public policy

Voidable
capable of being nullified by a court of competent jurisdiction

RELIGIOUS CONSIDERATIONS IN DIVORCE CASES

For some clients, religious recognition of the termination of a marriage may be even more important than a civil divorce. In some cultures, a divorce is both civil and religious in nature.

Divorce Under Jewish Law

Get
a "bill of divorce" in the Jewish religion

When a Jewish couple wants to divorce, they go to a Jewish court called a "Beth Din" presided over by a rabbi. In the presence of the Beth Din, the husband delivers to his wife a document called a **get,** a written "bill of divorce." Although the wife can refuse to accept the *get,* if she does so, she cannot remarry. If she does remarry in a civil ceremony, she is considered an adulteress, as she is still considered married under Jewish law. If a Jewish wife wants a divorce, the husband may refuse to give her a *get* and use her desire for one as a bargaining tool in the context of a civil divorce. If he deserts his wife or refuses to give her a *get* under any circumstances, she is called an *agunah* and cannot be married again by a rabbi even if she obtains a civil divorce. Some Jewish couples execute a *ketubah* (a religious agreement), or a premarital agreement in which the husband agrees to provide his wife a *get* in the event a civil divorce is eventually sought by either party.

The Muslim Religion

Talak
an Arabic word that means to release or divorce

As in the Jewish faith, an Islamic divorce generally is performed by a husband. He does this by pronouncing the word "talak." **Talak** is an Arabic word that means to release or divorce. It means to untie the marriage knot by stating the word that denotes divorce. Other requirements vary nation to nation and sect by sect. In some, the wife need not be present when the word is spoken, and in others, the *talak* must be spoken multiple times and/or in front of witnesses. In some, the husband is required to notify an arbitration council that he has spoken the *talak.*

THE DIVORCE PROCESS—A SKELETAL ROAD MAP

For the client, the decision to seek a divorce is often a monumental, life-altering event that takes place after months, even years, of deliberation. When the client comes to the attorney's office, he or she often feels the hard part is over and a divorce is just around the corner. However, it can be a rude awakening to discover that getting a divorce, even on an uncontested basis, takes months, and hotly contested divorces may drag on for years. Although the vast majority of divorce actions are settled and do not proceed to trial, approximately ten percent still do. This chapter first provides a description of the various stages of the full process in a contested case, along with a step-by-step review of the paralegal's role, and then addresses the process in uncontested cases. Every state establishes its own procedural rules for divorce/dissolution actions. In some states, they are the same as for civil actions in general. In others they are specific to domestic relations actions, and still others use a combination of the two. The basic steps in the process in a contested case are outlined in skeletal form in Exhibit 6.1. The role played by a paralegal in the process depends both on the specific paralegal's level of experience and also on the policies and procedures of individual law firms and supervisors. Even where it is not specifically stated in the material in this chapter, whenever actions are taken by a paralegal, such as filing a document or communicating with a client, it is presumed that the actions are taken only with a supervisor's approval.

EXHIBIT 6.1 A Skeletal Outline of the Divorce Process in a Contested Case

Conduct initial interview with client

Consider dispute resolution alternatives to

divorce or litigation, such as

mediation or counseling (if appropriate)

Plaintiff's Team:

Consider jurisdictional issues

and determine the proper forum

and court in which to file an

action for divorce

Identify the grounds for divorce

Draft and file the Complaint

Serve the Summons and Complaint

and complete Return of Service

Defendant's Team:

File an Answer (which may include a

Counterclaim for Divorce)

or

File a Motion to Dismiss

continued

<u>Both Teams</u>

File Motions for Temporary Orders

and other purposes, if necessary

Conduct discovery

Negotiate

Participate in Alternative Dispute Resolution,

if desired or required

Prepare Separation Agreement

covering undisputed issues

Prepare for and attend Pretrial Conference

Prepare for Trial

Trial

Court Issues Decree/Judgment

File Post-Trial Motions, if warranted

File Appeal, if warranted

Enforce Judgment

(Contempt Actions, etc.)

Seek Modifications of Judgment

(based on substantial change

in circumstances)

THE INITIAL INTERVIEW IN A DIVORCE CASE

An initial interview sets the tone for the working relationship between the client and the family law team. Some law firms and legal resources provide Client Questionnaires and Interview Checklists for suggested use in initial interviews. However, many practitioners find it more practical, productive, and economical to have the client complete a detailed Questionnaire at home. The interview can then be used to establish a relationship with the client, obtain answers to important threshold questions, and address fundamental preliminary matters. (See Paralegal Application 6.1.) Subsequent interviews can focus in more detail on particular issues such as the potential grounds for divorce, the nature and extent of the marital estate, completion of the financial statement, and child-related issues. An example of a basic client questionnaire for use in a divorce case is available on the companion website for this text in the material related to Chapter 6.

Paralegal Practice Tip
Occasionally, clients interview a series of attorneys before retaining specific counsel. In such situations, some attorneys will conduct brief, exploratory interviews at no charge. Others will charge a flat fee or full hourly rate. Once such an interview takes place, a conflict of interest may exist, should the attorney subsequently be contacted by the opposing party in the matter, a situation not uncommon in smaller communities.

PARALEGAL APPLICATION **6.1**

THE CLIENT'S INITIAL INTERVIEW WITH THE FAMILY LAW TEAM

An initial interview is usually conducted by the attorney with or without the presence and assistance of the paralegal. If the paralegal does participate, he or she is usually asked to take notes and prepare an intake memorandum confirming information gathered, agreements reached, and follow-up needed. If the paralegal is asked to interview the client, the following list can be used to guide the process, but it must be customized to avoid any unauthorized practice of law. Whatever role the paralegal plays, communications within the interview are confidential.

1. Get acquainted with the client. Establish a comfortable rapport, being sensitive to the emotionally charged nature of the topics discussed, the cultural background of the client, and any unique communication issues and/or barriers. Invite the client to ask questions at any point during the interview.

2. Obtain sufficient background information about each party and any children of the marriage (including ages and current addresses) so that basic jurisdictional questions can be assessed and a thorough conflicts check can be completed.

3. Learn more about why he or she has contacted the firm. Determine what the client's short- and long-term goals are. If the client appears to have unrealistic expectations, it is useful to establish at the outset that there are no winners in divorce and no guarantees about the outcome, no matter how hard the team works or how much the client pays. Discuss alternatives to divorce, including legal separation and annulment (if appropriate). Ask if the parties have engaged in counseling or mediation and/or are willing to do so. The attorney may suggest such options, especially if the client appears to be uncertain about whether or not the marriage really is irretrievably broken or if mediation eventually may be required by the court.

4. If the client is intent on seeking a divorce, identify the primary reasons for doing so (e.g., Have they simply "grown apart"? Is one or both of the parties involved in a new relationship? Are there financial problems?).

5. Inquire about the spouse's knowledge of the pending action and likely response. Will the action be joint or contested? Have any prior actions been filed? Is the spouse presently represented by counsel? If so, obtain contact information. If not, is he or she likely to be?

continued

6. Obtain a preliminary client history, basic financial information (major assets, employment of both spouses, dependence on public assistance, etc.), and additional information about any children of the marriage such as the existence of special needs, problems, or talents. Is either party responsible for additional children from other relationships? With whom are the children residing and what arrangements exist for visitation, if any? If participation in a parenting program is recommended or required by the court, explain the importance of the requirement and provide information about approved programs in the area.

7. Did the parties execute a pre- or postmarital agreement?

8. Identify any potential emergency issues. Are there any immediate financial or housing needs? If there is a history of abuse of either or both of the spouses and/or the children, have the police or social services been contacted? With what result(s)? Give the client a personal safety plan to complete if abuse of either the client or children is known or suspected.

9. Determine whether or not there will be any immigration issues as a result of the divorce.

10. Determine if there are any religious considerations involved.

11. Describe the firm's approach to cases, the roles played by various members of the family law team, fees, and billing policies and procedures. *Note*: Some attorneys address these topics at the outset before the nature and potential scope of the case is determined. However, that approach has a tendency to distract a client, who then may spend the balance of the interview quietly obsessing about cost rather than paying attention to the substance of the interview.

12. Does the client have any additional questions or concerns?

If the decision is made to accept the case and the client agrees to the terms of engagement, the attorney should outline the process of getting a divorce and identify the next steps to be taken by the client and members of the family law team. A contact person at the firm should be designated (customarily the paralegal rather than the attorney, partially in an effort to control costs).

Some firms give the client "homework" assignments to complete at this point, including, but not necessarily limited to, the following:

- Complete a Client Questionnaire.
- Complete a preliminary financial statement for review.
- Photograph the contents of the marital home.
- Keep a daily journal noting matters related to the case, such as parenting and financial issues (e.g., the dissipation of marital funds, etc.).
- Gather and/or make copies of important documents such as deeds, tax returns, passports, social security cards, bank account statements, etc.
- Remove valuable separate property (e.g., jewelry, family heirlooms, etc.) from the marital home for safekeeping lest they mysteriously disappear!

Some firms provide (or recommend that the client create) a notebook to organize documents related to the divorce, such as pleadings, financial affidavits, court orders, and discovery requests. If desired, the paralegal may be assigned to help the client organize his or her "notebook." If nothing else, assignments and a notebook may help to create in the client a sense of some control over the process.

Paralegal Practice Tip

If there is a history of abuse, copies of relevant documents should be obtained from appropriate law enforcement and social service sources.

Firms frequently have informational materials available for perusal in office reception areas including, for example, "Ten Most Commonly Asked Questions about Divorce" sheets; flow charts outlining the steps involved in the divorce process comparing contested and uncontested options; blank copies of personal safety plans for victims of abuse; lists of community resources for spouses and children; descriptions of alternative dispute resolution options; information regarding times and locations of state-approved parenting programs; blank financial statements; lists and descriptions of services available through the state's Title IV-D agency; and blank child support guideline worksheets. The paralegal may be responsible for ensuring that such material is up-to-date and in good supply.

After the initial interview, members of the family law team will perform a number of important follow-up tasks:

- **Complete and execute a *Fee Agreement* and a *Letter of Engagement.*** The attorney must establish the fees to be charged for services performed by various members of the family law team. The paralegal may draft or "fill in the blanks" on a boilerplate fee agreement used by the firm and ensure that two originals are signed by both the client and the attorney before placing one in the office file. The second original goes to the client. A sample fee agreement is provided on the companion website for this text in the resource material related to Chapter 1.
- **Establish a file and a tracking system.** The paralegal usually sets up "the file" and performs several related activities throughout the case:
  - marks all appropriate calendars with deadlines, appointment and hearing dates, etc.
  - develops a personal "tickler" (reminder) system
  - monitors follow-up activities and deadlines
  - maintains a chronology of activity on the case
- **Gather preliminary information and documents necessary to shape the nature and theory of the case.** The paralegal usually assists in gathering information, working with both the client and the supervising attorney, and then collects, organizes, and maintains a comprehensive filing system with appropriate subheadings (pleadings, witnesses, discovery, financial statements, research, etc.). The attorney uses this material to develop a theory of the case: What relief will the client seek? Why is the client entitled to that relief? What law and evidence support the client's position? What is the nature of the opposing party's case and how can it be countered?
- **Determine if there is a need to seek emergency relief.** It may be determined during conversations with the client that circumstances warrant the filing of *ex parte* motions, motions without advance notice to the defendant. Some, such as a restraining order to protect the client and/or the children or to prevent removal of the children from the jurisdiction, may need to be filed immediately. Others, such as motions to protect marital assets or for temporary custody and child support, may be filed with the complaint for divorce or shortly thereafter. The paralegal may:
  - suggest warranted forms of relief to the attorney
  - draft *ex parte* motions for review and signature (along with affidavits and proposed orders, if required)
  - help the client prepare an application for a restraining/protective order

Fee agreement
a contract between an attorney and a client regarding payment for the attorney's professional services

Letter of engagement
a letter from an attorney to a client confirming that the attorney agrees to represent the client in a particular legal matter

---

Paralegal Practice Tip
If the prospective client decides not to retain the attorney or the attorney elects not to accept the case, a *letter of nonengagement/ declination* should be drafted to confirm that decision in order to avoid any misunderstanding or a later malpractice action for failure to perform legal services. No reason needs to be given for declining the case. The person should be advised of any upcoming deadlines or matters requiring immediate attention with or without the assistance of another attorney. The paralegal may be assigned the task of drafting this letter.

Letter of nonengagement
a letter from an attorney to an individual confirming that the attorney will NOT be representing that individual with respect to a particular legal matter

DISPUTE RESOLUTION OPTIONS IN DIVORCE CASES

When a divorce case proceeds to trial, the parties essentially lose control over the making of decisions affecting not only their lives but also the lives of their children, if any. Given the cost of litigation in time, money, and emotional stress, nonjudicial means of resolving differences offer the parties potentially more productive alternatives that allow them to exercise more control over both the process and the end result. Although the alternatives to litigation also carry a price tag, they are usually considerably less costly financially. They are also more likely to lead to a mutually agreed-upon resolution of the parties' differences in a fraction of the time a fully litigated case would take. In addition, the rules governing most alternative dispute resolution (ADR) proceedings require, with limited exceptions, that information shared in that context remains confidential. On the other hand, court proceedings are open to the public and documents filed become part of a public record.

The courts strongly encourage the use of **alternative dispute resolution** options and in some circumstances require participation in court-affiliated mediation services, particularly with respect to child-related issues. In Texas, a party seeking a divorce is asked to sign a statement that he or she has been informed of the availability of ADR. In Massachusetts, the attorney signs a statement that he or she has advised the client of the availability of court-facilitated mediation.

ADR options can be used at any stage of the process, right up to trial. More than one option may be used and on more than one occasion, if desired. However, the earlier they are used, the more effective they are likely to be. Research also shows higher levels of satisfaction and compliance with mediated agreements than with litigated decrees. In the short run, the parties each play a greater role in shaping the outcome of their case, and, in the long run, in shaping their futures.

There are several dispute resolution alternatives to litigation. The most common are:

- Direct negotiation between the parties
- Mediation
- Collaborative law
- Negotiation through counsel
- Neutral case evaluation
- Arbitration

Direct Negotiation

In this option, the parties negotiate directly with each other in person, by telephone, and by mail (including e-mail). The parties initially operate without the assistance of any professional, legal or otherwise. Some couples are able to work out virtually all of the critical terms of their agreement, and others simply cannot sufficiently communicate to resolve any matters of significance. Attorneys are basically not involved until contacted by the parties when they have already reached their own agreement, or as many of its elements as they can. Unresolved issues may then be addressed through other options. Direct negotiation usually is not appropriate in high-conflict cases or cases in which there is a history of abuse between the parties because of the power imbalance in the relationship.

Alternative dispute resolution (ADR)
a procedure for settling a dispute by means other than litigation, such as mediation or arbitration

---

Paralegal Practice Tip
An emerging option for alternative dispute resolution in family law cases is parenting coordination. **Parenting coordinators** have a limited scope of responsibility. They are most commonly appointed by a court to deal with design and implementation of parenting agreements in high-conflict cases and cases in which children may be at risk. Parenting coordinators mediate disputes and, in some instances, are granted limited decision-making authority in an effort to reduce the numbers of return trips to court.

Parenting coordinators
individuals, usually appointed by the court, who assist with design and implementation of parenting agreements and enforcement of decrees in high-conflict cases involving minor children

Mediation

Sometimes called "assisted" negotiation, the parties may participate in *mediation* voluntarily or be ordered to do so by the court. In this process, a neutral third person, called a mediator, facilitates discussion of issues and negotiation between the parties and occasionally their attorneys. The mediator usually is trained in mediation, has strong communication skills, and often has relevant subject matter expertise in fields such as mental health and child development. A number of organizations and associations, such as the American Bar Association, have promulgated model standards of practice for family and divorce mediation. Some states have in place mediator certification programs, although certification may not be required.

The primary role of the mediator is to overcome barriers that prevent the parties from reaching agreement. Mediators focus on resolving issues rather than on winning and losing.

> First, the mediator acts as a buffer between the parties, moderating or eliminating many of the hardball tactics used. The mediator accomplishes this by translating the information exchanged and reframing it to remove threats or ultimatums. Second, the mediator learns to understand what is motivating each of the parties and what each hopes to achieve, giving a framework to subsequent negotiations. Third, the mediator uses this information to help the parties generate options. Last, the mediator works with the parties to build on these options by exchanging proposals and information to generate movement toward a resolution. During this process, the mediator relays the necessary information to each party, allowing the parties to find an acceptable solution. This works because each side feels safe to reveal its concerns, objectives, and supporting information, knowing that the mediator will not disclose the information to the other side without permission.[1]

The parties control many aspects of mediation, including scheduling, location, and selection of the mediator. Management of the mechanics of the process is largely relinquished to the mediator. However, the parties control the eventual outcome in terms of designing a settlement, although they are not required to reach an agreement. For the terms of any agreement to be incorporated into a decree, those terms must still be approved by the court.

The role of the parties' attorneys in mediation varies. They may or may not be present in actual mediation sessions, depending on the clients' preferences and levels of knowledge and confidence. Whether they actually attend and participate in the sessions or not, attorneys commonly brief their clients about the process, help define issues and goals for the mediation, and act as consultants before and after the sessions. They also review any draft agreements from the mediation before they are executed. However, absent some abuse or flaw in the process, the attorney's review should be limited to identifying any omissions of essential topics and pointing out terms that clearly are contrary to the client's interest.

The attorney's role is different from the mediator's in the sense that an attorney has an ethical duty to advocate zealously for the client and obtain the most favorable settlement possible. The mediator, on the other hand, is impartial, does not advocate the position of either side, and is committed to reaching a "fair deal," one that will serve both parties and the family as a whole in the long run. Given these differences, the roles of the mediator and attorney may work at cross-purposes in the mediation context. The attorney who participates in mediation may face an ethical dilemma—can an attorney simultaneously commit to zealous advocacy and to pursuit of a mutually agreeable, fair, and equitable settlement? One attorney has

Mediation
an approach to resolving differences in which a neutral third person helps the parties identify their differences, consider their options, and structure a mutually acceptable agreement

suggested that in the context of mediation, lawyers need to redefine what a "win" is and act as counselors rather than as blind advocates.[2] Attorneys who are

open to re-evaluating their views of "fairness" and who are willing to set aside their biases in favor of litigation will be amazed at how mediation can transform an often intractable, seemingly unresolvable conflict into a paradigm for successful resolution created by the parties themselves. In mediation, justice is not created by having the mediator act as a "pseudo judge." It is not the responsibility of the mediator to determine the appropriate remedy. Rather, it is the parties who are empowered to determine the remedy themselves. "The mediator must attend to the process, help the parties recognize the legitimacy of different perspectives of justice, and work towards a resolution that comports with the parties' views of a fair and acceptable outcome."[3]

Typically, the mediation takes place in one or a series of face-to-face meetings, as needed. Occasionally the mediator may "caucus" with each client individually within a session. The success of mediation is, to a considerable extent, dependent not only on the skill of the mediator but also on the parties' willingness to enter the process as equals prepared to respect each other, openly share information, and negotiate reasonably and in good faith. As a result, most attorneys and mediators do not consider mediation an appropriate option when there is a continuing history of concealing or destroying assets and/or abuse between the parties.

Collaborative Law

Collaborative law
an approach to reaching agreements and resolving differences that stresses cooperation, joint problem solving, and the avoidance of litigation

The **collaborative law** approach to addressing legal issues was introduced in Chapter 2 as a technique for developing premarital agreements. It is a relatively recent development in alternative dispute resolution methods that "combines the positive problem-solving focus of mediation with the built-in lawyer advocacy and counsel of traditional settlement-oriented representation. . . . In collaborative practice, specially trained lawyers agree to represent clients in negotiating a divorce with both parties and their lawyers committing to settle the case without litigation. While the clients cannot be prohibited from later switching to litigation, the lawyers are disqualified from representation should that happen."[4] This approach requires a strong commitment to NOT litigate. The lawyers jointly facilitate the process, and the focus is on creative problem solving designed to lead to a negotiated agreement tailored to the specific needs of the parties. The primary purpose of collaborative representation is to reach "a settlement that will work for the family."[5]

Negotiation Through Counsel

This is the traditional and most common model of negotiating divorce settlements. Proposals (written and/or oral) are usually exchanged between the attorneys until an agreement is reached or the parties come to an impasse with respect to unresolved issues. The attorneys coordinate the process and advise their respective clients throughout the process. No neutral party is involved. The parties participate in the process mostly through counsel and occasionally in four-way conferences (sometimes mandated by the court). Four-way meetings can be productive, but clients should be prepared for them in advance. Which issues will be discussed at the meeting? What are the client's goals with respect to the issues? Where is there room for compromise? What is the other side likely to propose? What kind of response will be called for? How should the client conduct him- or herself? Usually each topic is addressed separately, but no agreement is finalized on a single major issue until a comprehensive agreement is reached. Initial proposals rarely reflect the parties' bottom lines, and the negotiation process frequently involves considerable give-and-take and a series of compromises before a settlement is reached.

Neutral Case Evaluation

This option is customarily used later in the process, after completion of discovery and the parties' positions have been on the table for some time. Although those positions may have crystallized, there is a strong incentive for the parties to settle, given the stress and expense associated with an imminent trial. In a **neutral case evaluation,** an experienced trial attorney or judge provides the parties with a reality check. The evaluator listens to a summary of the conflict by each side and offers an opinion about settlement potential and a prediction about the likely outcome if the matter proceeds to trial. The evaluator then makes an attempt to resolve the case, sometimes using "shuttle diplomacy," meeting separately with each client and his or her attorney (if participating). The evaluator essentially controls the process and the proceedings are confidential.

Depending on how far the case has proceeded, the attorneys will provide various documents to the evaluator in advance of the actual case evaluation session(s), including the Complaint and the Answer, the parties' financial statements, pretrial memoranda, and the like. The attorneys may or may not attend the actual meeting(s). Whether they attend or not, they customarily brief the client regarding the nature of the process, its goals, and potential alternative outcomes. Although the evaluator controls the process and the attorneys provide information and documentation regarding their respective client's positions, the parties ultimately control the outcome and have complete discretion to accept or reject the opinion of the evaluator and to shape their own agreement or proceed to litigate the case.

Neutral case evaluation
a process in which a neutral third party, usually an experienced trial attorney or judge, listens to the parties' positions and offers an opinion about settlement potential and the likely outcome if the matter proceeds to trial

Arbitration

In **arbitration,** one or more neutral third parties who are trained arbitrators hear arguments, review evidence, and render a decision with respect to the issues identified by the parties for arbitration. The arbitrator is often an attorney and is usually affiliated with a professional organization such as the American Arbitration Association. The parties' attorneys describe the process to their clients and assist them in shaping the arbitration in advance to some extent by choosing the arbitrator, identifying the questions to be addressed, and limiting the range of remedies the arbitrator can consider. They can also decide whether the arbitration will be binding or nonbinding. In **binding arbitration,** the parties agree to abide by the arbitrator's decision. In **nonbinding arbitration,** the parties can accept or reject the decision. In the context of the actual arbitration, the attorney presents the client's position and the evidence. The parties have little control over the process itself or the outcome if they have agreed to binding arbitration. However, they may testify and respond to questions from both counsel and the arbitrator.

Any decision reached by the arbitrator remains subject to review by the court, which usually is unwilling to relinquish its decision-making authority, particularly with respect to child-related issues.[6] For example, the Michigan Supreme Court held in a 2005 case that even if parties submit to binding arbitration under the state's Domestic Relations Arbitration Act, the trial court has an independent duty to make a custody determination in the best interests of the children, and to do so by conducting an evidentiary hearing if necessary.[7] However, with respect to other kinds of issues, courts usually will not disturb an award that results from binding arbitration unless the arbitration process itself is flawed in some manner.

Arbitration
a process in which one or more neutral third persons who are trained arbitrators hear arguments, review evidence, and render a decision with respect to the issues selected for arbitration by the parties involved in a dispute

Binding arbitration
arbitration in which the parties agree to abide by the arbitrator's decision as final and unappealable

Nonbinding arbitration
arbitration in which the parties are free to accept or reject the arbitrator's decision

For example, under Michigan's Domestic Relations Arbitration Act (DRAA), "...
the court shall vacate an award under any of the following circumstances:

    a. The award was procured by corruption, fraud, or other undue means.

    b. There was evident partiality by an arbitrator appointed as a neutral, corruption of an arbitrator, or misconduct prejudicing a party's rights.

    c. The arbitrator exceeded his or her powers.

    d. The arbitrator refused to postpone the hearing on a showing of sufficient cause, refused to hear evidence material to the controversy, or otherwise conducted the hearing to prejudice substantially a party's rights."[8]

Arbitration is used less frequently than mediation prior to divorce. It is used more commonly post-divorce pursuant to a dispute resolution provision in the parties' separation agreement in which they agree to submit certain kinds of disputes to arbitration if they cannot be resolved by the parties or with assistance of counsel.

The paralegal's role in the alternative dispute resolution context generally includes the following:

- being familiar with the various forms of dispute resolution utilized in the jurisdiction
- maintaining lists of local ADR specialists, with pertinent information on each
- preparing any required forms relating to mediation
- scheduling ADR sessions/meetings
- helping the attorney prepare for conferences/meetings
- attending settlement meetings to listen and take notes on the parties' respective positions and any agreements reached
- communicating with ADR resources and arranging for payment
- drafting agreements based on understandings reached by the parties in various forms of ADR
- drafting provisions for inclusion in separation agreements pertaining to dispute resolution post-execution of the agreement

JURISDICTIONAL ISSUES IN DIVORCE ACTIONS— WHAT IS THE PROPER FORUM?

Jurisdictional questions must be addressed at the outset of every case. In many instances, the answers are straightforward—the parties and their children live in the same county within a single state and own minimal property beyond the marital home in which one of the parties is usually residing. In others, the answers are far more complex and eventually may have to be resolved by the court. For example, the whereabouts of a party may be unknown or the parties may be living in different states; have three children, two of whom are residing with the father and one with the mother; and each may own personal property, real estate, and business interests in multiple states. The paralegal's role with respect to jurisdictional issues usually involves researching the applicable statutory and governing case law and gathering the facts needed by the attorney to determine where a given action should be filed. In complex situations, the law of multiple states will need to be researched along with potential ***conflict of law*** issues.

Jurisdiction in a family law case is primarily a matter of state law and procedure subject to overriding federal constitutional limitations as interpreted by the U.S. Supreme Court. In a case involving dissolution of the marriage, property division, custody and support issues, the court hearing the matter needs to have subject matter jurisdiction over family law matters, personal jurisdiction over the parties, and *in rem* jurisdiction over the property in dispute. (See Exhibit 6.2.)

Conflict of law

a conflict arising out of a difference between the laws of two jurisdictions, such as two states or two nations

EXHIBIT 6.2 Jurisdiction in Divorce Actions

Type of Jurisdiction	How It Is Acquired	What the Court Can Do
Subject matter jurisdiction is the authority of a court to hear and decide a particular type of claim or controversy.	Subject matter jurisdiction is conferred by a state statute authorizing the court to hear and decide divorce actions. It cannot be created by agreement of the parties.	A court can hear divorce actions if authorized to do so by state statute provided (a) the plaintiff satisfies the state's applicable residency requirements, if any, and (b) the defendant is given proper notice of the action and an opportunity to be heard.
Personal jurisdiction is the authority of the court to issue and enforce orders binding a particular individual.	In order to exercise personal jurisdiction over a defendant, he or she must have notice of the action and an opportunity to be heard. Personal jurisdiction is acquired over a defendant by personal service of process, consent, or substituted service (e.g., by mail or publication in a newspaper) or under a state's long-arm statute if the defendant is a nonresident who has sufficient minimum contacts with the state.	The court can issue enforceable orders binding a defendant in a divorce action regarding alimony, child support, and property division.
In rem **jurisdiction** is the authority a court has over a thing (including the marital status in some states) rather than over a person.	A state court can exercise its powers over property located inside of that state's boundaries. In order to acquire *in rem* jurisdiction over a marital status, one of the parties must be domiciled in the state and reasonable notice of the action must be given to the defendant by a means authorized by state statute.	The court can issue orders affecting the parties' property located within the state's boundaries. However, even if the court has personal jurisdiction over a defendant, the court's power to distribute marital property located outside of the state may be limited.

There are basically two facets of divorce actions: (1) dissolution of the marital status and (2) corollary matters, such as division of the marital estate (property division), custody, and support issues. When the plaintiff satisfies applicable residency requirements, the appropriate court will be able to exercise subject matter jurisdiction over dissolution of the marriage, provided the defendant is given proper notice. The subject matter in the jurisdictional context is the marital status of the plaintiff. It is the *rem*, the basic "thing" being addressed in the action. It is possessed by each of the spouses and exists, for jurisdictional purposes, in any state where either of the spouses resides. Other related matters, such as property division and child-related issues, may also be addressed if additional jurisdictional requirements are met. Although it is not favored, occasionally a court may be willing to divide or bifurcate a divorce proceeding under unusual circumstances. In a **bifurcated divorce,** the court dissolves the marriage but does not adjudicate other issues, such as support and property division. It may reserve jurisdiction over those issues until a later date or leave them to be determined by the courts of another state that has jurisdiction over the defendant and/or the children. (See Case 6.1.)

Bifurcated divorce
a divorce in which the dissolution of marriage is resolved in one proceeding, and all other issues such as property division and child custody are resolved in one or more later, separate proceedings in the same or another state

CASE **6.1** *Von Schack v. Von Schack,* 2006 ME 30, 893 A.2d 1004 (2006)

BACKGROUND

Mary and Wesley Von Schack were married in New York State in 1976 and had one daughter born in 1991. While together, they lived in New York and Pennsylvania. In 2004, Wesley moved to Maine to accept an executive position in a corporation in that state. After living in Maine for six months, he filed for divorce, and Mary, who had no connection with the state of Maine, was personally served in New York. Wesley had been unable to file in Pennsylvania or New York, because he was not a resident of either state and he failed to satisfy other statutory grounds. "Mary moved to dismiss the complaint on the grounds that Maine was not a convenient forum and the court lacked personal jurisdiction over her and lacked *in rem* jurisdiction over the parties' property." The trial court denied her motion to dismiss. Although the court granted the divorce, it "left all property, spousal support, and parental issues to be litigated in a jurisdiction" with personal jurisdiction over both parties and over the child. Mary appealed, arguing that the court violated her due process rights under the Constitution when it granted the divorce when she was "not within the reach of the court's personal jurisdiction." The Maine Supreme Court then heard her appeal and upheld the lower court's ruling.

FROM THE OPINION

. . .

A. Personal Jurisdiction

Although Maine's divorce statute permits a plaintiff to file a complaint for divorce if "the plaintiff has resided in good faith in this state for 6 months prior to the commencement of the action." 19-A.M.R.S. § 901(1)(A) (2005), it does not speak to jurisdiction. To determine whether Maine has personal jurisdiction over a defendant, we apply Maine's long arm statute, 14 M.R.S. § 704-A (2005):...

. . .

Pursuant to this long arm statute, the court could have obtained personal jurisdiction over Mary in three possible ways: (1) if she "maintained a domicile in

continued

this State while subject to a marital or family relationship out of which arises a claim for divorce,"...; (2) if she "committed in this State...any act giving rise to such a claim,"...; or (3) if she "maintained any other relation to the State or to persons or property which affords a basis for the exercise of jurisdiction by the courts of this State consistent with the Constitution of the United States,"....

...Consistency with the Due Process Clause of the United States Constitution requires that: " '(1) Maine has a legitimate interest in the subject matter of this litigation; (2) the defendant, by...conduct, reasonably could have anticipated litigation in Maine; and (3) the exercise of jurisdiction by Maine's courts comports with traditional notions of fair play and substantial justice.' "...

...We agree with the trial court that Mary lacks any relation to the State that would permit the court to exercise personal jurisdiction consistent with this test....

B. Jurisdiction Over Marital Status

. . .

In Maine, we have not yet considered whether a defendant must have minimum contacts with the State for a court to enter a divorce judgment when no property, parental rights, or support issues are determined. Since the United States Supreme Court's adoption of the minimum contacts analysis, we have observed that a court may not entertain a divorce action if a *plaintiff* fails to establish her domicile in Maine when the plaintiff's spouse is also not domiciled in Maine. *Belanger v. Belanger,* 240 A.2d 743, 746–47 (Me. 1968);...

. . .

Presented with the same question, other state courts have consistently held that the forum court has jurisdiction to dissolve a domiciliary's marriage without distributing property or determining other rights that would require personal jurisdiction....

As the California Supreme Court has observed, "ex parte divorces are a striking exception to the rule that a court must have personal jurisdiction over a party before it may adjudicate his substantial rights." *Whealton v. Whealton,* 67 Cal. 2d 656, 432 P.2d 979, 982, 63 Cal. Rptr. 291 (Cal. 1967). A state's interest and that of the domiciliary spouse "justify subordinating the conflicting interests of the absent spouse and of any other interested jurisdiction." *Id.*

New York itself affords full faith and credit to a sister state's divorce judgment, entered without personal jurisdiction over the defendant, as long as the judgment determines only the marital status of the parties....

. . .

Because Maine has a unique interest in assuring that its citizens are not compelled to remain in such personal relationships against their wills and because no personal or real property interests would be determined in the proceeding, we conclude that Maine courts have jurisdiction to enter a divorce judgment without personal jurisdiction over the defendant upon compliance with 19-A.M.R.S. § 901(1)(A) and all other procedural requirements. We do not, however, alter or re-evaluate the requirement of personal jurisdiction in any other type of litigation affecting the parties' children, financial responsibilities, or property.

SIDEBAR

In the text of this opinion, the Supreme Judicial Court of Maine reviews the evolutionary history of U.S. Supreme Court jurisprudence regarding jurisdiction. It is worth reading and is available in its entirety on the companion website for this text in the material related to Chapter 6.

In this chapter we are concerned with jurisdiction as it relates to actions for divorce in particular and specifically with the answers to the following five questions as they apply in an individual case:

1. Does the plaintiff satisfy the state's residency requirements?
2. Which court has subject matter jurisdiction over divorce and related matters?
3. Does the court have personal (*in personam*) jurisdiction over the defendant?
4. Does the court have *in rem* jurisdiction over the property involved in the action?
5. In which specific court should the complaint for divorce be filed—i.e., where is venue proper?

Does the Plaintiff Satisfy the State's Residency Requirements?

Each state as a sovereign has a rightful and legitimate concern in the marital status of persons domiciled within its borders. . . . it is plain that each state can alter within its own borders the marriage status of the spouse domiciled there, even though the other spouse is absent."[9]

In order to file for divorce in a particular state, the general rule is that one of the parties must satisfy its domicile or residency requirement for bringing such actions. There is considerable variation in residency requirements, ranging from six weeks in states such as Idaho and Nevada to one year in approximately one-fifth of the states including, for example, Rhode Island and Pennsylvania. Even when there is a basic residency requirement, however, there are frequently exceptions that may or may not work to the client's advantage. For example, in Maryland, there is no residency requirement unless the cause of the marital breakdown occurred outside of the state (one year) or if the ground for the action is insanity (two years). Tennessee and Massachusetts have residency requirements of six months and one year, respectively, unless the party bringing the action is domiciled in the state and the cause of the marital breakdown arose within the state. Some states, such as Texas and California, also have county residency requirements.

Domicile
a person's legal residence; the place one considers his or her permanent home and to which he or she intends to return when away

The U.S. Supreme Court speaks of **domicile** when addressing the issue of a state's power to dissolve a marriage. The states speak in terms of residency (or, in some instances, both domicile and residency requirements). The distinctions can be confusing and have occasionally led to challenges with respect to the validity of a divorce. Your domicile is the place you consider your permanent home and to which you intend to return when away. Your residence may, in fact, be your domicile. However, you may have several residences where you reside on occasion, but only one domicile. Where one is domiciled is a question of law and fact. Evidence may need to be produced of a party's intent to remain indefinitely in the place claimed as his or her domicile. The court will look at several factors when determining an individual's domicile such as:

- how long the person has resided in a particular state
- whether the person has a long-term lease on the property where he or she is living
- whether the party owns property in the state
- where the party votes
- which state issued the party's driver's license
- where his or her car is registered and serviced
- where he or she pays income taxes
- what his or her mailing address is for billing purposes

- where the person is employed
- whether the person is an employee-at-will or has a long-term employment contract
- where the person's extended family lives

Which Court Has Subject Matter Jurisdiction Over Divorce and Related Matters?

Subject matter jurisdiction refers to a court's authority to hear and render a decision with respect to a particular type of case. All divorce matters are brought in state rather than federal courts. Subject matter jurisdiction is conferred by state statutes and the parties cannot confer it on a court by agreement. Each state determines the court authorized to grant divorces within its jurisdiction. In many states, there are specialized family courts, and in others, divorce actions are heard in courts of general jurisdiction such as a superior courts, chancery courts, or courts of common pleas that hear other kinds of matters as well. A court can have subject matter jurisdiction sufficient to dissolve a marriage, even if it lacks personal jurisdiction over a defendant, as long as the plaintiff is domiciled in the state. It is the plaintiff's relationship with the state where the action is filed that matters. However, if a plaintiff travels to another state solely for the purpose of obtaining a divorce, the defendant-spouse, particularly one who did not receive actual notice of the action, may be able to attack the validity of the divorce decree for lack of proper subject matter jurisdiction.

Does the Court Have Personal (*in personam*) Jurisdiction Over the Defendant?

It has long been the rule that a valid judgment imposing a personal obligation or duty in favor of the plaintiff may be entered only by a court having jurisdiction over the person of the defendant. The existence of personal jurisdiction, in turn, depends upon the presence of reasonable notice to the defendant that an action has been brought and a sufficient connection between the defendant and the forum State as to make it fair to require defense of the action in the forum. (Citations omitted.)[10]

In order for a court to issue an order that will be enforceable against a particular defendant (such as an order for property division or spousal support), it must have personal jurisdiction over that defendant. Given the Fourteenth Amendment's requirements of due process and procedural fairness, a defendant is entitled to reasonable notice and an opportunity to be heard in the matter at issue and is also protected from being hailed into court in a state with which he or she has no connection. There are four primary means of acquiring personal jurisdiction over a defendant in a domestic relations proceeding that are consistent with due process requirements:

- **Presence:** Personal service of process on a nonresident defendant while physically present in the state as a temporary resident, visitor, or otherwise. The U.S. Supreme Court has held that a nonresident of a state is subject to the jurisdiction of that state if he is properly served while physically present in the state.[11]
- **Domicile:** Actual service of process or substituted (or constructive) service over a defendant who is domiciled in the state by publication in the paper and mailing the summons and complaint to the defendant's last known address.

Long-arm statute

a state statute providing for
jurisdiction over a nonresident
defendant who has had sufficient
contacts in the territory where the
statute is in effect

- **Consent:**   The defendant, even a nonresident defendant, may voluntarily consent to the court's jurisdiction by accepting service or by appearing and defending the action.
- **Minimum contacts:**   Each state has a ***long-arm statute*** that identifies the kinds of minimum contacts a nonresident defendant may have with the state that are sufficient to give rise to personal jurisdiction over a nonresident defendant with notice of the action. The focus is usually on more recent contacts. The basic premise is that it is fair and reasonable to exercise personal jurisdiction in certain circumstances. State statutes vary but generally include provisions such as the following (some of which are tailored to domestic relations cases):
  - the defendant conducts business in the state
  - the defendant contracts to provide services in the state
  - the defendant has caused tortious injury by an act or omission in the state
  - the defendant has an interest in real property located within the state
  - the defendant has maintained a residence in the state (most often a marital residence)
  - the defendant is subject to an order of alimony, property division, parentage of a child, child custody, or child support issued by a court in the state
  - the litigation relates to some action of the nonresident defendant within the state
  - the defendant had sexual relations in the state that may have resulted in the birth of a child to the parties

Does the Court Have *in rem* Jurisdiction Over the Property Involved in the Action?

Paralegal Practice Tip
The *Russo* case provides an example of how important phrasing can be when requesting relief involving the disposition of out-of-state property in a divorce.

A state court with subject matter jurisdiction has authority over real property located within the state's boundaries and can issue orders with respect to that property. A court can distribute property within its jurisdiction pursuant to a divorce decree, but if the property in dispute is immovable (such as a piece of real estate or mining rights) and is located in another state, the court's powers may be limited.

The *Russo* case,[12] available on the companion website in the material related to this chapter, provides an illustration of what can be subtle differences in interpreting and applying personal and *in rem* jurisdiction. In *Russo*, a Pennsylvania trial court ordered the parties to sell real property located in the state of Ohio and divide the proceeds. The defendant husband appealed that portion of the divorce judgment, alleging that the court lacked jurisdiction to distribute property located outside of Pennsylvania. The husband argued on appeal that jurisdiction extended only to property located in Pennsylvania and that a Pennsylvania court could not exercise *in rem* jurisdiction over real or personal property located outside the state. The appellate court held that when the trial court ordered the parties to sell the Ohio property, it was not exercising *in rem* jurisdiction over the property. Rather, it was ordering the parties, over whom it had personal jurisdiction, to sell the property and distribute the proceeds. The court drew a distinction between a court's exercise of *in rem* jurisdiction by effectuating a transfer of out of state property and the exercise of personal jurisdiction over the parties by ordering them to take some action with regard to such property.

PARALEGAL APPLICATION **6.2**

JURISDICTIONAL ISSUES—WHAT DO YOU THINK?

CASE 1 FACT PATTERN

The parties in this case were married in Connecticut in 1979. In 1999, the wife filed for divorce in Connecticut, where she was domiciled. Her husband had left Connecticut in 1985. The parties had married, had a child, and received public assistance for several years in Connecticut. They had also filed joint tax returns in that state. The wife saw the husband when he visited family members in Connecticut in 1986 and 1989 but had not seen him since. The wife filed for divorce in Connecticut. The divorce was awarded, along with alimony and counsel fees. The husband appealed, claiming the court lacked personal jurisdiction over him.

SIDEBAR

Do you think it was fair and reasonable for the Connecticut court to exercise personal jurisdiction over the defendant? Why? See the case *Panganiban v. Panganiban*, 736 A.2d 190 (Conn. Ct. App. 1999), available on the companion website for this text in the material related to Chapter 6. Do you agree with the court's decision? Why?

CASE 2 FACT PATTERN

In 1987, a wife who was domiciled in Virginia went to Hawaii to marry a man who was a Marine stationed there. The parties subsequently lived at duty stations in Virginia Beach, Virginia, from 1996 to 1999 and in Guantanamo Bay for a year, at which time the husband was reassigned to Camp Pendleton in California. The wife, initially without the husband's knowledge, decided to return to live in Virginia because of the husband's admitted infidelity and a generally deteriorating marital relationship. She filed for divorce in Virginia and the husband was served with the summons and complaint while he was in Virginia visiting with the parties' children. The husband claimed that the Virginia court lacked both subject matter and personal jurisdiction. He alleged that neither party qualified as a bona fide resident or domiciliary of Virginia and that the court lacked personal jurisdiction over him because he was fraudulently induced to come to Virginia by the actions of the wife and would not have been there otherwise. The wife asserted that for purposes of subject matter jurisdiction, both parties were bona fide residents of Virginia based on the following evidence:

* one of the family's vehicles was still registered, licensed, and titled in Virginia
* each of them possessed a Virginia driver's license while they lived in Cuba
* they held accounts in Virginia banks
* the wife had a brother, sister, and brother-in-law living in Virginia
* prior to her marriage, the wife filed taxes in Virginia
* the parties lived in Virginia for three years prior to moving to Cuba, and the wife returned to Virginia to reestablish her residency
* when she left Virginia to go to Cuba, the wife left solely because of her husband's military orders

Under Virginia law, the issue of subject matter jurisdiction requires a determination of the plaintiff's domicile and bona fide residency in the state of Virginia for at least six months prior to the filing of the action for divorce.

continued

In Which Specific Court Should the Complaint for Divorce Be Filed?

Venue
refers to the geographical location within which a particular action should be filed

This question asks where venue will be proper. *Venue* refers to the particular geographical location within the state where the action should be filed—in which city, town, or county. As with subject matter and personal jurisdiction, the states establish rules governing venue. Typically, in a divorce action, venue will be proper in the county where the defendant resides, where the plaintiff resides, or where the parties last resided together as husband and wife.

GROUNDS FOR DIVORCE

Grounds for divorce
the reason for filing the action, the basis on which relief is sought

Divorce is a creature of statute, and each state establishes its own *grounds for divorce*, the reasons it considers sufficient to warrant the termination of a marriage. The statutory scheme in Tennessee (see Exhibit 6.3) is one of the most comprehensive. Similar to divorce statutes in just over sixty percent of the states, it includes both no-fault grounds (e.g., "irreconcilable differences" or living separate and apart) and fault grounds (e.g., adultery or cruel and abusive treatment). In several of the states, some of the statutory grounds for divorce are also potential grounds for annulment, such as impotency (e.g., in Massachusetts), bigamy (e.g., in Ohio), and fraud (e.g., in Connecticut). No-fault divorce is generally less costly, both emotionally and financially, and therefore few divorces now are brought on fault grounds. Although most divorces are granted on a no-fault basis, some clients insist on pursuing fault grounds for personal reasons such as anger, revenge, and a desire to publicly establish themselves as "blameless" for the failure of the marriage.

EXHIBIT 6.3 Tenn. Code Ann. § 36–4–101. Grounds for divorce from bonds of matrimony

From the Statute
The following are causes of divorce from the bonds of matrimony:
1. Either party, at the time of the contract, was and still is naturally impotent and incapable of procreation;
2. Either party has knowingly entered into a second marriage, in violation of a previous marriage, still subsisting;
3. Either party has committed adultery;
4. Willful or malicious desertion or absence of either party, without a reasonable cause, for (1) whole year;
5. Being convicted of any crime that, by the laws of the state, renders the party infamous;

continued

6. Being convicted of a crime that, by the laws of the state, is declared to be a felony, and sentenced to confinement in the penitentiary;

7. Either party has attempted to take the life of the other by poison or any other means showing malice;

8. Refusal, on the part of a spouse, to remove with that person's spouse to this state, without a reasonable cause, and being willfully absent from the spouse residing in Tennessee for two (2) years;

9. The woman was pregnant at the time of the marriage, by another person, without the knowledge of the husband;

10. Habitual drunkenness or abuse of narcotic drugs of either party, when the spouse has contracted either such habit after marriage;

11. The husband or wife is guilty of such cruel and inhuman treatment or conduct towards the spouse as renders cohabitation unsafe and improper, which may also be referred to in pleadings as inappropriate marital conduct;

12. The husband or wife has offered such indignities to the spouse's person as to render the spouse's position intolerable, and thereby forced the spouse to withdraw;

13. The husband or wife has abandoned the spouse or turned the spouse out of doors for no just cause, and has refused or neglected to provide for the spouse while having the ability to so provide;

14. Irreconcilable differences between the parties; and

15. For a continuous period of two (2) or more years that commenced prior to or after April 18, 1985, both parties have lived in separate residences, have not cohabited as man and wife during such period, and there are no minor children of the parties.

No-Fault Grounds

No-fault grounds for divorce are grounds that do not require a party to prove that the other party is to "blame" for the breakdown of the marriage. Marital misconduct is largely irrelevant. Each state establishes its own no-fault grounds or standards, and approximately forty percent of the states have eliminated fault grounds entirely and have only a single no-fault standard. The two most common no-fault grounds are:

- irreconcilable differences
- living separate and apart

Irreconcilable Differences (Also Called Irretrievable or Irremediable Breakdown of the Marriage or Incompatibility). Whatever it may be called, the core of this ground is that the marriage has broken down, is beyond repair, and one or both of the parties want to terminate it. Some jurisdictions require that the parties actually live separate and apart for a period of time prior to filing. Others recognize the economic challenges faced by many divorcing spouses and allow the parties to continue living under the same roof, provided they do not engage in "marital relations" during the period of "separation." When this ground is alleged on an uncontested or joint basis, the court's inquiry is generally limited. The parties may be asked to briefly describe the nature of the differences that have caused the breakdown, approximately how long they have persisted, whether the parties have sought counseling or participated in some

Irreconcilable differences
a no-fault ground for divorce, the essence of which is that the marriage has irreparably broken down due to serious differences between the parties

Paralegal Practice Tip
When parties have entered a
covenant marriage, a no-fault
divorce is generally not an option.

Covenant marriage
a type of marriage in which the
parties participate in counseling
prior to the marriage, accept marriage as a lifelong commitment,
and agree not to seek a divorce absent a total and complete breach of
the marriage covenant

Living separate and apart
a no-fault ground for divorce
based on the fact that, due to a
breakdown of the marriage, the
parties have lived apart from each
other for a requisite period of time

form of alternative dispute resolution in an effort to resolve their differences and save the marriage, and whether they believe the marriage has irretrievably broken down.

If a divorce action on this ground is contested, proof must be presented regarding the nature and extent of the parties' differences that have resulted in the alleged breakdown of the marriage. From a practical perspective, if one of the parties is intent on obtaining a divorce and the other is adamantly opposed, the breakdown is self-evident. However, that alone is not enough. The breakdown may be due to an inability to communicate; serious disagreements between the parties about finances, childrearing issues, value systems, or marital priorities; or the parties may simply have grown apart and developed such divergent interests and incompatible lifestyles that they can no longer live together in a "normal" marital relationship. Whatever the explanation is for the breakup, the court's task is to determine that the marriage is beyond repair without examining the individual conduct of the parties in fault terms.

Living Separate and Apart for a Specified Period of Time.   The essence of this no-fault ground is that the marriage has broken down and, as a result, the parties are living separate and apart. Marital fault is essentially irrelevant as long as the parties have lived apart for the requisite period of time. There is considerable variation in state statutes addressing this ground with respect to the length of time the parties must have lived separate and apart (commonly from one to three years), whether the period of separation must be uninterrupted by attempts at reconciliation, whether the parties are living apart pursuant to a court order, whether the decision to separate is mutual, whether the separation is voluntary (e.g., not due to incarceration, hospitalization, or military service), and whether or not the parties must actually have lived under separate roofs. The applicable Utah statute, for example, provides for a divorce on this ground "when the husband and wife have lived separately under a decree of separate maintenance of any state for three consecutive years without cohabitation."[13]

When this ground is alleged and contested, evidence should be produced to establish the nature and length of the separation. This is accomplished through the testimony of witnesses familiar with the parties' living arrangements and documents such as leases, rent receipts, telephone bills, etc.

Fault grounds

The most common fault grounds include:

- adultery
- desertion/abandonment
- cruelty
- habitual drunkenness or drug abuse
- criminal conviction and incarceration

Adultery.   Adultery as a ground for divorce commonly means voluntary sexual intercourse between a married person and a person other than his or her spouse, usually called the co-respondent. However, the language in state statutes varies. If the statute specifies intercourse with a "person other than the spouse," then it may encompass adultery committed with a person of either sex. If the statute is silent on this point, the courts usually look to relevant case law and/or criminal statutes. (See Case 6.2.) A majority of the states that have addressed this issue have concluded that adultery is not limited to heterosexual intercourse.

Adultery
voluntary sexual intercourse between a married person and a person other than his or her spouse

Paralegal Practice Tip
On rare occasions, a wronged
spouse may bring a tort action for
criminal conversation against
a third party who has committed
adultery with the plaintiff's spouse.

Criminal conversation
a tort action for adultery brought
against a third party who has
sexual intercourse with another's
spouse; abolished as a cause of
action in most jurisdictions

CASE **6.2** *In the Matter of Blanchflower and Blanchflower,*
150 N.H. 226, 834 A.2d 1010 (2003)

FROM THE OPINION

The record supports the following facts. The petitioner filed for divorce from the respondent on grounds of irreconcilable differences. He subsequently moved to amend the petition to assert the fault ground of adultery. . . . Specifically, the petitioner alleged that the respondent has been involved in a "continuing adulterous affair" with the co-respondent, a woman, resulting in the irremediable breakdown of the parties' marriage. The co-respondent sought to dismiss the amended petition, contending that a homosexual relationship between two people, one of whom is married, does not constitute adultery under RSA 458:7, II. The trial court disagreed, and the co-respondent brought this appeal.

Before addressing the merits, we note that this appeal is not about the status of homosexual relationships in our society or the formal recognition of homosexual unions. The narrow question before us is whether a homosexual relationship between a married person and another constitutes adultery within the meaning of RSA 458:7, II.

RSA 458:7 provides, in part: "A divorce from the bonds of matrimony shall be decreed in favor of the innocent party for any of the following causes:

. . . II. Adultery of either party." The statute does not define adultery. Id. Accordingly, we must discern its meaning according to our rules of statutory construction.

"In matters of statutory interpretation, this court is the final arbiter of the intent of the legislature as expressed in the words of a statute considered as a whole." . . . We first look to the language of the statute itself and, where terms are not defined therein, "we ascribe to them their plain and ordinary meanings." . . .

The plain and ordinary meaning of adultery is "voluntary sexual intercourse between a married man and someone other than his wife or between a married woman and someone other than her husband." *Webster's Third New International Dictionary* 30 (unabridged ed. 1961). Although the definition does not specifically state that the "someone" with whom one commits adultery must be of the opposite gender, it does require sexual intercourse.

The plain and ordinary meaning of sexual intercourse is "sexual connection esp. between humans: COITUS, COPULATION." *Webster's Third New International Dictionary* 2082. Coitus is defined to require "insertion of the penis into the vagina[]," *Webster's Third New International Dictionary* 441, which clearly can only take place between persons of the opposite gender.

. . .

We note that the current criminal adultery statute still requires sexual intercourse: "A person is guilty of a class B misdemeanor if, being a married person, he engages in sexual intercourse with another not his spouse or, being unmarried, engages in sexual intercourse with another known by him to be married." RSA 645:3 (1996)....

We reject the petitioner's argument that an interpretation of adultery that excludes homosexual conduct subjects homosexuals and heterosexuals to unequal treatment, "contrary to New Hampshire's public policy of equality and prohibition of discrimination based on sex and sexual orientation." Homosexuals and heterosexuals engaging in the same acts are treated the same because our interpretation of the term "adultery" excludes all non-coital sex acts, whether between persons of the same or opposite gender. The only distinction is that persons of the same gender cannot, by definition, engage in the one act that constitutes adultery under the statute.

The petitioner also argues that "public policy would be well served by applying the same law to a cheating spouse, whether the promiscuous spouse chooses a paramour

continued

of the same sex or the opposite sex." This argument is tied to the premise…, that "the purpose underlying [the adultery] fault ground is based upon the fundamental concept of marital loyalty and public policy's disfavor of one spouse's violation of the marriage contract with another."

We have not, however, seen any such purpose expressed by the legislature. As noted above, the concept of adultery was premised on a specific act. To include in that concept other acts of a sexual nature, whether between heterosexuals or homosexuals, would change beyond recognition this well-established ground for divorce and likely lead to countless new marital cases alleging adultery, for strategic purposes…. "we will not undertake the extraordinary step of creating legislation where none exists. Rather, matters of public policy are reserved for the legislature." *In the Matter of Plaisted & Plaisted,* 149 N.H. 522, 526, 824 A.2d 148 (2003).

The dissent defines adultery not as a specific act of intercourse, but as "extramarital sexual activity with another." This standard would permit a hundred different judges and masters to decide just what individual acts are so sexually intimate as to meet the definition….

We are also unpersuaded by the dissent's contention that "it is improbable that the legislature intended to require an innocent spouse in a divorce action to prove the specific intimate sexual acts in which the guilty spouse engaged."….the dissent notes that adultery usually has no eyewitnesses and therefore "ordinarily must be proved by circumstantial evidence." While this is true, it does not support the dissent's point…. That circumstantial evidence may be used to establish the act does not negate or undermine the requirement of proof that the act actually occurred….

Reversed and remanded.

FROM THE DISSENT

…To strictly adhere to the primary definition of adultery in the 1961 edition of Webster's *Third New International Dictionary* and a corollary definition of sexual intercourse,…is to avert one's eyes from the sexual realities of our world. While we recognize that "we first look to the plain and ordinary meaning of words to interpret our statutes [,]…it is one of the surest indexes of a mature and developed jurisprudence not to make a fortress out of the dictionary; but to remember that statutes always have some purpose or object to accomplish."…

. . .

From the perspective of the injured spouse, the very party fault-based divorce law is designed to protect, "an extramarital relationship…is just as devastating…irrespective of the specific sexual act performed by the promiscuous spouse or the sex of the new paramour." Indeed, to some, a homosexual betrayal may be more devastating. Accordingly, consistent with the overall purpose of New Hampshire's fault-based divorce law, we would interpret the word "adultery" in RSA 458:7, II to mean a spouse's extramarital intimate sexual activity with another, regardless of the specific intimate sexual act performed, the marital status, or the gender of the third party.

SIDEBAR

The full text of this opinion is available on the companion website. Do you agree with the position of the majority or the dissent? Explain your response. Was the dissent suggesting the creation of a new ground for divorce? Does the majority insist that the definition of adultery as a ground for divorce is forever fixed? How would a change come about? Do you think that the outcome in this case would be any different today, given the passage of a civil union law in New Hampshire that became effective January 1, 2008? (See Rev. Stat. Ann. § 457-A.)

PARALEGAL APPLICATION **6.3**

ADULTERY POST-SEPARATION—A GROUND FOR DIVORCE?

Clients who have already separated from their spouses often ask if it is okay for them to "date" while the divorce action is pending. The paralegal should refer the question to the attorney and avoid providing a response that might constitute the giving of legal advice to the client. For a case in which a New York court granted a divorce to a wife based on her husband's post-separation adultery, see *Golub v. Ganz*, 22 A.D.4d 919, 802 N.Y.S.2d 526 (2005). Although many courts would not view a "new" relationship in terms of a potential fault ground for divorce, they may look for dissipation of the marital estate that occurs in conjunction with the new relationship. Do you think post-separation relationships should be considered in the divorce context? Why?

Some states require that in order to claim adultery, both the petitioner and the respondent must be residents of the state where the divorce action is brought. Most states require that adultery involve actual sexual intercourse, although, because of its nature, the act may be proved by circumstantial evidence. Mere suspicions or the opportunity to commit adultery are not enough. Evidence of an "adulterous disposition" is usually established by evidence such as public displays of intimacy observed by others, e-mails and other forms of correspondence referencing sexual activity, unexplained absences and travel, and contracting of a venereal disease. In some states, the circumstantial evidence must be substantial, such as when a wife gives birth to a child genetically unrelated to her husband.

Desertion/Abandonment. To obtain a divorce on this ground, the petitioner usually must show that the defendant deliberately and without consent left the marital relationship with no intention to return, and that the absence has continued for a specified continuous period of time (customarily a year or more). The desertion must be unnecessary and without sufficient cause. Since it also must be voluntary, an absence due to military service, incarceration, or institutionalization in a mental or other facility such as a rehabilitation center will not constitute desertion.

When abandonment is alleged, it involves abandonment of the relation between the husband and wife and not necessarily the house in which they live. The desertion may be *"constructive" desertion* if a spouse's objectionable conduct is so abusive or otherwise intolerable that it renders continuation of the marital relationship impossible and forces the "innocent spouse" either to move out or to move into a separate area within the marital residence in order to maintain his or her health, safety, or self-respect. The spouse who leaves has a defense to a claim by the other party of desertion and also has his or her own ground for divorce.

Cruelty. Cruelty is frequently termed **cruel and abusive treatment,** cruel and inhumane treatment, indignities, physical and mental cruelty, or treatment that endangers health and reason. Although a single act may be sufficient if it is atrocious or severe, cruelty usually involves a course of conduct. In some states (such as Illinois), the cruelty must constitute "extreme and repeated physical or mental cruelty."[16] Particularly in states with a limited number of specific fault grounds, cruelty is often used as a catchall ground. For example, excessive

Paralegal Practice Tip

In some jurisdictions, if adultery is alleged, the name of the alleged co-respondent must be provided in the complaint for divorce, and the individual must be served. In others, the adultery may be alleged, but in order to name the third party, the petitioner must file a motion with the court for permission to disclose the name. The latter approach helps to reduce the number of baseless and malicious allegations.

Desertion/abandonment
a fault ground for divorce in some states; the plaintiff must show that the defendant deliberately and without consent left the marital relationship with no intention to return, and that the absence has continued for a specified continuous period of time (customarily a year or more)

Paralegal Practice Tip

A refusal of sexual relations and/or moving to a separate bedroom may form the basis of a ground for divorce (such as desertion or cruelty) depending on the facts of the case.[14] An unjustifiable refusal for an extended period (a year or more) may be sufficient unless the refusal is based on sexually abusive conduct of the defendant or a reasonable suspicion of his or her infidelity. For example, in a Virginia case, an appellate court held that a wife's refusal of sexual relations did not constitute desertion when the husband engaged in recurring extramarital sexual relations without using protection. His conduct was deemed to constitute cruelty.[15]

Constructive desertion
a situation in which a spouse's objectionable conduct is so abusive or otherwise intolerable that it renders continuation of the marital relationship impossible and forces the "innocent spouse" either to move out or move into a separate area within the marital residence in order to maintain his or her health, safety, or self-respect

Cruel and abusive treatment
a fault ground for divorce available in some states; conduct that is so physically or mentally damaging that it endangers the spouse's health, safety, or reason

drinking, drug addiction, or failure to provide for the needs of the family, when there is an ability to do so, may cause such severe emotional stress that a court may deem the conduct cruel and abusive.

Cruelty generally encompasses both acts of physical violence and the reasonable apprehension thereof and also "acts and conduct the effect of which is calculated to permanently destroy the peace of mind and happiness of one of the parties to the marriage and thereby render the marital relationship intolerable."[17] Nagging, temper tantrums, name-calling, rudeness, cursing, and criticism usually are not sufficient to constitute cruelty, although they may be, depending on the known vulnerabilities of a specific plaintiff and an intention to cause pain and anguish.[18] Some states require that the plaintiff demonstrate proof of the harm suffered as a result of the defendant's conduct, such as medical records, medications prescribed for stress, counseling sought, significant weight loss or gain, and sleep disturbances. (See Case 6.3.)

CASE **6.3** *Pfoltzer v. Pfoltzer*, 9 A.D.3d 615, 779 N.Y.S.2d 668 (N.Y. App. Div. 2004)

FROM THE OPINION

Appeal from an amended judgment of the Supreme Court... entered March 7, 2002... granting plaintiff a divorce, upon a decision of the court.

Supreme Court granted plaintiff a divorce following the parties' 15-year marriage on the ground of cruel and inhuman treatment. Defendant appeals, arguing that there was insufficient evidence upon which to grant plaintiff a divorce on this ground. Noting that Supreme Court's determination as the factfinder on this issue will not be lightly disturbed by this Court..., we disagree with the defendant's contention and accordingly affirm.

Domestic Relations Law § 170 (1) provides that a divorce will be granted on a theory of cruel and inhuman treatment after a showing "that the conduct of the defendant so endangers the physical or mental well being of the plaintiff as renders it unsafe or improper for the plaintiff to cohabit with the defendant." "[I]n order to make out a prima facie case of cruel and inhuman treatment, a party must show something more than 'mere incompatibility' and 'serious misconduct [must] be distinguished from trivial'" (citations omitted). While a high degree of proof of serious or substantial misconduct was required in this case owing to the long duration of the parties' marriage..., we are satisfied that plaintiff made such a showing....

The evidence revealed that defendant has engaged in a constant barrage of harassing and controlling behavior toward plaintiff, often underscored by harsh religious accusations. According to plaintiff, defendant has alienated him from certain members of his family and he was forced to obtain a temporary order of protection to remove his personal items from the marital residence following his departure therefrom. He also obtained an order of protection preventing defendant from continuing to make harassing telephone calls. The record further reveals that defendant has engaged in a course of verbal and mental abuse by harassing and embarrassing plaintiff with public accusations that he has loathsome personal hygiene, has engaged in sexual-related criminal conduct and that he suffers from a particular venereal disease, as well as Acquired Immune Deficiency Syndrome.

continued

The evidence also sufficiently established that the anguish and embarrassment suffered by plaintiff has had an effect on his physical and mental health thus providing a basis for finding that cohabitation with defendant would be either unsafe or improper....Plaintiff was receiving medical treatment for a stress-related ulcer at the time of the trial and had been receiving mental health counseling for some time to address his depression and to help him understand and overcome the abusive relationship between himself and defendant. Indeed for a one-year period in the latter part of the parties' marriage, plaintiff had been prescribed medication to treat his depression caused by the turmoil in the marriage.

Mercure, J.P., Crew III, Lahtinen and Kane, JJ., concur.

Ordered that the amended judgment is affirmed, without costs.

SIDEBAR

This opinion is available in its entirety on the companion website for this text in the material related to Chapter 6. Do you agree that the defendant's conduct was sufficient to warrant a divorce? Explain your response.

Habitual Drunkenness or Drug Abuse.   This ground is most commonly called habitual drunkenness, but the precise terminology may vary. In Massachusetts, it is called "gross and confirmed habits of intoxication."[19] The Georgia statute includes both "habitual intoxication" and "habitual drug addiction" as independent grounds for divorce.[20] Some states require that the abuse have continued for a certain period. The Illinois statute, for example, reads, "the respondent has been guilty of habitual drunkenness for the space of 2 years" and "the respondent has been guilty of gross and confirmed habits caused by the excessive use of addictive drugs for the space of 2 years."[21]

Criminal Conviction and Incarceration.   The state statutes that include criminal conviction and incarceration as a ground for divorce vary with respect to the type of crime committed, the jurisdiction in which the crime was committed, the length of the sentence, and whether or not the respondent is/was actually confined. The pertinent Maryland statute lists as a ground "conviction of a felony or misdemeanor in any state or in any court of the United States if before the filing of the application for divorce the defendant has: (i) been sentenced to serve at least 3 years or an indeterminate sentence in a penal institution; and (ii) served 12 months of the sentence."[22] The Georgia statute specifies that the offense be one that involves "moral turpitude."[23] In Ohio, the respondent must be incarcerated at the time the complaint is filed.[24] The Virginia statute addresses the potential impact of a subsequent pardon.[25]

Examples of some of the less common statutory fault grounds for divorce include the following:

- The respondent has inflicted the spouse with a sexually transmitted disease.[26]
- When either party has joined any religious sect or society that professes to believe the relation of husband and wife is unlawful and has refused to cohabit for a six-month period.[27]
- Insanity under certain conditions. For example, a ground in Connecticut is the legal confinement of a spouse "in a hospital or hospitals or other similar institution because of mental illness, for at least an accumulated period totaling five years within the period of six years next preceding the date of the complaint."[28]

- "Pregnancy of the wife by a man other than the husband, at the time of the marriage, unknown to the husband."[29]
- "Excessively vicious conduct toward the complaining party or a minor child of the complaining party, if there is no reasonable expectation of reconciliation."[30]
- "Willful neglect of the respondent to provide for the petitioner the common necessaries of life."[31] The Ohio statute lists "Any gross neglect of duty."[32]

DEFENSES TO A DIVORCE ACTION

Defenses to a divorce action commonly include:

- Lack of subject matter jurisdiction
- Lack of personal jurisdiction
- Lack of proper venue
- Forum nonconveniens
- Lack of proper service of process
- Failure of the complaint to state a claim upon which relief can be based. The plaintiff has alleged a ground for divorce that is not available in the jurisdiction.
- The matter is *res judicata*. The marital status previously has been dissolved as in an action for divorce or annulment in another state or country
- Invalidity of the marriage

When the divorce action is based on one or more fault grounds, additional defenses are available. These "traditional" defenses have their origins in common law and include the following:

- *Condonation:* This defense is used when the defendant asserts that the petitioner has, in effect, condoned the alleged blameworthy conduct, such as an adulterous affair, by forgiving it to the extent that he or she has resumed "normal" marital relations with the defendant spouse who, with forgiveness, regains innocence. As an Illinois court described it in a 2005 decision, "Condonation in the law of divorce is the forgiveness of an antecedent matrimonial offense on condition that it shall not be repeated and that the offender shall thereafter treat the forgiving party with conjugal kindness."[34]
- *Provocation:* When this defense is raised, the defendant is claiming that the plaintiff provoked the conduct alleged in the complaint. For example, if the alleged ground for divorce is desertion/abandonment, the defendant may defend by saying that the plaintiff's excessive drinking and drug use forced a departure from the marital home for the defendant's safety and protection.
- *Recrimination:* Eliminated in several states, this defense is raised when the defendant claims that the plaintiff has also committed a marital wrong such as adultery and thus should not be granted a divorce. Some states have adopted the *doctrine of comparative rectitude* to deal with situations in which both parties are at fault. Under the doctrine, a court grants the divorce to the party whose wrongdoing is least serious. Other courts occasionally award "*dual divorces*" in which each party is granted the divorce.
- *Connivance:* Connivance is an appropriate defense when the plaintiff allegedly consented to or created the opportunity for the defendant to commit the act complained of in the complaint. For instance, if the petitioner alleges habitual drunkenness as a ground for divorce, the

---

Paralegal Practice Tip

A single divorce action may involve assertion of multiple alternative grounds by one or both parties.[33]

Defense
a defendant's stated reason why a plaintiff has no valid claim or why the court should not grant the relief requested

Paralegal Practice Tip

The *marital communications privilege,* which prevents a spouse from testifying in court about confidential communications with the other spouse during their marriage, usually does not apply in divorce actions or cases in which the defendant is alleged to have committed a crime against the spouse and/or their children. However, if adultery is alleged and is still a crime in the jurisdiction, the defendant may claim a Fifth Amendment right against self-incrimination if questioned about the existence of an adulterous relationship that falls within the applicable statute of limitations period.

Marital communications privilege
the privilege that allows a spouse to refuse to testify, and to prevent others from testifying, about confidential communications between the spouses during their marriage

Condonation
the forgiveness of a matrimonial offense

Provocation
a traditional defense claiming that the plaintiff provoked the conduct alleged in the complaint and therefore should be denied relief

Recrimination
a defense raised when the defendant alleges the plaintiff has also committed a marital wrong and therefore should not be granted a divorce

defendant may defend stating that the plaintiff both participated in and promoted the defendant's drinking and actively sabotaged his or her efforts to seek treatment.

- *Collusion:* Collusion is less a defense than a legal bar to a divorce. Collusion is a determination by the court that the parties should not be granted a divorce because they had an agreement to, in effect, deceive the court as to the nature and true purpose of the action. Essentially they conspired to fabricate a reason for the divorce when no legally recognized ground existed. Although far more common in the fault era, collusion is not unheard of today. For example, in an Oklahoma case in 2005, a court vacated a divorce decree based on the fact that the husband and wife sought a divorce with no intention of separating and solely for the purpose of increasing the wife's public benefits in support of her chronic illness.[35]

DRAFTING AND FILING OF THE COMPLAINT

The litigation technically begins when the divorce Complaint/Petition is filed with the court and the defendant is served. The **Complaint** (or Petition for Dissolution) is the main pleading in a divorce case. It sets forth the nature of the action and the basis of the court's jurisdiction over the action. It usually calls for the following information:

- names and addresses of the parties
- date and place of the parties' marriage
- date when the parties separated/last resided together as husband and wife
- names and dates of birth of any minor children
- alleged ground(s) for the divorce
- declaration regarding property in a community property state
- the request (or "prayer") for relief (e.g., division of property, custody, child or spousal support, maintenance of insurance, sale of the marital home, resumption of maiden name, etc.), usually including a final open-ended request for any further relief the court deems fair and equitable

It should be prepared in a manner that complies with applicable state statutes and procedural rules re grounds, format, jurisdiction, venue, etc. In a Complaint, the parties are commonly referred to as the plaintiff and defendant. In a Petition they are usually called the petitioner and the respondent. If the petition for divorce is a Joint Petition, the parties are usually labeled petitioner and co-petitioner. A copy of a Complaint for Absolute Divorce used in the state of Maryland is provided in Exhibit 6.4.

The paralegal is often asked to draft the Complaint/Petition. Before doing so, the proper jurisdiction and venue should be confirmed with the attorney based on the facts of the case (where each of the parties resides, where the parties last lived together as husband and wife, where the children are located, etc.). The next step is to determine whether the court mandates the use of specific forms or formats. The paralegal then drafts the document using the appropriate form, e.g., Complaint, Joint Petition, etc. Many states now provide divorce forms online, and many practice manuals include disks with model forms. Careful attention must be given to using jurisdictionally appropriate terminology. For example, some states use the terms *divorce* and *dissolution* interchangeably. Others, such as Ohio, use *dissolution* strictly to refer to uncontested actions.

Doctrine of comparative rectitude
in the divorce context, the granting of a divorce to the party who is least at fault when both parties have committed marital wrongdoing

Dual divorce
a divorce granted to both parties

Connivance
a traditional defense in which the defendant alleges the plaintiff consented to, or participated in, the act complained of in the complaint

Collusion
a determination by the court that the parties should not be granted a divorce because they jointly deceived the court as to the true nature and purpose of the action

Paralegal Practice Tip
Before raising a common law defense, the paralegal needs to research whether or not such "traditional" defenses are still available to defendants in the jurisdiction. For example, in 1999, a Kansas appellate court held that recrimination and mutual fault could not be raised as defenses to a divorce action based on a failure to perform a marital duty or obligation.[36]

Complaint
the main pleading in a case that sets forth the nature of the action and the request for relief

Paralegal Practice Tip
Even in an uncontested Joint Petition, a ground must be indicated (e.g., the parties are seeking a divorce due to irreconcilable differences that have caused the irremediable breakdown of the marriage). Typically one party's attorney will complete the necessary documents for review by the other party's attorney and the clients prior to signing and filing.

EXHIBIT 6.4 Complaint for Absolute Divorce

Courtesy of the State of Maryland

Circuit Court for _____   **Case No.** _____

City or County

Name	Name
Street Address _____ Apt. #	Street Address _____ Apt. #
City State Zip Code Area Code Telephone	City State Zip Code Area Code Telephone
Plaintiff	*Defendant*

COMPLAINT FOR ABSOLUTE DIVORCE
(DOM REL 20)

I, _____ , representing myself, state that:

Your Name

1. The Defendant and I were married on_____

Month   Day   Year

     in_____ in a ☐ civil ☐ religious ceremony.

City/County/State where Married   (Check One)

2. *Check all that apply:*
   ☐ I have lived in Maryland since:_____

Month/Year
   ☐ My spouse has lived in Maryland since: _____

Month/Year
   ☐ The grounds for divorce occurred in the State of Maryland.

3. *Check one:*
   ☐ We have no children together (skip paragraphs 5 and 6) or
   ☐ My spouse and I are the parents of the following child(ren:)

Name	Date of Birth	Name	Date of Birth
Name	Date of Birth	Name	Date of Birth
Name	Date of Birth	Name	Date of Birth

4. I know of the following related cases concerning the child(ren) or parties (such as domestic violence, paternity, divorce, custody, visitation, termination of parental rights, adoption or other cases):

Court	Case No.	Kind of Case	Year Filed	Results or Status (if known)

5. I have been a party, witness, or otherwise involved in the following cases about custody or visitation of the child(ren) :

State	Court	Case No.	Date of Child Custody Determination

Attach the most recent court order for the above-referenced court cases.

continued

6. I know of the following people, not parties to this case, who have physical custody of, or claim rights of legal custody or physical custody of, or visitation with the child(ren) :

_____	_____
Name	Current Address
_____	_____
Name	Current Address
_____	_____
Name	Current Address

7. The child(ren) are currently living with:_____
Name

8. The child(ren) have lived in the following places, with the persons indicated during the last five years:

Time Period	**Place**	**Name(s)/Current Address of Person(s) with whom Child Lived**
_____	_____	_____
_____	_____	_____

9. It is in the best interests of the child(ren) that I have (*check all that apply*):

- ☐ joint ☐ sole physical custody of _____
  (Check One)   Name of Children
- ☐ joint ☐ sole legal custody of _____
  (Check One)   Name of Children
- ☐ visitation with_____
                                         Name of Children

10. I ☐ am ☐ am not seeking alimony because._____
     (Check One)

11. (You do not have to complete paragraph 11 if you are not asking the court to make decisions about your property.) My spouse and/or I have the following property (*check all that apply*)

- ☐ House(s)   ☐ Furniture
- ☐ Pensions   ☐ Bank account(s) and investment(s)
- ☐ Motor Vehicle(s)   ☐ Other_____
- ☐ Debts (attach list)

12. My grounds for absolute divorce are: (*check all that apply*)

- ☐ **Two-Year Separation** - From on or about_____, my spouse and I have lived
  Month/Day/Year
  separate and apart from each other in separate residences, without interruptions, without sexual intercourse, for more than two years and there is no reasonable expectation that we will reconcile.

- ☐ **Voluntary Separation** - From on or about_____, my spouse and I by mutual and
  Month/Day/Year
  voluntary agreement have lived separate and apart from one another in separate residences, without interruption, without sexual intercourse, for more than 12 months with the express purpose and intent of ending our marriage, and there is no reasonable expectation that we will reconcile.

- ☐ **Adultery** - My spouse committed adultery.

- ☐ **Actual Desertion** - On or about_____, my spouse, without just cause or reason,
  Month/Day/Year
  abandoned and deserted me, with the intention of ending our marriage. This abandonment has continued without interruption for more than 12 months and there is no reasonable expectation that we will reconcile.

continued

☐ **Constructive Desertion** - I left my spouse because his/her cruel and vicious conduct made the continuation of our marriage impossible, if I were to preserve my health, safety, and self-respect. This conduct was the final and deliberate act of my spouse and our separation has continued without interruption for more than 12 months and there is no reasonable expectation that we will reconcile.

☐ **Criminal Conviction of a Felony or Misdemeanor** - On or about_____, my
Month/Day/Year
spouse was sentenced to serve at least three years or an indeterminate sentence in a penal institution and has served 12 or more months of the sentence.

☐ **Cruelty/Excessively Vicious Conduct Against Me or my minor child** - My spouse has persistently treated me or my minor child cruelly and has engaged in excessively vicious conduct rendering continuation of the marital relationship impossible if I am to preserve my health, safety, and self-respect, and there is no reasonable expectation that we will reconcile.

☐ **Insanity** - On or about_____, my spouse was confined to a mental institution,
Month/Day/Year
hospital, or other similar institution and has been confined for 3 more years. Two doctors competent in psychiatry will testify that the insanity is incurable and there is no hope of recovery. My spouse or I have been a resident of Maryland for at least two years before the filing of this complaint.

FOR THESE REASONS, I request (*check all that apply*):

☒ An Absolute Divorce
☐ A change back to my former name:_____
Full Former Name

☐　　　☐ Sole ☐ Joint physical custody of the minor child(ren).
(Check One)

☐　　　☐ Sole ☐ Joint legal custody of the minor child(ren).
(Check One)

☐ Visitation with the minor child(ren).
☐ Use and possession of the family home for up to three years from the date of the divorce.
☐ Use and possession of the family use personal property for up to three years from the date of the divorce.
☐ Child support (Attach Form DOM REL 30 or DOM REL 31).
☐ Health insurance for the child(ren).
☐ Health insurance for me.
☐ My share of the property or its value.
☐ Transfer of family use personal property.
☐ A monetary award (money) based on marital property.
☐ Alimony (Attach Form DOM. REL 31).
☒ Any other appropriate relief.

I, _____ , solemnly affirm under the penalties of
Your Name
perjury, that the contents of this document are true to the best of my knowledge, information and belief.

_____ 　 _____
Date　　　　　　　　　　　　　　　　　Signature

Paralegal Practice Tip
The client may be able to seek a waiver of the filing fee by filing a motion and affidavit of indigency, if required. If granted, the person usually is said to proceed *in forma pauperis* (as a poor person).

Once completed, reviewed, and signed, the Complaint is filed, accompanied by the filing fee and any other required documents. Although the states vary with respect to the additional documents that must be filed, most require the following:

- Certified copy of the marriage certificate (with a certified translation if in a foreign language)
- Disclosure Affidavit concerning any orders in force or pending regarding care, custody, and support of the parties' minor children, if any
- Financial Statement (must be updated at trial and every time a motion with financial implications is heard)
- A Military Affidavit if the defendant/respondent is unlikely to appear or is in the service and will not be able to appear
- A Bureau of Vital Statistics Form used to collect data on divorcing couples

The attorney customarily also files an *appearance* at this point, indicating that he or she will be representing the plaintiff in the divorce action. The paralegal usually drafts the Appearance (or completes the court's appearance form) and files it after it is reviewed and signed.

The paralegal often gathers the necessary documents and files the Complaint along with the accompanying documents and a transmittal letter to the court when directed to do so by the supervisor. The paralegal needs to be familiar with filing requirements and practices in the jurisdiction (in person, by mail, electronically, etc.). Copies of all documents filed should also be placed in the client's file and sent to the client.

When the Complaint is filed, the clerk assigns a docket number and issues a summons. The docket number should appear on all subsequent documents and correspondence related to the action. Sometimes the summons is completed by court staff, but in some counties necessary information is filled in by a member of the family law team, usually the paralegal.

Occasionally, third parties may be joined in a divorce action. For example, if one of the spouses creates a sham trust, allegedly for someone else's benefit; makes a substantial "loan" to a sibling; holds property in the names of other persons; or otherwise transfers property in a scheme designed to deprive the other spouse of a fair share of the marital assets, the third party may be drawn into the divorce, usually by use of an "equity" complaint for a *declaratory judgment* and/or injunctive relief. Some states add financial institutions, putting them on notice that the assets they hold are subject to a court order, thereby facilitating discovery with respect to those assets.

SERVICE OF THE COMPLAINT AND RETURN OF SERVICE

Service of the Summons and Complaint must comply with all applicable local rules and customarily must be made within a specified period after the filing date (usually sixty to ninety days). The *summons* informs the defendant that he or she has been sued and needs to answer within a certain period (usually twenty to thirty days) or risk possibility of a default judgment. *Service of process* is usually accomplished by:

- **Acceptance of service**—If a defendant is aware (by whatever means) of the summons, he or she may, for example, go voluntarily to a courthouse, receive the summons, and sign a form acknowledging service.
- **Personal service**—An approved process server delivers the summons into the hand of the defendant. The server then completes the "return of service" information indicating it has been served (or that service was attempted on multiple occasions but not accomplished). The proof of service information on the summons must be completed by the process server, who certifies when, where, and how service was made. It is returned by the server to either the court or the attorney's office, depending on local rules. The original is kept in the court's file, and a copy should be placed in the client's file.
- **Publication in a local newspaper and mailing to the defendant's last known address** if the defendant is evading service or his or her whereabouts are unknown

The paralegal must be familiar with the rules and procedures governing service of process and will usually perform the following related tasks:

- Complete the summons, if required.
- Maintain a list of approved process servers and fees. Process servers usually include sheriffs, constables, marshals, etc. Some jurisdictions permit service by a disinterested adult.

Memorandum of *lis pendens*
a notice that ownership and disposition of certain real property is subject to a pending legal action, and that any interest acquired during the pendency of that action is subject to its outcome

Appearance
a document filed with the court by an attorney, indicating that he or she will be representing one of the parties in a divorce action

Declaratory judgment
a binding adjudication that establishes the rights, status, or other legal relations between the parties

Summons
a formal notice from a court informing a defendant of an action filed against him or her and ordering the defendant to respond and answer the allegations of the plaintiff within a certain period or risk entry of a default judgment

Service of process
delivery of a summons and complaint to a defendant in a manner consistent with state and federal law

Answer

a pleading filed by a defendant in response to a plaintiff's Complaint, setting forth the defendant's defenses and counterclaims

Counterclaim

a defendant's claim against the plaintiff

Motion to Dismiss

a request that the court dismiss the case because of some procedural or other defect

- Make arrangements for proper service and alert the client as to where and when it is likely to be made in case there are safety issues to address.
- If service is by publication, draft a Motion for Permission to Serve by Publication, if required. If approved, mail a copy of the order of notice of the action, the Complaint, and the Summons by certified mail to the defendant's last known address and arrange for publication in the appropriate newspaper(s).
- If the defendant is located in another state or nation, research and arrange to have him or her properly served in that location.
- Track and ensure that service is properly completed and documented and advise the supervisor and client to that effect.
- Return proof of service to the court, if necessary, keeping copies for the client and the file.
- Arrange for payment of the process server's fee.

DEFENDANT'S RESPONSE TO THE COMPLAINT

The Defendant's initial pleading is customarily an **answer** to the Complaint/Petition for Divorce, which must be filed within the period set by statute or procedural rule. In the Answer, the defendant admits, denies, or indicates lack of information sufficient to respond to each of the paragraphs/allegations in the Complaint. The defendant may also:

- Raise any **defenses** he or she has to the allegations in the complaint (such as condonation, existence of a binding premarital agreement, etc.).
- Include a **counterclaim** for divorce and his or her own request for relief.

If the defendant also wants a divorce, it is good practice to file a counterclaim (even if the grounds are the same as in the complaint, e.g., irreconcilable differences). In the event the other party subsequently withdraws his or her Complaint, the date the counterclaim is filed will be preserved and there is no need to start the process all over again. In the alternative, if the parties are able to reach an agreement, the contested claims may be converted to a joint uncontested action, and the parties can proceed on that basis.

When responding to a Complaint for Divorce on behalf of a nonresident defendant, careful consideration must be given to the nature of the response. In appropriate circumstances, in lieu of an answer, the defendant may file a **Motion to Dismiss** (for lack of subject matter or personal jurisdiction, improper venue, or deficiencies in service, etc.) and NOT an Answer. If a nonresident defendant files an Answer, he or she will trigger personal jurisdiction. If represented, his or her attorney should file a limited appearance for the purpose of contesting jurisdiction. Any personal appearance by a resident defendant will confer full personal jurisdiction on the court even if the defendant appears solely to seek dismissal of the action. The paralegal may be asked to draft whichever response will be filed. A copy of a Complaint and examples of alternative responses (Answer and Motion to Dismiss) are provided on the companion website for this text in the material related to this chapter.

Once notified that an opposing party has retained counsel, all communication from the firm should be with the attorney and not directly with the party he or she represents. Direct communication between the parties themselves is virtually impossible to avoid, even when restraining orders have been issued. Such communication is a double-edged sword. Voluntary resolution of differences and maintenance of a civil, even positive, relationship between the parties is encouraged, particularly when children are involved and resources are limited.

However, in high-conflict cases or when there is a considerable power differential between the parties, communication is best left to counsel. In either situation, a client should always consult counsel before signing or otherwise finalizing any agreements with the other party.

MOTIONS FOR TEMPORARY ORDERS AND OTHER PURPOSES

At this point in a divorce case, one or both of the parties may file a request for *temporary orders,* most often addressing custody and support issues. Usually the request is made in the form of a *Motion* (a request to the court for an order) accompanied by an *Affidavit.* In some states, requests for temporary relief may or must be made in one motion or in separate motions or may be contained in the initial Complaint or the Answer. Requests for temporary orders are driven by the needs and problems of each individual case. They are designed to maintain the status quo and protect the client, if necessary, **pendente lite** (while the matter is pending). Because of their potential to subtly impact "permanent" orders, absent an emergency, some attorneys prefer to postpone the decision to file for temporary orders until after sufficient discovery is conducted. A sample of a Motion for Temporary Orders is provided on the companion website for this text in the resource material related to Chapter 6. It is only a sample and uses terminology regarding child custody and support that is appropriate for some, but not all, jurisdictions.

The parties may file additional Motions as the action progresses, addressing other issues such as the following:

- removal of children from the state on a temporary basis while the litigation is pending
- protection of marital assets held by third parties, such as banks or investment firms (requires financial statement)
- preservation of marital assets requesting that the other party be enjoined from disposing of or encumbering a specific asset. An example of an Affidavit supporting a Motion for a Restraining Order to Preserve Marital Assets is provided on the companion website in the material related to Chapter 6.
- attorney's fees and costs *pendente lite* to allow the party to maintain the action (usually requires affidavit of attorney, schedule of anticipated expenses, financial statement, etc.)
- use and occupancy of the marital home and responsibility for related expenses (requires financial statement), including a request that one of the parties vacate the marital home, if necessary (See Exhibit 6.5 for a sample of a Motion to Vacate the Marital Home.)
- appointment of an investigator, custody evaluator, and/or guardian *ad litem* (If one of the parties is or becomes incompetent to handle his or her affairs, a guardian may be appointed to represent that person's interests.)
- restraining order for protection from abuse (may be based on a Complaint rather than a Motion, depending on the jurisdiction and circumstances)
- appraisals of major assets such as the marital home
- consolidation with the divorce action of one or more actions, such as a prior order from another court that is still in force relating to protection from abuse, child custody, and/or occupancy of the marital home

Temporary orders
orders designed to protect the parties and maintain the status quo while a matter is pending before the court

Motion
an oral or written request that the court issue a particular ruling or order

Affidavit
a first-person statement signed under oath laying out facts in support of the motion

Pendente lite
while the action is pending

Paralegal Practice Tip
The court will not be able to issue an enforceable temporary order for child and spousal support, etc., unless the defendant has been served and personal jurisdiction is established.

Paralegal Practice Tip
Some jurisdictions mandate that uniform forms be used for particular motions. If not, firms should have available templates, forms on disk, form and practice books, and motions in files from past cases that involved similar fact patterns that may be tailored to the case at hand.

EXHIBIT 6.5 Sample of a Motion to Vacate the Marital Home

STATE OF NEW HAMPSHIRE

HILLSBORO COUNTY

SUPERIOR COURT   **DOCKET NO. XXXXXXX**

JANE TURNER,	)	
Plaintiff	)	**PLAINTIFF'S**
	)	**MOTION TO VACATE THE**
v.	)	**MARITAL HOME**
	)	
JAMES TURNER,	)	
Defendant	)	
	)	

NOW COMES JANE TURNER, plaintiff in the above-captioned matter, and respectfully requests this Honorable Court order the defendant, JAMES TURNER, to vacate the marital home forthwith.

In support of her motion, the plaintiff states as follows:

1. The parties were married at Fort Myers, Florida, on November 16, 1998, and are presently residing in the marital residence at 306 North Dunstable Road, Nashua, New Hampshire, together with the parties' two minor children, Calvin Turner, age 6 years (DOB April 16, 2001), and Elizabeth Turner, age 4 years (DOB June 11, 2003).
2. The plaintiff has filed a Complaint for Divorce (Docket No. XXXXXXX) on the grounds of irreconcilable differences that have caused the irretrievable breakdown of the marriage.
3. The defendant's abusive behavior in the home has caused the plaintiff severe emotional stress and physical side effects. Moreover, tension caused by the defendant's actions and disagreements pertaining to the pending action for divorce are causing the parties' minor children emotional trauma and distress.
4. The relationship between the parties has significantly deteriorated in the five months since the Divorce Complaint was filed and conflict between the parties has escalated to a level that requires that the parties live apart.
5. It is in the best interests of the children that they remain in the marital home with the plaintiff, who has been their primary caretaker since birth.

In further support of this Motion, the plaintiff submits the accompanying Affidavit, which is herein incorporated by reference.

WHEREFORE, for the reasons set forth above and in the plaintiff's Affidavit, the plaintiff requests that this honorable Court order the defendant to vacate the marital home forthwith.

continued

Respectfully submitted,

Jane Turner

By her attorney,

Date:_____

_____

Attorney's name

Attorney's address

Attorney's telephone number

Attorney's Bar number

CERTIFICATE OF SERVICE

I, (*Plaintiff's Attorney*), hereby certify that I have today served the above Motion and accompanying Affidavit, and Proposed Order on the Defendant, James Turner, by first-class mail to the office of his attorney, (*name and address of defendant's attorney*), together with notice that the Motion has been marked for hearing before the presiding Justice sitting in the _____ Court at 8:30 a.m. on Monday, December 3, 2007.

Date: _____

_____

Name of Plaintiff's Attorney

Because of their nature, some of these motions may be filed **ex parte** (without advance notice to the opposing party). For example, the purpose of a motion for an order restraining transfer or dissipation of marital assets, or to prevent removal of the minor children from the jurisdiction, may be totally defeated if advance notice is provided. *Ex parte* motions usually must be accompanied by an affidavit setting forth the nature of the emergency and how the giving of notice would pose a substantial risk of harm.

Most states issue "automatic restraining orders" that are effective with regard to the plaintiff upon filing of the Complaint and to the defendant when served with the Summons and Complaint. The orders generally remain in effect while the matter is pending unless modified by agreement of the parties or by order of the court. These orders usually restrain transfer or disposal of any of the parties' property (except to cover reasonable living or ordinary business expenses), incurring of debt, and changing of any insurance or pension beneficiaries. The client may need to be alerted or reminded about the existence of these orders.

The court may choose to appoint a **guardian ad litem (GAL)** in cases where custody is contested, even if not requested by the parties. The guardian is likely to request from each party a variety of documents, such as pleadings, reports in the parents' possession, medical records, etc. Releases will need to be provided where necessary. The guardian usually interviews the parents, the children, school personnel, day care providers, pediatricians, and others to gather information about the child's history and

Ex parte **motion**
a motion made without advance notice to the opposing party; a motion considered and initially ruled on by the court without hearing from both parties, based on the urgency of the matter or the harm that might otherwise result

Guardian *ad litem*
a person, usually a lawyer, appointed by the court to conduct an investigation and/or represent a party who is a minor or otherwise unable to represent him- or herself in a legal proceeding; the guardian's role may be limited to a particular matter, such as custody

Stipulation

an agreement between the parties concerning some matter; may be filed with the court to be entered as an order

Military affidavit

an affidavit submitted by a party stating under pain and penalties of perjury that an absent party is currently not serving in the armed services

current home and school environment. The guardian may then make a custody recommendation to the court, which it may accept or reject. Counsel is customarily permitted to question the GAL at trial regarding the report and the basis for any findings and recommendations. The report is usually impounded and not part of the public record, to protect the privacy of the children and the parties.

Hearings on Motions

Motions are usually heard in what are called motion sessions, in which the court hears several motions in a sequence essentially controlled by the clerk. Sometimes the sequence will be determined in advance and specific time blocks will be allocated for each case. Usually, the docket is posted in the courthouse on the date of the hearing. Many courts require that all parties and attorneys expecting to be heard report at the same time (e.g., 8:00 a.m.). The clerk will "call the list" to confirm that all necessary individuals are present and determine whether there are any special needs, such as for an interpreter or a referral for mediation or a meeting with a family service worker.

In many states, if the parties have not already reached agreement with respect to the subject matter of the motion prior to coming to court, they will be required to meet with a family service worker or court-based mediator to see if the matter can be resolved prior to the hearing. If an agreement is reached by the parties, it is reduced to a written **stipulation** and submitted to the court for consideration. If the matter is not resolved, the family service worker may submit a recommendation, and the motion will be argued before the court.

Motion hearings are usually quite brief, and rules of evidence are rarely strictly followed, unlike in a trial. In some states, the parties are required to be present for hearings unless their absence is excused by the court. When a party fails to appear without explanation or excuse, the moving party must file a **military affidavit** in accordance with the Soldiers and Sailors Relief Act,[37] stating under pain and penalties of perjury that the absent party is currently not serving in the armed services.

The paralegal may perform the following tasks related to temporary orders and other motions:

- Gather information necessary to draft, support, and file the motion (or oppose it).
- Draft Motions, Supporting Affidavits, and Proposed Orders, if required, for review.
- File and send copies of the documents to the client and opposing counsel with transmittal cover letters when approved and signed.
- Assist with preparation of accompanying financial statement and child support guidelines worksheet if necessary.
- If the court permits scheduling in advance by counsel, check all appropriate calendars (including those of opposing counsel) and arrange to mark motions for hearing or diversion to court conciliation or mediation services, if appropriate (often the procedure with child-related motions). If the hearing date is known at the time of service, include it in the certification along with the time and place for the hearing.
- Be certain that hearing dates are marked on all appropriate calendars and on the firm's "docket control system" if applicable. The client should also be notified of the date. The attorney will usually describe the nature of the proceeding to the client and will review the roles of each party, counsel, and the court.
- Assist with preparation for motion hearings.

In order to carry out these responsibilities, the paralegal must keep current with respect to the rules governing various aspects of motion practice, including special rules of civil procedure for domestic relations courts, local court rules, and practices of various courts and judges. For example:

- Are uniform forms for motions, affidavits, and proposed orders required?
- How far in advance of a hearing must a motion be served? In an emergency, may a party request and be granted a "short order of notice" reducing the required notice period?
- Can motions be filed and/or served electronically?
- What are the procedures for scheduling motion hearings in the court where the motion is filed? Some courts permit counsel to schedule dates in advance and serve notice of the hearing date along with the motion if there has been prior consultation with opposing counsel. Other courts strictly control scheduling and mark motions only after they are filed with the court and without any opportunity for input from counsel.
- When a party opposes a motion for temporary orders, does the court require submission of a memorandum or affidavit in opposition to the motion, or does it simply rely on testimony presented at the hearing on the motion?
- Is the motion being filed governed by rules over and above those regulating domestic matters? For example, motions to protect marital assets may need to comply with nondivorce procedural rules (such as motions for **trustee process** that in effect freeze assets of the other party, directing a third-party holder of the assets, such as a bank, to hold them in trust, pending resolution of the action).

> **Paralegal Practice Tip**
> The paralegal should maintain a file of clerks/contacts in each court and agency with which the office has frequent contact. It is always helpful to establish a network and be able to refer to personnel by name. It also is a good idea to maintain a record of any of the "idiosyncrasies" of particular courts and special instructions and "pet peeves" of particular judges!

Trustee process
a legal process by which a third party holds the property of a party in trust at the direction of a court

DISCOVERY

Discovery is a pretrial process for obtaining information from the other side. Although it is sometimes used as a "fishing expedition," its proper focus is on relevant, unprivileged information pertaining to all issues involved in a case, such as custody, support, property division, etc. Its primary purposes are:

Discovery
the process of gathering information relevant to a matter at issue; includes both formal and informal methods

- to learn about the claims and defenses of the other side
- to understand the strengths and weaknesses of the case from the perspective of each of the parties
- to avoid surprises at hearings and at trial
- to promote settlement

Discovery is governed by procedural rules, limitations, and timelines that must be carefully followed. The paralegal must master these rules and any related amendments or variations county to county. The state may require certain basic kinds of mandatory discovery/production within a certain time period following service of the complaint (e.g., forty-five days). In addition, informal discovery may be completed by the entire family law team with the assistance of the client. Formal discovery methods available in every state include:

- Interrogatories
- Depositions
- Requests for Production of Documents or Things or Entry Upon Land
- Requests for Admissions
- Requests for Medical or Physical Examinations (These usually require permission of the court.)

There are several discovery-related motions that may be filed. The most common include the following:

- Motion for a Protective Order to limit discovery
- Motion to Compel Discovery (and impose sanctions, if appropriate)

- Request for Status Conference regarding discovery to clarify issues, resolve disputes, and outline a plan, methods, and timeline (Such conferences may be required by the court.)
- Motion for Fees to cover the costs of various discovery initiatives, such as accountants, appraisers, and the like

The paralegal's role in all kinds of discovery (formal, informal, electronic, etc.) is discussed at considerable length in Chapter 7 on Discovery and Financial Statements.

NEGOTIATION AND DRAFTING OF THE SEPARATION AGREEMENT

Separation agreement
an agreement made between spouses in anticipation of divorce or legal separation concerning the terms of the divorce or separation and any continuing obligations of the parties to one another

If the parties reach agreement on all unresolved issues following discovery, a *separation agreement* can be drafted, reviewed, and executed, and the case can move forward on an uncontested basis. If the parties have resolved some, but not all, issues, a partial separation agreement can be drafted that addresses all issues not in dispute. Whether the agreement is full or partial, the parties customarily request that the court incorporate it into the divorce judgment. Depending on its terms, the agreement either will "merge" into the judgment and lose its separate identity, or it will "survive" (with the exception of child-related provisions) as an independent contract with legal significance apart from the judgment. The concepts of "merger" and "survival" are discussed more fully in Chapter 12, which focuses entirely on the topic of separation agreements. It provides drafting advice, a comprehensive model of a complete agreement, and a description of the primary tasks the paralegal may perform with respect to separation agreements.

Paralegal Practice Tip
Given the potential that a case may settle at the time of trial, some attorneys prepare separation agreements for possible use at that time to avoid confusion, delay, and errors due to hasty drafting. The agreement will include undisputed issues and common "boilerplate" provisions and leave some spaces blank to be filled in with eventually agreed-upon amounts and/or terms. At least four copies should be brought to court "just in case" (one for the court, one for each attorney, and one for the client).

PRETRIAL ACTIVITIES

States vary with respect to the specific nature and sequencing of activities that take place between the time the parties reach an impasse regarding one or more issues and decide to proceed to trial and the date of the actual trial. Typically the following activities occur, although they may be labeled differently in various jurisdictions.

- The moving party files a **Request for Pretrial Conference/Hearing**, if required (may be in the form of a request for a trial that automatically triggers a court-ordered pretrial conference/hearing). The paralegal for the moving party may draft the request (or prepare the required form for signature and filing).
- The Court issues a **Pretrial Conference Notice and Order** indicating what is required at the pretrial conference/hearing. When the notice is received, the paralegal will mark the assigned pretrial conference date, place, and presiding judge on all appropriate calendars and advise the client of date and location in writing.
- Many states require that a **four-way conference** be held at this point prior to the formal pretrial conference.
- Each side prepares a **Pretrial Memorandum,** which customarily must address the following:
  - procedural history of the case
  - uncontested issues
  - contested issues, including contested issues of fact (finances, parenting skills, etc.) and contested issues of law (custody, alimony, attorney's fees, etc.), including the status of agreement with respect to each issue
  - status of discovery and time frame for completion (usually must be completed prior to filing a request for trial)
  - list of exhibits (including written objections, if any)

- list of proposed witnesses (including experts)
- property values (agreed on and disputed)
- estimated length of trial

An experienced paralegal may be asked to prepare the first draft of the Pretrial Memorandum.

- The **Pretrial Conference** is held and the court reviews the topics covered in the parties' memoranda. The judge/marital master who conducts the hearing usually strongly urges the parties to settle their differences and avoid the necessity of a trial. Some judges even will suggest how they are likely to rule on particular issues.
- Following the pretrial conference, if there is a need to complete further discovery and/or there is any potential for settlement, the court may, at the request of counsel or on its own initiative, schedule one or more **status conferences**.
- If and when the parties arrive at a clear impasse, one or both of them will file a **Request for Trial.** The paralegal may draft the Request or prepare the required form for signature and filing.
- The Court then issues a **Pretrial Order** and assigns a trial date. The paralegal should mark the trial date on all appropriate calendars and notify the client in writing.

THE TRIAL

Preparation for Trial

The opposing sides prepare for trial, although negotiations often continue in hopes the case can be settled "on the courthouse steps," thereby avoiding further litigation expenses and emotional trauma. The nature, extent, and cost of trial preparation depend on the type, number, and complexity of disputed issues to be addressed at trial. For example, some couples may be able to resolve all issues with the exception of the disposition of the marital home, an issue they can argue in a half-day trial with only the parties as witnesses and an agreed-upon appraisal of the property. Others may be unable to agree on any issues and maintain fixed positions with respect to the grounds for divorce, alimony, property division, and child custody and support. In such cases, the trial may take a matter of weeks and involve extensive testimony of witnesses (including experts, private investigators, employers, and GALs, among others), complex exhibits, sophisticated audiovisuals and computer graphics, business and property valuations, etc.

Whatever the scope of the trial, an experienced paralegal may play a major supportive role in all aspects of trial preparation. Some tasks are common to virtually all trials, no matter what their scope. The members of the family law team need to:

- **Verify that all required documents have been filed or are ready for filing**, including a current Financial Statement, Child Support Guidelines Worksheet, and Parenting Plan, if necessary.
- **Request and confirm a stenographer** to preserve the record for possible appeal. Some stenographic services now offer an option of plugging into the stenographer's computer and obtaining a simultaneous transcription during the trial.
- **Prepare witnesses** for questions likely to be asked in both direct and cross-examination. Witnesses cannot be told what to say, but they can be given advice with respect to how to most effectively answer questions and handle themselves in the face of various styles of questioning by opposing counsel. Preparation may include a trip to the courthouse to orient potential witnesses to the environment and nature of the proceedings. The client also needs to be familiar with and understand the exhibits to be presented and their significance to the case.
- Prepare/assemble a "*Trial Notebook.*" (See Paralegal Application 6.4.)
- **Draft Trial Memorandum of Law, Proposed Findings of Fact, Conclusions of Law, and Proposed Judgment, if required.** Counsel for each party is

Trial Notebook

a term used loosely to describe the organizational system used by an attorney to assemble all of the material needed for a trial

Paralegal Practice Tip
Increasingly, courts are requesting that certain documents, such as Trial Memoranda, Proposed Findings of Fact, Conclusions of Law, and Proposed Orders, be submitted in both hard copy and disk formats, partially in anticipation that the court may adopt all or a significant portion of a party's submission. The chances of this happening are significantly increased when the proposals are realistic and consistent with governing authority.

Proposed Findings of Fact
facts that a party asks a court to accept as true

Conclusions of law
statements as to how governing law applies to a case

customarily required to prepare these documents in anticipation of trial, with a focus on contested issues and the factors the court will consider when making decisions regarding those issues:

- **Trial Memorandum of Law**: The Trial Memorandum essentially lays out the basic facts of the case along with the client's arguments regarding contested issues supported by appropriate authority (statutory, case law, secondary resources, etc.). This document provides the court with references to potential authoritative support for its findings.

- *Proposed Findings of Fact:* In Proposed Findings of Fact, the attorney (on behalf of the client) asks that the court accept certain facts as true, such as the date and length of the marriage, the parties' ages and health status, their education and employability, their respective contributions to the marriage, etc. In most cases, the parties will stipulate, or agree to, a number of basic facts in advance of trial so that proof will not need to be presented with respect to those matters.

- *Conclusions of Law:* Conclusions of Law are statements for the court's potential adoption as to how governing law should apply to the case from the client's perspective. For example, the attorney may propose conclusions such as the following based on the facts of the case at hand:
  - That the court has jurisdiction over the case and the parties (based on the particular statute authorizing jurisdiction)
  - That a judgment of divorce should be entered when the court is satisfied that the parties' marriage is so irretrievably broken that it cannot be remedied and the parties can no longer live together (referencing the state's no-fault statute and possibly case law or other authority)
  - That, in dividing the parties' property, the court may consider the source of assets, particularly if acquired through inheritance or a party's family of origin (based on the applicable state statute and case law or other authority)
  - That custody decisions are to be guided by the best interests of the child standard and there is a presumption against awarding custody to a parent who has a documented history of abuse (based on statute and case law)

- **Proposed Judgment**: A Proposed Judgment is a judgment written from the client's perspective that the court is urged to adopt as its own. An example of a Proposed Judgment appears in Exhibit 6.6.

PARALEGAL APPLICATION 6.4

THE "TRIAL NOTEBOOK"

In all cases to be tried, no matter how uncomplicated, ORGANIZATION is critical. Thorough preparation is extremely important to the success of a case and leaves a favorable impression on the court (and the client!). The term "Trial Notebook" is used loosely to describe the organizational system used by an individual attorney to assemble all of the materials needed for trial. The physical form of the trial notebook may vary—it may truly take the form of an indexed loose-leaf binder or it may be in the shape of a series of well-labeled files organized in boxes if necessary. It often is comprised of multiple "notebooks":

- **The Trial Notebook:** This notebook essentially contains a script for the attorney that organizes materials according to each stage of the trial: an overall trial outline, an opening statement, outlines of witness examinations (and potential questions for cross-examination), identification and description of all exhibits, excerpts of deposition transcripts and interrogatories to be used, and a closing argument.

continued

- **Supplemental Notebooks:** These notebooks organize all of the material related to the case that may or may not be needed at trial, including, but not necessarily limited to:
  - a notebook containing all pleadings and rulings with those that are central to the case, clearly tabbed, and accessible if needed
  - a notebook containing tabbed discovery materials with accompanying summaries
  - a notebook containing clearly indexed financial information, including financial statements of each party, tax returns, bank records, credit card statements, mortgage applications, pay stubs, pension data, etc.
  - a witness notebook containing subfiles for each witness in alphabetical order including curriculum vita, deposition summaries/transcripts, correspondence, etc. This notebook may include appraisals of various assets (real estate, collections, businesses, etc.), medical reports, and reports of investigators, including court-ordered evaluations.
  - a notebook containing indexed research files by issue (for example, when a party can be granted a greater than fifty percent share of the marital assets, child support awards outside of the guidelines, or designation of certain assets as marital property). *Note*: If any seminal cases may be referenced, four copies should be available "just in case" (one for the court, one for the stenographer, and the other two for counsel).
  - an indexed notebook containing correspondence with the court, opposing counsel, the client, and others, organized separately and usually by date with the most recent appearing first
- Some courts, particularly in complex cases, require counsel to prepare indexed ***Exhibit Notebooks*** for the convenience of the court and to save considerable trial time sorting through and marking Exhibits during the trial. Four copies usually are prepared: one for each attorney, one for the court, and one for use with witnesses who are testifying. The Exhibit Notebook generally contains:

- The Plaintiff's Exhibits (disputed and undisputed)
- The Defendant's Exhibits (disputed and undisputed)
- Copies of current financial statements for each party
- The GAL's Report if the Guardian will be called as a witness by either party
- Stipulations of the parties with respect to such issues as tax matters, property values, business valuations, etc. (Depending on the court, these may be read into the record.)

Exhibit Notebook
notebook, prepared for the convenience of the court and counsel, containing all exhibits to be introduced at trial by either or both parties

---

EXHIBIT 6.6 Example of a Proposed Judgment

STATE OF_____

_____COUNTY   FAMILY COURT

                                        DOCKET NO:_____

TIFFANY HEALEY,   )

  Plaintiff   )

)   PLAINTIFF'S
v.   )   PROPOSED JUDGMENT
)

NOEL HEALEY,   )

  Defendant   )

continued

All interested persons having been notified in accordance with law and after hearing, it is adjudged *nisi* that a divorce be granted to the Plaintiff for the cause of irretrievable breakdown of the marriage (*cite statute*) and that upon the expiration of ninety (90) days from entry of this judgment it shall become absolute unless, upon application of any person within such period, the court shall otherwise order. It is further ordered that:

1. The Agreement of the parties dated April 1, 2008, is incorporated and merged in this judgment and hereafter shall have no independent legal significance.

2. The property located at 1125 Marlboro St., _____ shall be conveyed to the wife by the husband within one hundred and twenty (120) days of this date.

3. The parties shall have joint legal custody of the minor child, Bethany Healey, and physical custody shall be with the mother with reasonable rights of visitation to the father consistent with the parenting plan filed with this court and dated April 1, 2008.

4. The husband shall pay child support in the amount of $465.00 per month payable on the first day of each month commencing on June 1, 2008, said amount being consistent with this state's guidelines for child support.

5. Each party shall be responsible for his or her own health insurance and uninsured medical, dental, and/or psychiatric expenses and the father shall maintain health insurance for the benefit of the minor child.

6. Each party shall pay his or her own legal fees and costs.

_____

Presiding Justice

Dated:_____

Subpoena
a document ordering a witness to appear and provide testimony in a court hearing or trial

Subpoena *duces tecum*
a subpoena ordering a witness to appear in a legal proceeding such as a deposition, court hearing, or trial and to bring with him or her specified documents, records, or things

Motion *in limine*
a motion asking the court to exclude or limit the use of certain evidence at trial

In more complex trials, there are additional tasks that the family law team may need to complete prior to trial, including the following:

- Prepare **subpoenas** (for people including the GAL, if warranted) and subpoenas *duces tecum*. A subpoena is a document ordering a witness to appear and provide testimony in a court hearing or trial. A **subpoena duces tecum** requires the witness to bring with him or her certain documents such as bank, pension, or employment records.
- Obtain certified copies of public documents as appropriate, for example, certified copies of legal proceedings conducted in other jurisdictions.
- Gather documentation regarding any expert witnesses so that the court will be positioned to qualify them as "experts" able to render expert opinions.
- Prepare **Motions in limine** and memoranda in support of or in opposition to admissibility of particular evidence.

- Prepare Motion to Assess Counsel Fees, if warranted.
- Prepare a Complaint for any arrearages in payments due under temporary orders.
- Create PowerPoint presentations, illustrative graphics, etc., that will clearly illustrate major points and complex topics in a "simplified" form for the court.

The Trial

The trial in a contested case is a full trial involving opening and closing statements, presentation of each party's case through direct and cross-examination of witnesses, and introduction of evidentiary exhibits. The usual standard of proof in divorce cases is *preponderance of the evidence* (i.e., it is more likely than not that the facts alleged are true). The trial is intended to resolve all disputed issues. Divorce trials are open to the public although rarely attended except in higher-profile cases. Some states, such as New York and Texas, permit jury trials in divorce cases.

Although the attorney presents the client's case, the paralegal may perform several functions during the trial.

- With the court's permission, the paralegal may attend the trial and be seated at the counsel table with the client and the attorney. Counsel will introduce the paralegal by name and will indicate his or her paralegal status. The paralegal may then assist counsel by quickly locating needed documents, pointing out relevant materials, and providing support and encouragement to the client.
- Both the paralegal and the client may make notes during the trial regarding important issues, documents needed, ideas for additional questions, portions of exhibits to counter the defendant's testimony, etc.
- The paralegal is available to make needed copies and phone calls and confirm the arrival of a scheduled witness (or track down an absent witness!).

Preponderance of the evidence
a standard of proof that requires the evidence show that it is more likely than not that an alleged fact is true or false as claimed

The Judgment

After the case is presented, the judge reviews the evidence, testimony, etc., and makes a decision on the merits of the case. Some judges render decisions promptly, and others take a matter of weeks, even months, depending in part on the complexity of the case. Customarily, the judge then enters an *Interlocutory Decree* (or a *Decree Nisi*) along with accompanying findings of fact and conclusions of law. An interlocutory decree is not final, and the parties are technically still married until the final decree issues. If they reconcile in the interim period, a *Motion to Vacate the Judgment* may be filed. The *Final Judgment* (sometimes called the *Judgment Absolute*) usually enters automatically in most jurisdictions after a specified period of time (usually thirty to ninety days). The paralegal should obtain certified copies of the decree and send them to the client, who will need them for a variety of post-divorce matters, such as changing accounts and insurance policies, etc.

Interlocutory Decree/Decree *Nisi*
an interim decree; a decree that is not final

Motion to Vacate the Judgment
a motion requesting the court to nullify or cancel a judgment before it becomes final

Final Judgment/Judgment Absolute
the court's final decision determining the rights of the parties and issues in dispute

POST-DIVORCE PROCEEDINGS

Depending on the circumstances of each case, a variety of post-divorce proceedings may be necessary.

Post-Trial Motions

Post-trial motions may include the following:

- **Motion to Alter and Amend the Judgment** to correct factual and substantive errors
- **Motion for a New Trial**, alleging that prejudicial errors made during the trial affected the outcome. This motion usually must be brought promptly (e.g., within ten days).
- **Motion for Relief From Judgment**, based on fraud, mistake, or newly discovered evidence, etc. This kind of motion usually must be brought within a reasonable period (e.g., a year after entry of judgment). When the motion is allowed, the court may modify its initial judgment or vacate it and order a new trial.

The paralegal may be asked to draft these motions with careful attention to governing rules and strict timelines. Prior to doing so, he or she will need to obtain a copy of the transcript or portions of it, as necessary.

Appeal of a Final Judgment

Occasionally, a client will elect to appeal a final judgment or the portion of it that is adverse. The party filing the appeal is called the *appellant* and the opposing party is the *appellee.* The appeals process is governed by procedural rules and strict time standards that must be satisfied throughout the process, and an appeal can be dismissed for failure to meet a deadline. The appeal is usually heard by an intermediate appellate court unless the state does not have one, in which case it goes directly to the state's highest court. A decision of an intermediate appellate court usually can be appealed to the state's highest court.

An appellate court does not retry the case. The appeal is based on the record of what took place at the trial court level. New evidence is not introduced. The focus is on whether there were any errors made by the trial court in applying the law to the facts of the case and whether the trial court abused its discretion and made findings of fact unsupported by the evidence. Great deference is shown to the trial court's findings, because that court was in the best position to hear and assess the credibility of the witnesses.

The basic steps in the appeals process are the following:

- The appellant files a notice of appeal in the appropriate court within the required period after the final judgment (usually the date of the decree *nisi*).
- The appellant designates the portion of the trial court materials they want in the record on appeal (including any relevant portions of the transcript), and the appellee may cross-designate materials.
- The clerk assembles the record and then dockets the case with the appeals court.
- The parties submit briefs (first the appellant, then the appellee), and, after the submissions, the appellant has an opportunity to respond to the appellee's brief.
- The court may decide the appeal based on the briefs and the record or may hear oral argument.
- The appellate court affirms, reverses (in whole or in part), and/or remands for a new trial consistent with its opinion.

The paralegal may:

- Draft the notice of appeal for review, signature, and filing.
- Monitor the appeals process (deadlines, notice of appeal, submission of materials, etc.).

Appellant

the party bringing an appeal of a lower court's judgment

Appellee

the party against whom an appeal is brought

Paralegal Practice Tip

Appeals, etc., may be subject to statutes of limitations. For example, in a 2006 Texas case, following the death of her former husband, a woman sought relief when she learned that, shortly before he'd died, he had changed his will in favor of his current wife. The change violated a provision of the parties' divorce decree that required all finances and insurance policies through the time of divorce be granted to the ex-wife. A Texas appellate court held that her claim was subject to a two-year statute of limitations governing family law actions rather than by the longer six-year statute of limitations governing contracts.[38]

- Contact a stenographer and make arrangements to have the relevant portions of the transcript prepared and filed.
- Research and draft the appellate brief, although such assignments are generally given only to highly skilled and experienced paralegals.

Complaint for Modification

Either party may, at some point after judgment, find it necessary to file a Complaint (or Motion, depending on the jurisdiction) for Modification of child custody, child support, or spousal support (where permitted) based on a substantial change in circumstances (such as employment status, income, marital status, residence, and health). The court may issue temporary orders while the modification action is pending and discovery conducted, if necessary. The paralegal may be asked to research and draft the Complaint for Modification (or the Answer to a Complaint if representing the defendant) for review, signature, and filing. Absent an agreement between the parties, the court will issue its order after a hearing on the merits.

Complaint for Contempt

An existing order of the court remains valid until the court declares otherwise. However, it is not uncommon for clients simply to decide they should not have to comply with an order because of changed circumstances, such as the loss of a job or development of a serious medical problem, or because the other party is not abiding by the terms of the decree in some manner. For example, if the noncustodial parent fails to pay child support, the custodial parent cannot simply deny visitation. The client must understand that the appropriate response is to seek a modification rather than become a defendant in a contempt action!

When a party fails to comply with the terms of the judgment, the other party may file a Complaint for Contempt (sometimes called a Petition for Contempt or a Motion to Enforce Litigant's Rights). The paralegal may be asked to research and draft the Complaint for Contempt (or the Answer to a Complaint if representing the defendant) for review, signature, and filing. In addition to holding a defendant in contempt, several other remedies may be requested to enforce the decree, such as garnishment of wages and declaration of a *constructive trust* over property, depending on the nature of the defendant's noncompliance with the court's order. There may be a statutory presumption that attorney's fees will be awarded to the prevailing party in a contempt action but, if not, they should be requested. After hearing, the court will issue its order. The paralegal should ensure that a copy is sent promptly to the client.

Court of equity
a court that has authority to decide controversies in accordance with rules and principles of equity

Specific performance
a remedy for breach of contract in which the court orders the breaching party to complete the contract as promised

Constructive trust
a trust imposed by the court on an asset of a party who improperly or wrongfully acquired the property

FOLLOW-UP MATTERS

After the divorce is final, a number of follow-up tasks may need to be completed by one, the other, or both of the parties with or without the assistance of the attorney who handled the divorce. These actions may include, for example:

- Preparation of Deeds transferring real property interests
- Preparation and processing of a QDRO (See Chapter 11.)
- Transfer of stock ownership, etc.
- Closing of joint accounts
- Payment of joint debts

- Petition for name change if desired and not addressed as part of the divorce action
- Preparation of a new estate plan (may include a will, trust, health care proxy, etc.)

If any of these tasks fall within the attorney's scope of employment, the paralegal may monitor completion of those activities to ensure they are carried out in a timely manner.

The initial fee agreement/letter of engagement should specify the point at which the attorney's responsibility to the client with respect to the case will end and, specifically, whether or not it includes post-divorce activity. Even with a clear agreement, it is wise to send the client a letter of termination of services when the representation concludes, noting any need for follow-up in various areas. Some attorneys conduct closing interviews with the client in which they review the representation from start to finish, discuss the results obtained, identify matters requiring the client's attention, and answer any questions the client may have.[39]

THE UNCONTESTED SCENARIO

This chapter has focused in large part on the divorce process in a contested case. However, it is estimated that more than ninety percent of divorce cases proceed on an uncontested basis. Although generally considerably less costly in terms of time and dollars, an uncontested divorce can still be very costly emotionally. The two primary ways in which a divorce is uncontested are (1) when the divorce is sought jointly by the parties and (2) when the defendant does not oppose the divorce and either participates without opposition or fails to respond at all. The following material briefly outlines the process when the divorce is jointly sought by the parties, who may proceed *pro se* or with the assistance of counsel at each stage.

- The parties make the decision to dissolve their marriage on an uncontested (and usually no-fault) basis with or without having participated in counseling and/or contacting attorneys.
- The parties (with or without the assistance of dispute resolution options) negotiate the terms of an agreement resolving all of their marital rights and obligations and dividing their personal property and realty.
- The parties identify the proper forum in which to file their action for divorce.
- The parties draft and file their Joint Petition for Divorce, usually accompanied by the following:
  - Filing fee (or request for waiver, if eligible)
  - Certified copy of the parties' marriage certificate
  - Joint affidavit of irretrievable breakdown of the marriage
  - Financial statements
  - Fully executed separation agreement
  - Affidavit disclosing any care and custody proceedings, if the parties have minor children
  - Certificates of Completion of Parent Education Program, if required
  - Parenting Plan, if required
  - Child support guidelines worksheet, if there are minor children
  - Income assignment Worksheet, if applicable
- The parties request a Final Hearing (sometimes called a Request for Trial).
- The Final Hearing takes place, and the court renders a judgment.

Some courts require that both parties (or their respective attorneys) be present at the final hearing unless an absence is excused by the court. However, the trend is toward minimizing court appearances, and some jurisdictions no longer require either party to be present in a joint action. Hearings on joint petitions are customarily quite brief (five to fifteen minutes). However, a limited number of questions are usually asked so that it is apparent the court has made some inquiry and not simply rubber-stamped the parties' agreement. If the parties are represented, the court may have counsel question their clients. If a party is unrepresented, the court will conduct the questioning. The questions are very basic and usually address the following:

- parties' names and addresses
- facts about the marriage: when and where the parties married and when and where they last lived together as husband and wife
- names and ages of minor children, if any
- parties' shared belief that the marriage is irretrievably broken
- the separation agreement: Have the parties read it, discussed it with counsel, understood its terms, and signed it voluntarily?

The court may then ask specific questions on key issues such as insurance coverage, custodial arrangements, wage assignment, waivers of spousal support, etc. It is important that the parties understand the terms of the agreement so they can respond intelligently if asked about them.

Even in an uncontested divorce, post-decree activity is sometimes warranted, including:

- Post-Trial Motions
- Actions to enforce the judgment (Contempt actions, etc.)
- Modifications of the Judgment (based on substantial change in circumstances)

CHAPTER **SUMMARY**

"The culture of divorce" has changed dramatically over the past four decades from a fault-based system that made litigation inevitable to one that emphasizes the parties' capacity to resolve their differences without blame and courtroom battles. The focus has shifted from a preoccupation with fault and morality to one emphasizing economics and the nature of marriage, and particularly of parenthood, as a partnership that does not necessarily end upon divorce. The no-fault model recognizes the complexity of human relationships and the likelihood that in any given marriage, no one party bears full responsibility for its success or failure.

Couples who want to separate or dissolve their relationship have four potential legal options, depending on the facts of the case: divorce, legal separation, separate support, and annulment. For some individuals, it is also important to seek a religious termination of the marital relationship that will allow them to remarry within their faith.

Although the bulk of the content of this chapter describes the sequence of events in a contested case, approximately ninety percent of divorces are obtained without the necessity of a trial. To some extent, this is the result of an increasing emphasis by the legal profession, including the courts, on the use of alternative methods of resolving disputes such as direct negotiation between the parties, mediation, collaborative law, negotiation through counsel, neutral case evaluation, and arbitration.

The content of this chapter highlights the basic stages of the divorce process. Depending on his or her skills and experience, the paralegal may play a key role at virtually every stage of the divorce process in both uncontested and contested cases. Various aspects of that role are described in this chapter.

KEY **TERMS**

Adultery	Appellee	Complaint
Alternative dispute resolution	Arbitration	Conclusions of law
Annulment	Bifurcated divorce	Condonation
Answer	Binding arbitration	Conflict of law
Appearance	Collaborative law	Connivance
Appellant	Collusion	Constructive desertion

Constructive trust
Counterclaim
Court of equity
Covenant marriage
Criminal conversation
Cruel and abusive treatment
Declaratory Judgment
Defense
Desertion/abandonment
Discovery
Divorce
Divorce *a mensa et thoro*
Divorce *a vinculo matrimonii*
Doctrine of comparative rectitude
Domicile
Dual divorce
Exhibit Notebook
Ex parte motion
Fault grounds
Fee agreement
Final Judgment/Judgment Absolute
Get
Ground for divorce

Guardian *ad litem* (GAL)
In rem jurisdiction
Interlocutory Decree/Decree *Nisi*
Irreconcilable differences
Legal separation
Letter of engagement
Letter of nonengagement/declination
Living separate and apart
Long-arm statute
Marital communications privilege
Mediation
Memorandum of *lis pendens*
Military affidavit
Motion
Motions *in limine*
Motion to Dismiss
Motion to Vacate the Judgment
Neutral case evaluation
No-fault divorce
No-fault grounds
Nonbinding arbitration
Parenting coordinator
Pendente lite

Personal jurisdiction
Preponderance of the evidence
Proposed Findings of Fact
Pro se
Provocation
Recrimination
Separate maintenance
Separation agreement
Service of process
Specific performance
Stipulation
Subject matter jurisdiction
Subpoena
Subpoena *duces tecum*
Summons
Talak
Temporary orders
Trial Notebook
Trustee process
Venue
Void *ab initio*
Voidable

REVIEW **QUESTIONS**

1. Describe how the "culture of divorce" has changed over the past forty years.

2. Identify the four legal proceedings parties use to separate from each other or dissolve their marriage.

3. Describe the major distinction in the effect of a religious and a civil divorce or annulment in the United States.

4. Distinguish between a divorce *a vinculo matrimonii* and a divorce *a mensa et thoro.*

5. Define "bifurcated divorce" and identify a circumstance in which one might occur.

6. Describe at least three tasks that should be accomplished in an initial interview.

7. Identify the primary purposes of a letter of engagement, a letter of nonengagement or declination, and a closing letter.

8. Identify the six most common dispute resolution options used in divorce cases. What are the primary differences among them (particularly with respect to the role of the attorney)?

9. Define subject matter, personal (*in personam*), and *in rem* jurisdiction in the divorce context and indicate how each is acquired by a court.

10. Define "venue."

11. Identify the primary difference between a fault and a no-fault ground for divorce.

12. Identify and describe the two primary no-fault grounds for divorce.

13. Identify and describe a minimum of four fault grounds for divorce existing in some states.

14. Identify a minimum of five defenses to a divorce action.

15. Describe the nature and purpose of a complaint.

16. Identify the primary ways of serving process.

17. Describe the nature and purpose of a long-arm statute.

18. Identify the two most common responses of a defendant to an action for divorce and indicate the differences between them.

19. Describe the nature and purpose of temporary orders.

20. Identify a minimum of five kinds of motions sometimes filed in divorce actions while the litigation is pending.

21. Explain why a party might choose to file a motion on an *ex parte* basis. Give an example.

22. Define "discovery." What is its purpose? What are the primary methods of discovery?

23. Describe the nature and purpose of a separation agreement.

24. Describe the nature and purpose of a pretrial memorandum.

25. Describe what happens at a pretrial conference.
26. Identify and describe the four major documents prepared and filed in anticipation of trial.
27. Describe the nature and purposes of Trial Notebooks.
28. Explain what a stipulation is and indicate its effect when introduced at a hearing or at trial.
29. Identify the most common kinds of divorce-related legal proceedings brought post-divorce.
30. Describe the role of the paralegal in the various stages of the divorce process

FOCUS ON **THE JOB**

THE FACTS

David and Marie Rogers were married on July 17, 1993, in your city and state at St. Patrick's Church. Marie was born on September 7, 1973, and David was born on October 3, 1972. Both parties were born in your city and state and were raised as devout Catholics. David no longer practices his religion, but Marie has remained very active in her local church. The children often attend Mass with her, and this is a source of considerable tension between the parties.

David and Marie were high school sweethearts. After graduation from high school, Marie remained at home with her parents. She worked as a cashier in a local Starbucks and attended "beauty school" in the evenings at the regional vocational school. She was unable to complete her course of study because her mother became very ill and Marie had to stay home and take care of her. David went off to your state's university to study mathematics.

David and Marie initially planned to get married following David's graduation from college, and in the interim, they continued to see each other during his school vacations. During his senior year, David wrote to Marie and said he wanted to date other women. Marie was devastated. During spring break, they went to Florida and, while there, had sexual relations for the first and only time prior to marriage. Marie became pregnant and, as a result of the pregnancy, the couple decided to get married. Because of David's concerns that they were rushing into marriage prematurely, they executed a premarital agreement essentially providing that any assets or liabilities a party had entering the marriage would remain that party's, and any assets and liabilities accruing during the marriage would be divided equally. Despite his reservations about the timing, David thought getting married was what he wanted and should do. Now, in retrospect, he feels he had no choice. The wedding was held shortly after his graduation, and their son, Jon, was born on December 12, 1993. A second son, Charles, was born on May 12, 1996, and a daughter, Megan, was born on June 16, 2003.

Since their marriage, David has been employed as a math teacher at the local community college. Initially he had hoped to begin working on his master's degree in math following graduation while Marie continued her cashier's job, but the parties jointly decided it was important for Marie to stay home with Jon. Accordingly, to his great disappointment, he was unable to pursue his educational plans.

David earns $58,000 a year at his teaching job, and his family is covered on his insurance plan. He has paid into the state employees' pension fund since starting at the college in 1993 and became vested after ten years of service. He also does odd jobs for people during the summer months and on weekends and earns an additional $8,000 a year from that work. He is paid "under the table" for these odd jobs and the couple has never paid taxes on this income. They have filed a joint return every year since they married. David has been a good provider and a devoted father to his two sons, but, as discussed below, has had trouble relating to his daughter.

Since the birth of Jon, Marie has not been employed outside of the home. She maintains the home and is the primary caretaker of the children. At the time Marie became pregnant with Megan, David had been accepted into a master's degree program and Marie was going to return to work to help support the family. The plan was that when David completed his degree, he would then support Marie through beauty school and possibly a four-year-degree program if she wanted to go to college.

David believes that Marie got pregnant deliberately by failing to use birth control. He thinks that she was trying to sabotage his plans to return to school as she had done years before. He asked her to have an abortion, but she refused, given her strong religious beliefs. This was a major crisis in their relationship, and, during the pregnancy, the marriage began to fall apart. David's frustration kept building and he became increasingly more resentful that, once again, he would have to defer his educational plans because of Marie's pregnancy.

David remained bitter and, according to Marie, has never bonded with Megan. His interaction with her has been minimal, although he continues to engage in weekend activities with the boys. He acknowledges that he has difficulties with his daughter but says he was initially the same way with his boys until they got a little older and could talk and "do things."

Since Megan's birth, Marie has experienced several bouts of severe depression. She has been briefly hospitalized twice and is seeing a therapist regularly. She gained fifty pounds during her pregnancy with Megan and has put on an additional thirty pounds since giving birth. According to David, she also has begun to drink heavily and has neglected the household and the children. On several occasions, a neighbor has found her wandering around the neighborhood so inebriated that she was unable to find her way home.

Marie claims that David has become verbally abusive and has hit her on a few occasions. He denies hitting her, but acknowledges that he sometimes may have sounded "gruff" when he was particularly upset by her conduct. He says that she has closed herself off to any emotional support from him and has refused to engage in sexual relations since she became pregnant with Megan. He admits feeling trapped and overwhelmed by Marie's problems. This is particularly painful for him because he saw his own parents weighed down by the responsibilities of several children and vowed the same thing would never happen to him.

As for the children, Megan appears to be developmentally delayed. No one is quite sure why, but her pediatrician speculates that it may be due to the problems at home. A specialized play group has been recommended, but David and Marie have not followed through on the recommendation. The pediatrician has struggled with whether or not to file an abuse and neglect complaint, but so far has opted against doing this.

A few months ago, Jon was caught shoplifting CDs from a local store, but the store let him "work off" the offense without calling the police. David and Marie also learned recently that he and several other boys have been gathering at a friend's house after school to watch pornographic videos that an older neighbor rents for them. There is some concern that they may also have involved some younger neighborhood children in this activity at the man's request. Each parent blames the other for Jon's behavior. Marie is at a loss as to how to deal with him, and David tends to be quite strict and restricts the teenager's activities when Jon is with him.

Charles is doing extremely well in school academically but has limited social skills and no friends. He largely keeps to himself and Marie says he is a real computer "geek," spending hours at a time in front of the computer screen like his father. He says he likes being with his dad because they are interested in a lot of the same things.

Things finally reached the breaking point on February 1, 2008, and David moved out of the house at 412 Hale Street, your city and town (your area code-555–2712). He has refused to go to any kind of counseling despite Marie's request unless the whole family is involved. He has moved to a small apartment at 412 High Street, your city and town (your area code-555–3010). David sees the boys on a regular basis each weekend and has spent a little time with Megan, although Marie seems very nervous about him doing so. David claims that since he has moved out, the house has become a "pigsty" and on several occasions when he went to pick up the boys, the children were filthy, there were no clean clothes to pack for the weekend, and there was virtually no food in the refrigerator. On one Sunday, it was ten in the morning and the children asked him if they could go

get some breakfast before going to his apartment. Marie was at home, asleep on the couch in the living room, and David claims he smelled alcohol all around her. Marie claims he woke her up, shook her, and threatened to choke her if she did not get her act together. David doesn't deny shaking her but does deny threatening her. He said he shook her in a desperate effort to try and get through to her. Marie acknowledges that she has a problem dealing with caring for the home and the children on her own, but says that she is not neglectful and that David is just a compulsive "neatnik," a regular Mr. Monk who can't stand it when everything isn't just so.

Since he left the marital home, David has been dating a co-worker, Trisha Cronin. Marie suspects that he began dating her after she got pregnant with Megan, but David denies this. Trish is also a teacher and is working on a Ph.D. in comparative literature. She loves children and is unable to have any of her own because of a chronic medical condition. She and David are planning on moving in together at the end of the spring semester.

With respect to assets, the parties own the small condominium in which Marie presently resides with the children. They paid $140,000 for it shortly after their marriage with a $20,000 down payment. It is now assessed at about $200,000, but David claims the real estate market is greatly overinflated. They still owe about $77,000 on the mortgage. The money for the down payment came half from wedding presents and half from the proceeds of an insurance settlement from an automobile accident that Marie had been in. They have about $1,800 in a savings account and owe about $3,500 in credit card debt. David has about $19,000 in his retirement account and a government bond (with a present value of $15,000) that his father gave him before the parties married and that he has kept for a rainy day or an emergency. He also has a collection of seascape paintings by local artists that he began collecting as a small boy. Marie has a collection of figurines valued at about $3,500 and also a collection of Hummel figures she inherited from her grandmother as a young child. They own basic household furnishings valued at not more than $10,000 along with two cars, a Honda and a Toyota of relatively equivalent value, both of which are paid for.

David filed for divorce on March 15, 2008. The Docket number assigned to the case is 08D-1351-DI1 (or another docket number provided by your professor). David's attorney is: Juliana Wilson, Esq.

> 390 Main Street
> Your city, town, and zip code
> > Your area code-555–2354
> > Bar Number: 0283412

David's social security number is 022–34–1919.

Marie will eventually retain Attorney James Crivaro. His address is 30 Washington Street in your city and town.

His phone number is your area code-555-2424. His Bar Number is 346271. Marie's social security number is 044–43–6704.

THE ASSIGNMENT

The class should be divided into an even number of groups with up to six students in each group. Half of the groups will work as a family law team representing David and the other half representing Marie. The students on each team should develop a method for assigning the following tasks (e.g., by choice, drawing assignments, etc.), unless otherwise assigned by the course instructor.

David's Team	**Marie's Team**
Two students role-play David's initial interview, one as David and one as the paralegal	Two students role-play Marie's initial interview, one as Marie and one as the paralegal
Draft a Complaint for Divorce	Draft an Answer (and a possible Counterclaim for Divorce) in response to David's Complaint
Draft a Motion for Temporary Orders with a Supporting Affidavit and Proposed Order	Draft a Motion for Temporary Orders with a Supporting Affidavit and Proposed Order
Draft a Motion for Appointment of a Guardian *ad litem*, with a supporting Affidavit and Proposed Order	Draft a Motion for Attorney's Fees with appropriate Affidavits and a Proposed Order
Draft a Motion for Appointment of an Appraiser with a supporting Affidavit and a Proposed Order (to appraise the value of the marital home)	Draft a Motion for Appointment of an Appraiser with a supporting Affidavit and a Proposed Order (to appraise the value of David's art collection)

FOCUS ON **ETHICS**

Assume that you are the paralegal working for the attorney representing Marie in the above comprehensive fact pattern. You were present at the initial interview conducted with her by your supervisor, Attorney Crivaro. It was clear during that interview that Marie's top priority is to gain custody of all three children at all costs and that she is afraid David is going to try to take them away from her because of her psychological problems, alleged drinking, and poor house-keeping. Since the initial interview you have been asked to conduct a follow-up meeting with her to discuss a potential counterclaim for divorce and a motion for temporary orders including custody. In that interview, Marie tells you that she is prepared to falsely claim that the reason David is having trouble developing a relationship with Megan is that he has been sexually abusing her. She says in this day and age, no judge is going to take a chance awarding custody to a father who may be sexually abusing his daughter. Marie says she has heard from her divorced friends that if she can get temporary custody, she is a "shoo-in" for permanent custody. Attorney Crivaro does little family law work in her practice but is a respected attorney known for her diligent advocacy on behalf of her clients. She has asked you to report to her regarding the interview and to make recommendations regarding the appropriate actions to be taken with respect to the counterclaim, the motion for temporary orders, and Marie personally.

Review the ethical canons for paralegals promulgated by the National Federation of Paralegal Associations (NFPA), contained in Appendix B of this text. Also obtain a copy of the ethical standards governing attorneys in your state. You should prepare a memorandum to your supervisor reporting the result of the interview and your recommendations with this material as a backdrop or frame of reference. Use the following basic format:

INTEROFFICE MEMORANDUM

TO: *Your supervisor*

FROM: *Your name*

RE: *Follow-up Interview with Marie Rogers*

DATE:

CASE: *David Rogers v. Marie Rogers*

OFFICE FILE NUMBER/ DOCKET NUMBER:

Brief description of assignment: *What is it that you have been asked to do?*

Summary of interview: *Summarize the highlights of the interview.*

Ethical issues implicated: *Identify the ethical duties the paralegal and attorney have that are related to this situation and a future course of action.*

Analysis of the issues: *Discuss the applicability of the identified ethical duties to the facts of the case.*

Recommendations: *What actions do you recommend be taken? Suggestion: You may want to consider more than one scenario.*

FOCUS ON **CASE LAW**

The Oklahoma case *Barnes v. Barnes*, 2005 Ok 1, 107 P.3d 560 (2005), is located on the companion website for this text in the material related to Chapter 6. Locate and read the case and then respond to the following questions.

1. Describe the legal history of the case: What kind of a case is it? Where was it heard prior to reaching the Oklahoma Supreme Court and with what result?

2. What was the custodial arrangement pursuant to the divorce decree?

3. When, why, and based on what authority did the lower court enter the Order Appointing Parenting Coordinator?

4. Did the parents agree that the parenting coordinator should be appointed?

5. What were the responsibilities of the parenting coordinator and who spelled them out?

6. What was the mother's basic objection to the parenting coordinator after she was appointed by the court?

7. What issues did the wife appeal (ultimately to the Oklahoma Supreme Court)?

8. What was the outcome with respect to the issue of attorney's fees and why? What was the rationale provided by the court?

9. What was the outcome with respect to the issue of child care costs and why? What was the rationale provided by the court?

10. The wife in this case claims that the Oklahoma Parenting Coordination Act violates her right to equal protection under the U.S. and Oklahoma Constitutions. Does the court agree? Based on its analysis:

   a. What is the constitutionally protected fundamental right she claims is being taken away from her?

   b. What is the class of persons affected by the statute?

   c. Is the classification arbitrary or capricious?

   d. What governmental aim or purpose does the statute serve?

   e. Is the classification reasonably related to that end? How so?

11. The wife also claims that the statute violates her right to due process under the state and federal Constitutions. What interests does the court balance in determining whether or not her due process rights were violated? What does the Oklahoma Supreme Court conclude?

FOCUS ON **STATE LAW AND PROCEDURE**

1. Locate the section(s) of your state's statutes or rules of procedure governing service of process in domestic relations matters. What are the proper citations for those statutes and/or rules? How may service be effected on resident and nonresident defendants? Does the long-arm statute contain any provisions that specifically address family law actions? What are they?

2. What are the grounds for divorce in your state? Are both fault and no-fault grounds available?

3. What residency requirement, if any, must a plaintiff satisfy in your state in order to be able to file a complaint for divorce?

FOCUS ON **TECHNOLOGY**

WEBSITES OF INTEREST

http://www.abanet.org

This is the website of the American Bar Association. Go to the website and search for divorce charts containing state-by-state information, particularly Chart 4 Grounds for Divorce and Residency Requirements.

http://www.adrlawinfo.com

This site provides a wealth of information about family and divorce mediation state to state. It also provides links to various model standards for mediation and arbitration.

http://www.agunah.org

This is the website of an organization called Agunah, Inc., which functions as a support for orthodox Jewish women who are "chained to dead marriages" because their spouses have refused to grant them a Jewish divorce.

http://www.divorcelawinfo.com

This is the website for the Divorce Law Information Center. It offers "do-it-yourself divorce kits," and state-by-state divorce and family law information including child support calculators. Caution should always be exercised prior to actually using unofficial forms from commercial sites.

http://www.divorcelinks.com

This site offers links to state and federal divorce laws by topic.

http://www.divorcenet.com

This site offers links to state divorce laws, indicating statutory references and brief narratives on topics such as residence, grounds for divorce, approaches to division of property, alimony, and child custody, visitation, and support.

http://www.divorcesource.com

The site provides information on divorce laws by state.

http://www.findlaw.com

This is a particularly well-organized site with access to resources for both public and professional inquirers. It provides both general and state-specific information, including access to the laws of all fifty states on divorce and related topics.

ASSIGNMENTS

1. Determine which, if any, divorce-related forms are available online in the state in which you are studying family law. Several states (e.g., California, Colorado, Hawaii, Maryland, Massachusetts, New Hampshire, Wisconsin, etc.) have state-sponsored sites (through courts or law libraries) that provide basic family forms that can be printed or completed online. (See Appendix D: Websites of General Interest.)

2. Locate and visit a website that contains information about divorce laws in all fifty states and describe the range of information provided with respect to your state.

3. Many people believe that the institution and traditional significance of marriage is seriously threatened by the no-fault divorce and same-sex marriage movements in particular. A number of national organizations and initiatives such as the Alliance for Marriage, the National Marriage Project, and the covenant marriage initiative have emerged, seeking to "save" marriage. Locate online four websites, two supporting no-fault divorce and two opposing it. What are the arguments on each side? Do you think covenant marriage is a good vehicle for resolving the differences? Why?

chapter seven

DISCOVERY AND FINANCIAL STATEMENTS

IN THIS CHAPTER YOU WILL LEARN

- What discovery is—its nature, purpose, and scope
- What informal discovery includes
- What the various formal discovery methods are
- What e-discovery is
- What kinds of objections can be made to discovery requests
- How to locate and complete financial affidavits
- How to uncover hidden assets
- What the role of the paralegal is in the discovery process
- What the court's role is in discovery

Walt and Renee have been married for more than three decades. Throughout the marriage he has totally controlled the parties' finances and, it would appear, not always to his wife's benefit. Now that she has filed for divorce, he has no desire to share information with her or her attorney about whatever modest assets he may have accumulated.

Discovery is one of the working tools of the legal profession. It seems clear and has long been recognized that discovery should provide a party access to anything that is evidence in his case.[1]

DEFINITION OF DISCOVERY

Technically, ***discovery*** is the formal process by which parties engaged in litigation seek factual information and materials known by and available to other parties and potential witnesses in the action. More broadly viewed, it refers both to formal techniques of discovery governed by procedural rules and to less formal investigative initiatives, such as interviews with potential witnesses and the searching of public records.

Discovery
the process of gathering information relevant to a matter at issue; includes both formal and informal methods

PURPOSE OF DISCOVERY

The primary purpose of discovery is to gather as much information about a case as possible so that attorneys can make appropriate recommendations and clients can make informed decisions regarding their options, including whether they should settle a case or proceed to trial. In uncontested cases or cases involving few assets and no dispute with respect to custody, little or no discovery may be sought. In more complex or hotly contested cases in which it is appropriate, extensive discovery may be pursued.

Discovery can be very expensive, but a failure to conduct adequate discovery when it is warranted can be disastrous. In some instances, the family law team may fail to achieve the best possible result for the client. In the most egregious cases, a failure to conduct discovery may result in a malpractice action against an attorney. (See Paralegal Application 7.1.) In many cases, one of the parties may have significantly more resources than the other and be better positioned to conduct discovery. In such situations, the court may entertain a motion for attorneys' fees to allow the disadvantaged party to pursue or defend the action in order to avoid being forced to accept a settlement based on insufficient information.

PARALEGAL APPLICATION 7.1

WHAT IF THE CLIENT WILL NOT AUTHORIZE DISCOVERY?

In some circumstances, after conducting interviews and examining various documents, the attorney may tell the client that it appears the other party has removed funds from certain accounts and is "hiding" them. Further discovery could be used to trace and locate those funds, but not without expense. Even though discovery might well result in a significantly more favorable property division settlement in the long run, the client may say that he or she simply cannot afford additional legal costs and insist that no further discovery be conducted, despite the attorney's advice.

In such situations, it is wise for the attorney to have the paralegal draft a letter to the client reiterating the advice given and its potential benefits and costs. The letter also should confirm that, notwithstanding that advice, the attorney has been explicitly directed by the client not to conduct further discovery. To avoid any misunderstanding, the client may be advised that the letter is forthcoming and, in some circumstances, be asked to provide a written acknowledgment of receipt. Such a letter, promptly sent, documenting that the advice was given and specifically declined, would help defeat the client's later claim that he or she received inadequate representation to his or her considerable financial detriment.

SCOPE OF DISCOVERY

Technically, the scope of discovery is limited to information and material relevant to the subject matter of the case. For example, information regarding income and expenses is directly related to issues of spousal and child support as well as property division. In addition, the information or material requested must not be protected by a ***privilege*** such as the attorney-client or doctor-patient privilege. Although the information sought need not necessarily be admissible as evidence in its present form, it should be designed to lead to evidence that may be admissible at the time of trial.

In conducting comprehensive discovery, the family law team seeks information pertaining to each party and their respective claims, defenses, and requests for relief. As difficult as it is to explain to clients, consideration needs to be given to identifying the strengths and weaknesses of each of the parties and their respective positions.

Discovery is most commonly sought with respect to:

- financial assets and liabilities
- current income and expenses
- financial and nonfinancial contributions to the marriage
- dissipation of marital assets
- parenting history, skills, and weaknesses
- marital misconduct such as substance abuse, infidelity, or treatment that has endangered a party's health and safety if fault grounds for divorce continue to exist in the jurisdiction and/or conduct during the marriage is a factor the court considers when making property division decisions

Early in a case, a discovery strategy will be established. It will identify the kinds of information needed, the techniques to be utilized (both formal and informal), the sequencing of efforts, the assignment of tasks, and the projected cost. The plan may need to be modified after discussion with the client—particularly if there are cost constraints or if new informational needs are identified. Thorough research and preparation are essential, and the paralegal is often charged with considerable responsibility in the information-gathering effort. The nature and extent of an individual paralegal's role in this process is largely a function of his or her level of expertise. For example, an experienced paralegal may be asked to recommend a discovery plan and draft complex, sophisticated discovery requests. An entry-level paralegal is more likely to be asked to check "Blue Book" values, draft motions to compel, and prepare relatively standard discovery requests, such as Requests for production of employment contracts, insurance policies, or bank account statements. One of the most important tasks performed by paralegals is the marking of deadlines on all appropriate calendars. This includes both critical deadlines prescribed by rules governing discovery and related to scheduled court appearances, meetings and depositions, etc., and also self-imposed deadlines for completion of discovery-related tasks, allowing sufficient time for review and revision. Many paralegals find it useful to maintain a "tickler" file reminding themselves of upcoming review and submission dates.

INFORMAL DISCOVERY

Informal discovery may involve a variety of measures not usually governed by procedural rules. For example, a private investigator may be hired to document that a party who claims to be disabled and unable to work is actually attending

Privilege
a legal right or exemption granted to a person or a class of persons not to testify in a legal proceeding; generally based on the existence of a special relationship

---

Paralegal Practice Tip
Depositions in particular are sometimes used as open-ended "fishing expeditions" to obtain information, both admissible and inadmissible. Attorneys need to maintain a delicate balance between unethical questioning engaged in for an improper purpose (such as harassing or intimidating the ***deponent***) and strategic questioning conducted in the good-faith belief it will lead to admissible evidence.

Deposition
a method of pretrial discovery in which one party questions the other party or a third person under oath; responses to oral or written questions are reduced to writing for possible later use in a court proceeding

Deponent
the individual who is asked to respond under oath to questions asked in a deposition

Informal discovery
information gathering not governed by procedural rules, such as private investigations and searches of public records and "Blue Book" values

a gym "working out" and playing touch football with his old high school buddies. A search of public records may be conducted to establish that a party has purchased property in another state with his or her paramour. Marital property may be photographed to show that it has been allowed to fall into disrepair by the other party. Potential witnesses, such as coaches, counselors, school nurses, and teachers, may be interviewed to explore and document the impact of a parent's behavior on a child. The most useful resource is often the client. (See Paralegal Application 7.2.)

FORMAL DISCOVERY METHODS

Although *formal discovery* cannot be initiated until after a Complaint is filed, a considerable amount of informal discovery may be conducted while working with the client prior to filing. Such initial investigative efforts may shape the theory of a case and the action to be filed—for instance, a fault or no-fault Complaint for Divorce in states where both options are available. Once a Complaint is filed, some states initially require the parties to make *mandatory self-disclosure* of certain information before going to the effort and expense of the five traditional methods of formal discovery. (See Paralegal Application 7.3.)

Formal discovery
discovery methods that are subject to procedural and court rules

Mandatory self-disclosure
material specified by statute or court rule that each party in a particular legal action must provide to the other party within a certain period after filing and service of a summons and complaint

PARALEGAL APPLICATION 7.2

THE CLIENT AS A RESOURCE

When a client first seeks representation in a divorce action, he or she customarily is asked to respond to a Comprehensive Client Questionnaire (see sample available on the companion website for this text in the material related to Chapter 6). In addition, even before an action is filed, many attorneys ask clients to perform some initial informal discovery. The client may be asked to:

- Photograph the contents of the marital residence (house or apartment) with particular attention to any potentially valuable items such as jewelry, antiques, gun collections, and the like.

- Keep a journal concerning such topics as parenting situations reflecting the particular strengths or weaknesses of each parent, unexplained phone calls and absences from the home, incidents of abuse of any kind, work being performed "under the table," etc.

- Locate and make copies of important documents such as deeds, titles, registrations, bank account statements, credit card statements, travel materials (such as airline tickets and hotel invoices), employment records, brokerage account statements, state and federal tax returns, mortgage applications, etc.

- Make copies of relevant electronic documents such as e-mails and financial records.

- Make a list of the names, addresses, and telephone numbers of potential *lay witnesses* for the client and for the other party, and identify the matters about which they might testify.

- Make a list of the names, addresses, and contact numbers of any professionals, such as physicians, therapists, accountants, financial advisors, and appraisers, consulted by either or both of the parties for their benefit or the benefit of their children.

Lay witnesses
a witness who is not an expert on a matter at issue in a legal proceeding who testifies as to opinions based on firsthand knowledge

PARALEGAL APPLICATION 7.3

MANDATORY SELF-DISCLOSURE

In addition to financial statements, some states require by rule that each party auto-matically provide certain other documents to the opposing party within a certain period of time after the Complaint is filed and served. The Massachusetts rule gov-erning Mandatory Self-Disclosure of Financial Documents[2] provides that neither party can make discovery requests until mandatory disclosure is made. Absent agreement of the parties or order of the court, each party is required to deliver to the other, within forty-five days of service of the summons of an action for divorce or separate support, documents including the following:

- federal and state tax returns and supporting documentation for the past three years (individual, limited-partnership, and privately held corporate returns)

- bank statements for the prior three years for any bank accounts in the name of the party or jointly with another party for the benefit of either party or the parties' minor children

- the four most recent pay stubs from each employer for whom the party works

- documentation of the cost and nature of available health insurance coverage

- statements for the past three years for any securities, stocks, bonds, notes or obligations, certificates of deposit (for the benefit of either party or the minor children), 401(k), IRA, and pension plans (for all accounts listed on the party's financial statement)

- copies of any loan or mortgage applications filed within the past three years

- copies of any financial statements or statements of assets and liabilities prepared within the last three years

The five basic formal discovery methods are:

1. Interrogatories
2. Depositions
3. Requests for Admissions
4. Requests for Production of Documents or Things or Entry Upon Land
5. Requests for Physical or Mental Examinations

These methods are described in the following paragraphs, Exhibits, and Summary Table (Exhibit 7.3). The role of the paralegal is emphasized, given its potential im-portance in the discovery process.

Although the basic principles remain the same, the exact names for each of the discovery methods and the applicable procedural requirements may vary from state to state. For example, a Request for Production of Documents may be called a Demand for Documents or a Request for Production of Documents and Entry on Land, or it may be folded into a set of *interrogatories.* It may not be necessary to file any discovery documents with the court or to file only a certain type such as a **Request for Admissions** (in New Hampshire, for example) or a ***Request for a Physical or Mental Examination.*** In some states, such as Tennessee, the rules may vary from county to county. Because of these variations, it is critically important for the paralegal to be familiar with applicable terminology and rules governing discovery in general and domestic relations matters in particular.

In any given case, all, none, or some of the methods will be utilized, depend-ing on the nature and complexity of the case, how hotly it is contested, and the

Interrogatories
a method of discovery in which one party submits a series of written questions to an opposing party to be responded to in writing within a certain period of time under pain and penalty of perjury

Request for Physical or Mental Examination
a method of discovery in which one party requests that the court order the other party (or, in some instances, a third party) to submit to a physical or mental examination

financial resources of the parties. The sequence in which they are used may vary, but interrogatories are most commonly propounded first. Information obtained through most formal discovery methods is provided by the respondent under oath and is potentially very helpful to the requesting party. Customarily, states impose a duty to supplement responses if circumstances change, new information comes to light, or errors are discovered.

INTERROGATORIES

Interrogatories are written requests for information sent by a party to an opposing party in a lawsuit. Interrogatories must be responded to in writing under oath within a prescribed period, usually thirty days. The period for responding may be extended under the applicable rules of procedure if the interrogatories are served by mail. Jurisdictional rules of procedure typically provide when they may be served and limit the total number of interrogatories allowed (commonly fifty or fewer, not including subparts) absent permission of the court or agreement of the parties. They can usually be served all at once or in several sets, provided the total allowable limit is not exceeded. Many attorneys prefer to serve an initial set of fewer than the maximum number and hold the balance in reserve in case information is obtained warranting additional questions that initially could not have been anticipated. The primary strengths and weaknesses of interrogatories are described in Exhibit 7.3.

In order to be effective, interrogatories should be clear and concise, such that they produce specific and usable information. For example, a question such as "Do you have any retirement income" asked of a thirty-year-old working party tells us little. The question should request specific information with respect to any and all forms of retirement programs in which the respondent is participating. If the respondent is unaware of specifics, he or she is obligated to ascertain them prior to responding and to supplement responses later, if warranted.

Interrogatories (and depositions) commonly request specific information about the opposing party with respect to the following:

- basic background information, such as address, age, prior marriages, and children
- educational background, training, and job skills
- past and present employment as well as future plans
- real property owned individually or jointly with others before and during the marriage
- the nature and value of personal property, such as automobiles, jewelry, and collections (guns, artwork, collectibles, etc.), owned before and during the marriage
- how a party spends his or her leisure time (personal and social life and membership in any clubs, civic organizations, etc.)
- the other party's spending habits (what he or she spends money on, where he or she shops/dines, etc., whether he or she pays by cash or credit, etc.)
- income from all sources
- the responding party's investments, business interests, retirement accounts, interests in any trusts, anticipated inheritances, etc.
- bank accounts, safe deposit boxes, etc.
- financial liabilities
- the parties' respective strengths and weaknesses as parents, if applicable
- the opposing party's physical and mental health, treatment programs, physicians, and medications, etc.
- the history of the marriage, such as prior separations, counseling sought and obtained, conduct of the parties during the marriage, nature of changes in the parties' relationship during the marriage, etc.

As with all discovery requests, interrogatories should be tailored to the facts of each case. Caution needs to be exercised when relying on generic sets from form books or versions designed to meet the objectives in other cases handled by the office. Careful tailoring takes advantage of the opportunity to request relevant information. Failure to do so may give rise to accusations of harassment of the other party or to generation of unnecessary costs. A sample of the kinds of interrogatories that might be served in a fault case involving an allegation of adultery is provided on the companion website for this text in the resources related to this chapter.

PARALEGAL APPLICATION 7.4

INTERROGATORIES—THE POTENTIAL ROLE OF THE PARALEGAL

The paralegal must be familiar with the procedural rules in the jurisdiction governing each form of discovery in the family law context and with the established role of the paralegal in the firm where he or she is employed. **All discovery related tasks are carried out under the direction and supervision of an attorney**. The following reflects a common, but not necessarily universal, approach with respect to interrogatories.

IF SERVING INTERROGATORIES:

- Review the file to identify information needed (from the opposing party in particular).

- Discuss the information needs and discovery options with the supervising attorney, who will determine a discovery strategy (which methods will be used to obtain each kind of information).

- Draft proposed interrogatories for review by the client and the supervising attorney.

- Finalize interrogatories for review and signature(s) as required and then serve on the opposing party in the manner provided in local rules with a copy to the client.

- When answers are received, review them for completeness and, if incomplete, draft a letter for the supervising attorney's signature requesting that the responses be supplemented.

- If the responding party fails to respond or to supplement his or her answers, draft a motion to compel responses for review and possible filing.

- Summarize the responses and recommend follow-up measures, if warranted, such as questions for a second set of interrogatories or deposition questions.

IF RESPONDING TO INTERROGATORIES:

- Mark receipt and return dates on all appropriate calendars and also schedule draft and review dates for responses.

- Give a copy to the supervising attorney, who will make the legal determination as to whether any of the interrogatories call for privileged information and, thus, an objection rather than an answer, and, if appropriate, draft a motion for a *protective order*.

- Draft a letter to the client for the supervisor's signature explaining the process and enclose a copy of the interrogatories for review and preparation of initial responses within an appropriate timeline. The letter should also remind the client

continued

Paralegal Practice Tip

The paralegal should not serve the interrogatories until the supervising attorney has indicated his or her final approval. In addition to sending them to the other party, a limited number of states still require that interrogatories be filed with the court. Some states require the parties to file a notice of filing interrogatories and a notice of responding to and/or objecting to interrogatories.

Protective order
a court order restricting or prohibiting a party from unduly burdening an opposing party or third-party witness during the discovery process

that all answers must be true and accurate to the best of his or her knowledge, as they are provided under oath.

- Schedule a meeting for the client with the paralegal and/or the attorney as appropriate to review draft responses the client provides.

- Delete non-responsive answers, correct errors, complete incomplete responses, and note objections identified by the supervising attorney.

- If needed, draft a letter to opposing counsel requesting additional time to respond. If the request is denied, draft a motion asking the court to grant the requested extension in response time.

- Prepare final responses expressed in the light most favorable to the client, as long as the factual content is accurate and based on information provided by the client.

- Schedule a meeting in which the supervisor and the client review final responses and affix signatures in the required form.

- Serve the responses on the opposing party (and with the court, if required in the jurisdiction) along with a notice of responding to and/or objecting to interrogatories, if necessary.

DEPOSITIONS

In a deposition, one party asks the other party, or a third person who has or may have information and/or documents pertaining to the case, a series of questions to be answered under oath. The responses given are recorded verbatim by a court reporter or other individual licensed to record testimony. In some jurisdictions, depositions may be audio- or videotaped according to procedural rules.

The person being questioned is called the deponent. If the deponent is a party, a *Notice of Deposition* is sent to the deponent or his or her attorney, if represented, specifying the date, time, and location of the deposition. A party deponent is not required to bring any documents to a deposition unless specifically requested to do so. This is accomplished by combining a Notice of Deposition with a Request for Production of Documents. Even if the deponent does not bring documents to the deposition, his or her memory can be "refreshed" by being shown a particular document and asked if the document refreshes his or her memory about the topic of the question.

If the deponent is a third-party witness, such as an employer, the third party must be served with notice of the deposition by *subpoena.* A subpoena is a document signed by an officer of the court that requires the person who receives it to appear at the date, time, and place indicated under penalty of law. If it is requested that the deponent bring certain documents to the deposition, the subpoena is called a **subpoena duces tecum.** Sometimes the subpoena will specify that it can be satisfied by delivering the requested document(s) to the requesting attorney's office within a certain period of time, and then the actual deposition need not take place. In most, if not all, jurisdictions, third-party witnesses must be reimbursed for their related travel expenses.

Depositions usually take place in an attorney's office but may be scheduled at other locations that are mutually convenient. At the beginning of the deposition, the deponent is sworn in and promises to answer truthfully and to the best of his or her ability. Questions are usually asked orally (a deposition upon oral examination) but may be presented in written form. Counsel for the deponent has a limited role in the deposition and, depending on the jurisdiction, is usually restricted to clarifying information, registering objections, and indicating omissions to the deponent. However, the deponent customarily cannot consult with counsel prior to answering questions.

Notice of Deposition
the notification sent to an opponent (or his or her attorney, if represented) of an intention to depose him or her at a certain date, place, and time

Paralegal Practice Tip
As a courtesy and convenience, counsel will usually agree on a date, time, and place for the deposition in advance of notice to ensure the availability of counsel and the parties.

Subpoena
a document ordering a witness to appear and provide testimony in a legal proceeding such as a deposition, court hearing, or trial

Subpoena *duces tecum*
a subpoena ordering a witness to appear in a legal proceeding such as a deposition, court hearing, or trial and to bring with him or her specified documents, records, or things

Paralegal Practice Tip
Blank subpoenas can generally be obtained from the court and can be filled in with appropriate information as the need arises. They are then returned to the court to be issued.

Paralegal Practice Tip
In cases involving complex, large, and diverse marital assets or thorny custody and visitation issues, it may be necessary to schedule one or more "deposition days," during which a series of potential witnesses are deposed. This approach to scheduling is more efficient, convenient, and cost-effective for both parties and counsel than consuming several days over a more extended period.

Because of the costs associated with a deposition, once noticed, counsel for the parties may discuss the nature of the information sought and, if agreed, the deponent may voluntarily provide it without the need for the actual deposition. Although this happens occasionally, depositions are often designed to serve multiple purposes, such as observing the demeanor of the deponent when questioned under oath, assessing his or her credibility, creating a record that can be used at trial to impeach the deponent's testimony, and "fishing" for additional useful information. In such cases, depositions are unlikely to be canceled.

EXHIBIT 7.1 Sample Deposition Questions

The following questions are presented as a sampling of the kinds of questions commonly asked at depositions. One of the strengths of depositions as a discovery technique is that questions may be modified or expanded as responses lead to new areas worthy of pursuit.

1. Where are you presently employed?
2. What is your current salary?
3. Do you receive any additional compensation such as bonuses, tips, stock incentives, etc.?
4. Does your employer reimburse any of your expenses, such as meals or travel?
5. With respect to the marital residence, what do you estimate to be its present value?
6. Are there any mortgages or other liens on the property?
7. Do you recall what you paid for the house when you purchased it?
8. What was the amount of the down payment?
9. What was the source of funds for the down payment?
10. From what source of funds has the mortgage been paid during the marriage?
11. Do you presently have any credit card debt?
12. Is there a name on any of your credit card accounts other than your own?
13. I want to show you Exhibit 2. Do you recognize this credit card statement? Would you please identify the Exhibit for the record?
14. Let's look at some of the individual items on this statement starting with the $3,567 charge at the Casino Royale. . . .
15. Page 2 of the statement indicates a charge of $715 for a "bracelet" purchased at Shreve, Crump and High. For whom was this bracelet purchased?
16. Let's shift gears for a moment and look at your individual tax return for the 2007 tax year. Would you please identify this return for the record?
17. Calling your attention to Schedule B, do you see any interest income listed there?
18. How about dividends?
19. I have here a Financial Statement dated April 1, 2008, signed by you and filed with the court. Would you please identify this Statement for the record and verify that it was signed by you?
20. Looking at the statement, can you tell us where your interest and dividend producing assets appear?

PARALEGAL APPLICATION 7.5

DEPOSITIONS—THE POTENTIAL ROLE OF THE PARALEGAL

IF TAKING THE DEPOSITION:

- Make recommendations to the supervisor regarding witnesses who should be deposed.

- Prepare a notice of intent to take deposition if the person to be deposed is a party or a summons or summons *duces tecum* if the deponent is a nonparty.

- Arrange for service of the subpoena, if applicable, and later confirm that service has, in fact, been made. If the deponent is a party, serve notice on the opposing counsel.

- Draft recommended deposition questions.

- Organize information and documents, such as responses to interrogatories, witness statements, bank records, credit card statements, etc., that will be useful and/or referenced at the deposition. The materials should be organized in the order in which they will be addressed in the deposition.

- If the deponent was required to produce documents, review them for compliance with the request.

- If items are to be presented as exhibits at the deposition, they should ideally be marked by the reporter in advance of the start of the deposition. The supervising attorney will most likely want to have at least four parallel sets of documents available at the deposition: one clean copy to show to the deponent, one for the opponent's attorney, one marked up for personal use, and a fourth to give to the stenographer and have admitted as an Exhibit.

- Attend, listen carefully, and take notes during the deposition and be prepared to assist the attorney with locating any documents as appropriate or suggesting additional follow-up questions.

- Following the deposition, review the transcript (audiotape or videotape), prepare a summary (sometimes called a deposition digest), and make recommendations for follow-up.

- Arrange for any required payment to third-party deponents for travel expenses.

IF DEFENDING THE DEPOSITION:

- If the client is responding to a subpoena *duces tecum* and there is an objection to the requested production, draft a motion for a protective order and, if there is no objection, organize the document(s) he or she is asked to produce.

- If the client being deposed is a party, describe the process and assist the attorney in anticipating likely questions and preparing the client for questioning.

- Attend the deposition, listen carefully, take notes, and be prepared to assist the attorney with locating any documents as appropriate or suggesting clarifications, gaps, or errors in responses.

- Following the deposition, review the transcript for accuracy and correct mistakes as directed by the attorney in a manner consistent with applicable rules.

- Prepare a summary and recommendations for any necessary follow-up including the supplementing of responses if appropriate.

Paralegal Practice Tip

The paralegal should be alert to the rules governing a situation in which a subpoena is to be served in another state. A letter of request (sometimes called *letters rogatory*) is a document a court in one state issues to a court in another state requesting that the "foreign" court serve process on an individual or corporation within the foreign jurisdiction and return the proof of service for use in the pending case.

Letters rogatory
documents issued by a court in one state to a court in another state requesting that the "foreign" court serve process on an individual within the foreign jurisdiction

---

Paralegal Practice Tip

If taking the deposition the paralegal will usually be asked to schedule and arrange for payment of a qualified stenographer. If defending, the paralegal may be asked to order a copy of the deposition transcript.

Paralegal Practice Tip

Some attorneys choose to conduct mock depositions with their clients sufficiently in advance of an actual deposition to familiarize them with the process and the types of questions likely to be asked and to identify and address potential weaknesses in the deponent's performance.

REQUESTS FOR ADMISSIONS

Requests for Admission are written requests to an opposing party calling for an admission or denial of specific facts at issue or verification or denial of the genuineness of documents relevant to the case. Unlike Interrogatories, which are presented in the form of questions, Requests for Admission (or Requests to Admit, as they are termed in some jurisdictions) are presented as statements of fact. (See Exhibit 7.2.) Responses to requests are customarily short and include the following potential options:

- Admit the matter.
- Deny the matter.
- Indicate lack of sufficient knowledge to admit or deny the matter.
- State a specific objection to the request.
- Respond with a combination of the above (e.g., admit in part and deny in part).

A party who alleges lack of sufficient knowledge has a duty to look into the matter (examine his or her records, files, etc.) before responding. If a respondent denies a fact that is subsequently proven at trial, he or she may be assessed fees and costs incurred by the other party in proving the truth of the matter. If a party does

---

EXHIBIT 7.2 Sample Request for Admissions

STATE OF NEW HAMPSHIRE

HILLSBOROUGH, SS   **SUPERIOR COURT**

SOUTHERN DISTRICT   **DOCKET NO. 06-M-0000**

IN THE MATTER OF JOHN B. SMITH AND JANE SMITH

REQUEST FOR ADMISSIONS

John B. Smith, by his attorney, submits the following requests for admission to Jane Smith:

1. I admit that my husband and I separated on at least five (5) occasions during the five years of our marriage immediately preceding the filing of my pending action for divorce.
2. I admit that the attached deed to a property in Boring, Oregon, held in trust and bearing my name and signature, is authentic, genuine, and accurate.
3. I admit that the Bank North loan my husband and I obtained in 1999 was used to cover my tax liability (including interest and penalties) for previously undeclared income I earned as a waitress.
4. I admit that I have a joint bank account at First Third Bank with my friend, Alberto Bonilla.
5. I admit that I am now in good health and have been so throughout the past five (5) years.
6. I admit that my husband provided the initial down payment of $40,000 on the marital residence out of his own personal funds in 1995.
7. I admit that my husband performed all of the carpentry, plumbing, and electrical work completed over ten (10) full months when the marital home was fully renovated in 2002.

continued

8. I admit that the present value of the marital home is $250,000 based on an appraisal performed by a mutually agreed-upon appraiser in December of 2007.

9. I admit that I have contributed less than 30% of my income to the payment of joint expenses during the course of our marriage.

10. I admit that the signature on the attached application for a $150,000 mortgage from Citizen's Bank dated December 15, 2007 is my signature.

If any of the foregoing requests for admission is denied because of lack of information or knowledge, identify the request and give a detailed account of every effort made by you or your attorney to inquire into the subject matter of the request, including the date of each effort, the person making such effort, the substance of such effort, and the information obtained by such effort.

ANY PARTY, WHO WITHOUT GOOD REASON OR IN BAD FAITH, DENIES UNDER RULE 54 ANY SIGNATURE OR FACT WHICH HAS BEEN REQUESTED AND WHICH IS THEREAFTER PROVED, MAY, ON MOTION OF THE OTHER PARTY, BE ORDERED TO PAY THE REASONABLE EXPENSE, INCLUDING COUNSEL FEES, INCURRED BY SUCH OTHER PARTY.

Respectfully submitted,

John B. Smith

By his attorney,

_____

Juliana Wilson, Esq.

Address

Telephone No.: xxx-xxx-xxxx

Dated:_____

not object to the request and fails to respond to a Request for Admissions within the period prescribed by the applicable rules of procedure (usually thirty days), the content of the admissions is deemed admitted without further action, and the facts or authenticity of documents need not be proved at a subsequent hearing or trial.

Requests for admission are not often utilized. This is surprising, given their potential to help parties avoid significant time and expense and narrow the issues needing to be proved at trial. They may cover facts or documents about which no dispute is anticipated, clarify disputed issues, and confirm suspicions. Requests can cover a wide range of topics, but each individual request should address only one fact, document, or signature to avoid confusion and minimize denials. For example, a party may request that the other party admit

Paralegal Practice Tip
Attorneys are occasionally somewhat cavalier about responding in a timely manner to discovery requests. They may delay responding until a deadline passes and opposing counsel calls or files a motion to compel. This is not good practice in general, but with requests for admissions, it can have serious consequences.

Paralegal Practice Tip
If some or all of the requests are objected to, counsel may agree on a mutually acceptable revised request that can then be filed with the court if required. If a compromise cannot be reached, the court may consider the objections in a hearing at which both parties and their counsel are present.

PARALEGAL APPLICATION 7.6

REQUESTS FOR ADMISSIONS—THE POTENTIAL ROLE OF THE PARALEGAL

IF REQUESTING ADMISSIONS:

- Draft a proposed Request for Admissions based on facts, events, and documents involved in the case that may be suited to this technique.
- Review the draft with the client and the supervising attorney.
- Prepare a final draft that incorporates any corrections, additions, deletions, or edits.
- Serve the reviewed and signed request on opposing counsel and file it with the court in compliance with applicable procedural rules in the jurisdiction.
- Mark on all appropriate calendars the date when responses are due to be returned.
- If the response is incomplete or objections are raised, draft documents to implement the course of action determined by the supervising attorney. This may include a letter to and negotiation with opposing counsel or a motion to compel with an accompanying proposed order.
- If neither responses are received nor objections filed within the prescribed response period (usually thirty days), notify the supervising attorney, and the facts contained in the request will be deemed admitted in accordance with local governing rules.

IF RESPONDING TO A REQUEST:

- When a request is received, bring it to the attention of the supervising attorney and (if so directed) send a copy to the client, with a cover letter describing the nature, purpose, and effect of this form of discovery and asking that the client promptly review the requests and determine whether they are true and accurate.
- At the attorney's direction, schedule a meeting with the client in which the attorney will review the requests and potential responses and determine whether there are grounds for objecting to any of the requests.
- Draft a proposed final response for review by the client and the attorney.
- Serve the reviewed and signed response on the opposing party and file it with the court if required.

- that a Voluntary Acknowledgment of Parentage containing the parties' signatures is authentic, genuine, and accurate
- that the parties were married on a certain date at a certain location
- that one of the parties was the primary homemaker for the family during the marriage
- that one of the parties is in good health or has certain specified health problems
- that a deed to a property held in trust and bearing a party's name and signature is authentic, genuine, and accurate
- that a party removed a certain amount of funds from the parties' joint savings account on a particular date
- that the employee's insurance coverage provides for his or her children
- that the party has filed a pending wrongful termination suit against his or her employer
- that the party is receiving unemployment compensation
- that the party has been arrested for drunk driving on five occasions

When a request calls for authentification of a document or signature, a copy of the document at issue is attached to the request. If the responder admits that a document, a mortgage application, for example, is genuine, the application may be introduced at trial without having to be introduced through testimony of the mortgage broker. The party can then be questioned about the contents of the application, which may or may not contain accurate information. When applying for a mortgage, the applicant generally presents the most positive picture possible. That party will need to be able to explain discrepancies, if any, in the financial picture he or she presents at the time of the divorce action.

REQUESTS FOR PRODUCTION OF DOCUMENTS OR THINGS

A *Request for Production of Documents or Things* is a written request for documents or things in the possession, custody, or control of the opposing party or a nonparty third person (such as an employer) for inspection and copying, if necessary. Requests for production of documents most commonly seek financial records and information such as bank statements, tax returns, and employment records. They also can encompass other things as well, such as diaries, collections for appraisal, photographs, stock certificates, corporate by-laws, partnership agreements, trusts, deeds, wills, computers, hard drives and other files, e-mails, credit card records, airline tickets, deeds, and titles to motor vehicles, boats, and recreational vehicles, etc. Occasionally requests for production will ask that large items (vehicles, antique furniture, etc.) be made available for inspection, appraisal, and/or photographing.

Request for Production of Documents or Things
a method of pretrial discovery in which a party makes a written request that the other party, or a third person, produce specified documents or other tangible things for inspection and/or copying

As with all discovery requests, requests for production of documents and things should be tailored to the facts of each case. The request should state the time, place, and manner of production and be sufficiently specific that the responding party will be able to comply. For example, if requesting bank records, a request might read as follows: "Copies of all records of any accounts of any kind including, but not limited to, checking accounts, savings accounts, NOW accounts, Certificates of Deposit, and equity lines of credit with any bank, credit union, or other financial institution for the five years preceding the date of the request." A sample Request for Production of Documents or Things is in the Chapter 7 resources on the companion website.

The responding party must produce all documents or things requested unless there is a valid objection. For example, the items requested may be subject to a privilege or may not be in the possession or control of the responding party. Unreasonable and irrelevant requests may constitute harassment of the opposing party or a third party. On occasion, the materials requested may contain trade secrets or material about to be but not yet copyrighted or patented. In such situations, the responding party may file a motion for a protective order, or the parties may execute a confidentiality agreement (with or without the assistance of the court) warranting that confidentiality of certain information will be protected under penalty of law for failure to do so.

PARALEGAL APPLICATION 7.7

REQUESTS FOR PRODUCTION OF DOCUMENTS AND THINGS—THE POTENTIAL ROLE OF THE PARALEGAL

IF SERVING A REQUEST:

- Review the file to identify and compile a list of documents or things needed that are in the possession or control of the opposing party or of third parties such as the IRS, a banking institution, or an employer.

continued

- Discuss the information with the supervising attorney, who will determine a discovery strategy, including which documents and things to request and from whom.

- Draft a proposed Request for Production for review by the supervising attorney and the client.

- Finalize the request for review and signature(s) as required and then serve on the opposing party or third party in the manner provided in local rules.

- When production is received, compile a log and review production to confirm that it fully complies with the request and, if it does not, draft a letter requesting that the production be supplemented for the supervising attorney's review.

- If the responding party continues to fail to comply, draft a motion and proposed order to compel production for review and possible filing.

- Once received, organize the materials produced, summarize the response, and recommend follow-up measures, if warranted, such as questions for a first or follow-up set of interrogatories or deposition questions raised as a result of a review of the documents produced.

IF RESPONDING TO A REQUEST:

- Mark receipt and return dates on all appropriate calendars and also schedule response draft and review dates.

- Give a copy to the supervising attorney, who will make the legal determination as to whether any of the requests call for confidential or privileged information and thus a confidentiality agreement or objection rather than production.

- Draft a letter to the client, enclosing a copy of the request for review, and ask that he or she assemble as many of the requested materials as possible within an appropriate time frame.

- Schedule a meeting for the client with the paralegal and/or attorney as appropriate to review materials, filter out any not specifically requested, and remove any privileged documents based on the supervising attorney's instructions.

- If an extension is needed, notify the supervising attorney and draft a motion for extension of time for production (unless the supervising attorney negotiates a revised timeline with opposing counsel).

- Mark all appropriate calendars with revised draft, review, and return dates.

- Compile the production for delivery to the opposing party, being certain to limit it to material specifically requested and not privileged.

- Serve the materials on the opposing party in an appropriate manner after receiving authorization from the supervising attorney.

REQUEST FOR PHYSICAL OR MENTAL EXAMINATION

Unlike other discovery techniques, because of its intrusiveness a request to have a physical or mental examination conducted usually must be sought by motion. Generally, courts will grant such requests and compel attendance of a party or third person at an examination only after a hearing in which good cause is shown. There are sometimes circumstances in which a request may be appropriate, such as when

- A party raises his or her own or the other party's mental or physical health as an issue.
- The paternity of one or more of the parties' children is challenged.

- The mental instability or physical disability of a party is raised as a reason why he or she should be denied custody.
- One of the parties seeks alimony or a disproportional division of marital assets based on the alleged existence of a costly disability that makes it impossible for that party to be self-supporting.
- One of the parties seeks a divorce from the other on a fault ground that alleges the other party is a chronic alcoholic or abuser of other drugs.
- A party claims on his or her financial affidavit to have significant and continuing monthly costs for uninsured medical expenses or treatments of some kind.

Requests may also be made for examination of a third person in the custody of a party. For example, if a deviation from the child support guidelines is requested because of expenses associated with a child's medical condition, an examination and assessment of the child's treatment needs may be appropriate. An examination may also be appropriate in cases in which custody is at issue and a credible allegation of physical or sexual abuse of a child is raised. A sample Request for Physical or Psychiatric Examination is included in the Chapter 7 companion website resource material.

PARALEGAL APPLICATION 7.8

REQUESTS FOR PHYSICAL OR MENTAL EXAMINATION—THE POTENTIAL ROLE OF THE PARALEGAL

IF REQUESTING AN EXAMINATION:

- Review the case file and consider whether a physical or mental examination may be appropriate given the facts of the case and, if so, make a recommendation to the supervising attorney to that effect.
- Develop a list of proposed examiners (such lists often already exist in the resource files of a family law practice and may be maintained by a paralegal).
- If the attorney agrees, draft a Motion/Request for a Mental or Physical Examination and a proposed order as appropriate with an accompanying affidavit to be signed by the client in support of the motion.
- When approved and signed by the attorney, file the original request and proposed order with the court, serve it on the opposing party, and mark on the calendar the date of service and the date by which any objection to the request must be filed.
- If the opposing party does not file an objection within the period prescribed by the applicable rules of procedure, notify the supervising attorney for authorization to contact the office of the opposing counsel and make arrangements for scheduling the requested examination.
- If the opposing party does not submit to an examination within a reasonable period of time, notify the supervising attorney for authorization to prepare, file, and serve a motion to compel examination and a proposed order, with a copy to the client.
- When a hearing date is set, notify the attorney, mark the date on the calendar, and notify the client (by phone and in writing) that he or she should plan to be present for the hearing.
- If the examination subsequently occurs, be sure that the office receives a copy of the examiner's report and copies of the results of any tests for review and analysis, and suggest needed follow-up such as questions for the examiner if the report is introduced at trial.

continued

Paralegal Practice Tip
Before or after filing of a motion to compel, counsel for the parties may be able to negotiate an agreement covering the purpose and scope of the examination; the selection process for choosing the examiner; the date, time, and place of the examination; and the use to which the information obtained will be put. If the parties are unable to reach an agreement, the open hearing will proceed. The attorney and the paralegal will very likely prepare the client for the hearing and the kinds of questions that may be asked.

IF RESPONDING TO A REQUEST FOR AN EXAMINATION:

- When a request is received, the paralegal will customarily arrange a meeting for the attorney to discuss the request with the client and determine how to proceed.

- If there is no objection, the attorney will usually negotiate terms, which are confirmed in writing, limiting the nature, scope, and use of the examination.

- If there is an objection, draft the objection and supporting affidavit or memorandum for review.

- After review, finalize the objection, obtain the supervising attorney's signature, and file the objection with the court within the period provided by local rules (usually thirty days).

- When a hearing date is set on the objection, notify the attorney, mark it on the calendar, and notify the client (by phone and in writing) that he or she should plan to be present.

- If the examination is to take place, the paralegal may be asked to schedule it and ensure that the client keeps the appointment. On occasion, a paralegal may accompany the client to a medical examination. If questions arise (usually concerning the scope of the examination), the paralegal can contact the attorney for clarification and/or instructions.

- After the examination, a copy of the examiner's report and the results of any tests may be sought for review and analysis, but the client then is usually required to produce any similar medical reports in his or her custody or control. Under both state and federal law, the person examined may be required to execute releases waiving privacy rights with respect to medical records.

EXHIBIT 7.3 Summary Table Re Formal Discovery Methods

Expert
a person who, through education or experience, has developed special skill or knowledge in a particular subject

Interrogatories	Served on parties only	Strengths:
		Interrogatories are cost-effective.
		They can be designed to obtain information that can then be used as a basis for formulating other discovery requests.
		They may be used to identify potential witnesses, including *experts,* physicians, and co-respondents when adultery is alleged.
		Weaknesses:
		Interrogatories can usually be served only on parties and not on third persons.
		A responding party's responses are reviewed with counsel and carefully drafted to reveal as little potentially damaging information as possible.

continued

Responses to interrogatories are written. As a result, the requesting party does not have an opportunity to assess the respondent's credibility and potential weaknesses as a witness.

Depositions	Can be served on both parties and nonparty witnesses	**Strengths:**
		Depositions can be used with both parties and nonparty witnesses, including expert witnesses.
		Necessary information usually can be obtained more quickly than with other methods.
		The credibility and performance of the deponent under oath can be assessed.
		Follow-up and clarifying questions can be asked if further information is needed or if an answer is incomplete, evasive, or opens up a new area for inquiry.
		Weaknesses:
		Depositions are expensive. The costs are in the preparation, follow-up, and analysis time as well as in the conducting of the actual deposition, court reporter time, transcript preparation, and copying, each of which varies based on the length of the deposition.
		Deposition questions may reveal the deposing party's theory of the case and give the deponent a better chance to prepare for negotiation and/or trial.
Requests for Admissions	Served on parties only	**Strengths:**
		Requests for Admissions are cost-effective.
		They can be used to narrow the issues needing to be addressed at trial.
		They can be used to clarify disputed issues and to confirm suspicions.

continued

		Weaknesses: Requests may reveal the theory of the client's case and/or available defenses.
Requests for Production of Documents or Things or Entry upon Land	Can be served on both parties and nonparty witnesses	**Strengths:** These requests can be used with both parties and non-party witnesses. They allow a party to obtain critical information from entities such as employers and the IRS. They often yield a wealth of information that leads to further productive discovery.
		Weaknesses: They can be expensive, depending on the nature and extent of production.
Requests for Physical and Mental Examinations	Can be served on parties *Note*: The court may allow examinations of children in appropriate circumstances, such as when there are allegations of abuse.	**Strengths:** Requests may lead to discovery of otherwise privileged information.
		Weaknesses: Requests are highly intrusive and may exacerbate an already acrimonious dispute. Usually a request must be sought by motion, and such motions are granted only upon a showing of good cause.

ELECTRONIC DISCOVERY

Technology has greatly altered the manner in which businesses and individuals create, store, and retrieve information. The impact of this shift on a family law practice is dramatic and has particular implications for discovery. An attorney, paralegal, or computer forensics expert can potentially locate valuable information to support a case through *electronic discovery* (**e-discovery**). For example, in a case involving substantial assets including business interests, it may be necessary to access computer records of employees in one or more companies or partnerships in order to establish the value of a party's interest. Even in less complex cases, e-discovery may be useful. A case in point is a marriage in which one spouse has totally controlled the marital assets and has maintained detailed electronic records

Electronic discovery discovery of documents in electronic form; refers to any information created, stored, or utilized with computerized technology of any sort

of everything, from improvements on and maintenance of the marital home to income, investment, and tax records. (See Paralegal Application 7.9.)

The technology of e-discovery is complex and rapidly evolving. A paralegal who is well versed in and keeps abreast of developments in this area will be a real asset to any practice. An excellent overview of the current technology as of spring 2007 and its application is found in the winter 2007 "Family Advocate" published by the American Bar Association.[3] If you are a relative novice, it will be useful for you to be aware of some basics of computer information storage. Each "parcel" of information (letter, spreadsheet, picture, etc.) is stored in a file that also contains metadata—data that describes the file in terms of how large it is, what software was used to create it, when it was created, when it was last modified, etc. In addition, there can be (depending on the operating system in use) additional information that may be pertinent to your discovery. This additional information is stored outside the file and may include previous versions of the file (together with their metadata) as well as potentially recoverable, deleted versions or fragments. There may also be versions and/or related files stored on removable media such as floppy disks, tapes, memory "sticks," zip drives, etc. Finally, there are ways of encoding data and hiding it in otherwise innocuous files.

There is a broad range of costs in disruption, time, effort, equipment, and expertise that corresponds to the range of levels of complexity in electronic information retrieval. If all that is needed is a copy of a document from a trusted source, then a simple (and inexpensive) request for the document may suffice. At the other end of the spectrum, if what is needed are complex records concerning the values of multiple business interests of an uncooperative and deceptive opposing party, an e-discovery request may require the seizure of one or more computers and ancillary equipment for detailed inspection by forensic computing experts using sophisticated tools. It is important for the paralegal to understand what each situation requires and be prepared to specify it in appropriate discovery requests. (See Paralegal Application 7.9.)

PARALEGAL APPLICATION **7.9**

ELECTRONIC DISCOVERY

There are several steps that may be taken with respect to e-discovery. The three most common are the following:

- A letter may be sent to opposing counsel (or the opposing party directly if he or she is unrepresented) requesting that proactive steps be taken to preserve potential electronic evidence pending the divorce action. This approach presumes a positive relationship between the parties and an assumption that each will act in good faith.

- A request may be made for production of hard or electronic copies of documents, records, e-mails, files, etc., on the other party's computer and not otherwise accessible to the client.

- A request may be made for production/seizure of the other party's computer equipment, storage devices, etc. This request may be made by means of an *ex parte* motion to the court when there is a strong fear that the other party will destroy or alter the contents of the hard drive.

The approach taken depends in part on the nature of the documents sought, the reason for seeking them, the use to be made of them, and the relative likelihood of the other party altering or destroying them. For example, by obtaining the actual computer and its hard drive rather than hard copies of documents, one can obtain metadata that may reveal whether and how a particular document, account, or record has been altered.

OBJECTIONS TO DISCOVERY REQUESTS

A party who receives a request for discovery has a duty to respond to the request. In general, a party must respond to all questions and/or requests for which there is no legally accepted objection. Objections are commonly governed by procedural rules and common practice. If there is an appropriate objection, it is usually specifically stated in lieu of an answer. It is possible for a discovery request to call for information that is both relevant and unprivileged, and yet still be objectionable because it is unduly burdensome or cumulative, or because the information sought is not within the party's possession or control. Local rules may also structure the nature of responses. In some jurisdictions, in a deposition, for example, the question should be answered and the objection raised for consideration at trial.

The most common objections to discovery requests are the following:

1. **The request is unduly burdensome.**   For example, in a no-fault case involving minimal assets, the opposing party requests ten years of bank statements for an account that rarely held more than $2,000, and the parties have already essentially agreed on the division of their minimal property. Compliance with the request would be costly to the respondent and yield nothing productive for the party making the request.

2. **The request seeks discovery of material that is not relevant to the issues in the case.**   In a no-fault divorce action in a jurisdiction that does not consider marital fault as a factor in property division or spousal support decisions, requests for information pertaining to marital infidelity are very likely irrelevant. This would particularly be the case for questions related to an affair that took place ten years earlier, after which the parties reconciled and had three children together, or to an affair that occurred during a prior marriage.

3. **The document or information requested is not within the party's possession or control.**   In some marriages, one party has maintained control over the parties' finances, paying the bills, completing the tax returns, and maintaining records—often on a personal computer to which the other party has no access. In such circumstances, the other party may simply be incapable of complying with a discovery request calling for financial records.

4. **The document, thing, or information requested is protected by a privilege that is legally recognized within the jurisdiction.**   The most obvious privilege is the attorney-client privilege, which protects communications between the attorney and the client as well as the attorney's "work product." *Work product* customarily includes material prepared in anticipation of the litigation, such as comprehensive financial reports prepared by accountants. Most jurisdictions recognize additional privileges such as priest-penitent and doctor-patient privileges. A minority of jurisdictions recognize a social worker-client privilege and/or a parent-child privilege. A party may waive a privilege under certain circumstances. For example, if a spouse is seeking spousal support and/or a more favorable property settlement based upon an alleged health problem, information pertaining to that condition would likely be discoverable by the other party and would not be protected by a doctor-patient privilege.

5. **The information being sought is cumulative.** This objection is based on the argument that the party seeking the information previously has requested it in another request or format or already has the information in his or her possession or control.

Work product
written or oral material prepared for or by an attorney in preparation for litigation either planned or in progress

---

Paralegal Practice Tip
Because the paralegal is an agent of the client's attorney, acting under the attorney's direction and supervision, the paralegal's presence in client interviews or contributions to "work product" do not destroy the privileged character of those communications or materials.

6. **The form of the question is improper.** For example, the question is leading or redundant.

7. **The request is being made solely for the purpose of harassment.** For example, it is overbroad and asks for information unrelated to the period of the marriage, such as details about all income earned since the date the other party was first employed as a teenager. Such a request would be unreasonably broad in the context of most marriages contracted by adults. However, there may be rare instances in which such information would be relevant (e.g., if a child actor married at age seventeen).

8. **A respondent may raise a Fifth Amendment right against self-incrimination if appropriate.** For example, in a state where adultery still constitutes a criminal offense, a person may refuse to answer questions relating to an adulterous affair for at least the period falling within the applicable statute of limitations period.

FINANCIAL STATEMENTS

Every state requires each party to an action for divorce, separate support (or legal separation), or child support to exchange and file with the court a document containing basic financial information about his or her respective needs, resources, and liabilities. The document is commonly called a Financial Statement, a Financial Affidavit, or an Inventory of Assets and Liabilities, and it must be filed with the Complaint or within a certain period after the action is commenced. It is designed to provide the parties with data needed to inform their decisions, especially with respect to matters of support and property division. It also provides the court with a frame of reference for assessing the fairness of a proposed settlement or for making decisions in a contested case. The client is required to sign it under pain and penalty of perjury. Several states require that counsel also sign the document affirming that it does not contain information known to the attorney to be false. Clearly, a financial affidavit can be the single most important document presented to the court, as it not only provides essential information, but also reflects both the client's credibility and the attorney's level of preparedness.

The specific format of financial statements varies from state to state, but the basic information called for is essentially the same. All forms cover income, assets, expenses, and liabilities. Assets include both real property (real estate) and personal property (such as bank accounts, stocks and bonds, cash, collections, household furnishings/antiques, and notes payable to the party). Liabilities include such items as mortgages, equity loans, car loans, credit card debt, court judgments, debts owed, and the like. Some states, such as Massachusetts, have more than one form—one for parties of more modest means and a second, more detailed form for parties with more substantial income and assets. An example of a California Simplified Financial Statement is available on the companion website for this text in the material related to Chapter 7. A copy of a Financial Affidavit used in the State of Connecticut appears in the Exhibit 7.4.

The paralegal often is asked to coordinate preparation of financial statements. At first blush, completing an affidavit may appear to be a simple fill-in-the-blanks and tally-the-figures task. In cases involving few if any assets, completion of the form may be reasonably straightforward. Nonetheless, each affidavit requires careful attention, given its potential importance. Initially the client gathers the financial information for inclusion on the form provided by counsel or the court and completes a preliminary draft for review. Depending on the financial, organizational, literacy, and record-keeping skills of the client as well as the size and complexity of the marital estate, the paralegal may be assigned to work with the client on this task. The paralegal should

Paralegal Practice Tip
Many states now make divorce forms, including financial statements, available online. In addition, there are several software packages available that allow family law practitioners to create and print financial affidavits in approved formats, although it may be necessary to indicate that the form is computer generated and/or to print it on a particular color paper. Such programs are helpful because they automatically calculate the figures and store them for future use. However, considerable care must still be taken to ensure that the data input is accurate in initial and updated editions.

Paralegal Practice Tip

A helpful Guide to Documenting Asset Values is provided on the companion website for this text in the resource material related to Chapter 7.

verify that the figures provided are current, accurate, able to be documented to the greatest extent possible, and understood by the client. If necessary, the client needs to be able to respond to questions about the contents of the statement posed by the court or by the other party. For example, in the context of a deposition, it is not uncommon for a party to be questioned about:

- each and every expense item
- how each figure was calculated
- what documentary evidence exists to corroborate the figures
- how any discrepancies between income and expenses can be explained

EXHIBIT 7.4 Example of a Financial Affidvit—State of Connecticut

Courtesy of the State of Connecticut

FINANCIAL AFFIDAVIT
JD-FM-6 Rev. 1-08
P.B. 25-30

STATE OF CONNECTICUT
SUPERIOR COURT
www.jud.ct.gov

COURT USE ONLY
FINAFF

DOCKET NO.

FOR THE JUDICIAL DISTRICT OF | AT (Address of court) | NAME OF AFFIANT (Person submitting this form)

NAME OF CASE

☐ PLAINTIFF ☐ DEFENDANT

OCCUPATION | NAME OF EMPLOYER

ADDRESS OF EMPLOYER

A. WEEKLY INCOME FROM PRINCIPAL EMPLOYMENT (Use weekly average not fewer than 13 weeks)

DEDUCTIONS (Taxes, FICA, etc.)	AMOUNT/WEEK	DEDUCTIONS (Cont.)	AMOUNT/WEEK	
1.	$	4.	$	GROSS WKLY WAGE FROM PRINCIPAL EMPLOYMENT → $
2.	$	5.	$	TOTAL DEDUCTIONS → $
3.	$	6.	$	NET WEEKLY WAGE → $

B. ALL OTHER INCOME (Include in-kind compensation, gratuities, rents, interest, dividends, pension, etc.)

SOURCE OF INCOME	GROSS AMT/WK	SOURCE OF INCOME	GROSS AMT/WK	
1.	$	2.	$	GROSS WEEKLY INCOME FROM OTHER SOURCES → $
DEDUCTIONS	AMOUNT/WEEK	DEDUCTIONS	AMOUNT/WEEK	TOTAL DEDUCTIONS → $
	$		$	NET WEEKLY INCOME FROM OTHER SOURCES → $
	$		$	
	$		$	ADD "NET WEEKLY WAGE" FROM SECTION A, AND "NET WEEKLY INCOME" FROM SECTION B, AND ENTER TOTAL BELOW:
	$		$	
	$		$	A. TOTAL NET WEEKLY INCOME → $

1. WEEKLY INCOME

2. WEEKLY EXPENSES

1. RENT OR MORTGAGE	$			Gas/Oil	$	11. DAY CARE	$
2. REAL ESTATE TAXES	$	6. TRANSPORTATION		Repairs	$	12. OTHER (specify below)	
				Auto Loan	$		$
3. UTILITIES	Fuel	$		Public Trans.	$		$
	Electricity	$		Medical/ Dental	$		$
	Gas	$		Automo-bile	$		$
	Water	$	7. INSURANCE PREMIUMS	Home-owners	$		$
	Telephone	$		Life	$		$
	Trash Collection	$					
	Cable T.V.	$	8. MEDICAL/DENTAL	$		$
4. FOOD	$	9. CHILD SUPPORT (order of court)	$		$
5. CLOTHING	$	10. ALIMONY (order of court)	$	B. TOTAL WEEKLY EXPENSES → $

3. LIABILITIES (DEBTS)

CREDITOR (Do not include mortgages or loan balances that will be listed under assets.)	AMOUNT OF DEBT	BALANCE DUE	DATE DEBT INCURRED	WEEKLY PAYMENT
	$	$		$
	$	$		$
	$	$		$
	$	$		$
	$	$		$
	$	$		$
C. TOTAL LIABILITIES (Total Balance Due on Debts) →	$	D. TOTAL WEEKLY LIABILITY EXPENSE	$

(continued)

4. ASSETS	**A. Real Estate**	Home	ADDRESS	VALUE (Est) $	MORTGAGE $	EQUITY $
		Other:	ADDRESS	VALUE (Est) $	MORTGAGE $	EQUITY $
		Other:	ADDRESS	VALUE (Est) $	MORTGAGE $	EQUITY $

		YEAR	MAKE	MODEL	VALUE	LOAN BALANCE	EQUITY
	B. Motor Vehicles Car 1:				$	$	$
	Car 2:	YEAR	MAKE	MODEL	VALUE $	LOAN BALANCE $	EQUITY $

C. Other Personal Property	DESCRIBE AND STATE VALUE OF EACH ITEM	**TOTAL VALUE** $
D. Bank Accounts	BANK NAME, TYPE OF ACCOUNT, AND AMOUNT	**TOTAL BANK ACCOUNTS** $
E. Stocks, Bonds Mutual Funds	NAME OF COMPANY, NUMBER OF SHARES, AND VALUE	**TOTAL VALUE** $

	NAME OF INSURED	COMPANY	FACE AMOUNT	CASH VALUE	AMT. OF LOAN	
F. Insurance (exclude children)			$	$	$	**TOTAL VALUE**
			$	$	$	
			$	$	$	$

G. Deferred Compensation Plans	NAME OF PLAN (Individual I.R.A., 401K, Keogh, etc) AND APPROX. VALUE	**TOTAL VALUE (less loans)** $
H. All Other Assets		**TOTAL VALUE** $
I. Total	E. TOTAL CASH VALUE OF ALL ASSETS →	$

5. HEALTH INSURANCE	NAME AND ADDRESS OF HEALTH OR DENTAL INSURANCE CARRIER (Do not include policy number)
	NAME(S) OF PERSON(S) COVERED BY THE POLICY

SUMMARY
(Use the amounts shown in boxes A thru E of sections 1-4.)

TOTAL NET WEEKLY INCOME (A)	$	**TOTAL CASH VALUE OF ASSETS (E)**	$
TOTAL WEEKLY EXPENSES AND LIABILITIES (B + D)	$	**TOTAL LIABILITIES (TOTAL BALANCE DUE ON DEBTS) (C)**	$

CERTIFICATION
I certify that the foregoing statement is true and accurate to the best of my knowledge and belief.

SIGNED (Affiant)	Subscribed and sworn to before me on	DATE	SIGNED (Notary, Comm. of Superior Court, Assistant Clerk)

In cases involving complex assets and liabilities, it may be necessary to consult with accountants, financial advisors, appraisers, and other experts to establish values and appropriate figures to be included on financial affidavits. One of the greatest challenges, particularly in cases involving substantial assets, is to determine whether or not an opposing party (or a client for that matter!) is disclosing all of his or her assets and income. In some cases, *forensic accountants* may be retained at considerable expense. However, counsel and skilled paralegals are often able to uncover hidden assets by carefully reviewing and comparing financial affidavits, tax returns, and other documents produced through formal and informal discovery measures. Ultimate accountability rests with the supervising attorney, but a paralegal with appropriate knowledge, training, and expertise is an invaluable resource. (See Paralegal Application 7.11.)

Forensic accountant
an accountant who applies accounting principles and analysis to gather and present evidence in a lawsuit

PARALEGAL APPLICATION **7.10**

POINTERS ON COMPLETION OF FINANCIAL AFFIDAVITS

1. Instructions for completing financial affidavits should be followed carefully.

2. The Affidavit should be complete, with every space filled in with a figure, a 0, "none," or "NA" ("not applicable") as appropriate.

3. If allowed, footnotes or attachments should be used

   a. when necessary to supplement or more fully explain figures that might otherwise be confusing or misleading out of context

   b. if the form doesn't permit the party to adequately represent his or her specific circumstances

4. Although some attorneys might disagree, most believe it is better to provide a complete picture of the client's financial situation in an organized, coherent, and consistent manner. A failure to do so opens the door for attack by opposing counsel or questioning by a judge as to why certain information was not included.

5. The Affidavit should reflect a party's current financial circumstances. However, if a party's income varies seasonally, with market fluctuations or for some other reason, averages may usually be used.

6. If weekly or monthly income and expenses do not balance, the party must be able to explain how a shortfall is covered or where the excess income is placed. For example, if the party claims to be spending more than is earned, is he or she borrowing money, withdrawing from savings, selling assets, and/or receiving funds, gifts, or other subsidies from third parties?

7. Contested cases frequently drag on for months and involve multiple court appearances for temporary orders, motion hearings, discovery conferences, and the like. Whenever a hearing is for the purpose of addressing an issue with financial implications, such as child or spousal support or occupancy of the marital residence, a current financial affidavit is customarily required. A party must be able to explain any discrepancies between prior and current affidavits.

8. Care should be taken that figures appearing on affidavits can be documented wherever possible and that they are consistent with other documents that may be provided to the court or available to the other party.[4]

PARALEGAL APPLICATION **7.11**

THE SEARCH FOR HIDDEN ASSETS

In searching for hidden assets, a paralegal might explore the following:

1. Does a party report a modest income and yet live a lavish lifestyle with frequent vacations, an expensive residence with no mortgage, high-end motor vehicles, expensive clothing, and jewelry?

2. Has the other party deferred receipt of any income, bonuses, or other forms of compensation to a date subsequent to the divorce? A review of past income history is often helpful in this area.

3. If the other party is self-employed and claiming a reduction in business and income since initiation of divorce proceedings, is the decline in marked contrast to past history or market trends?

continued

4. Does the other party receive unacknowledged "perks" over and above direct salary at his or her job, such as a company car for business and personal use; subsidized housing or relocation costs; an allowance for uniforms or parking; an expense account for travel, dining, and entertainment; or club memberships?

5. Has the other party made sham or allegedly "bad" loans to a family member or friend?

6. Does the other party hold any as yet potentially valuable unexercised stock options in a company where he or she is or was employed?

7. Has the other party accumulated substantial sick, personal, or vacation time at work for which he or she may be compensated?

8. Has the other party accumulated a substantial number of frequent-flier miles?

9. Has the other party made substantial withdrawals from various accounts for unknown or unexplained purposes, funds that do not appear in another form on an affidavit? Does a credit card statement reflect an overnight trip to the Cayman Islands the day of or after the withdrawals?

10. Is cash being kept in a safe deposit box or in some other location?

11. What kind of business(es) is the other party engaged in? How is the income received? For example, does the party own or work at a gas station where receipts are tied to gas pump readings or in a convenience store or restaurant where large sums of cash and tips are received and may or may not be deposited in the business's accounts? Does the other party have a history of working "under the table"?

12. Does the opposing party's tax return indicate interest and dividend income while the same party's financial statement reflects no underlying asset generating that income?

COURT INVOLVEMENT IN THE DISCOVERY PROCESS

The courts generally affirm a party's right to conduct comprehensive and liberal discovery and prefer not to become involved in the process unless mandated by procedural rules (as in the case of Requests for Mental or Physical Examinations) or by the unique circumstances of individual cases or the conduct of counsel or the parties. The most common ways in which the courts become involved are:

1. **Discovery Conferences.**   A court may, on its own initiative, pursuant to court rule, or at the request of a party, order that a discovery conference be convened at which time a discovery plan is developed and agreed upon. The plan typically sets out the appropriate topics for discovery, the discovery methods to be used by each of the parties, and the timeline within which discovery must be completed. Most states have in place procedures for managing discovery under the court's supervision (through a "discovery master") to ensure that the parties make reasonable and timely requests and responses.

2. **Protective Orders.**   A court will entertain a motion for a protective order brought by a party who contends, for example, that one or more discovery requests seeks privileged information, is excessive and would lead to undue burden or expense, or is made in bad faith solely for the purpose of harassment. If the motion is granted, the court will establish limitations on discovery.

3. **Orders to Compel and Impose Sanctions for Noncompliance.** When a party fails to comply with a discovery request, the party making the request may file a motion to compel. If granted, the discovery request then becomes, in effect, an order of the court, and a failure to comply may result in sanctions. For example, the noncomplying party may be ordered to pay the fees the other party incurred in pursuing the matter. In especially egregious cases, if he or she is the moving party, the matter may be dismissed or the party may be prevented from introducing related evidence at trial. In some jurisdictions, prior to filing a motion to compel, the parties are required to exhaust efforts to settle the discovery dispute without the assistance of the court.

CHAPTER **SUMMARY**

This chapter provides a comprehensive survey of the discovery process—its nature, scope, purposes, and methods both formal and informal. Attention is given to the ways in which the client can contribute to the information-gathering efforts. The five major formal discovery methods are described and examples provided: interrogatories, depositions, requests for admission, requests for production of documents and things, and requests for physical and mental examinations. The nature, role, and importance of financial affidavits are also covered. The paralegal's role in the discovery process is heavily emphasized. Additional topics relevant to discovery are also considered, including: objections to discovery, the particular challenges of uncovering hidden assets, electronic discovery, and the court's involvement in the process.

KEY **TERMS**

Deponent
Deposition
Discovery
Electronic discovery
Expert
Forensic accountant
Formal discovery
Informal discovery

Interrogatories
Lay witness
Letters rogatory
Mandatory self-disclosure
Notice of deposition
Privilege
Protective order
Request for Admissions

Request for Physical or Mental
  Examination
Request for Production of Documents
  or Things
Subpoena
Subpoena *duces tecum*
Work product

REVIEW **QUESTIONS**

1. Define discovery.
2. Identify the purposes of discovery.
3. Distinguish between "formal" and "informal discovery."
4. Describe how the client can assist in the information-gathering process.
5. Describe the nature of interrogatories and identify their strengths and weaknesses.
6. Describe a deposition and indicate its strengths and weaknesses as a discovery method.
7. Describe requests for admissions and identify their strengths and weaknesses. What is the consequence of failing to respond in a timely way to a request for admissions?
8. Define and give two examples of requests for production of documents and things.

9. Identify three situations in which a request for a physical or mental examination might be appropriate. How is one customarily obtained?
10. Describe e-discovery and give an example of when and how it might be sought.
11. Identify the kinds of objections to discovery requests that can be raised.
12. Describe the nature and purpose of financial statements/affidavits.
13. Identify a minimum of five ways of concealing assets and how they might be detected.
14. Describe the role of the paralegal in the discovery process.
15. Describe the role the court plays in the discovery process.

FOCUS ON **THE JOB**

THE FACTS

Walt and Renee Albertson have been married thirty-seven years and have three adult children: Eleanor, Edward, and Walter, Jr. The marriage has been rocky and each party believes that the other has been "unfaithful" on several occasions. The only confirmed affair occurred in 1996 when Renee became involved with a next-door neighbor and at one point moved in with him after Walt "threw her out" of the marital home because of the ongoing and open affair. After a month he begged her to come home. She did, and they went to counseling, reconciled, and resumed their marital relationship. However, Walt never really trusted Renee after that. As a result, he kept all of his assets as separate as possible from hers, with the exception of a joint bank account out of which he paid all of the expenses related to the marital home as well as the food bills and car-related costs. Renee has been depositing her entire paycheck into this account, but Walter only matches what she puts into the account. He earns funds from four sources: social security, a modest salary as a school bus driver, an investment portfolio he established in 1980 and has maintained ever since, and money he earns doing electrical work "under the table" for which he is paid cash or "in-kind" (e.g., he does some wiring for his mechanic, and the mechanic repairs Walt's vehicle without charging him). He deposits his social security into the joint account along with about 20 percent of his check from the bus company. Throughout the marriage, he has maintained the couple's finances and largely kept Renee "in the dark," although he does give her a modest weekly "allowance." He has always kept extensive financial and business records on his computer. He pays his bills online and uses Turbo Tax to prepare the parties' joint tax returns.

The marital home (jointly held) is assessed at $350,000 for real estate tax purposes, but Walt claims it is worth closer to $500,000, based on work he has done building an addition that includes a den, bedroom, and bath with a hot tub in it. He spent the better part of a year doing the work in his free time. There is a $112,000 mortgage and a $20,000 equity loan secured by the property. The parties had to obtain the loan to cover income taxes (plus interest and penalties) due on previously undeclared income Walt had collected doing electrical work for friends and acquaintances. He asserts that he is not still doing this work, but Renee intends to hire a private detective to follow him in his free time, as she is certain he continues to work and not pay taxes on the funds collected or in-kind services received. He claims to never have any money but went to Aruba for a week in January of 2007, allegedly alone, and has a new Toyota convertible, for which Renee believes he paid cash. She also saw a credit card statement that listed expenditures at two local jewelry stores and several local restaurants that she has not been to with him.

In December of 2006, Renee became suspicious that Walt was having an affair with his old high school sweetheart, Valentina Ferrara, with whom he "reconnected" at his fiftieth high school reunion, which his wife refused to attend with him. Valentina had recently been widowed. Walt admits that he is "in touch" with her (particularly by telephone and e-mail) but that she would never consider having an intimate relationship with him as long as he is still married. Besides, he claims that at the age of seventy, he is no longer able to function sexually. Renee believes he is seeing a doctor and has a prescription for "that little blue pill." Renee's heart is broken, and she has filed for divorce on the ground of adultery in a jurisdiction that retains fault grounds.

THE ASSIGNMENT

Assume that in the jurisdiction where you reside and/or are employed, when making property division decisions, the court considers both conduct during the marriage and financial and nonfinancial contribution to the marital enterprise. Using an appropriate format, draft a set of twenty interrogatories. Assume that the firm where you work (Wilson and Tauson, LLP) represents Renee. The attorney handling the case is Juliana Wilson and the office is located at 390 Main Street in your hometown. What other forms of discovery do you think would be appropriate in this case and why?

FOCUS ON **ETHICS**

Assume that Walt is your supervising attorney's client. He has given you a completed draft of his financial affidavit/statement and claims that it accurately reflects all of his assets and liabilities. You are aware of all of the information presented in the above fact pattern and are concerned that Walt's affidavit is very likely not accurate, and yet he must sign it under oath. You are also in a jurisdiction where his attorney must also sign the affidavit indicating that to the best of his or her knowledge, the document contains no false information. Some of the things you are concerned about are that Walt has listed no credit card debt but does reflect a loan from his brother for $8,000, which he tells you should help him in the property settlement even though he doesn't really have to pay his brother back. He indicates his social security and bus driving income but reflects no income from investments or his work as an electrician, income you are reasonably certain he receives. He lists the joint account but no other accounts or cash assets. He has listed the value of the marital home as $500,000 less the mortgage and claims he doesn't have to list the equity loan because it was incurred to buy a car for Renee and he should not have to be liable for any of it. He also indicates that he pays 100 percent of the household expenses because, after all, he writes all the checks. As a paralegal, what course of action should you take, and how would you recommend the situation be addressed? Which of the ethical canons for paralegals promulgated by the National Federation of Paralegal Associations (NFPA), contained in Appendix B, are applicable in this context?

FOCUS ON **CASE LAW**

The Massachusetts case of *Pagar v. Pagar*, 9 Mass. App. Ct. 1, 397 N.E.2d 1293 (1980), is located on the companion website for this text in the material related to Chapter 7. Locate and read the case and then respond to the following questions.

1. What is the legal history of the case: What kind of a case is it? Where was it brought prior to reaching the Massachusetts Appeals Court and with what result?
2. What are the issues being appealed and by whom?

3. What concerns does the appellate court have about the wife's financial statement?
4. What concerns does the appellate court have about the husband's financial statement?
5. Does it appear that one or both of the parties is concealing and/or understating assets? How so?
6. What conclusion did the appeals court reach and what did it order?

FOCUS ON **STATE LAW AND PROCEDURE**

1. What forms of mandatory self-disclosure, if any, does the state in which you reside or are employed require of parties to a divorce action?
2. Obtain and review a copy of your state's financial affidavit form. Assume that Walt is the client in the case you are working on and the facts are the same as in the Focus on the Job hypothetical in this chapter. Make a

list of the kinds of documents and information you need to gather in order to help him complete his financial affidavit/statement.
3. Locate a case in your jurisdiction that addresses the issue of understating or concealing assets. How did the court address the problem?

FOCUS ON **TECHNOLOGY**

Website of Interest

http://www.findlaw.com

Findlaw's Legal Technology Center has instituted an Electronic Discovery Rule Wizard, an online interactive tool to help legal professionals understand the amended Federal Rules of Civil Procedure and improve their use of e-discovery methods and procedures.

Assignments

1. Locate online the financial statements for five states. A good place to start your search is with the websites for courts in various states. The list of websites provided in Appendix D may be helpful.
2. Assume that you are currently married and a party to a divorce action. Complete (online, if possible) the appropriate financial affidavit/statement you would need to submit in the jurisdiction where you reside. This assignment is designed to be an individual exercise, and not shared with fellow students or the instructor, absent consent.
3. Locate online a sample set of interrogatories.
4. Assuming the facts in the above Focus on the Job hypothetical, draft an *ex parte* motion on Renee's behalf seeking to stop Walt from using his laptop and storage devices (such as floppy disks, CD-ROMs, zip files, or

any other similar type of storage device) and requesting that he immediately produce and deposit the laptop and storage devices with the court in which the divorce action has been filed (your local family court) for examination by a recognized computer expert who will present subsequent testimony under oath regarding relevant contents. You should consider building in certain protections for the other party with respect to who and how the contents may be examined, stating that privileged contents will not be made public, indicating whether or not any provision will be made for temporarily replacing the laptop, and identifying who will bear related costs.
5. Of what use are the following websites with respect to discovery and financial statements, if any?

http://www.findlaw.com

http://divorcenet.com

http://divorcesource.com
6. Using *http://www.findlaw.com,*
   a. Locate the federal rules of civil procedure regarding electronic discovery.
   b. Identify three current issues relating to interpretation and application of these rules.

chapter **eight**
CHILD CUSTODY

George and Ethel Dosh are the grandparents of Melody and Darren, the children of their unmarried daughter, Christine, and her former boyfriend, Clark Brody. They believe they should be awarded visitation with the children so that they can save them from the influence of their sinful parents. Although Christine and Clark are no longer a couple, they both say, "No way. . . ."

IN THIS CHAPTER YOU WILL LEARN

- What the various types of custody are
- What the major jurisdictional issues are in child custody cases
- What standards have guided the courts when making child custody decisions
- What the "best interests of the child" means in various states
- What some of the major issues are that courts consider when making decisions about custody and visitation
- What visitation is and how it may be regulated
- What parenting plans and parent education programs are and why they are important
- When and how a custody order may be modified
- How custody and visitation orders are enforced
- What the rights of third parties are in the custody context
- Who speaks for the child in custody matters
- What the role of the paralegal is in a custody case

While this court has not had occasion to elucidate the nature of a child's liberty interests in preserving familial or family like-bonds, it seems to me extremely likely that, to the extent parents and families have fundamental liberty interests in preserving such intimate relationships, so, too, do children have these interests, and so, too, must their interests be balanced in the equation....[1]

Married parents whose marriages fail may divorce each other. Unmarried parents whose relationships break down do not have to divorce each other. But married or divorced, together or apart, parents cannot change the fact that they are parents. Justice Stevens' comment above reminds us that custody issues do not simply involve parents battling over inanimate pieces of property. Custody is about live children who have interests in the outcome of the battle. They are what the battle is supposed to be about.

INTRODUCTION

In the majority of divorces, there is no dispute with respect to which parent should have custody of the children or if custody should be shared between them. The parties establish an agreed-upon schedule and related provisions and present their agreement to the court for approval and incorporation in the decree dissolving the marriage. In some cases, however, before an agreement is reached, a considerable amount of negotiating may occur. One parent may even threaten the other parent with the loss of custody in an effort to obtain some advantage unrelated to custody, such as a more favorable property division.[2] In a small minority of cases, there is such hostility and disagreement between the parties that they are unable to reach an agreement even with the assistance of mediation.

At considerable emotional and financial cost, these high-conflict cases will go to trial to be decided by a judge. Each party will present evidence and testimony in support of his or her position and will have an opportunity to cross-examine the other party and his or her witnesses. Customarily, each party will testify about his or her relationship with the child, relating anecdotes about involvement in as many aspects of the child's life as possible—health, education, recreation, daily routines, medical care, religious training, discipline, and the like. Lay witnesses such as friends, neighbors, teachers, and counselors may be called to buttress a parent's testimony, and occasionally a battle of experts may ensue—especially if the child or either or both of the parents have health, psychiatric, or behavioral problems impacting on his or her fitness as a parent or if there is evidence that either parent is abusing the child in some manner. The court may also appoint its own resources, including a **guardian** ad litem to provide a neutral assessment of the situation, and may interview the child *in camera* as to his or her parental preference. The court then has to make a subjective decision about the course of action that will best serve the child's interests, based on objective evidence and a weighing of the credibility of the various witnesses. States afford judges broad discretion, and a trial court's decision will customarily not be disturbed on appeal absent a showing of an abuse of discretion, insufficient evidence to support the court's conclusion, or an error in declaring or applying the law.

TYPES OF CUSTODY

In general, **physical custody** (called residential custody or physical placement in some states) refers to where the child will live, and **legal custody** refers to decision-making authority. A **sole award** is vested primarily in one parent. A **joint award**

Guardian *ad litem*
a person, usually a lawyer, appointed by the court to conduct an investigation and or to represent a party who is a minor or otherwise unable to represent him- or herself in a legal proceeding; the guardian's role may be limited to a particular matter, such as custody

In camera
in the judge's chambers

Physical custody
custody relating to where and with whom the child resides

Legal custody
custody relating to decision-making authority with respect to major issues affecting a child

Sole award
an award made to one parent only

Joint award
an award made to both parents

involves shared responsibility. The various types of custody described in traditional terms are as follows:

Sole legal custody: one parent has the right and responsibility to make the major decisions regarding the child's welfare, including matters of education, medical care, and emotional, moral, and religious development.

Joint legal custody: both parents have continued mutual responsibility and involvement in the making of the major decisions regarding the child's welfare. Absent an emergency, when legal custody is joint neither parent should make a major decision related to the child without consulting the other parent. Although this arrangement sounds fine in principle, conflicts frequently arise, especially with respect to what constitutes a "major" decision. For instance, is getting a tattoo or dying one's hair purple a major or a day-to-day decision?

Sole physical custody: the child resides with and is under the day-to-day supervision of one parent, subject to reasonable visitation with the other parent unless a court determines that visitation would not be in the best interests of the child. The parent with whom the child primarily resides is commonly called the "custodial" parent and the parent with visitation rights is the "noncustodial" parent.

Joint or shared physical custody: the child has periods of residing with and being under the day-to-day supervision of each parent. The custody is shared in such a way that the child has frequent and continuing contact with each parent.

Split custody: each parent has legal and/or physical custody of one or more of the parties' children. Strong public policy supports keeping siblings together. Absent an extraordinary emotional, medical, or educational need or some other compelling circumstance (such as a significant age gap or severe conflict between the siblings), *split custody* is not favored by the courts.

Split custody
a custodial arrangement in which each parent has legal and/or physical custody of one or more of the parties' children

Although many states still use traditional terms to refer to custody, there is a move afoot to abandon the old terms such as *custody* and *visitation* in favor of a new terminology that emphasizes allocation of parental responsibilities[3] for the benefit of the child rather than the parents' struggle with each other. The premise is that if parents and counsel can come to view custody issues as mutual endeavors to address the needs of children rather than as contests between the parties, the best interests of all involved will be served.

The "new" approach to custody-related terminology is reflected in the "Parental Rights and Responsibilities Act" that went into effect in New Hampshire in 2005. Proposed by a Family Law Task Force after a two-year study, the Act is based on the premise that "children do best when both parents have a stable and meaningful involvement in their lives." Similar to other jurisdictions moving in this direction, it supports "frequent and continuing contact between each child and both parents" and encourages parents "to develop their own parenting plans" and "to share in the rights and responsibilities of raising their children...."[4] The Act replaces the term "custody" with the phrase "parental rights and responsibilities," requires parents to file parenting plans that allocate those rights and responsibilities, and codifies criteria for determining the best interests of the child. Legal custody is termed "decision-making responsibility" and physical custody, "residential responsibility."

Whatever terminology is used, there is no fixed formula for child custody determinations. Under the guidance of state statutes and case law, courts are free to create multiple forms of custody arrangements tailored to the unique needs and challenges of each family. This flexibility is especially useful in complex or high-conflict cases in which two equally fit parents are totally unable to communicate with each other. Courts often generate unique strategies in such cases in order to foster dispute resolution and avoid frequent and costly trips back to court.

The two most common forms of custodial awards are:

1. Joint legal custody with sole physical custody in one parent with reasonable rights of visitation in the other parent
2. Joint legal and physical custody

Prior to the 1970s, the first option was predominant and it continues to be common today. The noncustodial parent is customarily obligated to pay child support and as a result may feel disenfranchised when it comes to custody, even though he or she may become the custodial parent given a substantial change in circumstances at some future time. In the interim, he or she is entitled to "visitation" with the child, to participate in the making of major decisions pertaining to the child, and to have access to the child's medical and school records.

With the coming of no-fault divorce, gender-neutral custody laws, and equal rights movements in their many forms, joint physical and legal custody awards became increasingly more common. Most states now provide by statute or case law that joint awards are in the best interest of children, absent a history of domestic violence. However, joint awards have met with mixed success. The prospects for success are greatest when chosen by parties who are able to communicate effectively or when parents want to become or remain actively involved in their children's lives. They are less likely to be successful when imposed on disinterested parents, parties who cannot each afford to maintain a residence for the children, or parents who are unable to rise above hostility toward each other in order to commit to a shared role for the benefit of their children. Joint custody can also be difficult for children, particularly if they are forced to live in two different homes in two totally different communities.

JURISDICTIONAL ISSUES IN CHILD CUSTODY CASES

A court's authority to issue a child custody order is based on statute. Personal jurisdiction over a parent or a child is not sufficient for a court to make a custody determination. Subject matter jurisdiction is required. The parties cannot confer subject matter jurisdiction by agreement, and, therefore, a party must establish it by complying with governing statutes.

Jurisdictional problems are minimal in child custody cases when the parties' identities are known and both parties reside in the same state. However, problems can arise when multiple states are involved, particularly when variations in jurisdictional requirements exist. Prior to 1968, courts based jurisdiction for custody decisions on the child's physical presence in a state. This sometimes led to *forum shopping* by parents, some of whom would abduct their children and go to another state where they might receive a more favorable custody award. Interstate child custody disputes present the courts with complex problems, particularly in domestic violence and chronically high-conflict cases.

Forum shopping
seeking a court that will grant the most favorable ruling

Four Acts are of particular importance in the child custody context:

1. The Uniform Child Custody Jurisdiction Act (UCCJA)[5]
2. The Uniform Child Custody Jurisdiction and Enforcement Act (UCCJEA)[6]
3. The Federal Parental Kidnapping Prevention Act (PKPA)[7]
4. The Hague Convention on the Civil Aspects of International Child Abduction[8]

UCCJA

The National Conference of Commissioners of Uniform State Laws (NCCUSL) promulgated the Uniform Child Custody Jurisdiction Act (UCCJA) in 1968. The UCCJA is a model act designed to eliminate the incentive for a parent to remove a child to another state in order to obtain a more favorable custody order. By 1981, the Uniform Child Custody Jurisdiction Act (UCCJA) was adopted in all fifty states, the District of Columbia, and the Virgin Islands. Although the Act helped to reduce the filing of competing custody actions in multiple states, there still are problems and gaps with the UCCJA. Most notably, it includes no enforcement measures to put teeth into its provisions.

The UCCJA authorizes four independent bases of jurisdiction, none of which actually requires the presence of the child in the jurisdiction at the time of filing. The four potential jurisdictional bases for initial custody determinations are:

1. home state
2. significant connection
3. emergency
4. last resort

Home state jurisdiction: The home state is the state in which the child has lived with a parent (or a person acting as a parent) for at least six consecutive months immediately before the commencement of a child custody proceeding. If the child is less than six months of age, "home state" refers to the state in which the child has lived from birth. Periods of temporary absence from the state are included in the six-month period. Once the home state is established, if the child is removed from the state, a parent (or person acting as a parent) who remains there may bring a custody action within a six-month period.

Significant connection jurisdiction: A significant connection sufficient for jurisdiction exists when there is substantial evidence in a state concerning the child, at least one of the parties is present and available in that state, and exercising jurisdiction would be in the best interests of the child. The evidence might be in the form of school and medical records and the presence of potential witnesses familiar with the child's care.

Emergency jurisdiction: A state has emergency jurisdiction when the child is physically present in the state and requires emergency protection as a result of child abandonment, abuse, or neglect, even if the actual cause of the emergency did not occur in the state. States rely on this basis only in "extraordinary circumstances."

Last resort jurisdiction: A state can assume last resort jurisdiction if there is no other state that can or is willing to exercise jurisdiction under the Act, and it is in the best interest of the child for it to do so.

Under the UCCJA, a state could modify a custody order of another state only if the decree state no longer had continuing jurisdiction and the new state could assert

Home state jurisdiction
jurisdiction in custody matters based on where the child has lived for a specified period of time

---

Paralegal Practice Tip
Because the UCCJA does not prioritize home state and significant connection jurisdiction, it is possible for two states to claim initial jurisdiction simultaneously, resulting in conflicting custody orders. The Parental Kidnapping Prevention Act (PKPA) and the Uniform Child Custody Jurisdiction and Enforcement Act (UCCJEA) subsequently eliminated this loophole by prioritizing home state jurisdiction subject to the emergency jurisdiction provision.

Significant connection jurisdiction
jurisdiction based on the existence of substantial evidence in a state concerning a child

Emergency jurisdiction
jurisdiction based a child's physical presence in a state and need for emergency protection

Last resort jurisdiction
jurisdiction based on the fact no other state is willing or able to exercise jurisdiction, and it is in the child's best interest

jurisdiction in a manner consistent with the provisions of the UCCJA. As with initial jurisdiction under this Act, prior to passage of the federal Parental Kidnapping Act, it was possible for two states to claim modification jurisdiction simultaneously.

UCCJEA

Like the UCCJA, the Uniform Child Custody Jurisdiction and Enforcement Act (UCCJEA) is a uniform state law designed to avoid jurisdictional conflicts between states, deter child abductions for the purpose of obtaining jurisdiction in another state, avoid relitigation of decisions from other states, and ensure that custody matters are heard in the state that has the closest connection with the child and the family. It applies equally to initial jurisdiction and to later modifications.

The UCCJEA brings the UCCJA into compliance with more recent federal statutes, such as the Parental Kidnapping Prevention Act (PKPA) and the Violence Against Women Act (VAWA). By tightening the four jurisdictional bases, the UCCJEA addresses weaknesses in the UCCJA that have continued to result in costly litigation and inconsistent decisions in interstate custody cases. Major improvements in this Act as compared with the UCCJA include the following:

Forum *non conveniens*
the forum in which an action is filed is not convenient for one of the parties, and the court, in its discretion, may find that justice would be better served if the matter is heard in another court

- It avoids potential conflicts between states by making the child's home state the priority ground for original jurisdiction in interstate child custody cases, consistent with federal law. Under the UCCJEA, if the minor child has a home state, jurisdiction will be proper only in the home state unless that state declines jurisdiction.
- Under the UCCJEA, a state can exercise "significant connection" jurisdiction only if the "home state" declines jurisdiction, there are ***forum* non conveniens** or parental misconduct grounds, or there is no home state. It focuses on procedure and eliminates the "best interests" language of the UCCJA.
- It preserves exclusive, continuing jurisdiction in the decree state if that state has a basis for continuing jurisdiction. Consistent with the PKPA, jurisdiction continues in the decree state as long as the child, either of his or her parents, or any person acting as the child's parent continues to reside in the decree state.
- It expands protection for family members who are victims of domestic violence that occurred in the child's presence and authorizes courts to exercise emergency jurisdiction in such cases. The relief available in emergency cases is limited to temporary custody orders.
- It creates mechanisms for courts in different states to "communicate and cooperate" with one another and provides procedures for interstate registration and enforcement of a child custody and visitation order, provided the order was issued in substantial conformity with the UCCJEA. Although the UCCJA required states to enforce the decrees of sister states, it did not provide enforcement remedies to accomplish that end.
- It authorizes the issuing of warrants authorizing law enforcement officers to protect children at risk of being unlawfully removed from a state.
- Unlike the UCCJA, the UCCJEA is not applicable in adoption cases but does apply to tribal court proceedings.

The UCCJEA is designed to replace rather than to supplement the UCCJA and at the time of the writing of this chapter, it has been adopted and replaces the UCCJA in all but four states (Massachusetts, Missouri, New Hampshire, and

Vermont). A copy of the UCCJEA is available in the resource material for Chapter 8 on the companion website.

PKPA

The federal child custody jurisdiction act is the Parental Kidnapping Prevention Act (PKPA), enacted in 1980 to address interstate custody problems that continued to exist after the adoption of the UCCJA and before the UCCJEA was created. Its scope is not limited to "kidnapping" cases; rather, its primary purpose is to maintain jurisdiction in one court over custody orders pertaining to a given child in interstate cases. The PKPA has the same four jurisdictional bases as the UCCJA, but, like the UCCJEA, it fills a major gap in the UCCJA by giving priority in initial child custody determinations to home state jurisdiction. By doing so, it prevents a "significant connection" state from exercising jurisdiction over a custody matter as long as the child involved has a "home state." If it does exercise jurisdiction, its order will not be entitled to recognition by other states.

To avoid the issuing of conflicting custody orders, the PKPA mandates that states give full faith and credit to other states' custody determinations as long as they are made in conformity with the provisions of the PKPA. Subject to the emergency jurisdiction provision, it also provides for exclusive continuing jurisdiction over modification of custody actions involving the child as long as the original decree state continues to have jurisdiction. Jurisdiction continues in the decree state until such time as (1) the initial state has lost jurisdiction because it is no longer the home state and it no longer has a significant connection to the case because significant evidence is not present there or (2) neither the child nor either parent continues to reside in the decree state.

Although the UCCJEA is designed for adoption by the states and the PKPA is a federal act, the goals and procedures of the UCCJEA and the PKPA largely mirror each other. Whether a state has adopted the UCCJEA or still operates under a version of the UCCJA, when there is a conflict with federal law, the jurisdictional provisions of the PKPA will prevail, given the supremacy of federal law under the Constitution.

The Hague Convention on the Civil Aspects of International Child Abduction

International child custody disputes present highly complex, specialized, and challenging issues. The major challenge is that laws and court orders issued in the United States are not always recognized and enforceable internationally, and not all orders issued in foreign countries are necessarily enforceable in the United States.

There are a number of federal laws in place concerning custody, parental child abduction, and missing children, such as the National Child Search Assistance Act,[9] the International Child Abduction Remedies Act,[10] the International Parental Kidnapping Crime Act (IPKCA),[11] and the Fugitive Felon Act.[12] One of the most effective resources in the area of international child abduction is The Hague Convention on the Civil Aspects of International Child Abduction (Hague Convention), which became law in the United States in 1988. It has been endorsed by more than fifty nations. The Hague Convention provisions set forth detailed procedures to be followed when seeking the return of children who have been wrongfully removed from the United States.

WHICH STATE HAS JURISDICTION UNDER THE UCCJA, THE UCCJEA, AND THE PKPA?

FACT PATTERN

When multiple states are potentially involved in a case, a paralegal may be asked to research the jurisdiction issue. For example, assume that mom and dad get divorced in Illinois; dad is awarded physical custody and mom is awarded visitation with their five-year-old daughter. All three individuals remain in Illinois until the child is ten years old. At that point, dad moves to California with the child, who continues to visit mom in Illinois during the holiday vacations for the next three years. Then the daughter decides she really wants to live with her mom and claims her dad has been sexually abusing her. Mom, whose hostility toward dad is stronger than ever, meets her daughter in California and flees with her to Missouri, where she files a complaint for modification—delighted to have a chance to take custody away from dad.

SIDEBAR

On what basis(es), if any, can the Missouri court exercise jurisdiction under the UCCJA? Under the UCCJEA? Under the PKPA?

EVOLVING LEGAL STANDARDS FOR MAKING CUSTODY DECISIONS

Once the appropriate jurisdiction for bringing a custody action is identified, the standard used for making custody decisions in that state can be ascertained. Over the years, a variety of approaches to custody determinations have existed, depending on the state of society, economic forces, gender stereotypes, and prevailing public policies with respect to children. Some approaches have been fairly cut-and-dried; others are more flexible and open ended. The most prominent approaches have included the following:

- Paternal Preference
- Maternal Preference
- Tender Years Doctrine
- Best Interests of the Child
- Primary Caretaker Presumption
- American Law Institute's Approximation Rule

Paternal Preference

Paternal preference
the common law doctrine that fathers had an absolute right to the care and custody of their children

In the early history of child custody, a ***paternal preference*** was predominant in child custody awards. When the identity of the father was known, custody virtually always was granted to the father. Under the doctrine of *pater familias* (father of the family), he had an absolute legal right to custody (in effect, physical possession) of his offspring regardless of their welfare. In essence, custody was a matter of property law. The father had complete authority over his children and controlled all aspects of their lives, their education, their training, and their labor. This "paternal preference" under which mothers had no legal authority with respect to their children persisted in the United States until the late eighteenth century and is still evident in present-day patriarchal families and societies elsewhere in the world.

Maternal Preference and Tender Years Doctrine

By the early nineteenth century, the industrial revolution, urbanization, and the decline of an agrarian way of life brought about major societal changes and a redefining of roles within the family. Although the father remained the head of the family and the ultimate maker of major decisions, his primary role was that of breadwinner, and the mother's role was that of homemaker. She was viewed as the "heart" of the home and tended to all of the children's physical, emotional, and spiritual needs. Upon divorce, the father's role as breadwinner continued in the sense that he was customarily ordered to pay spousal and child support for his dependent wife and children. However, given a **maternal preference** for the mother as caretaker, the mother was most often granted physical custody, even over the father's objection.

Maternal preference
the concept that custody should be awarded to a mother over a father, provided she is fit

By the end of the nineteenth century, the common law doctrine of paternal rights had been firmly replaced by the **tender years doctrine.** Based on tradition and biological dependence, it was assumed that young children should be placed in the care of their mother as the natural custodian of the young and immature, provided she was fit to have custody. Occasionally, custody of older children, especially teenage boys, was awarded to fathers, particularly if the parties agreed and the children expressed a preference to that effect. The desire for "young men" to have "male role models" was commonly was a factor in the decision.

Tender years doctrine
the doctrine holding that custody of very young children should be awarded to the mother rather than the father unless she is found to be unfit

The maternal preference era lasted until the 1960s and the onset of the various "rights" movements. It was inevitable that the effects of the "civil rights," "women's rights," "children's rights," and "equal rights" movements would spill over into the custody context. "Fathers' rights" came to the fore at the same time as many women were choosing the world of work over homemaking as their primary focus (sometimes out of necessity). The father was no longer necessarily the primary breadwinner, and the mother was no longer the undisputed choice for physical custody. Custody laws in most states became gender neutral. Without a rule of gender preference to drive decision making, parents and the courts necessarily sought a more flexible standard that could accommodate diverse family models. Enter the "best interests of the child" standard, which is now the dominant standard across the country.

Best Interests of the Child

Applying the "best interests standard," the custody determination ideally involves an analysis of the child's needs and an assessment of which parent can most effectively meet those needs. Whether the arrangement is established by the parties or by the court, it must serve the best interests of the child. States identify by statute and/or case law a series of "best interest" factors that courts should consider, among others, in making custody determinations. The factors are not prioritized and the court is free to assign weight to them based on the facts of each case. The New Jersey statute in Exhibit 8.1 contains an extensive, representative list of these factors. Others appearing in various state statutes include but are not limited to the following:

Best interests of the child
the legal standard for resolving custody disputes that focuses on the needs of the child over the rights or wishes of the parents

- the ability of each parent to provide the child with nurture, love, affection, and guidance
- the mental and physical health of all individuals involved
- the child's adjustment to his or her home, school, and community
- the wishes of the child's parents as to his or her custody
- the ability of each parent to ensure that the child receives adequate food, clothing, shelter, medical care, and a safe environment
- the child's developmental needs and the ability of each parent to meet them, both in the present and in the future

- the relationship of the child with any other person who may significantly affect the child
- the love, affection, and other emotional ties existing between the parties and the child
- the capacity and disposition of the parties to continue the education and raising of the child in his or her religion or creed, if any
- the moral fitness of the parties involved[13]
- which parent is more likely to allow the child frequent and meaningful continuing contact with the other parent
- if one parent, both parents, or neither parent has provided primary care of the child[14]
- the length of time the child has lived in a stable, satisfactory environment and the desirability of maintaining continuity
- how the parents and child can best maintain and strengthen relationships with one another[15]
- the nature and extent of coercion or duress used by a parent in obtaining an agreement regarding custody[16]
- if a parent is incarcerated, the reason for and length of the incarceration and any unique issues that arise as a result of the incarceration
- the intention of either party to relocate the principal residence of the child

Customarily, there is a final catchall provision allowing the court to consider any other factors it deems necessary and relevant.

EXHIBIT 8.1 New Jersey Statute Re: Custody of Child, Rights of Both Parents Considered N.J. Stat. § 9:2–4

FROM THE STATUTE

The Legislature finds and declares that it is in the public policy of this State to assure minor children of frequent and continuing contact with both parents after the parents have separated or dissolved their marriage and that it is in the public interest to encourage parents to share the rights and responsibilities of child rearing in order to effect this policy.

In any proceeding involving the custody of the minor child, the rights of both parents shall be equal and the court shall enter an order which may include:

a.   Joint custody of a minor child to both parents, which is comprised of legal custody or physical custody which shall include: (1) provisions for residential arrangements so that a child shall reside either solely with one parent or alternatively with each parent in accordance with the needs of the parents and the child; and (2) provisions for consultation between the parents in making major decisions regarding the child's health, education and general welfare;

b.   Sole custody to one parent with appropriate parenting time for the noncustodial parent; or

c.   Any other custody arrangement as the court may determine to be in the best interests of the child.

In making an award of custody, the court shall consider but not be limited to the following factors:

- the parents' ability to agree, communicate and cooperate in matters relating to the child;

- the parents' willingness to accept custody and any history of unwillingness to allow parenting time not based on substantiated abuse;

continued

- the interaction and relationship of the child with its parents and siblings;
- the history of domestic violence, if any;
- the safety of the child and the safety of either parent from physical abuse by the other parent;
- the preference of the child when of sufficient age and capacity to reason so as to form an intelligent decision;
- the needs of the child;
- the stability of the home environment offered;
- the quality and continuity of the child's education;
- the fitness of the parents;
- the geographical proximity of the parents' homes;
- the extent and quality of the time spent with the child prior to or subsequent to the separation;
- the parents' employment responsibilities; and
- the age and number of the children.

A parent shall not be deemed unfit unless the parent's conduct has a substantial adverse effect on the child.

The court, for good cause and upon its own motion, may appoint a guardian ad litem or an attorney or both to represent the minor child's interests. The court shall have the authority to award a counsel fee to the guardian ad litem and the attorney and to assess that cost between the parties to the litigation.

d.   The court shall order any custody arrangement which is agreed to by both parents unless it is contrary to the best interests of the child.

The best interest test is child-centered and individualized and affords courts maximum discretion in making custody decisions.[17] In many respects, this is a positive development. A custody determination does not require a finding that one parent is a "better" or "worse" person than the other parent. The child's best interest is supposed to be paramount.[18] However, the test clearly is subjective and inevitably forces judges to make qualitative judgments into which they may subtly project personal views of what constitutes a "good parent." What is "best" varies by child and what a court considers "best" is not always what a parent may consider "best." A judge sitting in one family court may emphasize and reward parenting that is firm and regimented and emphasizes rules, discipline, and control. Another family court judge sitting in an adjacent courtroom may look more favorably on parents who promote individuality, creativity, and self-actualization of their children. Parents in this situation are faced with little predictability and potentially costly litigation.

The Primary Caretaker Presumption

In an effort to refine the best interests standard into a manageable test capable of producing predictable results, in the 1980s many courts began applying a "primary caretaker presumption" in making custody determinations.[19] A child's **primary caretaker** is the individual who has performed most of the significant parenting tasks for the child since birth or in the years preceding the divorce. The presumption builds on a wealth of child development research that suggests a child is likely to form the closest bond with the individual who is most involved in meeting

Primary caretaker
the individual who has performed most of the significant parenting tasks for the child since birth or in the years preceding the divorce

his or her daily needs and who is his or her secure base in times of stress. Child psychologists generally agree that maintenance of this relationship is essential to healthy development, supporting the presumption that custody should be awarded to the primary caretaker.

Rather than "custodial" and "noncustodial" parents, states applying this approach often refer to the parents as "the primary caretaker" and "the secondary caretaker."[20] Although both roles can be filled by either a father or a mother, many claim that the primary caretaker presumption is simply the maternal preference in disguise, as the determination focuses on activities traditionally performed by "moms." Paralegal Application 8.2 describes a sampling of the kinds of caretaking activities that are considered when trying to identify a "primary caretaker."

PARALEGAL APPLICATION 8.2

CARETAKING ACTIVITIES

Whether the standard applied is best interests, primary caretaker, or the ALI Approximation Rule, courts will consider the nature of each parent's relationship with the child in making custody determinations. Therefore, paralegals are often assigned to work with clients to gather information about the activities performed by each parent and the extent of his or her involvement with the child. Careful interviewing and preparation is critically important in preparing for a client's direct testimony and cross-examination at trial. For example, cross-examination can be very effective when a parent falsely claims to be the primary caretaker. The party might be asked when the child last went to the doctor, who took him or her, what the doctor's name was, how the child behaved, what the diagnosis was, what treatment was prescribed, who administered the treatment, etc. In relation to school, the party might be asked about the names of the child's teachers, the grades the child receives, the child's most and least favorite subjects, when the last parent teacher conference was, who attended it, who the child's best friend at school is, etc. An uninvolved parent is very unlikely to be able to answer these questions.

The kinds of caretaking activities most commonly considered are listed below. The extent to which any single activity is likely to be exercised by a parent will vary according to the age and developmental needs of the child. The list is drawn in large part from Section 2.03 of the ALI Principles of Marital Dissolution.

- Attending to the basic nutritional needs of the child
- Managing wake-up and bedtime routines
- Taking care of the child's personal hygiene needs, such as bathing, washing, and brushing teeth
- Attending to dressing and grooming
- Facilitating toilet training
- Attending to the child's needs when sick or injured and arranging for medical care
- Playing with the child
- Arranging for recreational activities
- Providing transportation to and from recreational and educational activities
- Protecting the child's physical safety
- Meeting the child's motor, cognitive, and socioemotional development needs
- Providing discipline and promoting moral and ethical development and self-discipline

continued

- Arranging for the child's education including remedial or other special services, communicating with school personnel, and working on homework
- Building the child's self-confidence
- Maintaining appropriate relationships with peers, siblings, and extended family members
- Arranging for and monitoring alternative care arrangements, including day care, babysitters, or other childcare providers

The American Law Institute's Approximation Rule

The ALI's *Approximation Rule* with respect to custody is that the custodial responsibilities of the parents at dissolution should be allocated in a manner that approximates the proportion of time each parent spent caring for the child when the family was intact.[21] Similar to the primary caretaker presumption, the focus of the ALI Rule is on concrete acts of parenting rather than on subjective judgments. It removes considerations of race, gender, religion, sexual preference, marital misconduct, and economic circumstances from the custody decision. As a result, to some extent it relieves judges of having to make subjective, relative judgments about parental fitness. The Rule assumes that after the divorce, each parent will be granted some level of access to the child, a level that will be comparable to his or her daily involvement with the child prior to the divorce. The Rule is not absolute, however. It allows for variation under certain circumstances, e.g., to keep siblings together, to accommodate reasonable child preferences, or to protect a child or parent from abuse.

The Rule is still essentially focused on the best interests of the child, but it provides parents the greater predictability and children the greater continuity in care afforded by the primary caretaker presumption. It has been cited favorably by courts in several states. West Virginia is the first state to adopt the ALI substantive custody standard over the primary caretaker rule, which it had adopted in 1981. Relevant excerpts from the West Virginia Child Custody statutes are accessible in the resource material related to Chapter 8 on the companion website for this text.

Approximation Rule
the rule that the custodial responsibilities of the parents at dissolution should be allocated in a manner that approximates the proportion of time each parent spent caring for the child when the family was intact

A CLOSER LOOK AT SOME OF THE ISSUES COURTS CONSIDER WHEN MAKING DECISIONS ABOUT CUSTODY AND VISITATION

Availability

Although not usually articulated as a discrete factor, availability is a consideration in custody decisions by implication. For example, courts look at activities parents participate in with their children, routines they perform (getting up and going to bed, etc.), attendance at school and recreational events, attending to medical and dental appointments, doing homework with the child, and providing religious training. To do these things, a parent has to be available, and therefore custody determinations are likely to favor the parent who has more time to devote to the children. Availability may be reduced or enhanced by work schedule, and a flexible work schedule may be especially attractive.

In today's busy world, most parents need to arrange with third parties for child care. Courts may consider the nature and extent of such arrangements when making custody decisions. For example, in a 2006 Idaho case (available on the companion website for this text in the material related to Chapter 8), an appellate court held that "consideration of a parent's work schedule and need for third-party child care is appropriate in a custody determination to the extent that these circumstances are shown to affect the well-being of the children" (*Silva v. Silva*, 136 P.3d 371 (Idaho App. 2006). When working on a case in which child care is an issue, the paralegal should research applicable law in the jurisdiction to learn when the courts are likely to decide the child's "well-being" is affected and why. For example, does it matter who provides the child care and how regular, how frequent, or how costly it is?

Stability

Stability is an important factor in custody deliberations. Recognizing that children's lives are seriously disrupted by divorce, courts often strive to maintain as much stability and continuity for them as possible. When fashioning custody agreements, the model that is likely to provide the greatest degree of stability for the child is one based on caretaking patterns during the marriage. Essentially, this amounts to the ALI or primary caretaker approach.

Although the ALI Approximation Rule provides that custodial arrangements during a period of temporary custody will not be considered by the court, the parent who has temporary custody pending a final order often has a subtle advantage in a contested custody case. If the child is doing well with that parent, the court may be very reluctant to disturb the status quo. In relocation cases, the parent with primary physical custody is likely to have an advantage, and, in some states, there is a presumption to that effect.

Gender

Gender-based presumptions have largely been abolished or declared unconstitutional as a violation of equal protection. The public policy of virtually all states is that fit parents have equal custody rights regardless of gender. Sometimes the policy is expressly referenced in court decisions, as in the following excerpt from a South Carolina case:

> In South Carolina, in custody matters, the mother and father are in parity as to entitlement to the custody of a child. When analyzing the right to custody as between a father and a mother, equanimity is mandated.... The parents stand in perfect equipoise as the custody analysis begins.[22]

Many states have codified a gender-neutral position, as Missouri has in its child custody statute: "As between the parents of a child, no preference may be given to either parent in the awarding of custody because of that parent's age, sex, or financial status, nor because of the age or sex of the child."[23]

However, the reality is that over 80 percent of custody awards are still made to mothers. Based on 2002 census data, 2.2 million men in the United States have primary custody of their children. That represents one-sixth of the total number of custodial parents, a very modest increase over the one-ninth proportion in 1970.[24] The bottom line is that regardless of what statutes may say with respect to the relevance of gender to custody decisions, gender stereotypes still persist. Five-sixths of custodial parents are women, and the functions considered as evidence of caretaking of children involve activities still performed predominantly by mothers. Mothers tend to be more highly penalized for extramarital affairs than men are,[25] and when they pursue careers, they are often viewed as self-interested and neglectful.

Race

The U.S. Supreme Court made clear in the landmark case of *Palmore v. Sidoti* that the equal protection clause of the Constitution prohibits the making of custody decisions based upon racial bias and a fear of potential harm to a child as a result of racial prejudice. (See Case 8.1.) Race of the parents or the child may not be used as the sole factor in determining what will be in the child's best interests. The issue remains open, however, as to what a court's proper course of action is if actual harm is occurring in response to a child's racial or ethnic heritage.

Religion

Under the Establishment Clause of the U.S. Constitution, the courts cannot favor or promote one religion over another. The court also cannot unduly restrict a party's freedom of religion absent a compelling state interest, such as the health or safety of a child. However, courts may properly consider which parent can best meet the religious needs of a child. Some states, such as Michigan,[26] include "the capacity and disposition of the parties to continue the education and raising of the child in his or her religion or creed, if any" as a statutory best interest factor. If a child has already begun to develop a religious identity, the court may look to which parent is best positioned to support continuation of that development.

CASE **8.1** *Palmore v. Sidoti,* 466 U.S. 429, 104 S. Ct. 1879, 80 L. Ed. 2d 421 (1984)

BACKGROUND

In this case, custody of the parties' minor daughter was granted to the Caucasian mother. The father (who also was Caucasian) subsequently petitioned for and was granted a modification of custody based on allegations of several instances of the mother's failure to properly care for the child and the fact that she was planning to marry an African-American man with whom she had been living. A lower court and the Florida District Court of Appeals affirmed that the change in custody would serve the best interests of the child. The mother appealed the decision to the U.S. Supreme Court.

The Supreme Court reversed and stated the following:

FROM THE OPINION

. . . The goal of granting custody based on the best interests of the child is indisputably a substantial governmental interest for purposes of the Equal Protection Clause.

. . . It would ignore reality to suggest that racial and ethnic prejudices do not exist, or that all manifestations of those prejudices have been eliminated. There is a risk that a child living with a stepparent of a different race may be subject to a variety of pressures and stresses not present if the child were living with parents of the same racial or ethnic origin.

. . . The question, however, is whether the reality of private biases and the possible injury they might inflict are permissible considerations for removal of an infant child from the custody of its natural mother. We have little difficulty concluding that they are not. The Constitution cannot control such prejudices, but neither can it tolerate them. Private biases may be outside the reach of the law, but the law cannot directly or indirectly give them effect.

SIDEBAR

The full opinion in this case is available on the companion website for this text in the material related to Chapter 8.

Paralegal Practice Tip

If two parents are equally qualified to parent a child, can race tip the balance in favor of one of the parents? In a 2006 Illinois case, an appellate court held that, given two such parents, the fact that the mother was African-American made her more qualified than the Caucasian father to parent their biracial child, as she was better prepared to help the child deal with hostility toward biracial individuals (*In re Marriage of Gambla,* 367 Ill. App. 3d 441, 853 N.E.2d 847 (2006)). Do you agree with this outcome, particularly in light of the *Palmore* decision? The case is available on the companion website for this text in the material related to Chapter 8.

The majority of courts that have addressed custody conflicts between parents arising from religious differences have affirmed each parent's right to freedom of religion and to parent a child by providing religious exposure and instruction as he or she sees fit. Conflicts most frequently arise in situations in which there is a dispute regarding medical care or disciplinary measures (particularly excessive corporal punishment), when a religion promotes illegal activities (polygamy, animal sacrifice, use of illegal drugs, etc.), or when one parent has no religious affiliation. Given that loss of custody is a high price to pay for exercising one's freedom of religion, courts generally are reluctant to intervene, even in cases involving medical treatment. However, if the conduct of the parent or a challenged belief or practice presents a substantial threat of present or future physical or emotional harm to the child, courts have been willing to restrict parental custody or behavior affecting the child in the least intrusive manner possible. The harm must be actual or highly likely and not simply speculative. For example, in a 1995 case, the Nebraska Court of Appeals declined to deprive a mother of custody, stating:

> . . . in order for Jeanne's religion to constitute a ground for awarding custody to Larry, we must be able to determine from the record that the Jehovah's Witness religion as practiced by Jeanne constitutes an immediate and substantial threat to the minor children's well-being. . . .
>
> As evidence of an immediate and substantial threat,. . . Larry makes reference to the fact that even in a medical emergency, Jeanne would refuse to consent to any of the children's receiving a blood transfusion. . . .
>
> No evidence was presented showing that any of the minor children were prone to accidents or plagued with any sort of affliction that might necessitate a blood transfusion in the future. We cannot decide this case based on some hypothetical future accident or illness that might necessitate such treatment.[27]

In a Pennsylvania case, the Superior Court opined that "For children of divorce in general, exposure to parents' conflicting values, lifestyles and religious beliefs may indeed cause doubts and stress. However, stress is not always harmful, nor is it always to be avoided and protected against. The key is not whether the child experiences stress, but whether the stress experienced is unproductively severe."[28] (See Paralegal Application 8.3.)

PARALEGAL APPLICATION 8.3

YOU BE THE JUDGE. . .

FACT PATTERN

Although such agreements are generally held to be unenforceable, a Jewish mother and a Catholic father agreed prior to marriage that their children would be raised in the Jewish faith. They subsequently had three children: Ari, ten, Moriah, six, and Rebekah, four. Three years after the parents married, the father joined a fundamentalist Christian church. The mother adopted Orthodox Judaism, the strictest of the Jewish movements. Ari was circumcised and was described as having a "Jewish identity," which is akin to having an ethnic identity as well as a religious faith. The two girls had traditional naming ceremonies, and all three children attended a Jewish school. The father testified at trial that he would never stop trying to save his children. His behavior toward them projected a negative image of the Jewish faith

continued

and culture, and he opposed their being taught about the holocaust. The father told the children that all individuals who do not accept his faith are sinners and will burn in hell. In addition, he cut off his son's payes (sideburns with religious significance) and threatened to cut off his tzitzitz (clothing fringe). The guardian *ad litem* reported that Ari's motivation and academic performance were declining and that he was uncomfortable and unhappy when visiting his father when he had "to do stuff he's not supposed to do on shabbas." The elder of the two daughters was experiencing stress relating to the ongoing conflict between the two parents. The mother is seeking to limit the children's exposure to their father's religion and the father responds that any limitation would constitute a restriction of his right to freedom of religion under the state and U.S. Constitutions.

SIDEBAR

What do you think the Court should do? Why? Read the case *Kendall v. Kendall*, 426 Mass. 238, 687 N.E.2d 1228 (1997) and see if you agree with the result. The case is available in its entirety on the companion website for this text in the material related to Chapter 8.

Parental Health or Disability

Poor physical or mental health of a parent will not necessarily render a parent unfit as a custodial parent. The court will examine the "nexus" or connection between the condition and the parent's capacity to provide proper child care. Stereotypes are hard to overcome, but some courts have come a long way. For example:

- In an Illinois case, an appellate court upheld the decision of a trial court to reject a custody evaluator's advice and granted custody of a child to a mother with an IQ of sixty-seven. The court found that the mother had been the child's primary caregiver, was capable of protecting the child from harm, and, with assistance, was able to foster the child's intellectual development.[29]
- In a Massachusetts case, the appeals court upheld a lower court's award of custody to a mother suffering from debilitating multiple sclerosis, contrary to the recommendation of the guardian *ad litem*. The court found that the lower court had properly considered the best interests of the child and noted that the mother had a full-time personal care assistant.[30]

But the results are not always positive for a parent with a disability. For instance, in the Illinois case above, the outcome may have been different if the child had a serious medical condition that required administering oxygen, balancing medications, and maintaining complicated dietary restrictions. In the Massachusetts case, the mother might not have been granted custody if she did not have her personal care assistant. Some courts even consider the disability of a parent's partner. A Kentucky court found, for example, that cohabitation of a custodial parent with an HIV-infected partner is, taken alone, a sufficient ground for modifying custody in favor of the noncustodial parent.[31]

Sexual Activity

The majority view is that a parent's sexual behavior or cohabitation with a heterosexual or same-sex partner is a proper factor to be considered by a court in making a custody determination, but that it should not play a role in the custody decision unless there is a connection between the behavior and the health and welfare of the child. However, some courts have held that extramarital cohabitation in the presence of children is contrary to a public policy of maintaining a stable environment for children and that "a parent's unmarried cohabitation with a romantic partner, or a parent's promiscuous conduct or lifestyle, in the presence of a child cannot be abided."[32] Courts have also enforced agreements between parties prohibiting either party from having "overnight guests of the opposite sex in front of the children" even if no adverse impact is shown.[33]

Historically, the level of tolerance has been higher for heterosexual relationships, but many states have applied a **per se rule** with regard to gay and lesbian parents. Harm was assumed to occur if a child were being raised by a gay or lesbian parent. In contemporary society, sexual orientation should not be a factor in custody decisions. However, despite the legalization of homosexual behavior and of same-sex marriage in two states as of June 2008, efforts sometimes still are made to argue that a parent's homosexuality has a detrimental impact on his or her children. Even if not expressly argued, old biases are hard to eliminate. Concern is expressed about the "stigma" of being raised by a gay or lesbian parent, particularly in a rural, conservative community where the parent may be perceived as immoral and the child is subjected to physical and psychological abuse as a result of the parent's sexual orientation. (See Case 8.2.)

Per se rule
by itself, without reference to additional facts

CASE **8.2** *McGriff v. McGriff,* 140 Idaho 642; 99 P.3d 111 (2004)

BACKGROUND

In this case, the Idaho Supreme Court affirmed a District Court's order denying a father's request for a modification in custody and granting custody of the parties' two children to his former wife. Among other claims in his appeal, Theron claimed that the court erred in basing its order modifying shared legal and physical custody on his sexual orientation. Although the order granted visitation to Theron on alternate weekends, it conditioned that visitation on his not residing in the same house with his male partner during those visits. The Idaho Supreme Court affirmed the lower court's decision.

FROM THE OPINION

. . . Admittedly, the allegations in Shawn's petition to modify were based largely on Theron's homosexuality and the magistrate judge did make specific reference to how Theron communicated his sexual orientation to the two children. However it does not appear that the magistrate's decision to modify custody was based on Theron's homosexuality. The magistrate stated:

> Father's homosexuality may not influence his/her (sic) parenting ability per se, and this Court does not decide custody and visitation issues on that basis. However, father's decision to openly co-habit with . . . , his partner, is a change of circumstances which needed to be jointly communicated to the girls in an appropriate manner. It is a change that will generate questions from the girls and their friends regarding their father's lifestyle. Moreover, Father has minimized this issue in regard to the conservative culture and morays (sic) in which the children live. Father has shown some insensitivity to the girls' needs regarding his lifestyle, even contrary to the recommendations of the Court-appointed evaluator. . . .

The majority of findings upon which the magistrate based his decision to modify custody . . . were unrelated to Theron's homosexuality. . . .

continued

In his decision, the magistrate found that Theron's choice of lifestyle should not be minimized in light of the conservative culture and values of the community in which the parties and the children reside. While we acknowledge that homosexuality is a sensitive issue and that a parent may feel he or she has a valid concern about the way in which the other parent communicates this to their children; whether or not a parent's sexual orientation will, in and of itself, support a change in custody of the children is a different issue altogether. It is important to observe that last year's landmark United States Supreme Court decision in *Lawrence v. Texas*, 539 U.S. 558, 156 L. Ed. 2d 508, 123 S. Ct. 2472 (2003) legalized the practice of homosexuality and in essence made it a protected practice under the Due Process clause of the United States Constitution. Justice Anthony Kennedy, writing for the majority, wrote:

> The petitioners are entitled to respect for their private lives. The state cannot demean their existence or control their destiny by making their private sexual conduct a crime. . . .

...This decision also has at least some bearing on the degree to which homosexuality may play a part in child custody proceedings. But even before the Lawrence decision was handed down, it was established in a number of state courts across the nation that a homosexual parent may not be denied custody of a child unless there is sufficient evidence presented to show that the parent's homosexuality is having a negative effect on the child and that the parent's custody is not in the best interests of the child. Only when there is a nexus between harm to the child and a parent's homosexuality, can that parent's sexual orientation be a factor in determining custody.... Sexual orientation, in and of itself, cannot be the basis for awarding or removing custody; only when the parent's sexual orientation is shown to cause harm to the child, such that the child's best interests are not served, should sexual orientation be a factor in determining custody.

SIDEBAR

This case is available in its entirety on the companion website for this text in the material related to Chapter 8. Read the case, including the dissent. Do you believe that the court's decision was or was not based on the father's sexual preference? Do you think the outcome would have been the same if the father were a heterosexual who was cohabiting with his girlfriend?

Parental Lifestyle

Judges are expected to rise above their own prejudices and to base their decisions on an objective analysis of the needs of children and the course of action best suited to meet those needs. However, we can never really know the extent to which subjective views about variations in lifestyle play a role in custody determinations. Judges are human. They have their own views of the world, and their own biases, moral codes, and levels of tolerance for what might be called "non-mainstream" behaviors or unusual beliefs. Some behaviors clearly are simply lifestyle choices, such as the decision to have pets or to engage in social drinking. Others are sufficiently extreme or potentially harmful that they may be viewed by the courts as lifestyle choices that cross an invisible dividing line between moral conduct and immoral conduct that may be harmful to children. The critical question is, "Does the behavior harm the child?"

A Florida court conditioned a father's right to visitation on his agreement to remove his cats from his home before his allergic sons would be allowed to stay overnight with him.[34] Courts in several states have either denied or conditioned custody on a smoking parent's agreement to not smoke in the presence or environment

Parens patriae doctrine
the doctrine holding that the government, as parent of the country, has standing to act on behalf of a citizen, particularly one who is a minor or under a disability

Judicial notice
a court's acceptance of a well-known fact without requiring proof

of a child suffering from respiratory problems. The behavior is usually raised by a nonsmoking parent as a risk to the child. However, in a highly unusual action, an Ohio court raised the issue of the danger of secondhand smoke on behalf of a healthy child under the **parens patriae *doctrine.*** The court took ***judicial notice*** of the dangers of secondhand smoke, citing overwhelming authoritative scientific evidence. It then issued an order restraining a custodial mother and her significant other from smoking in the presence of the mother's healthy eight-year-old child to protect her from having her health compromised by being forced to breathe secondhand smoke. The court held that the parent's right to privacy did not include the right to inflict secondhand smoke on the child.[35]

It is apparent from judicial decisions and state statutes that moral character and conduct count under some circumstances. The Michigan "best interest statute," for example, lists as a factor for consideration the "moral fitness of the parties involved."[36] A Georgia court has held that a parent may be denied custody of a child by putting "her own desires and perceived needs ahead of and to the detriment of her children" and lacking "the moral fiber" to be a role model for her children.[37] On the other hand, an Illinois statute reflects the general rule regarding the relationship between conduct and custody decisions that the "court shall not consider the conduct of a present or proposed custodian that does not affect his relationship to the child."[38]

Often the parents both have problems, and some states reflect this possibility in the statutory factors to be considered in custody determinations. For example, the applicable Wyoming statute calls for the court to consider the "relative competency and fitness of each parent."[39] However, the courts are often willing to grant considerable benefit of the doubt to parents who have had conduct issues such as drug or alcohol abuse, particularly if a parent is seeking treatment and making progress.

History of Abuse

Every state provides by statute or case law that a history of domestic abuse will be considered in custody determinations.[40] Although this has not always been the case, courts now take judicial notice of the research documenting the effect of being a victim of and witnessing domestic violence. Most especially, the courts recognize that children who have witnessed domestic abuse are at significantly greater risk of both becoming abusers and being abused in their intimate relationships as adults. Many states include a history of domestic violence as a statutory factor to be considered by the court when making custody determinations, as in the New Jersey Statute in Exhibit 8.1. Other states go further and establish a rebuttable presumption against granting custody to a parent who has been a documented perpetrator of domestic violence. (See Chapter 15.)

Child Preference

Historically, children's custodial preferences carried no weight, given children's lack of legal status and the existence of strong paternal and maternal preferences. This situation has changed dramatically over the years, and today children's wishes may be considered to some extent in all states. Even though it is permitted, however, most courts, attorneys, and even parents flatly oppose asking children to state a preference unless mandated by law. A small minority believes that children, even immature children, have a right to be heard, and, in some states, the child's preference will be determinative under certain circumstances.

The South Carolina Code reflects the majority view with respect to parental preferences of minor children: "In determining the best interests of the child, the court must consider the child's reasonable preference for custody. The court shall place weight upon the preference based upon the child's age, experience, maturity, judgment, and ability to express a preference."[41] Usually, minimal weight is given to the preferences of children under the age of seven. However, once children reach the teenage years, most courts have taken the position that the preferences of older children should be given serious consideration. (See Exhibit 8.2.)

If a child's preference is to be expressed, the challenge then becomes one of determining how to solicit it in a sensitive and age-appropriate manner: as a witness, through a guardian *ad litem,* through the child's attorney or other advocate such as a CASA (Court Appointed Special Advocate) volunteer (if one has been appointed), or through an interview with the judge in chambers. (See Exhibit 8.3 and Paralegal Application 8.4.) Most commonly, the GAL testifies as to the child's preferences unless the court allows either party to call the child as a witness or the judge is asked or elects to take testimony.

EXHIBIT 8.2 Statutory Provisions Re Child Preference in Custody
Context—Ga. Code Ann. §19–9–3

FROM THE STATUTE

(a)(4)... where the child has reached the age of 14 years, such child shall have the right to select the parent with whom such child desires to live and such selection shall be controlling unless the parent so selected is determined not to be a fit and proper person to have the custody of said child.

(a)(4.1) In all custody cases in which the child has reached the age of at least 11 but not 14 years, the court shall consider the desires and educational needs of the child in determining which parent shall have custody. The child's selection shall not be controlling. The best interests of the child standard shall apply.

EXHIBIT 8.3 Statutory Provisions Re Testimony in Custody Cases—
Utah Code Ann. §30–3–10(1)(c)(d) and (e)

FROM THE STATUTE

(c)   The children may not be required by either party to testify unless the trier of fact determines that extenuating circumstances exist that would necessitate the testimony of the children be heard and there is no other reasonable method to present their testimony.

(d)   The court may inquire of the children and take into consideration the children's desires regarding future custody or parent-time schedules, but the expressed desires are not controlling.... The desires of a child 16 years of age or older shall be given added weight, but is not the single controlling factor.

(e)   If interviews with the children are conducted by the court..., they shall be conducted by the judge in camera. The prior consent of the parties may be obtained but is not necessary if the court finds that an interview with the children is the only method to ascertain the child's desires regarding custody.

PARALEGAL APPLICATION **8.4**

PREPARING CHILDREN FOR COURT

One of the tasks paralegals are sometimes called upon to perform is to assist in preparing witnesses for court appearances. This does not involve telling the witness what to say, but rather explaining what is likely to happen in court and supporting them emotionally. Children, particularly young children, are rarely called as witnesses in custody proceedings, because of the potential trauma it may cause them. Occasionally, however, judges do "interview" children in chambers or in the courtroom. Parents are rarely present, but counsel for the parties are.

If called upon to orient a child for an interview, the following excerpt from a handbook for children published by the American Bar Association may be especially helpful and could easily be adapted for a conversation between a paralegal and a child rather than between the judge and a child. A copy of the Handbook may also be given to the parent for possible sharing with the child.

FROM THE HANDBOOK

Your Talk with the Judge

When I talk with a child, I do not use the courtroom. Often we sit in my office, also called my "chambers"—which is an old English term for office. Most of the time parents will not be present. A court reporter may be there to write down everything we say and type it up for me in what is called a "transcript." Lawyers for your parents may be present—as will your lawyer if you have one. While not exactly private, we try our best to provide a comfortable place for you to talk.

I never ask a child to choose with whom he or she wants to live. Divorce is hard enough on kids without that. My number one goal is to get to know you and what you are feeling so that I can make the best decision to help you grow into a healthy adult.

I may ask you lots of questions about your interests, school, and your living situation. I may ask about people in your life who matter to you, including your parents. I will ask you questions about the time you spend with your parents, before the divorce and now. I may ask who helps you when you have a problem or need help with school work or need a haircut or spending money. I may ask how you celebrate holidays and what you like to do on vacations. I will probably share some ideas I have about visiting schedules with your parents and get your ideas on the subject.

Sometimes a child tells me of a desire to live with one parent. Your wishes are very important for me to consider, particularly if you are older.... I must consider all the information I have heard. Sometimes I cannot honor a child's request to live with a parent because it is not the best decision for that child.

Not all judges will talk with the children in all cases. If the judge in your parents' case will not be talking with you, it is not because he or she does not care about you. Or the judge may decide that going to court would not be good for you. In that case, other witnesses will give the judge a good idea of what you think and feel.

Children's true feelings in custody conflicts are not always easy to discern. Their expressed preferences may be suspect, as they are often consciously or unconsciously influenced by a variety of factors and circumstances. Children may believe they are to blame for the breakup of the marriage and the ensuing conflict. They may be the pawns of one of the parents or subject to manipulation by both parents. They may be overtly angry in general or at one of the parties in particular. One of the parents may be viewed as more likely to "spoil" them with material benefits. One may be viewed as the more lax in setting and enforcing rules and administering discipline. The courts are especially cautious about expressed preferences in situations where there is a history of abuse, as a child may fear or identify with an aggressor who will not necessarily be the parent best suited to meet the child's needs. Whatever a child's preference, the overriding weight must be given to the best interests of the child.

Parental Alienation Syndrome

In assessing which parent would be the preferred custodial parent, the court will look at the extent to which each parent has the capacity to rise above his or her own desires and hostility to focus on the child's need to maintain a warm and positive relationship with both parents. For some parents, this is an impossible challenge, and such a parent will do everything within his or her power to disrupt visitation, denigrate the other parent in front of the child, and alienate the child from the other parent. In the extreme, some experts believe that a child who was close to both parents before the divorce will come to idealize one parent and demonize the other as a result of the former's pressure and manipulation. Some psychologists label this condition the *parental alienation syndrome.*

Parental alienation syndrome a condition in which a child involved in a custody dispute comes to idealize one parent and demonize the other parent as a result of the former parent's pressure and manipulation

VISITATION RIGHTS AND SCHEDULES

Although it is generally acknowledged that children benefit most when they have the sustained physical and emotional support of both parents, divorce often makes this ideal an impossible one to realize.

> Like Humpty Dumpty, a family, once broken by divorce, cannot be put together in precisely the same way. The relationship between the parents and the children is necessarily different after a divorce and, accordingly, it may be unrealistic in some cases to try to preserve the noncustodial parent's accustomed close involvement in the children's everyday life. . . .[42]

When joint custody is not desirable or feasible, visitation will customarily be awarded to a fit noncustodial parent, unless it would pose a threat to the child's health and welfare. There are no fixed formulas for visitation provisions. They assume a variety of forms, depending in large part on the degree to which the parents are able to communicate with one another regarding the children's needs and schedules and the extent to which they share a common vision as to appropriate parenting behaviors and goals for the children's welfare. The overriding goal is to provide a sufficient amount of time to enable the noncustodial parent to remain a significant part of the child's life. Schedules are tailored to a number of variables, most especially the relative availability of the parents, the proximity of the parents' residences to one another, and the ages, activities, and developmental needs of the children.

The schedule will ideally be agreed on by the parties and may reflect the results of consultation with the children, depending on their ages and levels of maturity. It will customarily be laid out in a "Separation Agreement" or a "Parenting

Plan." If the parties cannot agree, the court will determine the schedule and include it in its order or decree. Some courts rely heavily on model parenting schedules prepared by legal and mental health professionals that take developmental needs and milestones into account.[43] Assuming the parents live near each other and the children are in elementary school, a common schedule would be to have visitation Wednesdays after school, one to two weekends a month (or one day each weekend with an occasional overnight), alternating holidays, shared school vacation weeks, and an extended period during the summer months (at least one month). This schedule amounts to the child being with the noncustodial parent approximately 20 percent of the time.

Defined v. Flexible Visitation Schedules

Visitation schedules range from those defined in open-ended terms such as "visitation as the parties may reasonably agree," to highly detailed provisions such as the one contained in the Sample Separation Agreement in Chapter 12. Open-ended schedules tend to work best when parents have been separated for an extended period and already have worked out a mutually satisfactory plan. Detailed schedules usually address weekly/monthly visitation, holidays and vacations, pickup and delivery times and places, out-of-state travel with the children, illness and medical treatment of a child, transportation arrangements and costs (if incurred), telephone contact, guidelines for handling cancellations and other deviations from the schedule, provision of clothing and other supplies for the children during visitation, any conditions with respect to third parties being present during visitation, dispute resolution measures, etc.

Most visitation provisions fall somewhere between the two extremes. Some degree of structure is preferred by a majority of family law practitioners to minimize potential misunderstandings and disputes between the parties. The basic parameters are provided and provision is made for alterations as mutually agreed upon. This approach offers each parent a desirable degree of flexibility, while guaranteeing a basic level of involvement of the noncustodial parent that each parent and the children can plan on.

Several states now make parenting plan formats available online, generally through court websites. A number of computer programs also are available to help parties and counsel establish parenting schedules and courts to more easily and quickly review their nature and scope. These programs are especially useful in complex cases involving multiple children and frequent visitation. Some programs generate color-coded calendar graphics to help parties and children visualize the schedule and plan ahead.

Although specific visitation plans are useful, they may also give rise to disagreements, as high-conflict divorce cases often remanifest themselves in the form of high-conflict visitation cases. These cases are costly and burdensome to everyone involved—parents, attorneys, and the court—and they can be very stressful for children. Disputes may focus on technical violations (such as arriving late or failing to return the children exactly on time or making disparaging remarks about the other parent) or major issues (concealing the child's whereabouts or engaging in inappropriate behavior with a new sexual partner in front of the children). Courts make every effort to provide for traditional and innovative dispute resolution strategies short of having the parties return to court.[44] If the parties do keep returning to court, a visitation monitor or parenting coordinator may be appointed to oversee visitation on an ongoing basis with the cost to be divided between the parties. In the extreme, if the actions of one of the parents deprive the child of having any kind of relationship with the other parent, the court may remove the child from the custody of the uncooperative parent as a last resort, even if such an action is contrary to the preference of the child.[45]

Supervised and Unsupervised Visitation

Unsupervised visitation occurs when a parent is free to spend visitation time with children as he or she wishes without additional persons being present or being subject to conditions imposed by the court or the other parent. Most visitation is unsupervised.

Supervised visitation may be ordered in a variety of circumstances in which a question exists as to the fitness or competency of the noncustodial parent to appropriately or adequately care for his or her child. In extreme cases, there are situations in which a parent may be deemed unfit to parent, and his or her parental rights may be terminated. Even without a termination of rights, courts may deny not only custody but also visitation if such an action is in the best interest of the child. Short of termination of rights, the most common reasons why a court might order supervised visitation are that a parent has a history of substance abuse problems, mental illness, domestic violence, or failure to properly supervise and care for a child while in his or her custody, or when there is a reasonable fear that the noncustodial parent may try to abduct the child. The visitation may take place in an informal setting with supervision being by a friend or family member, or it may be in a facility equipped to monitor visitation in a controlled environment that charges a fee for services, such as a YMCA or Domestic Violence Center. A parent who has been denied unsupervised visitation may eventually ask the court to consider elimination of restrictions, a request that may or may not be granted, depending on the circumstances.

A court will not necessarily order that visitation be supervised, but rather on occasion will condition the right to visitation on a parent's agreeing to abstain from or engage in a particular behavior or activity. A parent may be ordered to attend parenting classes or participate in family counseling or treatment programs for anger management or substance abuse problems. A parent with a substance abuse problem may be required to agree to abstain from the use of drugs or alcohol as a condition of having visitation with his or her child.[46] Restrictions may also be placed on the kinds of activities the children can participate in while in the noncustodial parent's care, on the third parties who may be present during visitation, or on activities the parent may participate in with his or her child present.

Virtual Visitation

The potential of technology for promoting communication between parents and children during periods of absence is boundless. Technology offers benefits for parents who are separated from their children by blocks, counties, or state and national boundaries. E-mail, online games, and videoconferencing allow parents and children to interact and share information about what is happening in their respective daily lives or to work on projects or plans together. Courts have begun to include "*virtual visitation*" provisions in the parenting provisions of their initial decrees. For example, in a Connecticut case the court made the following order:

Virtual visitation communication between parents and children through the use of technology

> The Husband shall have "virtual visitation" with the children twice per week, on Tuesdays and Thursdays, from 6:00 P.M. to 7:00 P.M., and at such additional times as the parties may agree. To facilitate the virtual visitation each party shall forthwith purchase and install a video camera attachment and the related software for his or her computer.[47]

PARALEGAL APPLICATION 8.5

VIRTUAL VISITATION

When drafting documents relating to custody and particularly relocations and modifications, consideration should be given to including virtual visitation provisions in parenting agreements for incorporation in court orders. In addition to basic e-mail, some of the options presently available include text-to-speech capability, video e-mail, message-forwarding capability, creation of a website or a dedicated page on an existing website, videoconferencing, webcams, etc.

Courts in several states have noted in the context of relocation cases that despite physical separation, parents can maintain regular communication and significant contact with their child by applying the benefits of modern technology. For example, in the *McCoy* case in 2001, a New Jersey appeals court granted a mother permission to relocate from New Jersey to California with her nine-year-old disabled daughter over the objection of the child's father. The court praised the mother's "virtual visitation" proposal to develop an interactive website to facilitate the child's communication with her father as "creative and innovative." Through the use of camera-computer technology, the site would give the father and others the ability to communicate face-to-face with the daughter daily and to review her schoolwork and records on an ongoing basis.[48] Virtual visitation is a particularly valuable resource in cases involving parents residing in different nations or in international relocation requests. For example, a New York court included the following provision in its order granting a mother's request to relocate to Saudi Arabia with her six-year-old son.

> …Respondent shall hire, at her expense, a computer consultant in both New York and Dhahran to select, purchase and set up compatible computer systems with laser printers in both Petitioner's residence in New York and in Adrian's new residence in Dhahran to enable petitioner and son to communicate on the dedicated phone line. In addition, Adrian's room shall have a telephone with answering machine also with a separate dedicated phone line for Petitioner and Adrian to utilize. In the order to be settled, Respondent shall propose a reasonable schedule of communication by telephone, internet and fax and shall provide proof that the aforesaid systems and telephone have been installed, are fully operational, and that the dedicated phone lines are in place.[49]

(See Paralegal Application 8.5.)

PARENTING PLANS

Parenting plan
a written agreement in which parents lay out plans for taking care of their children post-separation or divorce

A *parenting plan* is now a critical component of a child custody case. In some states, parents are encouraged to develop plans covering their children's remaining childhood years. In other states, they are required to do so. In such states, if custody is a contested issue, each parent must submit a proposed custody implementation plan at trial. The court may issue an order that tracks the proposal of one or the other of the parties' plans or may reject both and create its own order. As indicated above, several states have developed guidelines or forms to assist parents in developing appropriate plans.[50] The court may waive the requirement of a parenting plan in a limited number of cases, such as those involving a history of domestic violence.

A primary goal of a parenting plan is to promote cooperative parenting and minimize disputes and continued hostility around parenting issues after dissolution of the marriage. Ideally, plans should reflect children's developmental needs at the time of the divorce and going forward into the future. By statute, the state of Washington has identified the following objectives of a parenting plan:

- Provide for the child's physical care
- Maintain the child's emotional stability
- Provide for the child's changing needs as the child grows and matures, in a way that minimizes the need for future modifications to the permanent parenting plan
- Set forth the authority and responsibilities of each parent with respect to the child
- Minimize the child's exposure to harmful parental conflict
- Encourage the parents to meet their responsibilities to their minor children through agreements in the permanent parenting plan, rather than by relying on judicial intervention
- To otherwise protect the best interests of the child.[51]

The range of topics covered in plans is reflected in the Wisconsin Proposed Parenting Plan, available on the companion website for this text in the material related to Chapter 8. The topics are similar to those contained in detailed child-related provisions of separation agreements. The essential differences are in process and focus rather than specific terms. The focus in a separation agreement is on contractual terms binding the adversarial parents with respect to each other. At least in spirit, a parenting plan is focused more on the children and on the importance of shared involvement and cooperation in meeting their ongoing needs.

PARENT EDUCATION PROGRAMS

Parents struggling with their own needs, conflicts, and stress during divorce proceedings often forget that it is not all about them. Parenting programs are designed to sensitize parents to the needs and feelings of their children, who are frequently victims of their parents' anger, frustration, and bitterness.

Many states require parents who are getting divorced to complete a parent education program, and virtually all of those who do not mandate participation recommend it. Some states also require that the parties' children in a certain age range also participate (between ages eight and sixteen in Delaware; six and seventeen in Florida). The programs for children are designed to help them cope with divorce and share their feelings with others in their age group. Courts make available information about approved program providers in pamphlets or Q&A sheets, and many do so online, including the names and locations of various programs by city and town. Some states grant waivers of participation under a limited number of circumstances, such as language barriers, institutionalization, or other unavailability of a party, or chronic and severe abuse that negates safe parental communication.

The primary purposes of parenting programs are to

- encourage parents to work cooperatively for the benefit of their children
- help children through the difficult period of divorce and separation
- reduce post-divorce litigation and court appearances

The curriculum of parent education programs varies from state to state and program to program, but commonly includes topics such as the following:

- the emotional effects of divorce or separation on parents and children
- what parents can do to help their children adjust
- harmful effects of parental conflict on children and how to avoid them
- communication and co-parenting skills
- developmental stages and needs of children
- factors that contribute to a child's healthy adjustment
- the function and value of parenting plans
- techniques of problem solving and conflict resolution
- warning signs that children are having problems
- community resources

In jurisdictions where participation in parent education programs is mandatory, failure to complete a program may have serious consequences. Among other options, the court may:

- refuse to move the case forward
- dismiss the case
- hold one or both parties in contempt

MODIFICATION OF CUSTODY ORDERS

At some time after the court issues its initial order, either parent may come to believe that a change in custody and/or visitation is warranted. Customarily, courts will not allow the parents to agree in advance to self-executing grounds for modification, as custody decisions are supposed to be based on a determination of the best interests of the child at the time of the modification. However, occasionally parties accomplish changes informally, and this may work as long as the parties are in agreement. However, an informal approach can be a problem if child support is an issue or if one of the parties later files for contempt, claiming he or she never agreed to a change.

The usual process for obtaining a modification involves filing a Motion for Modification of Custody (commonly accompanied by an affidavit in support of the Motion) in the court that has continuing jurisdiction, service of notice on the other party, possible filing of an affidavit in opposition to the Motion by the other party, and then a hearing before the court, at which time the parties each have an opportunity to testify, call witnesses, and present documentation in support of their respective positions.

A party seeking to modify a custody order generally must show that:

- there has been a substantial and material change of circumstances that affects the child's welfare,
- the change has occurred since entry of the decree and was not foreseeable,
- the change warrants a modification in custody, and
- the change will be in the child's best interests.

Although theoretically a Motion for Modification can be brought whenever a substantial change occurs that impacts the child's best interests, in states that have adopted the Uniform Marriage and Divorce Act (UMDA),[52] absent an emergency, a modification cannot be sought for at least two years from the date the decree or prior order was issued. The rationale for the rule is that children need stability in their lives, and changes in primary custody should be discouraged because they disrupt the child's life.

Motions will usually be granted if the parties agree to the modification, if it is apparent that an initial allocation of parental rights and responsibilities is not working, if there is clear and convincing evidence that the child's present environment is harming his or her physical, mental, or emotional health, or if the court finds that there is repeated, intentional, and unwarranted interference by one parent with the rights and responsibilities of the other parent. Commonly, the request for modification relates to a change in the circumstances of the custodial parent, but occasionally it results from a change in the noncustodial parent's circumstances that significantly alters his or her relative fitness as a parent. Case 8.3 illustrates a situation in which changes had occurred in the lives of both parents.

Relocations

Inevitably following divorce, at least one of the parents establishes a new place of residence. In today's mobile world, this initial relocation is often the first of several moves due to job changes, remarriages, economic conditions, extended family needs, and other life changes. In an initial determination to allocate parental responsibilities, courts generally have no authority to order a parent to live in a specific location. The court looks at where the parties live and factors geography into the allocation of parental responsibilities in a manner consistent with the best interests of the child. However, although courts have held that a parent has a constitutional right to travel and cannot be required to live in a particular place,[53] a problem often arises when a custodial parent wants to relocate with a minor child against the wishes of the noncustodial parent. When custody is shared and one parent wishes to relocate, there is an even higher hurdle to cross for the parent who wants to relocate if the move is opposed by the other parent. At the very least, relocation will call for a significant revision of the parties' parenting plan.

CASE **8.3** *Jackson v. Jackson*, 2004 WY 99, 96 P.3d 21 (Wyo. 2004)

DISCUSSION OF THE CASE

In this case, the mother had been awarded primary physical custody of the parties' two children at the time of divorce. From September to December 2002, the mother changed jobs five times. In February 2003, after being unemployed for over two months, she enrolled in cosmetology school. She subsequently dropped out of that program and enrolled in a different school a few months later. While she was at school the children attended day care.

During essentially the same time period, the father remained in the town where he had been living and continued working for a cable company. He made significant improvements in his lifestyle including quitting drinking and smoking and ended his association with "bad influences." He received a promotion at work and was able to provide health insurance for the children. He also developed a stable relationship with a woman whom he married shortly before the hearing on his request for modification of custody.

The court found that the balance had shifted in favor of the father and awarded him primary physical custody of the children. The Wyoming Supreme Court affirmed the change.

SIDEBAR

This case is available in its entirety on the companion website for this text in the material related to Chapter 8. Do you agree with the court's decision? Explain your response.

Relocation cases present a particular challenge for the courts, as they involve seemingly "irreconcilable conflicts in which the custodial parent's interest in building a new life with the children is often pitted against the noncustodial parent's interest in maintaining a close relationship with the children." They implicate "two legitimate interests—the custodial parent's interest in making unfettered decisions for the benefit of the new nuclear family and the noncustodial parent's interest in maintaining a close bond with the children."[54] The balancing act the court must perform occurs under the umbrella of the best interests of the child.

> The strong trend in family law is generally to allow the residential parent to move away with the child so long as satisfactory alternative parenting time arrangements with the nonresidential parent can be achieved and there are no bad faith motives for the geographical move. The basis for this new "permissive" relocation law in favor of the residential parent is a prioritizing of the "new family unit" constituted by the post-divorce relationship between the primary caretaker parent and child. It is assumed that the child's welfare and healthy development are dependent on continuity in this relationship. (citations omitted)[55]

Although the trend is toward allowing relocation and basic continuity in care, there is no uniform position among the states. Approaches run the gamut. In California, the custodial parent has a presumptive right to relocate with a minor child, subject to a court restraining a change on the ground that it would prejudice the rights or welfare of the child. In Minnesota, if a custodial parent seeks to move permanently to another state with the minor children over the noncustodial parent's objection, an evidentiary hearing is not required absent a prima facie case of endangerment to the child or a showing that the move was intended to deprive the noncustodial parent of visitation. The relevant Missouri statute presently provides that a person entitled to custody of a child shall not relocate the residence of the child for a period of more than ninety days except upon order of the court or with the written consent of the parties with custody or visitation rights. The applicable Colorado statute (available on the companion website) reflects a compromise approach in which the geographical extent of the relocation is critical. In determining whether to grant a custodial parent's relocation motion, the paramount concern is the best interests of the child. In effect, a parent may be forced to choose between custody and relocation.

ENFORCEMENT OF CUSTODY AND VISITATION ORDERS

When a parent fails to comply with court-ordered custody and visitation provisions, the other parent may be forced to return to court to enforce the order. The parent in violation may be found in contempt and be ordered to pay a fine, go to jail, or both.

Two especially difficult situations in this context occur when:

1. A parent who is failing to pay court-ordered child support insists on exercising his or her visitation rights. It is difficult for an attorney to explain to a client who is not receiving child support payments ordered by the court that he or she cannot refuse visitation and must comply with the court's order regarding custody and visitation. However unfair it may seem, the two orders are independent of one another, and each party's remedy is to pursue enforcement relief through the court.

2. A parent harbors a strong belief that the other parent is sexually abusing the child and refuses visitation or, in the extreme, flees with the child or conceals the minor's whereabouts, as in the high-profile case of Dr. Elizabeth Morgan, who at one point was incarcerated for more than two years for contempt of court because she refused to produce her daughter based on her fears of further abuse.[56]

THIRD PARTIES IN THE CUSTODY CONTEXT

Thus far in this chapter it may have seemed as if custody issues occur only in traditional families in the context of divorces between married biological parents of children. However, a basic theme of this text is that the "traditional family" has become the exception rather than the rule. Approximately one-third of families in this country have no father at all living in the home (in some urban areas, the figure is considerably higher). We have more step-parents than ever before. We have same-sex marriage, civil unions, and domestic partnerships. We have surrogate parents, adoptive parents, and *psychological parents* among other parental variations. Although a custody action most commonly is part of an action for divorce or legal separation, it may be brought by an unmarried parent or by a third party as a separate action, such as a Complaint for Custody or for Grandparent Visitation. Who are these individuals and what rights, if any, do or should they have?

> **psychological parent**
> the individual who has the strongest "parental" bond with the child, who has provided the most significant care for the child in quality and quantity, and whom the child often regards as the "parent"

"Third parties" generally fall into a limited number of categories:

- unmarried fathers whose legal status as parents is not established
- step-parents
- grandparents
- co-parents
- others, such as foster parents or extended family members

There are two primary and competing views regarding the custodial and visitation rights of third parties:

1. One school of thought holds that a biological parent has a presumptive right to custody of his or her child. This approach focuses on the fundamental rights of a fit parent to the care, custody, and control of his or her children and to direct the upbringing and education of those children.
2. The other school of thought believes it is in the best interests of a child to be placed in the custody of whichever adult will provide the healthiest and most stable environment. This approach focuses on the needs of the child and the nature and strength of the emotional bond between the child and the third party.

Historically, the courts have strongly protected parental rights, at times, some would argue, over the best interests of the child. However, as in so many other areas, the judicial winds of change have begun to blow. The decision of the U.S. Supreme Court in the *Troxel* case involving grandparent visitation rights (see Case 8.4) marks one of the rare instances in which the federal government has intervened in a family law matter traditionally left to regulation by the states.

> The opinion marks an evolution in parental autonomy protection.... By balancing the State's interest in protecting the child with the parent's interest in making child-rearing decisions free from unnecessary State interference, the Court no longer accords blind unquestioning deference to the decisions of presumptively fit parents. Ideally, when courts decide to balance the competing interests equally, the child's needs will be served and will prevail.[57]

When a third party seeks custody or visitation rights, the court must engage in a two-part inquiry:

1. Does the third party have standing to seek custody or visitation?
2. If the third party does have standing, would an award to that party be in the best interest of the child?

Standing

Standing
an individual's right to bring a matter before the court and seek relief based on a claim that he or she has a stake in the outcome of the case

Equitable parenthood
parenthood established on the basis of equitable principles of fairness rather than on biological connection

Parent by *estoppel*
an individual who has functioned as a parent with the approval of the legal parents

***De facto* parent**
an individual who performs a caretaking role without compensation for an extended period, knowing he or she is not a child's legal parent, often with the consent of the legal parents

Standing is a jurisdictional concept that refers to an individual's right to bring a matter before the court and seek relief based on a claim that he or she has a stake in the outcome of the case. Standing is usually based on statute (see Exhibits 8.4 and 8.5) but may be grounded in case law. Hawaii has one of the most liberal rules with respect to third-party standing to seek custody and visitation, extending it to "persons other than the father or mother whenever the award serves the best interests of the child."[58]

Legislatures and the courts have relied on a variety of theories of **equitable parenthood** to enable third parties to be granted rights to custody, visitation, and guardianship. The ALI Principles give the legal parents priority if they are able to care for their children, but state that custody ought to be available to individuals in addition to biological parents whose continued caregiving is presumed beneficial to a child. Specifically included are adults who have functioned in good faith as parents, believing they were legal parents; **parents by** estoppel (individuals who functioned as parents with the approval of the legal parents); and **de facto parents** (individuals who performed a caretaking role without compensation for at least two years, knowing they were not legal parents). Some jurisdictions recognize the concept of the "psychological parent," the individual who has the strongest "parental" bond with the child, who has provided the most significant care for the child in quality and quantity, and whom the child often regards as the "parent." Some states extend standing to third parties when the child has been in their custody for a certain minimum period. In extreme cases involving abuse and neglect, the state has third-party standing to seek custody of a child.[59]

EXHIBIT 8.4 Kentucky Statute KRS § 403.270 (2006) Pertaining to Custody Issues—Best Interests of Child Shall Determine— Joint Custody Permitted—De Facto Custodian

FROM THE STATUTE

(1) (a) As used in this chapter and KRS 405.020, unless the context requires otherwise, "de facto custodian" means a person who has been shown by clear and convincing evidence to have been the primary caregiver for, and financial supporter of, a child who has resided with the person for a period of six (6) months or more if the child is under three (3) years of age and for a period of one (1) year or more if the child is three (3) years or older or has been placed by the Department for Community Based Services. . . .

(b) A person shall not be a de facto custodian until a court determines by clear and convincing evidence that the person meets the definition of de facto custodian established in paragraph (a) of this subsection. Once a court determines that a person meets the definition of de facto custodian, the court shall give the person the same standing in custody matters that is given to each parent under this section. . . .

Unmarried Fathers.   Over the last four decades, increasing numbers of children have been born out of wedlock or to married women as a result of extramarital affairs. As a result, fathers might be legal fathers, biological fathers, or psychosocial/de facto fathers. Some fathers are unaware they even are fathers or have been deceived as to their children's existence. They have, for all practical purposes, become third parties.

In theory, unmarried fathers should have the same rights and obligations as married fathers and be entitled to petition the court for custody or visitation. However, that is not always the case. The U.S. Constitution guarantees biological fathers some rights to establish a connection with their offspring, but does not necessarily extend those rights to fathers who knowingly fail to acknowledge paternity in a timely manner.[60] The states vary in their approach to such situations, ranging from establishing a fixed window within which fathers must establish paternity to an approach tailored to the facts of individual cases, in hopes of reaching a fair result in each instance. The law also may impose obligations and extend rights to men who acknowledge paternity but who are ultimately determined to not be the biological father of a child. Under the Welfare Reform Act of 1996, with limited exceptions states are required to treat acknowledgments of paternity signed by mothers and "putative" fathers as establishing legal paternity. Issues related to such situations, including the establishment of putative father registries, are discussed more fully in Chapter 13.

Step-parents.   It is estimated that one in every four children will live with a step-parent before reaching the age of majority.[61] Although step-parents may have become part of American family life and are often as important in children's lives as (or even more important than) biological or legal parents, the law is unclear and inconsistent with respect to their rights and obligations. The majority view is that a step-parent's rights flow from marriage to the child's parent and do not survive dissolution of that marriage. A minority of states impose financial child support obligations on step-parents upon divorce in limited circumstances, such as when the step-parent voluntarily assumed a parental obligation to the child while married to the child's mother.[62]

EXHIBIT 8.5 Illinois Statute 750 Ilcs 5/601(b)(3) (2006) Pertaining to Jurisdiction; Commencement of [Custody] Proceeding

FROM THE STATUTE

(b) A child custody proceeding is commenced in the court: . . .

(3) by a stepparent, by filing a petition, if all of the following circumstances are met:

   (A)   the child is at least 12 years old;
   (B)   the custodial parent and stepparent were married for at least 5 years during which the child resided with the parent and stepparent;
   (C)   the custodial parent is deceased or is disabled and cannot perform the duties of a parent to the child;
   (D)   the stepparent provided for the care, control and welfare of the child prior to the initiation of custody proceedings;
   (E)   the child wishes to live with the stepparent; and
   (F)   it is alleged to be in the best interests and welfare of the child to live with the stepparent as provided in Section 602 of this Act [750 ILCS 5/602].

Paralegal Practice Tip
A federal law called the Servicemembers Civil Relief Act [65] is designed to protect military personnel on active duty by staying civil court actions or administrative proceedings during periods of military activation. Although child custody proceedings are civil in nature, some family court judges have held that in custody actions, state law must trump federal law. They argue that custody disputes are not comparable to civil property disputes, and such cases must proceed in the best interests of children. In effect, this means that parents may be forced to decide between custody and service to the country, unless they can regain custody once they are no longer deployed.

Step-parents who want to continue their relationship with their step-children often face considerable obstacles. Although a limited number of states afford them standing to petition for custody and visitation in some circumstances (see Exhibit 8.5), many do not. Absent statutory authority, courts sometimes struggle to find legal theories to support the good-faith desires of step-parents to continue to play a meaningful role in the lives of children they have lived with and care about. Equitable estoppel, *de facto* parenthood, the concept of the psychological parent, and the doctrine of *in loco parentis* have each been utilized on a limited basis to recognize a step-parent's history of parenting a child who is "not their own."[63]

Courts sometimes find ways to accomplish a desired end even if it stretches basic legal principles. For example, in a 2002 Kansas case, the Supreme Court of Kansas affirmed a lower court's denial of a noncustodial mother's motion for temporary custody for a one-year period, during which the custodial father would be on a tour of duty in Korea and would be unable to take his current wife and children with him. The children had been living with the father and his new wife, the children's step-mother, for four years. The mother claimed that under the parental preference doctrine, she should be granted custody during the father's extended absence. The father argued that the children had resided with him and their step-mother for an extended period, during which they had thrived and established a strong bond with their step-mother. The court denied the mother's motion for a temporary one-year change in custody, stating that it was in the children's best interests to remain in the primary residential custody of the father. The court essentially reasoned that the custody contest was between the mother and the father, not the mother and the step-mother, and that cases involving military families must be decided on a case-by-case basis.[64]

Grandparents.   In 2002, 4 percent of children lived in households with neither parent present, and, of those, almost half were living with their grandparents. A total of 5.6 million children in the United States (8 percent of all children in the country) were living in households with grandparents present.[66] Although under common law grandparents had no right of access to their grandchildren, legislatures in every state now have provided standing for grandparents to petition for custody and/or visitation rights under certain circumstances.[67]

In most states grandparents will have standing only under certain limited conditions, such as when the child's parents never married, the parents are divorced, one or both of the parents have died, or the parental rights of one or both of the parents have been terminated. Most states also provide that in order to have standing, there must have been a significant preexisting relationship between the child and the grandparents.

Once a grandparent establishes standing to seek visitation over the objection of a parent, he or she must satisfy the standard set out by the state for resolving visitation disputes between legal parents and grandparents. Based on the Supreme Court's decision in *Troxel v. Granville,* (see Case 8.4), the grandparent must establish something more than that visitation would be in the child's best interest. At the least in most states, the burden would be on the grandparents to show by clear and convincing evidence that a parent's denial of visitation with the grandparents is NOT in the child's best interests. A number of states interpreting *Troxel* have held that the courts must give presumptive validity to a fit parent's decision and, in order to rebut that presumption, the grandparents must show by a preponderance of the evidence that failure to grant visitation to the grandparents will cause the child significant harm by adversely affecting his or her health, safety, and welfare.[68]

CASE **8.4** *Troxel v. Granville*, 530 U.S. 57, 120 S. Ct. 2054, 147
L. Ed. 2d 49 (2000)

DISCUSSION OF THE CASE

At issue in this case was the state of Washington's third-party visitation statute that provided "Any person may petition the court for visitation rights at any time including but not limited to, custody proceedings." The U.S. Supreme Court described this language as being "breathtakingly broad." The case involved the two minor daughters of an unmarried couple, Tommie Granville and Brad Troxel, whose relationship ended in 1991. Brad committed suicide in 1993, but before doing so had established a relationship between his daughters and his parents. After the father's death, the mother had not entirely denied the grandparents visitation but wanted to limit it and not permit any overnight visits. The grandparents petitioned to continue their relationship with the children on a more extensive basis than the mother was willing to allow. On the mother's second appeal of a lower court's ruling allowing the visitation, the appeals court reversed the lower court's order on the grounds that the grandparents lacked standing to petition for visitation absent a pending custody action. The Washington Supreme Court reviewed the case at the request of the grandparents. It held that the Troxels did have standing but that visitation should not be ordered over the mother's objection, as such an action would infringe on the mother's fundamental right to parent her children as she sees fit. The grandparents then sought certiorari and the U.S. Supreme Court agreed to hear the case. The Court subsequently held that the statute was unconstitutional as applied to the facts of the case.

In a decision that many say raises as many questions as it answers, the Court at the least held the following:

- Parents have a fundamental liberty interest in the care, custody, and control of their children, which previously has been deemed by the Court to be protected by the Due Process Clause of the Fourteenth Amendment. The Washington statute was held to deprive the mother of this liberty interest without due process of law.

- Given this liberty interest, any decision made by a fit parent should be given special weight. There was no allegation that the mother in this case was unfit, yet the Washington statute contained no requirement that her decision be given any weight whatsoever.

- Courts should presume that a fit parent will act in his or her child's best interest. The Court did not indicate what kind of evidence is required to overcome the presumption.

- The courts are not free to simply substitute their view of what is in a child's best interest for that of the parent. The Washington statute placed the best interest determination solely in the hands of the judge rather than the parents.

The nine-justice court was divided four/two/three as to the specifics of the case. The majority opinion, written by Justice O'Connor was joined by Justices Rehnquist, Ginsburg, and Breyer. Separate concurring opinions were written by Justices Souter and Thomas. Dissenting opinions were written by Justices Stevens, Scalia, and Kennedy.

SIDEBAR

The lengthy and convoluted decision in this case is available in its entirety on the companion website for this text in the material related to Chapter 8.

PARALEGAL APPLICATION 8.6

YOU BE THE JUDGE

FACT PATTERN

In this 2005 case, contrary to the custody evaluator's recommendation, an Oregon court awarded custody to a father over a maternal grandmother with whom the children had lived, with his consent, for virtually their entire lives. The record indicated that during their marriage, the mother and father used illegal drugs and the father used alcohol. The father had been emotionally and physically abusive and had shown no interest in caring for the children. He had been convicted of two felonies and three misdemeanors and had been incarcerated on four occasions for periods ranging from thirty days to eighteen months. After his most recent release in 2002, the father had additional contact with the police and was convicted of improperly using 911 while he was intoxicated. While in prison and following his release, he completed counseling and treatment programs concerning domestic violence, anger management, parenting, drugs and alcohol, and bible studies. He earned his GED and had completed two terms at a community college at the time of trial. Although he had a job after his release from prison, he had been laid off for approximately a year prior to the custody trial. He has been diagnosed with attention deficit hyperactivity disorder (ADHD) and "possible alcohol dependency." For the three years prior to the trial, he had been living with a woman and her four children between the ages of five and thirteen, and they plan to marry. On most weekdays, the mother lives at the grandmother's. The mother also has been convicted of crimes including forgery and theft, and has been undergoing drug counseling. Her coping skills were described as poor. The father and grandmother have not gotten along well over the years, but he told the court he wants to improve that situation and maintain contact between the children and their grandmother on a regular basis.

In Oregon, to rebut the presumption that a legal parent's objection to custody or visitation by a grandparent is in the child's best interests, the court may consider factors including, but not limited to, the following:

A. The legal parent is unwilling or unable to care adequately for the child.

B. The petitioner is or recently has been the child's primary caretaker.

C. Circumstances detrimental to the child exist if relief is denied.

D. The legal parent fostered or consented to the relationship between the child and the petitioner.

E. The legal parent has unreasonably denied or limited contact between the child and the petitioner.

SIDEBAR

In light of the applicable statute, how would you have decided this case? The decision (*Dennis & Dennis*, 199 Ore. App. 90, 110 P.3d 607 (2005)) is available in its entirety on the companion website for this text in the material related to Chapter 8. Read the opinion and see if you and the appeals court reached the same conclusion.

Co-parent
a person engaged in a nonmarital relationship with the legal parent of a child who regards him- or herself as a parent rather than as a legal stranger to the child

Co-Parents.   A *co-parent* is a person engaged in a nonmarital relationship with the legal parent of a child who regards him- or herself as a parent rather than as a legal stranger to the child. The perception is usually based on a mutual intent to parent a child together, the performance of a variety of caretaking functions, and the provision of some degree of financial support for the child for an extended period of time. As with step-parents, co-parents have relied on a variety of legal constructs in an effort to maintain a relationship with a child they have helped to raise after the relationship with the child's legal parent has terminated. Most states deny parental status to co-parents, but may afford them third-party standing as persons such as grandparents and step-parents who bear a significant relationship to the child.

Decisions are mixed in cases involving same-sex co-parents in particular. (See related discussion in Chapter 13.) Case 8.5 illustrates an instance in which a Wisconsin court used the concept of *de facto* parenthood to grant visitation rights to a co-parent. However, some courts claim that recognizing co-parents' rights in the absence of statute, precedent, or well-established legal principle constitutes judicial lawmaking that denigrates fundamental parental rights and infringes on the province of the legislature. Despite such reservations, as this area of the law evolves, co-parents are likely to see an expansion of their rights, not only to visitation, but also to custody.

CASE **8.5** *Holtzman v. Knott (in re H.S.H-K)*, 193 Wis.2d 649, 533 N.W.2D 419 (Wis. 1995)

DISCUSSION OF THE CASE

In this case, the Wisconsin Supreme Court reversed the position it had taken in 1991 in the case of *In re Interest of Z.J.H*, 162 Wis.2d 1002, 471 N.W.2d 202 (Wis. 1991), in which it had firmly rejected the recognition of a lesbian co-parent as a parent by statute, as a *de facto* parent, or a parent by equitable estoppel. Relying on equitable principles rather than the visitation statute in this later case, the Court reached a favorable result for a petitioner who sought custody or visitation rights with the biological child of her former partner.

The Court held that a petitioner in such cases must first prove two factors:

1. That the petitioner had a parent-like relationship with the child:

    a. The relationship existed with the consent of or was fostered by the biological or adoptive parent.

    b. The parties lived in the same household.

    c. The petitioner assumed the obligations of care, custody, education, and development of the child without expecting compensation.

    d. The petitioner functioned in the parental role long enough to create a bonded and dependent relationship with the child that was parental in nature.

2. There was a significant triggering event that justified intervention by the state. In this case it was sufficient that the biological parent had substantially interfered with visitation and the petitioner sought visitation within a reasonable time after the interference.

Once the above two factors are established, the Court will consider whether or not visitation is in the best interest of the child in order to make a custody determination.

SIDEBAR

This case is available in its entirety on the companion website in the material related to Chapter 8.

Others.   Occasionally the third party is someone such as a foster parent, aunt or uncle, or friend of the family who has established a parent-like relationship with a child. These cases tend to particularly rely on the psychological parent doctrine. This doctrine asserts that an individual can assume the significance of a parent as a result of his or her relationship with a child. The status usually requires a long-term relationship in which the "psychological parent" interacts with and cares for the child on a day-to-day basis. Courts in several states have recognized the importance of a psychological bond between a child and a third party. As a Pennsylvania Superior Court has put it:

> …the need to guard the family from intrusions by third parties and to protect the rights of the natural parent must be tempered by the paramount need to protect the child's best interest. Thus, while it is presumed that a child's best interest is served by maintaining the family's privacy and autonomy, that presumption must give way where the child has established strong psychological bonds with a person who, although not a biological parent, has lived with the child and provided care, nurture, and affection, assuming in the child's eye a stature like that of a parent. Where such a relationship is shown, our courts recognize that the child's best interest requires that the third party be granted standing so as to have the opportunity to litigate fully the issue of whether that relationship should be maintained even over a natural parent's objections.[69]

New Jersey has established that when there is a conflict between a legal parent and a psychological parent, the case will be decided as if it involved two legal parents and the standard to be applied is the best interest of the child.[70]

WHO SPEAKS FOR THE CHILD IN CUSTODY MATTERS?

When minor children are involved in a legal matter, the law generally presumes that their interests will be represented by their parents, guardians, or others acting "in loco parentis" (in the place of a parent) on their behalf. Until children have the knowledge and maturity to act on their own, parents act and speak for them in virtually all contexts.[71] In custody cases, however, parents are often so wrapped up in their own concerns that they lose sight of their children's interests.

A guardian *ad litem* (GAL) is a neutral evaluator appointed by the court (often at the request of one or both of the parents) to attend to the interests of the children whose custody is in dispute (although GALs may be appointed in any matter involving children). Depending on the state, the guardian may be an attorney, a licensed social worker, a psychologist, or, in some instances, a volunteer trained and appointed by the court to assist with child-related issues. The primary role of the GAL is to objectively examine the child's situation as fully as possible, with special attention to the nature and quality of the child's relationship with each parent. At a minimum, the GAL usually will visit the parties' homes and interview each of the parents, the children, and any other individuals who may be able to contribute helpful information, such as schoolteachers, counselors, neighbors, or members of the clergy.

The GAL will present the court with his or her opinion in a written report as to the needs of the children, the strengths and weaknesses of each party as a parent, and the course of action most likely to serve the best interests of the children. The court considers, but is not necessarily bound by, the GAL's report, and the parties may cross-examine the GAL on issues related to the report and the basis for the recommendations made. The cost of the GAL is usually fully paid or heavily subsidized by one or both of the parties. However, the GAL is not intended to represent the interests of either of the parties, nor is the guardian technically an advocate for the child unless the state and/or court so labels the guardian. There are those who regard this as a flaw in the process and who believe that in especially complex cases involving parental manipulation, concealing of information, or allegations of abuse or parental unfitness, an attorney should be appointed to represent the child. The "child ought to be a player and not the football."[72]

The court may assign or approve additional responsibilities for a GAL as well. For example, a Wisconsin court approved a provision in a marital settlement agreement (later rejected by the mother) that a GAL and family counselor would have the right to break any impasse between the parties regarding decisions pertaining to their son's schooling.[73] In a Massachusetts case, a trial court judge provided in the parties' judgment of divorce that, in the event of a dispute concerning whether or not a particular religious belief or practice is harmful to the children, a GAL named by the court would be retained at the expense of the parties to investigate and evaluate the dispute.[74]

Because of the complexity of custody decisions, the courts may look to multiple resources for guidance over and above the GAL. Customarily, when custody is at issue on a contested or uncontested basis, the parties will be required to meet with a representative of a family services division located right at the courthouse. Family service personnel are usually not attorneys, but they generally are individuals with strong backgrounds in social work and developmental psychology who are trained in working through the maze created by disputing adults to come up with custody recommendations for the court. Although their recommendations are not binding, they are usually accorded considerable respect by judges.

Another important resource for children and the courts in every state is the **CASA Program** (Court Appointed Special Advocates). CASA is an organization that trains court-appointed volunteer advocates to work one-on-one with abused and endangered children. Much like GALs, CASA volunteers gather information in child abuse and neglect cases, assess each child's situation, and make objective recommendations to the court concerning the environment that will best ensure a particular child's safety and well-being.

CASA Program
a national program that trains court-appointed volunteer advocates to work one-on-one with abused and endangered children

The judge may also hear testimony from a variety of expert witnesses called by the parties on a variety of topics. In some states the court may designate a neutral court-appointed psychologist (sometimes called a "custody evaluator") and order that the parties and children cooperate with that individual by participating in interviews, producing relevant documents and records, and potentially submitting to psychological testing if deemed warranted. The parties must each waive their confidentiality rights in this context, thereby allowing the psychologist to reveal and discuss information that might otherwise be privileged.

WHAT IS THE PARALEGAL'S ROLE IN A CUSTODY CASE?

The most common tasks a paralegal performs in a child custody case are the following:

- researching the law governing custody actions in the jurisdiction
- preparing related memoranda based on research as requested
- gathering information and documentation essential to successful negotiation and resolution of custody cases
- scheduling and participating in interviews as assigned

- drafting correspondence, complaints/petitions, supporting affidavits, and proposed orders or responsive pleadings to complaints/petitions involving custody matters
- drafting discovery materials such as interrogatories, requests for admissions, questions for depositions, etc.
- drafting parenting plans/child custody provisions for inclusion in agreements
- assisting in preparation for temporary hearings or trials on the merits, including drafting pretrial memoranda for review and preparing subpoenas for potential witnesses if needed
- helping to prepare witnesses
- tracking the progress on the case to be certain timelines are met
- coordinating communication with the GAL, CASA volunteer, etc.
- making sure the client is kept informed of progress and upcoming deadlines, hearings, discovery matters, etc.

PARALEGAL APPLICATION 8.7

INFORMATION GATHERING IN A CONTESTED CUSTODY CASE

Contested custody cases are fact-intensive, and considerable information needs to be gathered about the relationship of the child or children with *each* of the parents. This is accomplished through client interviews; traditional discovery vehicles such as interrogatories followed by depositions, questionnaires, examination of documents and audiovisual materials; and interviews with individuals familiar with the child and the parents. In addition, the court may be gathering its own information through the use of a court-appointed psychologist, GAL, or other resources. The paralegal often plays a key role in the information-gathering effort as an integral member of the family law team.

Some of the kinds of information to be gathered include the following:

- The various caretaking functions performed by each parent need to be identified. Which parent has been primarily responsible for meeting the child's daily needs?

- Although clients are not always cooperative with the effort, the parenting strengths and weaknesses of each party need to be identified.

- Does either of the parents have any special problems or limitations that may interfere with his or her capacity to effectively parent? For example, does either parent have a mental health or substance abuse problem?

- The client's motivation for seeking custody needs to be assessed. Is it realistic? Is it based on revenge, a need to prove oneself, or some other unhealthy motive?

- Descriptions of the children need to be provided. What are they like? What are their favorite and least favorite activities? How are they doing in school? What are their parental preferences, if known?

- Any special needs, medical issues, or behavior problems of a child need to be identified along with an explanation of how they are being handled.

- It is useful to know if there are any major areas of disagreement between the parents with respect to the raising of the children, such as disciplinary measures, religious practices, or activities the children should be allowed to engage in.

- If there are siblings, step- or otherwise, the relationships between the child and those individuals should be explored.

- The nature of the relationship each parent has with the child needs to be described.

- In addition to basic parenting activities, what kinds of activities does each parent engage in with the child?

continued

- Questions should be asked about the child's friendships, role models, and involvement in community activities and organizations.

- It is important to know whether either parent has intentions to remarry or reside with another romantic partner (of either gender) and whether there will be any additional nonbiological children in that parent's home.

- If the parties have not already established new "permanent" residences, it is important to learn whether either parent plans to relocate in the near future and, if so, how far away. The potential impact of any relocation on proposed custody plans needs to be considered.

- The work schedules and relative availability of the parents need to be determined. Does either party's job require him or her to travel or be called out on emergencies at irregular hours? Will child care need to be provided by a third party when the child is with either parent? Does either party have a support system, such as parents, grandparents, friends, neighbors, etc.?

- Potential witnesses should be identified, including friends and relatives but more importantly, teachers, neighbors, childcare providers, coaches, medical professionals, clergy, probation officers, mental health professionals, etc. Issues of privileged communications may be raised, depending on the type of professional.

- Available documents should be identified and copies gathered, such as photos, videos, written reports of professionals, correspondence relevant to parental fitness and cooperation (attempts to visit, etc.), and materials produced by the child (with the child's knowledge and consent) such as e-mails, letters, creative work, journals, etc.

CHAPTER **SUMMARY**

Although children are no longer deemed the "property" of either parent, owned by them, and somehow subject to division upon divorce, this is not always apparent in contested custody battles in which parents duel with each other over their rights with respect to physical custody of their children and the authority to make decisions concerning their welfare.

In most cases, the parents themselves are able, with or without assistance of counsel or mediators, to arrive at an agreed-upon custodial arrangement and parenting plan. When they cannot, the courts are left to deal with the agonizing task of allocating responsibility between two very fit and committed parents, two parents who are not unfit but who have serious inadequacies, or two parents who both have parental strengths and weaknesses. The relative fitness of parents usually turns on the extent to which either parent has been the primary caretaker of the child and whether or not either parent has engaged in conduct that would negatively affect the welfare of the child.

The controlling consideration in a child custody case, be it an initial award or a modification, is the child's best interests. How will living with one parent and/or the other impact all aspects of the child's life: physical, psychological, cognitive, emotional, spiritual, familial, educational, and recreational? In order to make that decision, the court must examine and assess each parent's "fitness," character, parenting skills, and bond with the child. The court considers the weight of the evidence, the credibility of witnesses, and the recommendations of experts, GALs, and other resources. Each case must be decided on its own facts and the totality of the circumstances as perceived and interpreted by individual judges.

> The consideration and weighing of the factors in a custody dispute is essentially factual....Cases with very similar facts may be decided in divergent ways by courts of different states, and even by courts within the same state. The differing results often come from the hearts and emotions of judges, rather than from the facts of the case.[75]

In this chapter, the focus is primarily on custody decisions in the context of divorce. However, the nuclear family is no longer the dominant norm. It is reasonable to anticipate that in our rapidly evolving society with its multiplicity of "family" models, state courts will continue to explore creative ways of extending custodial and visitation rights to third parties as well as to biological parents. Some of these situations are discussed at greater length in Chapter 13. Although there is logic and justice to the results in such cases, there is a fear among advocates of family autonomy that they "open the door to virtually unfathomable exercises of judicial discretion, all in derogation of the constitutionally protected interests of natural parents with respect to their children."[76]

We have treated child custody in this chapter as if it were a discrete topic, but it is important to keep in mind the extent to which it is intertwined with other areas such as support and tax issues; property division and who remains in the marital home, if anyone; conflict of law when multiple states are involved; paternity questions; adoption; reproductive technology; domestic violence, abuse, and neglect; and constitutional rights of children and parents.

KEY **TERMS**

Approximation Rule
Best interests of the child
CASA Program
Co-parent
De facto parent
Emergency jurisdiction
Equitable parenthood
Forum *non conveniens*
Forum shopping
Guardian *ad litem*
Home state jurisdiction

In camera
Joint award
Judicial notice
Last resort jurisdiction
Legal custody
Maternal preference
Parens patriae doctrine
Parental alienation syndrome
Parent by estoppel
Parenting plan
Paternal preference

Per se rule
Physical custody
Primary caretaker
Psychological parent
Significant connection jurisdiction
Sole award
Split custody
Standing
Tender years doctrine
Virtual visitation

REVIEW **QUESTIONS**

1. Define and distinguish between legal and physical custody.
2. Define and distinguish between sole and joint legal custody.
3. Identify the two most common types of custodial arrangements.
4. Identify the four bases of jurisdiction under the UCCJA and indicate how the UCCJEA and PKPA refine them.
5. Identify the major purpose of The Hague Convention in custody cases.
6. Describe how the standards for making custody awards have evolved.
7. Describe the tender years doctrine.
8. Describe the best interest standard. Give examples of factors considered in implementing it.
9. Explain what a "gender-neutral standard" is in the context of custody decisions. Do you believe that custody decisions are, in fact, gender neutral? Why or why not?
10. Describe the primary caretaker presumption and explain how the courts determine the identity of a child's primary caretaker.
11. Describe the ALI Approximation Rule for making custody decisions and identify its advantages.
12. Identify the majority position with respect to each of the following in the making of custodial decisions:
    - availability
    - stability
    - gender
    - race
    - religion
    - parental health or disability
    - sexual activity
    - parental lifestyle
    - history of abuse
    - child preference
13. Define visitation and describe a common schedule.
14. Distinguish between supervised and unsupervised visitation.
15. Define "virtual visitation." Give an example.
16. Describe the nature of a parenting plan and indicate how it differs from a more traditional custody provision in a separation agreement.
17. Describe the nature and purposes of a parent education program.
18. Describe the circumstances under which a modification in custody is likely to be sought and granted.
19. Identify the important interests that must be balanced in relocation disputes.
20. Describe the majority rule with respect to each of the following categories of third parties seeking custodial and/or visitation rights:
    - step-parents
    - grandparents
    - co-parents
21. Explain what a guardian *ad litem* (GAL) is. What role do GALs play in custody cases?
22. Describe the role of the paralegal in a custody case.

FOCUS ON **THE JOB**

THE FACTS

Clark Brody and Christine Dosh are the unmarried parents of a daughter, named Melody, who was born on September 4, 2000, and a son, Darren, born on November 26, 2002. They lived together for a four-year period from 1999 to 2003, at which time they separated, largely due to arguments over Christine's drug use and Clark's suspicion that she was abusing their daughter. The daughter had experienced a series of unexplainable broken bones and bruises, and, on one occasion, the emergency room physician filed a report with the state's Social Services Agency, which is responsible for investigating complaints of suspected abuse. An investigation was conducted, but no conclusive finding was issued. The file has remained open, but no complaints have been filed for eighteen months since Christine completed a recommended parenting skills course. Christine lived with her parents, George and Ethel Dosh, on and off after she and Clark separated. She recently moved out of her parents' home because she had grown tired of their constant preaching to her about what an evil person they think she is. They are deeply religious people who have been trying to "heal" and "save" their daughter from the sinful life she has been living. They also want to "save" the children who they believe are the fruit of sinful unions. They are quite wealthy and have a lovely farmhouse in the country with animals, including horses and rabbits. There is also a swimming pool, a pond for skating in the winter, and an extensive exercise/play gym on the property. Christine has taken the children to visit her parents on several occasions (accompanied by Clark as a "supervisor"), and the children have enjoyed participating in all the activities available at the farm. They like going there as long as their grandparents don't lecture them about "sin and all that stuff." Neither Clark nor Christine wants to allow the grandparents to visit with the children.

Christine has had a series of jobs over the past few years but until recently has rarely managed to keep a job for more than three months at a time. She has been waitressing at a local restaurant and playing the organ in a local church, where she has become a regular member. She is also volunteering at a local shelter for abused women and children. Although she had participated in a number of treatment programs, she was still drinking heavily and using cocaine and heroin on a regular basis until about a year ago, when she seemed to get her act together. Shortly thereafter she was diagnosed as HIV-positive but shows no signs of full-blown AIDS. She continues to smoke cigarettes but is trying to give them up.

Clark works a regular job as a conductor on a commuter train. His regular shift is Wednesday through Sunday each week, ten hours a day. He recently married a woman who is a native of Uruguay. He met her when he began taking courses at a local community college where she was enrolled in an English-as-a-second-language program. She hopes eventually to master English and become a nurse. In the meantime she is working as an aide in a local nursing home.

When Clark and Christine split up, Clark took the children with him and refused to let Christine visit them for the first two years. She went to court and, over Clark's objection, obtained an order granting her supervised visitation at the local shelter where she is now volunteering. Her lawyer is reasonably confident that Christine will be able to successfully pursue primary custody of the children, now that her life has changed dramatically. The staff at the shelter say she is a very attentive and sensitive parent.

The children have been doing well living with Clark and his wife, Remigia. They have no health problems, with the exception of Melody's asthma, which is reasonably controlled with medication and inhalers. Melody says that she would like to live with her mother because she can talk with her, as she understands English. She also feels sorry for her because "everyone has been so mean to her." Darren does not seem to have bonded with his mother and appears largely indifferent toward her. He adores his dad and follows him around like a shadow. Clark is close to and very involved with both children. He enjoys taking care of and playing with them. He especially likes teaching them new games and skills.

THE ASSIGNMENT

Assume that both Clark and Christine are seeking custody of the children. They are in agreement that they should share the responsibility of making major decisions affecting the children, but they cannot agree on which parent the children should live with. Clark does not want Christine to have anything more than supervised visitation, given her history. Christine doesn't want Clark to have visitation because she believes he will take the children away from her, as he did when they split up years before. Assume that you are working for the judge who is hearing this case, Judge Solomon Stevens.

a. Outline in a memorandum to the judge the relative strengths and weaknesses of each of the parties' positions based on prevailing governing law in your state.

b. Draft a recommended parenting plan tailored to this case in a format used in your state. Courts in many states provide parenting plan forms online. As a default, you may use the New Hampshire Parenting Plan format, which can be accessed through the website for the courts in that state (*http://www.courts.state.nh.us*); the Permanent Parenting Plan Order form available online for use in the state of Tennessee; or the Wisconsin Proposed Parenting Plan format, on the companion website for this text in the material related to Chapter 8.

FOCUS ON **ETHICS**

Assume that you are a paralegal in the law office of Attorney Sofia Hidalgo, who is representing Christine Dosh in the above comprehensive fact pattern. While you were interviewing Christine recently about her parenting skills at your supervisor's request, she shared with you that she is quite certain that the court will not grant her custody of her two children. She says the only way she will ever be able to be with them is to take them to Canada, where her older sister and her husband live. They would welcome them and be able to provide for Christine and the children. She believes she could do this at the time of one of her visits with the children, as supervision has become very informal. This conversation is troubling you and over dinner, you tell your parents about what she said. Your father says he doesn't blame you for being concerned and that you should go to the police about this woman, who must be mentally unstable and a danger to the children if she would even think of doing such a thing. Your mother says she thinks you should keep your reservations to yourself and just do your job. Analyze this situation, applying the ethical canons for paralegals promulgated by the National Federation of Paralegal Associations (NFPA), which are contained in Appendix B of this text. Include in your analysis a description of what, if anything, you plan to do about this situation.

FOCUS ON **CASE LAW**

Review the *Troxel v. Granville* decision of the U.S. Supreme Court referenced in this chapter along with case law in your jurisdiction regarding grandparent visitation since that decision. If there is no subsequent case law in your jurisdiction, assume that the *Blixt* case (437 Mass. 649 (2002)) was decided by a court in your state and that the statute governing grandparent visitation in your state is the same as the one in Massachusetts. Assume that the firm where you are employed represents the grandparents in the comprehensive fact pattern provided in this chapter, George and Ethel Dosh. Your supervisor, Attorney Connie Mahoney, has asked you to review the applicable statute and governing case law and prepare a memorandum summarizing your research and indicating what you think the prospects are for the clients. Use the following format:

MEMORANDUM

TO: *Your supervisor*

FROM: *Your name and title*

RE: *Assessment of George and Ethel Dosh's Petition for Grandparent Visitation*

DATE:

Brief description of assignment: *What is it that you have been asked to do?*

Brief description of facts: *Describe the basic facts of the case*

Results of research: *Describe the applicable statute(s)/case law.*

Discussion: *Apply the governing law to the facts of this case.*

Conclusion: *What is your opinion about the prospect of the grandparents being granted visitation?*

FOCUS ON **STATE LAW AND PROCEDURE**

Assume that you are a paralegal working in the law firm of Wilson and Tauson, LLP and your supervisor is Attorney Tauson. Your firm represents Clark Brody in the comprehensive fact pattern provided in this chapter. He is seeking custody of his daughter. Your supervisor has asked you to research one of the issues that may be influential in the case.

Choose an issue such as domestic violence, religion, parental lifestyle, or health. Research the law in your jurisdiction regarding that issue and its role in custody determinations. Present your findings in a memorandum and include your conclusion with respect to the client's prospects, given the facts of this case and the governing law.

FOCUS ON **TECHNOLOGY**

Websites of Interest

http://www.abanet.org

This is the website for the American Bar Association. Go to the site and search for the custody chart. This chart, which is updated annually for the ABA Family Law Quarterly, includes a state-by-state summary of the following custody-related topics: statutory guidelines, children's wishes, joint custody, cooperative parents, domestic violence, health, and attorney or GAL.

http://www.childcustody.org

This site contains information about child custody organizations nationwide with links to topic- or state-specific discussion forums and "friendly" websites.

http://www.co.twinfalls.id.us/5thdistrict/Mediation/long.html

This is a court-sponsored site providing information about the psychological effects of divorce on children who are not physically close to their noncustodial parent. It offers age-specific suggestions on fostering the parent-child relationship through long-distance parenting.

http://www.courts.state.nh.us

Family law-related forms are available at this website, including a parenting plan.

http://www.dadsdivorce.com

This site has the flavor of a support system and contains a variety of tools and guides useful to those involved in custody disputes, including a newsletter.

http://deltabravo.net/custody/pplan3htm

The stated goal of this site is to ensure that children of divorce have access to both parents—regardless of marital status. It offers links to a rich variety of resources including an online parenting plan generator.

http://www.divorceinfo.com/kidsacrossmiles.htm

This site is offered by a rather upbeat divorce attorney/mediator who limits his work to people who want a divorce and are prepared to interact reasonably. The site offers guidance and tools to minimize difficulty and stress.

http://www.divorcenet.com

This site is similar to dadsdivorce.com but is broader in scope. It contains information on all aspects of divorce. It also provides a guide to finding resources and professional support by geographical area.

http://www.findlaw.com

This site provides links to the child custody laws of all states and the District of Columbia.

http://www.kidmate.com

This is a resource for joint custody software.

http://marion-court.ojd.state.or.us/unmarriedpar.htm

This is the Marion County (Or.) Circuit Court site. Forms to establish custody, parenting time, and support in Oregon are available at this site.

http://www.winchildcustody.com

This site contains material on winning and defending child custody cases.

Assignments

1. Assume that the mother in this chapter's focus on the job fact pattern is willing to agree at this point to virtual visitation between the grandparents and the children. Draft a provision for inclusion in an agreement between the parties that addresses this topic. A couple of recommended resources to review as you prepare to complete this assignment are the following:

   a. Shefts, Kimberly R., *Virtual Visitation: The Next Generation of Options for Parent-Child Communication*, 36 FAM. L. J., Number 2, Summer 2002.

   b. *In re Marriage of Thielges*, 623 N.W.2d 232 (Iowa Ct. App.) (2000)

2. Locate three websites providing support to fathers seeking custody of their minor children. In a brief report, describe the kinds of information available at each site.

3. Go to the following website for the Oregon Judicial Department: *http://www.ojd.state.or.us/familylaw*. Select the Parenting Plan Information link. Access and review the Basic Parenting Plan Packet for Parents containing information about parenting plans and the Oregon Parenting Plan Form and Instructions.

4. Working with another student in your class, locate the Permanent Parenting Plan Order Form for the State of Tennessee (available online). Each student should independently complete the form, with one student representing Clark and the other representing Christine in the comprehensive fact pattern above. After completing the form, each student should meet with his or her partner and identify any differences between the two proposed plans. The students should then negotiate a resolution to the differences. If the differences cannot be resolved, solicit the assistance of another classmate to function as a "mediator" (albeit untrained!).

5. Locate the CASA Program contact in your jurisdiction.

6. Locate the most current information in your state regarding parenting programs. Is participation required? Do minor children have to attend a program? Where is the nearest/most accessible program for you? Is there an online program option?

chapter **nine**

CHILD SUPPORT

William and Betty married three years ago after having had three daughters together. An accountant for ten years, William now has "found himself," quit his job, and decided to head to Africa to be a missionary. He says God will provide for Betty and the girls, since he will not be able to, and, besides, if he won't be seeing them, why should he have to pay child support?

WHAT CHILD SUPPORT IS AND WHEN, HOW, AND TO WHOM IT IS AWARDED

Child support refers to a parent's legal obligation to contribute to the economic maintenance of his or her child. It is usually in the form of a payment made by a *noncustodial parent* to a **custodial parent** for the benefit of a minor child for whom the parent is deemed legally responsible, including, for example, biological and adopted children. Historically, mothers were awarded custody of children, and *child support* was deemed to be the father's moral obligation—sometimes enforced under the **doctrine of "necessaries."** The duty of support was eventually codified as a legal duty, and nonsupport was made a crime in all states. Based on legislation in each of the states, the duty now is imposed equally on both parents regardless of who has legal or physical custody.

In What Contexts Do Child Support Issues Arise?

Child support issues arise in several contexts: Temporary and permanent child support are commonly sought in divorce or separate support actions. Support is also frequently an issue in abuse prevention actions, as well as in guardianship and paternity matters or cases in which a child is removed from a parent's home. A parent may be ordered to pay child support to a third party, such as a state agency or a grandparent acting as a custodian or guardian of a child.[1] When child support is ordered, subsequent modifications may be sought. Single or multiple states, even nations, and both state and federal law may be involved.

Temporary Child Support.   Temporary child support is designed to provide for children while an underlying action is pending. Temporary orders are usually issued after brief hearings with limited testimony. The court will customarily review the parties' financial affidavits, the parties' child support guidelines worksheets (which may differ from each other), the pleadings, and any supporting affidavits. In some jurisdictions, courts will issue temporary orders without a hearing based on the documents submitted. Requests for temporary child support orders must be taken seriously, as they often lay the groundwork and set a precedent for permanent orders.

"Permanent" Child Support.   In a contested case, a trial on the merits of a support issue is considerably more in-depth than a hearing on temporary orders. Counsel usually will address issues such as the reasons for any proposed deviation from the guidelines, unique needs of the children, and potential tax consequences related to the child support order. The case will be decided on the basis of the sworn testimony of the parties and witnesses (sometimes including experts), along with exhibits (including financial affidavits and documentation of expenses, work history, needs of the children, standard of living, etc.). The paralegal usually plays a key role in gathering and organizing the information essential at trial. On occasion the paralegal will attend the trial and assist counsel with locating documents when needed, checking numerical calculations, etc.

Who Has a Duty of Support?

In an era in which the concept of "family" is evolving and scientific technology is expanding, the question of who has a duty of child support is becoming increasingly complex. For example, some states impose a duty to pay support on a third party who is not the child's biological parent, but who acts **in loco parentis** (in the

Noncustodial parent
a parent who does not have sole or primary physical custody of a child but who is still a legal parent with enforceable rights and responsibilities

Custodial parent
the parent with whom the child primarily resides

Child support
a parent's legal obligation to contribute to the economic maintenance of a child until the age of majority or emancipation

Doctrine of necessaries
under common law, a husband's duty to pay debts incurred by his wife or children for "necessaries" such as food, shelter, and clothing

Paralegal Practice Tip
There is nothing like being organized and prepared. Many attorneys will prepare alternative versions of various documents in anticipation of the court's potential actions. For example, if there is a question with respect to whether or not a certain type of income will be includable in an obligor's income, alternative versions of the child support guidelines worksheet should be prepared. The one that best supports the client's case is offered first, but the second is available as backup.

Paralegal Practice Tip
Although often called "permanent" orders, the characterization really is not accurate, as child support orders remain subject to the continuing jurisdiction of the court and may be modified or terminated in a variety of circumstances.

In loco parentis
Latin for "in the place of the parent"; taking on some or all of the responsibilities of a parent

place of a parent). A person such as a step-parent may perform the role of a parent even if he or she has not formally adopted the child. However, the majority rule is that a step-parent will not have a legal duty to support the child absent an agreement or a court order. In some instances, a support duty may be imposed on a sperm or egg donor[2] or a man who has voluntarily acknowledged paternity but who is later proven by DNA evidence not to be a parent.[3] The parents' duty to support their child continues even if the child is in the custody of a government agency (a residential treatment program, a juvenile justice department, a department of social services, etc.) rather than in the custody of one of the parents. The agency that has custody may initiate an action for support.[4]

PARALEGAL APPLICATION **9.1**

ETHICS ALERT

An attorney has an ethical duty to carry out contracts to provide legal services and not to neglect or cause damage or prejudice to clients. A failure to file the documents necessary to secure child support for a client that results in a loss of payments to which that client would otherwise be entitled may result in a suspension from the practice of law.[5] One of the most important tasks a paralegal performs in a family law practice is to organize and monitor workflow and timelines in the office. It is thus important for a paralegal to have an effective reminder or "tickler" system in place.

EXHIBIT 9.1 Child Support and Spousal Support(Alimony)—
A Comparison

CHILD SUPPORT	**SPOUSAL SUPPORT (ALIMONY)**
Child support is a right of the child.	Alimony involves a spousal duty at the time of divorce or legal separation. It depends on a showing of need by one spouse and an ability to pay on the part of the other spouse.
Child support obligations cannot be permanently waived in premarital or separation agreements between the parties.	In most states, rights to spousal support can be waived in valid premarital and separation agreements between the parties.
Child support is calculated using federally mandated child support guidelines developed in each state.	In the majority of jurisdictions, there are no guidelines for courts to use when establishing amounts and duration of alimony awards.
Child support awards remain under the continuing jurisdiction of the court and can be modified upon a substantial change in circumstances.	Alimony awards may be modified upon a change in the parties' financial circumstances unless otherwise provided by statute, court decree, or a surviving agreement of the parties.
Child support obligations are not terminated as a result of the remarriage of either spouse.	In most jurisdictions, remarriage of the recipient spouse customarily will terminate an alimony award.

continued

Child support is neither deductible to the obligor nor includable in the income of the recipient.

Child support obligations are not discharged in bankruptcy and are entitled to priority in payment.[6]

Alimony is usually tax deductible to the obligor and taxable income to the recipient.

Spousal support obligations usually are not dischargeable in bankruptcy.

When Does the Child Support Duty End?

The duty to support a child most often continues until the child's emancipation. *Emancipation* usually means that the child has reached the *age of majority* (age eighteen in most states and twenty-one in a small minority of states). However, it can also refer to some other statutory, judicial, or agreed-upon indicator that the child should no longer be considered a minor, such as entering military service, getting married, moving out of the custodial parent's home, or becoming self-supporting. The award will also end if the obligor's parental rights are terminated or upon the death of the obligor, absent agreement or order to the contrary. The court may order, or the parties may agree, that the *obligor* will maintain a life insurance policy for the benefit of the child or establish a trust or some other vehicle to help ensure the child continues to receive an appropriate level of support during his or her minority in the event the obligor dies.

The termination of child support may not be automatic on emancipation. For example, in 2006, Pennsylvania amended its rule regarding termination of a child support award upon emancipation and established a requirement that the court conduct an "emancipation inquiry" within one year of the date a child who is the subject of a support order reaches age eighteen. If there is an order in place that applies to more than one child, the obligor may want or be required to file a petition for modification or a petition to terminate child support for a specific child upon emancipation if there would be a reduction in the support amount.

In some circumstances, the court has the discretion to order continuation of support beyond the age of majority, such as when a child is disabled and would otherwise become a *public charge.*

Emancipation
the age, act, or occasion that frees a child from the control of a parent and the parent from a child support obligation

Age of majority
the age, usually eighteen, at which a person attains adulthood and full legal rights

Obligor
in the child custody context, the parent who owes the duty of support

Public charge
a person dependent on public assistance programs for necessaries

INITIATIVES THE FEDERAL GOVERNMENT HAS UNDERTAKEN IN THE AREA OF CHILD SUPPORT

In order to understand the operation of child support procedures in the individual states, it is necessary to first be aware of how they are shaped, in many respects, by federal law. Historically, the federal government has largely left regulation of family law matters to the states. However, since the 1970s, it has assumed a powerful leadership role in order to accomplish several important objectives related to the establishment and enforcement of child support obligations:

- In order to contain the costs of *public assistance programs,* the federal government now holds both mothers and fathers accountable for support of their children.
- In an effort to address historical inadequacies and inconsistencies in child support awards from state to state, county to county, and judge to judge,

Public assistance programs
government programs providing financial and other forms of assistance to poor and low-income families

it has taken dramatic steps to promote uniformity in procedures used by the states to determine child support awards.

- Given the high rate of noncompliance with child support orders, a particular emphasis is placed on strengthening and streamlining enforcement of child support awards, especially when multiple jurisdictions are involved.

It is impossible to cover the many initiatives undertaken by Congress over the past four decades, but reference to some of them is appropriate to convey a sense of the nature and scope of federal involvement in the child support arena.

- **The Child Support Enforcement and Establishment of Paternity Act of 1974** (added Title IV-D to the Social Security Act).[7]
  a. This Act established the Office of Child Support Enforcement (OCSE), the federal agency now responsible for monitoring and helping states develop and manage their child support programs in accordance with federal law.
  b. It required states to develop comprehensive child support programs to be run by a single state agency (designated the state's *IV-D agency*) charged with facilitating parents' efforts to obtain and enforce child support awards. The primary tasks of the IV-D agency are to:
    1. when necessary, assist in establishing paternity through testing of *putative fathers*
    2. assist with location of noncustodial parents through state and federal parent locator services empowered by statute to search records of state and federal agencies
    3. facilitate entry of support orders after paternity is established and noncustodial fathers are located
    4. periodically review support awards
    5. enforce existing orders through an arsenal of resources, described later in this chapter under the topic of enforcement
- **The Child Support Enforcement Amendments of 1984 (CSEA)**[8]
  a. This Act required states to establish advisory numeric, formula-based child support guidelines for judges and other officials who set child support amounts in separation, divorce, and paternity cases.
  b. It required each state to have a law addressing procedures for establishing paternity of a child at any time before the child attains eighteen years of age.[9]
  c. It required state child support agencies to seek medical support as part of any petition to establish or modify support whenever health care coverage is available at a reasonable cost.
  d. It strengthened Title IV-D enforcement efforts by requiring the states to implement income withholding, state and federal tax intercepts, and liens against the property of obligors in default.
  e. It mandated that states receiving public assistance funds make the full range of parent locator and child support services available to all custodial parents and not solely to those receiving public assistance.
- **The Family Support Act of 1988**
  a. This Act mandated that by 1994, the states implement *presumptive* rather than advisory child support guidelines to be used in establishing initial awards and for any subsequent modifications.[10]
  b. The Act called for the National Commissioners on Uniform State Laws to create a new Uniform Act designed to improve the interstate collection of child support to replace and address problem areas in the prior Uniform Reciprocal Enforcement of Support Act (URESA) drafted in the 1950s and revised several times. The "new" Act, eventually called the *Uniform Interstate Family Support Act (UIFSA),*[11] was designed to promote uniformity in the processing of interstate cases; eliminate the potential for multiple, conflicting support orders; and expand

IV-D agency
the state agency charged with responsibility for enforcing child support obligations

Putative father
a man reputed or believed to be the father of a child

Presumptive child support guidelines
guidelines that are presumed to generate an appropriate amount of child support given a particular set of assumptions and circumstances

Uniform Interstate Family Support Act (UIFSA)
adopted in all fifty states; a model act designed to facilitate establishment and enforcement of interstate child support orders

long-arm jurisdiction to make it easier for a custodial parent to prosecute a child support case in his or her own state.[12]

- **The Personal Responsibility and Work Opportunity Reconciliation Act of 1996 (PRWORA)**[13]
  a. This Act abolished the former Aid to Families with Dependent Children Program (AFDC) and replaced it with the *Transitional Assistance to Needy Families Program (TANF).*
  b. The Act called for creation and maintenance of a *State Case Registry* containing basic information regarding all child support orders within the state and the creation and maintenance of state and national *Directories of New Hires* containing information from employers on new hires as well as applications for unemployment compensation.
  c. The Act required all states to adopt the Uniform Interstate Family Support Act (UIFSA) by 1998 in order to remain eligible to receive federal child support funds.
  d. The Act provides a mechanism for dealing with international child support cases.

By linking a state's compliance and effectiveness in child support enforcement with federal support for public assistance provided to the state, the government has been able to motivate the states' responsiveness to its initiatives regarding establishment and enforcement of child support awards. The changes made have promoted greater predictability of child support awards and enhanced child support collection efforts, although support still remains generally inadequate to meet the daily needs of many children.

THE MAJOR JURISDICTIONAL ISSUES IN CHILD SUPPORT CASES

The processes by which child support awards are established, modified, and enforced all involve jurisdictional issues. The court issuing, modifying, or enforcing an order must have subject matter jurisdiction over child support actions and also *personal jurisdiction* over the obligor.

Obtaining Personal Jurisdiction Over a Resident Defendant

Each state has its own statutes governing the ways in which personal jurisdiction can be obtained over a defendant. If the defendant in a child support action resides in the state where the action is brought, most often a copy of the complaint/petition and court summons will be personally served on the defendant. This is called *actual service of process.* If the defendant is believed to be in the state, but his or her precise whereabouts are unknown, the court may authorize an alternative mode of service, such as mailing the complaint to the defendant's last known address or service by publication in area newspapers. A defendant may also consent to the court's jurisdiction by voluntarily accepting service at the courthouse or filing a responsive pleading to a complaint.

Obtaining Personal Jurisdiction Over a Nonresident Defendant in the Petitioner's Own State

Approximately one-third of child support orders involve parents living in different states. Obtaining jurisdiction over a nonresident defendant and enforcing support orders across state lines can be challenging. If the defendant is a nonresident, a court

Long-arm jurisdiction
jurisdiction over a nonresident defendant on the basis of his or her contacts with the state seeking to exercise personal jurisdiction

Transitional Assistance to Needy Families Program (TANF)
the welfare system that replaced the former Aid to Families with Dependent Children Program (AFDC)

State Case Registry (SCR)
a statewide database containing basic information on all child support orders entered by courts within the state

State Directory of New Hires (SDNH)
a statewide database containing basic information regarding all newly hired employees and applicants for unemployment compensation within the state

Personal jurisdiction
the authority of the court to issue and enforce orders binding a particular individual

Actual service of process
actual delivery of notice to the person for whom it is intended

may be able to obtain personal jurisdiction over the defendant in the petitioner's own state under one of UIFSA's long-arm provisions. Under UIFSA, which now has been adopted in every state, if a defendant has one or more of the following eight kinds of "purposeful minimal contacts" with another state, it is considered fair and reasonable for a court in that other state to exercise personal jurisdiction over the individual and to adjudicate a child or spousal support dispute:

1. The nonresident is personally served in the state.
2. The nonresident submits to the jurisdiction of the state by consent, by entering a general appearance, or by filing a responsive document having the effect of waiving any contest to personal jurisdiction.
3. The nonresident once resided with the child in the state.
4. The nonresident once resided in the state and provided prenatal expenses or support for the child.
5. The child resides in the state as a result of the acts or directives of the nonresident.
6. The nonresident engaged in sexual intercourse in the state and the child may have been conceived by that act of intercourse.
7. The nonresident asserted parentage in the state such as through the putative father registry.
8. Any other basis consistent with the constitutions of the state and the United States for the exercise of personal jurisdiction.

(See Paralegal Application 9.2.)

PARALEGAL APPLICATION 9.2

JURISDICTION UNDER UIFSA

FACT PATTERN

Susan and her husband were married in Texas, by operation of common law, in 1997. Throughout their marriage, her husband (a known gang member) abused her both physically and psychologically. Susan also believed her husband was sexually abusing her daughter from a previous relationship. He threatened to kill her if she turned him in. Despite his threats, she contacted the police and reported both the death threats and the abuse, but the police did not investigate because she had not personally witnessed the abuse. She eventually left her husband and moved into a friend's trailer, but her husband continued to stalk her and slashed the tires on her car at work. She again reported the incidents to the police, and they told her she should move to a women's shelter. After that, her husband and a friend were seen armed with guns breaking into the trailer where she used to live. Her husband also made threatening phone calls to her father, who lived in Colorado. Early in January of 1999, pregnant by her husband and fearing for her life, she fled to her father's home in Colorado, where she gave birth to a son. In April of 2000, she filed for divorce in Colorado and sought child support, maintenance, and division of property and debt. After being personally served in Texas, her husband filed a motion to dismiss for lack of personal jurisdiction.

SIDEBAR

Should the Colorado court be able to exercise personal jurisdiction over Susan's husband under UIFSA? On what basis? To learn how the Colorado Supreme Court resolved this question, locate the case, *In re Marriage of Malwitz*, 99 P.3d 56 (Colo. 2004), available in its entirety on the companion website for this text in the material related to Chapter 9.

Obtaining Personal Jurisdiction Over a Nonresident Defendant in His or Her Own State

If the court cannot obtain personal jurisdiction in the petitioner's state, the matter cannot be adjudicated in that state. However, another avenue remains open to the petitioner working through the state's IV-D agency, with the agency acting on the petitioner's behalf or working with his or her attorney.

- The petitioner files a petition for child support in his or her own state.
- The IV-D agency in that state forwards the petition to the IV-D agency in the nonresident defendant's state.
- The appropriate court in the nonresident defendant's state obtains personal jurisdiction over the defendant and conducts an administrative or judicial hearing on the child support issue.
- The IV-D agency in the nonresident defendant's state then uses its enforcement powers to collect the child support amount from the defendant.

Continuing Exclusive Jurisdiction Under UIFSA

Under UIFSA, there should be only one valid support order between the parties that is enforceable in all states, and the states are required, under the Full Faith and Credit for Child Support Orders Act (FFCCSOA),[14] to respect properly issued orders from other states (including orders issued by tribal courts). By requiring other states to refrain from modifying those orders, the Act helps to prevent multiple and conflicting child support orders. Once a court issues a valid child support order under UIFSA, that court will have continuing exclusive jurisdiction over the case for purposes of modification, and no other state can modify the order as long as either parent or the child continues to reside in that state or the parties file written consents that another state assume jurisdiction. If neither of the parents nor the child continues to reside in the state that issued the initial order, that state loses its continuing exclusive jurisdiction and a court in another state can acquire it. It is conceivable that the parties may then simultaneously seek orders in different states, resulting in multiple orders. In this situation, under UIFSA, preference will be given to the child's **home state.** Home state is defined as the state where the child has lived for six consecutive months prior to the filing or since birth if the child is less than six months old. If neither state is the child's home state, the more recent order will control.

Home state
under UIFSA, the state where the child has lived for six consecutive months prior to the filing or since birth if the child is less than six months old

WHAT CHILD SUPPORT GUIDELINES ARE AND HOW THEY ARE APPLIED

Once the proper jurisdiction is determined, the paralegal can identify the appropriate child support guidelines and forms to utilize.

The Origin and Purpose of the Guidelines

In response to federal mandate, every state has put in place a system of child support guidelines designed to help parents and judges determine how much child support should be ordered in a given case. The basic requirements for each state's child support guidelines under federal law are as follows:[15]

- Application of the guidelines will produce a **rebuttable presumption** of the appropriate amount of support to be ordered.
- The guidelines must consider all earnings and income of the noncustodial parent.

Rebuttable presumption
an inference drawn from certain facts that can be overcome by the introduction of additional or contradictory evidence

- The guidelines must incorporate specific descriptive and numeric criteria.
- They must provide for children's health care needs.
- They must apply to all child support orders, whether at establishment or modification.
- Any order that deviates from the guidelines must include written findings of what the order would have been under the guidelines and why a deviation is warranted.
- Every four years each state's guidelines must be reviewed and revised, if necessary, to ensure that their application results in appropriate child support awards. The review must consider economic data on the cost of raising children and must analyze the application of, and deviations from, the guidelines to ensure that awards are consistent and deviations limited.

The Nature of State Guidelines

Although the federal government mandated their creation, it left the design of child support guidelines up to the individual states. As a result, no two states' guidelines are identical. Some provide for an exact computation of a support figure and others (such as Texas) establish a range within which the court has discretion to establish an amount of support. In addition to the overriding requirements of federal law, the guidelines of the various states:

> . . . reflect an intricate mix of estimated and actual expenditures on children; program provisions in related policy areas, such as child care, health care, tax policy and welfare reform; and research on the realities of life in separated families, such as shared parenting time and multiple families. . . . State guidelines vary with respect to the income basis for the determination of support; the estimate of spending on children upon which the guidelines are based; the treatment of child care costs; the treatment of medical insurance and out-of-pocket expenditures for medical care; provisions for other children to whom the parent owes a duty of support; adjustments for parenting time; and provisions for adjusting support when the obligor is low-income.[16]

Definition and Proof of Income

Guidelines are generally designed to calculate child support obligations when the parties' total combined income (net, adjusted, or gross, depending on the state) is under a certain maximum. For example, the maximum at the time this chapter was written was $150,800 in New Jersey and $80,000 in New York. Each state's formula establishes the base against which child support awards will be calculated:

Gross income
total income from all sources before any deductions are made

Adjusted gross income
income after nonvoluntary deductions are taken out, such as federal and state tax obligations, social security withholding, union dues, wage assignments related to prior support orders, etc

Net income
total income from all sources minus voluntary and nonvoluntary deductions

- *gross income* of the obligor (before any deductions are made);
- *adjusted gross income* (after nonvoluntary deductions are taken out, such as federal and state tax obligations, social security withholding, union dues, wage assignments related to prior support orders, etc.); or
- *net income* (after both nonvoluntary and voluntary deductions are subtracted).

Proof of income is often a central issue in a child support case. There are few types of income that continue totally unchanged from year to year. People lose or change their jobs, bonuses may be variable, interest rates rise and fall, and business conditions can result in inconsistent profits and losses, especially in cases where one or both of the parties are self-employed. The more something resembles a steady source of annual income that one can reasonably expect to receive in the future, the more likely it will be considered income for purposes of calculating a child support obligation.

If not controlled by federal law, the question of what should be included in income for purposes of calculating child support obligations will be determined by state statutes, administrative regulations, and case law. Most states define income broadly as "income from whatever source." All states include income from employment, including commissions, and virtually all include income from investment earnings, unemployment compensation, pensions, social security, and veterans' benefits. Treatment of occasional income (odd jobs, overtime, tips, bonuses, etc.) varies. Questions occasionally arise with respect to the following sources of income, among others:

- **Spousal or child support from a person not a party to the order:** Spousal support is usually considered income. Child support received by either party for children other than the child for whom support is being determined is not usually considered income.
- **Cash and gifts from family members:** An occasional modest gift may not be included, but if every year a party receives substantial gifts from his or her parents directly or from a family trust and does not have to repay or pay taxes on those sums, the amounts are likely to be included in income.[17]
- **Lump-sum severance pay:** Payments associated with compensation for employment are generally included in income. The same reasoning applies to severance pay and settlement amounts in suits for wrongful termination of employment that include compensation for lost pay.
- **Bonuses:** When bonuses are reasonably certain in the sense that they are awarded each year, even if in varying amounts, they are likely to be included in income. If a bonus is an occasional and uncertain event, a court may be reluctant to include it, depending on the circumstances.
- **Lump-sum personal injury settlements:** Although lump-sum personal injury settlements are often not considered an asset subject to property division between the parties, they are usually considered income in the child support context. The court may choose to prorate the award over a number of years.[18]
- **Lottery or gambling winnings, prizes, and awards:** Even though these are not customarily "continuing" sources of income, they are usually included.
- **Social Security Disability Benefits (SSD):** Because SSD benefits derive from prior employment, they are usually deemed includable in income.[19] A person becomes eligible to receive SSD benefits if he or she meets certain disability requirements and an employer has paid into the social security retirement system for his or her benefit. SSD is like an insurance policy intended to replace lost income when the employee is disabled and unable to work. Although the benefit will be included in his or her income, a disabled parent is ordinarily entitled to have Social Security Disability Benefits paid to a child (because of that parent's disability) credited against his or her child support obligation for that child.[20]
- **Means-tested sources of benefits, such as Pell grants, TANF benefits, food stamps, and Supplemental Social Security Income (SSI):** These usually are not considered income. Means-tested benefits are essentially social welfare programs designed to meet the basic needs of low-income persons. Congress has expressly exempted SSI from child support payments.[21]
- **Military allowances for housing (BAH) and subsistence (BAS):** Although these subsidies are not included in income for income tax purposes, several states (including Pennsylvania, Ohio, and Minnesota) have held them includable in gross income for purposes of calculating child support.
- **Military retirement benefits:** These benefits are includable as income, although under federal law there are limitations on the maximum percentage of the benefit that can be distributed pursuant to orders for property distribution, alimony, or child support.[22]
- **Reimbursements received in the course of employment:** When the reimbursements are significant and reduce personal living expenses, such as free housing, use of a company car, and reimbursed meals, they may be included. Louisiana, for example, specifically includes such reimbursements in income by statute.[23]

Imputed Income

Imputed income is income that is attributed to a party based upon his or her earning capacity rather than on actual earnings. Most states will impute income to one or both of the parties if appropriate. (See Case 9.1.) This practice is designed to prevent a party from avoiding a child or spousal support obligation by manipulating his or her income, for example, by voluntarily retiring early or remaining unemployed or underemployed. Most states will not impute income if there is a good-faith reason for unemployment such as physical disability or remaining at home for child-related reasons. However, many states will impute income when a party's wrongdoing results in the loss of gainful employment. Some states will also factor in the value of non-income producing assets such as boats, cars, and collections of such items as jewelry or artwork. If not considered by the formula, such assets may be used to justify a deviation from the guidelines if it appears a parent is deliberately trying to tie up funds that would otherwise be available to meet family obligations.

Some states establish by statute a formula for imputation of income. For example, in New Hampshire, RSA 458-C:2, IV(a) provides that, in cases in which a parent is determined to be voluntarily unemployed or underemployed, a trial court "in its discretion, may consider as gross income the difference between the amount a parent is earning and the amount a parent has earned." The court is also free to impute a lesser amount.[24] The amount set may depend in part on the noncustodial parent's educational background and job skills, as well as work history and job opportunities in the area. If the individual is unemployed and has no recent work history, the amount will be left to the court's discretion, absent governing statutory or case law. The North Carolina Guidelines provide that if a parent has no recent work history or vocational training, potential income should be estimated at not less than the minimum hourly wage for a forty-hour week.

Some states will impute income to affluent parents who have sufficient income-producing assets to support themselves and their child support obligations without working. The premise is that child support is not simply designed to meet children's reasonable needs but also that children are entitled to share in what would have been the total income and standard of living of the parties had the family remained intact.[25]

Courts will also consider averaging the income of a parent over a period of years, especially if the individual is self-employed in a highly volatile profession that is subject to market trends or when he or she has a windfall year that is totally inconsistent with an overall employment history. Income averaging imputes consistency in income rather than the income itself. In some jurisdictions, income averaging is specifically authorized by statute (for example, Alaska, Ohio, and Nebraska).

CASE **9.1** *McKenzie v. McKenzie*, 709 N.W.2d 528 (Iowa 2006)

BACKGROUND

The noncustodial parent, Timothy McKenzie, sought a modification of his child support obligation to his child by a first marriage based on a reduction in his actual income when he quit his job, moved to another state to be with his girlfriend (whom he subsequently married), and took a job that paid less than his prior position. The Iowa Supreme Court vacated the decision of the appellate court and affirmed the district court's denial of the modification petition. The denial was based on the findings that it was proper to impute income to Timothy

continued

at the level of the job he voluntarily left and that there had been no substantial change in circumstances sufficient to justify a change in his child support obligation. A variation of greater than 10 percent would have been required. In its opinion, the Court stated:

FROM THE OPINION

Timothy claims the reason he voluntarily left his employment at Gelita was to join Theresa in South Carolina, and not to avoid his child support obligation to Kilie. We have no reason to believe otherwise and recognize Timothy's desire to move and continue his relationship with Theresa is only natural. However, our first consideration under these circumstances is not what is in the best interest of Timothy, but what is in the best interest of his child. . . .

Timothy was not free to plan his future without regard to his obligation to his former wife and child. At the time Timothy left Iowa, he knew he had a preexisting duty to provide monthly child support in the sum of $495 for his daughter and that he could earn $45,260 annually if he stayed in Iowa. Even though he thought he could earn a comparable salary in South Carolina at the time he quit his job in Iowa, he had no idea what his earning capacity in South Carolina would be. Under these circumstances, Timothy's desire for self-fulfillment is outweighed by the preexisting duty he had to his former spouse to provide adequate support for his minor child.

SIDEBAR

Do you agree with the decision of the court in this case (available in its entirety on the companion website for this text in the material related to Chapter 9)?

PARALEGAL APPLICATION 9.3

CHILD SUPPORT GUIDELINE WORKSHEETS

Paralegals in a family law practice are frequently asked to complete child support guideline worksheets. A copy of the worksheet for the state of Tennessee is contained in Exhibit 9.2., and the instructions for completion of that worksheet are available on the companion website for this text in the material related to Chapter 9. A Worksheet must be completed for each action in which child support is an issue, as it presents the baseline for child support deliberations.

When preparing child support guideline worksheets, it is important to know what kinds of income will be considered includable for purposes of calculating child support in a given state and to identify and document all such sources of income. When any source of income is likely to be challenged or when income may be imputed, appropriate research needs to be done with respect to the issue in an effort to support the client's position.

Many firms have purchased software packages that can be used to calculate the amount of child support due under a given state's guidelines. Most states post worksheets on the web pages of their courts or IV-D agencies.

Because of the potential value of child support awards, it is important for the family law team to conduct adequate discovery with respect to the parties' respective incomes and any factors that may be used to argue for a deviation from the guidelines. If a deviation is going to be sought, the paralegal will very likely be asked to gather the information necessary to support that deviation based on the facts of the case.

EXHIBIT 9.2 Child Support Guidelines Worksheet For The State Of Tennessee

Courtesy of the State of Tennessee

Effective as of 6/26/2006

State of Tennessee - Department of Human Services
Child Support Worksheet

6/28/2006 - 1:07 PM

Part I. Identification

Indicate the status of each parent or caretaker by placing an "X" in the appropriate column

	PRP	ARP	SPLIT
Name of Mother:			
Name of Father:			
Name of non-parent Caretaker:			
TCSES case #:			
Docket #:			
Court name:			

Name(s) of Child(ren)	Date of Birth	Days with Mother	Days with Father	Days with Caretaker

---

Part II. Adjusted Gross Income

Use Credit Worksheet to calculate line items 1d - 1e

			Mother \ Column A	Father \ Column B	Nonparent Caretaker \ Column C
1		Monthly Gross Income	$	$	
	1a	Social Security benefit for child	+	+	
	1b	Self-employment tax paid	-	-	
	1c	Subtotal			
	1d	Credit for in-home children	-	-	
	1e	Credit for not-in-home children	-	-	
2		Adjusted Gross Income (AGI)	$	$	
2a		Combined Adjusted Gross Income			
3		Percentage Share of Income (PI)	%	%	

Part III. Parents' Share of BCSO

4	BCSO allotted to primary parent's household	$	$	$	
4a	Share of BCSO owed to primary parent	$	$		
5	Each parent's average parenting time				
5a	Equal parenting time				
6	Parenting time adjustment	$	$		
7	Adjusted BCSO	$	$		

Income Shares Worksheet - Page 1

Income Shares Worksheet V2 2006.xls

continued

Effective as of 6/26/2006   State of Tennessee - Department of Human Services   6/28/2006 - 1:07 PM
Child Support Worksheet

Part IV. Additional Expenses

		Mother \ Column A	Father \ Column B	Nonparent Caretaker \ Column C
8a	Children's portion of health insurance premium	$	$	$
8b	Recurring uninsured medical expenses	$	$	$
8c	Work-related childcare - Payroll Deducted	$	$	$
8d	Work-related childcare - Non-Payroll Deducted	$	$	$
9	Total additional expenses	$	$	$
10	Share of additional expenses owed	$	$	
11	Adjusted Support Obligation (ASO)	$	$	

** Reminder - Line 8d expenses are to be paid by the child's PRP or either parent in a 50-50 situation.

Part V. Presumptive Child Support Order

		OBLIGATION	
12	Presumptive Child Support Order (PCSO)	$	$

* Enter the difference between the greater and smaller numbers from Line 11.

Low Income? _____ (N=15% Y=7.5%)
Current Order Flat %? _____ (N / Y)

Modification of Current Child Support Order

13a	Current child support order amount for the obligor parent	$	$
13b	Amount required for significant variance to exist	$	$
13c	Actual variance between current and presumptive child support orders	$	$

Part VI. Deviations and FCSO

14	Deviations (Specify):	$	$

Deviations must be substantiated by written findings in the Child Support Order

15	Final Child Support Order (FCSO)	$	$
16	FCSO adjusted for SS benefit, Line 1a, Obligor's column.	$	$

Comments, Calculations, or Rebuttals to Schedule

Preparer's Use Only

Name: _____   Date: 6/28/2006
Title: _____

Deviations from the Guidelines

The Child Support Guidelines initially limit the discretion of the courts in a significant manner. They set a base from which a judge can then exercise discretion in a manner consistent with statutory, regulatory, and case law. In addition, federal regulations require that any deviation from the guidelines' amount be in the best interests of the child.[26] The presumption that application of the guidelines will result in an appropriate amount of child support is rebuttable. A court may deviate from the guidelines' amount if it is unjust, unreasonable, or inappropriate under the circumstances or not in the best interests of the child, provided the court issues findings regarding the reason(s) for the deviation in order to allow for effective appellate review. A copy of a Massachusetts form for documenting a deviation from the guidelines is available on the companion website in the material for Chapter 9.

To guide a court's exercise of discretion, in addition to basic child support guidelines the states also establish by statute, administrative regulation, case law, and/or practice the factors or circumstances that may justify a deviation from the guidelines. These factors may also form the basis for a modification of child support.

Extraordinary expense
an unusual, unanticipated child-rearing expense that is substantial in cost and/or duration

Extraordinary Expenses. In general, it is assumed that the custodial parent is responsible for payment of a child's ordinary day-to-day living expenses. These are costs that are reasonably predictable and consistent from child to child. On occasion, an unusual, unanticipated child-rearing expense may arise that is substantial in cost and/or duration. Such *extraordinary expenses* are often medical in nature. For example, a child may require either physical or psychological therapy on an ongoing basis or have a chronic medical condition, such as diabetes or cystic fibrosis. Such situations can involve costly medical care and medications, some of which may not be covered by insurance. Some conditions may require a custodial parent to make physical accommodations in the child's residence. Extraordinary expenses may be of other kinds as well. States vary with respect to how such costs will be treated. Most commonly, they are handled as a deviation from the guidelines for a temporary or extended period. A prorated amount may be added onto the child support obligation based on the respective incomes of the parties.

Multiple Families. According to the U.S. Department of Health and Human Services, almost 75 percent of people who divorce remarry. A new marriage often results in a his, hers, and ours situation when it comes to children. This can create both emotional and financial stress, and related problems often arise in child support cases. Although a new partner has no legal obligation to support his or her spouse's children from prior marriages or relationships, states may give consideration to such circumstances within the guidelines. For example, in New Hampshire, RSA 458-C:4 provides "When considering a request for an original support order or modification of a support order under this chapter, the court shall take into account any stepchildren for which either parent may be responsible."

However, the traditional rule is that "first families come first" in child support calculations, and an obligor usually cannot request a downward modification in support due a first family based upon his or her new obligations to a second family. In fact, should the later relationship fail, the guidelines in some states deduct the amount of support due to "first" or prior families from the income available to support potential obligations flowing from the more recent relationship. However, the obligor may be able to use obligations to the new family as a defense to a claim by a former spouse for an upward modification in child support to a prior family. For example, in 2002, the rules for the Nebraska Guidelines were amended to include the following provision:

> Limitation on Decrease: An obligor shall not be allowed a reduction in an existing support order solely because of the birth, adoption or acknowledgement of subsequent children of the obligor; however, a duty to provide regular support for subsequent children may be raised as a defense to an action for an upward modification of such existing support order.[27]

The contemporary view is that there is no precise, mathematical formula for calculating child support when multiple families are involved. The determination is left to the discretion of the court. As long as the court considers the obligations to both families and the income of the parent of the subsequent children and does not act in a manner that benefits one family at the expense of the other, a court's determination of a child support obligation is likely to be upheld.[28]

Educational Needs of the Children.   In the preschool, elementary, middle, and high school years, educational needs of the minor children may include enrollment in a private or alternative school, participation in extracurricular activities, tutoring and other forms of compensatory education for a child with disabilities, or special lessons for a gifted child who demonstrates unusual potential in a particular field such as music or athletics.

Several states set the age of emancipation and termination of child support at eighteen years but provide that if the child continues his or her high school education past age eighteen, the court, in its discretion, may order the continuation of support until the child finishes high school or reaches the age of nineteen. This is the approach taken in Idaho, for example. The Idaho Supreme Court described the rationale behind that state's statute in the 2005 *Busse* case as follows:

> There is a strong public policy in favor of providing support to students. A large population of educated persons greatly benefits society. All students should be encouraged to finish high school, regardless of whether they have reached the age of eighteen, and the absence of child support should not influence the decision to stay in school.[29]

The cost of higher education is not considered an extraordinary expense in the sense that it can be anticipated, and it is not viewed by some as a "necessary." The trend with respect to higher education is away from requiring parents to pay for college expenses absent an agreement, but there is a range among the states that address the issue by statute. At one end is New Hampshire, which revised its statute in 2004 to provide that "No child support order shall require a parent to contribute to an adult child's college expenses or other educational expenses beyond the completion of high school."[30] In 1997, Colorado also completely reversed its earlier position and terminated the court's authority to order postsecondary education support absent an agreement of the parties.[31] Massachusetts is at the other end of the spectrum. By statute, it provides that a court may order support "for any child who has attained age twenty-one but who has not attained age twenty-three, if such child is domiciled in the home of a parent, and is principally dependent on said parent for maintenance due to the enrollment of such child in an educational program, excluding educational costs beyond an undergraduate degree."[32]

Iowa is an example of a state that falls in the middle. Iowa Code section 598.21(5A) authorizes courts to order a postsecondary education subsidy under certain conditions for good cause shown. However, the amount to be paid by each parent cannot exceed one-third of the total cost of the postsecondary education. The court determines "the cost of postsecondary education based on the cost of attending an in-state public institution for a course of instruction leading to an undergraduate degree and shall include the reasonable costs for only necessary postsecondary education expenses." By case law, the Iowa courts have expanded the nature of what will be considered necessary educational expenses: "We recognized the reasonable and necessary costs of attending college surpass the costs of tuition, books, room, board, and supplies. A college education is not limited to what is learned in the classroom; it includes social, cultural, and educational experiences outside the classroom."[33]

Custodial and Visitation Arrangements.   Most early versions of state child support guidelines were based on a traditional custody model, with one parent having primary physical custody and the other parent having "reasonable visitation rights." It was estimated that the noncustodial parent would be with the child approximately 20 percent of the time. Deviations were sometimes allowed to accommodate alternative models, including joint and split custody. ***Joint physical custody*** refers to a custody arrangement in which a child spends a more or less equal amount of time living with each parent. In a ***split custody*** situation, for example, one involving four children, two of the children may live with one parent and the other two with the other parent.

As the concept of family has evolved and parents have adopted alternative models of physical custody, states and courts have had to recognize the need for deviations from basic child support guidelines. For example, a child may spend three continuous months with a noncustodial parent during the summer, and/or the child or noncustodial parent may have to travel a considerable distance to effect visitation. The child support amount may be adjusted based on such variations in visitation patterns or degrees of shared custody. In more than half the states, the deviation is left to the discretion of the court, but several states (such as Wisconsin) require the court to apply a different formula once visitation or shared custody reaches a certain level. Arizona,[34] Colorado,[35] and New Jersey[36] also are among the states that have established formulas to provide credit to a noncustodial parent for extended periods of visitation. The relevant Oklahoma statute provides for an adjustment in the base amount of child support when "shared parenting" time has been ordered by the court or agreed to by the parents. Shared parenting time means that each parent has physical custody of the child or children overnight for more than one hundred twenty (120) nights each year.[37] In 2003, the state of Maine enacted new child support guidelines that mandate an alternative method for calculating child support when the parties provide "substantially equal care for a child."[38] North Dakota also has a formula in place for calculating child support obligations in cases where parents have equal custody. (See Exhibit 9.3.) In determining what constitutes parenting, the courts may look beyond the quantitative number of days a child is technically in the custody of each parent, to qualitative factors such as participating in school activities and arranging for and attending extracurricular activities in which the child is involved, etc.

Joint physical custody
a custody arrangement in which a child spends a more or less equal amount of time living with each parent

Split custody
each parent has legal and/or physical custody of one or more of the parties' children

EXHIBIT 9.3 North Dakota Formula for Child Support with Equal
                 Physical Custody

FROM THE ADMINISTRATIVE CODE

Equal physical custody—Determination of child support obligation. A child support obligation must be determined as described in this section in all cases in which a court orders each parent to have equal physical custody of their child or children. Equal physical custody means each parent has physical custody of the child, or if there are multiple children, all of the children, exactly 50% of the time. A child support obligation for each parent must be calculated under this chapter, assuming the other parent is the custodial parent of the child or children subject to the equal physical custody order. The lesser obligation is then subtracted from the greater. The difference is the child support amount owed by the parent with the greater obligation.[39]

Occasionally, a custodial parent relinquishes possession and control of a child to a noncustodial parent without a formal change in custody. In doing so, the former custodial parent may well lose a right to child support previously ordered by the court. Texas addresses this situation by statute and provides that an obligor may plead, as an affirmative defense (in whole or in part) to a motion for enforcement of child support, that the *obligee* voluntarily relinquished to the obligor actual possession and control of a child in excess of the court-ordered possession and access.[40] In such situations, the most appropriate course of action is to seek an order of the court formally modifying both child custody and support based on the change in circumstances.

Obligee
under UIFSA, any person to whom a duty of support is owed

Cost of Living in a Geographical Area. The states vary with respect to whether or not cost of living will warrant a deviation from the guidelines when the parents live in different geographical localities. For example, an individual living in New York City is likely to have a considerably higher cost of living than one living in Littleton, New Hampshire. The Maryland Court of Appeals has held that "a lower cost of living in the child's locality is not a proper basis for deviating from the guidelines."[41] However, other courts have held that a noncustodial parent's higher cost of living may be an acceptable reason for deviating from the guidelines if substantiated by concrete evidence.

Standard of Living. The primary purpose of child support is to provide for a child's survival "needs." However, when feasible, an effort is made to provide the child with the standard of living he or she would have had if the family had remained intact. If either parent enjoys a higher standard of living, courts generally take the position that the child is entitled to enjoy that higher standard. The higher the income, the more likely a court will consider standard of living—the country club life, overseas travel, pedigree pets, private school, summer camp, etc. In effect, a child's needs are viewed as relative and directly related to the parents' incomes, and, therefore, support awards may vary accordingly. "To be sure, many people, adults and children alike, have far more than they truly 'need' to survive, or even to live comfortably.... Even among middle class populations, there is a range of tastes with varying costs.... Simply put, given a choice between rhinestones and rubies, many people opt for the latter if they can afford to do so."[42]

Additional examples of circumstances that may justify a deviation include, but are not limited to, the following:

- **Number and ages of the children:**   This information may be considered if not already factored into the guidelines formula.
- **The financial resources of the child(ren):**   A child may receive governmental benefits (such as social security disability income), be a beneficiary of a trust established by a grandparent, or be employed and earning limited or substantial income.
- **Needs and resources of the custodial parent:**   This may include income from a new partner if it frees up parental income. For example, the new partner may be covering the rent or mortgage payment and other household expenses.
- **Needs and resources of the noncustodial parent:**   This may include income from a new partner if it frees up parental income.
- **Financial misconduct of either parent:**   The court may consider whether either parent has failed to comply with discovery requests, made excessive expenditures, or fraudulently concealed or disposed of property in an effort to reduce a child support obligation. Under such circumstances a court may order child support in an amount that deviates from the guidelines and at a level substantially disproportionate to the guidelines amount or to the obligor's alleged ability to pay. (See Case 9.2.)
- **Existence of an agreement between the parties:**   Based on the strong public policy in favor of protecting the rights and needs of children, the courts retain jurisdiction over child-related issues such as child support and child custody. Parents cannot totally waive or relinquish support obligations by agreement, because the right to support is the child's right. However, an agreement of the parties' containing provisions relating to details pertaining to child support may be given considerable weight by the court if the terms are reasonable, are beneficial to the child, and do not provide for a level of child support below the minimum called for by the child support guidelines as applied to the parties. Courts in many states have enforced provisions in agreements in which noncustodial parents agree to pay child support amounts far in excess of the guidelines amount. For example, in the *Pursley* case, the Kentucky Supreme Court observed that parties to divorce frequently have valid motives for making what may appear to others to be "bad bargains." (See Case 9.3.)

CASE **9.2** *Farish v. Farish,* 279 Ga. 551, 615 S.E.2d 510 (2005)

DISCUSSION OF THE CASE

In this case, the Georgia Supreme Court affirmed a district court's order that a noncustodial parent of five children with a gross monthly income of $10,374 be required to pay $3,000 per month for support of the three minor children and $2,000 per month in alimony to his wife of twenty-six years. The court stated that, in determining the obligor's ability to pay, the district court had:

> . . . properly considered appellant's income, property in his possession, the fact that he appropriated for his own use $55,000 of joint or marital assets after the parties' separation for which he had not accounted at the time of trial, and the fact that the appellant accumulated substantial debt after the separation by providing monetary support for his paramour and her family to the detriment of his own children and wife.

SIDEBAR

This opinion is available in its entirety on the companion website.

CASE **9.3** *Pursley v. Pursley,* 144 S.W.3d 820 (Ky. 2004)

BACKGROUND

Under the parties' agreement in this case, the wife was awarded custody of the parties' two children. The husband agreed to pay thirty percent of all of his income from salaries and bonuses as child support until such time as the children turned eighteen or graduated from college or graduate school, whichever was latest. He also agreed to pay the cost of undergraduate and graduate educations for the children at any school that they chose in the United States. Additionally, he agreed to maintain the children's medical and health insurance and to pay any medical and dental expenses not covered by insurance.

In finding the agreement was not "unconscionable," the court noted the husband was "an educated and sophisticated businessman" with a strong moral desire to meet his obligations and that he was advised by counsel during extensive negotiations.

FROM THE OPINION

. . .One of the primary goals in enacting child support guidelines was to "increase the adequacy of child support awards." Unquestionably, Kentucky took a giant step towards this goal when it enacted the Guidelines. And the purpose of the Guidelines is not offended, but rather is aided by allowing divorcing parents to agree to provide greater support for their children. The Guidelines do not constitute the maximum support that a parent may agree to provide for his or her children. Although, as a rule, it is not in the best interests of the children when their parents agree to an amount of child support below the Guidelines, no one can convincingly argue that the best interests of children are not served when their parents agree to support in excess of the amount established by the Guidelines. Although a court is not bound by such agreements, . . . the Guidelines should not act as a barrier.

SIDEBAR

This opinion is available in its entirety on the companion website.

WHEN AND HOW A CHILD SUPPORT AWARD CAN BE MODIFIED

Modification of child support awards is governed by federal and state statutes, case law, and specific court rules. There are three primary bases for modification of a child support award:

1. modification triggered by a self-executing provision in an agreement of the parties that has been incorporated into a court's decree
2. modification based on proof of a substantial change in circumstances
3. modification based on a periodic review and adjustment of orders by the state's IV-D agency

Modification by Agreement

Modifications by agreement generally are accepted by the courts provided they do not waive the child's right to a reasonable level of support consistent with the guidelines and they are in the best interests of the child. (See Case 9.4.) Modification provisions in agreements should be tied to actual financial circumstances. For instance, courts have rejected provisions that call for a simple pro rata adjustment in the child support amount as each child reaches age eighteen.

CASE **9.4** *Lee v. Lee*, 2005 ND 129, 699 N.W.2d 842 (2005)

BACKGROUND

In this case, the Supreme Court of North Dakota awarded a custodial father child support despite a provision in his divorce agreement that he would receive primary physical custody of the child and pay a reduced amount of spousal support to his spouse in exchange for her not having to pay child support.

FROM THE OPINION

"The best interests of the children require child support obligors to provide adequate support and maintenance for their minor children." *Smith v. Smith*, 538 N.W.2d 222 (N.D. 1995).... For this reason, the court has said, "Parental agreements that prohibit or limit the power of a court to modify future child support are invalid." Id. This Court encourages settlements in divorce actions, but "takes a dim view of agreements purporting to sign away the rights of a child in support settings not from a contractual background but from a public policy one." Id.... Trial courts should not accept parental stipulations regarding child support if the court determines the stipulation is not in the child's best interests.

SIDEBAR

This opinion is available in its entirety on the companion website.

In the case of *Scott-Lasley v. Lasley*,[43] the Georgia Supreme Court held that when "an award of child support is made for several children and the trial court provides for reductions in child support as the children reach majority, the trial court may not reduce the child support on a pro rata per child basis, but must instead do so in accordance with the child support guidelines."

Modification Based on Proof of a Substantial Change in Circumstances

Either parent can bring a modification action based on a substantial change in circumstances. The moving parent has the burden of proving by a preponderance of the evidence that the requested modification is warranted. State IV-D agencies also can initiate requests for modification on a client's behalf. Although there is no guarantee that a motion for modification will be granted, it can still be brought in good faith. It will be granted if the court is persuaded that the change is substantial enough to make the prior award inequitable and the change is in the best interests of the child. In most states, the burden of showing a substantial change in circumstances will be satisfied if there is a given level of difference between the current presumptive guideline amount and the amount of the order then in force. The difference is usually expressed in a percentage. As of 2007, in Iowa, for example, the amount was 10 percent; in Tennessee, 15 percent (if the current support is $100 or greater per month); and, in Indiana, 20 percent.

Many states require the change to have been "unforeseeable" at the time the initial order was entered. The claims raised most often relate to unanticipated changes in the employment or financial resources of one or both of the parties, the impact of a subsequent family on either party's resources, a change in custody, a major change in the law governing some aspect of child support, or a change in a child's level of need. Generally, a parent may not rely on a claim of decreased income to obtain a modification of support if the parent's reduced earning capacity and inability to pay child support is voluntary. Parents who intentionally try to avoid payment of support or who do not consider their children's needs when changing employment, etc., may not be entitled to a change in child support.

Modification Based on a Periodic Review and Adjustment of Orders by the State's IV-D Agency

Under federal law,[44] the parties to a child support order may request a review every three years to determine whether the child support order in force continues to comply with the state's child support guidelines without having to show a change in circumstances. States are free to institute shorter review cycles but cannot extend the period beyond three years.

HOW AND BY WHOM SUPPORT ORDERS ARE ENFORCED

Changes instituted over the past three decades are designed to replace the traditional method of costly and inefficient case-by-case trips to court to enforce awards and to put in place a series of measures that can be handled in large part through administrative procedures outside the court system through each state's IV-D agency.

An action to enforce a support order may be brought by a custodial parent, a custodian or guardian of a child, a IV-D agency on behalf of a client, or an agency substantially contributing to the support of the child. There are three primary approaches to enforcement of child support orders:

- The custodial parent may proceed on his or her own with or without counsel using the resources available through the court system.
- The custodial parent may retain the services of a private child support agency that charges a fee for helping the parent recover the amount of child support owed to him or her.
- The custodial parent may use the services of the state's IV-D agency, which has a broad array of available resources and enforcement tools.

Paralegal Practice Tip

Although some courts have linked child support and custody/visitation orders, the majority view is that support and custody are independent issues and should not be linked. If the custodial parent denies the noncustodial parent visitation in retaliation for a failure to pay child support, he or she may be subject to a contempt action. If the interference is sufficiently extreme, such as concealing the child's whereabouts, the parent may even lose physical custody of the child. The better course of action is to seek enforcement of the support order.

PARALEGAL APPLICATION 9.4

AN ETHICAL ISSUE

The services of a state's IV-D agency are available to every parent with a child support issue at little or potentially no cost and without the need to have legal counsel. An attorney has an ethical duty to advise clients of the availability of free IV-D services before undertaking a child support enforcement matter on behalf of a client so that the client can make an informed decision with respect to the need for representation. The IV-D agency is not intended to eliminate the need for counsel but rather to complement it. If a client chooses to retain counsel, the family law team may explain IV-D procedures and assist the client in locating necessary information and completing required paperwork. It is not the paralegal's role to provide legal advice, but the paralegal should be aware of the policy in this area at the firm where he or she works. Some firms have information sheets that can be provided to clients describing various enforcement and representation options available.[45]

Whereabouts of the Noncustodial Parent

Often, the first major obstacle to enforcing a child support order is that the whereabouts of the obligor are concealed or unknown. Many obligors simply disappear. If the whereabouts of the noncustodial parent are unknown, counsel and the custodial parent can potentially benefit from the availability of a wide range of centralized databases that can be accessed through the state-sponsored IV-D agency or through a private company engaged in the business of collecting delinquent child support payments. As one of its mandated services, each state's IV-D agency provides a ***State Parent Locator Service (SPLS)*** that connects a variety of data sources at the federal, state, and local levels on addresses, income, and assets. The sources include vital statistics, state and local tax records, real and personal property records, records of occupational and professional licenses, employment security, and public assistance records. SPLS also has access to records of other state agencies such as the Division of Motor Vehicles, Unemployment Commission, Department of Revenue, and Bureau of Prisons. It also maintains the federally mandated State Case Registry (containing information about all support cases within the state's jurisdiction) and the State Directory of New Hires (containing information from employers within the state regarding new hires).

If unsuccessful at the state level, the state's IV-D agency can seek assistance from the ***Federal Parent Locator Service (FPLS)*** operated by the OCSE. The FPLS, in turn, can draw on the records of other federal agencies such as the Internal Revenue Service, Social Security Administration, Selective Service System, and the Departments of Defense and Labor, as well as the Federal Case Registry of Child Support Orders (FCR) and the National Directory of New Hires, which also includes information about individuals who have applied for unemployment compensation.

The Basic Title IV-D Process

When a custodial parent applies for public assistance, he or she is automatically referred to the state's designated IV-D agency for child support services. As a condition of receiving assistance, the parent must assign his or her rights to support to the state and must agree to cooperate with the state in identifying and locating the other parent unless a good cause for noncooperation can be established, such as a prior history of abuse that continues to pose a threat of serious violence.

State Parent Locator Service (SPLS)

a federally mandated service provided by each state for the purpose of helping to locate parents who are delinquent in meeting their child support obligations

Federal Parent Locator Service (FPLS)

a service operated by the OCSE for the purpose of locating parents delinquent in meeting their child support obligations when multiple states are involved

---

PARALEGAL APPLICATION 9.5

ALERT RE VICTIMS OF DOMESTIC VIOLENCE

Sometimes the resources of state and federal locator services are misused by individuals who have abused a former partner who has fled in order to protect him- or herself from further abuse. When a client is initiating a search, it is sometimes difficult to assess whether or not the search is being made in good faith. If the client is a victim and IV-D services will be used, it is important that the IV-D agency be advised of the history of abuse so that appropriate protective steps can be initiated at both the state and federal levels. In order to protect victims of domestic violence, a family violence indicator (FVI) is placed on the at-risk individual's name and the names of the children, indicating a restriction on disclosure of data. States are prohibited from releasing information on the whereabouts of "flagged" parents and children to anyone who has committed or threatened domestic violence. The address of the victim(s) will also be blocked out in paperwork pertaining to the enforcement action.

Once a support order is issued, the support obligation runs directly from the noncustodial parent to the state. Any support collected is then used to reimburse the state and federal governments for public assistance payments made to the custodial parent. Under federal law, states may elect to "pass through" to the custodial parent a modest portion of the amount collected.

Many custodial parents not applying for or receiving public assistance elect, but are not required, to receive assistance from the state's IV-D agency. At the time a child support order is obtained, the custodial parent, on his or her own or with the assistance of counsel, can ask the court to order that the payments be made through the state's designated IV-D child support enforcement agency, which operates under a complex set of state and federal laws and regulations. When the agency accepts the application, it assumes responsibility for collecting and disbursing payments, for monitoring compliance, and for initiating appropriate enforcement measures if a delinquency occurs. If the custodial parent does not initially accept services but later wants to seek them, he or she can apply for IV-D services by completing the appropriate application. The underlying rationale for providing this service is that, if parents receive their child support payments, their need for public assistance will be reduced. A copy of an application for IV-D services is provided on the companion website for this text in the material related to Chapter 9.

When an **arrearage** arises, the custodial parent may provide, either by request or on their own, the following kinds of information about the obligor to the IV-D agency:

Arrearage
a payment that is due but has not been made

- social security number
- place of birth
- last known residential address
- current marital status
- responsibility for additional children
- current and past employers' names and addresses
- nature, sources, and location of assets and income
- names and addresses of relatives and friends
- clubs and organizations the obligor has belonged to
- licenses held (driver's, professional, etc.)
- local banks, public utilities, and other creditors of the obligor

Enforcement of an Order Against a Nonresident Defendant

Traveling to the nonresident defendant's state, retaining counsel, and asking the court in that state to enforce the child support order can be time-consuming, costly, and inconvenient. In the alternative, under UIFSA, the petitioner can use the IV-D agency in his or her state to send the court order to an appropriate court in the state where the obligor resides. This is called "registering" the order with the second state, which can then enforce (but not modify) it as if it were an order of that state's court. The petitioner's state is called the "initiating state" and the defendant's state is called the "responding state." Once the order is registered, it is important to keep track of when the nonregistering party receives notice of the order. Generally, if the nonregistering party fails to contest the validity, enforcement, or modification of the registered order, or to seek to vacate the registration within twenty days after notice of registration, the order will be conformed by **operation of law**.[46]

Operation of law
automatically because the result is dictated by law; a party does not need to take any further action to bring about the result

Enforcement Methods

There are several mechanisms available to help the obligee enforce a child support order. Some flow from federal law and some from state law. Most can be initiated by a state's IV-D agency on behalf of a client, and some can be pursued privately without agency assistance and with or without the assistance of an attorney. The strongest and most comprehensive arsenal is available to the state's IV-D agency. The IV-D process is especially helpful in dealing with nonpayment of support by obligors whose identity or whereabouts are unknown or who have moved to another state or are traveling from state to state to avoid paying support.

A brief description of various enforcement methods is provided below. The success of many of these measures is possible because of the extensive linkages between various state and federal agencies that allow for sharing of data at an unprecedented (and, to some, alarming) level.

Criminal Prosecution.

In virtually all states, intentional failure to pay child support is a crime that can be prosecuted and punished by probation, fine, and/or incarceration. An intentional failure to pay is distinguished from an involuntary inability to pay. Before a delinquent obligor can be prosecuted at either the state or federal level, the obligor must be financially able to pay the overdue child support.

Under the federal Deadbeat Parents Punishment Act,[47] criminal nonsupport is a federal felony offense that can result in imposition of a sentence of from six months to two years. The nonsupport must have persisted for at least a year and be in an amount greater than $5,000. To trigger federal involvement, multiple states must be involved.[48] For example, the obligor and the child may reside in different states or the obligor may have left the state for an extended period to avoid paying his or her support obligations. Sometimes criticized as an unwarranted intrusion into matters best left to the states, this option is usually pursued only in the most egregious cases and, generally, when other federal offenses are involved, such as use of a false social security number. An action can be initiated by the state, the IV-D agency, or the individual.

Contempt Action.

An action may be brought against the delinquent obligor for civil or criminal contempt or both, depending on the circumstances. Although both potentially can result in fines, probation, or jail sentences, the purposes they serve are distinctly different. The purpose of *civil contempt* is remedial in nature. It is designed to encourage the obligor to comply with the child support order and catch up on payment of child support arrearages and thereby purge the contempt and avoid jail. The purpose of *criminal contempt* is punitive. It is designed to punish an individual for willfully disobeying an order of the court. The former serves the needs of the recipient of child support. The latter serves the dignity of the criminal justice system.

Income Withholding.

The most effective enforcement tool is *income (wage) withholding,* an automatic deduction from the paycheck of an obligor. All child support orders must include a wage-withholding provision, and an income-withholding order can be sent to an employer in any state. If it is a Title IV-D public assistance case, the wage withholding will take effect immediately absent good cause to suspend it or an alternative arrangement agreed to by the parties. If there is an arrearage, the income-withholding order may be increased on a percentage basis until the arrearage is paid off. If income withholding initially is suspended, it will go into effect when a month of support arrearages has accrued. Prior to this happening, the obligor is entitled to notice and a hearing.

More than half of all child support orders are enforced through this method. There are few defenses to income withholding other than a mistake in the amount of the support or arrearage due or in the identity of the noncustodial parent. Limits on the maximum amount that may be withheld are established

---

Paralegal Practice Tip

In several states, failure to pay child support is viewed as a "continuing" offense. However, actions to enforce child support orders in some jurisdictions are subject to **statutes of limitations.** For example, in Michigan, in a civil context the statute of limitations for bringing an enforcement action for failure to pay support "is ten (10) years from the date that the last support payment is due under the support order regardless of whether or not the last payment is made."[49] On the other hand, the crime of felony nonsupport is subject to a six-year period of limitations.[50] Such statutes protect defendants from having to defend against stale claims long after witnesses and evidence may have been lost through the passage of time.

Statute of limitations
a statute that bars a certain type of claim after a specified period of time

Civil contempt
a sanction for failure to obey a court order issued for another's benefit; a civil contempt proceeding is remedial in nature and designed to promote compliance with the order

Criminal contempt
a punishment for failure to comply with a court order; a criminal contempt proceeding is punitive in nature and designed to punish an attack on the integrity of the court

Income withholding
an automatic deduction of child support from an obligor's paycheck

by federal law. Failure to comply with an income-withholding order can subject an employer to sanctions including fines, and the employer may be held responsible for the amount of support that should have been withheld were it not for the omission.

Seizure of Assets.   Under federal law, states are required to create administrative procedures designed to automatically create a *lien* on the real or personal property of an obligor located within the state in the amount of unpaid child support. The lien arises by "operation of law" without any action having to be taken by the custodial parent. Under federal law, states must give full faith and credit to liens arising in another state.[51] The lien on the property restricts the ability of the obligor to sell, transfer, or borrow against the property until the arrearage is paid. The custodial parent may need to "perfect" the lien under some circumstances. For example, a lien against real estate should be recorded in the appropriate registry for public records of deeds in order for it to be effective against third parties. This measure is especially effective in cases in which the obligor lacks any income subject to withholding but does own property.

Title IV-D agencies can also attach and seize accounts of a delinquent obligor in financial institutions that operate in more than one state. The seizure can cover several kinds of accounts, such as checking and savings accounts, certificates of deposit, and mutual funds. The obligor will have a limited ability to sell or otherwise transfer those funds until the child support arrearage is satisfied.

Tax Refund Intercepts.   Both state and federal tax refunds due to obligors can be intercepted and offset up to the amount of an obligor's child support arrearage. State IV-D agencies submit to the Internal Revenue Service and state Departments of Revenue the names, social security numbers, and amounts of past due child support arrearages. If, for example, a federal tax refund is due the delinquent obligor, the Federal Tax Refund Offset Program can collect past-due child support payments from the refund after the obligor has received notice of the pending action and been given an opportunity to correct possible errors in a hearing. Only the IV-D agency has access to the federal intercept.

Unemployment Compensation Intercepts.   A state's IV-D agency can arrange to intercept social security or unemployment compensation benefits to meet both past-due and continuing child support obligations. Needs-based benefits, such as Social Security Supplemental Income (SSI), are not subject to interception or withholding.

License Denials or Revocations.   Under federal law, IV-D agencies can arrange to have a delinquent obligor's vehicle registration and/or driver's license suspended. They may be reinstated once the child support arrearage is paid. The agency can also seek denial or revocation of professional, recreational, or occupational licenses required by states to practice in a variety of professions, such as real estate, plumbing, and teaching. Virtually every state's Bar Association provides that the licenses to practice law of attorneys in contempt for failure to pay child support may be suspended. In particularly egregious cases, an attorney may be disbarred.

Passport Denial.   Under federal law, an individual owing over $5,000 in child support may be denied a passport or have an existing passport restricted or revoked.

Credit Reporting.   Under federal law, IV-D agencies must periodically report to credit bureaus the names of delinquent obligors whose support arrearages have reached a specific dollar amount.[52] Prior to the report being made, the obligor

---

Paralegal Practice Tip

The income-withholding notice can also include a requirement that the employer enroll the obligor's children in the group health insurance program available to the obligor, without the necessity of formally petitioning the court for a *Qualified Medical Child Support Order (QMCSO)*. Prior to federal legislation in this area, many insurance companies denied coverage unless the employee was the custodial parent or claimed the child as a dependent.

Qualified Medical Child Support Order (QMCSO)
a court order requiring provision of medical support or health benefits for the child of a parent covered by a group insurance plan

Lien
an encumbrance on the property of another that operates as a cloud against clear title to the property

must receive notice and have an opportunity for an administrative review. The reporting of child support debts creates a "cloud" on the obligor's credit and alerts potential creditors that an obligor may be a poor risk.

To encourage compliance with support orders, Title IV-D agencies use a variety of additional, less onerous preliminary techniques such as frequent delinquency notices and telephone reminders. Occasionally, states also implement creative measures such as intercepts of lottery winnings. Many states publish "wanted" posters in public buildings, such as town halls and courthouses, containing photographs of the state's most serious offenders for whom arrest warrants have been issued. The threat of prosecution and public humiliation sometimes provides a sufficient incentive to a delinquent obligor to pay arrearages.

Some enforcement measures raise issues of constitutional dimension. For instance, according to the U.S. Supreme Court, a state cannot deny a marriage license to a delinquent obligor.[53] However, in 2001, the Wisconsin Court of Appeals held, as a condition of probation, that a father who intentionally failed to pay child support for the nine children he'd fathered by four different women could be prevented from having additional children until he made sufficient efforts to support his current children![54]

In extreme cases, a failure to support a child may result in termination of parental rights under an abandonment statute. For example, under the Idaho abandonment statute, the court may terminate a parent-child relationship when it finds a parent has abandoned a child by willfully failing to maintain a normal parental relationship, including, but not limited to, reasonable support or regular personal contact without just cause for a period of one year.[55]

TAX IMPLICATIONS OF CHILD SUPPORT

Tax Treatment of Child Support Payments

Unlike spousal support payments discussed in the next chapter, child support is a tax-neutral event. Child support payments are not deductible by the payor and are not includable as income to the recipient for income tax purposes. However, when spousal and child support payments are lumped together in a single payment without any designation as to what portion, if any, constitutes child support, the entire unallocated support amount will be treated as alimony by the Internal Revenue Service (IRS). The full amount paid will then be deductible from the payor's gross income and will be includable in the recipient's income. As tempting as it may be to use this approach (assuming the recipient is in a lower tax bracket and unallocated payments result in a net tax gain for the parties), there may be costly consequences in the long run. As of 2007, the federal tax code retains specific provisions governing unallocated support payments. If, for example, any portion of the unallocated amount is associated in the parties' agreement with a child-related contingency such as a child's reaching the age of majority, getting married, or enlisting in the armed services, there is a rebuttable presumption that a portion of the amount is child support. The IRS may then disallow a previously claimed deduction for that portion and require the obligor to pay taxes, interest, and penalties on it. The obligee, in turn, should be entitled to a refund of the tax paid on that amount.

The Dependency Exemption

The general rule is that the custodial parent is entitled to claim the children as dependents for tax purposes, resulting in an adjustment to that party's gross income.[56] The amount of the exemption is subtracted from gross income before the tax is calculated. Because of the potential value of the exemption, parties to a divorce frequently negotiate other arrangements. The parties may agree, for example, to alternate years for claiming the exemption(s), or to divide the exemptions if there is more than one child. In any tax year in which the custodial parent agrees that the other parent may claim one or more of the minor children as dependents, the custodial parent must sign a written release, which is submitted with the tax return of the parent claiming the deduction (IRS Form 8332).

The Child Tax Credit

Since 1997, the parent claiming the exemption is also entitled to a child tax credit. This benefit provides the parent with a credit against his or her tax liability rather than an adjustment to gross income.[57]

THE ROLE OF THE PARALEGAL IN CHILD SUPPORT CASES

General Responsibilities

The most common tasks a paralegal performs with respect to child support cases are the following:

- Identifying and gathering information concerning any related jurisdictional questions
- Researching the law governing child support actions in the jurisdiction
- Gathering financial and other kinds of documentation necessary to complete appropriate forms and prepare necessary documents and pleadings
- Drafting complaints/petitions, supporting affidavits and proposed orders for child support, or responsive pleadings to complaints/petitions
- Completing child support guideline worksheets and preparing related memoranda if a deviation is at issue
- Assisting in preparation of the client's financial affidavit
- Recommending and drafting discovery materials such as interrogatories, deposition questions, etc.
- Drafting child support provisions for inclusion in separation agreements or parenting plans
- Assisting in preparation for temporary hearings or trials on the merits
- Tracking the progress of the case to be certain timelines are met
- Drafting Title IV-D correspondence and forms
- Making sure the client is kept informed of progress and upcoming deadlines, hearings, discovery matters, etc.

Specific Tasks Pertaining to Separation Agreements

Child support is frequently a hotly debated issue in a divorce case. Even though the guidelines provide some direction and are intended to be fair to both parents, the issue is not always simple enough to be distilled into a set formula. If the divorcing parties are able—either on their own or with the assistance of counsel and/or a mediator—to negotiate child support terms, they may develop a child support component for inclusion in their separation or parenting agreement. (See Paralegal Application 9.6 and the child support provision in the sample separation agreement in Chapter 12.)

PARALEGAL APPLICATION 9.6

DRAFTING POINTERS FOR A CHILD SUPPORT PROVISION IN A SEPARATION AGREEMENT OR PARENTING PLAN

A child support provision should address the following:

Amount of child support. The agreement may state that "child support will be in an amount consistent with the child support guidelines" or it may set an amount. If the parties want to deviate from the guidelines in their agreement, the child support amount must first be calculated according to the guidelines. Counsel must be prepared to provide evidence to show that application of the guidelines amount would be unjust, inappropriate, or not in the best interests of the child. If lower than the guidelines amount, it should be shown that the deviation was bargained for in exchange for some other benefit for the child under the agreement.

Timing of support payments. Will there be one or more payments per month and when are they due?

Method of payments. If neither the child nor the custodial parent is receiving public assistance, will payments be made directly to the recipient? In person? By mail? By direct deposit? If none of these, will payments be made through the state's IV-D agency?

Termination of child support. The agreement should specify the circumstances that will constitute emancipation and be sufficient to trigger termination of child support, such as a child moving away from home or getting a job and covering his or her own living expenses.

Escalation clause. Sometimes the parties build in an automatic-increase clause by tying increases in the child support amount to an official indicator, such as the Consumer Price Index. Some courts do not favor or permit this approach, because it is not sufficiently related to the parties' specific financial circumstances or to the best interests of the child. Another option is to provide that the parties will exchange basic financial information annually and recalculate the child support amount based on the guidelines. This approach takes into account fluctuations in the income of the respective parties but requires continuing contact and may be difficult to implement if the relationship is especially strained.

Income of the child. Will payments be influenced by resources that may become available to the child as a result of employment, trust income, inheritances, etc.?

Visitation/time with the noncustodial parent. Will any adjustment be made in child support payments during periods when the child is with the noncustodial parent? This is an especially important consideration if physical custody is shared or if a child will be spending extended periods (such as the entire summer) with the noncustodial parent.

Extended absences from the custodial parent's home. Will any adjustments be made in the child support amount if, for example, a child will be away at a private school for much of the year or at a summer camp for two months in the summer?

Costs of higher education. Although not permitted in some states, the general rule is that the parties may agree on coverage of the costs of higher education. The sample separation agreement provided in Chapter 12 contains a detailed provision addressing this issue. Consideration needs to be given to the resources of the parties, where the children will go to college, their special needs or abilities, the resources that may be available to them through scholarships and financial aid, and the costs associated with a basic program of study. For

continued

instance will "college expenses" cover tuition, room, board, books, computers, uniforms, fees, etc.? Will payments for educational expenses go to the custodial parent or directly to the educational institution?

Extracurricular activities. There are a host of activities available to children today, such as music, dance, art or drama lessons, athletic activities including sports clinics and camps, etc., but not without cost. The parties need to spell out how decisions will be made with respect to participation in these activities as well as how associated costs will be covered.

Medical insurance. Which party will pay for the coverage and how will uninsured medical expenses be handled? "Medical" should be broadly defined to include dental and eye care (glasses, etc.).

Income tax treatment of the child support payments. Assuming there will not be an unallocated support amount, the parties should indicate that child support payments will be nondeductible to the payor and nonincludable in the income of the recipient.

Dependency exemption. The parties should set forth their understanding regarding who will claim the exemption. If the noncustodial parent is going to claim the exemption, the agreement should provide that the custodial parent agrees to cooperate by executing IRS Form 8332 in a timely manner so that it can be filed with the obligor's return.

Security for child support payments. The parties may agree on some form of security for child support, such as a trust or insurance policy with the child as the named beneficiary.

Note: The general provisions of the parties' separation agreement usually include a **dispute resolution** provision, but if not, it is useful to indicate how the parties intend to resolve disputes pertaining to child support.

Prior to drafting a child support provision, information needs to be gathered regarding several preliminary questions:

- What are the financial resources of each of the parties? What is the presumptive figure when child support is calculated according to the guidelines? How long will support last? Is a deviation warranted?
- Do the children have any special needs? Will child support cover expenses like orthodontia, summer camp, clothing for when the child is with the noncustodial parent, dance lessons, private school or college expenses, uninsured therapy for psychological problems, etc.?
- Does either of the parents have any limitations with respect to being able to provide for the children?
- What was the family's standard of living before the parties' separation? Will each of the parties be able to maintain that standard following the divorce, or will the child's standard of living be negatively impacted by living with one parent or the other?
- What is the anticipated parenting plan? Will physical custody be shared or split? Will the children be with the noncustodial parent for significant portions of time? Do the parties live at a considerable distance from each other?
- What are the expectations and motivations of the parties? Is there any chance that a client feels threatened and is agreeing to a low amount of child support because of a fear that if he or she does not comply, custody will not be awarded in the manner desired?

CHAPTER **SUMMARY**

As much as the concept of family has evolved over the past four decades, one feature has remained constant: the belief that parents have a duty to provide for the children they bring into the world until such time as those children reach the age of majority or are otherwise emancipated. The economic impact of a parental failure to do so is sufficiently costly to society at large that the federal government has assumed a dramatic leadership role in an area historically left to regulation by the states. It has taken giant steps in the effort to hold parents accountable by mandating child support guidelines and the designation of Title IV-D agencies, facilitating interstate cooperation through UIFSA, creating massive interrelated databases, and strengthening enforcement strategies. Statistics suggest that progress is being made but that there is still much to be done to ensure that parents adequately provide for their children.

In order to establish and enforce an award, the court must have subject matter jurisdiction over custody matters and personal jurisdiction over the obligor. These requirements are not always easily satisfied. The child may have been moved from state to state. The identity of a child's father or the whereabouts of a noncustodial parent may be unknown. The parent may have gone to one or more other states to avoid paying support. The federal government has assisted in this area by mandating expedited procedures for establishing paternity, mandating the adoption of the Uniform Interstate Family Support Act, and creating databases such as parent locator services, child support registries, and new hire directories.

At the heart of a child support case is the establishment of a child support award through application of federally mandated guidelines designed to promote efficiency and fairness. However, no two states have exactly the same guidelines. Each state chooses an underlying model, its own approach to the definition of income, and the factors a court will consider in establishing and modifying child support awards. Deviations are commonly permitted to take into account special circumstances such as the existence of multiple families, shared parenting arrangements, or educational needs.

The courts permit modifications of child support in three major ways: The parties may stipulate (subject to the approval of the court) that a change in the support amount will be triggered by some mutually agreed-upon circumstance(s); a parent may show the court by a preponderance of the evidence that there has been a substantial change in the financial circumstances of one or both of the parties or in a child's level of need; or the order may be adjusted as a result of a periodic review mandated by state law or by federal law no less than every three years. Although the courts encourage agreements between the parents regarding details of the child support arrangement, parents are not permitted to permanently waive the right to request and receive support, as the right of support belongs to the child.

Whether dealing with an initial order or a modification, the order is essentially worthless if it cannot be enforced. Once again, the federal government has stepped into the arena, creating the federal crime of criminal nonsupport and mandating that the states put in place a variety of other enforcement strategies such as income withholding, tax intercepts, and denial of professional and driver's licenses, in addition to the more traditional methods of civil and criminal contempt.

Because of the complexity and fact-intensive nature of child support issues and the considerable variation in approaches from one state to another, the content of this chapter includes many illustrative examples. When working with a specific child support issue, it is important for the paralegal to be aware of, and to research as necessary, the governing law in the jurisdiction where the case arises. Other related responsibilities of paralegals are referenced throughout the chapter.

KEY **TERMS**

Actual service of process
Adjusted gross income
Age of majority
Arrearage
Child support
Civil contempt
Criminal contempt
Custodial parent
Directory of New Hires
Doctrine of necessaries
Emancipation

Extraordinary expense
Federal Parent Locator Service (FPLS)
Gross income
Home state
Imputed income
Income withholding
In loco parentis
IV-D agency
Joint physical custody
Lien

Long-arm jurisdiction
Net income
Noncustodial parent
Obligee
Obligor
Operation of Law
Personal jurisdiction
Presumptive child support guidelines
Public assistance programs
Public charge
Putative father

Qualified Medical Child Support
  Order (QMCSO)
Rebuttable presumption
Split custody

State Case Registry
State Parent Locator Service
  (SPLS)
Statute of limitations

Transitional Assistance to Needy
  Families Program (TANF)
Uniform Interstate Family Support
  Act (UIFSA)

REVIEW **QUESTIONS**

1. Define "child support" and explain the public policy behind requiring parents to pay child support.

2. Identify conditions under which the duty to pay child support commonly terminates. Under what kinds of circumstances might the duty of support continue?

3. Distinguish between child support and spousal support.

4. Describe the origin and purposes of Title IV-D agencies.

5. Describe the origin and primary purposes of the Uniform Interstate Family Support Act and identify three bases on which a court might obtain personal jurisdiction over a nonresident defendant under UIFSA.

6. Identify the primary purposes child support guidelines serve.

7. Define income. Identify three types of "income" that are usually not considered income in the child support context.

8. Define the term "imputed income." Give two examples of circumstances in which income might be imputed to a party.

9. Identify three circumstances in which a court might consider deviating from a child support amount that is presumptively appropriate under the guidelines.

10. Identify three ways in which a parent may obtain a modification of child support.

11. Define and give two examples of "extraordinary expenses." How do the courts generally deal with such expenses?

12. Describe how the majority of courts treat the existence of multiple families when making decisions about child support.

13. Identify some of the ways in which courts address parental responsibility for the cost of their children's higher education.

14. Identify at least five methods of enforcing child support obligations.

15. Identify and describe the major tax implications of child support.

FOCUS ON **THE JOB**

The Facts

William Pelletier and Betty Kelley began living together in the month of September nine years ago and got married three years ago on Valentine's Day. They have three daughters, Jennifer, Judie, and Jessica. Jennifer was born on June 26, 1999; Judie was born on June 24, 2001; and Jessica was born on July 4, 2003. William voluntarily acknowledged paternity at the time of each child's birth and has been a consistently adequate provider for Betty and the children. The three children are presently living with their mother in the home she inherited outright from her mother. The home is assessed at $375,000. Betty's father also has been very generous to her throughout her life. Over the past nine years, he has given her gifts of furniture, clothing, an automobile, several vacations with William and the children, and occasional cash gifts of up to $10,000 a year to help out with expenses, including special activities for the children. She hopes that he will continue to help her out when William is gone. She is aware that when her father dies, he plans to leave his entire fortune to a cancer research facility.

William has been working as an accountant for the entire period the parties have been together. His income has varied from a low of $24,000 in 2003 to a high of $97,000 in

2000. His income for last year was $62,000. Betty was a nurse before the children were born, and in her last year of full-time work, 1998, she earned about $42,000. She has occasionally worked night shifts since then but last year earned only $2,000. William and Betty agreed when Jennifer was born that Betty should stay home and care for the baby, and they have maintained that arrangement until the present time. Recently William decided to leave his job as an accountant working for wealthy people whose values and business ethics he found offensive. He has developed a fervent desire to become a missionary in Africa, where he will be receiving a token stipend of $5,000 a year. He will not have to pay for his food or housing, and his primary means of transportation will be a bicycle. He has not left the state yet but plans to leave before next Christmas. For now, he is living with a friend at 120 Bay Road in your town and state. Betty's address is around the corner at 250 Harrison Avenue, your town and state.

Betty is not certain what William has in the way of assets, as he has managed all the finances and paid all the bills during their relationship, saying it was "the least I can do, given that you take care of the kids all day." She knows at the very least that he has an investment portfolio valued at about $500,000, which generates interest and dividends of a minimum of $25,000 a year. They had a joint bank account with $17,000 in it, but William closed it out without notice to Betty. About $10,000 of that amount was a gift to Betty from her dad. Neither of the parties has any debts.

Betty says she doesn't care about herself but anticipates that she will continue to require the basic necessities for the children's benefit such as food, clothing, and housing costs (taxes, insurance, utilities, etc.), medical expenses, and education-related expenses. In addition, Jennifer shows considerable promise as a figure skater, and Betty hopes she can continue to keep up with her lessons and practice time, which costs about $250 a month. All three children are likely to require orthodontia work at some point down the road. Although he plans to stay in Africa for an indefinite period of time, William intends to retain his citizenship and residency in the state by using his sister's address. Although he realizes there are some negatives to this arrangement, such as having to pay taxes, he is a patriotic American citizen and wants to be able to complete absentee ballots and vote in each election.

William has filed a Complaint for Divorce in your local jurisdiction. He says that, since he will be in Africa and unable to visit the children, he doesn't think he should have to pay child support. Betty says the two of them brought the children into the world and each of them has a duty to support them.

THE ASSIGNMENT

Betty has contacted your supervisor, Attorney Tauson, and wants to seek child support. She feels she should at least get the amount she would receive under the state's child support guidelines but isn't sure she can do that given the circumstances. Attorney Tauson has asked you to draft the appropriate documents for your jurisdiction to accomplish this end, including a Motion for Temporary Child Support, a supporting affidavit for Betty's review and signature, and a proposed order. You should locate the statute in your jurisdiction that allows the court to order William to pay temporary child support. Locate models of all three documents, but be sure to tailor your documents to the facts of this particular case, applying the material covered in this chapter as appropriate.

FOCUS ON **ETHICS**

Assume that you are a paralegal in the law office of Christopher Pino, Esquire, a solo family law practitioner who represents William Pelletier in the above fact pattern. You are impressed with William and the personal sacrifice and commitment he intends to make as a missionary. While sitting with you in your lovely private office, William tells you that he expects Attorney Pino to represent him on a *pro bono* basis. In response, you tell him that Attorney Pino never accepts *pro bono* cases. William also tells you that he realizes that, because he has some substantial assets, he probably will be ordered to pay child support, but doesn't think he should have to under the circumstances. You sympathize with him and suggest that if he can get Betty to agree to let him satisfy

his child support obligation in the form of "alimony" rather than "child support," he will be able to deduct it from his income and at least receive that advantage. You also suggest that he should try to get the dependency exemptions for the three children. You later tell Attorney Pino about this conversation and he is very concerned. He gives you a copy of the ethical canons for paralegals promulgated by the National Federation of Paralegal Associations (NFPA) (contained in Appendix B) and directs you to prepare a memorandum to him in which you (a) describe the ethical issues the incident raises, (b) explain how you have violated the canons, and (c) recommend an appropriate course of action given your conduct.

FOCUS ON **CASE LAW**

The New Hampshire case *Donovan v. Donovan, Jr.*, 152 N.H. 55, 871 A.2d 30 (2005), is located on the companion website for this text in the material related to Chapter 9. Locate and read the case and then respond to the following questions.

1. What is the legal history of the case: What kind of a case is it? Where was it brought prior to reaching the New Hampshire Supreme Court and with what result?

2. What are the issues being appealed and by whom?

3. On what authority did the trial court impute income to the mother?

4. How was the figure for imputed income determined and by whom?

5. What did the New Hampshire Supreme Court decide with respect to this issue and why?

6. Do you agree with the trial court's or the Supreme Court's decision on this issue? Explain your reasoning.

7. Describe the respective positions of the parties regarding whether or not the basic support award covers the cost of extracurricular activities.

8. What did the New Hampshire Supreme Court decide with respect to this issue, and do you agree with that position?

9. What is the current state of the law in New Hampshire regarding the court's ability to order parents to pay for the college education of their children?

10. What was the parties' agreement with respect to coverage of college expenses in this case?

11. Did the New Hampshire Supreme Court modify the parties' agreement? Why?

12. What was the position of the dissent in the case regarding this issue?

13. Do you agree with the majority or the dissent on this issue? On what grounds?

14. What provision did the parties' agreement make with respect to an annual increase in child support?

15. Did the New Hampshire Supreme Court agree with this position? Why?

FOCUS ON **STATE LAW AND PROCEDURE**

Assume that the firm where you are employed represents William in the above Focus on the Job exercise. On his behalf, locate and complete the child support guidelines form/worksheet used in your state. For purposes of the guidelines calculation, assume that the parties have agreed on the following:

- The three children will live with their mother and the father will have no visitation for the foreseeable future, given his unique circumstances.

- Betty is caring for the children and there will be no childcare expenses.

- Betty's annual gross income is $2,000 and her adjusted gross income is $1,750.

- William's gross income is $59,000 and his adjusted gross income is $49,750.

- William has agreed to maintain health insurance coverage for Betty and the children at a cost of $320 per month. He will not carry insurance for himself, as he will be in a remote African village where medical services are minimal and available at no cost to missionaries.

- Betty's dad has agreed to make arrangements to cover Jennifer's ice skating program for as long as she remains involved.

FOCUS ON **TECHNOLOGY**

WEBSITES OF INTEREST

http://www.abanet.org

This is the website for the American Bar Association. The home page provides a search option where you can search for child support, child support guidelines, etc. You should be able to locate a number of excellent resources, including a chart that indicates the type of child support model used in each state (and the District of Columbia) and whether each state's guidelines address extraordinary medical expenses, child care expenses, college support, and shared parenting.

http://www.acf.hhs.gov

This is the site for the Administration for Children and Families (ACF), the federal agency that assists the states, territories, and tribal organizations through programs in support of children and families. It contains links to a number of topics related to family law including child support.

http://www.acf.dhhs.gov/programs/cse

This is the website for the federal Office of Child Support Enforcement (OCSE). There is a wealth of material available on this website including the publication "Essentials for Attorneys in Child Support Enforcement" (3rd edition 2002) and a listing of and links to child support (IV-D) agencies in each state.

http://www.alllaw.com

This site offers a feature called child support calculators for all states.

http://www.ancpr.org

This is the website of the Alliance for Noncustodial Parents' Rights.

http://www.census.gov

This site provides a number of statistical reports related to the topic of child support.

http://divorcenet.com

This site provides advice on family law-related issues including child support.

http://divorcesource.com

This site provides links to material on child support guidelines in all states.

http://www.findlaw.com

Click on legal professionals and then family law under practice areas and then search for child support guidelines. Relevant links are provided to information about child support in all states and the District of Columbia.

http://www.guidelines.com

This site provides links to child support guidelines in all states.

http://www.supportguidelines.com

This is a comprehensive resource on child support guidelines in the United States. It provides a number of useful resources and links.

ASSIGNMENTS

1. Locate three websites designed to help custodial parents receive the child support to which they are entitled and then summarize the information gathered from those sites.

2. If available, locate online a copy of the child support guidelines in use in your state. If you are a parent, complete the form using your own data.

3. Locate online information about your local IV-D agency and the services it provides. In particular, search for an Application to receive services.

chapter **ten**
SPOUSAL SUPPORT

J im, thirty, has been married to Julie, twenty-nine, for seven years. They have two children, ages four and six. When they married, Jim was going to college to become a teacher, but he dropped out, took care of the kids during the day, and waited on tables at night to support the family while Julie went to law school. Julie is now working at a large urban law firm and has decided that it is "time for her to move on." Jim says, "OK, but now you can support me." Julie says, "You have got to be kidding."

WHAT IS SPOUSAL SUPPORT?

Spousal support/alimony
an allowance for support and maintenance that one spouse may be ordered by a court to pay to the other spouse while they are living apart or divorced; also called alimony, maintenance, and separate support depending on the jurisdiction

Spousal support is an allowance for support and maintenance that one spouse may be ordered by a court to pay to the other spouse while they are living apart or divorced. What it is called depends on the jurisdiction and the circumstances of the case. If the parties are divorced, it is usually called *alimony,* maintenance, or spousal support. If they are legally separated, it is customarily called separate support or separate maintenance. Each state has developed its own approach to when spousal support will be awarded, what its purpose is, who will receive it, how much will be received, and for how long. This chapter provides an overview of the topic of spousal support along with several examples of jurisdictional variations. The terms *alimony* and *spousal support* will be used interchangeably.

Spousal support is distinct from child support. Parents have a legal duty to support their children. It is a requirement that parents cannot waive or bargain away. Spousal support, on the other hand, is a duty that flows from one spouse to the other. However, marriage does not create an "entitlement" to spousal support. It generally can be waived and bargained away, and it may not be awarded absent a demonstrated need on the part of one spouse and the ability to pay on the part of the other spouse.

Canon law
church law; the body of law developed within a particular religious tradition

HOW HAS SPOUSAL SUPPORT EVOLVED IN SOCIETY AND THE LAW?

An Historical Perspective: Before No-Fault Divorce

Divorce *a mensa et thoro*
a divorce from bed and board only; a legal separation

Legal separation
a judicial decree that allows the parties to live separate and apart without dissolving their legal relationship as husband and wife

Divorce *a vinculo matrimonii*
literally, a divorce from the chains or bonds of matrimony; an absolute divorce that frees the parties to remarry

Annulment
the legal procedure for declaring that a marriage is null and void because of an impediment existing at its inception

Absolute divorce
a total divorce of husband and wife that dissolves the marital bond

Married Women's Property Acts
state statutes that extended to women various property rights that were denied to them under common law, including ownership and control of property

The origins of alimony in the United States can be traced to the English legal system. In England, ecclesiastical or church courts initially had exclusive jurisdiction over family-related legal matters. The church courts applied **canon law,** the church's body of law. Ecclesiastical courts granted two kinds of "divorces": ***divorce* a mensa et thoro,** a divorce from bed and board that allowed the parties to live separate and apart but not remarry (as in a present-day **legal separation**), and ***divorce* a vinculo matrimonii,** essentially an **annulment** based on a canonical disability existing before the marriage (e.g., bigamy, etc.). Upon a divorce *a mensa et thoro*, an ecclesiastical court could require a husband to pay support to his wife (provided she was an innocent spouse) based on the belief that he had a lifelong duty to provide for her, even if they ceased living together.

The Divorce Act of 1857[1] (the Matrimonial Causes Act) relieved the ecclesiastical courts of their divorce jurisdiction and established **absolute divorce** by judicial decree under common law, allowing the courts to terminate valid marriages. The Act also granted judges jurisdiction to order a husband to provide for an innocent wife after the marriage ended. The amount he was required to provide was based on her wealth, his means, and their respective conduct during the marriage. The assumption was that innocent women who were abandoned by or separated from their husbands should be awarded alimony because they lacked the ability to provide for themselves. That assumption was reasonable, given that, upon marriage, women gave up their rights to enter into contracts, own property in their own names, and possess and control their earnings.

The English common law system adopted by the states brought with it this dual emphasis on fault and the economic dependence of wives on their husbands. A plaintiff seeking a divorce was required to allege some form of legally recognized fault, such as adultery, desertion, or mental or physical cruelty. The courts also continued to retain the remnants of a husband's duty of support into the early no-fault era, although **Married Women's Property Acts,** eventually passed in all fifty states, eliminated many of the economic legal disabilities that made it impossible for women to earn money or own property in their own names while married. The majority of states passed such acts in the 1850s.[2] However, in the United States, prior to the 1970s, men still tended to hold title to the majority of assets obtained during the marriage. Upon divorce, men kept their assets, and "innocent" wives often received substantial long-term alimony awards with which to support themselves. Divorce and alimony continued to be premised on the innocence of one party and the fault of another.

The Contemporary Perspective: No-Fault Divorce

Beginning in the 1970s, every state eventually made available at least one ***"no-fault" ground*** for divorce, recognizing that marriages often terminate because of "incompatibility" or "irreconcilable differences" between the parties rather than because of the fault of one or both of them. Although approximately half the states also retained fault grounds for divorce, the judicial and legislative fallout of the no-fault movement largely took fault out of the divorce equation.

No-fault ground
a ground for divorce based on an irremediable breakdown of the marital relationship rather than on the fault of one or both of the parties

The relationship between alimony and fault has evolved more slowly. After the onset of no-fault divorce and the revision of property division laws allowing women to be awarded a "fair" or equal share of the marital assets, alimony awards decreased in number and generally became limited in duration. Alimony became viewed primarily as a means of enabling a dependent spouse, usually the wife, to develop skills, enter or reenter the workforce, and become self-sufficient. The ultimate goal was, in a relatively short time, to cut permanently the economic cord between the husband and wife.

Today, a reasonable estimate of the frequency of alimony awards granted upon divorce is ten to fifteen percent, and the vast majority of these awards are to women. The general rule is that, even if marital fault is sometimes factored into alimony determinations, the purpose of alimony is no longer to punish an obligor for some alleged misconduct or to reward an "innocent" spouse. However, some states, such as Louisiana, still bar alimony awards to parties whose adulterous conduct caused the breakdown of the marriage. The *Mani* case in New Jersey reflects the challenge faced by a court in a heavily "no-fault" state struggling with the question of what role, if any, fault should play in alimony determinations. (See Case 10.1.)

CASE **10.1** *Mani v. Mani,* 183 N.J. 70, 869 A.2d 904 (2005)

DISCUSSION OF THE CASE

Unusual for several reasons, this case involved an alimony award to a husband. After a twenty-seven-year-marriage, the wife was ordered to pay her spouse $610 per week in spousal support. She had well over $2 million in assets, and her spouse had assets totaling a few hundred thousand dollars and a minimum earning capacity of about $25,000 per year. Both parties appealed. The husband sought more alimony, claiming he would otherwise be unable to meet his monthly expenses, and the wife argued he should receive no alimony whatsoever based on his "indolence" in meeting his own needs and his lack of noneconomic contribution to the marriage. The appeals court refused to eliminate the alimony award but also refused to raise it, based on the husband's alleged adulterous and abusive conduct during the marriage (which was not taken into account by the trial court). Both parties appealed to the New Jersey Supreme Court.

The New Jersey Supreme Court's opinion reflects a thoughtful review of the history of alimony in general and specifically in New Jersey. It reaffirmed that
continued

alimony is an economic right arising out of marriage that is designed to provide a dependent spouse with a standard of living generally commensurate with the quality of economic life that existed during the marriage. While noting that New Jersey can be characterized as a "no-fault" state in most respects, the court then proceeded to address the issue of what consideration, if any, should be given to marital misconduct in alimony determinations. The court ruled that marital fault is irrelevant except in two narrow instances:

1. when the fault affects the couple's economic life, as when one spouse gambles away the parties' assets

2. when the fault "so violates societal norms that continuing the economic bonds between the parties would confound notions of simple justice." Hiring someone to murder a spouse would constitute such a fault.

A dependent husband's extramarital affair standing alone was not viewed by the New Jersey Supreme Court as a sufficiently shocking violation of social norms as to deny him alimony in the context of a divorce.

SIDEBAR

This case is available in its entirety on the companion website. Do you agree with the court's decision? To what extent, if at all, do you believe marital fault should factor into the alimony equation?

In a no-fault environment, marriage is viewed largely as an economic partnership. The primary focus is on alimony as an economic event flowing from that partnership. Alimony is also now a gender-neutral concept. Most states gender-neutralized their alimony statutes on their own initiative in the 1970s. The issue was settled for the remainder of the states by the U.S. Supreme Court's 1979 decision in *Orr v. Orr.* In *Orr,* the Court declared an Alabama statute that imposed alimony obligations only on husbands unconstitutional as a violation of the Fourteenth Amendment's Equal Protection Clause.[3] Because the duty of support is reciprocal between husband and wife, either the husband or the wife may be ordered to pay alimony.

WHAT ARE THE DIFFERENCES BETWEEN ALIMONY AND PROPERTY DIVISION?

Relationship Between Alimony and Property Division

Decisions about alimony are generally not made until after the court has determined a suitable division of marital property. If each party is allocated sufficient assets to maintain the standard of living that characterized the marriage, alimony may not be an issue. Many argue there is merit to avoiding alimony and prolongation of contact between parties who are trying to move forward with their individual lives. Others argue that the reality is that many marriages continue to reflect a gendered division of labor, with a wife having devoted a disproportionate amount of time and effort to domestic responsibilities. When the marriage terminates, the woman is often left with a diminished future earning capacity in comparison with her spouse. As a result, she may be entitled to alimony or a greater share of the marital assets as a vehicle for addressing economic inequalities. Practically speaking, in many divorces the parties have more liabilities than assets, and there is rarely sufficient income for an alimony award to be considered at all.

Although an order for alimony cannot realistically be viewed apart from a division of marital assets, the considerations involved in each decision are different. The distinctions between alimony and property division are briefly summarized in Exhibit 10.1.

EXHIBIT 10.1 Alimony and Property Division—A Comparison

ALIMONY	PROPERTY DIVISON
Alimony originated in the common law duty of a husband to support his wife, a duty now deemed gender neutral.	Property division evolved with no-fault divorce and its emphasis on marriage as a partnership.
At the time of divorce, alimony focuses on what each party will need going forward into the future.	At the time of divorce, property division looks back to identify assets accumulated by the parties during the marriage that should be divided upon divorce.
Alimony awards are based on need and ability to pay, along with other factors considered relevant by statute and/or the court.	Division of property is based on the concept that both parties contribute to the marital enterprise and thus each party is entitled to a share of the partnership upon divorce according to community property or equitable distribution principles.
The court must have personal jurisdiction over the defendant, who must be provided with notice in order for an alimony order to be issued and be enforceable.	The court must have jurisdiction over the parties and the property to be divided.
Payment of alimony is usually in the form of cash payments payable on a periodic basis (e.g., monthly).	Property division usually involves transfers of property, such as an interest in a marital residence or a bank account.
Although lump-sum alimony is occasionally awarded, alimony is usually payable over a period of time. Payments are vested as they fall due.	A property division order is effective as of the date of divorce, at which time the rights to property are vested and enforceable against the other party's estate as a debt.
Alimony is usually modifiable upon a material change of circumstances that significantly affects the payee's need or the payor's ability to pay, although some jurisdictions consider alimony awards final absent a specific reservation of jurisdiction.	Absent fraud, etc., property division is rarely modifiable.
Alimony is tax deductible to the payor and income to the payee.	Payments or transfers made pursuant to a property division are not taxable events.
Alimony is generally not dischargeable in bankruptcy.	With limited exceptions, property division orders are generally dischargeable in bankruptcy.

continued

Death usually terminates alimony obligations (with the exception of arrearages) absent a judgment or agreement to the contrary.

Property division is not affected by the death of a party after the court has rendered a judgment. A property division is enforceable against the estate of a decedent.

Alimony obligations usually terminate on the recipient's remarriage, absent a statute, court order, or agreement to the contrary.

Property division is not affected by the remarriage of either party.

Alimony is no longer primarily punitive in nature, although in some states, the courts consider misconduct during the marriage, particularly economic misconduct, as a factor in calculating an alimony award.

In a divorce granted on fault grounds (still available in many states), a court may award a larger portion of the marital assets to the aggrieved party. Even in states where fault grounds are unavailable, serious misconduct during the marriage may influence the division of property in both community property and equitable division jurisdictions.

HOW DOES A PARTY OBTAIN AN ALIMONY AWARD?

Procedure

Customarily, the procedure for obtaining alimony/spousal support is either for the parties to agree to an alimony provision in a separation agreement or for one or both of the parties to petition the court for a suitable award given the facts of the case. In rare instances, however, a court will make an alimony award on its own initiative.

Initial Steps Toward an Alimony Award

Initial efforts of the family law team on behalf of a client in an alimony case usually focus on answering the following seven questions:

1. What is the governing law in the jurisdiction with respect to alimony awards?
2. Have the parties executed a premarital agreement and, if so, what does it provide with regard to alimony?
3. What are the needs of the parties?
4. Are there sufficient marital assets for there to be an alimony award?
5. What factors does the court consider in making an alimony decision?
6. Is one or both of the parties likely to file bankruptcy in the near future?
7. After the above questions are addressed, what should be the next step?

Paralegal Practice Tip
There is considerable variation across the states in terms of the types of alimony awards permitted in a given jurisdiction and favored by particular judges. Several of the cases and statutes referenced in this chapter reflect this variation. An understanding of the legal environment in which the client's case is filed will help guide interviewing, discovery, and drafting efforts.

What Is the Governing Law?   It is important to identify the current statutes and case law that govern alimony in the jurisdiction. The paralegal's research needs to take into account the tremendous variation among states and even among counties and individual judges within states. The kinds of questions needing to be answered include the following:

- Are waivers of alimony permitted?
- If alimony is allowed, what kinds of alimony awards are made? (See Exhibit 10.2.)
- Are awards of limited duration?
- Are there guidelines in place that need to be considered with respect to setting the amount of alimony to be paid?
- Is marital fault a bar to receiving alimony or a factor to be considered in the amount of the award?
- What other factors does the court consider important in the alimony context?

Have the Parties Executed a Premarital Agreement? If the parties have executed a ***premarital agreement,*** a copy needs to be obtained for review by the attorney. If the agreement contains a ***waiver*** of alimony, research may need to be done on the enforceability of such waivers in the jurisdiction. A majority of the states that have considered premarital agreements waiving spousal support have upheld them.[4] The Uniform Premarital Agreement Act, adopted in some form or another in just over half of the states, allows provisions in premarital agreements that establish or eliminate spousal support unless the agreement promotes divorce, was improperly executed, or enforcement would bring about an unconscionable result, such as causing a spouse to become a ***public charge.*** However, South Dakota, Iowa, and New Mexico are among the limited number of states that exclude alimony waivers from premarital agreements by statute or case law. (See Case 10.2.)

Premarital agreement
an agreement made by two persons about to be married defining for themselves their respective rights, duties, and responsibilities in the event their marriage terminates by death, annulment, separation, or divorce

Waiver
the giving up of a right or privilege

Public charge
a person dependent on public assistance programs for necessaries

CASE **10.2** *Sanford v. Sanford,* 2005 SD 34, 694 N.W.2d 283 (2005)

DISCUSSION OF THE CASE

The premarital agreement executed by the parties in this case included a single unallocated payment structure for alimony, support, and property division. The husband claimed that this provision not only protected his $55 million net worth, but also constituted a waiver of alimony by his wife.

Although the state of South Dakota had adopted the Uniform Premarital Agreement Act, it did not include its provisions allowing parties to contract regarding elimination or modification of spousal support. The legislature chose instead to exclude alimony waivers from prenuptial agreements by statute (SDCL 25–2–18), thereby protecting the rights of both men and women asked to sign away these rights.

The court noted that the agreement in question did not include specific reference to alimony and support, but that even if it did, a waiver would be of no effect. The Court held that provisions in a premarital agreement purporting to waive spousal support are void and unenforceable, as they are contrary to public policy and may be severed from valid portions of the agreement without invalidating the agreement in its entirety.

SIDEBAR

The opinion in this case is available on the companion website.

Separation agreement
an agreement made between spouses in anticipation of divorce or a legal separation concerning the terms of the divorce or separation and any continuing obligations of the parties to each other

Quid pro quo
an action or thing exchanged for another action or thing of relatively equal value

Forensic accountant
an accountant who applies accounting principles and analysis to gather and present evidence in a lawsuit

If the parties did waive their alimony rights in a premarital agreement but now wish to agree to an award, there is case law (in New York, for example) to the effect that they may be able to do so.[5] The general rule appears to be that "No public policy is violated by permitting enforcement of a waiver of spousal support executed by intelligent, well-educated persons, each of whom appears to be self-sufficient in property and earning ability, and both of whom had the advice of counsel regarding their rights and obligations as marital partners at the time they executed the agreement."[6]

Even if there is no premarital agreement, the parties may choose to waive their respective rights to alimony in their *separation agreement.* Notwithstanding the parties' freedom to contract to this effect, many judges will not permit such a waiver to survive the decree in a long-term marriage unless there has been a sufficient *quid pro quo.* For example, a spouse might be awarded a greater share of the marital assets in lieu of alimony.

What Are the Needs of the Parties?   Whether or not alimony will be sought depends in large part on the respective needs of the parties and their relative abilities to pay. Before the client makes the decision to pursue an alimony claim, a thorough review of the financial assets and liabilities of the parties needs to take place. In marriages involving substantial estates, this will generally require considerable discovery, evaluations of various kinds of assets by experts and appraisers, and possibly the use of a *forensic accountant* to assess and analyze the information obtained. It will also require that the client prepare a complete and realistic budget of his or her needs.

Are There Sufficient Marital Assets for an Alimony Award to Be Made?   The courts will usually divide the marital property first and then determine whether there is sufficient need and income to support an alimony award. In marriages with few assets, particularly those of short duration, alimony awards are rarely made. There simply are not enough resources "to go around" or the resources are limited in terms of how they can reasonably be divided. For example, if there is a marital home, its sale or division often must be postponed for the benefit of minor children.

What Factors Does the Court Consider in Making an Alimony Decision?   If it appears that alimony is needed and should be sought, information needs to be gathered regarding all of the factors potentially considered by the court in the jurisdiction to assess the strength of the client's bargaining position and case. Although need and ability to pay are threshold factors, courts usually consider a number of additional factors as well, such as duration of the marriage, the ages and health of the parties, and the standard of living maintained during the marriage. Based on the facts, counsel will consult with the client about the form or forms of alimony that may be appropriate, along with a desired amount and duration.

What if One or Both of the Parties Is Likely to File for Bankruptcy in the Near Future?   If bankruptcy looms in the future of the either or both of the parties, counsel will discuss with the client its potential impact on obligations flowing from a divorce. Particularly relevant is the fact that property division settlements in a divorce may well be discharged in bankruptcy, whereas spousal and child support generally will not. A client needing alimony may choose to settle for less in the way of an unprotected property award and seek a higher and potentially more secure award of alimony.

After the Above Questions Are Addressed, What Should Be the Next Step?   At this point, negotiations with the opposing party/counsel will begin or continue if already begun. If negotiations do not lead to an agreement, the parties may attempt to mediate their dispute. If that fails, a proposed alimony provision will be drafted by each party for the court's consideration. Paralegal Application 10.2, which appears later in this chapter, provides basic drafting suggestions for alimony provisions.

WHAT ARE THE VARIOUS TYPES OF ALIMONY AWARDS?

Although alimony is legally recognized to some degree in every jurisdiction, there is no consensus regarding its purpose, amount, or duration. Some states, such as Texas, are reluctant to make any awards at all and allow only short-term, limited-purpose maintenance except in certain circumstances. Others, like South Carolina, are flexible and creative in fashioning relief for parties deemed eligible to receive alimony. Unlike most states, South Carolina actually defines a number of alimony options by statute. Copies of the Texas Family Code provision governing duration of alimony and the South Carolina Code Section describing various types of alimony available in that state are accessible on the companion website in the material related to Chapter 10.

In general, spousal support awards are designed to meet a variety of needs. They vary primarily in terms of duration and nature of payment. A brief summary of the most common types is provided in Exhibit 10.2.

EXHIBIT 10.2 Types of Alimony/Spousal Support[7]

Temporary Alimony/Alimony *Pendente Lite*	Interim alimony ordered by the court pending an action for divorce or separation in which one party has made a claim for permanent alimony
Permanent/Traditional Alimony	Alimony usually payable in weekly or monthly installments, either indefinitely or until a time or circumstance specified in a court order
Term Alimony	Alimony payable in weekly or monthly installments for a specified period of time
Lump-Sum Alimony/Alimony in Gross	Alimony in the form of a single and definite sum not subject to modification
Rehabilitative Alimony (sometimes called limited or transitional alimony)	Alimony found necessary to assist a divorced person in acquiring the education or training required to find employment outside the home or to reenter the labor force
Restitution/Reimbursement Alimony	Alimony designed to repay a spouse who during the marriage made financial contributions that directly enhanced the earning capacity of the other spouse
Separate Maintenance	Money paid by one married person to the other for support if they are no longer living together as husband and wife

---

Temporary Alimony/Alimony *Pendente Lite*

Temporary alimony/alimony *pendente lite*

support awarded to a dependent spouse in order to maintain the status quo as to financial circumstances while a marital action is pending

Temporary alimony or *alimony* **pendente lite** is support awarded to a dependent spouse in order to maintain the status quo as to financial circumstances while a marital action is pending. The action could be one seeking an annulment, legal separation, or divorce. Temporary alimony generally continues until the matter is settled on the merits (an annulment is granted or a legal separation or divorce is awarded). In a limited number of jurisdictions, the amount of a temporary alimony award is based on guidelines similar to the guidelines used to calculate child support awards according to a basic formula. Motions for temporary alimony, like all motions for temporary orders, need to be taken seriously, as they often set the stage for permanent orders.

Motions for temporary alimony are not always granted. It is generally established that if the petitioning spouse has sufficient means to support himself or herself according to the parties' accustomed lifestyle and to prosecute or defend the pending action, that party's motion for temporary alimony may not be granted. There are also some specific circumstances that may bar alimony *pendente lite*, such as a voluntary departure from the household and abandonment of the other spouse, unless it can be shown that the other spouse's conduct justified the departure (abuse, threats, etc.). A defendant spouse may also raise as a defense a provision in a premarital agreement in which the parties both waived their respective rights to any form of alimony upon the filing of an action for divorce or legal separation. The agreement may bar temporary alimony unless the petitioning party has no other source or reasonable means of support.

The timing and procedure governing a filing for temporary support is established by statute. The request for alimony usually may be made in the initial complaint for divorce or by separate motion. If there is an urgent need, the request will be made early in the proceedings. However, if there are substantial assets, counsel may want to wait at least until initial discovery is conducted. Notice will be given to the other party, and a hearing will customarily be held. The burden is on the requesting party to establish that the parties are married; that a petition has been filed for divorce, legal separation, or annulment; and that facts exist justifying an award. The appropriate facts should be laid out in a supporting affidavit addressing the factors considered by the court in making alimony determinations. The respondent has the right to submit an affidavit in opposition to the motion for temporary alimony, and sometimes courts will make temporary alimony decisions based on the parties' affidavits without holding a hearing. A sample Motion for Temporary Orders can be accessed on the companion website in the material related to Chapter 6.

The general rule is that temporary alimony will not continue beyond the voluntary dismissal or abandonment of the underlying action or entry of the judgment and exhaustion of all appeals. In some jurisdictions, resumption of sexual relations between the parties will constitute a reconciliation warranting termination of the divorce action and the order.

Permanent alimony

alimony usually payable in weekly or monthly installments either indefinitely or until a time or circumstance specified in a court order

Permanent Alimony

Surviving agreement

an agreement of the parties incorporated into a court's divorce decree that also retains its existence as an independent contract enforceable under basic principles of contract law

Permanent alimony is somewhat of a misnomer, given that in most jurisdictions, a court-ordered award is not truly permanent, but rather customarily remains modifiable given a change in circumstances, unless the order incorporates a *surviving agreement* of the parties that specifically addresses duration. For example, the parties may agree that alimony payments will continue until either party dies or the recipient spouse remarries, cohabitates with another, or attains a certain age. Absent an agreement, permanent alimony usually terminates upon remarriage of the recipient or death of either party.

The primary purpose of permanent alimony is to provide financial assistance to the spouse in an economically weaker position. No duty is imposed on the dependent party to obtain employment and achieve economic self-sufficiency. When a permanent alimony award is granted, it is most likely to occur in a case involving a long-term marriage and a spouse who was a homemaker and primary caretaker of the parties' children for the bulk if not all of the marriage. The underlying premise is that, absent some extenuating circumstance, it would be unfair for one party's standard of living to remain high following divorce, while the other party's quality of life markedly declines as a result of mutual choices made during the marriage.

Although substantial permanent alimony awards were once common when men held title to the majority of the marital assets, they are relatively rare today. They are viewed as inconsistent with current assumptions about female economic independence. In addition, obligors, understandably, do not welcome permanent awards by which they will remain economically tied to a former spouse. They are also not favored by many courts. If there are sufficient marital assets subject to property division to accord both parties a standard of living comparable to that enjoyed during the marriage, courts usually prefer to facilitate a clean break and not make an award of permanent alimony.

Term Alimony

Term alimony continues for a set period of time or until a condition specified in a court order or agreement. It is customarily payable in weekly or monthly installments and usually remains modifiable upon a change in circumstances. In some states, the duration of term alimony will be limited by statute to no more than the length or some percentage of the length of the marriage.

> **Term alimony**
> alimony that continues for a set period of time or until a condition specified in a court order or agreement

Lump-Sum Alimony/Alimony in Gross

Lump-sum alimony, sometimes called ***alimony in gross,*** is alimony ordered payable in the form of a definite sum, usually in a single or limited number of installments. It has distinct advantages to each party. It may appear to be more in the nature of a component of a comprehensive property division settlement. However, because it is characterized as alimony, if structured properly, it usually will be deductible by the payor for income tax purposes. From the recipient's perspective, although it will be taxable as income, it ***vests*** in the recipient when awarded and thus usually may be recovered from the obligor's estate if necessary. It is also generally not subject to modification, elimination upon remarriage or cohabitation, or to discharge should the obligor declare bankruptcy. It also has the added advantage of "cutting the cord" and not dragging out the financial connection between the parties.

The *Thornley* case provides an example of how a court exercises its discretion, working with applicable statutory guidelines and case law to fashion an alimony award appropriate to the specific facts of a case—in this instance, a lump-sum award. This case is somewhat unusual, given that the court made the alimony award on its own initiative and not on the basis of a request of one of the parties. (See Case 10.3.)

> **Lump-sum alimony/alimony in gross**
> alimony ordered payable in the form of a definite sum, usually in a single or limited number of installments; usually not subject to modification

> **Vest**
> to give a person an immediate, fixed right of ownership and present or future enjoyment

CASE **10.3** *In re Marriage of Thornley,* 361 Ill. App.3d 1067, 838 N.E. 2d 981 (2005)

FROM THE OPINION

Stephanie and Jason Thornley married on June 30, 2001. They had no children as a result of the marriage. The couple separated in August 2003, and Stephanie filed a petition for dissolution of marriage on November 24, 2003. In the petition, she requested an order awarding her an equitable share of the marital property and "denying maintenance to the petitioner and respondent."...

Stephanie testified that during the marriage she was employed full time. She earned approximately $900 every two weeks. Jason was not employed, but attended Palmer College of Chiropractic. He periodically received money for living expenses. Stephanie believed that the amount averaged $2,500 on each occasion, but Jason testified that he received approximately $5,000 for living expenses per trimester, which he had to repay as part of his student loans. The couple had been married for seven trimesters before they separated, so Jason estimated that he had received about $35,000 for living expenses while they were together. However, Jason later stated that Palmer College charged him $120,000 for his 10 trimesters at the school, and he received $140,000 in student loans including the money for living expenses.

The couple deposited Stephanie's paycheck and Jason's living expenses funds into a joint checking account. Jason acknowledged that the majority of the deposits into the account were from Stephanie's employment. They paid some of Jason's school expenses from the account, including $350 for Jason's board exam and $2,190 and $5,835 payments to Palmer College....

Stephanie testified that during their marriage, she and Jason paid two loans that Jason had obtained prior to their marriage, estimating a $2,000 payment to Illinois State University and a $1,000 payment to Monmouth College....

Jason stated that he had finished his education and was employed as a teacher by Metropolitan Community College.... because he was waiting for the results of his board exam and license. His gross income was $2,143.76 per month.

...Though Stephanie and Jason's marriage was relatively short, the trial court found that other factors favored an unequal distribution to Stephanie. It noted that, during the marriage, Jason relied on Stephanie for support while he attended school, stating that "there was very little, if any, money from the loan proceeds over and above the cost of tuition and other school expenses. In addition, Ms. Thornley directly paid some of the chiropractic college expenses Mr. Thornley incurred." The court also found that when Jason receives his license, "he anticipates that his income will increase to $10,000 to $50,000 per month."...

Jason... argues that the trial court improperly awarded Stephanie maintenance. He contends that the court exceeded its authority because Stephanie's petition specifically requested an order "denying maintenance to the petitioner and the respondent." Stephanie claims that Jason forfeited this issue by not objecting at the hearing or filing a motion to reconsider.

In the present case, however, no formal waiver of maintenance occurred, only a suggestion to the trial court in the pleadings that it was best to resolve the matter by a distribution of property rather than an award of maintenance. The suggestion did not deprive the court of its discretion to award maintenance....

Section 504 of the Dissolution Act sets out a number of factors a trial court may consider in determining whether a maintenance award is appropriate. 750 ILCS 5/504(a) (West 2004). The section lists as relevant the income and property of each party, including marital property apportioned to the party seeking maintenance, the present and future earning capacity of each party, the duration of the

continued

marriage, and the contributions and services by the party seeking maintenance to the education, training, career or career potential, or license of the other spouse. 750 ILCS 5/504(a)(1), (a)(3), (a)(7), (a)(10) (West 2004). Though professional licenses and scholastic degrees do not constitute a property interest subject to division as a marital asset, "the contributing spouse must receive some form of compensation for the financial effort and support provided to the student spouse in the expectation that the marital unit will prosper in the future." *In re Marriage of Rubenstein*, 145 Ill. App. 3d 31, 38–39, 495 N.E.2d 659, 664, 99 Ill. Dec. 212 (1986). "There are three principal methods of affording compensation: (1) distribution of marital assets; (2) some form of maintenance or alimony; or (3) an equitable monetary award based on some equitable principle." *Rubenstein*, 145 Ill. App. 3d at 39, 495 N.E.2d at 664 (1986). An award of maintenance in gross may be proper where one spouse has supported the other as he obtained his license or degree. . . .

At the hearing, the trial court heard evidence regarding Jason's present and future earning capacity, the duration of the marriage, and the contributions Stephanie made toward Jason's education during that time. In its memorandum of opinion, the court wrote:

> The entire focus of this marriage was getting Mr. Thornley through chiropractic school. While much of the expense was borrowed, and this court has directed Mr. Thornley to repay those student loans, and while the court has disproportionately distributed the majority of the assets to Ms. Thornley, the allocation of property falls short of that which is needed to equitably divide the marital estate and recognize Mr. Thornley's career potential when he becomes Dr. Thornley.

Accordingly, the court awarded Stephanie $18,000 as maintenance in gross. Because the court properly considered relevant factors, . . . the court did not abuse its discretion.

SIDEBAR

The entire opinion in this case is provided on the companion website in the material related to Chapter 10. Do you agree with the court's decision? What are the arguments for and against such awards?

Rehabilitative Alimony

Rehabilitative alimony is usually awarded in situations in which one spouse has delayed or given up education or a career in order to remain at home and care for the children and the household. It is customarily awarded for a period sufficient in length to allow the dependent spouse to obtain education and training that will enable him or her to acquire greater earning power, reenter the workforce, and become self-sufficient with the exercise of reasonable effort. It is usually awarded for a fixed period and is generally not modifiable. Ideally, the recipient spouse should propose a plan for rehabilitation along with a timeline and an estimate of related costs.

In some states, a limit on the length of rehabilitative alimony is established by statute. More often, the court will set a time period within which the recipient is expected to make a realistic good-faith effort to complete a rehabilitative program and attain self-sufficiency. If either of the parties wants the award to be reviewable, the parties' agreement or the court order should include language to that effect. Circumstances in which a review might be

Rehabilitative alimony alimony designed to assist a divorced person in acquiring the education or training required to find employment outside the home or to reenter the labor force

warranted are, for example, when an educational program is interrupted due to a chronic illness or when the recipient fails to pursue an agreed-upon "rehabilitation" plan.

Consistent with no-fault reform, rehabilitative alimony represents a departure from the historical view of alimony as being fault based and unlimited in duration. The preferred approach in many jurisdictions, it accomplishes the dual purposes of (1) affording an economically dependent spouse an opportunity to build his or her job skills, obtain employment, and become economically self-sufficient and (2) setting a predictable end to the ongoing obligations of the parties to each other so that both of them can move forward with their lives. Despite these advantages, some courts are reluctant to make rehabilitative alimony awards, particularly in cases of long-term marriages in which one party has a dramatically reduced earning capacity due to the allocation of responsibilities during the marriage. It may also be denied if the planned rehabilitation is unrealistic or if the petitioner is already employed or employable and does not plan to change jobs.

In the *Anliker* case, the Iowa Supreme Court considered the state's alimony provision and weighed the relative merits of permanent "traditional" alimony awarded by the trial court against the appeals court position that rehabilitative alimony was more appropriate. (See Case 10.4.) The Iowa Supreme Court eventually deemed an award of permanent alimony most appropriate, given the facts of the case. This case reflects the extent to which judges may vary in approaching alimony decisions. It also demonstrates the importance of providing ample documentation in support of a client's position to inform the court's decision making.

CASE **10.4** *In Re Marriage of Anliker,* 694 N.W.2d 535 (Iowa 2005)

FROM THE OPINION

The factors in section 598.21(3) pertinent to this case include (1) the length of the marriage; (2) the age and physical and emotional health of the parties; (3) the property distribution; (4) the educational level of each party at the time of the marriage and at the time the action is commenced; (5) the earning capacity of the party seeking alimony, including educational background, training, employment skills, work experience, length of absence from the job market; (6) the feasibility of the party seeking alimony becoming self-supporting at a standard of living reasonably comparable to that enjoyed during the marriage, and the length of time necessary to achieve this goal; and (7) other factors the court may determine to be relevant in an individual case. Iowa Code § 598.21(3)(a)-(f), (j) (Supp. 2001)....

The district court considered these factors in deciding to award Donna traditional alimony as an appropriate form of spousal support. In applying these factors, we think the district court had it exactly right when it made the following findings:

> In this case, neither party is receiving a substantial amount of property. The property being divided relates to minimal household goods and furnishings as well as Donna's basic transportation. The debts being assigned to Scott are no more onerous to him than the debts being assigned to Donna pursuant to this decree....
>
> While Donna is only 51 years of age, the record supports a finding that her health has deteriorated since 1996 and is not likely to improve. She suffers ongoing pain and incapacity, and even Scott does not believe that she has exaggerated her testimony regarding her physical health. She is currently on

continued

several medications and is limited in her ability to alleviate her pain due to her loss of a kidney several years ago. Donna has been determined to be disabled by the Social Security Administration and her sole source of income at this point is her disability benefits, which net her $309 per month. Although Scott feels that any alimony award should be for rehabilitative purposes only, the record does not support such a conclusion. Due to her physical infirmities, Donna is an unlikely candidate for further education or training. She has never been able to put what training and experience she has accrued in 51 years to practical use in the job market. The Court does not find it to be realistic to think that Donna is employable in her current condition....

This is a long-term marriage of nearly 20 years. Scott has a substantially better earning capacity than Donna, who is permanently disabled. Donna's earning capacity appears limited to her social security disability benefits. Scott continues to have an earning capacity of $50,000 annually or more. Scott will have far greater social security retirement benefits than Donna. Additionally, Scott receives use of a vehicle as an employment benefit and does not currently have the expense of car payments....the Court takes note that the settlements she received for her injuries and future disabilities were invested in the marriage and are no longer available to Donna at the very time she needs the money.

In view of these findings, which are fully supported in the record and which we adopt, we think the spousal support award of $1,250 per month in traditional alimony until Donna attains the age of sixty-five or either party dies was equitable and should not be disturbed.

SIDEBAR

The entire opinion in this case is available on the companion website. Do you agree with the court's decision? Would any other form of alimony have been more appropriate?

Restitution Alimony

Restitution or reimbursement alimony is designed to repay a spouse who made financial contributions during the marriage that directly enhanced the future earning capacity of the other spouse. It is not based on need but rather on equitable considerations—considerations of fairness. The recipient spouse may have interrupted his or her education and earned and expended resources for the other party's benefit in the belief that the marital enterprise would be strengthened in the long term. If the marriage is terminated, it is considered fair that the contributing spouse be paid or reimbursed for the investment he or she made in the marriage. The typical fact pattern in which it might be awarded is when there is a short-term marriage, no children, limited assets, and one spouse has delayed or interrupted his or her education or career and worked to allow the other spouse to pursue graduate studies. Some courts may choose to use restitution alimony for the purposes served by rehabilitation alimony. Such an approach avoids the stigma that there is somehow something deficient or unhealthy in the recipient spouse that needs to be "rehabilitated."

Because it runs counter to traditional alimony principles, which base alimony on need, ability to pay, and standard of living of the parties during the marriage, restitution or reimbursement alimony is viewed with disfavor in some states and by some individual judges. It may be denied if the petitioner is self-sufficient, even if

Restitution or reimbursement alimony
alimony designed to repay a spouse who made financial contributions during the marriage that directly enhanced the future earning capacity of the other spouse.

CASE **10.5** *Mahoney v. Mahoney*, 91 N.J. 488, 453 A.2d 527 (1982)

FROM THE OPINION

In this case, the supporting spouse made financial contributions towards her husband's professional education with the expectation that both parties would enjoy material benefits flowing from the professional license or degree. It is therefore patently unfair that the supporting spouse be denied the mutually anticipated benefit while the supported spouse keeps not only the degree, but also all of the material benefits and rewards flowing from it.

. . . Also the wife has presumably made personal financial sacrifices, resulting in a reduced or lowered standard of living. Additionally, her husband, by pursuing preparations for a future career, has foregone gainful employment and financial contributions to the marriage. . . . She has postponed, as it were, present consumption and a higher standard of living, for the future prospect of greater support and material benefits. . . . The unredressed sacrifices . . . coupled with the unfairness attendant upon the defeat of the supporting spouse's shared expectation of future advantages, further justify a remedial reward. . . .

SIDEBAR

The entire opinion in this case is available on the companion website. Do you agree with the court's decision? Would any other form of alimony have been more appropriate?

only as a result of receiving disability benefits. It also may be deemed unwarranted if the requesting party already has a degree, does not require additional training, or is already employed in a good job and his or her earning capacity did not suffer as a result of contributions to the marriage.

The landmark decision of the New Jersey Supreme Court in the *Mahoney* case in 1982 illustrates a set of circumstances in which restitution or "reimbursement" alimony was considered appropriate to the facts of the case. (See Case 10.5.) The court in the *Thornley* case chose to call its award under similar facts an "alimony in gross" or lump-sum award. Although they are labeled differently, the two awards served a similar purpose. The labels chosen are largely due to judicial preferences. In the *Mahoney* case, the husband left the marriage shortly after attaining an advanced degree that he had earned with the wife's support. The court held that she was entitled to reimbursement for household expenses, educational costs, school travel expenses, and any other contribution she made enabling her husband to attain his degree.

WHAT FACTORS WILL A COURT CONSIDER WHEN MAKING AN ALIMONY DETERMINATION?

The power to award alimony is statutory, but unlike child support awards, which are essentially formula based, alimony decisions are left to the discretion of judges. Virtually all states, whether by statute or judicial decision, have identified the primary economic and noneconomic factors to be considered by the courts when making alimony determinations. These factors afford judges considerable flexibility in tailoring alimony decisions to the unique facts of each case. They also help guide the information-gathering efforts of the family law team on behalf of a client in an alimony case. The fundamental question in an alimony case is, does one of the parties have a need for financial support that the other party has the ability to meet?

Throughout this text, the importance of thorough preparation is empha-sized. In the *Adkins* case, the wife cast a wide net advancing a claim for an award of temporary, permanent, rehabilitative, and/or lump-sum alimony—a permissible, albeit unsuccessful, approach in this case due to a failure to support the claim with appropriate facts. (See Case 10.6.) Although her husband, an attorney, had the ability to pay, the court held that the wife failed to successfully demonstrate a need for alimony. It appears that the husband's counsel had conducted appropriate and thorough discovery and presented facts sufficient to inform the court's delibera-tion and defeat the wife's claim.

CASE **10.6** *Adkins v. Adkins,* 650 So. 2d 61 (Fla. App. 1994)

FROM THE OPINION

The wife on the main appeal. . . urged that the trial court erred in failing to award the wife alimony and attorney's fees. . . .

In the instant case, the parties married in 1978; it was the second marriage for both parties. There were no children born of the marriage and the husband filed for dissolution of the marriage in 1987. The trial court made the following relevant findings in the amended final judgment under review:

The Wife is 47 years of age. She is in good health, possesses various and valuable employment skills as reflected by her personal resume, and is currently unem-ployed. The Husband is 63 years of age. His health is problematic although, by his admission, not disabling. He currently is attempting to reestablish a law practice in Coral Gables, Florida, with a focus on the general practice of law. Each party entered this marriage with substantial assets. . . .

During the course of the marriage, the parties, by agreement, main-tained separate bank accounts, separate accounting records, and separate business interests. The Wife inherited from family members, substantial assets consisting primarily of real estate and tillable farmland and having a net worth of approximately Two Million Dollars. During this marriage, Wife managed her inherited property, churned her stock holdings profitably, and reinvested the profits of her labor in other property interests. . . . At no time did the Wife share with her Husband the fruits of her labor or the profits resulting therefrom. In fact, the Wife requested that the Husband reimburse her for any and all expenses she incurred from which the Husband and/or one of his assets may have derived a benefit.

The Husband worked diligently during this marriage to provide the Wife with a comfortable lifestyle. She was provided with a maid five days a week, a beautiful home, and an environment which included trips to Europe and elsewhere. In return for his labor, the Husband asked the Wife to abide by her premarital promise to provide a "nest", using the Wife's words, to be his companion and friend, and to be there when he returned from work. Instead, the Wife, for reasons unexplained, chose to lead a singular and self-gratifying lifestyle. For example, she would disappear from the home without notice or explanation for days, weeks, or even months at a time. She hesitated to be a homemaker in any of the traditional senses. Although these responsibilities are not required by today's environment, they were the responsibilities that were promised by the Wife to the Husband and they were the reasons that he was induced to marry her in the first instance. He had hoped to marry at last and forever and expressed to his Wife his need for a warm, comfortable, and stable homeplace. . . .

continued

With respect to the denial of the Wife's request for alimony, the trial court made the following relevant findings in the amended final judgment:

...In support of her request, she states that she has lost her job and is presently receiving unemployment compensation as a result. While receiving unemployment compensation, the Court finds that the Wife has a net worth in excess of Two Million Dollars. In fact, while completing the weekly form work required by the Bureau of Unemployment Compensation, the Wife has managed and maintained her stock portfolio, reinvested monies received through the sale of a small portion of real estate, effected a tax-free exchange of her South Carolina assets for investment property in North Carolina, and has acquired an interest in a Shoney's Restaurant. In short, the Wife is gainfully employed at this time, managing her substantial estate. The Court finds that the Wife fails to demonstrate the need or entitlement to receive alimony from the Husband....

Given the substantial wealth and income-producing property of the wife, the relatively high earning capacity of the wife, and the relatively short-term nature of this marriage, we see no abuse of the trial court's discretion in denying the wife's request for alimony....

SIDEBAR

The entire opinion in this case is available on the companion website. Do you agree with the court's decision? Explain your response.

The Florida court in the *Adkins* case relied primarily on three factors: income, earning capacity, and length of marriage. The Uniform Marriage and Divorce Act (UMDA)[8] lists the following factors as appropriate for consideration in the making of alimony determinations:

- the financial resources of the party seeking alimony, including marital property apportioned to him or her, the party's ability to meet his or her needs independently, and the extent to which a provision for support of a child living with that party includes a sum for that party as custodian
- the time necessary to acquire sufficient education or training to enable the party seeking alimony to find appropriate employment
- the standard of living during the marriage
- the duration of the marriage
- the age and physical and emotional condition of the spouse seeking alimony
- the ability of the spouse from whom alimony is sought to meet his or her needs while meeting those of the spouse seeking alimony

Additional kinds of factors that may appear in a given state's spousal support statute include the following:

- the relative needs of the parties and ability to pay
- the earned and unearned income of each party, including, but not limited to, earnings, dividends, and benefits such as medical, disability, retirement, or social security
- the relative current and future earning capacities of the spouses
- the respective liabilities of the parties
- the backgrounds of the parties in terms of education and training and the prospects of the spouse seeking alimony to become self-supporting within a reasonable period of time

- contribution of each of the parties to appreciation of the marital estate or to the education, training, career, and increased earning power of the other party
- contribution as a homemaker
- the misconduct/fault of either or both of the parties up to the time of the separation—most particularly fault with financial consequences
- the property brought to the marriage by the parties (or their families)
- the federal, state, and local tax ramifications of the alimony award
- a final catchall provision allowing the court to consider any additional factors it may consider relevant

A judge may be required to consider and make findings with respect to each of the statutorily defined factors in the jurisdiction but usually may assign whatever weight he or she believes is appropriate to any particular factor in light of the facts of each case. A decision can then be made with respect to the most appropriate form, duration, and amount of alimony, if any, to be awarded. Absent an abuse of discretion, an alimony decision will generally not be disturbed on appeal.

Although this approach maximizes flexibility for the courts when alimony is at issue in a case, it provides little predictability for counsel and clients and often escalates the cost of divorce as a result. Depending on the facts of the case, a family law team committed to effectively representing a client may be presented with a potentially monumental information-gathering challenge. The effort usually begins with a careful review of the applicable alimony statutes and controlling case law in the jurisdiction. An effort then is made in initial client interviews, formal discovery, and other information-gathering activities to identify the factors that will be most relevant to the case at hand in light of the client's goal (to negotiate a settlement and avoid trial, successfully litigate an alimony case, or defeat an alimony claim by the other party). It is not enough simply to identify the relevant factors. Each must be addressed and supported by provable facts backed up by admissible evidence. It is important to identify the merits and weaknesses of both the opposing party's and the client's case. For example, if seeking alimony, consideration needs to be given to whether or not the potential obligor can raise any defenses to the claim. Alimony cases are fact-intensive. THERE ARE NO SUBSTITUTES FOR CAREFUL LISTENING AND THOROUGH PREPARATION! Paralegal Application 10.1 contains information-gathering suggestions related to ten of the factors most commonly considered by the courts in alimony cases.

PARALEGAL APPLICATION **10.1**

THE FACT-FINDING MISSION IN AN ALIMONY CASE

LENGTH OF MARRIAGE:

How long have the parties been married? This is the customary starting point when assessing the potential of an alimony claim. There is consensus among the majority of states that marriages of different lengths should have different consequences with respect to alimony. For example, absent unusual circumstances, alimony is generally not an option in a short-term marriage of less than five years. The premise is that the parties have not as yet built up substantial economic reliance on one another or changed their premarital work patterns for a sufficiently

continued

extended period. In a long-term marriage of more than fifteen years, many courts agree that long-term support may be warranted if necessary to enable both spouses to maintain as closely as possible the standard of living that characterized their married life. Most litigation and inconsistencies in outcome occur with intermediate-length marriages of between five and fifteen years in duration. A small number of states have directly related length of marriage and spousal support by providing that alimony cannot last longer than the length of the marriage or some percentage thereof.

The answer to the question "How long have the parties been married?" is not always as simple as it might seem. Look behind the answer. Although it technically "doesn't count," how long were the parties together prior to marriage and were they simply dating or living together? Were there periods during the marriage when the parties were separated due to problems in the marriage or factors such as substantial work-related travel (as an entertainer, merchant mariner, etc.)?

Don't let "general rules" restrict thinking with respect to future prospects, given the facts of a specific case. If it is a short-term marriage and the client is seeking alimony, what unusual factors are present that argue for an award when it normally would not be granted? Illness? Abuse? If it is a long-term marriage and the client is fighting alimony, what distinguishes the case at hand from others in which permanent alimony would likely be awarded based on precedent?

Examples of Proof: Leases in either party's name, employment records, counseling or court records documenting periods of separation, medical records, etc.

INCOME:

A complete employment history should be compiled for each of the parties, including job titles, hours worked, salaries, job skills, and responsibilities. With respect to current employment, if any, is each party bringing in income to his or her full capacity, or is he or she intentionally decreasing income to an artificially low figure, refusing to seek gainful employment; quitting second jobs and part-time work performed while married; falsely claiming to be disabled; not reporting "under the table" income; postponing taking raises, bonuses, or commissions; or otherwise manipulating income? Under such circumstances, income may be imputed to the party who is deliberately reducing his or her earnings. On the other hand, is one party's income inflated in a given year by, for example, receipt of a substantial contingent fee, making it appropriate to average that party's income over a period of years? Is either party holding an unreasonable amount of assets in a low or non-income-bearing form to the detriment of the potential recipient? If either spouse is cohabiting with another person, does that other person contribute to support of the household, so that more funds are available to the spouse to meet an alimony obligation or less funds are needed by the recipient?

Examples of Proof: Resumes, tax returns, employment records, pay stubs, mortgage applications, documentation that the payor spouse will or has received appreciating assets in the property division, evidence of transfers made to third parties, evidence of purchases of luxury/non-income-producing items, logs of efforts to find work, etc.

NEEDS:

What are the REASONABLE needs of the parties as reflected in food, clothing, housing, and other basic living expenses as well as debts? Is either party living beyond his or

continued

her needs? The client should prepare a realistic budget of his or her living expenses for careful review. Keep in mind that "need" is a relative concept and cannot be considered apart from the parties' standard of living. What Madonna or your state senator "needs" is likely very different from what a laborer or teacher needs.

Examples of Proof: Financial statements, tax returns, credit card statements, bank statements, mortgage statements, bills, car payments, etc.

STANDARD OF LIVING DURING THE MARRIAGE:

In most cases, the level of assets in a marriage is such that it is simply not possible for both parties to maintain the marital standard of living post-divorce. The issue is more one of how the negative impact of divorce on lifestyle can be equally shared. However, in cases involving substantial assets, it is important to establish the nature of the parties' lifestyle during the marriage. What was the marital home like? Did it have a pool, tennis courts, or game room? What kind of neighborhood was it in? How did the parties spend their free time? Did they belong to golf, tennis, or yacht clubs? Did they take vacations and, if so, where? Did they own or have access to vacation homes? How often and in what manner did they entertain company? Did they make many charitable donations and attend prestigious fundraising events? What kind of a clothing budget did they have? Where did they shop? How did they pay their bills (cash, credit, loans, employment bonuses, gifts from parents, etc.)? How sustained was their lifestyle (were there a couple of good years and a decade of poor ones, or the reverse)? Was there a considerable amount of readily available cash that was put into savings for a later date rather than spent? Did they spend their funds on property, on tangible assets, or on events like lavish celebrations of birthdays and anniversaries? Were the parties unusually frugal?[9]

Examples of Proof: Photographs, receipts, credit card statements, bank statements, newspaper articles (society columns), membership records, invitations, employment records, expense accounts, etc.

CONTRIBUTION:

Identify and document to the fullest extent possible the financial and nonfinancial contributions of each of the parties to the marriage, including homemaking, home maintenance and improvement, childrearing, entertaining in support of one of the parties' careers, and/or vacations at retreats owned by the family of one of the spouses. Financial contributions should be broadly defined and may include trust income, inheritances, accident settlements, gifts from family members that were spent on marital expenses, etc.

Examples of Proof: Bank statements, credit card statements, appraisals, receipts, copies of trust instruments, photographs, etc.

FAULT:

Much to the consternation of wronged clients, approximately half the states do not consider fault when making alimony determinations. With those that do, the fault generally must have resulted in some form of economic loss. For example, the mere existence of an adulterous relationship usually is not enough. The family law team should research how the adultery impacted the marital relationship and estate. Were significant funds spent on gifts, travel, lodging, etc., that would otherwise have been available to support the marriage? Was the aggrieved spouse's emotional and physical health injured by the conduct?

Examples of Proof: Admissions, statements of the correspondent, photographs/videos, bank and credit card statements, reports of private detectives, phone

continued

records, e-mails and other forms of correspondence, hotel/motel records, medical records, etc.

Other types of fault also should be explored: criminal conduct; abusive behavior (physical and/or psychological); reckless spending, dissipation (such as through gambling), or diversion/concealment of assets; excessive use of alcohol or drugs; willful failure to provide essential support to the spouse and children. An isolated incident normally is not enough (unless especially egregious), so search for patterns in misconduct.

Proof: The specific type of supporting documentation needed will depend on the specific type of misconduct.

EDUCATION:

Compile histories for each of the spouses, covering all kinds of education and training received along with information about each party's career goals.
Examples of Proof: Resumes, job applications, certificates of completion, on-the-job training records, college applications, etc.

EMPLOYABILITY:

A party may have an impressive educational history and yet have obsolete job skills and be unemployable. What are the employment prospects for each party? Are there any factors that limit employment options, such as age, physical capacities, or chronic health problems? Has the party been terminated for cause at prior places of employment due to negative behavior, poor performance, or misconduct in the workplace? Is the party's level of employability the result of their own efforts, or to market forces?
Examples of Proof: Labor market forecasts produced by reputable sources, medical records, job descriptions listing required skills, testimony from employment counselors, etc.

AGE:

This factor seems to be straightforward, but its importance flows less from the number of years a person has lived than it does from how age influences employment prospects, health issues, capacity to acquire additional assets to improve living standard, etc. For example, a seventy-year-old attorney or stockbroker may be at the height of his or her career, whereas a professional football player may be barely hanging onto employment at age thirty-five.
Examples of Proof: Medical records, employment records, tax returns, etc.

HEALTH:

Does either party suffer or allegedly suffer from any illnesses or injuries that impede earning potential and result in additional uninsured medical costs?
Examples of Proof: Work absence records, medical records, etc.

The *Anliker* case provided an excellent example of a court's application of a wealth of documented facts provided by the petitioner to the statutory factors considered by the courts making alimony awards in Iowa. It is instructive to contrast *Anliker* with the *Ray* decision of the Supreme Court of Oklahoma, in which it vacated a Court of Civil Appeals opinion and reversed a trial court's award of alimony. (See Case 10.7.) This decision clearly illustrates the potential impact of failing to provide sufficient factual information on the client's behalf for the court's consideration.

CASE **10.7** *Ray v. Ray,* 2006 OK 30, 136 P.3d 634 (Okla. 2006)

FROM THE OPINION

The trial court's "quasi summary" dissolution hearing produced a paucity of facts serving as a basis for the alimony award....There is here no evidence of (a) the amount of money wife reasonably needs for readjustment of her lifestyle to a new economic situation, (b) her income-producing capacity, such as the number of hours she works per week and her monthly income; (c) her monthly expenses and future living plans and expenses, (d) her physical condition, (e) the cost of her desired education, (f) whether her station in life or standard of living has changed since the separation; (g) how much her cohabiting partner contributes to her monthly needs. Neither is there any evidence of (a) the husband's ability to pay support alimony, (b) the value of his home, (c) his net worth, (d) his physical condition, (e) his living standard based on monthly income and expenses. . . .

. . .Because the wife has failed to meet, before the trial court, her burden of affirmatively demonstrating the amount of needed support, if any, during the period of her economic readjustment, the trial court's alimony award is reversed and the cause remanded for further proceedings to be consistent with today's pronouncement.

SIDEBAR

The entire opinion in this case is available on the companion website. Do you agree with the court's decision? Why? Do you think the wife may have a malpractice claim against her attorney? Explain your response.

PARALEGAL APPLICATION **10.2**

DRAFTING POINTERS FOR AN ALIMONY PROVISION IN A SEPARATION AGREEMENT

This Application highlights the major topics that need to be addressed in an alimony provision of a separation agreement. The precise content needs to be tailored to specific client needs given the facts of each case.

- **Goal:** The goal of the alimony award should be stated. For example, if the award is in the nature of rehabilitative alimony, ideally a plan should be provided including a description of the program, a timeline for completion, and the associated costs. If the award will be in the form of restitution/reimbursement alimony, the expenses being reimbursed should be specified.

- **Designation of the payment as alimony:** The designation of the payment to be made as alimony should be clearly spelled out, along with a statement of the parties' intentions as to whether or not it will be includable in the taxable income of the recipient and deductible to the obligor.

- **Amount:** The amount should be established. Usually a fixed dollar amount is stated, which facilitates wage assignments, if warranted. However, if the payor's income fluctuates seasonally or otherwise, the amount may be set in the form of a percentage of that income. This approach has the disadvantages of uncertainty for the recipient and the need for periodic documentation and review of the payor's financial status.

continued

- **Duration:** The duration of the alimony should be established. Under what conditions will the obligation terminate? Some jurisdictions have specific limitations regarding the duration of alimony awarded by the court. The parties may agree on events that will terminate the alimony obligation, such as remarriage, cohabitation with another person for longer than a specified period, completion of an educational program, or obtaining full-time employment at a particular wage or higher.

- **Frequency and timing of payments:** The frequency and timing of payments should be laid out. Will there be a lump-sum or periodic payments? Will payments be made weekly or monthly?

- **Form of payments:** The form of payments may be agreed on. For example, alimony may be paid by check payable to the recipient spouse and sent by mail or by direct deposit. Each party should be required to notify the other of any change in address or applicable accounts. Payment can be made to a third party for the recipient's benefit to meet an obligation such as a mortgage on the marital residence. Another option is to have a court-ordered payroll deduction by the payor's employer (wage assignment or income withholding). Some states require payment through a state IV-D agency in a variety of circumstances. Whatever the method of payment, a party with an obligation to pay alimony should be advised by his or her attorney to keep detailed records and corroborative evidence of all payments to protect against a potential claim of contempt for nonpayment.

- **Modification of alimony:** The modifiability of the alimony award should be addressed in the agreement if permitted in the jurisdiction. The courts generally link changes to actual financial circumstances. However, the parties may agree on self-executing provisions that will result in an automatic modification based on an annual cost-of-living increase, a certain percentage increase or decrease in the payor's income, or receipt of an anticipated inheritance by either party. The triggering events should not be child-related, in order to protect deductibility of the alimony payment for income tax purposes.

- **Health care costs:** It is important for the client to be aware of any potential health insurance coverage issues prior to or upon divorce. If the client is insured through his or her employer, the state, or a private policy, there should be no interruption in coverage. However, if the client is covered through the spouse's employer, proactive steps may need to be taken. Some plans allow employees to remove someone from their health plan, including a spouse. Although the removed spouse may be eligible for COBRA extension coverage post-divorce, there may be a gap in coverage between the date of removal and the date of divorce, when COBRA eligibility commences. The topic of health insurance needs to be addressed in the agreement at some point. It should be expressly indicated if alimony is at least partly designed to cover medical, dental, and/or mental health expenses and, if the employee spouse is required by the divorce decree to pay COBRA premiums for his or her spouse, the employer should be promptly notified of the divorce.[10]

- **Security for alimony payments:** The recipient spouse will want to include security for the payment of alimony. Most states authorize courts to order the obligor spouse to maintain life insurance or some other form of security such as a trust for the recipient's benefit. Life insurance policies for the benefit of the recipient are the most common form of security for alimony payments.

- **Survival or merger of the alimony provision:** If alimony will be waived or paid pursuant to the terms of the parties' separation agreement, the attorney will consider with the client the issue of survival or merger of the alimony

continued

provision of the agreement. If the agreement survives, the provision will generally not be able to be modified by the court, absent a showing of something more than a change in circumstances (such as the likelihood the recipient will become a public charge absent modification). This is a difficult choice, but given the uncertainties in life, many practitioners believe it wisest to have alimony provisions merge in the decree. This way, in the event of a later economic downturn or windfall or the serious illness of either party, the option to modify the alimony award upon a material change in circumstances usually remains open to both parties. The concepts of survival and merger are discussed more fully in Chapter 12.

WHEN AND HOW CAN ALIMONY AWARDS BE MODIFIED OR TERMINATED?

The decision as to whether or not alimony can be modified or terminated is made on a case-by-case basis and is driven by statute, court order, case law, or the language of the agreement executed by the parties. Many of the cases addressing this issue demonstrate the importance of careful drafting.

Modification

If permanent or term alimony was awarded in the parties' divorce decree, most states allow a party to later file a Complaint or Petition for Modification based on a *material change in circumstances.* However, in most jurisdictions, absent extraordinary circumstances or extreme hardship, a lump-sum, rehabilitative, or restitution alimony award will not be modifiable. In some states, if alimony was not addressed in the divorce judgment, an alimony claim may not be able to be pursued at a later date unless the right to pursue alimony was preserved by a nominal award (e.g., $1.00 per year) at the time of the divorce. Some states allow a Complaint for Alimony to be filed subsequent to the divorce, given an unanticipated change in the parties' circumstances since the time of divorce.

Material change in circumstances a change in the physical, emotional, or financial condition of one or both of the parties sufficient to warrant a change in a support order; a change that, if known at the time of the divorce decree, would have resulted in a different order

The complaint for modification is usually filed in the court that issued the original order if it retains continuing jurisdiction over the matter. The burden of proving the change of circumstances rests with the party seeking the modification. The kinds of changes in circumstances that might justify an up or down adjustment in alimony include forced unemployment or early retirement, a windfall increase in income or assets, the onset of a serious medical condition resulting in permanent disability and increased uninsured medical expenses, a third-party mortgagee's exercising its option to accelerate payment of a mortgage loan on the marital home, or cohabitation with a person who assumes responsibility for many of the dependent spouse's living expenses.

The court will examine the nature of the change and assess whether or not the request is made in good faith. For example, if it is based on a reduction in the payor's income, is the reduction the fault of that individual? Has he or she engineered circumstances so that it appears there is a reduction in income or an increase in liabilities when there is not? Or is the increase in liabilities the result of spendthrift spending or an extravagant lifestyle? There are no fixed rules for determining what meets the threshold and each case is decided in the context of the surrounding circumstances.

In about half of the states, misconduct on the part of the recipient may constitute a sufficient change in circumstances to support a modification. For example, in the *Miller*[11] case in Massachusetts, the wife openly and intentionally conducted herself in a "scandalous" manner that embarrassed the husband, injured his reputation, and adversely affected his business. In response to the husband's motion for modification, the court reduced his alimony obligation to his former wife. The reduction was upheld on appeal. However, the courts are reluctant to modify payments when the change in circumstances underlying the request is the result of the petitioner's own wrongful acts, as illustrated in the *Willoughby* case. (See Case 10.8.)

If the parties have executed a separation agreement, it may provide that they will initially attempt to resolve modification issues through mediation prior to resorting to litigation. If the agreement is incorporated in the judgment of divorce and that agreement provides that alimony shall be unmodifiable or modifiable only under certain limited circumstances, the courts will usually hold the parties to their agreement absent extraordinary circumstances. The *Williams* case in Connecticut addresses a situation of this kind. It illustrates the potential impact of language in the parties' agreement; the interplay among statutes, case law, and agreements; and the importance of maintaining a complete case file. (See Case 10.9.) The court may also be constrained by provisions of a surviving agreement of the parties. In a few states, a court will have no power to modify spousal support unless the parties' agreement allows the court to do so. Other courts may refuse to honor a "no modification" clause in an agreement on public policy grounds if, for example, a spouse will be forced into dependence on public assistance as a result.

CASE **10.8** *Willoughby v. Willoughby,* 2004 PA. Super. 439, 862 A.2d 654 (2004)

DISCUSSION OF THE CASE

In this case, a former husband sought modification of his alimony payment after he was sentenced to three to seven years in prison for a variety of crimes including theft and forgery.

The court adopted a "no justification rule" that incarceration standing alone is not sufficient to warrant modification of an alimony obligation. The court reasoned that criminal activity that could lead to incarceration is clearly within the control of the individual obligated to make alimony payments. Incarceration for criminal offenses was distinguished from other obstacles to payment not within the control of the obligor such as injury, illness, job loss, or other involuntary obstacles.

Even if the alimony payments are not made while the obligor is incarcerated, the court stated, ". . . principles of equity dictate that he should not be relieved of his duty to pay the accrued arrearages upon his release."

SIDEBAR

The entire opinion in this case is available on the companion website. Do you agree with the court's decision? Should payments be stayed while the obligor is incarcerated?

CASE **10.9** *Williams v. Williams*, 276 Conn. 491, 886 A.2d 817
(2005)

DISCUSSION OF THE CASE

In this case, the parties executed an agreement that provided for weekly alimony for the wife for approximately ten years. The parties' agreement incorporated in the judgment stated the following with respect to modification:

> Husband shall not be entitled to receive a decrease in his alimony obligation unless he satisfactorily demonstrates to the court that he has suffered a substantial and significant decrease in income, such decrease was not due in any way to his voluntary change in lifestyle, career choice, place of residence or new responsibilities, and that he has taken affirmative steps and used his best efforts to maintain his income. Pursuant to General Statutes § 46b-86 (b), husband's alimony may be modifiable upon wife's remarriage or cohabitation.

The statute at issue provides as follows:

> In an action for divorce, dissolution of marriage, legal separation or annulment brought by a husband or wife, in which a final judgment has been entered providing for the payment of periodic alimony by one party to the other, the Superior Court may, in its discretion and upon notice and hearing, modify such judgment and suspend, reduce or terminate the payment of periodic alimony upon a showing that the party receiving the periodic alimony is living with another person under circumstances which the court finds should result in the modification, suspension, reduction or termination of alimony because the living arrangements cause such a change in circumstances as to alter the financial needs of that party.

When the husband's motion to modify the alimony terms of the dissolution judgment was denied, he appealed, claiming that the trial court improperly placed a burden on him to prove that the defendant's financial circumstances had been altered as a result of her remarriage. He claimed that the statute pertained only to cohabitation and that there was a presumption based on Connecticut case law that the alimony obligation should terminate because every marriage alters the financial needs of the party.

The husband relied on *Cary*, 112 Conn. 256, 152 A. 302 (1930), in which the Connecticut Supreme Court stated:

> The remarriage of the wife should relieve the husband from the obligation of supporting the wife of another man. To permit her to have alimony from the first husband as an equivalent for her support after she had secured the legal obligation from the second husband to support her would give her support from her present and her former husband and . . . would offend public policy and good morals. . . . Two husbands should not be liable for the obligation of support for a woman who is the divorced spouse of one and the wife of the other. Id. At 261.

The Connecticut Supreme Court took the position that *Cary* and subsequent cases did not deprive it of authority to award nonmodifiable alimony or in its equitable powers to award alimony that does not terminate even in the event of remarriage.

In a footnote, the court dealt with the obligor's assertion that the reference to the statute may have been a drafting error. It observed that the record was clear that

continued

the settlement agreement had undergone considerable scrutiny. The parties were represented by counsel when it was drafted, and the agreement itself indicated numerous handwritten changes, deletions, and substitutions, including several within the section at issue.

The state supreme court affirmed the lower court's decision.

> …in the absence of compelling reason to disregard the clear and unequivocal language set forth in the parties' settlement agreement, as incorporated into the judgment of dissolution. There is nothing inherently improper about requiring the plaintiff under the facts of this case, as the party with the alimony obligation, to demonstrate that remarriage of the defendant had a financial impact that should warrant a modification in his alimony obligation.…In the present case, the parties' decision to use the standard set forth in the statute as a basis for determining whether alimony should be modified was reasonable and clearly expressed. Therefore the trial court's decision was not improper as a matter of law.

SIDEBAR

The entire opinion in this case is available on the companion website. Do you agree with the court's decision? Explain your response.

Termination

Unless otherwise provided in a final divorce decree, or by its nature as in alimony in gross, an alimony obligation will usually terminate upon the earliest to occur of the following events:

- death of the recipient
- death of the payor
- expiration of a stated period of time
- remarriage of the recipient
- cohabitation of the recipient with another

The court frequently sets a termination date in the decree or incorporates one or more self-executing termination dates that the parties set forth in their agreement. For example, they may agree that cohabitation for greater than one month, recovery from a serious illness, retirement, completion of a specific educational program, or obtaining full-time employment will trigger a cessation of alimony. Regardless of how the alimony obligation terminates, the payor (or his or her estate in the case of death) generally remains liable for arrearages (i.e., unpaid back payments) unless otherwise ordered by the court.

Termination upon Remarriage. The general rule is that "permanent" alimony will terminate upon remarriage of the recipient or on whatever date or condition the parties agree to in their agreement. Many states, such as Alaska, Florida, Idaho, and Maryland, have automatic termination on remarriage rules but recognize an exception when the parties have expressly agreed to continue alimony upon remarriage. Provisions to that effect must expressly state that alimony survives the statutory presumption. Parties who know they want to remarry sometimes elect to choose this route and provide for a reduction in the amount of alimony to be paid upon remarriage. In this essentially win-win situation, the former spouse who wants to remarry does so without a total loss of alimony and the paying spouse is relieved of a portion of the full alimony obligation.

In states such as South Dakota and Massachusetts, remarriage establishes a **prima facie *showing*** supporting termination of alimony on remarriage unless the recipient is able to show the existence of extraordinary circumstances that require the continuation of alimony. If the obligor remarries, his or her alimony obligation will continue, absent a court order to the contrary. However, a court may entertain a complaint for downward modification if children are born to the subsequent marriage or for an upward modification if the recipient can show that the paying spouse has more of his or her income available as a result of the new spouse's contributions to his or her customary living expenses.

Prima facie showing
a legally rebuttable showing

Termination upon Death. If either of the parties dies, alimony payments customarily cease unless the parties' separation agreement expressly provides otherwise. For example, the parties may agree that payments will continue to be paid from the decedent's estate or from a trust. The American Law Institute's Principles of the Law of Family Dissolution provides that the alimony obligation may survive the obligor's death if the court makes written findings establishing that the termination of the award would work a substantial injustice because of facts not present in most cases. A more common approach is for the divorce decree to include an order requiring the obligor to maintain an insurance policy for the recipient's benefit.

Termination upon Cohabitation. The majority rule with respect to cohabitation in jurisdictions without a specific statute on point is that cohabitation can result in the reduction or elimination of a spousal support award only if it improves the financial circumstances of the recipient spouse enough to substantially reduce the need for support. This requirement of proof of a substantial change in need level rather than an automatic termination reflects the fact that cohabitation, unlike marriage, does not create a reciprocal and continuing support obligation between the cohabiting parties. The court will look at facts such as the following:

1. Does the cohabitant provide housing for the recipient?
2. Does the cohabitant contribute financially to rent/mortgage and household operating expenses? Is the contribution consistent?
3. Was the benefit received unanticipated at the time of the divorce decree?
4. Has the recipient made substantial purchases, such as vehicles, a boat, property, etc., since the period of cohabitation began?

HOW ARE ALIMONY AWARDS ENFORCED?

In most jurisdictions, the primary enforcement vehicle for nonpayment of alimony is a ***contempt*** action, ***civil*** or ***criminal,*** depending on the circumstances. When court-ordered alimony is not paid, the aggrieved recipient is entitled to file appropriate paperwork in the applicable court (usually a Motion or Complaint for Contempt or a Citation with an Order to Show Cause) to enforce the order. If the obligor is found to be in civil contempt of an alimony order, the court will usually order payment of the overdue amount according to a schedule tailored to the obligor's ability to pay. Although the court has the authority to impose a jail sentence for an indefinite period to compel payment, usually the defendant in a civil contempt case will be given the opportunity to pay the arrearages and thereby purge the contempt and avoid jail. Usually the obligor will not be found in contempt if there was an inability to pay at the time the delinquent payments were due or if the recipient contributed to the nonpayment, for example, by failing to provide the obligor with notice of a change of address. In a criminal contempt case, a sentence may be imposed for a fixed period, and the arrearage cannot be purged by payment.

Civil contempt
a sanction for failure to obey a court order issued for another's benefit; a civil contempt proceeding is remedial in nature and designed to promote compliance with the order

Criminal contempt
a punishment for failure to comply with a court order; a criminal contempt proceeding is punitive in nature and designed to punish an attack on the integrity of the court

If the alimony recipient is also receiving court-ordered child support, he or she may also seek assistance from the state's Title IV-D agency and its arsenal of enforcement measures, such as income withholding and tax refund intercepts. States may also provide additional enforcement support for individuals not eligible for IV-D assistance. If the obligor presently resides in another state, the recipient can also seek enforcement across state lines under the Uniform Interstate Family Support Act (UIFSA).

In some circumstances, the recipient may seek to place a lien on property owned by a defendant found in contempt. In many states, statutes that protect property from legal process for collection of debts (attachment, etc.) do not apply to alimony or support claims. Another, more extreme measure, abolished in many states, is for the aggrieved party to file for a **Writ ne exeat,** a court order restraining a person from leaving the jurisdiction until the petitioner's claim has been satisfied.

The general rule is that when the alimony obligation is based on an agreement of the parties not merged in the divorce judgment, the agreement continues to exist as an independent contract, which the family court has no power to modify. If, given unusual circumstances, the family court imposes or varies the alimony obligation notwithstanding the agreement establishing different alimony obligations, the aggrieved party can pursue traditional breach of contract remedies, such as a suit for damages (to recover the difference between the alimony paid under the court order and the amount, if any, provided for in the parties' agreement).

If the obligor dies while there are outstanding alimony payments due, the recipient can seek to recover the accrued amount of arrearages from the decedent's estate if payment has not otherwise been secured by agreement of the parties or by order of the court.

Writ *ne exeat*
a court order restraining a person from leaving the jurisdiction until the petitioner's claim has been satisfied

WHAT ARE THE TAX AND BANKRUPTCY IMPLICATIONS OF ALIMONY?

The material that follows provides a very basic description of the relationship between alimony or spousal support obligations and tax and bankruptcy law. Each of these areas is a complex and specialized area of law, and determinations made by the Internal Revenue Service and Bankruptcy Courts will depend on the facts of each individual case.

Tax Implications

In general, the parties cannot come up with their own private agreement dictating the deductibility and includability of alimony payments unless the agreement satisfies applicable tax regulations. Under federal and state tax law, alimony is deductible from gross income by the payor and is income to the payee provided the following criteria are satisfied:[12]

1. The payments are made to a spouse or former spouse incident to a divorce decree or separation agreement. (An order for temporary alimony *pendente lite* will also qualify.)
2. The parties do not file a joint tax return for the period during which alimony payments are made.
3. The parties are not living in the same household when the payment is made. (This requirement applies only if the parties are legally separated under a decree of divorce or separate maintenance.)

4. The payments are made in cash (bank check, money order, etc.) and not in-kind (services rendered).
5. The payor has no liability for payments after death.
6. The payment is not improperly disguised child support (as when there are children but no child support is agreed to, and reductions in alimony amounts are tied to child-related events such as a child reaching the age of eighteen, graduating from high school, moving out of the custodial parent's home, or entering the military service, etc.).
7. The parties have not designated the payments as non-includable in the recipient's income.

When alimony payments are made to a third party for the recipient's benefit (typically for payment of a mortgage), to be deductible, the payment to the third party must be at the written request of the recipient to the payor. The writing must specify that the payments are in lieu of alimony payments directly to the recipient and that both spouses intend the payments to be treated as alimony.

The IRS requires the payor deducting alimony to provide on his or her tax return the social security number of the recipient spouse. This information allows the IRS to verify that the recipient is including alimony received as income. Failure to provide the number can result in a disallowance of the deduction and/or a penalty.

The ***alimony recapture rule*** found in Section 71(f) of the Internal Revenue Service Code is designed to prevent parties to divorce from disguising what is actually part of a property division settlement as alimony in order to obtain the benefit of a tax deduction. It applies when there appears to be a "front-loading" of alimony payments that decrease substantially or end during the first three calendar years following the divorce. The determination of whether or not the rule will apply is based on a formula. Essentially, "front-loading" of alimony is deemed to occur when the alimony payments made in the first year following the divorce (year one) are significantly higher than the payments in years two and three and there is more than a $15,000 decrease in alimony payments between years two and three. If the Internal Revenue Service determines that the alleged support payments are actually in the nature of a property settlement, the negative consequences can be especially dramatic for the payor. Any claimed deduction on previously filed tax returns in the applicable period is disallowed, and the amount of "alimony" previously deducted is "recaptured" and subject to taxes, interest, and penalties. The recipient spouse becomes entitled to a corresponding refund for taxes previously paid on "alimony" declared as income.

Alimony recapture rule
the IRS rule that the government can recover a tax benefit (the prior taking of a deduction for payment of alimony) by taxing the income that no longer qualifies for the benefit

Bankruptcy

In general, individuals who are deeply in debt have the right to file for bankruptcy in federal bankruptcy court in an effort to be relieved of full or partial payment of as many of their debts as possible. However, relatively recent changes in bankruptcy law have made relief far more difficult and complicated to obtain for individuals earning more than the mean annual income in the state where they live.[13]

In the event that a bankruptcy petition is successfully filed, the Bankruptcy Court has the authority to ***discharge*** some debts (relieve the debtor of the obligation to pay them), but other debts cannot be discharged, based largely on public policy grounds. In the bankruptcy context, the focus of attention with respect to spousal support is on whether or not a particular court-ordered payment from one spouse to the other constitutes "support." Although property division orders

Discharge
to extinguish a legal obligation; a discharge relieves an obligor of the duty to pay a debt

pursuant to a divorce usually will be dischargeable except under certain limited conditions, the general rule in bankruptcy is that alimony obligations are not dischargeable.[14] Every provision in a judgment of divorce or separation made solely for the purpose of support will be considered alimony, whether it is expressly labeled as such or not, and irrespective of whether it is paid in a lump sum or in intervals. The Bankruptcy Court looks at a number of factors in determining whether or not an award is in the nature of support. The bottom line is "…if it looks like a duck, walks like a duck, and quacks like a duck, then it probably is a duck"[15] and a party cannot avoid paying alimony simply by filing bankruptcy.

TRENDS

As the content of this chapter indicates, approaches to spousal support vary considerably from state to state and court to court. Clearly, it is awarded far less frequently than it was prior to 1970, and some believe that it has lost its rationale in a no-fault era. Despite inconsistencies and conflicting viewpoints, however, most continue to believe that alimony has a role to play at the dissolution of a marriage. Several general trends with respect to spousal support are becoming apparent.

The Role of Fault in an Alimony Determination

Slightly more than half the states continue to consider marital fault relevant to an alimony determination. Virginia is among the states that still specifically include adultery in their statutes governing maintenance and support as a factor to be considered.[16] In 1995, the Utah Legislature amended the Utah Code to include a subsection allowing trial courts to consider fault in determining alimony awards.[17] In the *Riley* case in 2006, a Utah appellate court opined that the "Husband's engagement in extramarital affairs and his prolonged deceitful conduct that led to the divorce—present precisely the type of situation where the legislature intended the trial court to consider fault. Indeed, Husband's fault goes a long way in explaining the propriety of a $900 per month alimony award, even though such an award would be too high if only economic factors were considered."[18]

At the other end of the spectrum are the states that have adopted the Uniform Marriage and Divorce Act.[19] Section 308 of the Act provides that maintenance awards should be set "without regard to marital misconduct." Although adopted in only a minority of states to date, the Act has been cited as persuasive authority in many jurisdictions as the trend is generally away from a consideration of "moral fault" of either partner. For example, as of October 1995 in the state of North Carolina, both post-separation spousal support and alimony became available to financially dependent spouses without having to prove that the supporting spouse was at fault for the breakup of the marriage.[20] Even among the states that consider marital fault as a factor, the primary focus is on economic fault. The basic inquiry to be made is, did the misconduct have financial consequences that took resources away that would otherwise have been available to the spouse and children? For example, did the philandering wife spend thousands of dollars on gifts, trips, clothing, meals, and perhaps even an apartment for her "lover"? Did the compulsive gambler deplete the parties' savings account and mortgage the marital home to support his habit?

The Use of Guidelines in Alimony Determinations

Unlike child support awards, which are based on guidelines in all states in response to a federal mandate, there is no requirement that states adopt guidelines for spousal support. As a result, there is little consistency among the states, or even among individual judges, with respect to alimony awards. To address this lack of consistency and predictability, the American Law Institute recommends, and some jurisdictions and individual judges[21] have moved toward, the adoption of computational guidelines for spousal support awards. An increasing number of states (and counties within states) have experimented with and implemented guidelines in an effort to improve efficiency, decrease litigation, and provide predictability in this area.[22]

The Rise and Fall of Rehabilitative Alimony?

In the early 1970s at the outset of no-fault reform, the assumption was that if a wife received an equal or equitable share of the marital property and was employed, she should be able to be self-supporting. If not, the most she should require would be short-term transitional support allowing her to strengthen her job skills and reenter the workforce. On the surface, reliance on short-term rehabilitative alimony made sense.

But the reality is that despite the movement and the constitutional mandate that alimony statutes be gender neutral, traditional ways of thinking still persist, and both marriage and alimony remain heavily gendered in practice. Even though women have made great strides since the 1970s, they are still on the underside of the glass ceiling, on average earn less than men, receive the overwhelming majority of alimony awards, and are disproportionately represented on the welfare rolls. Women continue to be more likely than men in the context of marriage and the family to make sacrifices that reduce their earning potential when they exit the marriage. As a result, they are also more likely to experience a decline in their standard of living post marriage than are men, who have been less hampered by domestic contributions during the marriage. Consistent with this perspective, legislators in states that have historically placed restrictions on the duration of alimony have begun to reexamine their statutes. Perhaps the Massachusetts appellate court expressed this view best in the *Bak* case:

> In a marriage during which the wife has remained out of the work force for some time and has been the primary caretaker of the children (while the husband advanced his career), her likelihood of becoming self-sufficient has to be considered with care. Unless rehabilitation is proved probable, the husband's support responsibilities may be of extended duration. . . . This has nothing to do with feminism, sexism, male chauvinism or any other trendy social ideology. It is ordinary common sense, basic decency and simple justice.[23]

The shift to a view of alimony as compensation is reflected in an Illinois maintenance statute that requires a court to consider, among other factors, "any impairment of the present and future earning capacity of the party seeking maintenance due to that party devoting time to domestic duties or having forgone or delayed education, training, employment or career opportunities due to the marriage."[24] The *Sutphin* case in Ohio (see Case 10.10) falls short of actually endorsing a loss-of-income-production-capacity method to determine a maintenance obligation, but the trial court clearly took such an approach, labeling the award to the wife "compensatory spousal support."

CASE **10.10** *Sutphin v. Sutphin*, 2004 Ohio 6844 (Ohio App. 2004)

DISCUSSION OF THE CASE

Prior to the parties' marriage, they had signed a premarital agreement in which the wife agreed to be a stay-at-home parent. Per the agreement, the wife quit her job and did not work outside the home until their one minor child graduated from high school. At the time of the divorce, the husband earned about $500,000 a year. At trial, the court heard testimony from an economist about the value of the wife's total projected earnings. Ann Crittenden, author of the book *The Price of Motherhood*, also testified regarding lost income opportunities of stay-at-home mothers.

In its award, the trial court took the total projected earnings of the wife, subtracted the projected earnings for the period after the minor child graduated from high school, and subtracted an amount attributable to the duration of the parties' marriage. Based on this calculation, the court awarded the wife $1,415,620 in what it termed "compensatory spousal support" payable in $9,000 monthly installments over approximately thirteen years. The husband appealed, and the Ohio intermediate appellate court affirmed the lower court's decision, albeit with reservations about the characterization of the award as "compensatory." The reservation was based on the fact that the phrase "compensatory spousal support" was not found anywhere in the state's maintenance statute.

SIDEBAR

The entire opinion in this case is available on the companion website. Do you agree with the court's decision? Explain your response.

THE ROLE OF THE PARALEGAL IN A SPOUSAL SUPPORT CASE

The tasks most commonly performed by a paralegal in a spousal support case are:

- researching current governing law (statutes and case law) regarding spousal support in the applicable jurisdiction
- scheduling and participating in interviews as assigned
- making discovery-related recommendations and drafting discovery requests as instructed, with particular attention to the factors the court will consider when making the spousal support decision
- drafting complaints, motions, supporting affidavits, and proposed orders (including motions for temporary support)
- drafting spousal support provisions for inclusion in separation agreements
- assisting in identification and preparation of prospective witnesses
- drafting a pretrial memorandum, if required, advising the court of the merits of the client's request for alimony
- assisting with gathering and preparation of exhibits related to spousal support requests for use in negotiations and at hearings and trial
- drafting proposed findings of fact and conclusions of law addressing each of the factors to be considered by the court
- tracking progress on the case to be sure all deadlines are met
- making sure the client is kept informed about progress on the case, upcoming deadlines, and hearings, etc.

CHAPTER **SUMMARY**

Alimony awards are allowances ordered by a court for support and maintenance of one spouse payable by the other spouse. Parties to a marriage now frequently create their own agreements with respect to spousal support and often waive their respective rights to alimony in those agreements. Since the onset of the no-fault era in the 1970s, the primary vehicle for allocating marital resources upon divorce is property division, and only a small percentage of divorce decrees provide for alimony. The majority of those awards are made to wives, although women are now generally viewed as capable of providing for their own needs. At least by law, alimony has become gender neutral based on the U.S. Supreme Court ruling in the 1979 case *Orr v. Orr.*

Although there is considerable variation across the country, it appears that most state legislatures and courts are willing to explore creative ways of providing for dependent spouses and especially for those who would otherwise end up on public assistance. The most common types of alimony are temporary, permanent, term, lump-sum, rehabilitative, and restitution. The types vary primarily with respect to purpose, duration, and conditions governing termination and modification.

Unlike child support awards, which are based on guidelines established in each state, there are few guidelines for determining when alimony will be awarded, in what amount, and for what purpose or duration. Alimony decisions are largely left up to the discretion of individual judges, and awards cannot be overturned absent an abuse of discretion. In making alimony determinations, courts consider a variety of factors established by statute and case law and assign weights to the factors according to the facts of each case. Given the limited assets in most marriages, the initial focus is usually on relative need and ability to pay. Other commonly considered factors include the length of the marriage, the age of the parties, the employability and earning capacity of each spouse, and the standard of living that characterized the marriage. About half of the states consider marital fault, particularly misconduct with economic consequences, relevant to alimony decisions.

Given the complexity of this topic and the diversity in its treatment among the states, this chapter initially describes a generic approach to the issue of alimony and then references a number of jurisdictional variations and cases. Because alimony cases are fact-intensive, the paralegal applications focus on locating governing law and procedure and gathering and organizing information to support the client's position in the context of that law. A limited number of tax and bankruptcy issues related to alimony are briefly described, although the family law paralegal's role in these complex areas is likely to be limited.

This chapter began by tracing the evolution of spousal support from its origins under ecclesiastical and common law as a lifetime duty of a husband to support his wife. It concludes with a view to future trends with respect to alimony. The current lack of predictability in this area results in increased labor for the family law team, uncertainty for the client, and escalated costs—both emotional and financial. The combination of these pressures is likely to lead in the future to a decreased emphasis on fault and an increased development and use of guidelines.

KEY **TERMS**

Absolute divorce
Alimony
Alimony recapture rule
Annulment
Canon law
Civil contempt
Criminal contempt
Discharge
Divorce *a mensa et thoro*
Divorce *a vinculo matrimonii*
Forensic accountant

Legal separation
Lump-sum alimony/alimony
   in gross
Married Women's Property Acts
Material change in circumstances
No-fault ground
Permanent alimony
Premarital agreement
Prima facie showing
Public charge
Quid pro quo

Rehabilitative alimony
Restitution/reimbursement alimony
Separation agreement
Spousal support
Surviving agreement
Temporary alimony/alimony
   pendente lite
Term alimony
Vest
Waiver
Writ *ne exeat*

REVIEW **QUESTIONS**

1. Define spousal support/alimony and identify its purpose.
2. Contrast the approaches to alimony in the fault and no-fault contexts.
3. Describe how a premarital agreement might influence whether or not a spouse obtains alimony.
4. Describe the significance of the *Orr* decision.

5. Distinguish between alimony and property division.

6. Describe the nature and purpose of "permanent" alimony.

7. Describe lump-sum or alimony in gross. How is it different from other forms of alimony in its nature and effect?

8. Define rehabilitative alimony and identify its primary purpose.

9. Define restitution/reimbursement alimony and indicate how it differs from other forms of alimony.

10. Identify the type or types of alimony that might be granted to a spouse who supported his or her spouse while the latter pursued a graduate degree during the marriage.

11. Identify the kinds of factors courts will consider when making alimony determinations.

12. Describe the kinds of evidence that need to be gathered to document the parties' standard of living during the marriage when significant assets are involved.

13. Identify the general rule governing modifications of alimony awards.

14. Identify a minimum of three events that commonly result in the termination of an alimony obligation.

15. Describe the basic tax rule applicable to alimony awards with respect to includability and deductibility.

16. Describe how bankruptcy law treats property division and spousal support awards.

FOCUS ON **THE JOB**

THE FACTS

Jim Jones, thirty, has been married to Julie Jones, twenty-nine, for seven years. They have two children, Morgan, age four, and Freeman, age six. When they got married, Jim was in his senior year of college and planning to graduate the following June and go on to get his master's degree in education. His lifelong dream has been to be a teacher. However, Julie got pregnant right after they were married and stopped working for a year. As a result, Jim dropped out of college and went to work in a local steak house, waiting on tables. He continues to work part-time waiting tables and earns about $500 per week. He gets no employment benefits.

Freeman was born on January 12 six years ago, and right after he was born, Julie enrolled in law school. She received some financial aid and took out substantial student loans to support the cost of most of her tuition and books. Jim paid the remainder of her educational expenses as well as the household expenses for the three years she was in law school. Julie did not work at all because she wanted to put all her energy into her studies. She graduated with high honors and was promptly hired at a major urban law firm where she had interned for a semester. Her supervisor was Marcus Tye, a senior partner in the firm. She and Mr. Tye became very close and Jim has reason to believe that he and Julie are having an affair, given that Attorney Tye's wife recently filed for divorce. Although he doesn't know for sure, Jim believes Tye's wife is claiming that her husband is having an affair with some new employee at the office.

While Julie was going to school and for the couple of years she has been working, the parties agreed that Jim would stay home and manage the household and be primary caretaker for the children. He really didn't mind, because he loves the children and always figured that his turn would come once Julie got settled in her $170,000-a-year job, where she receives bonuses of varying amounts each year and benefits including medical insurance and a pension plan. Jim and the children are presently covered by her insurance.

The parties' only asset is the marital home, which is valued at $350,000, and they are carrying a $150,000 mortgage.

Jim's parents gave them the $50,000 for the down payment when Jim and Julie bought it. They have been very generous to the couple and frequently picked up the slack when debts piled up and upset Jim. They figured he had enough stress. The way Jim dealt with his stress (to no one's knowledge) was to gamble, and his gambling often ate up his paychecks. He also ran up substantial credit card debt taking cash advances. He did have a few big hits, though, and has hidden away about $70,000, which no one knows about.

Jim recently told Julie that he feels the time has come for him to go back to school and resume his career goals. He said she is making plenty of money now and could support their expenses along with day care for the kids. In response, Julie said she had been meaning to talk with him about her desire to get a divorce and move on. It was nothing personal, she said, just that their individual lives have evolved in different directions. The life they had shared was too "low-end" for her. She said she wants to start living "the good life." He can plod along watching DVDs and going to amusement parks with the kids for vacations, but she wants more. Jim is very hurt and angry but said he will make the best of a bad deal, and she can pay him support so that he can get his life back on track. She told him that he had to be kidding and then left the house and hasn't come home since. He is not sure where she is.

THE ASSIGNMENT

Jim has decided to file for divorce and is hoping to negotiate an agreement with Julie, who will be representing herself in the divorce. Although his initial bargaining position may be tougher, your supervisor, Attorney Tauson, has asked you to draft a reasonable alimony provision for inclusion in a potential separation agreement. The provision should be tailored to the facts of the case and be sufficiently defensible that a court in your state would approve it. You should research some models and be sure to reflect what you have learned reading this chapter about the nature of alimony provisions and the various types of alimony that may be available.

FOCUS ON **ETHICS**

The family law firm where you are employed (Wilson and Tauson, LLP) represents Jim in the above fact pattern. You have been interviewing Jim and gathering information from him regarding his divorce and claim for alimony. You and Jim have become quite friendly, and he apparently trusts you. Today, when the two of you met regarding the case, Jim asked if you could "grab a bite to eat" with him at the local delicatessen. It was lunchtime and you needed to eat, so you decided to go and insist on paying for your own lunch so that Jim would not get the wrong impression. While eating lunch, Jim shares with you the fact that as a result of his gambling, he has accumulated nearly $70,000 in cash, which he has kept at home in a bureau drawer. He tells

you that Julie doesn't know about the cash and he doesn't plan to tell her about it or declare it on his financial statement, because he doesn't want her to get any of it. He is going to move to a small apartment in a tough neighborhood and doesn't want to take the money with him. He asks if you would be willing to hold it in safekeeping for him and says that he will give you 10 percent of it if you do. He tells you not to answer right away and to think about it. You tell him that if you do not agree to hold the cash, your supervisor will. What are you going to do? Why? Relate your response to the ethical canons for paralegals promulgated by the National Federation of Paralegal Associations (NFPA), which are contained in Appendix B.

FOCUS ON **CASE LAW**

The Iowa Supreme Court case, *In re the Marriage of Olson,* 705 N.W.2d 312 (Iowa 2005), is located on the companion website for this text in the material related to Chapter 10. Locate and read the case and then respond to the following questions.

1. Describe the legal history of the case.
2. What issue is addressed in the appeal to the Iowa Supreme Court?
3. Briefly describe the facts of the case.
4. How did the district court treat the husband's overtime income? Was it included in his income for purposes of calculating alimony? Did the state's high court agree with this approach?

5. What factors are considered by Iowa courts when determining whether or not an award of alimony is appropriate? Where are those factors set forth?
6. Describe the types of alimony considered by the court in this case.
7. Which type of alimony did the court conclude was appropriate and why?
8. Explain how the court factored the wife's gambling into the alimony decision, if at all.
9. What was the decision of the Iowa Supreme Court in this case?
10. What was the essence of Justice Carter's concurring opinion?

FOCUS ON **STATE LAW AND PROCEDURE**

Locate the statute(s) and/or case law in your jurisdiction governing initial alimony awards. Identify the factors considered by the courts in making alimony determinations. Assume that in your capacity as a paralegal in the firm of Wilson and Tauson, LLP, you have been asked by your supervisor, Attorney Tauson, to assess Jim Jones' prospects for receiving an alimony award in your state based on those factors. Present your findings in an internal memorandum using the format below. Be sure to include a list of the factors. Is marital fault relevant, and, if so, under what circumstances? Do any of the sources you located specify the kinds of support that can be awarded? If yes, which kind would be appropriate in this case, if any?

MEMORANDUM

To: *Your Supervisor*

From: *Your name, paralegal*

Re: *Assessment of James Jones' Claim for Alimony*

Date:

Description of assignment: *What is it that you have been asked to do?*

Results of Research: *Describe the applicable statute(s)/ case law.*

Discussion: *Apply the governing law to the specific facts of Jim's case.*

Conclusion: *What is your opinion about the client's likelihood of success with respect to his claim for alimony?*

FOCUS ON **TECHNOLOGY**

Websites of Interest

http://www.divorceonline.com

This site provides a wide range of articles and information on various aspects of divorce. It includes links to state divorce laws. Click on Professional Resources and then on State Divorce Laws.

http://www.divorcehelp.com

This site is operated by a lawyer. One of the resources it provides is a copy of "A Short Divorce Course" for people considering and/or going through a divorce.

http://www.divorcenet.com

This site offers family law advice on divorce. It provides links to state resource pages that contain a wealth of articles and links on a variety of topics, including alimony.

http://divorcelinks.com

This site provides direct links to state and federal divorce law by topic.

http://www.findlaw.com

A search on "spousal support" will prove fruitful. The site offers alimony information by state along with articles on types of alimony and criteria for awards.

Assignments

1. Using online resources, locate the factors considered by the court when making alimony determinations in three states: California, New York, and Pennsylvania.

2. Go to the website for the U.S. Department of Labor (*www.dol.gov*) and locate information about COBRA health insurance coverage post-divorce.

3. Go to *www.abanet.org,* the website for the American Bar Association. Search for the chart on alimony/spousal support factors (Chart 1) that contains a state-by-state summary indicating:

   • which states have a statutory list of factors for courts to consider when making alimony decisions

   • which states consider marital fault

   • which states consider standard of living

   • which states consider a party's status as a custodial parent

   • what did you learn about your state from this resource?

chapter **eleven**

PROPERTY DIVISION

Jimmy and Alice had been married for ten years and lived a comfortable life with their three children—that was until Alice had an affair with her boss and Jimmy found out about it. He says he will make her pay for hurting the family like that. He tells his lawyer he wants to file for divorce on the grounds of adultery and that he intends to win at all costs. She will walk away with nothing.

IN THIS CHAPTER YOU WILL LEARN

- What the differences are between alimony and property division

- What the five phases of the property division process are

- What the differences are between separate and marital property

- What kinds of property are subject to division when a marriage dissolves

- How the community property and equitable distribution approaches to property division differ from each other

- What role conduct plays in the division of marital property

- What some of the options are for dividing major marital assets, such as pensions and the marital home

- How liabilities are allocated when a marriage dissolves

- What some of the tax implications of property division are

- What the paralegal's role is in the property division process

INTRODUCTION

Jimmy makes a naïve assumption in the opening scenario. It is naïve in the sense that no one really "wins" in a divorce. Each party ends up materially with less than he or she had during the marriage and is often emotionally bankrupt as well. The old idea that a wronged spouse can somehow punish his or her former partner, "get everything," and make him or her pay forever largely passed from the legal scene more than three decades ago with the coming of no-fault divorce.

Marriage is now viewed more as an economic partnership than as a romantic, lifelong union. Complaints for divorce on the grounds of irreconcilable differences are rarely denied, and marriages are dissolved as if they were business partnerships. Marital Property is divided between the spouses based on an assumption that, since marriage is a partnership, when it dissolves both parties have an interest in the marital assets and should be held accountable for the liabilities incurred during the process. Generally, courts first divide the marital estate and then, if allowed in the jurisdiction, make a determination with respect to whether or not an alimony award is also appropriate. A comprehensive comparison of property division and alimony is provided in Chapter 10 in Exhibit 10.1. The major distinctions between the two are as follows:

Alimony

- originated in the common law duty of a husband to support his wife
- requires personal jurisdiction over the parties
- is based on need and ability to pay
- is no longer primarily punitive in nature
- vests as payments fall due
- is usually in the form of periodic cash payments
- is modifiable in most states, given a material change of circumstances
- is tax deductible to the payor and income to the recipient
- is usually not dischargeable in bankruptcy
- usually terminates upon remarriage of the recipient
- usually terminates with the death of either party (except for arrearages)

Property Division

- evolved with no-fault divorce and an emphasis on marriage as a partnership
- requires jurisdiction over the parties and the property to be divided
- is based on the concept that both parties contributed to the marital enterprise and each party is entitled to a share of the partnership upon dissolution
- may be influenced by serious misconduct during the marriage
- vests as of the date of the divorce
- usually involves transfers of property
- is rarely modifiable absent fraud
- involves nontaxable transfers of property
- is dischargeable in bankruptcy with limited exceptions
- is unaffected by the remarriage of either party
- is enforceable in favor of or against a decedent's estate

THE FIVE PHASES OF THE PROPERTY DIVISION PROCESS

Property division is a complex and often emotionally charged topic. Although specific approaches, procedural rules, and case law vary from state to state, the basic process remains constant. It essentially involves five phases, each of which addresses a specific task:

Paralegal Practice Tip

Although the parties may not appreciate the distinction between alimony and property division, it is especially significant in the tax or bankruptcy context. In most circumstances it is best to label payments or transfers as either alimony or property division to avoid confusion and post-divorce litigation. However, language in the parties' agreements or labels in family court orders are not necessarily determinative in every context. The IRS and bankruptcy courts make their own determinations as to the character of each transaction.

Paralegal Practice Tip

A list of definitions relating to types of property (real and personal, tangible and intangible, etc.) and forms of ownership is available on the companion website for readers seeking an introduction to or review of basic property concepts.

1. Definition of property: What is "property" and what property do the parties have?
2. Classification of property: Is the property "separate" or "marital" property?
3. Identification of property subject to division upon divorce: Which property can the courts reach to effectuate a division of property?
4. Valuation of property: What is the property worth—how and when is it valued?
5. Division of property: How is property divided—what approaches do the courts apply?

Definition of Property

The threshold question in a property division case is, "Does a particular asset fall within a definition of 'property'?" In most cases, this question does not even arise because the parties' only assets are clearly property, such as automobiles, household furnishings, bank accounts, or a marital home, but some cases involve assets that are less clearly "property." Assets that are mere expectancies (such as possible inheritances or future earning capacity) or that have no presently determinable value (such as a patent on an obscure engine part) will generally not be considered property subject to division.

It is important that all actual and potential assets and liabilities be identified. A failure to identify, value, and seek distribution for the client may amount to malpractice if significant assets are overlooked. Before even filing for divorce, counsel will usually ask the client to identify (and document where possible) the tangible and intangible "property" the parties may have. Clients often initially fail to recognize the nature and extent of property they and/or their spouses may own that has value. They need, therefore, to be encouraged to think in broad terms. This process can be facilitated by the completion of a client questionnaire, such as the sample provided on the companion website for this text in the material related to Chapter 6. Exhibit 11.1 provides some examples of "property" that may be subject to division upon divorce. Some of the types of property listed are not uniformly considered property, but a sound and creative legal argument can often be persuasive.

EXHIBIT 11.1 Property Potentially Subject to Division

- annuity contracts
- antiques, heirlooms
- appreciation in the value of property during the marriage, depending on whether it involves separate or marital property and active or passive appreciation (See Paralegal Application 11.2.)
- artwork
- bank accounts (checking, savings, credit union, etc.)
- boats
- bonuses
- business interests (sole proprietorships, corporations, partnerships, etc.)
- cash
- certificates of deposit
- clothing (including furs, etc.)
- club memberships (social, golf, tennis, yacht, etc.)[1]
- collectibles (guns, china, figurines, stamps, coins, baseball cards, etc.)[2]
- contingent fee agreements[3]

continued

Paralegal Practice Tip
For a court to issue an enforceable order dividing the **marital estate,** the court must have personal jurisdiction over the parties and jurisdiction over the property to be divided. If the court lacks jurisdiction, its order can be attacked on jurisdictional grounds and may not be entitled to full faith and credit. As indicated in Chapter 1, the paralegal often gathers the information the attorney needs to address such jurisdictional issues.

Marital estate
the property acquired during the marriage other than by gift or inheritance that is subject to division at the time of marital dissolution

- contracts (such as a professional athlete's contract)[4]
- copyrights, patents, and trademarks
- deferred compensation
- disability awards (See Paralegal Application 11.2.)
- employment "perks" (housing, car, parking space, etc.)
- frequent-flier miles
- furniture and appliances
- gifts
- goodwill of a business (See Case 11.1.)
- governmental benefits
- inheritances
- insurance policies with cash-surrender values
- jewelry
- licenses (e.g., pilot's license or a taxi medallion)
- lottery winnings[5]
- motor vehicles including cars, trucks, recreational vehicles, motorcycles, trailers, etc.
- mutual funds
- pending lawsuits and judgments
- pension plans (IRAs, 401(k)s, etc.)
- personal injury awards (See Paralegal Application 11.2.)
- pets/companion animals (See Case 11.2.)[6]
- professional degrees (See Case 11.3 and Paralegal Application 11.1.)
- profit sharing plans
- real estate (residence, vacation homes, rental property, time-shares, cemetery lots, deeded rights to parking spaces, etc.)
- season tickets to athletic events, theaters, concerts, and other cultural events
- silverware
- social security benefits[7]
- stocks and bonds
- stock options (vested and unvested)[8]
- tax refunds and overpayment of state and federal taxes
- trusts (beneficial interests)
- vacation or sick leave time (See Paralegal Application 11.2.)
- worker's compensation benefits[9]

Paralegal Practice Tip

Occasionally, despite the best efforts of a client and the family law team, an asset concealed by the other party will not be discovered until after entry of the judgment dissolving the parties' marriage and dividing their assets. Although property distributions are generally held to be final and not subject to modification, courts will sometimes reopen a case based on discovery of additional assets concealed at the time of the divorce.[10]

PARALEGAL APPLICATION 11.1

TO BE OR NOT TO BE PROPERTY

There are some things that look like property but that may or may not be considered property, depending on the jurisdiction: Consider, for example, the following:

THE PROFESSIONAL GOODWILL OF A BUSINESS:

Goodwill has been defined as "the favor which the management of a business has won from the public and probability that old customers will continue their patronage."[11] The financial value of goodwill sometimes can be determined by an

continued

expert. When goodwill is based on personal characteristics of a party or is intrinsically tied to the attributes and skills of a particular individual, most states do not consider it to be property subject to division, because the value of the goodwill cannot be sold—it does not survive the disassociation of the individual from the business. However, goodwill that is wholly attributable to a commercial business, such as a hardware store, the business itself, its location and customer lists, etc., may be considered property subject to valuation and division upon divorce.[12] (See Case 11.1.)

PETS:

Family pets can present an emotionally challenging issue for parties to a divorce. Some spouses provide for "custody and visitation" with treasured pets by formal agreement and others do so by informal cooperative arrangements. When disputed, most of the few courts that have considered this issue have determined that pets are personal property subject to division but that there is no authority for a trial court to grant custody or visitation of pets.[13] (See Case 11.2.)

A PROFESSIONAL DEGREE OR LICENSE:

A majority of jurisdictions hold that a professional degree (J.D., M.D., Ph.D., etc.) does not possess the basic characteristics of marital property. "It is personal to the holder; it cannot be sold, transferred, pledged, or inherited. It does not have an assignable value, nor does it represent a guarantee of receipt of a set monetary amount in the future...."[14] "A degree only gives the owner a speculative increase in future earnings, which is affected by so many other influences and factors that it can hardly be considered more than a future expectancy. It certainly does not award the holder any guaranteed monetary amount or current specific rights of an ascertainable value, which may be distributed equitably."[15] Even if the degree was earned during the marriage and marital funds were used to pay for related expenses, the degree is still not necessarily a marital asset. Most states choose to consider degrees earned during marriage in the spousal support context. For example, a court may choose to award reimbursement or restitution alimony to a spouse who worked to support the family unit while the other spouse earned a degree. Case 11.3 presents the minority view that professional degrees constitute marital property that should be assigned a value based on evidence offered through an expert witness if not agreed upon by the parties.

CASE 11.1 *Traczyk v. Traczyk*, 1995 OK 22, 891 P.2d 1277 (1995)

BACKGROUND

In this case, a husband appealed a trial court's consideration of the goodwill of his medical practice as an element of the marital property to be divided between the parties. He testified that the reason clients came to the clinic was because of him and that few would remain as patients if he sold his foot clinic practice. He claimed that such goodwill could not be valued and sold as part of the business, because it was personal to him. The Oklahoma Supreme Court affirmed the decision of the trial court. This case also addresses the distinctions among property division, alimony, and alimony in lieu of property division.

continued

FROM THE OPINION

The professional practice of one spouse is an appropriate element of the marital property to be divided between the parties where it is jointly acquired property. *Ford v. Ford,* 766 P.2d 950 (Okla. 1988);... The issue before us is whether goodwill of Husband's podiatry practice may be considered in determining the value of the practice.

Pursuant to 60 O.S. 1991 §§ 315 and 316, goodwill of a business is defined as "the expectation of continued public patronage," and is considered property transferable like any other property....

In determining the value of the Bethany Foot Clinic, the expert witness consulted the Goodwill Registry, "an accumulation of information concerning sales of medical related practices by experts." From this publication, the expert determined that of the most recent purchases of podiatry clinics, an average of thirty-two percent (32%) of the podiatry patients stay with the clinic after it is sold to a new doctor. The range from which he obtained the average was 21% to 44% of clients staying.

Noting that the traditional method used in valuing a medical practice is the previous year's gross income, the expert then took the previous year's gross income at the clinic ($324,201.51) and multiplied it by the 32% figure to arrive at a goodwill value of $103,744.00. Adding this to the value of the remaining business assets, the expert found the total value of the Bethany Foot Clinic to be $152,605.44. The trial court accepted this valuation and used it in determining how much alimony in lieu of property division to award.

We find that the trial court did not err in considering the goodwill of the Bethany Foot Clinic as a factor in determining the value of the clinic as marital property. The goodwill of the Bethany Foot Clinic is distinct from the personal reputation of Dr. Traczyk. Although many of Dr. Traczyk's patients would not continue to patronize the Bethany Foot Clinic were Dr. Traczyk to sell to another podiatrist, competent evidence indicates that many would stay. Indeed, Dr. Traczyk may use the goodwill as a selling point to potential purchasers.

If goodwill is to be divided as an asset, its value should be determined either by an agreement or by its fair market value. Both of these methods are widely accepted for valuing goodwill. See annotation, 78 A.L.R.4th 853, 860–71 (1987). Mocnik, 838 P.2d at 505.

The goodwill of the Bethany Foot Clinic was valued as an asset and was a factor in determining the total value of the business for property division purposes. This goodwill was part of the property which should be divided between the parties; Wife had a right to receive her share of the property. 43 O.S. 1991, §121. On the other hand, the award of support alimony was a separate determination based upon Husband's ability to pay and Wife's demonstrated need.... Although the property division is permanent and irrevocable, the award of support alimony is subject to modification upon a showing of substantial change in circumstances, i.e. Husband's ability and/or Wife's demonstrated need. 43 O.S. 1991, §134; *Clifton v. Clifton,* 801 P.2d 693 (Okla. 1990).

By awarding support alimony and including goodwill in the value of the business for property division purposes, the trial court did not "double dip" into Husband's future income. Both awards, one for support alimony and one for alimony in lieu of property division were proper and distinct from the other....

SIDEBAR

The entire opinion in this case is available on the companion website. Do you agree with the court's decision? Explain your response.

CASE **11.2** *Bennett v. Bennett,* 655 So.2d 109 (Fla. App. 1995)

BACKGROUND

In this case, a Florida appellate court considered a husband's appeal of a trial court's decision to award his wife visitation with the parties' dog.

FROM THE OPINION

...[T]he trial court's ruling...reads:

7. *Dog. Roddy:* The former husband...shall have custody of the parties' dog "Roddy" and the former wife...shall have visitation every other month beginning October 1, 1993. The visitation shall begin on the first day of the month and end on the last day of the month.

Based on the history of this case, there is every reason to believe that there will be continued squabbling between the parties concerning the dog.

While a dog may be considered by many to be a member of the family, under Florida law, animals are considered to be personal property.... There is no authority which provides for a trial court to grant custody or visitation pertaining to personal property....

While several states have given family pets special status within dissolution proceedings (for example, see *Arrington v. Arrington,* 613 S.W.2d 565 (Tex. App. 1981)), we think such a course is unwise. Determinations as to custody and visitation lead to continuing enforcement and supervision problems (as evidenced by the proceedings in the instant case). Our courts are overwhelmed with the supervision of custody, visitation, and support matters related to the protection of our children. We cannot undertake the same responsibility as to animals.

While the trial judge was endeavoring to reach a fair solution under difficult circumstances, we must reverse the order relating to the custody of "Roddy," and remand for the trial court to award the animal pursuant to the dictates of the equitable division statute.

SIDEBAR

The entire opinion in this case is available on the companion website. In the family law context, do you believe pets should be treated as personal property and distributed like other assets or treated more like children for whom custody and visitation determinations need to be made? Explain your answer.

CASE **11.3** *Woodworth v. Woodworth,* 126 Mich. App. 258, 337 N.W.2d 332 (1983)

BACKGROUND

In this case, a Michigan appeals court considered the issue of whether a law degree is subject to distribution and adopted the minority view that it is. During their marriage, the plaintiff, Michael Woodworth, and his wife, Ann, had relocated their family to Detroit so that Michael would be able to attend law school and increase his earning capacity for the benefit of the family. He subsequently graduated, passed the bar, and practiced law, first as an attorney with the court of appeals and later as a partner in a Lansing law firm. The trial court held that the law degree was property valued at $20,000 and awarded this amount to the wife in payments of

continued

$2,000 over ten years, the length of the period between the parties' wedding and date of separation. The husband appealed the order, contending that the degree was not a marital asset subject to division.

FROM THE OPINION

The basic issue in this case is whether or not plaintiff's law degree is marital property subject to distribution....

The facts reveal that plaintiff's law degree was the end product of a concerted family effort. Both parties planned their family life around the effort to attain plaintiff's degree. Toward this end, the family divided the daily tasks encountered in living. While the law degree did not pre-empt all other facets of their lives, it did become the main focus and goal of their activities....

We conclude, therefore, that plaintiff's law degree was the result of mutual sacrifice and effort by both plaintiff and defendant. While plaintiff studied and attended classes, defendant carried her share of the burden as well as sharing vicariously in the stress of the experience known as the "paper chase."

We believe that fairness dictates that the spouse who did not earn an advanced degree be compensated whenever the advanced degree is the product of such concerted family investment. The degree holder has expended great effort to obtain the degree not only for himself or herself, but also to benefit the family as a whole. The other spouse has shared in this effort and contributed in other ways as well, not merely as a gift to the student spouse nor merely to share individually in the benefits but to help the marital unit as a whole.

...a marriage is not intrinsically a commercial enterprise. Instead it is a relationship sanctioned by law governed at its essence by fidelity and troth. Neither partner usually expects to be compensated for his or her efforts. But that consideration does not end the discussion. We are not presently concerned with how best to characterize a marriage while it endures. Instead, we are concerned with how best to distribute between the parties what they have once the marriage has for all intents and purposes dissolved. In other words:

> "To allow a student spouse *** to leave a marriage with all the benefits of additional education and a professional license without compensation to the spouse who bore much of the burdens incident to procuring these would be unfair ***." O'Brien, supra, 452 NYS2d 805.

...Defendant is not asking us to compensate for a failed expectation that her husband would become a wealthy lawyer and subsequently support her for the rest of her life. Instead, she is merely seeking her share of the fruits of a degree which she helped him earn. We fail to see the difference between compensating her for a degree which she helped him earn and compensating her for a house in his name which her earnings helped him buy.

...Clearly, in this case, the degree was a family investment, rather than a gift or a benefit to the degree holder alone. Treating the degree as such a gift would unjustly enrich the degree holder to the extent that the degree's value exceeds its cost....

SIDEBAR

The entire opinion in this case is available on the companion website. The holding reflects the minority position on the question of whether or not professional degrees earned during a marriage constitute marital property subject to division. Do you agree that degrees should be considered marital property? Why? If they are deemed property, what factors should a court consider when placing a value on the degree? How else might they be handled?

Classification of Property as Separate or Marital

Generally, the parties begin acquiring ***marital property*** at the commencement of the marriage and cease to do so at the time of separation, the filing of the complaint for divorce, or as of the date of the divorce decree. Many states have legislatively established statutory definitions of marital and separate property.[16] The section of the West Virginia Code defining marital and separate property is available on the companion website. The South Carolina legislature has defined marital property as "all real and personal property which has been acquired by the parties during the marriage and which is owned as of the date of filing or commencement of marital litigation...."[17] Marital property excludes ***separate property*** but usually includes property classified as marital regardless of how title to that property is held. For example, the deed to the marital home may be in the name of both parties as tenants by the entirety, joint tenants with rights of survivorship, or solely in the name of one spouse. Most states exempt from marital property gifts and inheritances received by either of the parties from third parties during the marriage, but some consider interspousal gifts purchased with joint funds to be marital property. Some states distinguish between segregated separate property and separate property supported, maintained, and improved with marital funds and time.

Sometimes classification of property as separate or marital is especially challenging. (See Paralegal Application 11.2.) When a division of property action involves immovable property such as real estate in another state, the basic choice of law rule is that the law of the *situs* (the place where the property is situated) will govern all rights, title, and interests in and to the property. Depending on the location of the property, it may be necessary for the paralegal to research the governing law of another jurisdiction to determine whether a particular asset is likely to be treated as separate or marital.[18]

Marital property
property that is acquired by either or both parties during the marriage, other than by inheritance or gift from a third party

Separate property
property that a spouse owned before marriage or acquired during the marriage by inheritance or gift from a third party; may include property acquired during marriage in exchange for separate property

---

PARALEGAL APPLICATION 11.2

SEPARATE OR MARITAL PROPERTY?

Some kinds of property may be difficult to classify as separate or marital. Consider the following:

DISABILITY AWARDS:

"The majority of courts contemplating the proper classification of disability benefits have adopted an approach which focuses on the underlying purpose of the specific disability benefits at issue. Thus, benefits that actually compensate for disability are classified as separate property because they are personal to the spouse who receives them. However, where justified by the particular facts of a case, courts adopting this approach have separated the benefits into a retirement component and a true disability component, classifying the retirement component as marital property and the disability component as separate property."[19] In determining the character of disability benefits in a specific case, courts usually will look at several factors:

- Does a state statute specifically exclude them from marital property?
- Are the benefits the result of a private disability policy paid for with marital funds?
- Are the benefits compensation for past services rendered during the marriage?
- Did the right to receive benefits result from employment during the marriage?

continued

- Do the benefits replace future income?
- Does the benefit compensate for lost earning capacity?
- Does the benefit represent retirement pay earned during the marriage?
- Did the parties discuss the benefit and view it as a joint investment to secure their future?

PERSONAL INJURY AWARDS:

As with disability payments, the courts will customarily look at the purpose(s) served by the award. The West Virginia Supreme Court of Appeals expressed it this way: "…to the extent that its purpose is to compensate an individual for pain, suffering, disability, disfigurement, or other debilitation of the mind or body, a personal injury award constitutes the separate nonmarital property of an injured spouse. However,…economic losses, such as past wages and medical expenses, which diminish the marital estate are distributable as marital property when recovered in a personal injury award or settlement."[20]

APPRECIATION IN THE VALUE OF SEPARATE PROPERTY:

Property owned by one of the parties prior to marriage often appreciates in value during the marriage. For example, assume that the husband had a stock portfolio worth $10,000 prior to the marriage. He knew little about managing stocks and had essentially let the market take its course. During the marriage, the wife read several books and enrolled in two workshops addressing investment strategies. The husband let her "play" with the account and over the course of their ten-year marriage, the account increased in value to $100,000. Thirty percent of that increase ($30,000) was attributable to market trends and would have occurred had the parties taken no action whatsoever (known as *passive appreciation*). However, $60,000 of the increase was a direct result of the wife's effective management of the account (known as *active appreciation*). Although the stocks are not registered in the wife's name, the increase in value (particularly the $60,000) derived during the marriage may well be considered marital property subject to division. In most jurisdictions, the husband's share would be $70,000 (his initial $10,000, the $30,000 passive appreciation, and half of the $60,000 active appreciation during the marriage). The wife's share would be $30,000 (half of the active appreciation during the marriage). A minority of jurisdictions would consider the full amount of appreciation to be separate property based on the nature of the underlying asset as separate.

ACCRUED VACATION OR SICK LEAVE TIME:

The courts that have considered these assets are divided. If an employee will be paid the value of accrued vacation or sick leave time at some point, courts may construe time credits that accrued during the marriage as a marital asset divisible upon divorce. However, if accrued sick time cannot be cashed in but rather only applied toward the employee's post-retirement health insurance premiums, it may not be deemed marital property because it is personal, intangible, difficult to value, and impossible to transfer.[21]

NOTE:

Classifying a property as marital rather than separate does not mean that the particular property must be divided or that the holder of title to the property will not be permitted to keep it. It just means that the family court has the authority to divide it if necessary to effect an equal or equitable division. The paralegal may be involved in gathering the information necessary to support the classification and the distribution most favorable to the client.

Passive appreciation
increase in the value of an asset that results without effort and as a result of market forces and the passage of time

Active appreciation
increase in the value of an asset that results from effort rather than simply market forces or the passage of time

An argument is sometimes made that separate property has lost its identity as separate and has become marital property during the course of a marriage, that a *transmutation* or change has taken place in the characterization of the property due to certain circumstances:

- After ten years of "a wonderful marriage," in a state that permits them to do so, the parties may decide to execute a *postmarital agreement* in which they mutually designate their separate property as marital.
- For estate planning purposes, they may decide to jointly title the marital home or certain other property.
- The parties may use or treat a separate asset as a marital asset by spending both marital time and funds on the asset. For example, the husband may own a home in his name prior to marriage. After marriage, he and his wife live in the home for twenty years. During the marriage they both participate in remodeling, redecorating, and landscaping initiatives paid for with marital funds, and they warmly refer to the residence as "our home."
- The transmutation may result from a *commingling* of separate resources with marital resources. For example, the wife sells a condominium she owned prior to the marriage for $250,000, and the parties then buy a new marital residence with that amount plus $10,000 from the husband's savings account that he held prior to the marriage, $100,000 in marital funds, and a mortgage in both their names.

Given such fact patterns, the majority of courts are likely to assume that basic fairness requires the property involved be treated as marital property available for division upon divorce.

Courts have adopted a variety of approaches to establish ownership of commingled property. The two most prominent theories are *inception of title* and *source of funds/pro rata.* Inception of title theory bases ownership on whichever spouse first acquired title to the property: A party acquires property at the time of initial purchase, and postmarital contributions are of no effect. The preferred approach to establishing ownership, source of funds theory, bases ownership on contribution toward acquisition of the property. The two theories can lead to opposite results in the same situation. For example, if the marital home cost $150,000 and was initially titled in the wife's name but the husband paid the down payment and all of the mortgage payments, under inception of title theory, the property is viewed as owned by the wife despite her lack of financial contribution. Under source of funds theory, it is the husband's property. If the wife contributed 40 percent of the down payment and mortgage payments, the property would be considered 40 percent hers and 60 percent his based on their respective contributions. Courts may even consider the contributions of third parties when relevant to determining each party's interest in the marital property. For instance, if in the above fact pattern the entire down payment came from the wife's parents, then the wife's share may be greater.[22]

If either party seeks to establish that he or she did not intend for his or her separate property to lose its identity as separate, that party must be able to *trace* his or her contribution to what appears to be marital property back to separate property. The property may retain its separate identity even if it is refinanced and the proceeds of the refinancing become marital property .[23] If all or part of the transmuted property can be retraced to separate property, the burden usually shifts to the other party to establish that there was an intention to make a gift of the separate property to the marital estate.

Transmutation
a change in the classification of an asset from separate to marital or marital to separate

Postmarital agreement
an agreement made by two people already married to each other who want both to continue their marriage and also to define their respective rights upon separation, divorce, or death of one of them

Commingling
mixing together a spouse's separate property with marital property, or mixing together the separate property of both spouses

Inception of title theory
a theory that fixes ownership of property at the time a property is acquired and holds that postmarital contributions are of no effect

Source of funds/*pro rata* theory
a theory that bases ownership of property on contribution; an asset may be characterized as both separate and marital in proportion to the respective contributions of the parties

Tracing
the process of tracking ownership of a property from the time of inception to the present

Identification of the Property Subject to Division

When parties to a marriage sever their relationship, they necessarily must divide their property. The general rule is that only the property acquired during the marriage is subject to division by the court. Property belonging to a spouse prior to marriage usually remains the property of that spouse unless the parties otherwise agree (as in a premarital agreement or separation agreement) or the property has undergone a transmutation from separate to marital property as described above and in Case 11.4. Jurisdictions that classify property as separate or marital and allow only marital property to be distributed at divorce are called **dual property** jurisdictions. The limited number of states, such as Massachusetts and Connecticut, in which the court may assign any of a spouse's property to the other spouse are called **all property** states. If necessary to accomplish an equitable division in these states, the courts are permitted to disregard the distinction between separate and marital property and to reach all of the parties' assets regardless of when, how, and by whom they were acquired. A copy of the applicable Connecticut statute is available on the companion website.

Dual property states
states that distinguish property for distribution purposes and permit only marital property to be divided and distributed at divorce.

All property states
states in which divorce courts may distribute property at divorce without distinguishing between separate and marital property; all property is considered, however acquired, in order to achieve greater equity

CASE 11.4 *Miller v. Miller,* 105 P.3d 1136 (Alas. 2005)

BACKGROUND

The parties in this case were divorced in 2003 after fifteen years of marriage. The wife, Violeta, was a mother and homemaker during much of the marriage, and the husband, Chad, worked as an electrician and occasionally for his family's business. In this appeal, the husband contested the findings of the superior court that the marital home was transmuted into a marital asset during the thirteen years the parties lived there and that a cash gift from Chad's mother also was transmuted into marital property when he intentionally placed the funds into a joint account and used it for marital purposes. The Alaska Supreme Court affirmed the decision.

FROM THE OPINION

During the marriage, the family lived in a home given to Chad by his mother, Molly Miller, one week before his marriage to Violeta. The parties lived in this home until they separated in March 2001. In 1998 Molly Miller also gave a large cash gift to Chad. Although Chad initially placed this money in an investment account bearing his name alone, he later transferred the funds to a joint account bearing both his and Violeta's names. The investment account grew from an initial investment of $230,000 in 1998 to $290,000 in 2000, but the balance had dropped to $173,729 by the time the parties separated in March 2001. Chad testified that this decline was due to market losses. After the parties separated, however, Chad began to spend vast sums of money on personal items, living expenses, gifts and internet gambling, depleting the account by more than $94,000 by the end of May 2001, the month he filed for divorce. By October 31, 2001 this account had a zero balance, despite a pretrial order issued on May 16, 2001 enjoining the parties from using marital property for any purpose other than personal and necessary expenses. Chad Miller testified that he spent the money because his investments were declining in value and he wanted to use the money himself rather than lose it in the stock market. He claimed that he saw nothing wrong with spending this money after separation because he thought the money was his separate property and no one had informed him that it was inappropriate to do so if he was contemplating a divorce.

continued

1. Marital Home

...Chad Miller argues that the superior court erred in classifying the family home as marital property subject to equitable distribution. While he acknowledges that a premarital home owned by one spouse can transmute into marital property if it is used as the primary marital residence, he claims that the home remains his separate property because the parties always viewed it as such....

Property owned by one party as separate property becomes marital property if the parties demonstrate an intent to treat the property as marital. In determining whether a home should be treated as marital property, a court will consider factors such as: (1) the use of the property as the parties' personal residence, (2) both parties' participation in ongoing maintenance and management, (3) placing title in joint ownership, and (4) using the credit of the non-titled party to improve the property.

The superior court found that although the home was originally a gift to Chad from Molly Miller prior to his marriage to Violeta, the residence was transmuted from separate to marital property by the actions of the parties over the thirteen years that they lived there together. The court found that taxes, insurance, and maintenance expenses were paid from the marital property; that Violeta cleaned and maintained the house during the marriage; and that Chad made no attempts to maintain the separate character of this property. These factual findings are supported by the record....

Chad also argued...that, if any portion of the home is marital property, it would be only that portion representing its appreciation in value during the time the parties lived together. He claimed that the court should at the most award Violeta only one-half of the increased value rather than one-half of the total value of the home. This argument ignores the differences between the theories of transmutation and active appreciation. While separate property can become marital property under either theory, transmutation converts an asset entirely from separate to marital, while active appreciation converts to marital property only the increase in an asset's value due to a contribution of marital funds or efforts. These theories are mutually exclusive, and we have previously held that if separate property is transmuted into marital property, the trial court must allocate the entire equity in the property rather than just the appreciation in value.... and thus the superior court correctly determined that the full equity value was marital property....

2. Investment Account

Chad also argues that the court erred in classifying as marital property an investment account opened with funds given to him by his mother. He claims that this gift was an advancement on his inheritance that remained his separate property throughout the marriage. The superior court found that these funds were transmuted into marital property when Chad transferred them from an account in his name alone into an account in the parties' joint names. This finding is not clearly erroneous.

Molly Miller gifted Chad $230,000 in 1998. With these funds he opened an investment account in his own name..., listing Violeta and his children as beneficiaries of equal shares in the event of his death. Approximately one year later, these funds were transferred to a joint account in the names of both Chad and Violeta. Under this account the parties were joint tenants with rights of survivorship, so if one party died before the other, the surviving spouse would receive the entire account balance. At trial, Chad testified that he transferred the funds to a joint account so that if he died before Violeta the

continued

funds would transfer to her without going through probate, but that he was fully in control of the account because it was his inheritance.

Inherited property is separate, even if received during marriage, though it can be transmuted into marital property where that is the intent of the owner. There is a strong presumption that placing separate property into a joint account demonstrates an intent to treat the property as marital. Thus absent evidence to the contrary, Chad's decision to move the funds into a joint account will be viewed as a demonstration of his intent to treat the property as marital. Chad argues that this presumption is rebutted by Violeta's testimony that the joint account was created strictly for probate purposes.

When Violeta testified that she never attempted to access funds from the joint account, she also stated that she considered the account to be marital property because her name was on it, and that the parties used these funds for ongoing household expenses such as taxes. The trial court found that the fact that Violeta never made withdrawals from the account was insignificant given Chad's general unwillingness to allow Violeta to participate in major decisions or to exercise control over the family's finances.

Furthermore, the evidence does not support Chad's claim that account ownership was changed solely for probate purposes. At trial Chad testified that he put the account in joint ownership in 1999 on the recommendation of his mother because of the delays and costs the family experienced dealing with the probate process after the death of Chad's father. Chad claimed that joint ownership would ensure that Violeta got the funds automatically upon his death. But earlier he also testified that the house was put into his name alone based on the advice of his mother because she "knows about probate" and "it would be best if [the house] was in my name free and clear, before I get married, so that if something did go wrong later with the marriage, that [Violeta] couldn't try to take the whole thing."... If the ownership decisions were made to avoid problems with probate, it would make little sense to maintain sole title to the home while placing the investment account in joint ownership.

The trial court's finding that the investment account transmuted to marital property was not clearly erroneous.

C. The Superior Court's Valuation of the Marital Estate Was Not Clearly Erroneous

...In the weeks after separation, Chad spent an enormous amount of money, depleting the account by $68,503.49 in the month of April alone. He used the funds on items such as an $18,000 all-terrain vehicle, a $32,000 custom-made travel trailer, an $11,750 emerald ring for Violeta, and thousands of dollars of internet gambling. Chad also testified that he took the children out to dinner nightly, spending at least $100 each night.

...Chad also argues that the court erred in valuing the property he purchased from this account at its purchase price rather than its fair market value at the time of trial. As Violeta's counsel noted at trial, much of this property is of a type that depreciates rapidly, such as tools, electronic equipment, recreational vehicles, camping gear, exercise equipment, and automobile upgrades. While a trial court should normally value property at the time of trial it can, in special circumstances, value property at the time of separation, so long as the court makes specific findings regarding why the earlier date is proper. Dissipation of marital assets justifies a valuation at the time of separation.

...For the foregoing reasons we AFFIRM the decision of the superior court in all respects.

continued

SIDEBAR

This opinion is available in its entirety on the companion website. Do you agree with the court's decision with respect to the marital home? The investment account? Valuation of the marital estate? Explain your responses.

Valuation of Property

When dividing marital property, courts seek to allocate the parties' property, with each spouse receiving a portion of an equal and/or equitable value depending on the jurisdiction. In order for the court to do so, the value of each major piece of property to be divided needs to be determined. **Valuation** is the process of assessing the financial worth of property, real or personal. If contested, the value of a particular piece of property is a question of fact to be determined by the judge based on testimony and evidence presented by the parties. Few statutes specify how a particular asset is to be valued, and a wide variety of approaches are used. There is no "right" answer to a valuation question, but rather a range of possible answers, each supported by a rationale and documentation whenever possible. If opposing parties use different approaches or propose conflicting values using the same method, the court has the discretion to accept the valuation of either of the parties or to establish its own. Technically, it may constitute reversible error for a trial court to order a division of property without first determining values. However, if a party fails to present evidence as to the value of a contested asset, he or she may waive a right of appeal on the issue. Thorough preparation is thus essential!

There are three basic issues in valuation cases:

1. Which property of the parties should be valued?
2. What is the appropriate date for valuation?
3. Who will conduct the valuation and how?

Which Property of the Parties Should Be Valued? In some cases, the parties have few if any assets, and valuation is not an issue. In other cases, the parties may be able to agree on a division of property without engaging in valuation. If so, they can avoid a costly and time-consuming process, but they will have no way of knowing whether the agreed-upon settlement really is fair. Absent agreement on a fair allocation of assets and liabilities that a court will be willing to approve, property subject to division may need to be valued. This includes, but is not necessarily limited to, all of the property identified at the beginning of this chapter in Exhibit 11.1. Sometimes the parties will agree that only property above a certain threshold amount will be valued. That amount may be $500, $5,000, or even $50,000 or more, depending on the nature and extent of the marital estate.

The kinds of property most commonly warranting valuation are retirement plans (**vested** or unvested), business interests, and the marital home (and any other real estate such as a rental or vacation property). If there is a mortgage and/or a loan secured by the real estate, the amount of **equity** in the property needs to be determined. Equity is the **fair market value** of the property less any encumbrances (mortgages, loans, tax liens, etc.). Fair market value is commonly defined as the price a willing buyer would pay a willing seller in an arm's-length transaction (e.g., not between friends or family members) when neither party is under any compulsion to buy or sell.

Valuation
the process of assessing the financial worth of property, real or personal

Vested
fixed or accrued; unable to be taken away by subsequent events or circumstances

Equity
the fair market value of a property less any encumbrances (mortgages, loans, tax liens, etc.)

Fair market value
the price a willing buyer would pay a willing seller in an arm's-length transaction when neither party is under any compulsion to buy or sell

PARALEGAL APPLICATION 11.3

WHO GETS THE HOUSE?

Once the value of a marital asset has been established, additional information may be needed to develop a compelling rationale for why the asset ought to be awarded to the client. For example, assume the marital home is valued at $250,000. There is a $50,000 mortgage and a $20,000 equity loan secured by the property, and thus the equity in the home is $180,000. The parties obtained the equity loan in order to pay off gambling debts the husband incurred during the marriage. The parties purchased the property in 1990 for $125,000 and took title as tenants by the entirety. The wife provided a down payment of $40,000 out of funds she had accumulated prior to marriage. She paid the mortgage and taxes throughout the marriage, landscaped the property, and redecorated the interior, making it a virtual showplace. She is emotionally very attached to the home and both of the parties' two children were home-birthed there. She is seeking custody of the children and wants to continue to raise them in the only home they have ever known. This scenario provides a strong case for awarding the home to the wife and illustrates that property division decisions are not just about dollars and cents.

What Is the Appropriate Date of Valuation? Some states establish by statute or case law the date as of which marital assets are to be valued, but most prefer a flexible approach. Common options include the date when the parties separate, the date on which the divorce complaint (or action for division of property) is filed, the date when discovery is completed, the trial or final hearing date, or the date when the decree of dissolution is entered. The issue can be critical, for example when:

- there is a long period between the date of separation and the filing for divorce;
- the marriage is terminated in one proceeding and other issues (such as custody, support, and division of property) are decided at a later date in the same or a different state;
- the value of an asset is highly volatile and likely to change during the pendency of the divorce litigation due to rapid shifts in the real estate market or broader economic climate; and/or
- one of the parties dissipates or increases the value of assets while the case is pending.

When there is flexibility regarding the date for valuation, multiple alternative dates should be explored so that the attorney can determine which will work to the client's best advantage.

Paralegal Practice Tip

The paralegal should also be alert to the fact that, in some states, contribution to property during a period of premarital cohabitation may be considered by the court when fashioning a division of marital assets. (See Paralegal Application 11.4.)

PARALEGAL APPLICATION 11.4

DOES COHABITATION COUNT—WHAT DO YOU THINK?

FACT PATTERN

This case involves an eight-year marriage preceded by a ten-year period during which the parties lived together. They had no children. When the parties first met, the husband had a small jewelry business with an inventory of approximately $5,800 and gross annual sales of $62,769. The wife learned and worked in the business on a full-time basis for the nine years preceding the marriage. Through their joint efforts, the business thrived, and by the time they married it had an inventory of nearly

continued

$100,000 and gross annual sales of over $400,000. Each party had accumulated considerable savings and retirement benefits. Notwithstanding their success in business both before and after the marriage, their personal relationship deteriorated. The husband was verbally and physically abusive to the wife, and she, in retaliation, engaged in an extramarital affair. At the time of the divorce, the trial court awarded the wife approximately one-third of the marital assets. In calculating the award, the judge included, within the assignable estate, the parties' premarital pension and retirement benefits. The husband appealed.

SIDEBAR

Do you think that premarital contributions to marital assets should be considered as marital property upon dissolution and, if so, under what circumstances? Read the case *Moriarty v. Stone,* 41 Mass. App. Ct. 151, 668 N.E.2d 1338 (1996), available on the companion website. Do you agree with the decision of the Massachusetts Court of Appeals? Explain your answer.

Who Will Conduct the Valuation and How?   Valuation of assets such as bank accounts is reasonably straightforward and can usually be accomplished by the client, who is in a position to obtain account statements. Paralegals can research the value of several kinds of property such as automobiles, recreational vehicles, stock values, and the like, by checking "blue book" values and stock listings in the business section of the newspaper. Some family law practitioners and paralegals are skilled at other kinds of valuation, but because valuation issues may sometimes be beyond their expertise, most maintain lists of *experts,* including their respective areas of expertise, fee schedules, and current resumes. The task of maintaining these resource lists may be assigned to the paralegal. Experts may include, among others, appraisers, accountants, *actuaries,* financial planners, and investment counselors able to assess the values of such things as real estate, jewelry, pensions, degrees, a party's interest in a professional practice or ongoing business, a pending lawsuit, a copyright, the value of a spouse's contribution as homemaker and caretaker for the children, etc.

> **Paralegal Practice Tip**
> Available on the companion website for this text in the material related to Chapter 7 is a Guide to Documenting Asset Values. It provides a list of several common types of assets, some of the kinds of documentation and resources that are available with respect to valuation of those assets, and the basic data elements regarding them that may be useful in preparing financial statements, conducting negotiations, or preparing exhibits for hearings or trial.

> **Expert**
> a person who, through education or experience, has developed special skill or knowledge in a particular subject

> **Actuary**
> a statistician who determines the present value of a future event; one who calculates insurance and pension values on the basis of empirically based tables

PARALEGAL APPLICATION 11.5

PROTECTING THE FIRM

The standard approach to a property division case is to identify assets and liabilities, value them, factor in the client's goals, and then propose an appropriate allocation. Throughout the process, the family law team works in consultation with the client, always mindful of an ethical obligation to provide competent and zealous representation. In turn, the client needs to understand the strengths and weaknesses of his or her case in order to make informed decisions after reviewing governing law and the risks and benefits of various courses of action.

Sometimes a client will not agree to follow the legal advice provided. He or she may direct that the firm not search for concealed property or value a significant asset or may insist on settling for less than he or she reasonably would be entitled to in order to avoid a trial or as a trade-off for some other objective. Under such circumstances, the client should be sent a letter reiterating the recommendations made and noting that, notwithstanding that advice, the attorney has been explicitly directed by the client not to pursue the recommended course of action.

Division of Property

In cases involving few if any assets or liabilities, property division is a relatively simple matter often settled by the parties without advice of counsel. Agreements are usually based on the parties' relative needs, personal preferences, and emotional attachments to particular possessions. The primary task of the attorney in such cases is to advise the client with respect to whether or not he or she has settled for the share to which he or she may be legally entitled. Sometimes this is a challenge, as clients often exaggerate or deflate the values of property based on their own subjective appraisals. For example, in exchange for getting to keep the family pet, a client may "give away" all of the household appliances and furnishings.

If the parties are unable to agree on how their property should be divided, it falls on the courts to determine the distribution. In the no-fault era, an equal division of the marital estate is implicit in the community property approach and strongly favored in equitable distribution jurisdictions, particularly given a long-term, traditional marriage in which the husband contributed primarily as the "breadwinner" and the wife as the homemaker, and there is a reasonably conventional mix of assets. However, the courts may deviate based on the facts of an individual case, and one can never totally predict a certain outcome.

There are three primary ways in which the property of parties to a divorce may be divided:

1. The parties may have executed a **_premarital agreement,_** a contract in which they mutually agree as to how their property will be divided in the event of divorce, annulment, or death. The court hearing the divorce case will first determine the validity of the agreement, which should be brought to its attention at the outset of the divorce proceeding. If held to be valid, property will be distributed according to the terms of the agreement.

2. If there is no premarital agreement or it is held to be invalid, the parties may negotiate a mutually agreeable property division for inclusion in a settlement or **_separation agreement_** (see Chapter 12) and submission to the court for approval. Courts will usually accept the parties' agreement, provided its terms do not violate public policy and are not unconscionable.

3. Judges strongly urge attorneys and counsel to settle cases in order to save costs and conserve judicial resources. However, if the parties are unable to reach an agreement with respect to the distribution of their assets and liabilities, the matter will be tried before the court. Guided by case law and either **_community property_** or **_equitable distribution_** statutes (see Exhibits 11.2 through 11.4), trial courts have considerable discretion in resolving property division disputes on a case-by-case basis, given the evidence and testimony presented by the parties. A trial court's decision regarding property distribution generally will not be reversed on appeal absent an **_error of law_** or an **_abuse of discretion._**

The Equitable Distribution Approach.   A majority of the states are equitable distribution jurisdictions, in which the courts apportion marital property between the parties in a manner that is fair and "equitable" (albeit not necessarily equal) based on a consideration of factors laid out in case law and/or statutes.

Premarital agreement

an agreement made by two persons about to be married defining for themselves their respective rights, duties, and responsibilities in the event their marriage terminates by death, annulment, separation, or divorce

Separation agreement

an agreement made between spouses in anticipation of divorce or a legal separation concerning the terms of the divorce or separation and any continuing obligations of the parties to each other

Community property

assets owned in common by a husband and wife as a result of having been acquired during the marriage by a means other than an inheritance or a gift to one spouse generally holding a one-half interest in the property no matter in whose name it is held; usually divided equally between the parties upon dissolution of the marriage absent an agreement to the contrary

Equitable distribution

the legal concept that upon divorce property accumulated during a marriage should be divided between the parties equitably, but not necessarily equally, based upon principles of fairness

Error of law

a mistake made by a court in applying the law to the facts of a case

Abuse of discretion

the failure of a court to exercise sound, reasonable, and legal decision making

EXHIBIT 11.2 Summary Table Re Equitable Distribution and
              Community Property Approaches

Equitable Distribution Approach	**Equitable distribution** is the legal concept that property accumulated during a marriage should be divided between the parties based upon principles of fairness. • The majority of states apply this approach to property division upon dissolution of a marriage. • Each state adopts by statute and/or case law a series of factors to be considered by the court in making a property distribution.
Community Property Approach	**Community property** refers to any assets acquired during the marriage with the exception of gifts and inheritances. It generally includes all earnings, assets, and liabilities accumulated during the marriage by either or both of the parties. • Under the community property approach, the parties' marital property is divided equally between them. • This approach is applied by a minority of the states: Arizona, California, Idaho, Louisiana, New Mexico, Nevada, Texas, and Washington. *Note:* Wisconsin[24] and Alaska[25] are also sometimes characterized as community property states.

(See the Illinois statute in Exhibit 11.3 and the Mississippi guidelines, initially established in case law and now codified, accessible on the companion website.) The courts are not required to give equal weight to each factor but rather to consider them in light of the facts of each case, recognizing that both parties contributed to the marriage in a variety of ways (financially, maintaining and improving the home, raising the children, etc.). In some equitable distribution states there is a presumption that the division will be equal; but the presumption is rebuttable.

Although some property (such as gifts to or inheritances of an individual spouse) may be exempt from division as separate property, generally, all property in which a party acquires an interest during the marriage through an expenditure of funds or effort of some kind is subject to division. As mentioned earlier, in "all property" states, the courts may even reach separate property when effecting a distribution. Some refer to this as "dipping into" separate property to achieve an equitable distribution. It has been argued that equitable distribution statutes deprive an individual of property without due process of law, but such statutes have been upheld as constitutional.[26]

EXHIBIT 11.3 Illinois—An Equitable Division Jurisdiction—750 ILCS 5/503 (8)(d)

FROM THE STATUTE

(d) In a proceeding for dissolution of marriage or declaration of invalidity of marriage, or in a proceeding for disposition of property following dissolution of marriage by a court which lacked personal jurisdiction over the absent spouse or lacked jurisdiction to dispose of the property, the court shall assign each spouse's non-marital property to that spouse. It shall also divide the marital property without regard to marital misconduct in just proportions considering all the relevant factors, including:

(1) the contribution of each party to the acquisition, preservation, or increase or decrease in value of the marital or non-marital property, including the contribution of a spouse as a homemaker or to the family unit;

(2) the dissipation by each party of the marital or non-marital property;

(3) the value of the property assigned to each spouse;

(4) the duration of the marriage;

(5) the relevant economic circumstances of each spouse when the division of property is to become effective, including the desirability of awarding the family home, or the right to live therein for reasonable periods, to the spouse having custody of the children;

(6) any obligations and rights arising from a prior marriage of either party;

(7) any antenuptial agreement of the parties;

(8) the age, health, station, occupation, amounts and sources of income, vocational skills, employability, estate, liabilities, and needs of each of the parties;

(9) the custodial provisions for any children;

(10) whether the apportionment is in lieu of or in addition to maintenance;

(11) the reasonable opportunity of each spouse for future acquisition of capital assets and income; and

(12) the tax consequences of the property division upon the respective economic circumstances of the parties.

The Community Property Approach. A minority of the states are community property jurisdictions in which property acquired during the marriage is viewed as belonging equally to the spouses and, therefore, rightfully divided equally between them upon divorce. Predominantly located in the American Southwest, most community property states were originally settled by Spanish colonists and adopted a system of law rooted in Spanish (or French, in the case of Louisiana) civil law rather than English common law, which based ownership on title. From the outset, the system grounded in civil law valued both financial and nonfinancial

CASE 11.5 *Wade v. Wade*, 2005 VT. 72, 178 Vt. 189, 878 A.2d 303 (2005)

BACKGROUND

In this case, a Vermont family court applied the factors set forth in the state's equitable division statute and awarded 90 percent of the marital estate to the wife. The Vermont Supreme Court upheld the award.

FROM THE OPINION

Husband and wife were married in 1991, had one child together, and separated in 2002. The parties, their daughter and husband's son from a prior relationship lived in the town of Waitsfield in a home that wife purchased before the parties married. Since 1985, wife used part of the home to run the Sunshine Montessori School, Inc., a nursery school she founded and continues to operate. Husband has a landscaping business. During the marriage, the husband took on seasonal work in the restaurant, construction and ski industries. Over the last four years, husband earned between $13,000 and $23,000 annually. Wife's income from the Sunshine School averaged $21,824 in 2000–2002.

In 1996, wife received a series of gifts from her mother. She was given title to her mother's home, which wife rented out until 2002 when she sold the property. Wife also received $22,000 in cash and put $40,000 from her mother into a VUGMA account for the parties' minor daughter. The $22,000 went into an account in her name only. Wife subsequently exhausted the money in the account by using it to pay for various family expenses....

After wife sold the home her mother gave her in 2002, the parties each received $10,000 from the proceeds. The remaining proceeds of $59,000 were placed into escrow pending distribution in the divorce proceeding. After her mother died, wife used some of her inheritance to purchase a twenty-nine foot sailboat and a catamaran for the family. Husband spent time repairing and maintaining the boats for the family, and used his carpentry and other handyman skills to maintain and improve the parties' residence. The family also owned a camper, and husband held a half interest in a seasonal camp in Rochester, Vermont.

Throughout the marriage, wife paid the mortgage on the marital residence and most of the household expenses. Husband paid half of the utilities and charged many of his own expenses, and those of his landscaping business to credit cards. At the time the parties separated, husband had over $23,000 in personal and business credit card debt. Wife's credit card debt was a fraction of the husband's. After separating, wife remained in the marital home, and husband moved into a friend's home where he acts as a caretaker.

Wife filed for divorce in October 2002. She sought primary custody of the parties' daughter and most of the parties' property.... Husband... asked the court to split their property roughly fifty-fifty. Both parties hired expert witnesses to testify about the value of the Sunshine School. It was undisputed that the husband's business had no value.

The court issued a written order following a hearing in December 2003. Wife received approximately ninety percent of the marital property, including the parties' home and all of its equity, the catamaran, the camper, and the escrowed proceeds from the sale of her mother's home. The court awarded husband the sailboat, $10,000 from the sale proceeds that he had already received, his interest in the Rochester camp, and his tools. Crediting wife's expert witness, the court found that the Sunshine School, while valuable to the wife personally, had no market value....

In support of the property award, the court explained that wife had lived in the parties' home since 1985, six years before the parties married. Wife paid the

continued

mortgage and property taxes. She also paid for the parties' two boats and contributed all of her income to other household expenses. The court acknowledged that what money husband earned was spent primarily on the household, but it noted that husband "never earned much in any year." The court found that the husband had not "followed a conventional career; instead he has enjoyed the freedom of working on a seasonal basis and taking time when he wishes to work on his own business." The court found that husband could earn more money working a full-time job in construction or some other business if he chose.

Husband...argues that the court awarded a disproportionate share of the marital property to wife by ignoring some of the statutory factors in 15 V.S.A. §751 and giving too much weight to others. Section 751 of Title 15 directs the family court to divide the marital estate in an equitable manner after considering several factors:

(1) the length of the marriage

(2) the age and health of the parties

(3) the occupation, source and amount of income of each of the parties

(4) vocational skills and employability

(5) the contribution by one spouse to the education, training, or increased earning power of the other

(6) the value of all property interests, liabilities and needs of each party

(7) whether the property settlement is in lieu of or in addition to maintenance

(8) the opportunity of each for future acquisition of capital assets and income

(9) the desirability of awarding the family home or the right to live there for reasonable periods to the spouse having custody of the children

(10) the party through whom the property was acquired

(11) the contribution of each spouse in the acquisition, preservation, and depreciation or appreciation in value of the respective estates, including the nonmonetary contribution of a spouse as a homemaker

(12) the respective merits of the parties

...The family court has broad discretion when analyzing and weighing the statutory factors in light of the record evidence....When fashioning an equitable award, the court must explain the underlying rationale for its decision..., which we will not disturb absent a showing that the court abused its discretion....

Husband asserts that the property division lacks equity because the court did not consider the length of the marriage; husband's lack of a college education and his contribution to wife's business; husband's inability to acquire capital assets or additional income; husband's sweat equity in maintaining and improving the marital home and the rental property acquired from wife's mother; and the lack of a proper home for their daughter when she spends time with husband. We find no merit to husband's contention because the text of the court's decision reflects that it considered all of those factors.

The court found that the parties were married for twelve years. It determined that in light of all the factors the length of marriage did not weigh in favor of either party. The court acknowledged husband's lack of a college degree, but it found that husband could increase his annual income by taking a full-time position in the construction industry or in another industry in the Mad River Valley. Husband is healthy and his age—forty-eight-years old—at the time of the divorce did not preclude him from acquiring his own home or other assets in the future. On the issue of maintenance, husband did not

continued

request maintenance in lieu of property, and cannot now fault the family court for not considering this factor.

As for husband's suggestion that the property award left him without an ability to obtain a suitable residence where his daughter can stay when she is in his care, there is no factor in §751 that directly addresses this issue.... the court must consider the "desirability of awarding the family home... to the spouse having custody of the children."... The court considered that factor when it determined the child's best interests were served by allowing her to remain in the marital residence—the only home the child has ever known—under wife's primary care.

According to the family court, the statutory factors that weighed most heavily in its decision were numbers (10) and (11): through whom the assets were acquired, and which party contributed more to their preservation.... All of the assets in this case came through wife, either because she acquired them before marriage or purchased them after marriage with money wife's mother provided. All of wife's income, as well as her inheritance, went to support the family and the family's recreational interests. She paid the mortgage and property taxes on the marital home. Husband's financial contribution was recognized through the $10,000 he received from the sale of the wife's mother's home and the sailboat court awarded husband. The court declined to allocate the parties' debt because it found that husband's larger share of credit card debt was due to the relatively low income he earned by choice. In light of the wife's substantial monetary contribution to the family's expenses, the court determined that it would be unfair to saddle her with a portion of husband's personal and business debt....

We recognize that wife received ninety percent of the parties' assets. Had the family court failed to explain in detail the reasons for the facially disproportionate property distribution, the outcome of this case would likely be different. But the family court carefully explained why it weighed factors (10) and (11) more heavily in reaching its decision. As trier of fact, the family court was in the best position to assess the merits of the parties' contentions, and its decision addresses the relevant statutory factors. Therefore we cannot say that the court abused its discretion in fashioning the property award in this case....

SIDEBAR

Do you agree with the Vermont Supreme Court's holding? Read the entire case, which is available on the companion website. Be sure to read the strong dissent by Justice Skoglund in which he states his belief that the "lopsided award" in this case would not have been affirmed "if it had been the wife and not the husband who received the paltry ten percent share of the parties' marital estate." Do you agree with the majority or with the dissenting justice? How would you have decided the case? Explain your response.

contributions such as maintaining the home and caring for the children. Although early community property law recognized the husband and wife as separate and not a single entity upon marriage, it still did not consider them equal partners. For example, women could own property, but only men could manage and control it.

The contemporary community property approach is based on a view of marriage as a partnership and an assumption that both the husband and the wife contribute to the acquisition and accumulation of marital assets and liabilities. It assumes that each spouse acts for the benefit of the marital unit and is, therefore, entitled to an interest in half of the property acquired during the marriage through the expenditure of marital funds or the efforts of either or both spouses. Separate property remains separate property in community property jurisdictions, and it generally includes assets brought into the marriage, property acquired in exchange for separate property, and gifts and inheritances received by a spouse during the marriage. A copy of the Nevada community property statute is provided on the companion website. Although only about one-fifth of the states are community property states, approximately one-quarter of the population of the United States lives in those states (which include both Texas and California). Whether employed in a common law or community property jurisdiction, the family law team needs to be aware of the laws of any community property states in which the parties have resided, given the potential consequences for clients during marriage, upon divorce, and at death. (See Exhibit 11.4.)

EXHIBIT 11.4 Community Property—Ten Commonly Asked Questions

QUESTION 1: What are the community property states?

ANSWER: The traditional community property states are Arizona, California, Idaho, Louisiana, Nevada, New Mexico, Texas, and Washington. Wisconsin is also sometimes classified as a community property state and is recognized by the federal government for tax purposes as such. Alaska is technically not a community property state; however, under Alaska's Community Property Act, "...property of the spouses is community property...only to the extent provided in a community property agreement or a community property trust."[27]

QUESTION 2: Is the law governing community property the same in all the community property states?

> **Common law property state**
> a state in which property is generally owned by the party who acquired it during the marriage; property acquired during the marriage is divided equitably upon divorce in common law property states

ANSWER: No. The marital property laws of the community property states differ significantly, not only from the marital property laws in **common law property states,** but also from one another's laws. Although the federal government recognizes community property for tax purposes, it has established no mandatory definition of community property for use by all of the states. There are variations among the community property states, for example, in terms of how they define community property, how they treat income from separate property, and when they hold that the "marital community" terminates for purposes of accummulation of community property.

QUESTION 3: How is community property treated upon divorce?

ANSWER: Under community property theory, when the parties marry, they form a "marital community." Absent an agreement of the parties to the contrary, upon dissolution, the courts start with a presumption that all property acquired (and liabilities incurred) during the marriage and still existing at the time of divorce is community property and subject to a fifty-fifty division regardless of the relative contributions made by each of the parties. In Wisconsin, for example, by statute, "An obligation incurred by a spouse during marriage, including one attributable to an act or omission during the marriage, is presumed to be incurred in the interest of the marriage or the family."[28] The time period in which the debt was incurred is more relevant than the name on the account under which the debt was created. This does not mean that each individual asset or liability must be divided equally, but rather that each spouse should receive 50 percent of the net community estate after deducting the joint obligations. If one of the parties contests the characterization of a particular asset or liability as belonging to the marital community, that person will have the burden of proving the claim.

continued

QUESTION 4: How is community property treated at death?

ANSWER: The primary advantage of the community property system is evident, upon the death of one of the spouses, in the form of a "double step-up" in **basis** for the surviving spouse. Basis is defined as the value assigned to a taxpayer's investment in property. It is the reference point used for calculating a gain or a loss when the property is transferred to another. Assuming assets increase in value while they are owned, there is a tax incentive to hold property as community property because the share of both spouses receive a "step-up" in basis, and not solely the shares of the decedent. A higher basis translates to a smaller gain (or greater loss) if the surviving spouse sells the property. If the asset is depreciable, larger depreciation reductions will be available. These advantages are lost if the property has decreased in value between the date it was acquired and the date of death of the first spouse to die.[29]

Basis
the value assigned by the IRS to a taxpayer's investment in property

QUESTION 5: Does conduct have any impact on the division of community property?

ANSWER: The general rule is that conduct will not play a role in a no-fault divorce. However, in most community property states, the courts may consider conduct when dividing the marital estate, particularly economic misconduct. For example, if a party has committed "community waste" by concealing assets or disposing of them in a fraudulent or irresponsible manner (such as through excessive gambling), that party's share of the community property upon divorce may be reduced.

QUESTION 6: What are the primary disadvantages of holding property as community property?

ANSWER: The two primary disadvantages are:
- The former/surviving spouse may receive a larger share of the assets upon divorce or death than desired or intended by the other spouse.
- A spouse does not have complete management or control over the community property. Some of the kinds of restraints that may be imposed include prohibitions against:
  - Devising or bequeathing by will more than one-half of the community property
  - Gifting community property without the express or implied consent of the other spouse
  - Selling, conveying, or encumbering community real property without the other spouse's participation and acknowledgment
  - Purchasing or contracting to purchase community real property without the other spouse joining.[30]

QUESTION 7: What happens if spouses move from a common law property state to a community property state and later divorce?

ANSWER: In some community property states (such as Arizona and California), if the parties are both residents of the community property state at the time of the divorce, the court will treat property acquired during the marriage in a common law property state as if it were acquired in the community property state and apply the concept of quasi-community property.

QUESTION 8: What happens to community property if spouses move from a community property state to a common law property state?

ANSWER: The general rule is that property acquired with, or traceable to, community funds will continue to maintain its character as community property in

continued

most states. However, if an asset (such as a vacation home) is actually located in the common law property state, the common law state may decline to treat that particular asset as community property, based on public policy.[31]

The Restatement (Second) of Conflicts of Laws rule is that, absent an effective choice of law by the parties, the law of the spouses' domicile at the time of acquisition will usually determine the rights of each spouse in tangible and intangible personal property.[32] For example, in an Iowa case in which the parties had made no agreement regarding governing law, an appellate court held that Texas community property law should govern disposition of a brokerage account created and funded when the spouses lived in Texas, a community property state. The court held that greater weight should be given to the law of the state where the spouses were domiciled when the movable property was acquired.[33]

QUESTION 9: Can the parties change the nature of property from separate to community or community to separate during their marriage?

ANSWER: Yes, in most states. Spouses often choose to change the characterization of property by means of agreements (e.g., a pre- or postmarital agreement where permitted) or by gifting an interest in property to the community or to the other spouse in his or her sole name. The spouses may also, intentionally or unintentionally, convert a separate asset to community property by commingling separate property with community assets such that the separate property loses its identity. The burden of tracing the asset is on the spouse who claims a separate interest.

QUESTION 10: Can the parties influence the division of community property upon divorce?

ANSWER: Yes, by executing a separation agreement or by proposing a division to the court in contested cases. A copy of a California Property Declaration form is accessible on the companion website.

THE ROLE OF CONDUCT IN THE CONTEXT OF PROPERTY DIVISION

A majority of the states have adopted the position advocated in section 307 of the Uniform Marriage and Divorce Act, which provides that decisions about property division should be made "without regard to marital misconduct." In general, the courts have little patience with a party rambling on about how his or her spouse "cheated and lied." However, in keeping with a view of marriage as a partnership, many states still consider misconduct—particularly extreme instances of abuse or economic misconduct, which can come in many forms:

- Incurring excessive credit card debt for unnecessary expenses that do not support the family unit
- Failing to make a contribution of any kind (financial or otherwise) to the marital partnership over an extended period
- Using marital funds or assets to entertain or support an adulterous relationship
- Gambling excessively during the course of the marriage
- Making sham loans and transfers for less than fair market value to friends and family members, etc., in anticipation of divorce[34]

- Transferring or concealing assets after being served with notice of an impending divorce and while under a court order not to do so (Upon filing and serving of a divorce complaint, many states automatically restrain the parties from disposing of assets subject to division during the pendency of a divorce action unless otherwise agreed by the parties or ordered by the court.)
- Intentionally destroying marital or the other spouse's separate property
- Making high-risk or speculative investments during the marriage
- Cashing out joint accounts without the consent of the other party
- Engaging in criminal conduct that results in the imposition of fines that must be paid during the course of the marriage[35]
- Refusing to cooperate in the discovery process

When dissipation of assets is demonstrated at trial based on evidence and testimony, the court in its discretion may choose, among other options, to award a greater percentage of the assets to the innocent spouse or assign the bulk of the liabilities to the offending spouse. In some situations, the court may require that it be shown only that assets disappeared and not necessarily how they were spent. A Kentucky appeals court took this position when it held that a wife "did not have any information as to how the dissipated funds were spent, or the means to discover such information. It would be inequitable to require the party claiming dissipation to show exactly what use was made of the marital assets, because this information is not as readily available to the complaining party as it is to the dissipating party."[36] In the *Miller* case (Case 11.4), the husband largely acknowledged how he had spent funds in an account he regarded as separate property even though he had previously placed his wife's name on the account, allegedly only for purposes of probate. That case effectively illustrated **dissipation,** appreciation, and transmutation of marital resources in the property division context. Case 11.6 directly addresses the topic of dissipation.

Dissipation
the use of an asset for an illegal or inequitable purpose, such as when a spouse uses marital property for personal benefit when a divorce is pending

CASE **11.6** *Szesny v. Szesny,* 197 Ill. App.3d 966, 557 N.E.2d 222 (1990)

FROM THE OPINION

... [I]n the case here the trial court specifically found that respondent was solely responsible for the over $82,000 in debt. There was testimony that after they purchased the marital home, petitioner drastically reduced her expenditures while respondent maintained or increased his. The trial court noted that respondent would go out at night without his wife and child; that he belonged to a health club; that respondent opened charge accounts without petitioner's knowledge or permission; that respondent spent money on clothing for himself and at fine restaurants; that he gave money to his mother; that respondent borrowed money but he did not use it to reduce marital debt; and that he "in effect kited his account in consumer debt." The trial court also found that petitioner spent minimal amounts on clothing, ate in fast food restaurants, and in one year was responsible for less than one-twelfth of their total expenses.

Dissipation can occur prior to dissolution.... The key is whether one spouse uses marital property for his or her own benefit for a purpose unrelated to the marriage.... When one party is charged with dissipation, he must prove by clear and convincing evidence that the questioned expenditures were made for a marital purpose....

The trial court here noted that respondent claimed to have spent the money for family expenses but that he could produce only a few credit card

continued

statements for insignificant amounts. The court also noted that respondent opened credit card accounts without petitioner's permission, even though her name was used, and that respondent retained total control of these accounts, having the statements sent to his mother's house. Where one spouse has sole access to funds or incurs debt without the knowledge of the other, that spouse can be held to have dissipated marital assets and can be held responsible for the entire debt....

...We affirm the distribution of marital debt as ordered by the trial court....

SIDEBAR

This opinion is available in its entirety on the companion website.

DIVISION OF MAJOR ASSETS

It is virtually impossible to divide each piece of marital property equally, and it is seldom practical to liquidate all of the parties' assets so that the proceeds can be equally divided. Rather, the courts try to assign property of an appropriate value and type to each party. If there are sufficient assets, the court will assign to each party a variety of different properties up to a determined value. For example, one party may be awarded the marital home and the other a vacation property; each party may retain his or her pension; a stock portfolio may be divided; joint bank accounts might be split; etc.

The Marital Residence

Given the fact that it is often the parties' only major asset, many emotionally charged property disputes focus on the marital residence. Disposition is especially complicated when minor children are involved. Some statutes (see Exhibit 11.3) specifically require consideration of custodial issues when effecting a property division. The most common options for dispositional treatment of the marital residence are the following:

- If neither spouse wishes to keep the house, the residence may be sold and the proceeds divided equally or in some other agreed-upon or court-ordered proportion.
- When the marital home is the only asset the parties have, the court may be forced to order the sale of the residence and division of the proceeds so that the parties can receive cash awards and move forward with their respective lives.
- One spouse may buy out the other spouse's interest (often refinancing the property) and keep the home.
- One spouse may be awarded the marital home, while the other spouse is awarded offsetting assets such as a bank account or pension.
- The house may continue to be held jointly, with one party having the right to exclusive use and occupancy until a future date (usually connected with a child-related contingency), at which time the property will be sold and the proceeds divided. The precise terms of such an arrangement need to be laid out carefully in the parties' agreement or the court's order (i.e., who is responsible for payment of the mortgage, taxes, insurance, maintenance, and repairs; what will be deducted from the proceeds prior to distribution; how will the proceeds eventually be divided; and how will appreciation or depreciation be treated?).

Pensions, Retirement Benefits, and Qualified Domestic Relations Orders (QDROs)

Individuals in a position to do so usually anticipate and plan for eventual retirement from the world of work. Acquired either individually or through an employer, retirement plans come in a variety of forms such as pensions, individual retirement accounts (IRAs), 401(k) plans, deferred compensation, profit sharing, and stock option plans. Retirement plans are generally tax deferred, which means that the income produced will not be taxed until the income is paid during retirement. Along with the marital home, retirement plans are commonly one of the only large assets available for division upon divorce.

A *pension* is a job-related retirement benefit acquired by an employee and funded through contributions by the employer, the employee, or a combination of both. It is a form of deferred compensation. There are two primary types of pension plans:

- In a *defined-benefit plan,* the amount of the benefit is usually determined according to a formula based on the participant's earnings, length of service, or target monthly benefit. The value of a defined benefit plan (a "traditional" pension) is usually established by an actuary, who determines the total benefits the employee is likely to receive based on his or her life expectancy and then calculates the present cash value of the right to receive that amount in the future. Upon retirement, the employee is entitled to receive the defined benefit in a lump sum or in periodic payments (depending on the definition of the benefit).

- In a *defined-contribution plan,* each employee has his or her own individual retirement account, such as a 401(k) plan. Such plans may involve purchase money arrangements, profit sharing, stock bonuses, etc. The eventual benefit is based on the amount of contributions and investment earnings in the years during which the employee is covered by the plan. The value of a defined contribution plan is based on its current value without any adjustment for income taxes and/or penalties if the balance were withdrawn early. Because a defined-contribution plan has an account value in the participant's name, its value can be determined without actuarial assistance, for reference in property division deliberations. Upon retirement, the employee is entitled to withdraw the pension funds as he or she sees fit (subject to certain constraints imposed by the government).

In either plan, the employee is entitled to receive the pension funds that he or she contributed. In addition, the employee is entitled to receive those contributed by the employer, provided the pension is vested. A pension vests when an employee has met certain threshold requirements—for example, being employed for a certain period of time such as ten years. If an employee has not satisfied the minimal threshold requirements, the pension is unvested. When employees leave employment prior to vesting of their pensions, they generally are entitled to receive only the funds contributed personally and none of the funds contributed by the employer.

A vested pension is customarily considered marital property, although the general rule is that only that portion of the pension attributable to the period of the marriage is subject to division upon divorce. For example, if the husband's pension is based on twenty-five years of employment and he was married to his wife for ten of those years, she may be awarded 40 percent ($10/25 = 2/5 = 40\%$) of "her half" of his pension (20 percent of the total pension ($2/5 \times 1/2 = 1/5 = 20\%$)), especially if the pension is the parties' only major asset. If there are other assets, the pension may be left intact and the wife may be awarded other assets equivalent in value to 20 percent of the pension. Courts vary in their treatment of unvested pensions.

Pension
a job-related retirement benefit acquired by an employee and funded through contributions by the employer, the employee, or a combination of both

Defined-benefit plan
a retirement plan in which the amount of the benefit is usually determined according to a formula based on the participant's earnings, length of service, or target monthly benefit

Defined-contribution plan
a retirement plan in which the eventual benefit is based on the amount of contributions and investment earnings in the years during which the employee is covered by the plan

Some consider them future expectancy interests not subject to division. Others consider the amount of the contribution made by a party to the pension fund during the marriage to be marital property.[37]

State law generally establishes how property will be divided upon divorce, but federal law largely controls retirement benefits. Most employers must comply with the Employee Retirement Income Security Act (ERISA), a federal statute passed in 1974 and amended by the Retirement Equity Act (REA) of 1984. The Act is designed to protect employee pensions in the event an employer goes out of business or declares bankruptcy. Under ERISA, a qualified retirement plan is one that does not discriminate in favor of highly compensated employees. Although most are, not all retirement plans are subject to ERISA. For example, some governmental and church-offered plans are not. Military pensions are also subject to their own rules and regulations at the state and federal levels. Generally, the federal government will honor domestic relations orders dividing military pensions if the parties have been married for at least ten years and the award to the alternate payee does not exceed 50 percent of the net pension.

When one or both of the parties are participants in pension plans, it is necessary to obtain from each plan administrator (through the client or during the discovery process) copies of the plan and a record of contributions. The plan should then be valued. As indicated above, depending on the nature of the plan, valuation may require the assistance of a pension valuation expert/service. If a client waives valuation, the waiver should be in writing and preferably expressly stated in the parties' separation agreement to avoid a later malpractice claim against the attorney advising the client.

Pension plans can pose complex challenges for the family law team including, but not limited to, the following:

- As noted above, the value of a participant's interest in a retirement plan may not be ascertainable without expert advice. For example, it is hard to predict a specific retirement date, the life expectancy of the participant, the amount of contributions that eventually will be made by the employer and the participant, or the ultimate value of the account at some future date.
- The participant may choose not to retire at his or her earliest retirement age unless required to do so. Continued employment beyond the age projected at the time an agreement is negotiated may result in the other party receiving less of a benefit than he or she bargained for![38]
- Pensions of various kinds (e.g., the military and public and private employers) are governed by an array of federal, state, and employer rules and regulations. The rules governing distribution of pensions are complex and must be followed scrupulously.
- As indicated earlier in this chapter, questions may be raised as to whether disability retirement pensions constitute property divisible as marital property.[39]

Pensions may be divided in a variety of ways depending on the parties' preferences, assets, needs, and circumstances. Commonly employed options include the following:

- Assume that a wife has a pension presently valued at $120,000, which she does not wish to have divided. She has other assets totaling $60,000 that she is willing to liquidate and use to "buy out" her husband's share and thereby leave the pension intact.
- Assume the husband has a pension presently valued at $300,000. He and his spouse own a marital home as tenants by the entirety. The home is valued at $300,000 and is owned outright. He does not wish to divide his pension and is willing to offset the pension by transferring his interest in the marital home to his wife. She, in turn, is pleased with this arrangement, as

she wants to remain in the home and sell it at a later date after the children have graduated from high school.

- Assume the parties met when they began teaching at a Midwestern, state-funded community college, where they have continued to teach for the last twenty years. Each has been contributing to the state retirement system for the full period. Although their contributions have not been exactly equal, the parties are willing to waive valuation and their respective potential rights in each other's pensions.

- Applying an "if, as, and when" approach, a non-employee spouse may be awarded a share of an employee spouse's pension funds if, as, and when the employee spouse receives them. The share is most often determined according to a "marital fraction" formula based on the ratio of the years of marriage to the number of years of employment at the time of distribution. The present value of the pension does not need to be determined and no offsetting award is required.

- Assume the parties have been married for over twenty years and that the husband's General Electric pension is their only major asset. The non-employee spouse may seek to directly reach the pension funds by obtaining a **Qualified Domestic Relations Order (QDRO).** A QDRO is a court order directing the administrator of a pension plan to pay a specified portion of the pension to an alternate payee, the non-employee spouse. Considerable care must be taken to specify whether the QDRO includes only the retirement benefit or also the death benefit as well.[40] The QDRO must be approved by counsel for each party, the Plan Administrator, and the court in order to be effective. A sample QDRO is available for review on the companion website.[41]

DIVISION OF LIABILITIES

Although we have primarily focused in this chapter on the division of assets when a marriage terminates, it is equally (and sometimes more) important to consider personal and business debts. Often substantial debt has contributed to the breakdown of the relationship between the parties, and they have come to view divorce as the only way to bring an end to an escalating debt that is spiraling out of control. The parties' debts should be classified as separate and marital. **Marital debt,** like marital property, is usually specifically identified, valued, and apportioned between the parties. The general rule is that debt incurred prior to marriage is a separate debt, as it was presumably not incurred for the benefit of the marriage, although that assumption may be rebutted by the facts and circumstances. Debts for **necessaries** for the family unit (such as shelter, food, clothing, and medical care, for example) are considered marital debts. For purposes of equitable distribution, the South Carolina courts have defined a marital debt as a debt incurred for the joint benefit of the parties regardless of who incurred the obligation.[42]

Qualified Domestic Relations Order (QDRO)
a court order directing the administrator of a pension plan to pay a specified portion of the pension to an alternate payee

---

Paralegal Practice Tip
Under federal law, the employee is required to designate the employee spouse as the beneficiary of his or her retirement benefits. If there is no QDRO upon divorce, the employee should be advised to change the designee following dissolution, assuming he or she wishes to do so. A certified copy of the judgment should be filed with the additional paperwork required by the plan.

Marital debt
debt incurred during the marriage for the benefit of the marital enterprise regardless of which party incurred the obligation

Necessaries
things that are indispensable to living, such as food, clothing, and shelter

---

PARALEGAL APPLICATION **11.6**

IDENTIFICATION OF DEBTS

The paralegal may be asked to work with the client in an effort to compile a summary of the parties' debts, both individual and joint. For each debt, the summary should indicate:

- the amount of the debt
- the amount and frequency of payments

continued

- who is making the payments and out of what source of funds
- who incurred the debt
- why the debt was incurred (i.e., for what purpose)
- when the debt was incurred (before the marriage, during the marriage, post separation, or after commencement of the divorce proceeding)
- whether or not the debt is secured (for example, a mortgage secured by the marital home, a car loan secured by the vehicle, etc.)
- the duration of the obligation

As with marital assets, there are three primary ways in which separate and marital debts are divided.

1. The parties may have executed a premarital agreement that addresses responsibility for separate and marital debt.
2. The parties may allocate responsibility for debt in their separation agreement.
3. Absent an agreement of the parties, the issue may be presented to the court for resolution.

The courts use a variety of approaches to allocating responsibility for debt, such as the following:

- The court may require payment of the parties' debt out of existing assets and then allocate the remaining assets, if any.
- The debt may be factored into the overall property division. For example, rather than awarding a wife $15,000 of property, the court may order the husband to pay $15,000 of the wife's outstanding student loans.
- The courts may make an equal allocation of debt.
- The court may decide to assign all of the debt to one of the parties. In an Illinois case, an appellate court did precisely that when it upheld a trial court's award of all assets to a wife and all debts to the husband, given the nature and extent of his dissipation of marital assets. (See Case 11.6.)

Although a divorce decree may allocate responsibility for marital debt between the parties, the family court does not have the power to limit the rights of third-party creditors. For example, if both parties took out a car loan and the judgment provides that the wife will pay the balance of the loan and she fails to do so, the lender is free to try to collect from either spouse individually or both spouses jointly. To help protect against such situations, it is important to include a **hold harmless provision** in the parties' separation agreement. A hold harmless provision specifies that a particular spouse will be solely responsible for payment of certain debts and that the other spouse shall be free and clear of any obligation regarding those debts and will be indemnified by the debtor spouse if forced to pay the debt.

Sometimes the debt burden is so extensive and overwhelming that, subsequent to divorce, one of the parties declares personal bankruptcy. Bankruptcy involves complex issues and procedures usually handled by attorneys who

Hold harmless provision
a provision specifying that a particular spouse will be solely responsible for payment of certain debts and that the other spouse shall be free and clear of any obligation regarding those debts and will be indemnified by the debtor spouse if forced to pay the debt

specialize in this area of the law, but there are two basic points of particular relevance to the topic of property division:

- With the exception of debts in the nature of child support and spousal maintenance, bankruptcy law may provide for discharge of the bulk of a petitioner's debts. If a jointly held debt is discharged in this context, the creditor is still free to pursue the other spouse to collect on the remainder of the debt.
- Although child support and alimony generally are not dischargeable in bankruptcy, payments due to a former spouse under a court-ordered division of property usually are dischargeable.

TAX CONSEQUENCES OF PROPERTY DIVISION

Under current federal tax law, transfers of real or personal property between spouses during a marriage or at dissolution as incidents of divorce are not taxable events.[43] A transfer is "incident to a divorce" if it occurs within one year after the date on which the marriage ends or if it is related to the ending of the marriage. However, this does not mean that there are no tax issues to be considered. In fact, several jurisdictions require that the court consider the tax implications of a property division for each of the parties.[44] An attorney's failure to advise a client regarding related tax issues may give rise to a malpractice claim in some circumstances. For example, assume that a wife is awarded a substantial number of shares of Starbucks stock worth $150,000 at the time of the divorce. If and when she elects to sell the stock, she may receive a rude awakening when she learns that she is liable for payment of a significant *capital gains tax* because the stock was initially purchased at a mere fraction of its current worth. She will actually realize much less than the $150,000 she thought she'd bargained for and would receive. Of course, if the stock sells for less than its purchase price, a loss may be claimed.

Some other tax-related issues that may arise include:

- If the property division is such that a party must withdraw funds from a retirement plan before he or she is entitled to in order to "pay off" the other spouse, the value of the retirement plan is reduced, and the participant is likely to face an early withdrawal tax penalty.
- The parties may attempt to disguise as alimony a portion of the property division in order for one party to receive a tax deduction for the transfer. This is usually accomplished by "front-loading" the first two or three years of "alimony" payments, i.e., making them significantly larger than in subsequent years. The IRS will determine whether the transfer is alimony or property division based on its own criteria, not on others' labels or titles. If the IRS determines that the "alimony" paid was in fact property division, it will *recapture* the tax deduction claimed by the payor, who will then have to pay taxes, interest, and penalties on the improperly deducted amount. The recipient, on the other hand, will now be able to deduct the amount on which he or she previously paid taxes as alimony income.
- Sometimes, part or all of a division of property is paid to a third party. For example, a husband may pay off his wife's mortgage on her condominium. The Internal Revenue Service will still allow the transfer between the spouses to be a nontaxable event between them if:
  1. the transfer is made pursuant to a divorce or separation agreement,
  2. the transfer is made pursuant to a written request of the beneficiary spouse, and
  3. the transferring spouse receives a written acceptance of the property after it has been transferred.

Paralegal Practice Tip
Attorneys have an ethical duty to advise clients of the tax consequences of divorce. In complex cases, accountants may be retained to calculate costs and benefits for the client. Although attorneys' fees in general are not tax deductible for income tax purposes, the portion of fees attributable to services pertaining to tax matters is tax deductible, and the client should be advised in writing as to that amount.

Capital gains tax
a tax on income derived from the sale of a capital asset (a long-term asset) as defined by the Internal Revenue Code

Alimony recapture rule
the IRS rule that the government can recover a tax benefit (the prior taking of a deduction for payment of alimony) by taxing the income that no longer qualifies for the benefit

ADDITIONAL PROPERTY RELATED TAX ISSUES

There are several additional tax issues related to division of property, debt, and spousal support. Of particular importance is the designation of who will be obligated to pay any taxes due and who will be eligible to claim tax benefits. For example, the following issues should be addressed in the parties' separation agreement:

- Have the parties failed to file any required state or federal tax returns for any year(s) during their marriage?

- Who will be responsible for paying any tax deficiencies, interest, and penalties should the Internal Revenue Service or a state department of revenue impose them for any prior years during which the parties filed joint tax returns?

- If both parties signed joint tax returns in the past, but only one of the parties prepared the form, controlled the information that went into it, and is responsible for errors, omissions, and/or fraud committed, resulting in significant penalties, Congress now provides some relief for an ***innocent spouse*** under certain circumstances. The spouse must be able to prove that at the time the return was signed, he or she did not know and had no reason to know that the spouse understated taxes that were due. Otherwise, the parties will be jointly and individually liable for the deficiency, meaning that the IRS can collect from one or both of them. An "innocent spouse" will want to include language in the agreement that the spouse who prepared the returns will indemnify the innocent spouse against any taxes and penalties arising out of any joint returns filed during the marriage.

- Will the parties file joint or separate tax returns for the year in which they separate and sign their agreement, and who will pay the taxes due, if any? Who will be entitled to any tax refund that may be due to the parties?

- If the parties are going to continue to jointly own the marital home post divorce, who will be responsible for paying property taxes, and who will be entitled to claim any related mortgage interest and taxes as deductions?

- If the marital home is subsequently sold, how will the capital gains tax be handled should any be due?

Innocent spouse
a spouse who may be relieved of liability incurred if the other spouse prepared the tax forms, controlled the information that went into them, and is responsible for errors, omissions, and/or fraud that resulted in imposition of significant taxes, interest, and penalties

THE PARALEGAL'S ROLE IN THE PROPERTY DIVISION PROCESS

The tasks most commonly performed by a paralegal in a property division case are:

- compiling a list of the parties' assets indicating how the property is titled, its value, and how the value was calculated
- scheduling and participating in interviews as assigned
- drafting complaints/petitions, motions, supporting affidavits, and proposed orders, as well as correspondence related to the case
- making discovery-related recommendations and drafting interrogatories, depositions, and requests for production of documents as directed to assist in identifying and valuing assets and the parties' respective contributions to those assets. In equitable distribution jurisdictions, discovery efforts may also be designed to gather information relating to factors to be considered by the court when making property distributions.
- researching current law (statutes, case law, and secondary sources) to support the client's position with respect to contested assets so that the court will have a rationale on which to base a decision.[45] In some cases, this may mean both state and federal law need to be considered.[46]

- suggesting issues on which expert testimony may be necessary, such as valuation of pensions, and maintaining lists of experts qualified to assist with and potentially testify as to specific issues, such as valuation of a business interest or the marital home
- drafting a pretrial memorandum, if required, informing the court of the nature and extent of the marital estate and the merits of the client's claim as to property distribution
- assisting in preparation for motion hearings
- drafting a property article/paragraph/exhibit for inclusion in a separation agreement if the parties negotiate a mutually agreed-upon division
- assisting with gathering and preparing evidentiary exhibits related to each of the property-related issues for trial, including, where applicable, statutory factors to be considered by the court
- helping to identify and prepare prospective witnesses
- drafting proposed conclusions of law and findings of fact, which, in an equitable distribution jurisdiction, should address each of the factors to be considered by the court
- making sure the client is kept informed of progress and upcoming deadlines, hearings, discovery matters, etc.
- tracking progress on the case to be certain timelines are met
- if within scope of expertise, preparing preliminary draft of a QDRO

Many of these tasks have already been referenced in this chapter and elsewhere in the text. Examples of property division provisions addressing real property, personal property, and debts and liabilities in a separation agreement are contained in the sample agreement provided in Chapter 12.

CHAPTER **SUMMARY**

The division of marital property upon divorce is one of the most hotly contested and emotionally charged issues addressed in a family law practice. The discussion in this chapter reflects the contemporary view of marriage as a partnership to which each party is presumed to make economic and noneconomic contributions. When that partnership dissolves, both assets and liabilities need to be allocated between the parties. This may be accomplished via an enforceable premarital agreement, a separation agreement negotiated by the parties and approved by the court, or a court order following a trial on the merits of the parties' respective proposals.

After describing the differences between alimony and property division, this chapter explores in some depth the five basic phases of the property division process:

1. Definition and identification of the parties' "property"
2. Classification of the property as separate, marital, or both
3. Identification of the property subject to division upon divorce
4. Valuation of major assets and liabilities
5. Division of the parties' property according to the appropriate jurisdictional standard: community property or equitable distribution

The chapter devotes particular attention to some of the more challenging issues confronted in the property division context. For instance, are assets such as a professional degree or the goodwill of a business actually property on which a dollar value can be placed, and, if so, do they constitute separate or marital property? Does separate property lose its identity as separate when it becomes commingled with marital property? Should the conduct of the parties (such as dissipation of assets) be considered when allocating marital property? Should one party be permitted to access the other party's pension? What are some of the potential tax issues related to property division?

This is an area in which the role played by a paralegal will vary considerably based on training, skills, and experience. A property division case provides an opportunity for the paralegal to do some creative thinking about assets, development of arguments and theories to support a request for division, and organization of materials (exhibits, charts, PowerPoint presentations, etc.) to persuade a court to adopt the client's position at trial. However, a paralegal should not undertake a task beyond his or her expertise. There is no shame in acknowledging a need for guidance and supervision. A failure to do so does a disservice to the client, and in the extreme, may give rise to a malpractice claim against the firm if an assignment is not thoroughly researched and properly prepared. Even a supervising family law attorney may choose to consult with an expert on a particularly complex issue beyond his or her expertise.

The chapter (including the end notes) references a broad array of statutes and case references illustrating the various topics covered. However, it must be emphasized that courts vary considerably in their approaches, and the paralegal needs to be attentive to the current governing law in his or her jurisdiction and in other jurisdictions, when appropriate. There simply are no guidelines a family law attorney can use with a client to predict the precise outcome of a property distribution upon divorce. Particularly in equitable distribution jurisdictions, even though judges may be required to consider certain factors in reaching a decision, no specific formula applies, and they are free to exercise broad discretion and weigh the various factors as they see fit in each individual case. Their decisions are rarely overturned absent an abuse of discretion or an error in application of the law.

KEY **TERMS**

Abuse of discretion
Active appreciation
Actuary
Alimony recapture rule
All property state
Basis
Capital gains tax
Commingling
Common law property states
Community property
Defined-benefit plan
Defined-contribution plan
Dissipation

Dual property state
Equitable distribution
Equity
Error of law
Expert
Fair market value
Hold harmless (indemnity) clause
Inception of title theory
Innocent spouse
Marital debt
Marital estate
Marital property
Necessaries

Passive appreciation
Pension
Postmarital agreement
Premarital agreement
Qualified Domestic Relations Order
 (QDRO)
Separate property
Separation agreement
Source of funds/*pro rata* theory
Tracing
Transmutation
Valuation
Vested

REVIEW **QUESTIONS**

1. Describe the partnership view of marriage prevalent in contemporary society.
2. Identify the major differences between alimony and property division.
3. Identify the five phases of the property division process.
4. Explain the effect of including professional goodwill in the definition of property.
5. Identify the majority view regarding professional degrees as "property."
6. Distinguish between separate and marital property. Give an example of each.
7. Identify the general rule with respect to the classification of personal injury awards as separate or marital property.
8. Distinguish between active and passive appreciation of property and explain why this difference is significant in the context of property division.
9. Define and give an example of transmutation.
10. Define commingling and give an example of its potential effect.
11. Distinguish between the source of funds and the inception of title rules and explain how they can lead to opposite results.
12. Define tracing and give an example.
13. Explain the difference between a "dual property" and an "all property" approach to effecting a division of property upon divorce.
14. Define valuation and indicate why it is important and when it occurs.
15. Define fair market value.
16. Describe the primary differences between a community property approach and an equitable division approach to property division.
17. Identify a minimum of six factors generally considered by courts dividing property in equitable property jurisdictions.
18. Describe the role, if any, played by conduct in the context of property division.
19. Identify the basic difference between a vested and an unvested pension.
20. Describe the nature and purpose of a QDRO.
21. Identify the nature and purpose of a hold harmless provision.
22. Describe how the courts generally treat debt in a property distribution.
23. Identify three tax issues related to property division cases.
24. Describe the paralegal's role in a property division case.

FOCUS ON **THE JOB**

THE FACTS

Jimmy and Alice have been married for ten years and have three children. They appeared to have a good life and a decent marriage until recently, when Alice had an affair with her boss and Jimmy found out about it. He is filing for divorce and says he wants to "take Alice to the cleaners so she walks away with nothing." His lawyer appreciates his feelings, but has told him that that's just not the way it works anymore.

The assets involved in this case include the following:

- When the parties married, the wife had a jewelry collection valued at approximately $10,000. During the marriage she received as gifts an additional $15,000 worth of jewelry. The collection is now valued at $35,000, $10,000 of which is attributable to appreciation in the value of the rings, watches, and necklaces included in the collection.

- Before marriage, the husband had a baseball card collection valued at $7,300 that is now worth approximately $29,100. Half of the increase is the result of the purchase of new cards with marital funds and the balance is due to appreciation in the value of the cards owned prior to the marriage.

- The parties have resided in the marital home since their marriage ten years ago. The property has been appraised at $225,000. The down payment of $40,000 came from the wife's mother and father, who insisted that the home be titled solely in their daughter's name. The purchase price was $170,000 and there is a mortgage on the property with a remaining balance of $72,000. The husband added a den to the property through his own labor over a six-month period. It is estimated that this increased the value of the home by approximately $15,000. The remainder of the increase in value is attributable to market forces. The parties have contributed equally throughout the marriage to payment of the mortgage, insurance, property taxes, and household expenses. The wife wants to remain in the marital home for the next five years until the parties' youngest child graduates from high school, and she doesn't figure this is any problem because the house is in her name.

- The wife is a nurse and the husband is a physical therapist. They have each worked throughout the marriage and contributed to their respective pension plans. Both plans are vested but neither has been valued. The parties believe they are relatively equal in value and do not want to go to the expense of having them valued. They have each advised their respective attorneys to this effect. They each want to keep their own pension intact.

- The parties bought two pets during their marriage: a seven-year-old beagle named "Spike" and a five-year-old cat named "Kaspar." They both adore the pets and have contributed to their care throughout their marriage. Both pets were obtained from a local pet shelter at no cost other than the cost of an initial medical examination and shots.

- The parties have an investment portfolio that they opened together and have funded equally in the total amount of $60,000. The account is presently worth $92,000; $12,000 of this amount is due to market trends (passive appreciation), and the balance appears to be the result of the husband's sound management of the asset (active appreciation).

- The parties have a joint bank account used for necessaries. The balance in the account is presently $2,632.18. They have contributed equally to the account.

- The parties have a joint savings account to which they have both contributed, but neither has maintained any records regarding their respective contributions to the account over the years. They each acknowledge that this account was established to support the marital enterprise in the event of an emergency or a special opportunity. The account presently contains $16,234.

- The wife has credit card debt in the amount of $1,368, and the husband has credit card debt in the amount of $4,786.

- Although they each had their educational degrees prior to marriage, the wife has been paying back student loans throughout the marriage. The balance on the loans is now only $924. She has paid off approximately $7,000 during the marriage out of joint marital funds.

THE ASSIGNMENT

Working with another student in your class, negotiate an appropriate division of the property given the above fact pattern. You will need to:

1. Determine whether you are in an equitable distribution or community property jurisdiction.

2. Create a chart depicting what you believe to be marital property and the separate property of each of the spouses. The chart should reflect the value of each asset (and the amount attributable to each spouse). Note that some assets may be part separate and part marital/community property.

3. Create a chart indicating the results of your negotiation with respect to how the property should be divided between the parties, given the standard in your state and the facts of this case. Remember to factor the parties' liabilities into your deliberations.

FOCUS ON **ETHICS**

Assume that you are a paralegal in the law office of Attorney Karen Goldberg. Attorney Goldberg represents Alice in the above hypothetical but is presently away on her honeymoon with her fourth husband. She has told you that the client just wants what is fair. Alice feels bad about the affair but does not think it should be held against her. Attorney Goldberg has directed you to negotiate a property settlement with representatives of the law firm representing Jimmy. As a paralegal, what course of action should you take, and how should the situation be addressed? Which of the ethical canons for paralegals promulgated by the National Federation of Paralegal Associations (NFPA), contained in Appendix B, are applicable in this context?

FOCUS ON **CASE LAW**

Edelman v. Edelman, 3 P.3d 348 (Alas. 2000), a case decided by the Supreme Court of Alaska, is located on the companion website. Locate and read the case and then respond to the following questions.

1. What is the legal history of the case: What kind of a case is it? Where was it brought prior to reaching the Alaska Supreme Court and with what result?
2. What are the issues being appealed and by whom?
3. What is the Alaska Supreme Court's standard of review of a lower court's ruling of this nature?
4. According to the opinion, what are the three steps the lower courts take when making decisions about property division?
5. Based on this case, would you conclude that Alaska is an equitable distribution or a community property state?
6. What factors did the Supreme Court indicate should be considered by the superior court when making decisions concerning property division? What is the source of those factors?

7. Identify the assets in dispute in this case.
8. What did the court decide with respect to the "set net permit"? Was it deemed to be separate or marital property? Why?
9. What was the primary issue with respect to valuation of the marital home?
10. How did the court deal with the wife's post-separation payments of the mortgage on the marital home?
11. What was the nature of the tort claim in this case? Did the Court consider this claim to be in the nature of separate or marital property or both?
12. What did the Alaska Supreme Court decide with respect to the superior court's ruling regarding the husband's pension?
13. What did the court decide with respect to the wife's claim for alimony?
14. Although the court remanded the issue of attorney's fees to the superior court, how did it view the wife's appeal on this issue in particular?

FOCUS ON **STATE LAW AND PROCEDURE**

Locate the property distribution statute in your jurisdiction and then respond to the following questions:

1. Is your state an equitable distribution or a community property jurisdiction?
2. How is marital/community property defined? How is separate property defined?

3. If you are in an equitable distribution state, do the courts apply a dual or all property approach?
4. What factors does a court consider when dividing marital property?
5. Are the nonfinancial contributions of spouses considered?

FOCUS ON **TECHNOLOGY**

WEBSITES OF INTEREST

www.abanet.org/family/familylaw/table5.html

This is the site of the family law section of the American Bar Association. It contains a wealth of information including a chart summarizing the approaches of the various states to property division. The chart provides a state-by-state summary of a variety of factors related to the topic of property division including:

- Identification of both traditional and nontraditional community property states
- Whether only marital property is divided
- Whether or not the state has a statutory list of factors to be considered by the courts when dividing marital property
- Whether the state considers nonmonetary contributions, economic misconduct, or contributions to education when dividing marital property

This chart also appears in the *Family Law Quarterly* published by the ABA on an annual basis.

http://www.dol.gov/ebsa

The U.S. Department of Labor has produced an informative forty-eight-page publication regarding QDROs: The Division of Pensions through Qualified Domestic Relations Orders (QDROs). It can be located at this site.

http://www.findlaw.com

The site provides links to state laws concerning a variety of divorce-related topics including property division.

ASSIGNMENTS

1. Locate online the statutes governing division of property in the states of California, Louisiana, Maryland, Massachusetts, Pennsylvania, and Texas. What are some of the significant differences among them?

2. Locate online an example of a property division provision/exhibit for a separation agreement.

3. Locate online an example of a QDRO.

4. Locate online information about a firm/company that values pensions and prepares QDROs, such as at *http://www.pensionappraisers.com* and *http://www. qdrosolutions.com*.

5. Of what use are the following websites with respect to the topic of property division, if any?
   a. *http://www.divorceinfo.com*
   b. *http://divorcelinks.com*
   c. *http://www.divorcenet.com*
   d. *http://divorcesource.com*

chapter **twelve**

SEPARATION AGREEMENTS

Herman, an elderly multimillionaire, and Anna, a relatively young "model," have been married for twelve years and have a minor son, Theodore. The couple has decided to seek a no-fault divorce because they no longer seem to have anything in common. Anna believes she is getting a pretty good settlement, given that she came into the marriage with little more than good looks. She figures she recognizes a good deal when she sees it and doesn't need some high-priced attorney telling her what she already knows.

WHAT IS A SEPARATION AGREEMENT?

Separation agreements are relative newcomers to the family law legal scene. For centuries, and even after the passage of married women's property acts, a husband and wife could not execute a valid contract with each other. Separation agreements, in particular, were considered contrary to public policy favoring the preservation of marriage, because they appeared to promote divorce by providing financial incentives for terminating the marital relationship. As late as the 1960s, state legislatures and courts were still in the process of lifting such restrictions.

A *separation agreement* is a contract that sets forth the understanding reached by parties to a divorce or *legal separation* regarding their individual rights and obligations with respect to matters relating primarily to finances, property, and minor children, if any. The name given to the document varies by jurisdiction. For example, it may be called, among other options, a marital agreement, marital dissolution agreement, marital property settlement, or a permanent stipulation of the parties. In theory, a separation agreement addresses any and all rights arising out of the marital status. In an increasing number of states, the agreement is divided into two parts: a parenting plan that addresses child-related provisions and a stipulation/property settlement agreement that covers all other issues.

Since the agreement is a contract, it must meet all the requirements of a valid contract:

- The parties must have the legal capacity to contract—they must be able to understand the nature and effect of the agreement.
- The parties must enter the contract of their own free will—they must not be acting under duress.
- There must be an offer and an acceptance—there must be a *meeting of the minds* with respect to the terms of the agreement.
- There must be *consideration* for the agreement—a separation agreement is a bilateral contract in which the parties have reciprocal obligations, and the consideration is the mutual promises of the parties contained within the agreement.

In an uncontested divorce, the parties' agreement must customarily be filed with the divorce petition or shortly thereafter. Timing of the submission is based on procedural rules or local practice in each state. In a contested case, the parties may file no agreement or may file a partial agreement that addresses the issues they agree on. The remaining issues are left for the court to determine following a trial. For example, the parties may agree on custody, visitation, and child support but be at loggerheads when it comes to division of their property.

WHAT IS THE PURPOSE OF A SEPARATION AGREEMENT?

In today's legal climate, separation agreements are welcome. From the court's perspective, they conserve judicial resources by eliminating the need for lengthy, costly, and bitter trials. From the clients' perspective, they allow the parties to privately negotiate the terms of their separation or divorce without governmental interference. The separation agreement provides a blueprint for them to follow as their marriage terminates and they move forward into the future. A carefully

Separation agreement
an agreement made between spouses in anticipation of divorce or legal separation concerning the terms of the divorce or separation and any continuing obligations of the parties to each other

Legal separation
a judicial decree that allows the parties to live separate and apart without dissolving their legal relationship as husband and wife; sometimes called a limited divorce

Meeting of the minds
a shared understanding with respect to the terms and conditions of a contract

Consideration
a bargained-for exchange or mutual promises underlying the formation of a contract

drafted agreement, which the parties negotiate, review, and understand, not only allows the case to proceed on an uncontested basis, but also helps minimize post-divorce confusion, aggravation, disagreements, and litigation.

WHAT ARE THE CHARACTERISTICS OF AN EFFECTIVE SEPARATION AGREEMENT?

The primary characteristics of an effective separation agreement are as follows:

Unearned income
income derived from investment rather than labor

Parol evidence rule
when a writing is intended to embody the entire agreement between the parties, its terms cannot later be varied or contradicted by evidence of earlier or contemporaneous agreements

- **The agreement is comprehensive.** In order to minimize disputes and avoid costly post-divorce litigation, the agreement should address all of the rights and obligations that arise out of the marital status including, for example, property division, spousal support, insurance, taxes, and matters pertaining to minor children, if any. (See Exhibit 12.1.)
- **The terms of the agreement are clearly defined.** For example, if a provision of the agreement will vary with a party's income, does "income" include both earned and **unearned income**? Does a reference to a party's "pension" include both the pension and the related death benefit?
- **The terms of the agreement are stated fully so that the parties know what is expected of each of them.** For example, if one party will continue to reside in the jointly owned marital home, the agreement should specify who will be responsible for payment of the mortgage (if any), property taxes, insurance, utilities, and maintenance expenses such as repairs, landscaping, painting, or snow removal, if warranted.
- **The agreement accurately reflects the parties' intentions.** Each attorney must carefully review the agreement with his or her client to be certain it reflects what the parties actually have agreed to and that there are no extraneous oral or written agreements between the parties. When an agreement is intended to embody the parties' entire understanding, the **parol evidence rule** provides that its terms cannot later be varied or contradicted by evidence of earlier or contemporaneous agreements.
- **Although the parties are free to settle for less than they might be entitled to under the law, the agreement still should be fair and freely entered** (although it inevitably reflects considerable compromise on both sides). When courts assess whether or not an agreement is fair and reasonable at the time of separation, divorce, or post-divorce litigation, they consider several factors:[1]
  - Are the financial provisions fair and reasonable when the agreement is viewed as a whole? For example, is one party left nearly destitute while the other receives substantial assets?
  - Is the agreement consistent with the statutory or case law factors governing alimony, property division, and custody issues in the jurisdiction? Does it appear to relieve one parent of his or her statutory duty to support a child?
  - Under what circumstances did negotiations take place? Was one party under considerable duress, such as a threat of abuse or loss of custody of the children?
  - How complex are the issues? Were experts consulted to assist with complicated valuation problems?
  - How legally sophisticated are the parties? What kinds of education and professional background do they each have?
  - Was each party represented by separate counsel competent in family law matters? Was one party not represented? Did both parties believe themselves to be represented by the same attorney?

EXHIBIT 12.1 Checklist of Basic Topics Covered in Separation Agreements

Identification Clause/Opening Paragraph

> Date of execution
>
> Names and addresses of the parties and names used to refer to the parties in the agreement

Recitals/Statement of Facts

> Date and place of marriage and the number of marriage for each party
>
> Names and birthdates of all children born to or adopted by the parties
>
> Date of separation and location where the parties last resided together
>
> Reason for separation (e.g., irreconcilable differences)
>
> Current living status (usually separate and apart)
>
> Identification of any pending action for divorce or legal separation (separate maintenance) with name of court and docket number
>
> Purpose of the agreement and parties' intent with respect to its effect
>
> Confirmation of participation in negotiation of agreement and knowledge of rights and liabilities
>
> Confirmation agreement is signed freely and voluntarily
>
> Consideration for agreement (mutual promises)

General Provisions

> Separation
>> Intention to live separate and apart
>> Nonmolestation provision (an agreement not to restrain or interfere with each other)
>
> Mutual/General Release (acceptance of the agreement in full satisfaction of all claims against each other except those arising from the agreement and subsequent divorce)
>
> Waiver of Estate claim with exceptions (a waiver of any rights in the other's estate upon death)
>
> Execution of Documents necessary to implement agreement (e.g., deeds, QDROs, etc.)
>
> Acknowledgments
>> Independent representation of choice (or opportunity for it or an acknowledgment that one or both of the parties proceeded *pro se*)
>> Full disclosure made or opportunity to do so
>> Parties have read and understood terms of the agreement
>> Agreement is free from fraud or coercion
>> Agreement is fair and reasonable
>
> Situs/Governing Law (designation of the state's law that will govern interpretation and enforceability of the agreement)
>
> Validity/Severability/Savings Clause (a clause stating that if any provision of the agreement is declared void, the remaining provisions will continue to be valid)

continued

Entire Agreement (statement that the agreement embodies the parties' complete understanding with respect to resolution of the rights and responsibilities flowing from their marital relationship)

Effective Date

Binding Effect on heirs, assigns, etc.

Intention with respect to merger or survival of agreement (Will the agreement merge in the divorce decree or survive as an independent contract?)

Modification (Under what circumstances, if any, can the agreement be modified?)

Strict Performance (Can a party waive an occasional "breach" by the other party without waiving other breaches or will strict performance of the terms of the agreement be required?)

Dispute Resolution (method; process for selection of mediator, arbitrator, etc.; coverage of costs; binding effect)

Breach of Agreement

Attorneys' Fees

Number of counterparts executed, each constituting an original

Signature and Acknowledgment/Certification

Specific Exhibits

Alimony
Waiver(s) OR
Payment of alimony
Type (permanent, lump sum, restitution, etc.)
Amount and form of payment
Payment schedule and duration
Termination contingencies—cohabitation, death, remarriage, etc.
Modifications/cost-of-living adjustments
Intended income tax consequences (intention that payments will be tax deductible to the payor and includable in the income of the recipient)
Security (insurance policy, trust, etc.)
Interest on unpaid balance

Child Custody and Visitation ("parenting time") (unless covered in a parenting plan)
Physical and legal custody—joint/sole
Allocation of decision-making responsibility (major and day-to-day)
Identification of topics considered "major" and requiring consultation (e.g., religious upbringing, education, major surgery, and participation in hazardous activities)
Parental cooperation
Access to school, medical, and dental records, etc.
Visitation/parenting time schedule
Reasonable rights based on mutual agreement
Structured
Days, weekends, weeks
Holidays

continued

Birthdays, Mother's Day, and Father's Day
Transportation arrangements and cost
Illness—emergency medical treatment
Removal/absence from the state—temporary, long term
Contact by phone, e-mail—virtual visitation
Visitation with extended family
Adjustments to schedule—cancellation provisions
Supervised visitation, if warranted
Agreement with respect to children's surname

Child Support (unless covered in a parenting plan)
Amount—relationship to guidelines
Payment schedule
Form of payment—wage assignment, if appropriate
Duration—definition of emancipation
Child care (built into child support formula in several states)
Modification
Expenses related to special activities
Education—elementary, secondary, postsecondary if permitted
Public, private
Costs covered
Allocation of responsibility
Use of children's assets, scholarships, etc.
Decision-making process and cooperation in seeking financial assistance
Access to records
Security for obligation (trust fund, etc.)
Dependency exemption
Treatment for tax purposes, execution of necessary tax forms
Effect of bankruptcy (not dischargeable)
Security for child support (insurance, trust for benefit of children, etc.)

Property Division
Personal property
Waiver of any rights to each other's property
Delivery of documents evidencing ownership
Vehicles
Schedule of property already divided, if appropriate (See Chapter 11 for a list of kinds of property potentially subject to division.)
Property remaining to be divided—time frame and process for division
Retirement funds—Qualified Domestic Relations Order(s)

Real property
Identification/description of all real property
Disposition of each parcel—timing of conveyances, treatment of proceeds, closing costs, commissions, fees, encumbrances, shares to parties, etc.
Assumption and/or payment of mortgages and operating expenses
Marital home—exclusive right to occupy, responsibility for related expenses, mortgage, right of inspection, etc.

continued

Rights to purchase/agreements to sell
Execution of deeds
Tax treatment and capital gains distribution

Liabilities
Allocation of joint debt
Hold harmless provisions for past and future debts
Responsibility for individual debt

Insurance
Medical insurance
Medical insurance for parties
Medical insurance for children
Name of insurer—policy number(s)
Notice of changes
Payment obligations
Duration of coverage
Release from obligation (remarriage, change of employment, emancipation, etc.)
Responsibility for uninsured medical costs of spouses
Responsibility for uninsured medical costs of children
Scope of expenses included (e.g., dental, orthodontic, psychological, optical, prescriptions, etc.)
Agreement regarding elective and cosmetic surgery
Claim and reimbursement procedures
Rights under state/federal law (COBRA, etc.)

Other kinds of insurance
Life
Identify policy(ies) and ownership
Amount
Beneficiaries
Responsibility for payment
Proof of policy
Changes
Right to provide alternative coverage
Property
Liability
Automobile
Other

Taxes
Status of all prior returns (state and federal)
Allocation of refunds
Liability for past-due taxes, interest, and penalties
Notification of audits or assessments, etc.
Innocent spouse language, if appropriate
Cooperation in preparation, etc.

Bankruptcy Filing (if appropriate)
Notice of intention to file
Support obligations not dischargeable

HOW IS A SEPARATION AGREEMENT DEVELOPED?

In the majority of cases, the parties to a divorce or separation reach an agreement with or without the assistance of counsel and/or mediation. This may be accomplished in a variety of ways including the following:

- The parties may reach an agreement on their own and proceed **pro se** or present it to their respective attorneys for review and submission to the court.
- The parties may retain counsel and discuss with their respective attorneys what each considers his or her goals and ***bottom-line*** terms. Financial information will be exchanged, and necessary documents, such as bank statements, deeds, mortgages, etc., will be gathered. If there is no need for formal discovery, counsel may negotiate an agreement via telephone, correspondence, and four-way conferences. In relatively uncomplicated cases, one attorney will generally prepare a draft reducing the agreement to writing for the other's review and input. Successive drafts will be exchanged until an agreement is reached that reflects a "meeting of the minds."
- In more complex cases, drafts will not be prepared until discovery is completed and each party has an opportunity to consider his or her options after carefully examining the full nature and extent of the ***marital estate.*** In high-conflict cases, the attorneys often draft and exchange initial proposals outlining their clients' respective positions on issues such as child custody, visitation, support, alimony, health insurance, property division, distribution of debts, attorneys' fees, etc. Areas of agreement, if any, will be identified and negotiation will proceed with respect to the remaining issues. Once the agreed-upon terms are framed, a partial or full agreement is prepared. If the agreement does not address all of the issues, the remaining topics may be referred for mediation. The issues that remain unresolved after exhaustive efforts will be presented to the court for resolution. More often than not, even those issues may be settled "on the courthouse steps" by parties not wishing to incur the risk or full expense of a trial.

The client ultimately controls the case in the sense that he or she has the final word on terms, on the scope of discovery, and on whether or not a case will proceed to trial. With respect to agreements, the client must have input and approve all proposals communicated to the other party and also must have an opportunity to review and consider all counterproposals.

Pro se
the condition under which a person represents himself or herself in a legal proceeding without the assistance of an attorney

Bottom line
the limit beyond which a party will not go in a negotiation

Marital estate
the property acquired during the marriage other than by gift or inheritance that is subject to division at the time of marital dissolution

PARALEGAL APPLICATION **12.1**

INFORMATION GATHERING FOR SEPARATION AGREEMENTS

Except in cases involving few if any assets, before an agreement is actually drafted, a considerable amount of information should be gathered from the client, the other party, and third parties as well, if appropriate. The parties should have a comprehensive picture of their circumstances before negotiating an agreement or agreeing to a single term in isolation. For example, a party initially opposed to paying spousal support eventually may prefer to pay tax-deductible alimony over time if it means his or her pension will remain intact.

What follows is a summary of the kinds of documents and information that should be collected and compiled in summary form for easy reference when drafting an agreement. The paralegal generally plays an active role in gathering this information through informal and formal discovery, if necessary.

continued

- Personal data:
  - Names
  - Addresses (home and business)
  - Social security numbers
  - Home, business, and cell phone numbers
  - E-mail address (for communication purposes)
  - Details regarding the date and location of the marriage
  - Names and birthdates of the children (of both or either of the parties)
- Contact information for all attorneys involved in the divorce and any other potentially related matters, such as abuse complaints, pending claims, etc.
- Summary of all property owned by the parties indicating how it is held (by husband, wife, jointly, with third parties, in trust, etc), when it was acquired (before or during the marriage, before or after the date of separation), the value of the property, and the means by which the value was established
- Income from all sources of both parties
- Liabilities of both parties: identity (and relationship) of each creditor, amount of debt, who incurred the debt and for what purpose, whose name the debt is in, etc.
- Documents to collect (not intended as an exhaustive list):
  - Pre- or postmarital agreements
  - Deeds
  - Leases
  - Titles
  - Contracts for purchase or sale of property
  - Mortgage/loan applications
  - Insurance policies
  - Wills and trusts
  - Tax documents
  - Financial statements (current and past)
  - Business and professional licenses
  - Pension/retirement account plans, statements, etc.
  - Bank account statements
  - Appraisals
  - Medical reports
  - Pending claims (personal injury, etc.)
  - Court orders or judgments affecting the rights and liabilities of either or both of the parties (including decrees from previous divorces, if any)
  - Credit card statements
  - Royalty statements
  - Articles of Incorporation, corporate by-laws, etc.

THE FORM OF THE SEPARATION AGREEMENT

The actual document is generally in one of three formats:

1. **A two-part format** consisting of:
   A main body containing:
   - a recital of pertinent facts (names and addresses of the parties; names and ages of the parties' children, if any; date and place where the parties were married; and when and where they last lived together)

- several general provisions common to most agreements (clauses relating to waivers, disclosure, interpretation, implementation, modification, severability, nonmolestation, and enforcement of the agreement) A series of "exhibits" that are *incorporated by reference,* each of which addresses a specific topic (such as spousal support, child custody and visitation, or property division) (See Exhibit 12.2.)

2. **An integrated document** that has numbered sections (Articles I, II, III, etc.) following the introductory "recitals" of pertinent facts. Each Article is customarily labeled, for example, General Provisions, Custody and Visitation, Personal Property, etc.

3. **A format recommended or prescribed in the jurisdiction.** Several states provide forms online on state/court-sponsored websites. For example, the New Hampshire courts provide standard forms online for parenting plans and permanent stipulations, which contain numbered paragraphs on all major topics. Several options are provided under each main topic, with boxes for the parties to check indicating their choices. This approach vastly simplifies the process for parties proceeding *pro se*, who lack knowledge about the scope of issues that need to be resolved when their marriage dissolves. If the parties are represented by counsel who choose to develop their own agreements, those agreements must use the same topical numbering system as is used in the court's format. This requirement facilitates review by judges so that they do not have to struggle with the organization of each individual agreement to locate the terms (such as custody, spousal support, or health insurance) that most concern them.

> **Incorporation by reference** adoption by reference; made a part of the agreement by including a statement in the agreement that the Exhibits are to be treated as if they are part of the agreement

> **Paralegal Practice Tip**
> It is unusual, but some jurisdictions permit agreements to be made by oral stipulation of the parties in court rather than by written agreement. If the agreement is read into the record under oath and determined by the court to be fair, reasonable, and freely entered, it may be approved, made a part of the judgment, and be just as binding on the parties as a written agreement.

Whatever the basic format, there is considerable similarity agreement to agreement. However, each separation or divorce involves two parties, each with his or her own unique goals, needs, and circumstances. Therefore, considerable care must be taken to ensure that the agreement is tailored to those circumstances and meets the client's goals and needs to the greatest extent possible (understanding that there are rarely any fully satisfied customers in the divorce context).

THE PARALEGAL'S ROLE IN DRAFTING THE SEPARATION AGREEMENT

Paralegals are often asked to draft separation agreements based on the specific terms provided by the supervising attorney after consultation with the client. A basic approach generally includes the following steps:

- The supervising attorney will first review the client's priorities and expectations as well as his or her rights and responsibilities under governing law. In order to establish the basis for an agreement, the attorney must identify the client's position on fundamental issues, such as child custody, pensions, and the division of any real property, including the marital residence. After discovery is completed and the basic terms are negotiated and agreed upon (or formulated as proposals), an outline of the basic terms is prepared. The paralegal is sometimes present for these initial discussions and may be asked to take notes and develop an outline for review.

- The paralegal should review (or already have knowledge of) basic (case or statutory), rules, and procedures governing content and format of agreements. For example, does the court mandate specific numbered paragraphs and topics? Are child-related provisions addressed in the agreement or in a separate parenting plan?

Paralegal Practice Tip
Successive editions of the agreement, including copies of those marked up by counsel for the other party, should be retained in the client file. Occasionally, questions arise as to whether the opposing party knew about or had input into a particular provision. **Forensic** material can help establish that he or she clearly was aware of the challenged provision and may even have proposed it.

Forensic
gathered as potential evidence in a lawsuit

- The paralegal will review available "model agreements" in firm files, both paper and computer. Form books, state practice manuals, and other resources may also be consulted. Previously drafted agreements in closed divorce files may be especially useful when cases present similar fact patterns (for example, a high-conflict child custody and visitation situation or cases in which bankruptcy or tax audit issues are looming in the immediate future). There are many online resources for agreements—some are helpful, but all need to be carefully assessed, adapted to reflect jurisdictional terminology and formats, and tailored to the facts of the case.
- The paralegal carefully drafts an agreement for review based on an outline provided/approved by the supervising attorney. Drafting generally involves considerably more than filling in the blanks or simple cut-and-paste activity. Although there is no need to reinvent the wheel, the content must reflect the facts and intentions of the parties in the particular case and comply with current governing law and procedure. Caution always must be exercised when using **boilerplate** provisions. For example, there may be a recent change in the state's treatment of some issue in agreements such as whether or not the court will approve a provision pertaining to responsibility for college expenses.
- The paralegal may be asked to review an agreement or feedback received from the opposing party. Generally the paralegal will check to be sure all of the appropriate terms are included, identify any differences from the client's position, and, if necessary, recommend potential alternative language for review by the supervising attorney.
- The complete Final Draft must be carefully reviewed prior to signature and submission to the court for incorporation into the judgment. Before signing, counsel should walk through the entire document with the client and address any questions that may arise.

SAMPLE SEPARATION AGREEMENT

The following sample separation agreement is based almost entirely on an agreement executed and filed in a divorce case in the Commonwealth of Massachusetts. The names of the parties have been changed and other identifying information is omitted. Some brief additions have also been made to the actual text of the agreement for instructional purposes. Specific terms of the agreement are tailored to the needs of a middle-income couple married for twenty years who have two minor children. They have been separated for approximately eighteen months. The parties have filed a joint petition for divorce on the grounds that irreconcilable differences have caused an irremediable breakdown of their marriage. They have reached agreement on all issues after an extended period of negotiation, initially in the context of mediation without counsel present and then with counsel. The most challenging issues for these parties involved the specific provisions concerning custody and visitation, disposition of the marital home, payment of substantial joint debt, and the parties' respective retirement funds.

The content of the sample agreement is written in "plain English" and avoids excessive use of "legalese" wherever possible. Note that after the initial statement of facts/recitals, headings are used for each major topic. Each Article is designated with a Roman numeral and each Exhibit with a letter. Whatever system is used, it should afford easy reference for the parties, counsel, and the court. Exhibit 12.1 provided a summary of the basic elements that should be considered for inclusion in the agreement. Drafting Tips appear throughout the agreement to indicate possible variations, explanations, cautions, etc. Places in the agreement where specifics (e.g., name of the court, county, state, etc.) need to be filled in are indicated.

EXHIBIT 12.2 Sample Separation Agreement

NAME OF STATE

NAME OF COURT

NAME OF COUNTY   Docket No. *07D-XXXX-DVI*

SEPARATION AGREEMENT

Drafting Tip
The title will vary according to local custom, practice, and procedure.

This Agreement ("Agreement") is made this *date* day of June 2008 by and between **Stephen Morgan** (hereinafter referred to as **"Stephen"**) of *address* and **Juliana W. Morgan** (hereinafter referred to as **"Julie"**), of *address*. The term "parties," as used in this Agreement, refers to Stephen and Julie.

Drafting Tip
This is the "Identification Clause" of the Agreement. The date is often filled in by hand on the specific date of signing. The parties' names and current addresses are included, along with the names that will be used to refer to each of the parties throughout the agreement. The two most common approaches are to use the first names by which the parties are commonly known or to use "husband" and "wife." In the case of same-sex marriages, the parties may be referred to as "spouse A" and "spouse B." The use of "plaintiff" and "defendant" has fallen into disfavor with the institution of no-fault divorce, and given the potential for confusion when multiple actions are filed involving the parties.

Drafting Tip
If there is a history of serious abuse and/or a restraining order in force against one of the parties, the address of the other party may not appear in the agreement and also may be ***impounded*** in court records.

Impounded
kept in the custody of the court and not available to the public, and, in some instances, to other parties

Drafting Tip
Some attorneys include the parties' social security numbers in the agreement. Most no longer do so, however, because of the potential for identity theft, given that agreements filed in divorce actions are part of a public record.

STATEMENT OF FACTS

The parties were married on May 16, 1988, in Fort Lauderdale, Florida. This was the first marriage for both parties.

Two children have been born of this marriage, both minors: Robert G. Morgan, born 1/14/95, and Jennifer Ruth Morgan, born 04/10/98. Julie has borne no other children during the marriage.

Due to serious and irreconcilable differences that have arisen between the parties, causing the irretrievable breakdown of their marriage, Stephen and Julie separated on January 16, 2007. They continue to live separate and apart, and it is their wish and intent to remain living apart from each other.

The parties have filed a Joint Petition for Divorce (Docket No. # *number*), which is currently pending in the *name of court*.

The parties have decided to confirm their separation and effect this Agreement to settle between themselves all of the issues relating to their respective property and

continued

estate rights, spousal support, care and custody of their minor children, and all other claims and demands each might have against the other by reason of their marital relationship.

Each of them fully understands the facts, each has been fully informed of his or her legal rights and liabilities, and each signs this Agreement freely and voluntarily.

NOW, THEREFORE, in consideration of the mutual promises and covenants contained herein, the parties agree as follows:

Drafting Tip

This section is often referred to as the "Recitals." It includes the basic facts of the case. In some models, the section begins with the heading "Witnesseth," and each paragraph begins with "Whereas. . . ."

Drafting Tip

One of the recitals confirms that the parties have separated. Historically the courts looked with disfavor on agreements negotiated while the parties were still living together, particularly when the agreement provided that if one party subsequently filed a complaint for divorce, the other party would not appear or defend against that action (even if he or she had a valid defense). Such promises constituted a form of **collusion** or fraud on the court in order to obtain a divorce. Courts have been less concerned about such provisions since the arrival of no-fault divorce.

Drafting Tip

If no complaint for divorce has yet been filed, the agreement should indicate what effect, if any, a subsequent filing will have on the validity of the agreement. If the complaint has been filed, the agreement may indicate the effect of a reconciliation between the parties.

Drafting Tip

The fact that one of the recitals states that the agreement was signed freely and voluntarily is evidence that it was so signed, but is not necessarily dispositive. Abused spouses frequently sign agreements out of fear and a desire to escape a threatening situation, but may later challenge them once in a safe environment.

Collusion
an agreement by the parties to a divorce action to jointly deceive the court as to the true nature and purpose of the action

ARTICLE I SEPARATION

From this date forward, Stephen and Julie will continue to live separate and apart from each other, as if sole and unmarried, and free from the authority of or interference from the other. Each agrees to respect the other's privacy. However, the parties hereby do not intend to create a restraining order or intend that either of them be entered on the computer tracking system for restraining orders on account of this provision or any other provision hereof.

Drafting Tip

This provision is sometimes called a "Nonmolestation Clause." It does not constitute a restraining order and is not designed to prevent all contact between the parties. Rather, it serves as a confirmation that each party is free to live his or her individual life as if never married, without interference or unwanted contact with the other party. If there is a restraining order in place, the language in this paragraph would be modified to reflect that fact.

ARTICLE II MUTUAL RELEASES

Subject to other provisions of this Agreement, each party, individually, and for his or her heirs, legal representatives, executors, administrators, and assigns, releases and discharges the other of and from all causes of action, all claims, rights, or demands in either law or in equity, which either of the parties ever had or now has against the other or which may hereafter arise by reason of their marriage. This does not apply to any or all causes of action for this divorce, and such liabilities as may accrue or any payments due under the terms of this agreement.

continued

Drafting Tip

This general mutual release is designed to prevent post-decree litigation between the spouses for any cause of action arising out of or occurring during the marriage. For example, this provision could foreclose a wife who was physically abused during the marriage and never raised the abuse as an issue during the divorce proceeding from filing a post-divorce civil complaint seeking damages for assault and battery and intentional infliction of emotional distress. Although this may serve the interests of judicial economy and bring some closure to the parties, it does not take into consideration the dynamics of an abusive relationship. Until free and clear of the marriage, an abused spouse may not dare risk raising such an issue, and may later claim that he or she signed the agreement under duress.

ARTICLE III WAIVER OF ESTATE CLAIM

Except as otherwise provided in this Agreement, each party hereby waives and releases any and all rights that she or he may now have or hereafter acquire as spouse under the present or future laws of any jurisdiction:

a)   To elect to take against any will or codicil of the other party now or hereafter in force;

b)   To share in the party's estate in case of intestacy; and

c)   To act as executor or administrator of the other party's estate.

Both parties intend that their respective estates shall be administered as though no marriage between them ever existed. However, each is specifically not waiving any rights he or she may have in: (1) claims against the other's estate by reason of a breach of this Agreement; (2) any testamentary provisions that are voluntarily made for his or her benefit by the other; and/or (3) Any rights either may have to social security benefits by virtue of their marriage to the other.

Drafting Tip

Generally, a divorce automatically revokes bequests to a former spouse unless otherwise provided in a will. However, the revocation is not effective until the divorce is granted and the parties are no longer "spouses." It is therefore wise for the parties to cover the time period between the date of separation and the date of divorce in their agreement, especially if there will be an extended period of separation.

Drafting Tip

The personal representative of a decedent (executor, administrator, etc.) may be required to satisfy remaining alimony, child support, and property division obligations under the agreement from the assets of the estate.

ARTICLE IV EXECUTION OF IMPLEMENTING DOCUMENTS

Within a reasonable time after this Agreement has been signed, each party will execute, seal, deliver, file, or record such bills of sale, deeds, leases, waivers, or other instruments or documents as the other party requests and may reasonably require to effectuate the terms of this Agreement.

Drafting Tip

Some agreements expressly provide that if either party fails to comply with the provisions of this paragraph, the agreement itself will constitute a satisfactory substitute for the unexecuted document. Third parties, however, may not be satisfied with this alternative to an executed deed or transfer of title of a vehicle or boat, etc. A party's failure to comply with this Article that results in damages to the other party may constitute a breach of the agreement.

ARTICLE V ACKNOWLEDGMENT OF THE PARTIES

Each party to this Agreement acknowledges and agrees:

a)   that each is represented by a competent attorney of her or his own choosing or has freely chosen not to be represented;

continued

b) that each of the parties has made full disclosure of his or her respective assets and liabilities and that this Agreement is entered into with knowledge of the financial circumstances and needs of the other party;

c) that each has carefully read this Agreement, has discussed it with his or her respective counsel, understands the provisions contained within it, and considers the Agreement to be fair and reasonable;

d) that this Agreement is not the product of fraud or coercion; and

e) that this Agreement is fair and reasonable at the time it is being signed and at the time it is being submitted to the court as part of the parties' divorce proceedings.

Drafting Tip

The "acknowledgments" in this Article are sometimes called "representations" and may appear in separate Articles to highlight their importance.

Drafting Tip

When only one party is represented by counsel, courts may be reluctant to approve or enforce an agreement if it appears that the unrepresented party did not understand the effect of the agreement or was pressured to sign it under duress. In such circumstances, it is wise to include language such as the following: "Husband acknowledges that this agreement was drafted by wife's attorney, that he has been advised to seek independent counsel, and that he has declined to do so of his own volition."

Drafting Tip

Occasionally, when one party is represented by counsel and the other is not, the agreement is lopsided in favor of the represented party. Before issuing a decree, the court may require the unrepresented party to seek counsel for the limited purpose of reviewing the agreement and ensuring that he or she understands its terms and the impact of any rights that may be waived, etc.

Drafting Tip

Article V b) provides an example of when boilerplate can be dangerous. In this case, the parties believed there was full disclosure. However, if a party has been concealing assets that have not been located despite due diligence or if a client has refused to permit adequate discovery despite counsel's recommendation, this language may be modified to provide for later discovered assets presently "unknown" to either party. For example, "The parties further agree that any intentional material misrepresentation by either of them in his or her financial statement shall be grounds to seek *rescission* or other equitable relief. In the alternative, it will constitute grounds for seeking modification of any court order or judgment incorporating the terms of this agreement or for objecting to consideration of the agreement in any subsequent legal proceeding between the parties or their personal representatives, heirs, or assigns."

Drafting Tip

Either here or elsewhere in the agreement, there usually is a reference to attorneys' fees, e.g., "Except as herein otherwise provided, each party agrees to pay his or her own attorney's fees incurred in negotiation, preparation, and execution of this agreement." (See Article XIV.)

Rescission
the cancellation or unmaking of a contract for a legally sufficient reason

ARTICLE VI SITUS

This Agreement shall be construed, governed, and enforced in accordance with the applicable laws of the state of _name of state_.

ARTICLE VII VALIDITY

In the event that any provision of this Agreement is held to be invalid and unenforceable, such invalidity shall not invalidate the whole agreement, but the remaining provisions of this Agreement shall continue to be valid and binding to

continued

the extent that such provisions reflect fairly the intent and understanding of the parties at the time of execution.

Drafting Tip

This clause is a "severability" or "savings" provision. It provides, for example, that if the Exhibit pertaining to alimony is held to be invalid as violating public policy, the rest of the Agreement will still be valid and effective.

ARTICLE VIII ENTIRE AGREEMENT

There are no representations, warrantees, conditions, promises, or undertakings other than those set forth in this Agreement, which contains the entire agreement of the parties.

Drafting Tip

Any "side" agreements between the parties are unenforceable and in the extreme may invalidate the entire agreement if they appear to constitute a fraud upon the court.

ARTICLE IX EFFECTIVE DATE

This Agreement shall be effective upon execution by the parties.

ARTICLE X BINDING EFFECT

Except as otherwise stated herein, all the provisions of this Agreement shall be binding upon the respective heirs, next of kin, trustees in bankruptcy, personal representatives, executors, administrators, and assigns of the parties.

ARTICLE XI INDEPENDENT CONTRACT

This Agreement may be submitted to any court before which any Complaint or proceeding for divorce or dissolution of marriage shall be tried, and in the event that a Judgment of Divorce shall be entered, the same shall incorporate in full or in substance the provisions of this Agreement and the Agreement shall be incorporated and not merged but shall survive as a document having independent legal significance, and the property settlement and any alimony provisions herein shall forever be binding upon the parties. Notwithstanding the foregoing, any provisions of this Agreement relating to children who are not emancipated shall remain modifiable by the court upon a material change in circumstances of a party or a child, or if a modification is consistent with the best interests of the child.

Drafting Tip

The parents cannot bargain away the rights of their children, and all child-related provisions remain subject to the continuing jurisdiction of the court.

ARTICLE XII MODIFICATION

A modification or waiver of any of the provisions of this Agreement shall be effective only if made in writing and executed with the same formality as this Agreement or by order of a court of competent jurisdiction.

Drafting Tip

If the agreement merges in the decree, this paragraph will reflect that distinction. For example, "After approval of this agreement and entry of a final judgment of divorce, this agreement may not be altered or modified except pursuant to the court's order."

ARTICLE XIII STRICT PERFORMANCE

The failure of either party to insist upon strict performance of any of the provisions of this Agreement shall not be construed as a waiver of any subsequent default of the same or a similar nature.

continued

Drafting Tip

This paragraph provides that if, for example, Julie chooses to excuse Stephen's failure to pay child support for the month of December because he is experiencing a temporary financial crisis, she is not agreeing to excuse his failure to pay support in any other past or future months. Rather, she can insist that this provision of the agreement be enforced with respect to those other periods. Such "informal" waivers of breach do not deprive the court of its ultimate jurisdiction over child-related issues and may occur at the risk of either or both parties.

ARTICLE XIV RESOLUTION OF DISPUTES, BREACH OF AGREEMENT, AND ATTORNEYS' FEES

Except as herein otherwise provided, Stephen and Julie will each pay their own attorneys' fees incurred in connection with negotiation of this Agreement and the pending Joint Petition for Divorce.

In the event that a dispute arises between the parties regarding any of the provisions of this Agreement that Stephen and Julie are unable to resolve on their own or with the assistance of counsel, they agree that prior to filing any legal action in court, they will make an effort to resolve the dispute through mediation at Thomas Kelley and Associates or another similar agency mutually agreed upon. The fees and costs of the mediation shall be borne equally by the parties unless the court later determines that the actions of one party were so unreasonable as to require such mediation, in which case, the party responsible for the unreasonable action shall be responsible for that portion of the fees and costs that the court deems equitable. Nothing in this paragraph shall prevent either party from proceeding directly to court or pursuing any other legal remedy if either party defaults on a financial obligation under this Agreement.

If either party commits a breach of any provisions of this Agreement and legal action is reasonably required to enforce such provisions and is instituted by the non-breaching party, the party in breach shall be liable to the party who prevails in the court action for all statutory interest from the date of breach and for all court costs and reasonable attorney's fees incurred in instituting and prosecuting such action. If either party brings legal action against the other on frivolous, insubstantial grounds or in bad faith, and does not prevail in that action, then the prevailing party shall be awarded reasonable attorney's fees and other costs and expenses incurred in defending against such action.

Drafting Tip

If one of the parties promises in the agreement to pay the fees of the other party, the attorney for that other party becomes a creditor of, and can seek to recover fees directly from, the promisor as a ***third-party beneficiary*** of the contract between the parties.

Drafting Tip

Another option for conflict resolution is arbitration. The provision should state who the arbitrator will be (or how she or he will be selected) and how the related costs will be paid.

Third-party beneficiary
a person who, though not a party to a contract, benefits from performance of the contract

ARTICLE XV ARTICLE HEADINGS OF NO EFFECT

The headings at the beginning of each Article and Exhibit of this Agreement are included for convenience and reference purposes only and do not constitute terms or conditions of the Agreement.

ARTICLE XVI EXHIBITS

There are annexed hereto and incorporated by reference Exhibits A through K. Stephen and Julie agree to be bound by and to perform and carry out all of the terms contained in said Exhibits to the same extent as if each Exhibit was fully set forth in the text of this Agreement.

continued

Exhibits A through K are enforceable and may not be discharged in any bankruptcy action brought by or against either of the parties, as they are necessary provisions for the support and maintenance of the other as a consequence of possible disparities in income, the special needs of the parties, and the allocation of resources.

Drafting Tip

Although bankruptcy court rulings will ultimately control in the event that a bankruptcy action is subsequently filed, this is an attempt to protect as many of the obligations created under this agreement as possible by designating them as being in the nature of "support" and thus generally not dischargeable in bankruptcy.

IN WITNESS WHEREOF the parties have signed, sealed, and acknowledged this Agreement in three (3) counterparts, each of which shall constitute an original.

Witnesses to Husband's Signature

_____   _____

                                 Stephen Morgan

_____   Date:_____

Witnesses to Wife's Signature

_____   _____

                                 Juliana W. Morgan

_____   Date:_____

Drafting Tip

The signature section should comply with any governing procedural requirements. For example, some states require each signature to be witnessed by two disinterested parties. Others require counsel to sign the agreement as well as the client. The names used by the parties should conform to the names used in the underlying action for divorce or legal separation.

CERTIFICATION
STATE

COUNTY_____

On this _____ day of June 2008, personally appeared JULIANA W. MORGAN, known to me to be the person whose name is subscribed to the within instrument and acknowledged that she executed the same for the purposes therein set forth, as her own free act and deed, before me.

IN WITNESS WHEREOF, I hereunto set my hand and official seal.

continued

_____

Notary/Justice of the Peace

(Seal)

STATE

COUNTY_____

On this _____ day of June 2008, personally appeared STEPHEN MORGAN, known to me to be the person whose name is subscribed to the within instrument and acknowledged that he executed the same for the purposes therein set forth, as his own free act and deed, before me.

IN WITNESS WHEREOF, I hereunto set my hand and official seal.

_____

Notary/Justice of the Peace

(Seal)

EXHIBIT A
ALIMONY

A.1   Each party currently receives income and incurs expenses at a level consistent with the financial statements filed at the time of the final hearing on this matter, which statements are incorporated herein.

A.2   Each party is able to provide for his or her own needs without any support or contribution from the other party.

A.3   Julie waives any and all right to alimony, past, present, and future from Stephen.

A.4   Stephen waives any and all right to alimony, past, present, and future from Julie.

A.5   Each party understands that this waiver of alimony can be forever binding and intends that his/her waiver be so binding on him/her even if the circumstances of either party change with the passage of time.

Drafting Tip

Depending on the jurisdiction, alimony may be referred to as spousal support, separate maintenance, or by some other designation.

Drafting Tip

Because of the parties' limited resources and the fact that each of them is presently employed and able to be self-supporting if necessary, Stephen and Julie have chosen to permanently waive alimony. Assuming they remain healthy and employed, this may not present a problem, but what if one of them should hit the lottery and the other become indigent? Some courts do not look favorably on permanent waivers even if they are "voluntary, knowing, and intelligent." Counsel must make every effort to ensure that the parties understand the potential consequences of such waivers and, in the alternative, that ultimately they may be unenforceable under certain conditions (e.g., extreme hardship, debilitating illness, the likelihood of one of the parties becoming a public charge, etc.).

---

continued

Drafting Tip

For a discussion of terms commonly included in alimony provisions in separation agreements, see Chapter 10.

Drafting Tip

In some situations, the parties may agree to a flexible approach to alimony payments. For example, if the obligor's sole income is from an ice cream stand he owns and operates twelve hours a day from April 1 through October 1 each year, the parties may agree that alimony will be paid only during that six-month period when there is a steady flow of income.

Drafting Tip

Some jurisdictions hold that if alimony is not awarded in the final decree, it cannot be sought at a later date. In such circumstances, the parties may agree to a nominal alimony award of $1.00 simply to preserve their options.

Drafting Tip

Largely depending on the jurisdiction, an alimony provision may designate the type of alimony to be paid (rehabilitative, permanent, restitution, etc.).

EXHIBIT B
CHILD CUSTODY AND VISITATION

B.1   Stephen and Julie shall have joint legal custody of the children. Julie shall have physical custody of the children. The parents agree that it is of paramount importance for each of them to remain involved in the major parental decisions and guidance of the children, for the children to feel deep affection for each parent, and for each parent to foster and nurture in the children respect and affection for the other parent, to the end that each parent's relationship with the children will remain as close as possible. Accordingly, each parent agrees to keep the other well and promptly informed of the academic, physical, emotional, and social status and activities of each child. Each parent may, without further permission of the other, review all school, medical, dental, and other reports or written communications concerning the welfare of the children, and consult with individuals providing medical, psychological, dental, educational, or other services for the children. Each may give authorization for provision of emergency services for the children. Each also may exercise sole authority and responsibility for decisions concerning the daily living needs and activities of a child while in his or her physical custody.

B.2   The parties shall consult on significant issues concerning the welfare of each child, including, but not limited to, medical, mental health, and dental treatment, religious education, educational choices and alternatives, social and recreational activities, including participation in any inherently dangerous or unusual activities, and the time spent with each of the parties. The parties agree that in all such matters, the interests and the desires of the children shall be determined and given primary consideration.

B.3   Stephen's visitation rights shall remain open and liberal at all reasonable times and places as agreed between the parties, subject to reasonable advance notice to Julie and the school schedule and activities of the children. However, in the event that the parties are unable to agree as to reasonable visitation rights, the following schedule will define minimum visitation rights for the present.

   a) Stephen will pick up the children at Julie's residence at 6:00 p.m. on the second and fourth Fridays of each month (unless otherwise agreed) for the weekend, and will return them on Sunday afternoon at 4:00 p.m.

continued

b) On each Wednesday evening, Stephen will pick up the children at Julie's residence at 5:30 p.m. and return them at 8:30 p.m.

c) The parties agree to alternate the major holidays such that if the children spend Christmas Day of 2008 with one parent, they will spend Christmas Day of 2009 with the other parent and so on. This provision will affect the following holidays:

    Christmas Eve
    Christmas Day
    Thanksgiving
    Easter
    Independence Day
    Halloween

d) In 2008, the children will be with Julie on Thanksgiving Day and Christmas Eve and with Stephen on Halloween and Christmas Day from 9:00 a.m. to 9:00 p.m. In 2009, they will be with Julie on Independence Day, Christmas Day, and Halloween and with Stephen on Easter, Thanksgiving, and Christmas Eve from 5:00 p.m. to 9:00 a.m. Christmas morning.

e) The children will spend Father's Day with Stephen and Mother's Day with Julie (from 10:00 a.m. to 8:00 p.m. if there is a conflict with another visitation provision). Stephen and Julie will make arrangements such that the children are able to spend some portion of each parent's birthday with that parent.

f) Stephen and Julie agree that they each should be able to spend time with them on the children's birthdays. They agree that each child should have a single birthday party at which both parents will be present. The parent who has physical custody of the child on the day of the birthday will be responsible for planning and paying for the costs of the party.

g) The children shall spend a total of four weeks with Stephen during the summer months (July and August) in two uninterrupted two-week periods in addition to the full week of the February school vacation.

h) Unless otherwise agreed, Stephen will be responsible for any transportation of the children necessary to implement the visitation provisions of this Agreement.

B.4 During any period when a child is in the physical custody of the other parent, the absent parent shall have the right to communicate with the child by telephone and/or electronic mail at all reasonable times. The parties agree that they will not use the children as the means of communicating with each other and that they will communicate directly.

B.5 Stephen and Julie acknowledge that at some future time, either or both of them may marry again. Until that time, when the children are present, neither parent will entertain overnight guests with whom he or she has an intimate sexual relationship.

B.6 In the event of any serious illness of a child, the parent with whom the child is then staying shall immediately notify the other parent and, under such circumstances, shall permit the other party to visit the sick child upon reasonable notice and request.

B.7 Neither party shall permanently remove the children or change the children's principal residence more than twenty-five miles from the

continued

children's current residence in _location_ without obtaining prior written consent of the other party, or, if said consent is denied, the permission of the _name of court_ pursuant to applicable state law.

B.8 Both parties shall have the right to take trips with the children, including the right to take the children out-of-state for trips and vacations that are temporary in nature, but shall notify the other parent in advance of such trips and vacations. This provision shall include the making of a "safe call" after arrival at the destination, advising the other parent of the arrival, where the children will be staying, and how the other parent may reach the children by telephone.

B.9 The parties agree that it is important for the children to maintain an ongoing relationship with each of their extended families, including, among others, grandparents, aunts, uncles, and cousins, and each will seek to foster and support those relationships.

B.10 The parties acknowledge that there will be occasions when something occurs that may require an adjustment in the visitation schedule, such as illness, a school trip, a major work-related commitment, etc. When such situations arise, Stephen and Julie agree to make every effort to accommodate them and ensure that Stephen does not experience any loss in overall visitation time.

Drafting Tip

The agreement should use the appropriate terminology pertaining to custody in the jurisdiction, for example, primary/secondary parent, custodial/noncustodial parent, residential/nonresidential parent, etc. Many states require that a primary caretaker be designated.

Drafting Tip

Any agreement made by the parties concerning child custody remains subject to the continuing jurisdiction of the court and is modifiable based upon a change in circumstances and what will serve the best interests of the child.

Drafting Tip

Although the courts cannot realistically enforce parental cooperation clauses, they may penalize a parent who actively seeks to alienate a child from the other parent or who obstructs the other parent's custodial or visitation privileges. Some states such as Tennessee require that Marital Dissolution Agreements and Parenting Plans include a list of the statutorily guaranteed rights of noncustodial parents.

Drafting Tip

The nature of a custody and visitation provision depends heavily on the extent to which the parties are able to communicate with each other. The provisions in this particular agreement are quite specific, in an effort to minimize questions and misunderstandings between parties who have a history of conflict on child-related issues.

Drafting Tip

When the parties have been separated for an extended period and communicate effectively with each other, they may already have in place an acceptable custody and visitation plan. In such situations, the Custody and Visitation Exhibit may simply state that the noncustodial parent shall have reasonable visitation with the child at all times mutually agreed upon by the parties.

Drafting Tip

The right to access medical and school records in B.1, etc., may be restricted if an abuse order is in effect or to otherwise protect a parent or the children.

Drafting Tip

This sample agreement involves a situation in which the parties reside within ten miles of each other. Significant variations necessarily occur when parents reside at a considerable geographic

continued

distance. Although the noncustodial parent may have as much visitation in real time as he or she would have if the parents lived in close proximity, it is likely to occur in large blocks of time. In such situations, provisions may also address telephone access, virtual visitation, and transportation costs, if not already factored into child support.

EXHIBIT C
CHILD SUPPORT

C.1   Commencing the first month after execution of this Agreement and continuing each month thereafter until the children are emancipated, as hereinafter defined, Stephen will pay $_____ per week to Julie as child support, said amount being consistent with the state's child support guidelines. The payment should be sent or delivered so that it is received by Julie no later than the first day of each month.

C.2   Currently, the child support obligation is based on the parties having two children who are not emancipated. The parties agree that, when either child becomes emancipated, as defined below, the amount of child support Stephen pays will be adjusted accordingly without need for intervention from the _name of court_. The adjusted Child Support obligation shall remain within the amount proposed for the remaining one child under the state's Child Support Guidelines in effect at the time of the first child's emancipation.

C.3   Emancipation with respect to each minor child shall occur on the earliest to happen of the following:

a) At age eighteen (18) or graduation from high school, but not later than at age 20, whichever occurs later, unless the child is pursuing postsecondary schooling as a full-time student as defined in b) below.

b) At age twenty-three (23), if a child is then attending an accredited postsecondary educational training school or a two-year or four-year college program as a full-time student, such schooling has not been completed, and the child is still a dependent of the parents;

c) At the completion of schooling as it is defined in b) above;

d) Death or marriage of the child;

e) Permanent residency away from the custodial parent's home. (Residency at boarding school, camp, or college is not to be deemed a permanent residence away from the custodial parent's home if the child is engaged in activities pursuant to a) and b) above);

f) Engaging in full-time employment, including the military, after the age of eighteen (18), except that full-time employment during vacation and summer periods shall not be deemed emancipation. Such emancipation shall be deemed to terminate upon cessation by the child for any reason of full-time employment, including the military, provided the child thereafter becomes engaged in activities pursuant to a) or b) above, or other applicable provisions of this paragraph.

C.4   Any payment of support as required by this Agreement may be made in cash or by check or money order payable to Julie. Child support shall not be paid by wage assignment, except as may hereafter be required by a court of competent jurisdiction or any applicable federal or state statute, rule, or regulation, or in the event that Stephen breaches this provision of the Agreement. If Stephen falls behind in child support payments by three or more months, Julie will utilize the services of the state's IV-D agency to secure payment of past-due and future payments.

continued

C.5   Upon request of either party, before February 15 in any year in which Stephen is obligated to pay child support, the parties agree to exchange W-2 forms. Either party may seek a change in the amount of the child support obligation upon a material change in circumstances.

C.6   The parties agree that they will consult with each other regarding extracurricular activities and agree to share equally the mutually agreed-upon expenses of said activities for the children, which shall include but not be limited to music and dance lessons, sports and sports-related equipment and clothing, and camp.

C.7   The parties agree that their children should receive the best education available to them including education at the college level. They further agree that choices of educational institutions for the children shall be made on the basis of joint consultation with due regard for the parties' financial circumstances and the children's aptitudes and interests. It shall be the children's and the custodial parent's obligation to consult with the other parent and come to an agreement regarding reasonable and affordable postsecondary schooling for the children. To the extent that they are then financially able to do so, the parties shall contribute equally to the net expenses of postsecondary education for their children who are not emancipated to the extent that educational expenses are not otherwise covered by scholarships, grants, loans, and the children's savings and earnings. For purposes of this Exhibit, the term "expenses" shall include application fees and related before-college expenses, tuition, board, room, books, uniforms (if required), basic computer equipment, usual and normal student activity fees and other expenses normally charged on college or university bills, and a reasonable allowance for transportation to and from such institution. The parties agree to cooperate with each other in applying for financial aid. However, it shall be the children's obligation to pursue scholarships, grants, loans, and other financial aid, as well as to contribute earnings from summer jobs and other part-time employment. The parents' obligation shall extend only to those costs not covered by the foregoing and shall be capped at the tuition level of the highest-cost in-state university. The obligation to contribute to schooling shall terminate upon a child's emancipation.

C.8   The parties hereby agree that all payments designated for the support and maintenance of the minor children under the terms of this Agreement are exclusively for child support and maintenance, and further agree that such payments shall be excludable from Julie's gross income and nondeductible by Stephen subject to the law governing such deductions on any future federal or state income tax returns.

C.9   The parties agree that for the tax year beginning on January 1, 2009, and as to any tax year thereafter, Julie shall be entitled to claim the dependency exemption for Robert, and Stephen shall be entitled to claim the exemption for Jennifer, subject to applicable federal and state laws. When Robert becomes emancipated, the parties will claim the exemption for Jennifer in alternate years. Julie agrees to execute annually any tax forms necessary to enable Stephen to claim this exemption.

C.10   Stephen's obligation to make payments for the support and maintenance of the minor children under this section of the Agreement is an obligation in the nature of support as defined under the relevant

continued

provisions of the United States Bankruptcy Code, as amended, and the said obligation shall not be dischargeable in bankruptcy. In the event that any arrearages for support due to Julie under this Exhibit, or any obligation to make future payments due under the Agreement, shall be discharged in bankruptcy, Julie shall have the unrestricted right to seek appropriate relief in any court of competent jurisdiction to obtain further orders of support.

Drafting Tip

Because of the circumstances and conflict between the parties in this case, this is an extensive and detailed child support provision.

Drafting Tip

Although it is not necessarily stated in an agreement, clients paying child or spousal support are usually advised to make all payments by check or money order (NOT in cash) so that their payments are documented.

Drafting Tip

Child support provisions remain subject to the continuing jurisdiction of the court. Modifications are governed by state law. If permitted in the jurisdiction, some parties build an annual review process into the agreement. Even if the parties agree to a change, child support is an order of the court, and any changes should be approved by the court to avoid a later contempt claim.

Drafting Tip

Occasionally, child support and alimony/spousal support payments are lumped together ("unallocated"). To minimize potential tax problems, it is often better to differentiate between them. For tax purposes, alimony is deductible to the payor and income to the recipient, and child support is neither.

Drafting Tip

Many agreements provide that the obligor will maintain a life insurance policy in a set amount for the benefit of the minor children. It is designed to guarantee an income source for the children in case the parent with the child support obligation should die prematurely. Another option is to establish a trust fund as in Exhibit H of this agreement.

Drafting Tip

Courts in several states will no longer order a parent to pay a child's college expenses. This particular agreement reflects the law in Massachusetts, a state that still strongly supports a parental duty to provide the costs of a child's basic college expenses, up to the age of twenty-three under some circumstances. Although the agreement references educational contributions by the children, it does not bind them to those obligations, because they are not parties to the agreement.

Drafting Tip

If the minor children are enrolled in private school, related expenses should be addressed in the agreement.

Drafting Tip

In some states, childcare costs are factored into the child support formula. If not, they should be addressed in the agreement.

EXHIBIT D

DIVISION OF PERSONAL PROPERTY

D.1   Except as otherwise specifically provided in this Agreement, Stephen and Julie have already divided their personal property. Each agrees that from now on each shall continue to possess, own, have, and enjoy independently of any claim of right of the other, all of his or her personal

continued

property of every kind, nature, and description with full power to dispose of the same as fully and with such effect in all respects and for all purposes as though he or she were unmarried.

D.2 Julie specifically waives any right, title, interest, or claim she may have to the proceeds, if any, of a settlement or judgment obtained by Stephen in connection with a pending personal injury action filed by him relating to a motorcycle accident on January 1, 2005, in which he received extensive injuries.

D.3 The parties agree that all of the personal property (books, records, tools, etc.) currently stored in the shed in the yard at the marital home located at _location_ presently belongs to Stephen. With reasonable notice to Julie, he will remove the property within thirty (30) days of the execution of this Agreement. After thirty (30) days, the property will belong to Julie, who will be free to keep, sell, or destroy it as she sees fit.

D.4 Each party shall deliver to the other all property or documents evidencing ownership of property that, by the terms of the Agreement, is to remain or become the property of the other. All property acquired from now on by either Stephen or Julie and all income and earnings of each party shall constitute and be the sole and separate property of the person by whom the said property is acquired or earned.

D.5 Each party shall retain as his or her sole property free of any claim of right of the other the vehicle in his or her possession and shall be solely obligated for payment of any expenses incurred for use, operation, maintenance, and financing thereof. Each shall indemnify and hold the other harmless from any liens or debts in connection with the vehicle he or she is retaining.

Drafting Tip

Depending on the nature and extent of the parties' personal property, the various items assigned to each party may be listed to avoid confusion (e.g., husband receives his Roth IRA account _identifying information_ ; the joint savings account at First Third Bank, account # _number_ ; his General Electric pension _identifying information_ ; and his baseball card collection. Wife receives 401(k) account _identifying information_ ; her pension _identifying information_ , her china collection, her jewelry, bank CD _identifying information_ , and three checking accounts: bank account # _number_ , bank account # _number_ , and bank account # _number_). When the assets are specified in such a manner, it makes it more difficult for a party to claim later that a particular asset on the list was not disclosed and distributed at the time of divorce.

Drafting Tip

Ideally, the parties should divide their personal property prior to executing the agreement, to avoid post-divorce problems. Paragraph D.3 gives the husband the opportunity to collect his possessions that are still stored on the marital property where the wife now resides. However, by establishing a reasonable time frame, it does not grant him an unlimited opportunity to do so. If the property remaining to change hands is not all conveniently located in one place (the shed, in this instance), the items should be specifically listed, if possible, to avoid disputes and misunderstandings. In extremely high-conflict cases in which a restraining order is in force, the agreement may set a particular time for the pickup and require that a police officer be present.

Drafting Tip

The personal property of most divorcing couples is of modest value. If the parties own substantial assets (business interests; antiques; artworks; stock portfolios; rights to receive funds in the future, such as royalties on works created during the marriage or contingent fees for work performed during the marriage), these assets should be specifically addressed to avoid confusion. A schedule reflecting the division of property may be appended to the agreement.

---

continued

EXHIBIT E
REAL ESTATE

E.1 Stephen and Julie own real property, the marital home, located at *location*, as tenants by the entirety, having taken title by deed dated May 17, 1987, recorded in the *name of county* Registry of Deeds in Book 7539, page 031. The property is encumbered by two mortgages on which Stephen and Julie are co-signors and co-mortgagors, dated May 17, 1987, and June 13, 1997, both to Berger Mortgage, Inc., and each secured by the marital home. The first is a purchase money mortgage with a remaining principal balance of $124,000 and recorded at the above referenced Registry in Book 7539, page 045. The second mortgage was obtained on May 13, 1997, in order to pay jointly incurred marital debt of the parties. It is in the principal amount of $21,900, recorded at Book 9887, page 331.

E.2 The parties agree that Julie shall have exclusive possession, use, and control of the marital home effective upon the execution of this Agreement.

E.3 Within ninety (90) days of execution of this Agreement, Stephen shall convey his interest in the above property to Julie by quitclaim deed.

E.4 Julie agrees that within ninety (90) days of execution of this Agreement, she shall obtain financing sufficient to:
   a) pay off both of the outstanding mortgages referenced in E.1 above; and
   b) pay Stephen the sum of thirty thousand dollars ($30,000) for his equity interest in the marital home, which the parties agree is currently valued at $205,000 based on the appraisal completed by Marjorie Anderson, a mutually agreed-upon licensed appraiser.

E.5 Julie further agrees that from the time of her receipt of the deed from Stephen, she shall indemnify and hold him harmless from any responsibility for all sums due, and that may become due in the future, on the two outstanding mortgages.

E.6 Both Stephen and Julie understand that Sections 1041(a) and (b) of the U.S. Internal Revenue Code of 1980, as amended, are applicable to the conveyance and transfer described in E.3 above; that no gain or loss will be recognized by Stephen upon his conveyance or transfer of any property interest to Julie; and that Julie will have a carryover basis in said property and receive Stephen's interest at his adjusted cost basis. Each party will provide the other with any and all documentation in his or her possession and control establishing the cost basis of the property.

Drafting Tip

In this case, the wife was able (with assistance from a "friend") to buy out the other party's interest in the property. If resources had been more limited and the marital home was the only major asset, the agreement would likely have provided that the custodial parent continue to remain in the home with the parties' children until the youngest reaches the age of emancipation. At that time, the house would be sold, with the parent in residence having a "right of first refusal" to buy the home at fair market value. The net proceeds would be divided between the parties in agreed-upon percentages.

Drafting Tip

All kinds of "real property" should be covered in the agreement including residences, vacation homes, business properties, leases, time-shares, contracts to purchase or sell property that may impact the nature and extent of the marital estate, etc.

---

continued

Drafting Tip

Part of this provision spells out the tax consequences of the transfer so that the party receiving the property cannot later claim she was unaware of a related capital gains tax possibly being due.

EXHIBIT F

JOINT AND SEVERAL DEBTS

F.1 Stephen and Julie have four (4) jointly held credit card accounts on which they are co-signors with balances that remain outstanding. Each party acknowledges that they are equally responsible for incurring this debt and that the balances owed constitute joint marital debt. The following is a complete list of the joint credit card accounts that remain outstanding, in the amounts owed at the time of execution of this Agreement:

Creditor	Indebtedness
a) MBNA America	$21,000.
b) Citizens	$22,300.
c) ATT Universal	$ 7,500.
d) Discover Card	$ 2,350.
	$53,150.

F.2 Julie agrees that from the date of this Agreement forward, she will hold Stephen harmless for these four debts and she will indemnify Stephen for all sums remaining to be paid on these four unsecured credit card accounts.

F.3 Julie agrees that she shall assume the indebtedness for all four of the above jointly held credit cards and that, as soon as practicable after the execution of this Agreement, she will obtain sufficient financing to pay off the remaining balances on all four cards and close the accounts. Julie has agreed to these terms because in January of 1997, Stephen liquidated his entire retirement annuity from his employer in order to pay off part of the joint marital debt the parties had incurred. At that time, Julie had a retirement account through her employer that was approximately equal in value to Stephen's. Julie did not then, and has not since, withdrawn any of her retirement funds—her account remains entirely intact and has since grown in value and become vested due to her years of service. The parties acknowledge that they jointly agreed that Stephen's retirement annuity should be used to pay down the joint marital debt and that Julie could have contributed one-half of that amount from her own funds but did not do so per their agreement. Julie's assumption of the remaining credit card debt will fairly compensate Stephen for liquidating his retirement savings in 1997. Assumption of the debt by Julie will allow Stephen to make a fresh start and continue to prepare for his future retirement needs.

F.4 Neither Stephen nor Julie may hereafter incur any debts or obligations on the credit of the other, and shall indemnify and hold the other harmless from any such debt or obligation incurred.

F.5 Except as provided in paragraph F.1 above, and as may be otherwise provided herein, and as set forth on each party's Financial Statement filed at the time of the final hearing on this matter, each of the parties represents to the other that he or she knows of no other debts for which the other may be liable, and each shall be responsible for and hold the other harmless for any liability incurred by the other as a result of the

continued

breaching party's nondisclosure. If either party violates this Agreement and the other party becomes obligated to make payment to any third party as a result of such breach, then the non-breaching party shall have the right to be indemnified by the breaching party and the breaching party shall pay all of the non-breaching party's costs and attorney's fees in connection therewith.

F.6 Except as provided in paragraph F.1 of this Exhibit and as may be otherwise provided herein, Stephen shall be solely responsible for and indemnify Julie for all of the debts set forth on his financial statement filed with the Court at the time of the final hearing on this matter.

F.7 Except as provided in paragraph F.1 of this Exhibit and as may be otherwise provided herein, Julie shall be solely responsible for and indemnify Stephen for all of the debts set forth on her financial statement filed with the Court at the time of the final hearing on this matter.

Drafting Tip

The heading of this section may vary, but whatever it is called, it addresses liabilities of the parties.

Drafting Tip

It is important to include *"hold harmless" provisions* in this Exhibit. (See F.4, F.5, F.6, and F.7.)

Drafting Tip

Paragraph F.3 is somewhat unusual. However, in this case, the judge specifically required that the agreement address the rationale for why the wife was assuming a seemingly disproportionate percentage of the marital debt.

Hold harmless provision
a provision specifying that a particular spouse will be solely responsible for payment of certain debts and that the other spouse shall be free and clear of any obligation regarding those debts and will be indemnified by the debtor spouse if forced to pay the debt

EXHIBIT G
MEDICAL INSURANCE, UNINSURED MEDICAL EXPENSES

G.1 For the benefit of the children, Julie shall maintain in full force and effect her current health insurance coverage, or its equivalent, as long as it is available through her employer, and as long as each child is not emancipated as that term is defined herein.

G.2 For the benefit of Stephen, Julie shall maintain in full force and effect her current health insurance coverage, or its equivalent, as long as it is available through her employer, and as long as the cost or premium is not in excess of that which Julie is required to pay to maintain such coverage for herself and the children who are not emancipated.

G.3 Stephen agrees that maintaining health insurance coverage for the children is a duty that he bears equally with Julie. Therefore, as long as Julie maintains family health insurance coverage through her own employer for the benefit of the children, or for the benefit of both Stephen and the children, Stephen agrees that he shall pay Julie a sum equal to one-half the difference between what Julie would pay for individual health insurance coverage and what she must pay for family health insurance coverage. This contribution from Stephen shall be paid by him in addition to and at the same time as his base child support payment as per the child support guidelines. Upon Stephen's request, Julie shall provide him with evidence of the cost of the premiums for coverage.

G.4 In the event that Julie remarries and thereby affects Stephen's eligibility for continued coverage, or in the event that Stephen can no longer be covered by Julie on her plan without additional cost to her, Stephen shall have the right, pursuant to state and other applicable law, to

continued

continue to receive benefits as are available to Julie by any means then existing, including by rider to the existing policy or conversion to an individual policy. If Stephen elects to continue such coverage, Julie shall cooperate with him in making the necessary arrangements for, and shall execute any documents necessary to effectuate, the continuation of said coverage. If such coverage results in an additional cost or premium to Julie and Stephen elects to continue such coverage, then Stephen shall pay to Julie the additional cost or premium incurred as a result of his election as such payment comes due. In addition to any obligation imposed by applicable law upon the insurer to notify Stephen of cancellation of coverage, Julie shall forthwith notify Stephen as soon as she becomes aware of any circumstance that would affect his eligibility for, the availability of, or the nature of his continued health insurance coverage.

G.5   Each party shall be responsible for payment of his or her own uninsured medical, dental, psychiatric, prescription, hospital, and other expenses of a medical nature.

G.6   The parties shall share equally the payment of the reasonable and necessary uninsured medical and dental expenses of the minor children. Each party shall consult with the other in advance about any need for uninsured medical expenses of the children beyond a total of $500 per year, per child, and shall obtain the other party's prior consent for any such expenditure, which consent shall not be unreasonably withheld.

G.7   In the event that individual or family insurance coverage is no longer available through Julie's current employer or that she is no longer eligible, insurance coverage for the children will be secured through Stephen's employer or Julie's subsequent employer as mutually agreed upon by the parties. If said insurance incurs a cost, the cost will be borne equally by the parties.

Drafting Tip

This Exhibit should cover medical insurance for both the parties and the children and should address insured and uninsured expenses. If a parent and/or child has any extraordinary medical needs, these should be considered (e.g., physical therapy, counseling, home care, etc.). In circumstances in which the parties are unemployed and have few assets, the parties may go without medical insurance or apply for government benefits.

Drafting Tip

The courts tend to be especially interested in this provision, particularly as applied to any minor children. In some states, including Massachusetts, the cost of medical insurance for the children is factored into the child support formula.

EXHIBIT H
LIFE INSURANCE

H.1   Stephen shall maintain a total of $250,000 of term insurance on his life to be allocated equally for the benefit of each of the minor children. Stephen shall maintain said insurance for the benefit of each child until such time as that child becomes emancipated and Stephen is no longer obligated to pay child support for the benefit of that child.

H.2   At Stephen's option, the life insurance provided for the benefit of the minor children in paragraph H.1 above shall be held in trust by a trustee of his choosing selected by him in a form of trust to be approved by Julie, whose approval shall not be unreasonably withheld.

continued

H.3   Stephen will, from time to time, and as requested by Julie, furnish her with satisfactory evidence that said insurance policies are in full force and effect.

H.4   Except as otherwise provided in H.1 and H.2 above, after execution of the Agreement, Julie and Stephen shall each have the right to make any changes in his or her respective insurance policies including, but not limited to, changing his or her beneficiary, increasing or decreasing coverage, or canceling such policies.

Drafting Tip

This provision is designed to guarantee an income stream for the benefit of the minor children and often appears in the Exhibit pertaining to child support. The designation of the children as beneficiaries should be irrevocable as long as the child support obligation continues.

Drafting Tip

The parties often have several kinds of insurance in addition to life insurance, such as health, homeowners', automobile, liability in connection with a business or professional practice, etc., that may be covered in one Exhibit or separately.

EXHIBIT I
RETIREMENT ACCOUNTS

Except as otherwise herein provided, from the date of this Agreement forward, all 401(k), IRA, and other retirement-type accounts and state and federal retirement plans standing individually in a party's own name shall be retained by that party as his or her sole property free of any claim of any right of the other, with full power in that party to dispose of the same as fully and with such effect in all respects and for all purposes as though he or she were unmarried. However, either party may voluntarily name or retain the other as a beneficiary, or as trustee of said funds for the benefit of the parties' children.

EXHIBIT J
BANKRUPTCY FILING

J.1   In the event that either party to this Agreement decides to petition for bankruptcy under the provisions of Title 11 of the United States Code, that party must notify the other of his or her intention to file such a petition. Such notice shall be in writing and shall be given to the other party at least ninety (90) days prior to the filing of such petition. The notice shall be given by certified first-class mail, return receipt requested. The notice must include, but is not limited to, the name, address, and telephone number of the attorney, if any, who has been retained to represent the petitioning party in the bankruptcy action and must identify the court in which the petition will be filed. The receipt of such notice shall not in any way limit, restrict, or prevent the right of the party receiving notice from seeking any appropriate remedy or relief available to him or her under existing law or this Agreement prior to the filing of the petition in bankruptcy, nor shall the receipt of such notice limit, restrict, or prevent the party receiving the notice from asserting any claim available to him or her under law after such petition has been filed.

J.2   In the event that a party to this Agreement petitions for bankruptcy under the United States Code, that party shall be liable for attorney's fees incurred by the other party in protecting his or her rights under this Agreement to the extent that they are incurred as a consequence of the filing.

continued

Drafting Tip
This is not a common provision in most agreements, but in this case, one of the spouses was seriously considering filing for bankruptcy.

EXHIBIT K
TAXES

K.1 Stephen and Julie hereby warrant to each other that all income taxes, local, state, and federal, on all joint returns filed by the parties have been paid, and that to their knowledge, no interest or penalties are due and owing, and no tax deficiency proceeding or audit is pending or threatened.

K.2 If there is a deficiency assessment in connection with any of the joint returns, the party receiving notice of such deficiency shall notify the other party immediately in writing. The party responsible for the act or omission that caused the deficiency assessment shall be solely liable for any deficiency assessment, penalty, and interest, and shall hold the other harmless against any loss or liability in connection therewith. In the event that neither party is responsible for the act or omission that caused the deficiency assessment, then the parties shall pay the assessment in proportion to their income in the tax year for which the assessment is due.

K.3 In the event that there is a refund, the parties shall divide the amount of the refund equally.

THE COURT'S ROLE

The courts encourage the parties to resolve their differences and negotiate agreements whenever possible. However, this does not mean that courts play no role. In fact, the courts play a variety of roles with respect to separation agreements. The most common are the following:

- Reviewing the agreement at the time of the final hearing or trial for possible incorporation into the decree
- Modifying the agreement
- Enforcing the agreement
- Setting aside the agreement

Review of the Agreement at the Time of Trial or Final Hearing

When a complete or partial separation agreement is presented for approval, the court generally exercises one of three options (the first two at the choice of the parties):

- It may incorporate and merge the terms of the agreement into the decree; or
- It may incorporate the terms of the agreement into the decree, including the provision that it will not merge but rather survive as a separate contract with *independent legal significance;* or
- It may reject the agreement in whole or in part because it violates the law or a strong public policy. (In contrast to negotiation of a commercial contract, the parties' freedom to contract the terms of the dissolution of their marriage is more limited.)

Independent legal significance
a contract that is a separate, legally binding contract in its own right

EXHIBIT 12.3 Distinction between Merger and Survival as an
Independent Contract

A separation agreement is a contract that is effective upon signing unless otherwise
provided. If a judge eventually approves the agreement at the request of the parties, it is either incorporated and merged into the court's decree OR it is incorporated by reference in the decree but does not merge. Rather, it continues to survive
and retain its independent legal significance as a contract separate and apart from
the divorce decree. Often, the distinction between merger and survival is confusing for clients, but its consequences can be dramatic. Counsel needs to explain the
options clearly to the client so that he or she can make an informed decision about
which route to pursue. The two options are represented graphically below.

Separation Agreement
is presented to the court
with one of the following two results:

Agreement incorporated and merged into the decree	**OR**	Agreement incorporated into divorce decree and also survives as an independent contract

DECREE   **DECREE**

The decree includes the terms   The decree includes the terms of
of the agreement that are   the agreement that are incorporated
incorporated by reference and   by reference and made part of the
merged into the decree. The   decree. The decree is enforceable by
terms are enforceable only by   the family court according to its
the family court.   terms and applicable law.

                                       AND

AGREEMENT   **AGREEMENT**

The agreement merges into the   The agreement continues to exist
decree and no longer exists as   as a contract, with independent
an independent contract.   legal significance separate from
                                       the decree and is enforceable as
                                       a contract in court of equity.

In an uncontested case, neither spouse objects to the granting of the divorce, and the parties execute a mutually agreed-upon separation agreement. However, even in an uncontested case, the court customarily holds a brief hearing with one or both of the parties present. The judge/magistrate does not simply rubber-stamp the agreement (even if it resulted from arbitration) but rather reviews and occasionally asks questions about it. Particular attention is usually given to the conditions for payment of child support (e.g., will there be a wage assignment?); the arrangements made for continuing health insurance; the presence of waivers of alimony, if any; and whether the agreement will merge with the divorce or separation decree or survive as an independent contract. (See Exhibit 12.3.) Usually each of the parties is asked whether he or she has read, understood, and freely signed the agreement; whether each has exchanged and reviewed relevant financial information and agrees that there has been full disclosure of assets and liabilities; and whether each believes the agreement is fair.

In a contested case, if a partial agreement is submitted, the court may approve it and incorporate its terms into the divorce decree along with its determinations regarding the contested issues following a trial. As in an uncontested case, the partial agreement may be incorporated and merged into the decree or survive as an independent contract.

It is important that the parties understand what the terms of the agreement mean and what they have agreed to. Occasionally, a judge will address a question directly to a party in a hearing. It is a poor reflection on counsel if the client is able only to stare blankly at the court or look helplessly to the attorney in response! Given that no one "wins" in a divorce and that agreements invariably reflect compromises between what a party wants and what she or he can reasonably expect to have, clients are rarely 100 percent satisfied with agreements. Given a chance to speak, inadequately prepared clients occasionally vent such dissatisfaction, to the end that a court may send the parties back to the drawing board! When helping to prepare a client for court, the paralegal must be careful to leave explanations of the legal effect of various provisions to the attorney, but the paralegal can be a source of moral support to the client.

Modification of the Agreement

If the agreement is incorporated and merged into the divorce decree, the court retains the authority to modify it based on a substantial change in circumstances. If the agreement is incorporated but survives as an independent contract, the general rule is that it can be modified in only a limited number of circumstances:

- The agreement itself may provide for modification under certain circumstances, such as cohabitation or remarriage of one of the parties or a substantial increase or reduction in income.
- Since the court retains jurisdiction over child-related matters, provisions relating to the parties' children remain modifiable given a change in circumstances.
- If there has been a more-than-substantial change in circumstances such that one of the parties will become a public charge if a modification is not granted, many courts will order a modification rather than have the indigent person be supported by the taxpayers.

Enforcement of the Agreement

If the agreement is incorporated and merged into the divorce decree, then enforcement is pursued in the family court because the "breach" is a violation of an order of that court. The aggrieved party generally files a contempt action.

If the agreement is incorporated into the decree and also survives as an independent contract, the courts generally make every effort to enforce the terms of the agreement, unless doing so would violate the law or contravene a strong public policy. With a surviving agreement, the aggrieved party has two routes to use to obtain relief. As with a merged agreement, he or she may file a contempt action in the court that issued the decree. In addition, however, because the agreement retains its existence as an independent contract, contract remedies are also available. For example, the aggrieved party may sue for breach of contract, seeking damages or specific enforcement of a term of the agreement.

A confusing situation can develop when a family court modifies a provision of a surviving agreement that was incorporated into its decree. For example, assume the parties' agreement provides that wife will pay husband $500 per month in spousal support. She does so for the first two years following the divorce but then stops paying after losing her job. She seeks and is granted a modification by the family court based on a more-than-substantial change of circumstances. The court reduces her payment to $100 a month and she resumes making payments. Since the original agreement survives, technically the husband can sue in contract to recover the $400 difference between the amount of court-ordered alimony ($100) and the contractually agreed-on amount ($500).

The agreement may also be enforced in the context of other kinds of actions. For example, a party to a divorce who has been ordered to transfer property to a former spouse and to pay child support and alimony may try to avoid these obligations by filing for bankruptcy. The bankruptcy court will determine which of the obligations are in the nature of "support" and not **_dischargeable_** in bankruptcy. Agreements may also be considered in probate proceedings. For example, a spouse who has remarried may have been ordered to maintain an insurance policy for the benefit of his children but changes the beneficiary to his new wife. Upon his death, the children may seek to recover from the estate the amount they should have received from the policy.[2]

Discharge
the method by which a legal duty to pay a debt is extinguished

Action to Vacate the Agreement

After the divorce is "final," a party may file an action to have the court vacate or set aside the judgment incorporating the agreement. For example, six months after the decree has issued, one of the parties may discover that, despite his or her best efforts to obtain full disclosure before negotiating their agreement, the other party successfully concealed a substantial asset. Had the asset been brought to light in a timely manner, the property settlement would have been significantly different. Another scenario involves the situation in which an agreement was executed under duress. For example, an abusive husband may have threatened physical harm to both his wife and their children if she did not sign an agreement granting him custody of the children and a disproportionate share of the marital assets. Several months after the divorce when the wife feels more confident and safe from harm, she may seek a settlement that is truly fair and reasonable, including custody of the children and a greater portion of the marital assets.

PARALEGAL APPLICATION 12.2

YOU BE THE JUDGE

The following hypotheticals are excerpted from cases in which the courts have rendered decisions concerning issues related to separation agreements. Assuming you are the judge, what would your decision be in each case? Why? Would you require any additional information? What does the case teach you about the drafting of agreements—what could have been done to avoid the problem, if anything? Each of the cases is available in its entirety in the companion website.

CASE **12.1** *Larson v. Larson,* 37 Mass. App. Ct. 106, 636 N.E.2d 1365 (1994)

Judy and Richard were divorced in 1983. Their separation agreement provided that he would pay her $2,500 per month in unallocated alimony and child support until emancipation of the youngest of the parties' three children and thereafter at the rate of 30% of his annual gross earned income. The agreement was incorporated by reference in the judgment but also survived as an independent contract. The youngest child became emancipated in May 1991. The husband paid no alimony after that time claiming that he had no earned income. He had decided, on his own, to retire in good health from a successful career some years before his normal retirement age and thus stopped earning income. In January 1992, Judy filed a petition for modification alleging changed circumstances and seeking alimony. Richard claimed that the surviving agreement barred modification.

CASE **12.2** *Milark v. Meigher,* 17 A.D.3d 844, 793 N.Y.S.2d 581 (2005)

Hollis and Timothy were divorced in 2002. Their comprehensive separation agreement was incorporated but did not merge into the judgment of divorce. Among other provisions, their agreement provided that "the parties shall equally divide all primary and secondary school tuition, the cost of all school supplies, all mutually acceptable extracurricular activities, all reasonable clothing expenses for the children, all mutually acceptable summer programs for the children, all mutually acceptable sporting goods for the children, [and] all child care incurred by either party." At the time the agreement was executed, the children were enrolled in private school. Hollis subsequently failed to pay her share of the private school tuition claiming, among other things, that she should not be compelled to pay private school tuition when the community makes available a public school.

CASE **12.3** *In re Marriage of Grossman,* 338 Ore. 99, 106 P.3d 618 (2005)

Linda and Richard executed a marital settlement agreement, separated briefly, and then reconciled and lived together for another ten years before seeking to dissolve their marriage. Richard sought to enforce the agreement that the parties had already made. Linda argued the court should divide their property in a "just and proper" manner under the applicable state statute without enforcing the earlier agreement.

CASE **12.4** *In re Marriage of Wassom,* 352 Ill. App. 3d 327, 815 N.E.2d 1251 (2004)

Kelly and Rita were divorced in 1997. They had one son, Jessie. They executed a marital settlement agreement that was incorporated in the judgment. Article III of that agreement titled "Support of Children and Related Matters" provided in part:

> WIFE will carry the child on her health insurance, and the parties will equally divide any uncovered medical, dental, or orthodontic expenses on a 50/50 basis.... In addition to child support in Article III, paragraph 1, the HUSBAND will reimburse the WIFE for 50 percent of the health insurance premiums currently being paid by the WIFE.

Kelly claimed he should only be responsible for 50% of the health insurance premiums paid for Jessie and not for those paid for Rita's benefit.

CASE **12.5** *Brennenstuhl v. Brennenstuhl,* 169 N.C. App. 433, 610 S.E.2d 301 (2005)

Daniel and Karen were divorced in 1999 after executing a separation agreement in 1997. An amended version of the agreement was incorporated in the divorce judgment. A section of the property division settlement provided as follows:

> F. Retirement Benefits: Issues of retirement will be addressed at a later date.

In May 2003, Daniel retired from the military. In March 2004, Karen filed a motion requesting the trial court to award her a share of his military retirement pay. Daniel asserted that the provision was too vague to establish a right in the defendant to seek a portion of his military retirement pay subsequent to the divorce.

CASE **12.6** *Reaser v. Reaser,* 2004 S.D. 116, 688 N.W.2d 429 (2004)

David initiated divorce proceedings against his wife, Jami, in January of 1999. David was represented by counsel, Jami was not. The parties entered a stipulation prepared by David's attorney that addressed child custody, child support, alimony, and property division. Under the agreement, David was to have custody of the children. Jami waived any claim to alimony and David relieved Jami of any claim for child support. The judge refused to grant the divorce because the stipulation did not provide for child support. The parties then modified the stipulation to establish a child support obligation for Jami. Prior to submitting it to the court, David's attorney drafted a "document of private agreement" in which Jami "was to have no duty to pay ongoing [child] support despite the language of the Divorce Decree." This "private agreement" was kept in the lawyer's office and was not disclosed to the judge who subsequently approved the second stipulation. In 2002, Jami sought a change in custody and child support. During the course of the hearing, the "private agreement" came to light.

CHAPTER **SUMMARY**

We devote an entire chapter to the nature, purpose, modification, and enforcement of agreements in the context of divorce and separation because of their importance in bringing closure to a couple's marriage and shaping the parties' future. In a real sense, this chapter brings together many of the other chapters in the text, given the topics covered in agreements such as marital rights and responsibilities, child custody, child support, spousal support, and division of property both real and personal. The primary focus of the chapter is on the structure and components of agreements that must be tailored to the facts of each individual case. Particular attention is given to preparing paralegals for the important role they play in drafting effective separation agreements.

KEY **TERMS**

Boilerplate
Bottom line
Collusion
Consideration
Discharge
Forensic
Hold harmless provision

Impounded
Incorporation by reference
Independent legal significance
Legal separation
Marital estate
Meeting of the minds
Parol evidence rule

Pro se
Rescission
Separation agreement
Third-party beneficiary
Unearned income

REVIEW **QUESTIONS**

1. Describe how the courts historically viewed separation agreements and why.
2. Describe what a separation agreement is and identify the purposes it serves.
3. Identify the characteristics of an effective separation agreement.
4. Identify the factors the courts consider when determining whether or not a separation agreement is fair and reasonable.
5. Describe how most separation agreements are developed and identify the role commonly played by the paralegal.
6. Define "boilerplate." Identify at least five sections of an agreement that generally consist of boilerplate.
7. Identify the major topics commonly addressed in separation agreements.
8. Describe the nature and purpose of a severability clause.
9. Distinguish between a separation agreement that merges into a divorce decree and one that survives as an independent contract, and explain the significance of the distinction.
10. Describe the various ways in which the courts become involved with separation agreements.

FOCUS ON **THE JOB**

THE FACTS

Anna and Herman Nicole were married on August 16, 1995, in San Diego, California. It was the first marriage for Anna and the fourth for Herman. At the time of their marriage, Anna was twenty-seven years old and Herman was eighty-two. The parties have one minor child, Theodore Carleton Nicole, born on November 16, 1995. Anna presently lives at 23 Chandler Street in Chicago, Illinois, and Herman lives at 1102 Country Club Drive in your city and state. They separated on Christmas Day 2007 after opening gifts at the Country Club Drive residence and intend to continue to live separately for the rest of their lives. They have filed jointly for a no-fault divorce because irreconcilable differences have arisen between them. The action has been filed in your county in the appropriate court.

Both parties want to remain actively involved in their son's life but agree that Anna will be his primary caretaker, particularly during the school year so that there will at least be continuity in that aspect of his life. He is presently enrolled in a private school and is very active in a variety of sports. He is taking trumpet lessons and shows considerable musical talent. Herman will pay reasonable child support in an amount consistent with the state's child support guidelines (if they apply) based on an unearned income of $400,000 a year. It will be payable monthly.

The parties have exchanged financial statements but have engaged in no additional discovery. Anna earns approximately $125,000 a year as a "model" and intends to continue her career. She has no retirement fund. Herman has been retired for some time but is independently wealthy. His assets are valued at approximately $5.5 million. Herman has managed all of the couple's financial affairs, and his accountant has prepared all of the joint tax returns submitted during the marriage based on the information Herman provided.

Herman was both physically and emotionally abusive to Anna during their twelve-year marriage, but she is willing to forget all that if he pays her alimony of $10,000 per month for the rest of her life and lets her have their apartment in New York City, their summer home in Newport, Rhode Island, and the condo where she is presently residing. All of the properties are owned outright by Herman. (Anna owns no real estate in her own name.) He has also agreed to split his General Electric pension with her (requiring preparation of a QDRO) and to make her the sole beneficiary of a $500,000 Prudential life insurance policy. She will receive the Rolls-Royce and he will keep his collection of vintage automobiles. For understandable reasons, Herman is willing to waive any rights to ever claim alimony and wants the alimony provisions of the agreement to be non-modifiable by any court under any circumstances. He has no objection to paying his own debts but refuses to pay Anna's credit card debts, which have been a constant source of tension between them. (Anna is somewhat of a shopaholic.) Anna figures he will end up paying some of the debt anyway, because two of her three cards are in their joint names. The accounts are a Bank of America account numbered 1772-2356-7631-8976 (balance $7,980), a Jet Green Master charge account numbered 028-3456-93 (balance $13,569), and an American Express account numbered 1357-2468-0864 (balance $22,567).

The parties have already divided their personal property, except that Herman needs to remove from the New York and Newport properties all the works of art he has collected over the years.

Herman says he feels sort of bad about the divorce and that he may decide to provide for Anna in his will, but she is not counting on that. However, she is happy that he will pay for comprehensive medical insurance for her until his death and for Theodore until his emancipation. That is important to her because she has heavy bills for psychiatric treatment and medications. Anna figures that she is "making out like a bandit" and has chosen not to obtain legal advice because she doesn't want to waste any of the funds she is receiving on an attorney.

The Assignment

Assume that you are a paralegal in the family law firm representing Herman in this matter. Draft a separation agreement tailored to the above fact pattern. Use a format that is appropriate in the jurisdiction where you are studying family law. This may mean that, instead of an integrated separation agreement, you will be preparing a parenting plan and a marital property settlement/stipulation. You should also be sure to use the appropriate terminology in your jurisdiction for child-related and spousal support matters.

FOCUS ON **ETHICS**

Edward E. Edwards, III, is the attorney who represents Herman in the above fact pattern. His office is located at 12 Beacon Street in your city and state. You are his paralegal. Edward is thrilled to be handling this case and has told you to prepare monthly invoices for as long as the case continues; he figures he will be able to "drag it out for a while." He tells you to keep track of your hours as well as his and to bill them all at his regular hourly rate of $250. He says he is happy to split the fee with you because you are such a good employee. You are uneasy about this—it just doesn't feel right but you really need the money. Besides, you are aware that Herman has abused all of his wives and you figure he deserves to pay. As a matter of fact, when you saw Anna at a local club recently, you told her she really ought to get a lawyer because she could probably "do better."

Discuss this situation from an ethical perspective. Relate your response to the ethical canons for paralegals promulgated by the National Federation of Paralegal Associations (NFPA), which are contained in Appendix B of this text.

FOCUS ON **CASE LAW**

The case *In re Marriage of McInnis,* 199 Ore. App. 223, 110 P.3 639 (2005), is available on the companion website. Read the case and then respond to the following questions.

1. Describe the legal history of the case. What kind of a case is it? Where was it first brought and with what result?

2. What are the issues on appeal?

3. Was the parties' agreement approved by the court? Did it merge into the judgment or did it survive as an independent contract?

4. What did the agreement provide with respect to spousal support?

5. What did it provide with respect to modification of spousal support?

6. What was the basis of the trial court's decision not to enforce the agreement with respect to modification of spousal support?

7. What was the basis of the appellate court's decision to enforce the agreement with respect to modification of spousal support?
8. What remedies do the courts in Oregon provide to support the enforceability of marital agreements?

9. Do the courts in Oregon always enforce marital settlement agreements?
10. What did the appellate court decide regarding both the requested modification and the trial court's award of attorneys' fees, and do you agree with the decision?

FOCUS ON **STATE LAW AND PROCEDURE**

Locate and brief a recent case in the state where you are studying family law regarding the enforceability of separation agreements.

FOCUS ON **TECHNOLOGY**

WEBSITES OF INTEREST

http://www.divorcelawinfo.com

This is the website for a commercial service that provides, for sale, online interactive preparation of a variety of forms having to do with divorce. The service comes in two forms, a do-it-yourself format and a paralegal-assisted format. Forms and services are purportedly state-specific. The site also has a frequently asked questions feature.

http://www.divorcesupport.com

This site provides material related to a broad range of divorce-related topics. For separation agreements, there are generic informational features such as Frequently Asked Questions (FAQ), online discussion forums, and state-specific separation agreement preparation services. The site also provides links to state divorce law information.

http://www.findlaw.com

This site provides a sample separation agreement (which is not state-specific) for a short-term marriage with no children. It also provides links to divorce forms by state. Several of the state links contain sample separation agreements and parenting plans.

http://www.LawDepot.com

This site provides fill-in-the-blank forms for a variety of legal situations including separation. The forms are not jurisdiction-specific.

http://www.uslegalforms.com

This is the website for a service that provides, for sale, either downloadable or hard-copy forms for a variety of legal situations that are purportedly state-specific. For each state, it offers a number of different separation agreement forms that are tailored to the requirements of various general separation situations.

Note: Caution needs to be exercised when considering using commercial packages.

ASSIGNMENTS

1. Locate three online resources related to separation agreements in your state.
2. Locate at *www.courts.state.nh.us* the Parenting Plan and Permanent Stipulation Forms used by the New Hampshire courts.
3. Locate the sample *pro se* parenting plan and separation agreement forms provided by the Colorado courts at *www.courts.state.co.us*.

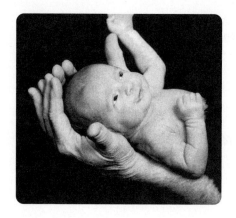

chapter **thirteen**

PARENTHOOD

Stephen and Mary are in their early thirties. They have been seeing each other for four years and want to share a life together. The only thing needed to complete the picture is a child, but Stephen carries a rare genetic disease, and Mary had a hysterectomy due to uterine cancer when she was twenty-five years old. They have decided to search for egg and sperm donors who carry traits they consider desirable and then have Mary's best friend, Carol, serve as a surrogate mother. Carol and her husband, Chip, are all for the idea.

What started out as an effort to help married couples fulfill their dreams of having genetically related children has, within a few short years, triggered a revolution about how we think about parentage, marriage and even gender identification.... Not long ago, religious leaders were calling for the criminalization of sperm donation. In the not-too-distant future, the issues will be about the cloning of human beings, "sexual" reproduction using artificially produced gametes, and...eugenics.[1]

INTRODUCTION

In its coverage of the topics of parentage and assisted reproductive technology, this chapter further extends a basic theme of this text: Society and the law are confronting changes in the way people define parenthood, create families, and assign responsibility for children. Nontraditional means of conceiving and giving birth now make parenthood possible for thousands of people who would otherwise be childless and, in so doing, expand the diversity of nontraditional families in society. Although preference for the "traditional family" is still strong, doors have opened to new bases for establishing, and in some cases, disestablishing, legal parenthood.

The content of this chapter supplements material in Chapter 8 on child custody and anticipates Chapter 14 on adoption. It begins with a brief historical perspective on the child's legal status, identifies the three major interested parties in parentage determinations, describes the most common ways in which parentage is established and may be "disestablished," and then addresses key topics and issues in the evolving area of assisted reproductive technology.

THE CHILD'S LEGAL STATUS

Under early common law, the child's legal status essentially depended on the marital status of his or her parents. Children were regarded as legitimate if born to married parents and illegitimate if born to unmarried parents. The child of unwed parents was deemed a "***filius nullius,***" a child of no one, a bastard with a legal bond to neither parent—essentially a public ward. If the mother were married and the child was the product of an illicit affair, then legal parentage was established based on a ***marital presumption*** of legitimacy rather than on biological parenthood.

By the nineteenth century, the states began to move away from penalizing children for their parents' sexual misconduct and toward treating them as innocents warranting protection, support, and nurturance rather than punishment and the stigma of illegitimacy. Given the relative ease of establishing maternity based on the biological realities of pregnancy and birth, the legal bond between an unwed mother and her child was the first to be recognized, rendering children "legitimate" at least with respect to their mothers.

Establishment of the father-child relationship outside of the marital unit has been slower to evolve. However, recognizing the negative impact of illegitimacy on unwed fathers and their children, states began enacting legislation in the early 1800s providing for acknowledgment of paternity and legitimization of children whose parents subsequently married. Progress was slow but was energized in the 1960s by that era's focus on equal rights and elimination of discrimination in many areas. In a piecemeal fashion and with mixed results, scrutiny has gradually extended to laws that treat unwed fathers and mothers

Filius nullius
Latin for "the son (child) of no one"

Marital presumption
the presumption that when a woman gives birth to a child while married or within three hundred days of termination of the marriage, her husband is presumed to be the child's legal father

differently and unwed parents and their children differently from married parents and their children based solely on marital status. Consider the following landmark cases:

- In the 1968 *Levy* case, the U.S. Supreme Court held that Louisiana's wrongful death statute violated the equal protection clause of the Constitution by denying children the right to recover for the death of their mother because they were "illegitimate."[2] The Court stated:

  > Legitimacy or illegitimacy of birth has no relation to the nature of the wrong allegedly inflicted on the mother. These children, though illegitimate, were dependent on her; she cared for them and nurtured them; they were indeed hers in the biological and in the spiritual sense; in her death they suffered wrong in the sense that any dependent would.[3]

- Beginning with *Lehr v. Robertson*[4] in 1983, the Supreme Court basically established a ***"biology-plus" approach*** to extending rights to unwed fathers in the adoption context. Under this approach, a biological connection alone is not enough to establish an unwed father's parental rights. Unlike an unwed mother, whose legal parentage is established at birth, a man must also act as a father. According to the Court:

  > The significance of the biological connection [between father and child] is that it offers the natural father an opportunity that no other male possesses to develop a relationship with his offspring. If he grasps that opportunity and accepts some measure of responsibility for the child's future, he may enjoy the blessings of the parent-child relationship and make uniquely valuable contributions to the child's development.[5]

- Gender-based discrimination against and between unwed mothers and fathers has been permitted in some contexts when a statute is deemed to serve important governmental purposes and the discriminatory means employed are substantially related to the achievement of those objectives. In *Nguyen v. Immigration and Naturalization Services*,[6] for example, the Supreme Court upheld a provision of the Immigration and Naturalization Act[7] applicable to children born outside of the country when only one parent was a citizen. The statute imposed different requirements for a nonmarital child's acquisition of citizenship based on whether the citizen parent was the unwed mother or the unwed father. According to the Act, the child of an unwed mother acquires citizenship if the mother, prior to the birth, was a citizen and met a one year residency requirement.[8] If the father was the citizen parent, he must have been a citizen when the child was born, have established a blood relationship to the child by clear and convincing evidence, have agreed to support the child until age eighteen, and have acknowledged paternity or been adjudicated the father before the child turned eighteen.[9] The Court reasoned:

  > Fathers and mothers are not similarly situated with regard to the proof of biological parenthood....In the case of a citizen mother and child born overseas, the opportunity for a meaningful relationship between citizen parent and child inheres in the very event of birth.... The same opportunity does not result from the event of birth, as a matter of biological inevitability, in the case of the unwed father.[10]

In a strong dissent, Justice O'Connor, joined by Justices Souter, Ginsburg, and Breyer, opined that the majority's opinion may have reflected a stereotype of "male irresponsibility" with respect to children "that is no more a basis for the validity of the classification than are stereotypes about the 'traditional' behavior patterns of women."[11]

Biology-plus approach
the approach that holds that an unwed father's parental rights are worthy of constitutional protection if the father grasps the opportunity to develop a relationship with and accept responsibility for his child

WHO ARE THE INTERESTED PARTIES?

The three parties most interested in parentage determinations are children, parents, and the government.

The Child

"In 2002, according to a U.S. Census Bureau Report, 13.8 million children were living alone with their single mothers."[12] The precise number of these and other children who do not know the identities of their biological fathers is virtually impossible to establish, but the numbers are significant. The impact of not knowing the identity of a parent can be monumental for a child as he or she grows into adulthood. The answer to the question, "Who am I?" inevitably rests, at least in part, on the answer to the question, "Where did I come from?" Even if the answer is not entirely satisfactory, it has many potential emotional, social, economic, and legal advantages for a child:

- the opportunity to form a bond with the parent and other relatives
- the chance to discover and appreciate his or her cultural heritage
- eligibility for a wide range of economic benefits, including, for example, child support, insurance coverage, inheritance rights, worker's compensation allowances for dependents, social security death benefits, veterans' and employer educational and pension survivor benefits, etc.
- standing to bring certain causes of action, such as for a parent's wrongful death
- medical benefits, including access to the medical histories of parents and members of their extended families, particularly with respect to potential inheritance and transmission of genetically based diseases and identification of donors for blood transfusions and bone marrow and organ transplants, if needed

Although some courts have acknowledged that children have a natural desire to feel rooted, to find themselves, and to know their origins, children often confront legal obstacles when they attempt to discover their true parentage. (See Paralegal Application 13.1.)

PARALEGAL APPLICATION **13.1**

OBSTACLES TO DISCOVERING PARENTAGE

- **The Marital Presumption:** Under the marital presumption, a man married to a child's mother at the time of birth (or within three hundred days of termination of the marriage) is presumed to be the child's father, a presumption that still carries considerable weight in many jurisdictions.

- **The Doctrine of Estoppel:** The doctrine of estoppel holds a mother and/or a man accountable for their conduct regarding paternity in some circumstances. If they act as if the man is the child's father, he may be deemed by the courts to be the father, and neither the mother nor the "father" may be permitted to request genetic testing to deny paternity at a later date.

- **Issue Preclusion/*res judicata*:** Issue preclusion and *res judicata* principles prevent parties from relitigating in a subsequent suit an issue that was

continued

fully litigated and decided in an earlier action. For example, if the issue of paternity of a particular child is raised and decided in the context of a divorce proceeding, in most states neither party is permitted to file a later paternity action seeking to have someone else designated the father of the child.

- **Reproductive Technology Statutes:** Depending on the method of assisted reproductive technology used to produce a child, states may dictate by statute who will or will not be deemed a legal parent. For example, the Uniform Parentage Act of 2000 (as amended in 2002), adopted in some states, provides that the donor of semen to a licensed physician for use in artificial insemination (of a woman other than the donor's wife) will be treated as if he were not the father of a child thereby conceived.

- **Sealed Records/Confidentiality Statutes:** After an adoption is finalized, many states require that all records of the adoption be sealed, including the child's original birth certificate and any other documents that identify the child's birth parents. In most states, no one can have access to identifying information about the biological parents absent a showing of good cause, such as a medical emergency.

SIDEBAR

Do you believe all children are entitled to know who their "real" parents are, no matter how complex or disturbing their origins may be?

The Parents

The threshold question is who are the child's parents? "Who's your mother?" was once a reasonably simple question to answer. Even "Who's your father?" was not that complicated, depending on the mother's marital status. However, with the emergence of reproductive technologies, even the answer to "Who's your mother?" is not so simple anymore. For example, the Uniform Parentage Act of 2000 (as amended 2002) recognizes both genetic consanguinity and giving birth as legitimate means of establishing a mother-and-child relationship. But, what should happen if the two means do not coincide in one woman? (See Case 13.3 later in this chapter.) And what if, in a state that recognizes the marital presumption, the mother's husband and the child's biological father are different men? (See Paralegal Application 13.2.)

Once established, a parent's status as a mother or a father automatically brings with it a variety of rights and obligations that, for the most part, attach whether or not one exercises them. Although much of the legislation and litigation on parenthood focuses on the obligations of parenthood (primarily economic responsibilities), parenthood also brings with it a variety of rights as well as the potential joys and satisfactions of raising children. Parental rights for married parents include, for example, the shared rights to discipline and educate their children and to make decisions regarding medical treatment, religion, place of residence, and social contacts. For unmarried or divorced parents, these rights may be more limited, because they often are shaped by law and established by the courts.

PARALEGAL APPLICATION **13.2**

MICHAEL H. V. GERALD D., 491 U.S. 110, 109 S. Ct. 2333, 105 L. Ed. 2d 91 (1989): WHEN BIOLOGY-PLUS AND MARITAL PRESUMPTION COLLIDE[13]

THE FACTS

In this case, the Supreme Court dealt with two fathers, each with a bona fide claim to paternity. In 1981, a woman named Carol gave birth to a daughter named Victoria. Carol's husband, Gerald, was identified on the birth certificate as the child's father, and he lived with the mother and child on and off during the years following the birth. However, the child actually was the product of Carol's extramarital affair with a man named Michael, who was genetically determined (within a 98.7 degree of probability) to be the child's father. He, too, lived with Carol and Victoria on and off following the child's birth, during which time he established a relationship with his daughter. However, Gerald and Victoria subsequently reconciled. When Michael filed a paternity action seeking to be declared the child's father and to establish a right to visitation, Gerald opposed, claiming that, under California law, he was the child's father based on the marital presumption. The child filed a cross-complaint asserting that she should be entitled to maintain her relationship with both *de facto* fathers.

SIDEBAR

Faced with the forced choice between two fathers in this case, what do you think the court should do? Explain your response. Should it matter that the child is the product of an affair? Should the biological father be permitted to rebut the marital presumption? Must one father be rejected in favor of the other father, or do you think the courts should recognize both fathers as the child requested? To learn what the Supreme Court decided in this case, check the full opinion available on the companion website. Do you agree with the outcome? Compare the major arguments of the plurality and the dissent.

In an era in which several individuals may have legitimate claims to parentage in a given case, courts are called upon to address challenging questions:

- Should parenthood flow on a strict liability basis, solely from the performance of a sexual act regardless of the circumstances or intent of the parties to create a child? If so, how do we deal with cases involving nonconsensual sexual relations, statutory rape,[14] or partners who lie about the use of birth control measures?
- Should parenthood "by accident" be treated differently from parenthood by deliberate choice?
- Should parents have to act as parents in order to be considered parents?
- Should the mother's marital status determine parentage?
- Should individuals be able to assign parental status by contract?
- Should parenthood be a fixed status—once a parent, always a parent?
- Should children be permitted to have more than two parents?
- Should same-sex partners be permitted by law to be parents (by contract, adoption, etc.)? (See Paralegal Application 13.3.)

PARALEGAL APPLICATION 13.3

DOES A CHILD NEED A MOTHER AND A FATHER?

One of the arguments often raised in opposition to legal recognition of gay co-parents is that a child needs both a mother and a father, as opposed to simply two parents, be it two mothers or two fathers. The claim is that "A child needs both a mother-figure and a father-figure in order to develop to his (or her) maximum potential. Implicit in this argument…is the assertion that fathers have certain traits that mothers cannot utilize or model as well as fathers can, and that mothers have certain traits that fathers cannot utilize or model as well as mothers can."[15]

Clearly, sex is controlling during gestation and birth, because, at least at this point, a man cannot carry and deliver a child. However, post birth, must caretaking be gendered? Do you think there is a difference between fathers and mothers as parents? Can fathers mother and mothers father? Is the sex of the person performing the role more important than the role he or she performs?[16]

The Government

The government's interest in establishing parentage is essentially economic.[17] It is motivated less by a desire to provide for the needs of an individual child than by an interest in controlling the costs of public assistance. This interest is well founded, given that under the federal definition of poverty, approximately one in five to six children in the United States lives in poverty. This statistic is at least in part due to a lack of economic support from unknown and absent fathers.[18]

As discussed at length in Chapter 9, the federal government plays a prominent role in the area of child support in an effort to contain the costs of public assistance in all its forms: support, food stamps, health insurance benefits, etc. The child's entitlement to support exists without regard to the parents' marital status or the nature or extent of his or her relationship with the parents. Pursuant to a variety of federal statutes, the states must:

- require mothers receiving public assistance to cooperate with the state's IV-D agency in identifying and locating the child's father, who may then become a defendant in an action to recoup child support
- allow children (and, in most cases, their mothers) to sue for paternity until the children's eighteenth birthday
- require mothers who receive prenatal and post-partum medical assistance under the Social Security Act to assist the Social Security Administration in recovering the cost of that care from the child's biological father
- meet specified paternity-establishment percentages as a condition of federal funding for child support enforcement programs

HOW IS PARENTAGE ESTABLISHED?

As suggested earlier in this chapter, the concept of parentage was once reasonably straightforward. A child had two parents, and they were presumed to be a biological mother and her husband. Today there are many kinds of parents including, but not limited to, those described in Exhibit 13.1. There are also multiple ways of establishing legal parentage, particularly fatherhood, which vary considerably among the states.

EXHIBIT 13.1 When is a Parent a Parent?

- **Acknowledged parent:** a parent who has acknowledged parentage by executing an affidavit acknowledging parentage
- **Adoptive parent:** a person who, by means of legal process, becomes a parent of a child to whom he or she is biologically unrelated
- **Biological parent:** a blood-related parent who contributes half of the child's genetic material by means of a reproductive cell (egg or sperm); sometimes called a genetic or "natural" parent
- **Co-parent:** a person who shares childrearing responsibilities with a partner with or without benefit of a legally recognized parent-child relationship
- *De facto* **parent:** a person who has been a primary caregiver and financial supporter of a child, usually with consent of the legal parent and for a requisite period of time
- **Egg or sperm donor:** a person who donates genetic material (sometimes for a fee) to help others have a child; donors often remain anonymous and usually give up any parental rights they may have to a child they may help to create
- **Foster parent:** a person who takes care of a child for a temporary period of time, usually for a modest payment through a child welfare agency
- **Gestational mother:** a woman who carries and delivers a child to whom she may or may not be biologically related
- **Intended parent(s):** a person or couple who intend to take custody of and assume all parental rights and responsibilities for a child as a result of an adoption, a surrogacy arrangement, or some other technique of assisted reproduction; an intended parent may or may not be genetically related to the child
- **Legal parent:** a person who is recognized as a child's parent under state or federal law
- **Natural parent:** a mother or father who is a biological (genetic) parent of a child
- **Parent by estoppel:** an individual who, although not a legal parent, lives with and accepts parental responsibilities for a child and on whose support the child and the other parent have relied
- **Presumed father:** a man who is presumed to be the father of a child who is conceived/born during the course of his marriage (or within a certain period thereafter) to the mother
- **Psychological parent:** the individual who has the strongest "parental" bond with the child, who has provided the most significant care for the child in quality and quantity, and whom the child often regards as a "parent"
- **Putative father:** a man who may be the father of a child but who was not married to the child's mother at the time of birth and whose paternity has not yet been established through legal process
- **Step-parent:** a person who marries the legal mother or father of a child to whom he or she is biologically unrelated
- **Surrogate mother:** a woman who agrees to carry and deliver a baby with an understanding that she will surrender the child to the intended parents at birth or shortly thereafter; a surrogate mother may or may not be genetically related to the child

Traditionally, motherhood and a mother's constitutionally protected rights to parent her child flow from the critical role she plays in nourishing the child in her womb and enduring the pain and risks of childbirth. The Supreme Court has described the relationship as "verifiable from the birth itself."[19] Because fatherhood has posed more of a challenge, the following material focuses primarily on establishment of paternity. There are three major ways in which legal parentage is established:

- The marital presumption
- Acknowledgment of parentage
- Adjudication of parentage

The Marital Presumption

As mentioned earlier, under common law, parentage was based on the marital presumption (sometimes called the legitimacy presumption) that when a married woman gave birth to a child while the parties were married or within three hundred days of termination of the marriage, the woman's husband was presumed to be the child's legal father. In the interest of preserving marriages, the general rule was that all of the potentially interested parties (the husband, the mother, the child, and the biological father) were precluded from bringing a paternity action. Lord Mansfield's Rule of evidence prohibited either spouse from giving testimony that the husband was not the father, even in the face of strong biological evidence to the contrary. When challenges were allowed, the presumption could be rebutted only with evidence of the husband's sterility, impotency, or non-access to the wife at the time of conception. The interests served by the presumption were described in 2006 by a Michigan Supreme Court Justice as follows:

> The presumption that children born or conceived during a marriage are the issue of that marriage is deeply rooted in our statutes and has been consistently recognized throughout our jurisprudence....This presumption vindicates a number of interests, not the least of which include the interest of the child in not having his or her legitimacy called into question, the interest of the state in ensuring that children are properly supported, and the interest of both in assuring the effective operation of intestate succession. The presumption also reflects the recognition that "'[t]here is no area of law more requiring finality and stability than family law.'"[20]

The states now generally set forth by statute or case law the rules for if, when, and by whom the marital presumption can be rebutted. Courts in several states still uphold it, even when conclusive scientific proof of biological paternity is available, at least as long as the marital unit is intact. However, in most states, a putative biological father or a husband who has reason to believe he is not the child's biological father, may rebut the presumption, but must do so within a limited period of time. Case 13.1 illustrates a court's application of the marital presumption, estoppel principles, and fraud in the context of a child support action.

Acknowledgment of Parentage

Under federal law, all states must have in place simple procedures enabling parents to voluntarily acknowledge parentage by completing an appropriate notarized acknowledgment, stipulation, or affidavit. The document is most often called a voluntary acknowledgment or affidavit of parentage. It may be executed at a hospital at the time of birth or at some point thereafter. In addition to

CASE **13.1** *Doran v. Doran,* 2003 PA Super 129, 820 A.2d 1279 (2003)

BACKGROUND INFORMATION

In this case, the Appellant, Pamela Doran (a.k.a., Smigiel), appealed an order of a Court of Common Pleas granting her former husband's petition for dismissal of a child support order dated August 24, 1994, but denying his request for restitution of previously paid support. At the time of the Petition to Dismiss, the child was almost eleven and a half years old. He was born during the parties' marriage and was about five years old at the time of the parties' divorce in 1995. The husband, William, had raised and supported the child as his own and the wife, when asked, had assured him that the child, Billy, was his. Without his knowledge, however, Pamela had been sexually involved with another man at the time of conception and for a decade thereafter. In early 2001, Billy's appearance and mannerisms caused William to question that he was the child's biological father. He asked his wife to agree to DNA testing, the results of which indicated a zero percent probability of paternity. Despite his request that they talk with the boy together, the mother chose to tell him the truth herself. William then "gently" removed himself from the child's life, hoping to cause him as little hurt as possible under the circumstances. He also then sought relief from the court based on his former wife's infidelity and deception, which had caused him to believe he was Billy's biological father. His Petition was granted in June 2002. In July, Pamela raised the following issues on appeal:

1. Was it reversible error for the lower court to grant the petition to dismiss, given that the parties were married and living together at the time of the child's birth and continued to do so for almost four years thereafter?

2. Was it reversible error to grant the petition to dismiss, given that William had maintained suspicions as to the child's paternity and yet continued to hold the child out to the public as his son even after he knew for certain that he was not the child's father?

3. Was it reversible error to grant the petition to dismiss where the decision to do so was contrary to established precedent with respect to the doctrines of "presumption of paternity" and "estoppel" for purposes of paternity and support matters?

FROM THE OPINION

Discussion

Smigiel essentially argues that the trial court should not have granted Doran's petition to dismiss child support since the presumption of paternity applies to the instant case. However, she further argues, if the presumption does not apply to the instant case, estoppel does.

"In matters involving support, a reviewing court will not disturb an order of the trial court unless there has been an abuse of discretion." *Diehl v. Beaver,* 444 Super. 91, 663 A.2d 232, 233 (Pa. Super. 1995) (citations omitted)....

In *Brinkley v. King,* 549 Pa. 241, 701 A.2d 176, 180 (Pa. 1997), the Pennsylvania Supreme Court set forth the analysis required to determine the paternity of a child conceived or born during a marriage:

The essential legal analysis in these cases is twofold: first one considers whether the presumption of paternity applies to a particular case. If it does, one then considers whether the presumption has been rebutted. Second, if the presumption has been rebutted or is inapplicable, one then questions

continued

whether estoppel applies. Estoppel may bar either a plaintiff from making the claim or a defendant from denying paternity. If the presumption has been rebutted or does not apply, and if the facts of the case include estoppel evidence, such evidence must be considered.

We must first determine if the presumption of paternity applies to the instant case. "The policy underlying the presumption of paternity is the preservation of marriages." *Fish v. Behers*, 559 Pa. 523, 741 A.2d 721, 723 (Pa. 1999). "The presumption only applies in cases where that policy would be advanced by the application; otherwise, it does not apply." *Id.* (citation omitted). In this case, there is no longer an intact family or a marriage to preserve. Smigiel and Doran separated and a divorce action was pending prior to the hearing in the support matter instituted by Smigiel against Doran. Accordingly, the presumption of paternity is not applicable.

Having concluded that the presumption is inapplicable, we must determine whether Doran is estopped from denying paternity. "A (former) husband may be estopped from denying paternity of a child born during a marriage if either he or his wife holds the child out to be the child of the marriage." *Weidman v. Weidman*, 2002 PA Super 308, 808 A.2d 576, 577–78 (Pa. Super. 2002) (citation omitted).

> Estoppel in paternity actions is merely the legal determination that because of a person's conduct (e.g., holding out the child as his own, or supporting the child) that person, regardless of his true biological status, will not be permitted to deny parentage, nor will the child's mother who has participated in this conduct be permitted to sue a third party for support, claiming that the third party is the true father. As the Superior Court has observed, the doctrine of estoppel in paternity actions is aimed at "achieving fairness as between the parents by holding them, both mother and father, to their prior conduct regarding the paternity of the child."

Fish, 741 A.2d at 723 (citation omitted).

In the instant case, Doran admitted that he held the child out as his own from the child's birth in 1990 until DNA testing excluded him as the father in … June 2001, he exercised visitation with the child and continued to support the child. Doran also stated that he continued to see the child after the DNA testing excluded him as the father. Therefore, it appears that Doran is estopped from denying his paternity.

Nevertheless, Doran argues that Smigiel's fraudulent conduct was the basis for his treating the child as his own; therefore, estoppel is precluded. Specifically, Doran argues that Smigiel assured him that he was the natural father and deceived him by failing to inform him of the truth of her unfaithfulness when he first had doubts about his paternity.

"When allegations of fraud arise in a paternity action, an estoppel analysis must proceed in a different manner than it would without such averments." *McConnell v. Berkheimer*, 2001 PA Super 224, 781 A.2d 206, 211 (Pa. Super. 2001) (citation omitted). Evidence of fraud "must be considered by the trial court in whether to apply paternity by estoppel." *Sekol v. Delsantro*, 763 A.2d 405, 410, 2000 PA Super 351 (Pa. Super. 2000) (citation omitted).

> The presumption that a child born during a marriage is a child of the marriage and the doctrine of paternity by estoppel grew out of concern for the protection of the family unit; where that unit no longer exists, it defies both logic and fairness to apply equitable principles to perpetuate a pretense. In this case, application of estoppel would punish the party that sought to do what was righteous and reward the party that has perpetrated a fraud.

continued

Id. . . . "The test for fraud is: (1) a misrepresentation, (2) a fraudulent utterance, (3) an intention by the maker that the recipient will thereby [be] induced to act, (4) justifiable reliance by the recipient upon the misrepresentation, and (5) damage to the recipient as a proximate result." Sekol, 763 A.2d 405 at 411 n. 7 (citation omitted).

In its decision, the trial court found that:

> . . . Mr. Doran had been operating for more than a decade under the misrepresentation that he was, indeed, the child's father. This subterfuge was a direct result of the mother's intentional misstatements and deceptions to him. She deluded herself by refusing to even consider that her child might be fathered by the man with whom she had an illicit affair. She never once mentioned her meretricious relationship with this third party to her husband. Instead, she fallaciously led him to believe, at the same time as she was seeking child support from him, that he was, in fact, the child's father. Had she been forthright to her spouse and explained what she had done at the time of the child's conception, her husband may certainly have acted differently. Unfortunately, her deceit, falsehoods and misrepresentations gave Mr. Doran no reason but to treat the child as his own—with love, care and respect, as only a decent human being would do under the circumstances.

Decision, 6/13/02, at 5–6.

. . .

Based on our limited standard and scope of review, we affirm. We hold that the trial court's factual findings are supported by competent evidence which is sufficient to sustain the trial court's order. Smigiel testified that she had sexual relations with Doran and another man at the time the child was conceived. When Doran became suspicious in 1996 that the child was not his, she assured him that it was even though she did not know for sure. It was not until 2001, when Doran questioned her again, that she finally admitted that she was not sure and agreed to the DNA testing. We, therefore, find that the trial court did not abuse its discretion in granting Doran's petition to dismiss the support order.

SIDEBAR

This opinion is available in its entirety on the companion website. Do you agree with the holding in the case? Why? Do you believe that Doran did "as only a decent human being would do under the circumstances"? Explain your response.

hospitals, acknowledgment forms are also commonly available at IV-D agencies, social service agencies, and other locations where children and their parents receive services. The form contains, or is accompanied by, a description of the legal consequences of executing the document with respect to child support, custody, and visitation rights, and obligations. A copy of the Illinois Voluntary Acknowledgment of Paternity Form and Instructions is accessible on the companion website. Once executed, the document becomes the equivalent of a legal finding of paternity subject to a sixty-day rescission period.[21] The acknowledgment then is entitled to full faith and credit in all states. Thereafter it is binding and can be challenged only on the grounds of fraud, duress, or mistake of fact. Congress has also provided that the unmarried father's name may appear on a birth certificate only if the mother and father have executed an acknowledgment of parentage or there has been an adjudication of paternity.[22]

Paralegal Practice Tip
Unmarried fathers often voluntarily acknowledge paternity without legal counsel and without benefit of the scientific certainty afforded by genetic (DNA) testing. When counsel is consulted, the client commonly is advised to confirm paternity through testing. This is especially the case in jurisdictions in which, once a functional parent-child relationship is established, parentage is no longer an issue that can be challenged, even given maternal fraud.

Adjudication of Parentage

Historically, paternity actions were primarily criminal in nature and were designed to punish sexual misconduct. Today, they are largely civil in nature and commence with the filing of a Complaint to Establish Paternity (see Exhibit 13.2) or a Petition for Declaration of Parentage. They are most often brought by mothers seeking child support, IV-D agencies on behalf of a recipient of public assistance, or men

---

EXHIBIT 13.2 Complaint To Establish Paternity

Courtesy of Commonwealth of Massachusetts

Commonwealth of Massachusetts
The Trial Court
Probate and Family Court Department

Division _____

Docket No. _____

COMPLAINT TO ESTABLISH PATERNITY

_____ , Plaintiff   v.   _____ , Defendant

1. Plaintiff, who resides at _____
   _____ / _____ / _____
   (Street Address)   (City/Town)   (County)

   _____ _____ , is
   (State)   (Zip)

   ☐ the ◯ mother ◯ father of a child born out of wedlock.

   ☐ a child born out of wedlock.

   ☐ the ◯ guardian ◯ custodian of a child born out of wedlock.

   ☐ the ◯ parent ◯ personal representative of the ◯ mother ◯ father of a child born out of wedlock.

   ☐ the ◯ Department of Social Services   ◯ agency licensed under G.L. c. 28A.

   ☐ the Department of Revenue.

2. The child who is the subject of this complaint is:

   Name _____ Date of Birth _____

   _____ / _____ / _____ / _____
   (Street address)   (City/Town)   (State)   (Zip)

3. Defendant, who resides at _____
   _____ / _____ / _____
   (Street Address)   (City/Town)   (County)

   _____ _____ , is the ◯ mother ◯ father of the above-named child who was born out of wedlock.
   (State)   (Zip)

4. The plaintiff and defendant are not married.

5. The mother of the child was not married at the time of the child's birth and was not married within three hundred days before the birth of the child.

6. Wherefore, the plaintiff requests that the Court:

   ☐ adjudicate the ◯ plaintiff ◯ defendant to be the father of the child.

   ☐ order a suitable amount of support for the child.

   ☐ order the ◯ plaintiff ◯ defendant to ◯ maintain ◯ provide health insurance for the benefit of the child.

   ☐ prohibit the defendant from imposing any restraint on the personal liberty of the ◯ plaintiff and/or ◯ the child.

   ☐ grant the ◯ plaintiff ◯ defendant custody of the child.

   ☐ grant the ◯ plaintiff ◯ defendant visitation rights with the child.

   Date _____

   _____
   (Signature of attorney or plaintiff, if pro se)

   _____
   (Print name)

   _____
   (Street address)

   _____
   (City/Town)   (State)   (Zip)

   Tel. No. _____

   CJ-D 106 (4/07)   B.B.O. # _____   C.G.F

PARALEGAL APPLICATION 13.4

KNOW YOUR PATERNITY BASICS

There is considerable variation among the states with respect to paternity actions and the rules that govern them. The following are questions a paralegal may need to address when working on a paternity case:

- What are the various ways in which parentage can be established in the state? Acknowledgments? Paternity actions? Legitimation actions?

- Which court(s) in the state have subject matter jurisdiction over paternity proceedings?

- Does the court in a given case have personal jurisdiction over the defendant?

- Which statutes of limitations govern the bringing of various kinds of paternity actions (domestic relations, probate, tort, etc.)?

- Are there mandatory forms to be used when filing paternity actions?

- Who has standing to bring a paternity action: mother, husband, putative father, child, IV-D agency, third parties (such as co-parents, grandparents, personal representatives, etc.)?

- What is the standard of proof in paternity actions? Preponderance of the evidence? Clear and convincing evidence?

- When and how can genetic testing be used?

- Is the marital presumption recognized and, if so, when and how is it rebuttable?

- Does the state recognize the equitable parent doctrine? (See Case 13.2.)

seeking to establish or disestablish paternity. Under federal law, when paternity is contested, states must require genetic testing of the parties and the child, if requested. If the tests indicate paternity to a high degree of probability, a rebuttable presumption of paternity is established, and the burden shifts to the **_putative father_** to prove nonpaternity if he chooses and is able to do so. A copy of an Affidavit in Support of Establishing Paternity (initiating a IV-D case) is accessible on the companion website.

The courts also sometimes base parentage determinations on nonbiological grounds. In addition to the marital presumption, courts apply a variety of legal theories to justify decisions finding that a person is, for example, a _de facto_ parent, a psychological parent, a co-parent, or a parent based on equitable estoppel. Such theories are used when the courts recognize the rights of individuals who have functioned as parents to maintain their relationships with the children they have helped to raise. For example, in Case 13.2, the Wisconsin Supreme Court applied the **_equitable parent doctrine_** against a biological father in favor of a nonbiological father in a custody case.

Parenthood by estoppel essentially provides that a man may be designated the legal father of a child if he has held himself out as the child's father and has supported the child emotionally and financially. It is assumed that both the child and the mother have come to rely on that support and that it would be inequitable to deprive them of its continuation. A paralegal may be called on to gather information to support a claim that a father has held a

Putative father
a man reputed or believed to be the father of a child but who was not married to the mother when the child was born and who has not established his paternity through legal process

Equitable parent doctrine
a doctrine used to extend parenthood to an individual who is willing and able to assume parental rights and responsibilities and/or who has done so in the past

Parenthood by estoppel
essentially provides that a man may be designated the legal father of a child if he has held himself out as the child's father and has supported the child emotionally and financially

CASE **13.2** *A.J. v. I.J.*, 2002 WI App 307, 259 Wis. 2d 120, 655 N.W.2d 195 (2002)

BACKGROUND

In this case, a mother, Norma, gave birth to a child in January 1998 while she was married to her husband, Randy. Randy did not learn until he filed for divorce in October 1999 that the child's biological father was actually the mother's boyfriend, Brendan. The child knew only Randy as her father, although the mother did take her to Brendan's for weekly visits prior to her being sentenced to eight years in prison in May 1999. After the mother's incarceration, the child lived with Randy. In December 1999, Norma filed a counterclaim in the divorce action and alleged Brendan was the child's father. Brendan filed a motion to intervene and sought to be adjudicated the child's natural father and requested legal custody and primary physical placement of the child. The trial court denied the motion to intervene and declared Randy the child's equitable parent and awarded him custody. Norma and Brendan appealed.

FROM THE OPINION

This divorce case presents an unusual factual scenario. Randy A.J. is willing to continue supporting and providing care for a child that is not biologically his own. He seeks to maintain the parent-child relationship he established with a child born during his marriage to the natural mother, Norma I.J., despite the fact that genetic tests have established to a 99.99% degree of certainty that Brendan B. is the child's father. Norma and Brendan argue that because the genetic tests showed that Brendan is the biological father of the child, the trial court had no authority to determine that establishing Randy as the legal father and awarding him custody were in the best interests of the child. We conclude that Randy is the equitable parent of the minor child and affirm the trial court's decision that otherwise awarded Randy custody of the child.

. . .

On appeal, Brendan and Norma assert that once the parties submitted to genetic testing and the tests showed Brendan to be the biological father, the trial court erred in concluding that Wis. Stat. §§ 767.463 and 767.458 (1m) granted it the authority to conduct a best interests of the child hearing and dismiss the paternity action. Brendan and Norma further contend that once the genetic tests demonstrated that Brendan was the biological father…, he overcame the marital presumption.

. . .

The statute explicitly permits the court to dismiss an action to establish the paternity of a child based upon the best interests of the child only if genetic tests have not yet been taken.

. . .

The trial court next concluded that despite the fact that the genetic tests had established Brendan's parentage to a 99.99% degree of certainty, Brendan had not rebutted the marital presumption.…The presumption is rebutted by the results of a genetic test establishing by a statistical probability of 99.0% or higher the parentage of a man other than the man presumed to be the father under subsec. (1). Sec. 891.41(2).

. . .

While the trial court may have used the incorrect vehicle in the law, the court clearly felt compelled by the evidence to declare that Randy, not Brendan, should be the child's father. The trial court made unmistakable, but implicit, findings that Brendan should not be entitled to whatever foothold he had gained by reason of

continued

the genetic tests....the trial court was wrong on the law, but its factual findings supported the correct result, had the proper standard been applied.

...

We first reiterate what we have already written—that the marital father is presumed to be the natural father unless rebutted. A genetic test showing another man to be the natural father rebuts that presumption. But that does not end the matter. Under Wis. Stat. § 767.48(1m), the natural father then only gains a *rebuttable presumption* that he is the child's parent. Thus, it is evident from the law that even if a test shows a man to be the natural father, his legal fatherhood is only presumed. Next, we must consider "how" such a presumption may be overcome. In our view, the presumption may be overcome by evidence that the marital father has so bonded with the child as to be considered the "equitable parent."...

Wisconsin has recognized the equitable parent doctrine. See *J.J. v. R.J.*, 162 Wis. 2d 420, 429–30, 469 N.W.2d 877 (Ct. App. 1991). The equitable parent doctrine extends the rights and responsibilities of a natural parent to a nonbiological parent seeking custody or visitation.... Once a court determines that a party is an equitable parent, there is no distinction between the equitable parent and any other parent; each is endowed with the same rights and responsibilities of parenthood.... We have permitted a mother in a divorce action to estop a nonbiological father from denying paternity in order to avoid child support obligations.... We have also held that for the purposes of establishing a right to a relationship with the child born to his wife but fathered by another man, the husband may utilize the status of "equitable parent" to assert an equitable estoppel defense against the child's mother instituting paternity proceedings against him.... Here we face the unusual situation where the mother is in prison, the child does not recognize the biological father as being her parent, and the nonbiological father not only wants to continue the parent-child relationship, but also wishes to support the child emotionally and financially by maintaining custody of the child.

The Michigan Court of Appeals faced a somewhat similar situation in *Atkinson*....

...[T]he court concluded that the husband was entitled to be treated as a natural father under the equitable parent doctrine.... Thus, the custody dispute between the husband and the wife would be settled as if it were between two natural parents, based upon the child's best interests....

While we acknowledge that the equitable parent doctrine has not been invoked in Wisconsin against a natural parent for the purpose of awarding custody to a nonparent, we have invoked the doctrine set forth in *Atkinson* against a natural parent for the purpose of awarding visitation to a nonparent in a situation that bears some factual similarity to this case....

... In this case, the trial court held several days of hearings concerning the best interests of the child in which all parties participated.... we acknowledge that in exercising its equitable powers, the trial court did not expressly use the equitable parent doctrine to declare Randy the legal father and otherwise award him custody. However,...the trial court made substantial and careful findings of fact regarding the relationship each party had established with the child and the

continued

conduct of the parties concerning the child's paternity and we use these findings in our analysis of the equitable parent doctrine as applied to this case. Whether the facts as found permit the application of equitable estoppel is a question of law that we review independently of the trial court's determination....

During the pregnancy and up until Norma's incarceration, Randy, Norma and the child lived together. After Norma's incarceration, Randy became the sole custodian of the minor child and has continued to assume responsibility for her. The child considers Randy to be her only father and, up until the divorce proceedings, Randy believed her to be his biological daughter. The trial court found that "there clearly is a-what would otherwise be viewed as a normal parent-child relationship and bond between [Randy] and [the child], and, in fact, he has been her only parent from the standpoint of regular and daily contact and custodial care since May of 1999."...

Prior to the divorce proceeding, and with Norma's cooperation, Randy believed he held the status of a natural parent and assumed the rights and responsibilities of fatherhood. Norma and Brendan never took any steps to change Randy's belief despite the fact that they had suspected Brendan was the father of the child. The trial court found that it was in both Norma's and Brendan's best interests not to take any action concerning the child's paternity. Norma was involved in significant criminal legal difficulties at the time and needed Randy's financial backing. During legal proceedings, Randy supported Norma and funded the costs of her legal representation, using all of the family's cash and equity in their home. It was not until Norma was incarcerated and Randy filed for divorce that Norma raised the paternity issue.

The trial court also found that Brendan had the opportunity and ability to assume parental responsibility for the child and chose not to do so. The court determined that while Brendan saw the child on a weekly basis prior to Norma's incarceration, the relationship established between the two was not that of father and daughter. The relationship arose simply upon the event of Norma's relationship with Brendan. The trial court further determined that Brendan, having to purchase such things as diapers, formula, and some clothing for the child during her extended weekend stays prior to Norma's incarceration, in no way constituted support of the child either emotionally or financially. Finally the court noted that Brendan did not raise the issue of his paternity in this state until the child was well over three years old....

The trial court also relied upon the testimony and recommendations of the psychologist,... She recommended that Randy remain the father of the child.... Finally, the court also gave due consideration to the substance abuse problems of the parties.

We have ... determined that Brendan may not assert his parentage based on the facts as found by the trial court and the applicable law.... We affirm the trial court's determination that it was in the child's best interests that the court estop Norma from asserting the child's parentage. We hold that Randy is the legal father and affirm the trial court in that regard. We also hold that Randy is entitled to custody and affirm the trial court's determination on that issue.

SIDEBAR

The opinion in this case is available in its entirety on the companion website. How would you define the equitable parent doctrine? Do you agree with the court that it properly applied to the facts of this case? Explain your response.

child out as his own. Some of the kinds of conduct to be considered include the following:

> A man is deemed to have held out a child as his biological offspring when he engages in parental conduct such as: changing the child's diapers; feeding him; taking him to the doctor; bathing him; taking the child on visits away from the mother's home; allowing the child to call him daddy; giving the child gifts or cards; attending parent-teacher conferences or school events; giving the child his surname; voluntarily providing financial support for the child; and providing or building a loving relationship with the child. He can also put the child on his insurance, claim governmental benefits for the child under his name, or claim to be the child's father to the public at large, such as the child's school, daycare or even to friends, relatives and neighbors.[23]

Uniform Parentage Act

The Uniform Parentage Act (UPA) was first adopted by the National Conference of Commissioners on Uniform State Laws in 1973. It was subsequently revised in 2000 and amended in 2002. As of July 2007, the revised UPA has been enacted in whole or in part in a small number of states, including Delaware, Texas, Washington, and Wyoming, and is under consideration in others, some of which presently recognize the 1973 edition of the Act. The current version creates a single, coherent act regarding parentage by integrating the 1973 UPA with the Uniform Putative and Unknown Fathers Act and the Uniform Status of Children of Assisted Conception Act. Its provisions are also consistent with the principles and requirements of two other key uniform acts, the Uniform Child Custody Jurisdiction and Enforcement Act (UCCJEA) and the Uniform Interstate Family Support Act (UIFSA), both of which are available on the companion website in the material related to Chapters 8 and 9 respectively. It is also consistent with paternity requirements of federal child support enforcement law in general.

The Act addresses both paternity and maternity determinations and treats marital and nonmarital children equally with respect to their legal status and rights. Under the Act, a father-child relationship may be established in the following ways:[24]

- An unrebutted presumption of paternity based on (a) the common law marital presumption that a married woman's husband is the father of a child born during the marriage, or (b) openly holding out a child as his own and residing in the same household as the child for the first two years of his or her life
- An effective acknowledgment of paternity, with the agreement of the mother, in a written document that has the same force and effect as an adjudication of paternity
- An adjudication of paternity in a judicial proceeding
- Adoption of the child by the man
- An adjudication confirming the man as a parent of a child born to a gestational mother if the agreement was validated...or is enforceable under other law

The Act recognizes the availability of genetic testing to determine parentage. It also includes provisions governing parentage of children born as a result of assisted reproduction and includes optional provisions for allowing judicial approval of gestational/surrogate parent agreements.

HOW IS PARENTAGE DISESTABLISHED?

A natural consequence of the availability of DNA testing is that some putative fathers learn with scientific certainty that they are not the biological fathers of children they have been raising and supporting in good faith as their own. In many instances, they have mistakenly formally acknowledged paternity or been adjudicated fathers by the court. Although paternity judgments are binding and not easily challenged, an increasing number of states have determined by statute or case law that, in the interest of fairness, a father faced with such circumstances should be permitted to seek an order vacating an earlier paternity judgment, in effect disestablishing an existing father-child relationship.

Several states, such as Alaska,[25] Georgia,[26] Maryland,[27] and Ohio,[28] have established statutory procedures by which an otherwise legally recognized father can disestablish paternity. The Alaska Paternity Set-Aside statute is accessible on the companion website. Based on the potentially devastating effect of **disestablishment** on the child, legislatures and courts in some other states have taken a more cautious approach and have expressly not permitted petitions to disestablish paternity. The child, rather than the nonbiological father, is viewed as the victim. Courts in still other states weigh the relative benefits of knowledge of the truth against disruption in the child's life. Factors these courts consider include:

- the nature and stability of the present home environment
- whether or not there is an existing relationship with a nonbiological father figure
- the desire and willingness of the biological father to assume parenting responsibilities
- whether the child already has established a bond with the biological parent
- the motive of the party bringing the paternity or disestablishment action
- the age of the child
- whether or not the child is uncertain of his or her parentage
- the child's physical and emotional needs
- whether or not there exists a compelling medical need to establish the father's identity

The law with respect to disestablishment actions continues to evolve. When they are permitted, there is considerable variation state to state in terms of when they may be brought and by whom, whether genetic testing must be conducted prior to or as part of the petition to set aside paternity, and whether or not restitution of past child support payments will be granted.[29]

Disestablishment of paternity
a court order vacating an earlier paternity judgment or child support order based on evidence the man is not the child's father, in effect disestablishing a previously existing father-child relationship

Paralegal Practice Tip
The state has a statutory right to, in effect, "disestablish" parentage in some contexts. For example, the state may terminate a parent's rights if it proves parental unfitness by clear and convincing evidence, although parental rights may not be terminated merely to advance the parents' convenience and interests, either emotional or financial.

PARALEGAL APPLICATION 13.5

TO DISESTABLISH OR NOT TO DISESTABLISH—THAT IS THE QUESTION

In your opinion, which of the following three approaches to disestablishment should legislatures and courts adopt and why? Should they:

1. act in the interests of the nonbiological father seeking to be relieved of parental responsibility for a child he did not procreate by allowing disestablishment?

   Under Maryland law, for example, in proceedings to modify or set aside paternity declarations, a "determination of the best interests of the child in ordering … testing, or in the consideration of paternity,

   continued

whether original or revised, is inappropriate."[30] "Simply stated, the fact of who the father of a child is cannot be changed by what might be the best interests of the child."[31] Finality of paternity determinations is outweighed by fairness to a man who is not a child's biological father. The "law will not compel one who has stood in the place of a parent to support the child after the relationship has ceased."[32]

2. act in the best interests of the child by maintaining an existing parent-child relationship and not allowing disestablishment?

The Vermont Supreme Court has described this position as follows:

> … [T]he financial and emotional welfare of the child, and the preservation of an established parent-child relationship, must remain paramount. Where the presumptive father has held himself out as the child's parent, and engaged in an ongoing parent-child relationship for a period of years, he may not disavow that relationship and destroy a child's long-held assumptions, solely for his own self-interest.… Whatever the interests of the presumed father in ascertaining the genetic "truth" of a child's origins, they remain subsidiary to the interests of the state, the family, and the child in maintaining the continuity, financial support, and psychological security of an established parent-child relationship.[33]

3. act in the best interests of the child by allowing disestablishment on the ground that the child should have the opportunity to know his or her biological father?

> … [C]hildren have a profound right to know their father. They have an interest in their father's care and companionship.…In certain cases, it will be in the child's best interest to know the father's identity. Moreover, it is in the child's best interest to have the opportunity to establish a relationship with him.[34]

Paternity Fraud

In some cases, a misunderstanding with respect to biological parenthood may be innocent. A mother truly may not know the identity of the father, or a man may choose to perpetuate a falsehood about the identity of a child's biological father out of love for his spouse and/or a child. However, in other cases, for a variety of reasons, the mother may have deliberately withheld information and/or fraudulently misled both the child and a man believing himself to be the child's father with respect to the biological father's true identity:

- She may not want contact with the biological father because of the circumstances of conception (e.g., rape).
- There may be a history of abuse by the father and she fears for her safety and/or the safety of the child.
- If she is married, she may not want to jeopardize marital harmony or financial security by revealing that the child is the product of an adulterous affair.
- She may want to place the child for adoption and fears that if the father has notice, he will delay or block the adoption.
- In an effort to receive needed public assistance, she may have responded to pressure to designate someone as her child's father by naming a man she knows is not the father.

Paternity fraud
fraud in which a mother has intentionally misled a man into believing he is the father of a child to whom he is genetically unrelated

Although **paternity fraud** is old news, paternity fraud actions are a relatively new phenomenon made possible by advances in genetic testing. "In 1999 alone, almost one-third of 280,000 paternity cases evaluated by the American Association of Blood Banks excluded the individual tested as the biological father of the child. In a period of only one year, that is almost 100,000 men who were falsely accused of being the father of a child which, they simply did not father."[35] Paternity fraud actions may involve husbands, ex-husbands, or unmarried fathers, but they all essentially have one thing in common: a man has discovered that he has no genetic relationship to a child he formerly believed was his offspring and he no longer wants to be legally obligated for support. Much like wrongly convicted felons, some fathers greet DNA testing as a route to freedom. The U.S. Citizens Against Paternity Fraud website goes so far as to display the motto, "If the genes don't fit, you must acquit."[36] But is the cure worse than the disease? "Unlike Pinocchio, a fairy tale ending is neither guaranteed nor likely.... Marriages, relationships, and families end. Children are abandoned by the only fathers they ever knew. Fathers are bitter and fight to disown the nonbiological child. Children lose their sense of identity. And the damage cannot be undone."[37]

The focus of this chapter now shifts dramatically from the often painful collapse of family bonds through disestablishment to the joyful promise of assisted reproductive technology as a means of creating families once not possible. Each opens doors and presents challenges for an expanding legal horizon.

ASSISTED REPRODUCTIVE TECHNOLOGY

Assisted reproductive technology (ART)
treatment or procedures designed to make parenthood possible for persons with fertility problems or individuals who are otherwise unable or personally unwilling to reproduce

In a family law text, a discussion of the contemporary concept of parenthood is incomplete without some consideration of the fascinating, and, for some, alarming, topic of **assisted reproductive technology (ART)**. One commentator has described the evolution of the use of this technology as follows:

The technology of assisted reproduction, developed primarily to aid married couples with infertility, has been made available to people who are physically unable to engage in coitus, or who have an aversion to coitus....It has been made available to people for whom gestation and childbirth pose unacceptable risks, and extended further toward the more controversial use of gestational mothers so that the genetic and/or intended mothers can avoid the inconvenience of going through a pregnancy. It has been made available to people who wish to avoid the risks of having children with genetically determined diseases, and extended further to sex selection and perceived enhancement of the genome of the intended child, in a word to eugenic practices. ...ART has been utilized to enable procreation by dead people, by the use of gametes obtained with their knowledge and consent, and sometimes without, and sometimes obtained only after their death. It can potentially be used to enable procreation by fetuses who will never be born.[38]

Since the 1970s, hundreds of thousands of children have been conceived through ART rather than "naturally" through coitus. Most state legislatures have been reluctant to tackle this development. However, some have begun to do so, and family law practitioners addressing ART issues need to monitor developments and be aware of any applicable governing laws and regulations. What does exist is limited, fragmented, and far from uniform. For example, Illinois has a comprehensive set of statutes regulating surrogacy;[39] New Hampshire has passed legislation regarding evaluation of gamete donors and use of gametes;[40] Massachusetts criminalizes experimentation on embryos before or after implantation;[41] Pennsylvania requires "all persons conducting or experimenting with *in vitro* fertilization" to file quarterly

PARALEGAL APPLICATION 13.6

SHOULD ART BE AVAILABLE TO EVERYONE?

Procreation is a fundamental right that enjoys constitutional protection, but does that right extend only to reproduction through traditional means (sexual relations) or also to assisted methods as well? As indicated above, ART provides a valuable resource for a variety of individuals and couples seeking to have children: infertile couples, couples engaged in same-sex relationships, parties seeking to avoid transmission of disease (such as sickle cell anemia, tay sachs, or sexually transmitted diseases), or individuals wanting to produce a child with particular characteristics. Do you believe everyone should be able to make use of the technology available, or should access be restricted? Consider the following:

> William Gerber is a forty-one year old inmate at Mule Creek State Prison in California serving a sentence of one hundred years to life plus eleven years. Given the length of his sentence it is unlikely that he will ever be paroled. He and his wife want to have a child. To that end, Mr. Gerber has requested that he be allowed to provide his wife with a sperm specimen she can use to be artificially inseminated. He argues that a refusal to permit him to do so would constitute cruel and unusual punishment and violate his fundamental right to procreate.

How do you think the warden should respond to this request? Why? A copy of a sharply divided opinion dealing with this fact pattern is available on the companion website. (See *Gerber v. Hickman*, 291 F.3d 617 (9th Circ. Ct. of Appeals 2002).)

reports with the state;[42] Arkansas requires that facilities that provide *in vitro* fertilization services be certified and achieve a "reasonable success rate with both fertilization and births";[43] and several states have passed legislation addressing insurance coverage for persons undergoing assisted reproductive technology procedures. A few states, such as Maryland,[44] mandate coverage but limit the mandate to particular procedures.

The remainder of this chapter is devoted to identification of some of the ethical issues associated with this technology and a review of the state of the law, as of the fall of 2007, with respect to surrogacy, cryopreservation of embryos and gametes, posthumous reproduction, the use of ART by same-sex couples, and areas of potential liability. A concerted effort is made to reference cases and statutes from many states to illustrate the tremendous variation that exists in this rapidly evolving area. Exhibit 13.3 provides definitions of some basic ART terms for initial reference.

EXHIBIT 13.3 Assisted Reproductive Technology—Basic Terminology

Artificial insemination/ intrauterine insemination	This procedure involves insertion of the sperm of a donor into a female's reproductive organs by a means other than sexual intercourse with the intent to bring about a pregnancy.
Cloning	Cloning is the genetic replication of a living organism.
Cryopreservation	This process involves the freezing of gametes or embryos to preserve them for use at a later date.

continued

Cytoplasmic egg donation	In this procedure, genetic material is extracted from the eggs of a donor and injected into the eggs of another woman. In effect, the process technically results in the potential for a child to have two genetic mothers.
Donor	A donor is an individual who produces eggs or sperm for use in assisted conception. The donor may or may not receive compensation.
Embryo adoption	Embryo adoption is not technically an adoption. It occurs when an embryo donor(s) gives an embryo to a recipient with the intention that the recipient become pregnant. The recipient (and her spouse, if any) may subsequently adopt the resulting child.
In vitro fertilization (IVF)	An egg is fertilized by sperm outside the womb with the intention that the resulting zygote be transplanted into the reproductive system of the genetic mother or a surrogate or that it be available for cryopreservation, donation, or research.
Posthumous reproduction	Posthumous reproduction occurs after the death of one or both of the gamete contributors.
Pre-implantation genetic diagnosis (PGD)	This technique involves the biopsy of a single cell or embryo prior to implantation, usually to determine sex, detect genetic disorders, or custom-create or select embryos with desirable traits.
Surrogacy Agreement/Contract	In a surrogacy agreement, a woman agrees to conceive a child through natural or artificial insemination or to implantation of an embryo and to relinquish her parental rights to the resulting child.
Surrogate	A surrogate is a woman who agrees to serve as the birth mother of a child for another individual or couple. She may or may not receive compensation.
Traditional surrogate	A traditional surrogate is artificially inseminated with the sperm of a man other than her husband. She is genetically related to the resulting child, whom she agrees to surrender post birth to the intended parents. Customarily she agrees to relinquish all of her parental rights to the child.
Gestational surrogate	A gestational surrogate agrees to serve as the birth mother of a child to whom she is genetically unrelated. The genetic parents may be the intended parents, gamete donors, or a combination of the two.

ETHICAL ISSUES

The science of assisted reproductive technology tends to evoke strong reactions from the general public, religious leaders, legislators, and legal and medical professionals, among others. It has been the focus of many groups, such as the President's Council on Bioethics, the National Conference of Commissioners on Uniform State Laws, the American Bar Association's Reproductive and Genetic Technologies Committee, the Federal Center for Disease Control and Prevention, the Federal Food and Drug Administration, the American Society for Reproductive Medicine, and the American College of Obstetricians and Gynecologists, among others. Despite the attention, no consensus or clear public policy has emerged. Little regulatory legislation exists at either the federal or state level, and no concerted effort is in place to gather data on standards and practices that might inform decision making.[45] The science of ART clearly has not developed without generating considerable controversy and monumental ethical challenges. Exhibit 13.4 provides a brief introduction to some of these ethical challenges.

EXHIBIT 13.4 Ethical Considerations in Art[46]

Ethical considerations in ART essentially fall into two separate and distinct areas of concern:

1. **Considerations that concern laboratory standards, procedures, and accountability** address the underlying question, "Is this technical process being performed according to acceptable standards?"

2. **Considerations that concern the application of ART** address the broad question, "Should a particular application of ART be undertaken at all and, if so, under what constraints or conditions?" That is, is it in the best interests of those involved and of society at large?

Each of these is already complex and challenging enough, given the status of ART today. The continuing evolution of the technology makes these considerations moving targets that are likely to become even more challenging in the future.

Laboratory Standards, Procedures, and Accountability: This is an exceedingly complex and many-faceted area. Its origins lie in several diverse regulatory bodies dating back to the 1970s and in industry and ethics bodies first represented by the Society for Assisted Reproductive Technology (SART), established in 1987 as an affiliate of the American Society for Reproductive Medicine (ASRM) founded in 1944. Today, many government, industry, professional (medical and legal), academic, religious, and patient advocate groups are "stakeholders." The National Coalition for Oversight of the Assisted Reproductive Technologies (NCOART) is a body spawned by SART in which membership is available to any of the "stakeholders" and in which they can each have a voice. Although it has no formal authority, NCOART has emerged as an effective forum for the introduction and discussion of issues and for the preparation of consensus-based recommendations to standards, regulatory, and legislative bodies.

The Ethical Application of ART: The questions here are fewer, easier to ask, but profoundly more difficult to answer. The answers will likely eventually come in the form of legislation establishing boundaries on how ART may be used. No

continued

matter what answers are legislated, some groups (and, in some cases, perhaps all groups) will be dissatisfied. Various related debates stimulate fervor akin to that surrounding abortion. Six of the more prominent debates focus on the following issues:

1. **Pre-implantation Genetic Diagnosis (PGD):** The idea here is that the genetic structure of an *in vitro* fetus can be examined. The possibilities range from those as fundamental and critical as simple assessment of the fetus's survivability to those as superficial as selection of personal characteristics such as sex and eye color. Critical intermediate possibilities include important health issues such as the identification of genetic markers for various diseases. The question, then, becomes, "Given that each fetus deserves 'profound respect' and 'special status' even if not 'the full legal and moral rights attributed to persons,' to what extent is it ethically permissible to select a fetus to be implanted based on PGD?"

2. **Posthumous Children:** With ART it is possible to have a child conceived, carried, and born even if one or both of his or her parents are dead. Ethical questions arise regarding consent of the (deceased) parents, creation of a viable "parenting plan," financial support for the child, the role of the state, etc.

3. **Marketing of Ova and Sperm:** With ART, it is possible for a prospective parent (whether fertile or not) to go shopping (for example, on college campuses or websites) for "high-quality" sperm and ova as candidates for *in vitro* fertilization and subsequent implantation.

4. **Surrogacy:** ART provides an opportunity for a couple to have a child who is genetically theirs without having to carry the child through gestation. The idea of "commercial" surrogacy has given rise to considerable public opposition. The picture painted is one of a wealthy couple hiring a poor woman to suffer the discomfort and risks of pregnancy.

5. **"Savior Siblings":** Consider the couple who has a child with a disease that might be cured (or at least mitigated) by a bone marrow transplant from a genetically suitable donor. Using PGD it is now possible to select an embryo that is genetically suitable and have a child for the sole purpose of its being a donor for its afflicted sibling.

6. **Human Cloning:** Ever since the cloning of "Dolly" in 1997, the cloud of human cloning has hovered over us and given rise to considerable debate. While there presently is no credible evidence for successful cloning of humans, there is little doubt that the technology will eventually emerge. If fetus selection based on PGD is questionable, then cloning is profoundly more so. Of particular interest is the question of the rights of the cloned person *vis a vis* expectations based on the nature of the person being cloned. For example, if Celine Dion were cloned, there would likely be inordinate pressure placed on the clone, based on expectations that she would become an outstanding vocalist with tremendous earning potential. What if she wanted instead to be a missionary or a teacher or a physician at a free clinic?

continued

What is your position with respect to human cloning? Should priority be given to its potential for alleviating human suffering or to the dignity of the human embryo? Assuming that its potential as a reproductive option is eventually realized, do you think it should be available to assist infertile couples to reproduce? Should gay and lesbian couples be permitted to use it, thereby allowing them to reproduce without having to use a third-party donor? If the right to privacy encompasses reproductive decisions, should the government be permitted to deprive citizens of the right to make use of this option?

SURROGACY

Surrogacy law in the United States is at best unsettled as of the spring of 2008. Most states have no controlling statutory or case law. On one end of the spectrum of those that do is the state of Michigan, which presently bans surrogacy contracts,[47] compensated or not, and sentences anyone convicted of inducing, arranging, procuring, or otherwise assisting in the formation of a surrogacy contract with up to five years in prison and a fine of up to $50,000.[48] At the other end of the spectrum are states such as Florida, which permits unpaid surrogacy agreements in which at least one intended parent is genetically related to the child and the parties follow several statutory requirements. (See Exhibit 13.5.) Other states have enacted legislation specifically pertaining to surrogacy that varies greatly in content. For example:

- Illinois provides considerable protection for parties to surrogacy agreements and permits pre-birth establishment of the legal parentage of children of assisted conception.[49]
- In New Hampshire, parties to a surrogacy agreement must have their agreement judicially approved prior to impregnation.[50]
- Under Utah law, the intended mother cannot be receiving Medicaid or other state assistance, and she must be married to the intended father.[51]
- Although generally a surrogacy-friendly state, Virginia prohibits surrogacy "brokers."[52]
- The state of Washington will not give full faith and credit to a compensated surrogacy agreement executed in another state.[53]
- Nevada and several other states permit compensation of a surrogate, provided the payment is limited to necessary medical and living expenses.[54]
- Kentucky prohibits compensation to attorneys for negotiating and drafting agreements regarding payment of surrogates.[55]

Although "*forum shopping*" is generally discouraged and, in some instances, not permitted by the courts, parties from one state may be permitted to execute an agreement in a more surrogacy-friendly state, provided that state has at least some connection with the matter and the result is not contrary to a strong public policy. For example, in one case, the Massachusetts Supreme Judicial Court allowed a pre-birth judgment of parentage when the intended parents resided in Connecticut, the surrogate and her husband lived in New York, and the baby was scheduled to be born in Massachusetts.[56] The governing law of the jurisdiction in which a surrogacy agreement is executed must be carefully reviewed to better ensure the likelihood that the terms of the agreement will be enforceable.

Forum shopping
seeking a court in a jurisdiction that will provide the most favorable ruling in a case

---

EXHIBIT 13.5 Fla. Stat. § 742.15 Gestational Surrogacy Contract

FROM THE STATUTE

§ 742.15. Gestational surrogacy contract

(1) Prior to engaging in gestational surrogacy, a binding and enforceable gestational surrogacy contract shall be made between the commissioning couple and the gestational surrogate. A contract for gestational surrogacy shall not be binding and enforceable unless the gestational surrogate is 18 years of age or older and the commissioning couple are legally married and are both 18 years of age or older.

(2) The commissioning couple shall enter into a contract with a gestational surrogate only when, within reasonable medical certainty as determined by a physician licensed under chapter 458 or chapter 459:

    (a) The commissioning mother cannot physically gestate a pregnancy to term;

    (b) The gestation will cause a risk to the physical health of the commissioning mother; or

    (c) The gestation will cause a risk to the health of the fetus.

(3) A gestational surrogacy contract must include the following provisions:

    (a) The commissioning couple agrees that the gestational surrogate shall be the sole source of consent with respect to clinical intervention and management of the pregnancy.

    (b) The gestational surrogate agrees to submit to reasonable medical evaluation and treatment and to adhere to reasonable medical instructions about her prenatal health.

    (c) Except as provided in paragraph (e), the gestational surrogate agrees to relinquish any parental rights upon the child's birth and to proceed with the judicial proceedings prescribed under § 742.16.

    (d) Except as provided in paragraph (e), the commissioning couple agrees to accept custody of and to assume full parental rights and responsibilities for the child immediately upon the child's birth, regardless of any impairment of the child.

    (e) The gestational surrogate agrees to assume parental rights and responsibilities for the child born to her if it is determined that neither member of the commissioning couple is the genetic parent of the child.

(4) As part of the contract, the commissioning couple may agree to pay only reasonable living, legal, medical, psychological, and psychiatric expenses of the gestational surrogate that are directly related to prenatal, intrapartal, and postpartal periods.

In states such as California that permit parties to obtain pre-birth parentage orders, an effort should be made to do so.[57] Even though the parties may execute a surrogacy agreement that provides the surrogate will relinquish the child and her "parental rights" at birth and/or an agreement is not required by statute, it is generally advisable for the intended parents to formally adopt the child post birth in a manner consistent with state law. For example, in a Connecticut case,[58] an intended mother who never formally adopted a child born to a surrogate was treated as a third party, rather than a parent, in a custody dispute in the context of a divorce action.

When disputes involving surrogacy agreements reach the courts, the parties may include the surrogate mother and her husband, gamete donors, and the intended parents, who may or may not be married and who may be of the same or different sexes. The courts customarily apply one of the following four tests to determine parentage, each of which may produce a significantly different result.

- An *intent test:* Under this test, the individual or individuals who want to become parents and put the birth process in motion will be considered the legal parents of the resulting child. "[B]ut for the acted on intentions of the parties, the child would not exist."[59] The California Supreme Court was the first to adopt the intent test in *Johnson v. Calvert,* a case that involved a "contest" between an intended and a gestational mother in which the court held that "she who intended to bring about the birth of a child that she intended to raise as her own is the natural mother."[60] (See Case 13.3.)

  Intent test
  the individual(s) who set the procreative process in motion with the intent of raising any resulting children should be deemed the legal parent(s) of those children

- A *genetic test:* Courts that apply a genetic test in parentage determinations give priority to genetic heritage, based on the premise that genes contribute to the greatest extent in shaping the child's nature and future life. A genetic parent will be deemed a legal parent under this test. In cases in which the surrogate mother is also the genetic mother, courts are especially reluctant to terminate her parental rights. In some states, absent an enforceable agreement to the contrary, the individuals who contribute the genetic material are considered the child's legal parents.

  Genetic test
  the individuals who contribute a child's genetic material should be considered his or her legal parents

- A *gestational test:* This test places the greatest emphasis on the significance of the fact that the birth mother is responsible for the health and safety of the fetus for the nine months of pregnancy. Her lifestyle, habits, and physical and psychological condition potentially have a permanent effect on the child. This test is consistent with the traditional common law approach to the establishment of maternity.

  Gestational test
  the woman who carries and gives birth to a child should be deemed the child's legal mother

- A *best interest of the child test:* This is the standard traditionally applied in the family law context with respect to matters pertaining to the custody of children. It serves to ensure that in resolving disputes affecting minor children, protection of the child will be the primary consideration. The court looks to who is best able to fulfill the social and legal responsibilities of parenthood, including not only financial support but also physical and psychological nurturing of the child, intellectual and moral guidance, and stability and continuity of care.

  Best interests of the child test
  determinations of legal parentage should be based upon who is best able to fulfill the social and legal responsibilities of parenthood

CASE **13.3** *Johnson v. Calvert,* 5 Cal. 4th 84, 851 P.2d 776, 19 Cal. Rptr. 2d 494 (1993), cert. denied 510 U.S. 874, 114 S. Ct. 206, 126 L. Ed. 2d 163 (1993)

FROM THE OPINION

In this case, we address several of the legal questions raised by recent advances in reproductive technology. When, pursuant to a surrogacy agreement, a zygote formed of the gametes of a husband and wife is implanted in the uterus of another woman, who carries the resulting fetus to term and gives birth to a child not genetically related to her, who is the child's "natural mother" under California law? Does a determination that the wife is the child's natural mother work a deprivation of the gestating woman's constitutional rights? And is such an agreement barred by any public policy of this state?

continued

We conclude that the husband and wife are the child's natural parents, and that this result does not offend the state or federal Constitution or public policy.

Mark and Crispina Calvert are a married couple who desired to have a child. Crispina was forced to undergo a hysterectomy in 1984. Her ovaries remained capable of producing eggs, however, and the couple eventually considered surrogacy....

On January 15, 1990, Mark, Crispina, and Anna signed a contract providing that an embryo created by the sperm of Mark and the egg of Crispina would be implanted in Anna and the child born would be taken into Mark and Crispina's home "as their child." Anna agreed she would relinquish "all parental rights" to the child in favor of Mark and Crispina. In return, Mark and Crispina would pay Anna $10,000 in a series of installments, the last to be paid six weeks after the child's birth. Mark and Crispina were also to pay for a $200,000 life insurance policy on Anna's life.

The zygote was implanted on January 19, 1990. Less than a month later, an ultrasound test confirmed Anna was pregnant.

Unfortunately, relations deteriorated between the two sides. Mark learned that Anna had not disclosed she had suffered several stillbirths and miscarriages. Anna felt Mark and Crispina did not do enough to obtain the required insurance policy. She also felt abandoned during an onset of premature labor in June.

In July 1990, Anna sent Mark and Crispina a letter demanding the balance of the payments due her or else she would refuse to give up the child. The following month, Mark and Crispina responded with a lawsuit, seeking a declaration they were the legal parents of the unborn child. Anna filed her own action to be declared the mother of the child, and the two cases were eventually consolidated. The parties agreed to an independent guardian ad litem for the purposes of the suit.

The child was born on September 19, 1990, ... The parties agreed to a court order providing that the child would remain with Mark and Crispina on a temporary basis with visits by Anna.

At trial in October 1990, the parties stipulated that Mark and Crispina were the child's genetic parents. After hearing evidence and arguments, the trial court ruled that Mark and Crispina were the child's "genetic, biological and natural" father and mother, that Anna had no "parental" rights to the child, and that the surrogacy contract was legal and enforceable against Anna's claims. The court also terminated the order allowing visitation. Anna appealed from the trial court's judgment. The Court of Appeals for the Fourth District, Division Three, affirmed. We granted review.

Discussion
Determining Maternity Under the Uniform Parentage Act

The Uniform Parentage Act (the Act) was part of a package of legislation introduced in 1975....to eliminate the legal distinction between legitimate and illegitimate children.

...

continued

... The "parent and child relationship" means "the legal relationship existing between a child and his natural or adoptive parents incident to which the law confers or imposes rights, privileges, duties, and obligations. It includes the mother and child relationship and the father and child relationship." (Civ. Code, §7001.) ...

Passage of the Act clearly was not motivated by the need to resolve surrogacy disputes, which were virtually unknown in 1975. Yet it facially applies to *any* parentage determination, including the rare case in which a child's maternity is in issue. We are invited to disregard the Act and decide this case according to other criteria, including constitutional precepts and our sense of the demands of public policy. We feel constrained, however, to decline the invitation.... We therefore proceed to analyze the parties' contentions within the Act's framework.

These contentions are readily summarized. Anna, of course, predicates her claim of maternity on the fact that she gave birth to the child. The Calverts contend that Crispina's genetic relationship to the child establishes that she is his mother.

...

... In this case, there is no question as to who is claiming the mother and child relationship, and the factual basis of each woman's claim is obvious.

...

Disregarding the presumptions of paternity that have no application to this case, then, we are left with the undisputed evidence that Anna, not Crispina, gave birth to the child and that Crispina, not Anna, is genetically related to him. Both women have thus adduced evidence of a mother and child relationship as contemplated by the Act.... Yet for any child California law recognizes only one natural mother, despite advances in reproductive technology rendering a different outcome biologically possible.

We see no clear legislative preference in Civil Code Section 7003 as between blood testing evidence and proof of having given birth.... It is arguable that, while gestation may demonstrate maternal status, it is not the sine qua non of motherhood....

Because two women have each presented acceptable proof of maternity, we do not believe this case can be decided without enquiring into the parties' intentions as manifested in the surrogacy agreement. Mark and Crispina are a couple who desired to have a child of their own genes but are physically unable to do so without the help of reproductive technology. They affirmatively intended the birth of the child and took the steps necessary to effect in vitro fertilization. But for their acted-on intention, the child would not exist. Anna agreed to facilitate the procreation of Mark's and Crispina's child. The parties' aim was to bring Mark's and Crispina's child into the world, not for Mark and Crispina to donate a zygote to Anna. Crispina from the outset intended to be the child's mother. Although the gestative function Anna performed was necessary to bring about the child's birth, it is safe to say that Anna would not have been given the opportunity to gestate or deliver the child had she, prior to implantation of the zygote, manifested her own intent to be the child's mother. No reason appears why Anna's later change of heart should vitiate the determination that Crispina is the child's natural mother.

continued

We conclude that although the Act recognizes both genetic consanguinity and giving birth as means of establishing a mother and child relationship, when the two means do not coincide in one woman, she who intended to procreate the child—that is, she who intended to bring about the birth of a child that she intended to raise as her own—is the natural mother under California law.

Our conclusion finds support in the writings of several commentators.

. . .

In deciding the issue of maternity under the Act we have felt free to take into account the parties' intentions, as expressed in the surrogacy contract, because in our view the agreement is not, on its face, inconsistent with public policy.

. . .

Anna urges that surrogacy contracts violate several social policies. Relying on her contention that she is the child's legal, natural mother, she cites the public policy embodied in Penal Code section 273, prohibiting the payment for consent to adoption of a child. She argues further that the policies underlying the adoption laws of this state are violated by the surrogacy contract because it in effect constitutes a prebirth waiver of her parental rights.

We disagree. Gestational surrogacy differs in crucial respects from adoption and so is not subject to the adoption statutes. The parties voluntarily agreed to participate in in vitro fertilization and related medical procedures before the child was conceived; at the time when Anna entered into the contract, therefore, she was not vulnerable to financial inducements to part with her own expected offspring. . . . Anna was not the genetic mother of the child. The payments to Anna under the contract were meant to compensate her for her services in gestating the fetus and undergoing labor, rather than for giving up "parental" rights to the child. Payments were due both during the pregnancy and after the child's birth. We are, accordingly, unpersuaded. . . .

It has been suggested that gestational surrogacy may run afoul of prohibitions on involuntary servitude. . . . We see no potential for that evil in the contract at issue here, . . .

Finally, Anna and some commentators have expressed concern that surrogacy contracts tend to exploit or dehumanize women, especially women of lower economic status. Anna's objections center around the psychological harm she asserts may result from the gestator's relinquishing the child to whom she has given birth. Some have also cautioned that the practice of surrogacy may encourage society to view children as commodities, subject to trade at their parents' will.

. . .

We are unpersuaded that gestational surrogacy arrangements are so likely to cause the untoward results Anna cites as to demand their invalidation on public policy grounds. Although common sense suggests that women of lesser means serve as surrogate mothers more often than do wealthy women, there has been no proof that surrogacy contracts exploit poor women to any greater degree than economic necessity in general exploits them by inducing them to accept lower-paid or otherwise undesirable employment. . . .

The argument that a woman cannot knowingly and intelligently agree to gestate and deliver a baby for intending parents carries overtones of reasoning that for centuries prevented women from attaining equal economic rights and professional status

continued

under the law. To resurrect this view is both to foreclose a personal and economic choice on the part of the surrogate mother, and to deny intending parents what may be their only means of procreating a child of their own genes. Certainly in the present case it cannot seriously be argued that Anna, a licensed vocational nurse who had done well in school and who had previously borne a child, lacked the intellectual wherewithal or life experience necessary to make an informed decision to enter into the surrogacy contract.

. . .

Constitutionality of the Determination that Anna Johnson is not the Natural Mother

Anna argues at length that her right to the continued companionship of the child is protected under the federal Constitution.

. . .

Anna relies mainly on theories of substantive due process, privacy, and procreative freedom, citing a number of decisions recognizing the fundamental liberty interest of natural parents in the custody and care of their children....

Anna's argument depends on a prior determination that she is indeed the child's mother. Since Crispina is the child's mother under California law because she, not Anna, provided the ovum for the in vitro fertilization procedure, intending to raise the child as her own, it follows that any constitutional interests Anna possesses in this situation are something less than those of a mother....

... Society has not traditionally protected the right of a woman who gestates and delivers a baby pursuant to an agreement with a couple who supply the zygote from which the baby develops and who intend to raise the child as their own; such arrangements are of too recent an origin to claim the protection of tradition.

. . .

Drawing an analogy to artificial insemination, Anna argues that Mark and Crispina were mere genetic donors who are entitled to no constitutional protection. That characterization of the facts is, however, inaccurate. Mark and Crispina never intended to "donate" genetic material to anyone. Rather, they intended to procreate a child genetically related to them by the only available means. Civil Code section 7005, governing artificial insemination, has no application here.

Finally, Anna argues that the Act's failure to address novel reproductive techniques such as in vitro fertilization indicates legislative disapproval of such practices. Given that the Act was drafted long before such techniques were developed, we cannot agree. Moreover, we may not arrogate to ourselves the power to disapprove them. It is not the role of the judiciary to inhibit the use of reproductive technology when the legislature has not seen fit to do so; any such effort would raise serious questions in light of the fundamental nature of the rights of procreation and privacy. Rather, our task has been to resolve the dispute before us....

SIDEBAR

This opinion remains one of the best expressions of the "intent standard" applied in a case in which the gestational mother has no biological relationship to the child born as a result of a surrogacy arrangement. But what if she is not only the gestational mother but also the genetic mother as well? Should the result be different? Explain your response. See the full opinion of the high-profile
continued

Baby M. case (referenced earlier and below) decided by the New Jersey Supreme Court in 1988 involving this set of facts and available on the companion website. (*In the Matter of Baby M.*, 109 N.J. 396, 537 A.2d 1227 (1988)). What role, if any, should "the best interests of the child" play in such cases? The dissent in *Johnson v. Calvert* opined that the best interests of the child test, rather than an intent test, should be applied by the courts in surrogacy cases in the absence of legislation. For example, what if the intended parents are unstable or substance abusers or their circumstances change dramatically during the course of the pregnancy?

Application of various tests to individual fact patterns can lead to widely diverse and unusual results. For example, in the high-profile case *In the Matter of Baby M.*,[61] the New Jersey Supreme Court held that a surrogacy "contract" between a biological father and a genetically related surrogate mother was against public policy and unenforceable as a matter of law. The court created a new "family" configuration for the child by awarding physical custody to the intended/biological father and visitation to the surrogate mother, who was also the child's genetic mother. In describing its reasoning for not enforcing such agreements, the court commented:

> The long-term effects of surrogacy contracts are not known, but feared—the impact on the child who learns her life was bought, that she is the offspring of someone who gave birth to her only to obtain money; the impact on the natural mother as the full weight of her isolation is felt along with the full reality of the sale of her body and her child; the impact on the natural father and the adoptive mother once they realize the consequences of their conduct....The surrogacy contract is based on principles that are directly contrary to the objectives of our laws. It guarantees the separation of a child from its mother; it looks to adoption regardless of suitability; it totally ignores the child; it takes the child from the mother regardless of her wishes and her maternal fitness; and it does all of this, it accomplishes all of its goals, through the use of money.[62]

CRYOPRESERVED EMBRYOS

As more and more couples utilize ART to create and freeze embryos for use at a later date, it is inevitable that the courts will increasingly be called upon to resolve controversies involving the parties' rights and responsibilities with respect to those embryos. It is estimated that there are already hundreds of thousands of unused embryos in cryopreservation.[63] Two of the contexts in which the courts have begun to address this development are when frozen embryos need to be disposed of upon divorce, and when they are used posthumously (after the death of one or both of the parties).

Disposition of Frozen Embryos Upon Divorce

After three decades of experience applying this technology, it has become apparent that, in addition to planning for use of *in vitro* fertilization and freezing of surplus embryos, couples also must anticipate and provide for the disposition of those embryos in the event of separation, death, divorce, or changes in plans or circumstances. Options for disposition include storing them for use at a later date, donating them for "embryo adoption"[64] or research, preserving them for an indefinite period, or thawing and discarding them.

A limited number of states have enacted legislation addressing issues specifically relating to use, storage, and disposition of preserved embryos. New Hampshire and Louisiana, for example, have provisions addressing some aspects of maintenance and duration periods for storing pre-zygotes outside of the body.[65] Under Louisiana law, the embryos are considered legal persons[66] and embryo donations are essentially regulated by adoption statutes. Florida requires by statute that couples execute written agreements addressing disposition of pre-embryos in the event of death, divorce, or other unforeseen circumstances.[67] Oklahoma law refers to embryo donation as "human embryo transfer donation." Only biological parents may donate embryos; both the donor and donee couples must be married; and the donee couple, the physician, and a judge in a court with jurisdiction over adoption must execute a written consent form.[68]

In the absence of legislation, courts in some states have been forced to judicially address disposition upon divorce with and without written agreements between the parties. The courts generally select from among five approaches to such cases:

1. In the absence of an agreement, favor the party seeking to avoid forced parenthood.
2. Enforce agreements of the parties.
3. Enforce agreements, but allow the parties to change their minds and modify their agreements up until implantation or destruction of the embryos.
4. Enforce agreements, but not for non-reproductive use unless permitted by state law.
5. Refuse to enforce agreements based on state law, public policy, or other considerations.

Related case law reflects a fact-based approach and a general trend toward not compelling unwanted parenthood. A sampling of these cases includes the following:

- In the landmark *Davis* case,[69] the Tennessee Supreme Court considered disposition of seven frozen embryos belonging to an already divorced couple, each of whom had remarried. The wife sought to donate the embryos to another childless couple, but the husband wanted them destroyed. The Tennessee Supreme Court determined that the lower court had erroneously applied a "best interests of the child" test (appropriate for a custody determination) and ruled that "pre-embryos are not, strictly speaking, either 'persons' or 'property,' but occupy an interim category that entitles them to special respect because of their potential for human life."[70] In reaching its decision, the Court recognized that "the right to procreational autonomy is composed of two rights of equal significance—the right to procreate and the right to avoid procreation."[71] The wife's interest in donating the embryos was viewed as less significant than the husband's interest in avoiding parenthood. The court noted that the outcome might have been different if the wife had wanted them for her own use and had no other reasonable opportunity to conceive a child. Although the parties in this case had not executed a written agreement, the court indicated in dictum that such agreements should be upheld in the event of separation or divorce, stating, "the state's interest in the potential life of these preembryos is not sufficient to justify any infringement upon the freedom of these individuals to make their own decisions as to whether to allow a process to continue that may result in such a dramatic change in their lives as becoming parents."[72] The court stated:

  > [W]e recognize that life is not static, and that human emotions run particularly high when a married couple is attempting to overcome infertility problems. It follows that the parties' initial 'informed

consent' to IVF procedures will not be truly informed because of the near impossibility of anticipating, emotionally and psychologically, all the turns that events may take as the IVF process unfolds. Providing that the initial agreements may later be modified *by agreement* will, we think, protect the parties against some of the risks they face in this regard. But, in the absence of such agreed modification, we conclude that their prior agreements should be considered binding.[73]

- In the *Kass* case,[74] New York's highest court addressed a situation in which, post-divorce, a wife sought sole custody of five cryopreserved "pre-embryos" so she could thaw and use them. The husband opposed their removal from storage and sought enforcement of the consent form executed by the parties at the IVF clinic where the embryos were stored. The form provided that the frozen embryos would not be released from storage without the written consent of both parties, and, if the parties could not reach a mutual agreement, the embryos would be donated for research purposes.[75] The trial court granted custody of the "pre-zygotes" to the wife for implantation within a reasonable time, holding that a female progenitor has "exclusive decisional authority over the fertilized eggs...just as a pregnant woman has exclusive decisional authority over a non-viable fetus."[76] The appellate court reversed and found that the agreement should control. The high court affirmed the appellate court's holding, stating:

  ...[P]arties should be encouraged in advance, before embarking on IVF and cryopreservation, to think through possible contingencies and carefully specify their wishes in writing. Explicit agreements avoid costly litigation....Advance directives, subject to mutual change of mind that must be jointly expressed, both minimize misunderstandings and maximize procreative liberty by reserving to the progenitors the authority to make what is in the first instance a quintessentially personal, private decision. Written agreements also provide the certainty needed for effective operation of IVF programs.[77]

Posthumously Conceived Children

Given advances in assisted reproductive technology, it is now possible for children to be conceived after the death of one or both of their genetic parents through the use of cryopreserved gametes or embryos. (See Paralegal Application 13.7.) Section 707 of the Uniform Parentage Act of 2000 as revised in 2002, adopted in some states (such as Colorado, Delaware, Texas, Washington, and Wyoming), acknowledges this option, providing that:

If an individual who consented in a record to be a parent by assisted reproduction dies before placement of eggs, sperm, or embryos, the deceased individual is not a parent of the resulting child unless the deceased spouse consented in a record that if assisted reproduction were to occur after death, the deceased individual would be a parent of that child.[78]

Most disputes regarding posthumously conceived children arise in connection with probate matters and claims for Social Security Benefits. As of the fall of 2007, several states including Colorado, Delaware, Florida, Virginia, Washington, and Wyoming identify the intestate inheritance rights of posthumously conceived children by statute. For example, the applicable Florida statute requires that the intended parents and treating physician must have signed a written agreement regarding disposition of cryopreserved eggs, sperm, and pre-embryos in the event

Paralegal Practice Tip
Clients contemplating cryopreservation should be encouraged to anticipate the possibility of posthumously conceived children and prepare wills that spell out their intentions with respect to children born as a result of assisted reproductive technology.

> ### PARALEGAL APPLICATION 13.7
>
> #### WHAT DO YOU THINK?
>
> Do you think that people who are terminally ill, going off to combat, or participating in inherently dangerous activities should be permitted to freeze gametes for use post-death? What are the arguments for each side of the question? Would it make a difference in your opinion if the eggs or sperm are harvested post-death? Without prior consent of the decedent? For use by parties other than the donors?

of the death of one of the spouses. The decedent also must have provided for the child in his or her will.[79] In Louisiana, a posthumously conceived child has inheritance rights, provided the child is born to the surviving spouse within three years of the death of the decedent.[80]

Posthumously conceived children may be eligible for Social Security Benefits if the child is entitled to inherit under the intestacy law in the state where the decedent was domiciled at death.[81] Courts in New Jersey[82] and Massachusetts have addressed the rights of posthumously conceived children to Social Security Survivor Benefits. In the Massachusetts case, a man who was dying from leukemia had some of his sperm cryopreserved so that his wife could conceive after his death. She was subsequently successfully inseminated and gave birth to twins about two years after he died. On appeal, the Supreme Judicial Court reversed the Social Security Administration's decision denying the children survivors' benefits on the basis that they were not the husband's children under the Social Security Act. The court held that posthumously conceived children can inherit in Massachusetts (and be eligible to receive survivor benefits) under certain conditions:

- The child's paternity is established.
- The decedent consented to posthumous reproduction and to support the child.
- All parties interested in the estate are given notice.
- An unreasonable period of time has not elapsed since the decedent's death.[83]

CHILDREN BORN TO SAME-SEX COUPLES THROUGH ART

When ART is utilized by same-sex couples to produce children, another dimension is added to the complex array of issues considered in parentage determinations. In the past, courts in states such as Florida, Illinois, Michigan, New York, Ohio, and Tennessee[84] determined that only the birth parent was a legal parent to a child born to a lesbian couple that had a child together through artificial insemination. In effect, the other partner was considered a legal stranger, even if she lived in a committed relationship with the parent and child for several years, participated fully in the decision to have a child, supported the reproductive process and birth, helped to raise the child, provided financial support, and was referred to by the child as "mom."[85] The consequences for a child can be severe when such relationships are not acknowledged. In the extreme, the child may be sent to live with relatives or become a ward of the state. Even if the legal parent nominates the second parent as the child's guardian in his or her will, there is no guarantee that the courts will approve the nomination, especially if challenged by blood relatives.

Not all courts have been unreceptive to recognizing joint parental rights for same-sex partners, however. In Chapter 14, the topic of co-parent adoption is discussed as an option available in an increasing number of states. In Chapter 8, the coverage of child custody includes a review of several of the legal theories being used by some courts to attribute parental rights and responsibilities to same-sex co-parents. In finding that both members of a same-sex couple are responsible for financial support of a child they have together through ART, the California Supreme Court held in a 2005 case that "A person who actively participates in bringing children into the world, takes the children into her home and holds them out as her own, and receives and enjoys the benefits of parenthood, should be responsible for the support of those children—regardless of her gender or sexual orientation."[86] The trend toward recognizing such parental rights and responsibilities is consistent with Section 2.03 of the ALI Principles,[87] which provides that a person who is not an adoptive or biological parent may be deemed a parent by estoppel with all the rights and responsibilities of a legal parent if he or she:

> Lived with the child since the child's birth, holding out and accepting full and permanent responsibilities as a parent, as part of a prior coparenting agreement with the child's legal parent...to raise a child together each with full parental rights and responsibilities, when the court finds that recognition of the individual as a parent is in the child's best interests.

The 2000 Uniform Parentage Act (as amended in 2002) recognizes that two people who procreate with the intention of raising the resulting child together should be considered co-equal parents from the time of the child's birth.[88]

PARALEGAL APPLICATION 13.8

EGG AND SPERM DONORS: PARENTS OR LEGAL STRANGERS?

When donors participate in ART initiatives, it is important that they confirm in writing their intent with respect to the legal parentage of any children resulting from their donations.

- Under the Uniform Parentage Act, an egg or sperm donor is not a parent of a child conceived by means of assisted reproduction.[89]

- If the parties do not comply with statutory requirements in a given state, a donor may later be able to claim parental rights, particularly when the donor is known to the intended parents. For example, in a California case, *Jhordan C. v. Mary K.*,[90] a lesbian couple chose a sperm donor from among several potential donors. Contrary to a requirement of a state statute of which the couple was unaware, the sperm was supplied directly to the couple and not to a physician, which would have allowed the donor not to be treated as the father of the resulting child. The parties also acted without legal advice and did not execute a contract regarding their arrangement. As a result, the donor was eventually able to have the rights of a legal father, entitling him to visitation.

- Contracts with known donors that exempt them from support obligations but provide for visitation are unlikely to be upheld as a matter of public policy. If it can be established that the donor had no intent to become a legal parent, he may be relieved of the support obligation.

- Agreements that a donor will remain anonymous may not always be enforceable against a physician, clinic, or hospital. For example, it may be necessary to reveal the identity (or at least the characteristics) of the donor in the event of a medical emergency involving the child. It is not outside the realm of possibility that even a posthumously conceived child of a deceased donor could discover the donor's identity and make a claim to his or her estate.

PARALEGAL APPLICATION **13.9**

KING V. S.B. (*IN RE A.B.*), AN INDIANA CASE TO CONSIDER

The facts as provided in *King v. S.B. (In re A.B.)*, 818 N.E.2d 126 (Ind. Ct. App. 2004):

The complaint reveals the following relevant facts. Dawn and Stephanie shared their home and their lives for nearly nine years, beginning in 1993. During their relationship, the couple shared joint finances and held themselves out to their families, friends, and community as a couple in a committed loving relationship....

After several years together, the couple jointly decided to bear and raise a child together. They mutually determined that Stephanie would be impregnated by artificial insemination and....Stephanie suggested using Dawn's brother as the semen donor because she wanted both herself and Dawn to be genetically related to the child....All parties involved (Dawn, Stephanie and the brother) intended for Dawn and Stephanie to be co-parents of the resulting child, assuming equal parental roles in the child's care and support. Stephanie was artificially inseminated with semen donated by Dawn's brother ... and A.B. was born on May 15, 1999. Dawn was present for and participated in A.B.'s birth. Further, all expenses associated with the pregnancy and birth that were not covered by insurance were paid from the couple's joint bank account.

At some point following A.B.'s birth, Dawn, with Stephanie's consent, filed a co-parent petition to adopt A.B. While the adoption was pending, the parties separated for approximately three months, and Stephanie withdrew her consent to the adoption. During this brief period of separation, Dawn paid child support for A.B.'s benefit and enjoyed regular visitation. For reasons not apparent in the record, the adoption was not pursued any further after Dawn and Stephanie reconciled and resumed living together as a family. The relationship ... eventually ended in January 2002. Thereafter, Dawn paid monthly child support and continued to have regular and liberal visitation with A.B. until late July 2003. At that point, Stephanie unilaterally terminated visitation and began rejecting Dawn's support payments.

From A.B.'s birth until July 2003, Dawn and Stephanie acted as co-parents, with important decisions concerning A.B. being determined by them in concert. Dawn has cared for A.B. as a parent, feeding and bathing her, attending doctor's appointments, providing health insurance coverage, and generally providing the financial and emotional support of a parent. She held A.B. out to family, friends, and the community as her daughter. Stephanie consented to and encouraged the formation of a parent-child relationship between Dawn and A.B. Dawn and A.B. have established a bonded, dependent parent-child relationship, and A.B. knows Dawn as her mother in the same manner that she knows Stephanie as her mother. A.B. calls Dawn Momma.

On October 31, 2003, Dawn filed the instant declaratory judgment action, seeking to be recognized as A.B.'s legal second parent with all of the attendant rights and obligations of a biological parent. Alternatively, the complaint asserted that even if Dawn is not A.B.'s legal second parent, she nonetheless acted in loco parentis and in a custodial and parental capacity entitling her to, at a minimum, continued visitation with A.B. Stephanie moved to dismiss the complaint for failure to state a claim upon which relief may be granted....on June 1, 2004, the trial court, with apparent reluctance, dismissed the complaint....

continued

SIDEBAR

Assume that you are working on a case with very similar facts. The client is in the same position as Dawn and wants to know if she has standing in Indiana to seek recognition as a second parent with all the attendant rights and obligations. Your supervisor recalls this earlier case but does not remember whether or not it was appealed. You have been assigned to track the history of the case. Was it appealed? If so, to which court(s) and with what result(s)? What will the answer be to the client's question based on the case?

THE LEGAL LIABILITY FALLOUT FROM ASSISTED REPRODUCTIVE TECHNOLOGY

The eventual range and forms of liability associated with the availability and use of assisted reproductive technology are unknown. Thus far, courts have addressed liability issues primarily through the application of traditional tort, negligence, contract, criminal, and consumer protection law. A sampling of actual and potential areas of liability include the following:

Wrongful birth
an action brought by parents claiming that the defendant's negligent conduct resulted in the birth of a child with serious defects or disabilities, thereby causing the parents serious emotional distress and expense

Wrongful life
an action brought by a plaintiff who claims he or she was brought into the world with a disability that was foreseeable and could have been prevented by a competent physician exercising due care

- *Wrongful birth:* This is an action brought by parents claiming that the defendant's conduct (negligence, failure to advise, etc.) resulted in the birth of a child with serious defects or disabilities, thereby causing the parents serious emotional distress and expense.
- *Wrongful life:* In an action for wrongful life, the plaintiff claims that the fact he or she was brought into the world with some form of physical, mental, or social disability is a compensable wrong that could have been prevented by the provision of competent medical advice to the mother prior to or during pregnancy. Courts do not favor wrongful life claims, given an inability to determine "what defects should prevent an embryo from being allowed life"[91] and a perception that "measuring the value of an impaired life as compared to non-existence is a task beyond mortals."[92] However, some courts are willing to award special damages for costs associated with the disability, such as extraordinary medical and educational costs.
- **Failure to warn:** There are risks associated with the various forms of assisted reproductive technology. For example, a physician or clinic may be held liable for a failure to warn patients about potential side effects of fertility-enhancing drugs, such as the possibility of multiple pregnancies and births, premature births, and higher risks of birth defects.[93]
- **Failure to properly screen donors for significant health risks:** The failure of a fertility clinic to properly screen a gamete donor that results in harm may give rise to a negligence action. For example, in a sixth circuit case, a surrogate mother sued a clinic for failing to test the man for whom she served as a surrogate for a particular sexually transmitted disease that resulted in her child being born with cytomeglic inclusion disease, a condition characterized by mental retardation and other defects.[94]
- **Wrongful implantation of gametes or embryos:** The state of California penalizes wrongful use or implantation of sperm, ova, or embryos as a felony punishable by three to five years in state prison and up to $50,000 in fines.[95] The statute was enacted following misappropriation of embryos at the In Vitro Fertilization Clinic at the University of California at Irvine. Embryos produced by and for some clients were used for research and use by other well-paying clients without consent of the owners.[96]

- **Negligent implantation of gametes or embryos:** A New York *in vitro* fertilization clinic accidentally implanted in a Caucasian woman an embryo of an African-American couple participating in the same program. The Caucasian woman subsequently gave birth to two children, one of whom was African-American. Four months after the birth, the Caucasian couple was required to transfer the child to the other couple and was denied visitation rights.[97] Both couples sued the physician responsible for the negligent implantation. The African-American couple's case was based on a theory of emotional distress due to the lost opportunity to experience pregnancy and the birth process and the loss of the companionship of their child during its first four months of life.[98] The Caucasian couple claimed both physical and emotional injury resulting from the necessity of a caesarian delivery and having to make the difficult decision to give up a child.[99]
- **Failure to obtain, update, or comply with consent:** Ideally, written consents should be obtained from all appropriate parties including donors, surrogates, and intended parents. The consent should clearly state the circumstances under which it can be withdrawn and whether it is a general consent or only a consent to an initial procedure, which needs to be renewed prior to any subsequent procedures.
- **Unauthorized disclosure of confidential information:** The potential for this problem to arise is especially great when gamete donors have been promised anonymity.
- **Deceptive advertising:** Assisted reproductive technology is a big, largely unregulated business. Among other forms of false advertising, clinics and physicians providing assisted reproduction services may artificially inflate success rates to attract clients.
- **Wrongful death:** Fertility clinics may be sued for wrongful death if they intentionally or negligently destroy frozen embryos and embryos are defined as persons under state law or a court elects to so treat them.
- **Breach of fiduciary duty and bailment contract:** Clinics that store and "lose" embryos have been held liable for breach of contract.[100]
- **Malpractice:** The potential scope of liability for attorneys who handle ART cases is unknown, but it presents a virtual minefield. Potential conflicts of interest are rampant; legal risks and obligations for clients are not fully known; "agreements" are not necessarily enforceable; and state statutes and case law vary, leaving no clear road maps for counsel to follow.

THE ROLE OF THE PARALEGAL

The paralegal's role in this area will be determined largely by the prevailing law in the jurisdiction where the paralegal is employed and the degree to which the firm handles cases involving parentage determinations and assisted reproductive technology. Tasks performed are likely to include the following:

- researching controlling statutes and case law governing parentage determinations and/or techniques of assisted reproduction
- gathering information in preparation for drafting pleadings and/or documents related to arrangements involving parentage issues
- maintaining a list of reputable test banks and arranging for DNA testing, if required
- drafting pleadings and/or agreements (See Paralegal Application 13.10.)
- drafting discovery materials such as proposed interrogatories, deposition questions, and requests for admission and production of documents
- maintaining a file of experts on related topics
- coordinating communication with experts and other witnesses, if necessary

- preparing affidavits, exhibits, memoranda, correspondence, etc., as assigned
- assisting with preparation for hearings and/or a trial on the merits
- organizing materials for appeals, if necessary
- making sure the client is kept informed of progress and upcoming deadlines, hearings, discovery matters, etc.

PARALEGAL APPLICATION 13.10

ASSISTED REPRODUCTION DOCUMENTS

As a general rule, when parties enter into assisted reproduction arrangements, they should execute written agreements and consent forms documenting their intentions and expectations. Contracts may be between several different sets of parties, such as the following:

- between donors and intended parents
- between intended parents and surrogate parents
- between the intended parents
- between various parties and the clinics or physicians who facilitate the pregnancy and delivery
- between parents and clinics harvesting and/or storing gametes and embryos

Agreements necessarily will vary depending primarily on the type of arrangement and the residence of the parties. Because the law of assisted reproductive technology is largely unsettled, these agreements should anticipate various potential scenarios.

In preparing these documents,[101] attention must be given to complying with any controlling statutory requirements and prohibitions and to carefully choosing the law to govern the agreement. Some potentially important provisions to consider including in a surrogacy agreement in particular are the following:

- a description of the arrangements, including a timeline within which the agreement must be performed before it expires
- a provision that the parties participate in psychological and medical screening (required in some states)
- a surrogate celibacy provision to remain in effect until the fertilization process is concluded
- an indemnification clause identifying the risks involved in the process and protecting the attorney and client from liability
- a clear statement with respect to insurance coverage for the surrogate and child
- a clause addressing any compensation to be paid to the surrogate, including the amount and purpose(s) for which it is being paid (time, pain, inconvenience, medical expenses, etc., and NOT for releasing parental rights)
- a provision indicating the circumstances under which the agreement may be terminated or modified, including the surrogate mother's right to abort the pregnancy (and the inability of the intended parents to compel an abortion)
- language consistent with state law addressing the surrogate's (and her spouse's, if applicable) relinquishing of parental rights and release of the child to the intended parents post birth
- a provision requiring the intended parents to accept the child even if their circumstances change or the child is born with serious health issues, etc.
- if donors are involved, a clause indicating that donors have waived any and all parental rights

continued

- a clause covering any agreement regarding confidentialty/disclosure of information

- a clause addressing the parties' agreement with respect to post-birth contact, if any

- a provision regarding disposition of any surplus gametes and/or embryos

- an affirmation that each party has been represented by independent counsel

- a provision regarding the respective parties' rights in the event of a breach, particularly since specific performance is not available as a remedy

- a provision addressing the timing and effect of "changes of mind"

- a severability clause so that if one clause in an agreement is deemed unenforceable, it can be severed from the remainder of the agreement

CHAPTER **SUMMARY**

This chapter focuses on the concept of "parenthood" in an era in which the structure of the American family is undergoing dramatic change. Traditional nuclear families are in decline, as both individuals and couples turn to reproductive technology to create parent-child relationships. The "best interests of the child" are increasingly sacrificed in the wake created by battling adults, fiscally conservative legislatures, and overwhelmed courts.

The statutes and cases regarding determination of parentage referenced throughout this chapter reflect the controversy and tension currently permeating this rapidly evolving area of family law. As one commentator has phrased it:

Despite heightened…emphasis on biological connection in the paternity fraud context, more courts are recognizing the rights of functional parents to establish legal relationships with the children they have parented….Moreover, advances in reproductive technology have caused courts to evaluate the legal parenthood of nonbiological parents who contract with either a surrogate, egg donor, and/or sperm donor and to make a determination of legal parenthood. Several of these courts have recognized that the "intended" parent should trump the parent with a biological connection to the child. Significantly, courts are recognizing that biology is not the only means by which to establish legal parenthood and parental rights.[102]

Moral, religious, ethical, and legal considerations confront the courts as they struggle to fit cases into a legal system ill-equipped to accommodate fact patterns involving parentage determinations and reproductive technologies. Practitioners have opportunities to shape public policy in the courtroom, as judges are compelled to draw from a patchwork quilt of contract, constitutional, criminal, property, adoption, probate, and family law to resolve disputes, all the while urging legislatures to step up to the plate and provide guidance.

… we must call on the Legislature to sort out the parental rights and responsibilities of those involved in artificial reproduction. No matter what one thinks of artificial insemination, traditional and gestational surrogacy (in all its permutations), and—as now appears in the not-too-distant future, cloning and even gene splicing—courts are still going to be faced with the problem of determining lawful parentage. A child cannot be ignored…courts will still be called upon to decide who the lawful parents really are and who—other than the taxpayers—is obligated to provide maintenance and support for the child. These cases will not go away.[103]

KEY **TERMS**

Artificial insemination	Co-parent	Foster parent
Assisted reproductive technology (ART)	Cryopreservation	Genetic test
	De facto parent	Gestational mother
Adoptive parent	Disestablishment of paternity	Gestational test
Best interests of the child test	Donor	Intended parent
Biological parent	Equitable parent doctrine	Intent test
Biology-plus approach	*Filius nullius*	*In vitro* fertilization
Cloning	Forum shopping	Legal parent

Marital presumption
Natural parent
Parent by estoppel
Paternity fraud

Posthumous reproduction
Presumed father
Psychological parent
Putative father

Step-parent
Surrogate mother
Wrongful birth
Wrongful life

REVIEW **QUESTIONS**

1. Describe the significance of the term *"filious nullius."*

2. Describe the nature and significance of the "biology-plus" approach to establishing parental rights for unwed fathers.

3. Identify the three parties with the strongest interests in parentage determinations and describe the nature of those interests.

4. Identify and describe the three primary ways of establishing legal parentage.

5. Describe the equitable parent doctrine and explain how it was applied by the Wisconsin Supreme Court in *A.J. v. I.J.*

6. Explain what it means to "disestablish" paternity. Identify some of the common arguments in favor of and against disestablishment.

7. Identify three circumstances in which assisted reproductive technology is most likely to be utilized as a reproductive option.

8. Identify some of the ethical issues that arise in the context of assisted reproductive technology.

9. Describe the nature and purpose of a surrogacy agreement.

10. Identify and describe the four tests most often applied by the courts to resolve disputes arising out of surrogacy arrangements.

11. Identify the primary purposes of cryopreserving embryos.

12. Describe approaches used by the courts to resolve disputes regarding disposition of cryopreserved embryos upon divorce.

13. Define posthumous reproduction and give an example of circumstances in which it might be utilized.

14. Describe the current state of the law in the United States with respect to recognition of same-sex partners as parents of children born through assisted reproductive technology.

15. Identify at least four kinds of liabilities arising out of the use of reproductive technologies.

16. Describe the role of the paralegal in this area of the law.

FOCUS ON **THE JOB**

THE FACTS

Stephen and Mary recently married after dating each other for four years. They want to share a life together and have a child, but Stephen carries a rare genetic disease, and Mary has had a hysterectomy due to uterine cancer. They have decided to execute a surrogate parent agreement with their friends Carol and Chip. Chip feels he and Carol could use the money they would receive. Carol really doesn't care about the money and just loves having babies. She and Chip are raising their three daughters in their small five-room home, which they are hoping to remodel.

Carol signs a contract with Stephen and Mary in which she agrees to have an embryo implanted into her womb, to carry it full term (absent severe medical complications), and to release the child and execute a consent to adoption one week after the child's birth. Chip also signs the agreement consenting to the agreement in his capacity as Carol's husband.

The embryo will result from *in vitro* fertilization using egg and sperm from two unmarried donors identified by Stephen and Mary following exhaustive research concerning their backgrounds and characteristics. The donors, John and

Kay, each take great pride in their genetic heritage and are very honored to be selected as donors. Each is professionally successful and independently wealthy. Neither will accept payment for services as a donor. No formal, written contract is executed with the donors.

Over the course of the gestation period, several events occur:

1. Stephen and Mary develop marital problems when Stephen becomes intimately involved with his best friend, David. Mary and Stephen agree to separate and consider their respective options for the future. Each of them wants custody of the baby about to be born, and David is looking forward to co-parenting with Stephen.

2. John and Kay begin dating and decide they should get married and seek custody of the baby about to be born. They want to protect the product of their genes and ensure that the child has the best opportunity to develop his or her potential. They claim separate and joint rights to be declared the child's parents.

3. Chip gets a promotion at work and decides he can move his family to a much nicer and more spacious home, spacious enough to accommodate a fourth

child. He decides that if the baby his wife is carrying is a boy, he wants to keep it. Carol also has had a change of heart. She has bonded with the fetus she is carrying and wants to keep it post birth with or without her husband's consent.

One week after Carol gives birth to a seven-pound, eight-ounce healthy baby boy (Baby B), each of the seven parties seeks a declaration of legal parentage, and the cases are consolidated.

THE ASSIGNMENT

The members of the class should be divided into seven groups, with each group working for an attorney representing the interests of one of the parties in this case: Stephen, David, Mary, Carol, Chip, John, and Kay. Each group should research governing law (both statutory and case law) in the jurisdiction and develop an argument in support of his or her client's claim to legal parentage of Baby B.

FOCUS ON **ETHICS**

Assume that you are a paralegal in the large firm where Attorney Jane Newton is employed. Attorney Newton represents Carol in the above fact pattern. You work for Attorney Karen Kelly, who has represented Chip and Carol in the past on a variety of matters. An ethical wall presently insulates both Attorney Kelly and you from the present case. However, as you are riding down the elevator to go to lunch, you realize that Carol and a friend of hers are also in the elevator. You say "hi" but Carol does not recognize you and continues to carry on a conversation with her friend.

She "confides" to the friend that, even though there was a celibacy clause in the surrogacy agreement, she engaged in a "one-night stand" with a stranger around the time when she conceived. She says there is a slight chance that Baby B is the product of that incident, but she doesn't intend to risk Chip's and her chances for legal parenthood by admitting it. How should you address this situation? In preparing your response, refer to the canons of the National Federation of Paralegal Associations (NFPA) contained in Appendix B for guidance.

FOCUS ON **CASE LAW**

The opinion of the Iowa Supreme Court in *Witten v. Witten*, 672 N.W.2d 768 (Iowa 2003), is available on the companion website. Locate and read the case and then respond to the following questions.

1. What is the legal history of the case? What kind of a case is it? Where was it heard prior to reaching the Iowa Supreme Court and with what results?
2. What were the issues being appealed and by whom?
3. What were the basic facts of the case?
4. What agreements/contracts/consent documents did the parties execute? What, if anything, did they provide regarding disposition of stored frozen embryos?
5. What was each party seeking with respect to the embryos?
6. What arguments did Tamera use to support her position?
7. Is a frozen embryo a "child" in the context of a dissolution action in Iowa?

8. According to the Iowa Supreme Court, should the "best interest" standard be applied in resolution of disputes involving frozen embryos?
9. According to the court, what are the primary approaches used by courts in various states when resolving disputes over the disposition of frozen embryos? Which approach is the prevailing view, and what does the court see as the primary strengths and weaknesses of each approach?
10. What is Iowa's public policy with respect to judicial enforcement of agreements concerning personal decisions about marriage, family, and reproduction?
11. What purpose(s) are served by "disposition" agreements?
12. What was the court's holding, and which approach did it use to resolve the dispute in this case?

FOCUS ON **STATE LAW AND PROCEDURE**

Appendix A of the *Baby M.* case referenced in this chapter contains a copy of the Surrogacy Parenting Agreement executed by the parties in that case. Appendix B contains the agreement between the genetic father, William Stern, and the Infertility Center of New York (ICNY), which facilitated the surrogacy arrangement. In this assignment, you need to:

• Locate a copy of the Surrogacy Agreement of the parties in the *Baby M.* case and review it.

• Determine whether it contained all of provisions recommended in Paralegal Application 13.10 that are applicable given the facts of the case
• Research the applicable law in your state (both statutory and case law), if any, governing surrogacy agreements.
• Determine the likelihood that the Agreement would be enforceable in your state if executed today.

FOCUS ON **TECHNOLOGY**

Websites of Interest

http://bioethics.gov/

Sponsored by the President's Council on Bioethics, this site offers a rich variety of sources including transcripts, reports, background materials, and books. The reports may either be downloaded or ordered in print form. Of particular interest are three reports: *Reproduction and Responsibility: The Regulation of the New Biotechnologies* (March 2004); *Beyond Therapy: Biotechnology and the Pursuit of Happiness* (October 2003); and *Human Cloning and Human Dignity: An Ethical Inquiry* (July 2002). This website is particularly user-friendly.

http://family.findlaw.com/paternity

This site has links to state paternity laws.

http://www.ncsl.org/programs/cyf/paternitylegis.htm

NCSL is the site of the National Conference of State Legislatures. This particular link will take you to a summary of enacted and proposed legislation on disestablishment of paternity.

http://www.paternityfraud.com

This is the website of the New Jersey Citizens Against Paternity Fraud, an organization founded by Patrick McCarthy, a man who unsuccessfully sought to disestablish paternity after learning post-divorce that he was not the biological father of his fourteen-year-old daughter.

http://www.resolve.org/main/national/embdon/guide1.jsp

See Dianne Clapp and Jennifer A. Redmond, eds. *Embryo Adoption: An Online Guide for Potential Embryo Donors.*

Assignments

1. Locate three sites on the Internet that market eggs and/or sperm for use in assisted reproductive technology methods. Describe each of the sites. What quality-control measures are in place, if any? How does one donate? How does one make a purchase? What costs are indicated?

2. Go to the site listed above for the National Conference of State Legislatures and compile a list of the states that have enacted legislation permitting disestablishment of paternity.

3. Locate the website for the Title IV-D agency in your state. Describe the information and forms you find there regarding establishment of paternity.

chapter **fourteen**
ADOPTION

Scott and Hayley Martinelli want Scott's son, Mike, to be a part of their family, and so they plan to have Hayley adopt him....Mike's mother, Jessica Olivio, doesn't feel that she can handle the responsibility of raising Mike and sees adoption as a good solution, as long as she can maintain enough contact to watch him grow up....

IN THIS CHAPTER YOU WILL LEARN

- What adoption is and the purposes it serves
- What the various types of adoption are
- What the differences are between an open and a closed adoption
- What the major steps are in the adoption process
- What the rights of biological parents are in the adoption context
- If unwed mothers and unwed fathers stand on an equal footing with respect to parental rights
- What a putative father registry is and what purposes it serves
- Under what circumstances a parent's rights may be terminated
- Who must consent to an adoption and what the characteristics of an effective consent are
- What a safe haven law is
- Who can adopt and who can be adopted
- What a home study is
- Under what circumstances an adoption may be challenged and by whom
- What the role of the paralegal is in an adoption case

Adoption is a fundamental family relationship and not simply a privilege created by state law.... Adoption has been a part of human society since prehistoric days and fulfills a key function in knitting together the fabric of parent-child relationships, especially in times of need.... Like marriage, adoption is a means of family formation that is no less fundamental because it is characterized by choice and commitment rather than blood ties and procreation.... Adoption is as crucial to children seeking parents as marriage is to adults seeking partners.[1]

INTRODUCTION

Historical Perspective and Purpose of Adoption

Adoption has existed in one form or another for centuries and has served a variety of purposes. In other times and cultures, it primarily served the needs of adults seeking to maintain political power, ensure heirs, and transfer wealth. Historically, the primary purpose of adoption in this country was to protect children and ensure their futures within the context of a family unit. Although Mississippi and Texas recognized informal adoptions prior to the 1850s, Massachusetts passed the nation's first comprehensive adoption statute in 1851, and other states promptly followed suit. The acts essentially formalized the parent-child relationship for children already living in **de facto** family relationships. They also advanced welfare reforms targeted at abandoned and orphaned children living in institutions and providing a source of cheap labor as apprentices.

Definition of Adoption

Adoption is the judicial process by which a new parent-child relationship is created. It constitutes, in effect, a birth by legal process in which an adoptive parent assumes the legal rights and duties of a biological parent. Adoption is essentially a two-step process in which an existing parent-child relationship (usually between the child and one or both of his or her birth parents) is terminated and a new parent-child relationship is judicially created. The birth parents may voluntarily surrender their rights and consent to the adoption, or their parental rights may be involuntarily terminated by the court. An adoptive parent may be a stranger to the child, a relative, a step-parent, or a known but unrelated adult, as is usually the case in an adult adoption. The adoption may, and in some states must, be coordinated by a state-approved public or private agency, and in the context of the most recent forms of reproductive technology, may be facilitated by a contractual agreement enforceable in the courts. According to U.S. Census Bureau estimates, there are more than two million adopted children in the United States.[2]

Legal Effect of Adoption

Once an adoption is finalized, the relationship between the **adoptee** (the child who is adopted) and his or her adoptive parents is as permanent as the relationship between a child and a biological parent in the sense that it does not end with divorce or the death of a parent. Only the court can end the relationship by invalidating or revoking the adoption or terminating the parental rights and responsibilities of the adoptive parent for cause. Adoption brings to the child the wide range of benefits that flow from the parent-child relationship, including, for example, the right to be supported by the adoptive parent(s) while a minor,

---

De facto adoption

an adoption that does not meet formal statutory requirements but is considered an adoption based on the conduct of the parties and the surrounding circumstances; sometimes called an equitable adoption or adoption by estoppel

Adoption

the judicial process by which a new parent-child relationship is created and an adoptive parent assumes the legal rights and duties of a biological parent

---

Paralegal Practice Tip

Throughout this chapter, we generally refer to the adoptee as "the child." Although the adoption process establishes a parent-child relationship, an adoptee may be an adult. In this limited context, the term "child" refers to an adult adoptee.

Adoptee

the individual who is adopted

to inherit by and through the adoptive parent(s), entitlement to adoptive parents' worker's compensation benefits, and *standing* to bring a wrongful death action on the death of an adoptive parent.

Standing

an individual's right to bring a matter before the court and seek relief based on a claim that he or she has a stake in the outcome of the case

TYPES OF ADOPTION

Types of adoption are classified in terms of:

> Who is adopting the child
> Who facilitates the adoption
> The extent of post-adoption contact between the biological and adoptive parents

(See Exhibit 14.1.)

Types of Adoption Based on Who Is Adopting the Child

Children may be adopted by family members, step-parents, married couples, single persons, and co-parents.

Family Member. Several states establish by statute or administrative regulation a preference for adoption by family members such as aunts, uncles, and grandparents, ostensibly to minimize disruption and maintain some degree of family connectedness for children. However, states also may place restrictions on adoptions of family members. For example, the Massachusetts adoption statute provides, "A person of full age may petition the probate court…for leave to adopt as his child another person younger than himself, unless such other person is his or her wife or husband, or brother, sister, uncle or aunt, of the whole or half blood."[3]

EXHIBIT 14.1 Types of Adoption

TYPES OF ADOPTION BASED ON WHO CAN ADOPT
> Family member adoption
> Step-parent adoption
> Married couple/joint adoption
> Single parent adoption
> Co-parent adoption

TYPES OF ADOPTION BASED ON WHO FACILITATES THE ADOPTION
> Independent adoption
> Agency adoption
> International adoption
> Equitable adoption/adoption by estoppel
> Illegal/black market adoption

TYPES OF ADOPTION BASED ON EXTENT OF POST-ADOPTION CONTACT
> Closed
> Open

Cut-off rule
the rule requiring that a biological parent's rights to his or her child be terminated prior to adoption of the child by a third party; not applicable when a step- or co-parent is adopting the child

Step-parent.   A step-parent adoption occurs when the spouse of a divorced or widowed and remarried custodial biological parent or the spouse of a parent of a nonmarital child seeks to adopt the child. The child retains a legal relationship with one parent, but his or her other parent (if living and known) generally must consent to the adoption or have his or her parental rights involuntarily terminated as in other adoptions. Unlike a typical adoption, in which both biological parents' rights are extinguished, the **cut-off rule** does not apply to the custodial biological parent who remains in the new family unit. Although the adoption still must be approved by the court, most states have in place simplified procedures designed to expedite step-parent adoptions. Depending on the circumstances and extent of the relationship between the child and the parent whose rights are being terminated, the court may grant some degree of post-adoption contact similar to that provided in an open adoption agreement.

Joint petition for adoption
a petition to adopt a child that is brought by both parties to a marriage

Married Couple.   The most common form of adoption is one in which a married couple seeks to adopt a child who is biologically unrelated. The couple is usually required to file a **joint petition for adoption.** Several states expressly prefer married couples as adoptive parents and are reluctant to grant adoptions to unmarried couples (heterosexual or homosexual) seeking to adopt a child. Some biological parents condition placement of their child with an agency on eventual adoption by a married couple.

Single Parent.   Today, both single persons and married couples are eligible to adopt in virtually all states. However, historically, some states have prohibited single persons (regardless of sexual orientation) from adopting and others have not considered them desirable candidates as adoptive parents. Old attitudes die hard, and some agencies still have biases, expressed or masked, in favor of placing children with married couples.

Co-parent
a person engaged in a nonmarital relationship with the legal parent of a child who regards him- or herself as a parent rather than as a legal stranger to the child

Co-Parent.   In co-parent adoptions (sometimes labeled second-parent adoptions), one partner in an unmarried couple has or adopts a child and the other partner seeks co-parent status. That status affords the second partner parental rights, including the right to make decisions regarding the child's health, education, and welfare, along with the responsibility of providing financial support. Should the parties' relationship terminate, both parties have custodial and visitation rights.

Some states are slow to accept and accord rights to nontraditional family units. For example, a Utah statute provides as of 2008, "it is not in a child's best interest to be adopted by a person or persons who are cohabiting in a relationship that is not a legally valid and binding marriage under the laws of this state."[4] However, courts in a number of states have granted adoptions to unmarried partners, either heterosexual or homosexual, when they find them to be in the best interest of the children involved.

Types of Adoption Based on Who Facilitates the Adoption

Adoptions may be facilitated independently (privately), by agencies licensed by the state, by international adoption providers, by order of the court under its equitable powers, or by use of illegal resources on the black market.

Independent adoption
an adoption usually facilitated by a third party such as a physician or attorney, rather than by a licensed state agency; sometimes called private or designated adoption

Independent Adoption.   In an independent or private adoption, the biological parent(s) transfer custody of the child directly to the adoptive parents. The process is usually facilitated by a third party—such as a physician, member of the clergy, and/or an attorney specializing in adoption law—who performs most of the tasks usually handled by an agency. This type of adoption generally allows biological parents to designate adoptive parents or to prescribe more fully the characteristics they would like prospective adoptive parents to possess. Sometimes the parents are brought together as a result of ads or by adoption exchange organizations and entrepreneurs listed in the yellow pages or posted on the Internet.

Although a majority of the states permit independent adoptions, some states do not, due to concerns that they are not regulated and screened as carefully as agency adoptions. Birth parents usually do not receive counseling regarding their options, and pre-placement home studies are not necessarily required. As a result, even in states where they are permitted, independent adoptions may be subject to regulations regarding the fees that may be charged by intermediaries, and adoptive parents may need to be approved or certified by the state. Although independent adoptions are privately arranged, they still must be approved by the court.

Agency Adoption.   Each state has a designated state agency responsible for regulating adoptions within the state. In an agency adoption, a public or private agency licensed by the state takes temporary custody of a child for subsequent placement in a permanent adoptive home. Children come into the custody of an agency through two primary routes: (1) the parent(s) voluntarily transfer custody of the child to the agency by executing a written surrender relinquishing their parental rights, or (2) a court terminates parental rights for cause based on clear and convincing evidence of parental unfitness and places the child in the temporary custody of an agency pending an adoption.

All states permit agency adoptions and, in some states, all adoptions must be facilitated by an agency except when the adoption is by a step-parent or close family member. The agency is essentially responsible for all phases of the adoption process including, among other tasks, recruiting foster care and adoptive homes, screening prospective parents, conducting comprehensive home studies, locating potential adoptees, and securing proper consents/terminations of parental rights.

International Adoption.   An *international adoption* takes place when a child residing in one country is adopted by a resident of another country. This is a highly specialized area of practice and usually involves a costly and protracted process. In some instances, the adoptive parents may be required to live in the child's birth country for a requisite period of time. Careful attention must be given to complying with the laws of both countries, including any applicable Immigration and Naturalization Service regulations.

Equitable Adoption.   An *equitable adoption,* sometimes called an *adoption by estoppel,* is not technically an adoption. It refers to a situation in which prospective adoptive parents accept a child into their home and raise the child as their own without ever formally finalizing an adoption. Some states allow a child in such circumstances to inherit from the "adoptive" parents should they die intestate (without a will) even though the adoption process was never completed. The adoption is treated by the court as if it took place, and the "adoptive" parents' estates are estopped (prevented) from denying the child's claim.

Illegal/Black Market Adoption.   Illegal adoptions are often referred to as baby selling. They are brokered by individuals who collect a substantial fee for locating a child who is transferred from one person or couple to another without proper legal process. Historically, black market adoptions have been pursued by individuals who do not qualify as adoptive parents under agency standards, or who seek to adopt children in high demand (commonly infants). Such "arrangements" are high risk and likely to be deemed void if challenged at a later date. Some courts have held that surrogacy agreements constitute a form of baby selling. Before approving or enforcing a surrogacy agreement, most courts will scrutinize it to determine whether or not the gestational mother was paid for anything beyond reasonable medical costs such that the agreement constitutes the sale of a baby in violation of public policy and the law.

Paralegal Practice Tip
Although many adoptions are by relatives and step-parents, adoption has become a big (nearly $2 billion a year) business.[5] Competition is stiffening for traditional facilitators of adoptions, as profit-making adoption entrepreneurs enter the scene and use the Internet extensively to find and bring together financially and emotionally challenged pregnant women and prospective adoptive parents. Birth mothers under stress are prime targets of adoption brokers seeking to satisfy the needs of paying customers. For pregnant women with deeply held religious and moral beliefs, adoption is promoted as a morally acceptable alternative to abortion, one that achieves a positive result for children who are "unwanted" for any of a host of reasons.

Agency adoption
an adoption facilitated by a licensed state agency

International adoption
an adoption in which a child residing in one country is adopted by a resident of another country

Equitable adoption
refers to a situation in which prospective adoptive parents accept a child into their home and raise the child as their own without ever formally finalizing the adoption; treated by some courts as an adoption to promote fairness and serve the ends of justice; sometimes called an adoption by estoppel

Illegal/black market adoption
an adoption brokered by an individual who collects a substantial fee for locating a child who is transferred from one person or couple to another without proper legal process

Types of Adoption Based on Extent of Post-Adoption Contact

Adoptions in the United States fall along a continuum from closed to open. In a **closed adoption,** the biological and adoptive parents essentially know nothing about each other, and adoptees have no access to their original birth certificates or any identifying or nonidentifying information about their biological parents. In an **open adoption,** the biological parents, adoptive parents, and the adoptee have varying degrees of contact with each other.

Closed Adoption. Most adoptions are still initially closed adoptions, in which the biological and adoptive parents do not know each other's identities. The general rule is that once an adoption is finalized, the court orders the record sealed, and a new birth certificate is issued in an effort to protect the privacy of the birth parents and the security of the adoptive parents from interference with the new family bond. However, these interests have not stopped adoptees from challenging the constitutionality of confidentiality laws. (See Case 14.1.)

Closed adoption
an adoption in which biological and adoptive parents essentially know nothing about each other, and adoptees have no access to their original birth certificates or identifying information about their biological parents

Open adoption
an adoption in which biological parents, adoptive parents, and the adoptee have varying degrees of contact with each other

CASE **14.1** *Alma Society Inc v. Mellon,* 601 F.2d 1225 (2d Cir. 1979)

BACKGROUND INFORMATION

The appellants in this case were an association of individual adult adoptees who challenged the constitutionality of the New York statutes that required the sealing of adoption records. They claimed that upon reaching adulthood they should be entitled, without a showing of cause, to obtain their sealed adoption records, including the names of their natural parents. Some appellants argued that lack of access caused serious psychological trauma, pain, and suffering; potential medical problems and misdiagnoses due to a lack of medical history; the danger of unwitting incest; and an impairment of religious freedom due to not being reared in the religion of their natural parents. The District Court dismissed their Complaint, and the second circuit appellate court affirmed that decision.

FROM THE OPINION

The attack on the New York statutes is three-fold. Appellants first argue that the interests of an adult adoptee in learning from the State (or agencies acting under…state law) the identity of his natural family is a fundamental right under the Due Process clause of the Fourteenth Amendment….

Second, appellants argue that adult adoptees constitute a suspect or "quasi-suspect" classification under the Equal Protection clause of the Fourteenth Amendment….

Finally, appellants argue that the Thirteenth Amendment also applies to this case because the statutes that require sealing of the adoption records as to adults constitute the second of the five incidents of slavery namely, the abolition of the parental relation….We will discuss each of appellants' three arguments in turn.

Substantive Due Process

What appellants assert is a right to "personhood." They rely on a series of Supreme Court cases involving familial relationships, rights of family privacy, and freedom to marry and reproduce. As they put it, "an adoptee is someone upon whom the state has, by sealing his records, imposed lifelong familial amnesia…injuring the

continued

adoptee in regard to his personal identity when he was too young to consent to, or even know, what was happening," …

…

…we must look to the nature of the relationships and…choices made by those other than the adopted child…involved.…[T]he State may take these choices into consideration and protect the natural mother's choice of privacy…even if appellants are correct, … , that many mothers would be willing in this day and age to have their adult adopted children contact them. So, too, a state may take into account the relationship of the adopting parents, even if, … , many of them would not object to or would even encourage the adopted child's seeking out the identity of or relationship with a natural parent. The New York statutes in providing for release of the information on a "showing of good cause" do no more than take these other relationships into account. As such they do not unconstitutionally infringe upon or arbitrarily remove appellants' rights of identity, privacy, or personhood. Upon an appropriate showing of psychological trauma, medical need, or of a religious identity crisis [and] though it might be doubted upon a showing of "fear of unconscious incest" the New York courts would appear required under their own statute to grant permission to release all or part of the sealed adoption records.

Equal Protection

Appellants begin their equal protection analysis with the argument that adult adoptees are a suspect classification (and the correlative argument that the State has no compelling interests to support the validity of the sealed records laws).… [A]ppellants suggest that they are at least entitled to the same level of constitutional scrutiny as illegitimates who have been termed a "sensitive" or quasi-suspect category for which the appropriate level of scrutiny is "intermediate," not "strict" …

…

Even assuming that the classification here were subject to intermediate scrutiny, it would not violate equal protection; for we conclude that it is substantially related to an important state interest.…

…The statutes, we think, serve important interests. New York Domestic Relations Law § 114 and its related statutes represent a considered legislative judgment that the confidentiality statutes promote the social policy underlying adoption laws.…Moreover, the purpose of a related statute, Section 4138 of the Public Health Laws, was to erase the stigma of illegitimacy from the adopted child's life by sealing his original birth certificate and issuing a new one under his new surname. And the major purpose of adoption legislation is to encourage natural parents to use the process when they are unwilling or unable to care for their off-spring.…These significant legislative goals clearly justify the State's decision to keep the natural parents' names secret from adopted persons but not from non-adopted persons.

To be sure, once an adopted child reaches adulthood, some of the considerations that apply at the time of adoption and throughout the child's tender years no longer apply or apply with less force. Illegitimacy might stigmatize an adult less than a child, and the goal of encouraging adoption of unwanted and uncared for children might not be significantly affected if Adult adoptees could discover their natural parents' identities. But the state does have an interest that does not wane as the adopted child grows to adulthood, namely, the interest in protecting the privacy of the natural parents.…

Thirteenth Amendment

Appellants make the novel argument…that the Thirteenth Amendment's prohibition of slavery and involuntary servitude gives them an *absolute* right to release of their adoption records.…The argument is…that in abolishing slavery and involuntary

continued

servitude, the Framers also intended to abolish five "necessary incidents of slavery." ... [W]e find that the Amendment is entirely inapplicable to this case.

...

...Appellants liken their situation...to that of the antebellum South where a slave child was "sold off" while too young to remember his parents and grew up separated from them by inability to communicate as well as by distance. The analogy according to appellants is that however literate they may be, they cannot write to their natural parents, cannot visit them, and thereby wear a "badge or incident" of slavery.

...

...Although it is doubtless true that an "incident" of slavery (in the original sense) was the abolition of the parental relation, i.e. the offspring of a slave was deprived of the care and attention of parents, ... the New York sealed records laws do not deprive appellants of their parental relation. It is the New York adoption laws themselves and not the sealed records laws that recognize the divestment by natural parents of their guardianship because of formal surrender, abandonment, or forfeiture by unfitness or jeopardy of the child's best interests; and it is the adoption laws that create a new parent-child relationship between appellants and their adoptive parents. Appellants do not challenge the constitutionality of the adoption laws; thus their challenge to the sealed records laws, ... , is misdirected....

SIDEBAR

The full opinion in this case is available in its entirety on the companion website. The policy of closed adoption is a source of controversy among adoption professionals. What are the primary arguments on each side of this issue? What is your position? The court suggests that the proper target for the appellants' claim is the adoption laws themselves rather than the sealed records laws. Do you believe the appellants would prevail in that context? Explain your response.

Generally, the child's desire to establish his or her roots and identity is not deemed sufficient for the records to be opened by court order although over the years some exceptions to the rule of secrecy have developed in unusual or emergency circumstances.

Adoption registry
a vehicle available in some states that allows adoptees after a certain age (usually eighteen) to try to contact their biological parents and siblings

- Some states have established an exception for medical reasons when the adoptee or a child of the adoptee requires information about inherited diseases and medical conditions or is in need of a bone marrow or organ transplant.
- Several states (including Colorado, for example)[6] maintain **adoption** or **reunion registries** that allow adoptees after a certain age (usually eighteen) to try to contact their biological parents and siblings. Once contacted by the adoptee, the registry attempts to contact the birth parents, and, if they consent, arrangements are made to put them in touch with each other. If a birth parent refuses, no further contact is made.
- Some states have statutes providing for the release to adoptees of nonidentifying information about their biological parents. Such information usually includes medical, ethnic, socioeconomic, and educational information and, in some cases, information about the circumstances under which the adopted person became available for adoption.[7]
- A small number of states including Alabama, Alaska, Kansas, and Oregon[8] have legislated that an adoptee, upon reaching the age of majority (usually eighteen), may request a copy of his or her original birth certificate.

Open Adoption.   An open adoption is a form of adoption in which the birth parents, the adoptive parents, and the adoptee maintain a degree of post-adoption contact with each other. The contact may assume a variety of forms including, for example, the sending of annual or seasonal photographs, written or electronic correspondence with or about the child, and visits. In states where open adoptions are permitted, the terms of the agreement are customarily expressed in a contract submitted for approval by the court. The applicable statute in Oregon governing such open adoption agreements is accessible on the companion website.

THE ADOPTION PROCESS

Adoption is a creation of statute and is subject to applicable state and federal laws. Each state has enacted its own adoption procedures and practices, which vary considerably from one jurisdiction to another. Although the National Conference of Commissioners on Uniform State Laws approved a new Uniform Adoption Act (UAA) in 1994 in an effort to standardize adoption law, it has thus far been adopted in only a small handful of states.

The basic steps in the adoption process in virtually all states include the following:

1. Determine rights of biological parents
2. Terminate biological parents' rights
    By consent
    By involuntary termination
3. Identify potential adoptive parents and adoptees
    Who can adopt?
    Who can be adopted?
4. Conduct home study(ies) (depending on the jurisdiction and type of adoption)
5. Determine proper jurisdiction and venue
6. File Petition for Adoption
7. Serve Notice on all interested parties
8. Conduct Preliminary Hearing
9. Issue Interlocutory Decree granting temporary custody to the adoptive parents
10. Arrange Pre-adoption Placement of the child with the adoptive parents
11. Issue Final Decree
12. Consider challenges to Adoption Decree

> **Paralegal Practice Tip**
> The states vary with respect to whether dual representation of biological parents and adoptive parents is permitted. Very few states expressly permit it, but several states, including Kentucky, Maine, Minnesota, New York, and Wisconsin, expressly prohibit dual representation.

These steps are carried out by several actors whose precise roles and relationships depend on governing law and the facts of the case: the biological parents, the adoptive parents, attorneys, agency personnel, third-party facilitators, and the courts.

THE RIGHTS OF BIOLOGICAL PARENTS IN THE ADOPTION CONTEXT
The Biological Mother

As discussed in Chapter 13, a mother's parental rights are essentially already established at birth. The biological mother has the right to choose to place her child for adoption by voluntarily surrendering her parental rights to an agency and/or consenting to an adoption. If the state seeks to terminate her parental rights involuntarily, it can do so only based upon clear and convincing evidence of parental unfitness.

The Married Father

If the biological mother is married, under a marital presumption, her husband commonly is deemed to be the father of any child born during their marriage or within three hundred days of its termination. If no other man has been ruled the legal father of her child, an adoption cannot take place unless the married father's rights are terminated or he surrenders his parental rights and/or consents to the adoption.

The Father Whose Identity or Whereabouts Are Unknown

In the event the mother does not know the identity of the father, she (or the agency to which she has relinquished custody) usually must file an affidavit attesting to that fact before the adoption can proceed. If the identity of the father is known but he cannot be located, a diligent search must be made to locate him, and proof of the effort may be required by the court. The effort may involve a search of telephone, military, and post office records; driver and voter registration rolls; and publication of notice in newspapers published in areas where the father has been known to reside. A number of locater services are now available online. A failure to conduct a proper search may result in a later challenge to the adoption on the grounds that the father did not receive proper notice to which he was constitutionally entitled.

The Nonmarital Biological Father

Under common law, the father of an illegitimate child had no standing to intervene in an action to adopt his biological child, and, prior to 1972, there was little case law specifically addressing the rights of unwed fathers with respect to their children in the adoption context.

The Uniform Adoption Act (UAA)

> …distinguishes between fathers who willfully abandon their children and those whose attempts at fatherhood have been thwarted. The thwarted father has somehow been prevented from meeting his parental responsibilities, because the mother either never informed him of her pregnancy or the child's birth, lied to him about her plans for the child, disappeared with the child, named another man as the birth father, or was married to another man in a state that presumes the legitimacy of a child born to a married woman. According to the UAA, the unmarried father in these circumstances has not willfully abandoned his child but has instead been externally prevented from carrying out his parental responsibilities. Thwarted fathers can assert parental rights during the pendency of adoption proceedings, but they must prove a compelling reason for not having performed their parental duties. The thwarted father must also defend against other parties who try to prove that termination of his rights is necessary to avoid "detriment or a risk of substantial harm to the child."[9]

Four key cases decided by the U.S. Supreme Court between 1972 and 1983 began to define the rights of unwed fathers. Beginning with the *Stanley* case in 1972,[10] the Court established that fathers of nonmarital children have constitutionally protected legal rights as parents under the Equal Protection clause of the Fourteenth Amendment and a privacy interest in children they have sired and raised, such that the state cannot terminate their parental rights without affording them notice and an opportunity to be heard. However, the unmarried father's rights are neither automatic nor unlimited. Under the **biology-plus rule**, an unmarried father must take affirmative steps to demonstrate his parental commitment.

Biology-plus rule
the rule that the biological connection between father and child is worthy of constitutional protection if the father grasps the opportunity to develop a relationship with and accept responsibility for the child

Depending on the jurisdiction and the extent of demonstrated commitment, the rights of an unmarried father may include the following:

- He may be entitled to notice of an adoption proceeding as an interested party who may not be able to block the adoption but who can speak to whether it will be in the best interests of the child.
- He may be entitled to an opportunity to prove to the court that his consent should be required because he has taken sufficient steps to establish a relationship with his child, because his efforts to do so have been actively thwarted, or because his failure to do so should be excused for some other legitimate reason.
- Once his right to consent is established, he may have the capacity to block the adoption unless he is determined to be unfit and his parental rights are involuntarily terminated.

A description of each of the four landmark Supreme Court decisions addressing the rights of nonmarital fathers is available on the companion website:

- *Stanley v. Illinois,* 405 U.S. 645 (1972)
- *Quilloin v. Walcott,* 434 U.S. 246 (1978)
- *Caban v. Mohammed,* 441 U.S. 380 (1979)
- *Lehr v. Robertson,* 463 U.S. 248 (1983)

The unifying theme emerging from these decisions is summarized in the following quote from the *Lehr* case:

> The significance of the biological connection [between father and child] is that it offers the natural father an opportunity that no other male possesses to develop a relationship with his offspring. If he grasps that opportunity and accepts some measure of responsibility for the child's future, he may enjoy the blessings of the parent-child relationship and make uniquely valuable contributions to the child's development. If he fails to do so, the Federal Constitution will not automatically compel a State to listen to his opinion of where the child's best interests lie.[11]

Although the Supreme Court has begun to address directly the rights of unwed fathers with respect to adoption of their children, several questions remain unanswered:

- What, if any, criteria should be used to measure when an unwed father has sufficiently grasped the "opportunity interest" in fathering his child such that his parental rights warrant constitutional protection?
- Can an unwed father lose his parental rights by failing to establish a relationship with his newborn child by, for example, failing to support the mother emotionally and financially during the pregnancy, failing to be present at the birth, and failing to visit the mother and child in the hospital?[12]
- Can an unwed father who has established a parent-child relationship lose that relationship as a result of failing to comply with technical requirements such as those imposed by putative father registries?[13]
- Can an unwed father's parental rights be lost as a result of the birth mother's deceit and/or concealment of a pregnancy until after an adoption is approved? (See Paralegal Application 14.1.)
- What constitutes meaningful notice to an unwed father of a petition for adoption?[14]
- At what point do a fit parent's rights to notice give way to the best interests of a child, particularly one who has been in an adoptive family for an extended period of time?
- Does the child have a right of association with a fit biological parent?

PARALEGAL APPLICATION **14.1**

A "NEW" CAUSE OF ACTION—TORTIOUS INTERFERENCE WITH PARENTAL RELATIONSHIPS

THE FACTS

What remedy should an unwed father have when he diligently seeks to exercise his parental rights when the birth mother conceals her whereabouts and places the child for adoption against his wishes and with knowledge of a judgment determining him to be the child's natural father? What if she accomplishes this with active and knowing assistance from members of her family and her attorney? In 1998, a West Virginia father who was confronted with these circumstances sued the mother, her parents, her brother, and her attorney for fraud, civil conspiracy, tortious interference with parental relationships, outrage, and violation of constitutional rights. In a 118-page opinion, a West Virginia appellate court affirmed a $7.85 million judgment against all of the defendants (including the attorney) and, in its opinion, created a new cause of action imposing civil liability on anyone who conspires to conceal the whereabouts of a newborn from a parent seeking information about the child's location:

> …where a person has knowledge of information concerning a newborn child's birth or physical location, or indicating where and in whose care the child may be found, and the child's parent inquires of such person regarding his or her child's birth or physical location, and/or where and in whose care his/her child may be found, such person may be held liable for fraudulently concealing information if he/she affirmatively, intentionally, and willfully fails to provide such information to the child's parent pursuant to his/her request for such information, and such concealment unduly hinders or otherwise irreparably harms the parent's ability to establish a parent-child relationship with his or her child.[15]

SIDEBAR

The cause of action established in this case opens the door to considerable civil liability by imposing an affirmative duty on the public at large. Do you agree with the court that such a cause of action is appropriate? How far do you think that liability should extend? What challenges do such actions pose for a plaintiff?

Putative father
a man who may be the father of a child but who was not married to the child's mother at the time of birth and whose paternity has not yet been established by legal process

Putative father registry
a vehicle available in several states that is designed to protect a putative father's parental rights by giving him notice of a pending adoption proceeding without his having to rely on the birth mother or prospective adoptive parents for such information

State Initiatives

There is a lack of uniformity among the states with respect to the level of support available to nonmarital fathers in the adoption context beyond the limited protection afforded by federal law. Many states have taken steps to protect their interests in assuming a role in the future of their children. The two primary methods used to do so are putative father registries and publication notice requirements.

Putative Father Registries.   A **putative father** is a man who may be a child's father but who neither married the child's mother before the child was born nor has established that he is the father in a court proceeding. When a putative father registers with a putative father registry, he is registering his intent to assert his rights and responsibilities as a parent. If he registers within a specified time frame, he will be given notice of a proposed adoption of his child and petition for termination of his parental rights. The notice advises the putative father that the action has been filed and includes the date, place, and time of any scheduled hearing.

Putative father registries of one form or another have been established by law in a majority of states. Although the states vary with respect to the information maintained in their registries, they typically include the following:

- Registration date
- Name, address, social security number, and date of birth of both the putative father and the birth mother
- Child's name and date of birth, if known, or anticipated month and year of birth

A copy of the Ohio Application for Search of Putative Father Registry "Registration Form for Fathers" is accessible on the companion website.

The features of putative father registries vary state to state, particularly with respect to:

- the time frame within which a putative father must register (ranging from prior to the child's birth to any time prior to the filing of an adoption petition)
- the consequences of a failure to register (usually an irrevocable implied consent to adoption and/or loss of the right to notice)
- the permissible exceptions to the registration requirement, if any (such as a failure to register due to the mother's concealment of the pregnancy)
- whether or not a putative father who registers can subsequently revoke or rescind a notice of intent to claim paternity

The information contained in the Registry is essentially confidential and usually is available only to "interested parties," such as birth mothers, adoption agencies, state departments of social services and child support enforcement, adoptive parents, courts, attorneys for parties in a case, and others for good cause shown.

Registries are ostensibly designed to protect the parental rights of a putative father who has registered by giving him notice of a pending adoption proceeding without his having to rely on the birth mother or prospective adoptive parents for such information. By default or design, they serve a number of additional purposes:

Paralegal Practice Tip
Putative fathers serving in the armed forces may have additional protections under the Sailors and Soldiers Relief Act. This resource should be considered if a client is serving in the armed forces at the time an adoption of his or her child is pending.

- They help reassure the birth mother and prospective adoptive parents that an adoption will not be disrupted at a later date when the father, whose whereabouts or identity was previously unknown, appears and challenges the validity of the adoption.
- Consistent with Supreme Court decisions, they satisfy in part the requirement for an assumption of responsibility by a putative father who wants to establish a relationship with his child.
- They allow the birth mother to protect her privacy by not having to publish details of her personal life, and relieve the pressure on her to perjure herself if she is unwilling or unable to identify the putative father and wants to receive public assistance.
- They generate revenue for the states through modest filing fees and potential establishment of paternal responsibility for child support and the expenses of the mother's prenatal and birth expenses.

Although touted as a protection for the rights of unknown fathers, the long-term impact and effectiveness of registries are yet to be measured. Critics argue that registries unreasonably restrict realization of the rights of putative fathers and serve instead to facilitate adoption and promote early bonding with adoptive parents. One commentator phrased her concerns in these terms:

The draconian nature of most registry acts protects neither the interests of responsible fathers nor the long-term emotional interests of the child. In actuality, the function of most registries is usually to cut off the birth father's rights, often before he knows of the child's birth or whereabouts. In an astonishing number of instances, the unwed father has been actively deceived by the birth mother into believing that the baby died. In other cases, the birth mother leads the father to believe the baby is not his, or she never allows him to know that she is pregnant. Such statutes' interest in identifying the father is suspect and borders upon the pretextual, considering the absurdly short periods of time in which the father's rights are terminated for failure to file with the correct registry. The result is catastrophic for the child....[16]

- In Alabama, for example, the Putative Father Registry has been designated by the legislature as the exclusive vehicle entitling a putative father to notice of and the opportunity to contest an adoption proceeding.[17] In addition, under the Alabama pre-birth abandonment statute, a father can be deemed to have abandoned his child and impliedly consented both to termination of his parental rights and to an adoption by failing, with reasonable knowledge of the pregnancy, to offer financial and/or emotional support to the mother for a period of six months prior to the birth, OR failing to file with the putative father registry within thirty days of the birth.[18]
- No registry presently requires the mother to inform a putative father of her pregnancy, although some state registries have a provision recognizing that some mothers may intentionally conceal their pregnancy to deceive the father. Such registries allow him to register when he discovers the existence of the baby. For example, the applicable Minnesota statute provides that a putative father will be considered to have timely filed if he proves by clear and convincing evidence that (1) it was not possible for him to register timely; (2) his failure to register was through no fault of his own; and (3) he registered within ten days after it became possible for him to do so.[19]
- Some states such as Arizona,[20] Florida, Minnesota, Ohio, Texas, and Utah do not accept a putative father's ignorance of a pregnancy or birth as an excuse for not registering. For example, a Utah statute provides that "[a]n unmarried biological father, by virtue of the fact he has engaged in a sexual relationship with a woman: (i) is considered to be on notice that a pregnancy and an adoption proceeding regarding that child may occur; and (ii) has a duty to protect his own rights and interests."[21]
- The burden is placed on the unmarried biological father to establish his claim of paternity by registering, and yet many putative fathers are unaware of the existence of putative father registries and may lose their parental rights by default, as most states provide that failure to register in a timely manner constitutes a waiver and surrender of any parental rights to notice. A small number of states make a special effort to publicize the existence of their putative father registries. Missouri does so through public service announcements and by requiring the Department of Health and Senior Services to provide, on request, pamphlets describing the Registry to hospitals, libraries, medical clinics, schools, universities, and other providers of child-related services.[22]

Publication Notice Requirements.   Publication requirements are not in place in all states and in states that do have them, they vary widely. At one extreme is a Utah adoption statute that provides: "... an unmarried mother has a right of privacy with regard to her pregnancy and adoption plan, and therefore has no legal obligation to disclose the identity of an unmarried biological father prior to or during an adoption proceeding, and has no obligation to volunteer information to the court with respect to the father."[23] At the other extreme is Florida's "Scarlet Letter law," enacted in 2001 and subsequently held unconstitutional on privacy grounds in 2003[24] and replaced with that state's Putative Father Registry. The Florida District

Court essentially held that the Florida Constitution protects the privacy rights of individuals to avoid disclosure of personal matters and to make certain decisions independently. In effect, the law had required a genetic mother who could not identify or locate the father of the child she wanted to place for adoption to publish detailed information about dates and places where she had engaged in sexual relations and descriptions of partners who might be the child's father.[25]

Some states, such as Kansas,[26] require the court in which the adoption petition is pending to provide publication notice to unknown putative fathers, while other states leave it to the court's discretion. Still other states, such as North Carolina,[27] place the burden of publication on the individual petitioning for adoption.

PARALEGAL APPLICATION 14.2

A DOUBLE STANDARD?

Consider the following:

> What becomes evident about unwed fathers from case law is that many times they are vitally interested in their children, only to find that their parental rights have been terminated before they have had an opportunity to assert them. A fit unwed father may have his paternal rights terminated for "abandoning" a child pre-birth or for merely failing to sign the correct form, in the correct court, within the correct number of days after his child's birth. Society's dismissive, often summary, legal approach to the child-father dynamic is in startling contrast to the deference states typically afford to the child-mother relationship.[28]

In a Connecticut case, a birth mother continued to use cocaine during her pregnancy "even after being warned that such use posed potential harm to the unborn child. After the child was born addicted to cocaine, the state sought to terminate the mother's parental rights. The court declined to terminate the mother's rights, despite her long drug history and the serious injury inflicted upon the child, concluding that the infant was not a child prior to birth and the mother's pre-birth conduct could neither be considered abuse or neglect."[29] However, in some states, an unwed father who fails to provide emotional and financial pre-birth support to the mother of their child may forfeit his parental rights to the child.

SIDEBAR

What is your opinion with respect to the following questions?

1. Does an unwed mother's right to privacy outweigh an unwed father's paternity opportunity interest? What are the arguments supporting each parent's interest?

2. Should putative fathers have as long to establish their paternity rights as the states have to establish fathers' paternity for purposes of imposing financial obligations (i.e., at any time before the child attains eighteen years of age)? Explain your response.

3. Should all unwed genetic fathers be treated alike with respect to affording them an opportunity to develop a parent-child relationship with their offspring? How about a rapist? A statutory rapist? A male participant in a "one-night stand"? An abusive spouse who rapes his spouse? A man who has sexual relations with a woman after giving her a "date rape" drug without her knowledge? A man who solicits a prostitute or who has relations with a woman in exchange for drugs?

TERMINATION OF PARENTAL RIGHTS

Prior to the 1960s, public policy in the United States favored preservation of the biological family as a priority. When a child was removed from a home, voluntarily or involuntarily, the move was considered temporary whenever possible. The priority articulated by state legislatures and social services agencies was reunification of the biological family after effective completion of a service plan for the parents and children. For better or worse, today the focus is on permanency planning for the thousands of children in state care who have lost their parents to death, abandonment, incarceration, and/or abuse and neglect. ***Permanency planning*** is designed to move children as soon as possible into healthy, stable, and "permanent" homes.

The Adoption and Safe Families Act of 1997 (ASFA)[30] requires state agencies to petition for termination of parental rights when a child has been in state care for fifteen of the prior twenty-two months. Although appearing to serve the best interests of children by not leaving them in limbo indefinitely, some commentators contend that this requirement does a disservice to poor families in particular. "Formerly, poor parents encountering housing, marital, economic, or health crises had foster care as a 'safety net' to provide temporary substitute care at public expense while they got back on their feet. Now, even voluntary placements by good parents in difficult times can rapidly lead to disintegration of a family and permanent loss of family ties."[31]

In order for an adoption to proceed, the groundwork usually is laid for extinguishing the biological parents' rights, through voluntary consent or involuntary termination, in one of four ways:

- The parents voluntarily surrender their parental rights, and the court transfers custody of the child to an agency, which then places the child in foster care or some other residential setting, depending on the circumstances. If and when the child is subsequently adopted, it is the state agency that consents to the adoption. In some states, the voluntary surrender effectively terminates the parents' rights. In other states, the surrender allows the agency to petition the court for a termination.
- The biological parents consent to the adoption directly, and their consents are filed with the petition for adoption.
- The biological parents' rights are terminated by the court for cause, and the state is granted custody of the child pending adoption.
- One of the biological parents, a third party, or a prospective adoptive parent asks the court to dispense with parental consent given the circumstances of the case. For instance, the mother of a child who has been in long-term foster care may be willing to consent to adoption, but the father who is serving an extended sentence in prison for battery on the child unreasonably refuses to consent.

Ideally, the rights of both biological parents are extinguished by consent or court-ordered termination, in order to minimize the risk that the validity of the adoption may be challenged at a later date. However, this is not always possible, particularly in cases involving abandoned newborns, unknown fathers, and children left at ***safe havens.*** (See Paralegal Application 14.3.) Virtually all states permit ***at-risk adoptions*** of children in such circumstances as an alternative to having children remain in permanent foster care placements. Parents who adopt at-risk children knowingly assume the risk that a biological parent may later appear and attempt to challenge the adoption.

Permanency planning
planning designed to place children who have been removed from their homes into, healthy, stable, "permanent" homes by either returning them to their biological parents or placing them in adoptive homes as soon as possible

At-risk adoption
an adoption that is at risk of being challenged at a later date because the rights of one or both biological parents have not been terminated; an alternative to permanent foster care

PARALEGAL APPLICATION 14.3

SAFE HAVEN LAWS: STATE-SPONSORED ABANDONMENT OF NEWBORNS? WHOM DO THEY PROTECT AND WHOM DO THEY HARM?

Beginning in 1999 when Texas passed its "Baby Moses" law, a majority of the states enacted safe haven laws allowing a parent, or an agent of a parent, of an unwanted newborn to anonymously leave the baby at a "safe haven" center without fear of legal charges of abandonment or child endangerment, etc., provided there is no evidence of abuse. The applicable Florida statute provides: "Except where there is actual or suspected child abuse or neglect, any parent who leaves a newborn infant...has the absolute right to remain anonymous and to leave at any time and may not be pursued or followed unless the parent seeks to reclaim the newborn infant."[32] Safe haven centers are usually located at medical facilities and police and fire stations. The center subsequently delivers the newborn to the appropriate child-protective agency. Although the parent is not required to provide or accept any information, some states require the safe haven provider to whom the newborn is relinquished to ask the parent for medical and family information and to give the parent information regarding adoption resources. No two states' safe haven laws are exactly the same, but all set maximum age limits for babies that can be left, with most ranging from three to thirty days of age (although Missouri and North Dakota cover children up to a year old). In some states, the parent may be able to reclaim the child within a certain period of time by following prescribed procedures. In the case of abandoned babies, the identity and whereabouts of both biological parents are unknown, and the burden of making a good-faith effort to identify and notify them of a petition for adoption eventually rests with the state's primary social services agency.

SIDEBAR

Safe haven laws protect newborns from infanticide and abandonment in dumpsters, high school lavatories, and other sites where they are at considerable risk. They provide an incentive to mothers to bring their babies to locations where they will receive appropriate care and medical attention and be placed in nurturing homes pending adoption. This serves mothers and babies well, but what about the fathers of these children? Do safe haven laws violate their rights to notice and an opportunity to be heard and consent before their children are effectively abandoned and placed for adoption?

Safe haven law
a law that allows a parent, or an agent of a parent, of an unwanted newborn to anonymously leave the baby at a safe haven center, such as a hospital emergency room, without fear of legal charges of abandonment or child endangerment, etc., provided there is no evidence of abuse

Consent

Each state establishes by statute or administrative regulation the requirements governing consent to the kind(s) of adoption permitted in the jurisdiction: who must consent, the form of the consent, when the consent can be given, and under what circumstances it can be revoked. The rules are designed to respect and balance the constitutionally protected rights of birth parents and the rights of the adoptive parents who are seeking to establish a new family unit with confidence in its permanence.

Who Must Consent?   Absent involuntary termination, the mother's consent (or surrender of parental rights) is required, and the father's consent may be required depending on the circumstances (whether he is married to the mother, has an established relationship with the child, etc.). Depending on the jurisdiction, the consent may be solely to a termination of parental rights or both to termination of parental rights and to the specific adoption, as in an independent adoption. In the case

Surrender

a formal document in which a legal (usually biological) parent gives up his or her parental rights to a specific child

of a step-parent adoption, the consent of the custodial spouse/parent is solely to the adoption and not to a termination of his or her parental rights. If the adoptee has attained the age of majority, parental consent is not required. In most states, courts will consider the wishes of the child and, in some states, the adoptee's consent may be required if he or she has reached a certain age (usually twelve to fourteen).[33] If the parental rights of the biological parents have been terminated, parental consent to the adoption is not required, and the parent(s) cannot block an adoption of their child.

In What Form Is the Consent Given? If the birth parents are willing to relinquish their parental rights, this is usually accomplished by their executing a formal document commonly called a **surrender** of parental rights or a consent to adoption and termination of parental rights. The consent must be in an impartially witnessed and notarized writing that clearly identifies the child and the parental rights being terminated. To be valid, it must be fully informed and free from duress, fraud, and undue influence. In some states, a voluntary surrender must be followed by a court order confirming the termination of parental rights.

PARALEGAL APPLICATION 14.4

MAKING CONSENT COUNT

The Child Welfare League of America and other advocates and practitioners recommend that, in order for a mother's consent to adoption to be meaningful and binding, certain precautions be taken even if not mandated by state law or administrative regulation. Such steps protect both the biological mother by informing her decision and also the prospective adoptive parents by promoting finality in adoptive placements. They also help to balance the power relationship between mothers with few resources who are experiencing maximum stress and adoptive parents who are more likely to be economically secure, emotionally stable, and eager for the adoption to proceed. Suggested measures include:

- **Counseling:** More than half the states require that the mother participate in some degree of counseling before placing her child for adoption. "Counseling for parents, ... can help parents to 'own' their decisions.... Counseling for mothers should include providing information about alternatives to adoption, options within adoption, legal steps and consequences involved in adoption, and possible effects of adoption on themselves and their children. Ideally, counseling will also help mothers resolve issues that arise with the fathers and family members."[34] The counselor should be a neutral third person who has no interest in the mother's ultimate decision.

- **Legal advice:** Mothers should be given copies of all documents they will be asked to sign and have an opportunity to review them and raise questions with an attorney. They should be advised about "whether they may give binding consent before the birth, after the birth, or only after the passage of a certain number of days or hours after the birth. They should be informed about whether they have any right to revoke their consent and, if so, when and how to do so and whether revocation means automatic return of the child or a judicial best-interests determination. If any agreements are contemplated between the mother and the prospective adoptive parents, such as agreements concerning providing information about the child's development, they should be informed about whether and under what circumstances the agreements are enforceable."[35]

- **Sufficient time:** Mothers relinquishing their parental rights and consenting to adoption should not be rushed into the decision, a luxury most state laws do not afford them.

When Can the Consent Be Given? Ideally, if the consent is voluntary, it should (and in some states must) be given prior to or simultaneously with filing of the adoption petition. If the adoption is of a newborn, some states permit consent to be given prior to the birth of the child, but the majority of states specify that it can be given only after a certain period following the birth (generally three days). The rationale for such restrictions is to minimize the situations in which a birth mother experiencing the emotional impact of delivering the child changes her mind and claims that an earlier consent was given under duress. Once the consent is given, some states provide a time limit within which it can be revoked.

Under What Circumstances Can Consent Be Revoked? Most states provide that a consumer has seventy-two hours to rescind an ordinary business contract and yet, in many states, a mother's consent to adoption may be given and become irrevocable in fewer than four days after a child's birth. The general rule is that a consent to adoption that is given voluntarily, knowingly, and intelligently cannot be revoked absent proof that the consent was obtained by means of fraud, duress, or undue influence. Absent such circumstances, many states do not permit revocations.

When revocation is permitted, it usually must be written, witnessed, and notarized and given within a limited period of time. Generally, the revocation must be submitted to the court and may or may not be approved, based on the court's discretion and standards, which vary from state to state. Simple changes of heart are usually insufficient, but a minor's claim that she received no counseling, was provided with no information about other options, and was coerced to consent by her parents may well prevail. (See Paralegal Application 14.5.) When the matter is considered by the court, the adoptive parents may contest the revocation and ask that the court dispense with the parental consent requirement in the best interests of the child.

Paralegal Practice Tip
The Indian Child Welfare Act prevents a mother from consenting to an adoption until ten days after the child's birth and allows her to revoke her consent until the adoption is final.

PARALEGAL APPLICATION 14.5

YOU BE THE JUDGE

THE FACTS

When T.F. was sixteen years old, she and her boyfriend, R.O., had A.L.O., a baby girl. T.F. correctly indicated her age to her doctor and on the certified paternity acknowledgment she and R.O. executed. They initially planned to raise A.L.O., but, after three weeks, decided they were not able to handle the responsibility. The father then asked if his sister and brother-in-law, Jennifer and Branch Martin, would consider adopting the child, and they agreed to do so.

During the relinquishment and adoption process, the mother misrepresented her age as over eighteen on all the documents, and everyone apparently believed her. However, when she went through counseling and signed the papers, she was actually only seventeen and still a minor. Under Montana law (MCA Section 42-2-405(2)), "In a direct parental placement adoption, a relinquishment and consent to adopt executed by a parent who is a minor is not valid unless the minor parent has been advised by an attorney who does not represent the prospective adoptive parent" and the legal fees "are an allowable expense that may be paid by prospective adoptive parents...." The Martins were aware of the requirement but claimed they did not know T.F. was a minor, and T.F. stated she was unaware the Martins would have paid for an attorney for her.

continued

Despite the Montana law prohibiting revocation of consent more than thirty days after termination of parental rights, T.F. filed a motion to set aside the adoption because she was a minor without legal representation at the time she signed the relinquishment papers. She testified that she had trouble understanding the paperwork and that it all looked the same to her. She also claimed that Jennifer Martin and Jennifer's mother called her daily, encouraging her to sign the papers and assuring her that she could see A.L.O. any time she wanted, but later, after signing, she learned she would not be able to do so.

The District Court set aside the termination of parental rights and voided the decree of adoption. The Martins appealed the order and sought a reversal and return of A.L.O. to their care, claiming equitable and judicial estoppel among other theories.

SIDEBAR

How do you think the Montana Supreme Court should decide this case? Does it make a difference that it involves an independent/private adoption? Why? What are the arguments in favor of T.F.? The Martins? What would be in the best interests of the child, or don't the child's interests matter in this context? Read the case (*In re Adoption of A.L.O.*, 2006 MT 59, 331 Mont. 334, 132 P.3d 543 (2006)) on the companion website to see what the court did.)

Termination of parental rights the judicial severing of the legal relationship between a parent and child and associated rights; may be voluntary or involuntary

---

Paralegal Practice Tip
Adoptive parents, like biological parents, may have their parental rights terminated if they prove to be unfit to care for their adopted children.

Involuntary Termination of Parental Rights

Because parents have a constitutionally protected right in the parent-child relationship, their rights as parents generally cannot be terminated without notice and an opportunity to be heard in a termination proceeding. Although there is no parallel constitutional requirement that they be provided with counsel if they cannot afford an attorney, in most states, "parents have a right to counsel when the state seeks to terminate their parental rights. The ethical duty to provide competent and zealous representation extends to all clients, including those faced with potential termination of their parental rights. Personal biases cannot compromise advocacy on behalf of the client. The vast majority of parents in termination proceedings are indigent, which often means that their counsel is appointed by the court or provided through a public defender or contract system. The representation of parents by overworked and underpaid attorneys results in claims by parents that their counsel was ineffective."[36]

The states establish by statute, administrative regulation, and case law the circumstances in which termination may occur given clear and convincing evidence of parental unfitness and the best interest of a child. Paralegals are often surprised and troubled about the degree of "unfitness" that must be present in order for a parent's rights to be terminated. Given that parental rights are afforded a high degree of constitutional protection, before they can be terminated there must be clear and convincing evidence of severe inadequacies in parenting that place the child at risk. It is not necessarily enough that parents are overly strict or lax in discipline; that they fail to supervise their children and "let them run wild"; that the home is messy; that "negative" influences are present; or that the parents drink to excess, use "recreational" drugs, or have been convicted of crimes. Circumstances that may result in a termination include:

- Failure to support the child's basic needs, although nonsupport alone may not be enough
- Failure to see or contact the child for a specified period of time

- Failure to provide a safe environment for the child
- Incarceration of a parent for serious crimes against the child and/or the other parent of the child(ren)
- Failure to participate in a court-ordered rehabilitation or family-reunification plan
- Legal determination of incompetence of the parent and placement under guardianship

Even if these factors all are present, before rights can be terminated, the parent must be given a reasonable opportunity to address his or her parental deficiencies with or without the child being present in the home. In the final analysis however, the best interests of the child standard is the paramount consideration as the courts weigh the impact of parental inadequacies on the child's physical, emotional, and mental welfare and need for a stable home and continuity in care. To the extent feasible, many courts will consider "the child's opinion of his or her own best interests in the matter."[37]

PARALEGAL APPLICATION 14.6

WOULD YOU GIVE MOM ANOTHER CHANCE?

THE FACTS

A mother of five children had an extensive history of substance abuse and dysfunctional relationships with a series of men, three of whom had abused both her and some of the children. Her problem with drugs over the years impaired her ability to parent and exposed the children to drugs, drug paraphernalia, and other drug users. She had come to the attention of the Department of Social Services on multiple occasions, based on complaints that she was neglecting the children, and the children were removed from the home. For two years, she failed to cooperate in the service plan designed to reunify the family. The department eventually changed the goal of the plan for the family from reunification to adoption. Six weeks before the initially scheduled trial on termination of her parental rights, the mother entered a four- to six-month residential treatment program from which she successfully graduated. The mother presented evidence that she had participated successfully in a drug rehabilitation program. She was responding well to therapy and had submitted to required drug screens, all of which were negative. She was actively involved in outpatient services including substance abuse programming that encompassed five AA meetings a week, early recovery and relapse-prevention counseling, and domestic violence therapy. She was living with her mother, working two jobs, and visiting her five children once a month.

SIDEBAR

When deciding whether to terminate the rights of a parent, what factors do you think the court should consider? What if the parent's lack of fitness is "temporary" rather than chronic? What if the parent is taking steps and making significant progress toward addressing his or her inadequacies as a parent? How much leeway should be given to parents when an indeterminate period of time will be required for their recovery? Would you terminate the mother's parental rights in this particular case? To see what the Massachusetts Supreme Judicial Court decided to do and why, see the case *Adoption of Elena*, 446 Mass. 24, 841 N.E.2d 252 (2006), available on the companion website.

Paralegal Practice Tip

For many years, several states did not allow foster parents to petition to adopt a child in their care. That bar has now been lifted in virtually all states. Although foster parents now have standing to petition for adoption, they cannot block an adoption. However, in some states, a ***foster parent*** has standing to petition for termination of the parental rights of one or both parents of a child in foster care, on the grounds that the parent has abandoned the child. The highly publicized *Kingsley* case (*Kingsley v. Kingsley*, 623 So. 2d 780 (Fla. Dist. Ct. App. 1993)) initially involved the effort of a minor child to, in effect, divorce his mother by petitioning to have her parental rights terminated. The court denied the child's petition based on a minor child's lack of standing to initiate legal proceedings in his or her own name. However, the child's foster parent subsequently was able to accomplish the desired result and eventually adopted the child.

Foster parent

a person or persons who provide a temporary home for a child when his or her parents are temporarily unwilling or unable to do so

The Americans with Disabilities Act (ADA)[38] provides: "… no qualified individual with a disability shall, by reason of such disability, be excluded from participation in or denied the benefits of the services, programs, or activities of a public entity, or be subjected to discrimination by any such entity."[39] Under the Act, a disability includes a physical or mental impairment that substantially limits one or more of a person's major life activities. The states are divided with respect to the question of whether or not the ADA applies to termination proceedings. Courts in states such as Iowa, Maine, and Washington have held that it does apply, whereas courts in Connecticut, Vermont, and Wisconsin have concluded that it does not. If it does apply, the state may be required to accommodate the special needs of parents with recognized disabilities that impact their parenting skills when those individuals are threatened with termination of their parental rights.

IDENTIFICATION OF POTENTIAL ADOPTIVE PARENTS AND ADOPTEES
Who Can Adopt?

Basic threshold requirements for potential adoptive parents vary but customarily relate to age, marital status, race, religion, health, and sexual orientation. Additional factors relating to parenting skills, emotional stability, financial resources, and nature of the home environment are also scrutinized—generally in the context of home studies conducted prior to placement and finalization of an adoption. (See Exhibit 14.2 later in this chapter.)

Age.   Adoption statutes usually require that the petitioner be an adult under state law (typically at least eighteen to twenty-one years of age). Although there is customarily no maximum age set, given the basic purpose of adoption, adoptive parents usually must be older than the adoptee and of such an age that they are able to provide continuity of care to adoptees until they reach the age of majority. (See Paralegal Application 14.7.)

PARALEGAL APPLICATION **14.7**

CAN A PERSON EVER BE TOO OLD TO BECOME AN ADOPTIVE PARENT?

THE FACTS

This case involves a seventy-seven-year-old paternal great-aunt's petition to adopt a four-year-old child who has lived with her since the age of two months. Evidence was presented that the child's mother:

- had evicted the child and her father from the family home when the child was an infant and put their belongings in the street in inclement weather

- had neglected the child and failed to protect her from sexual abuse by her half-brother

- had failed to cooperate with the child's treatment plan or the service plan designed to address the neglect

- used marijuana and cocaine and was convicted of distributing cocaine prior to the child's birth

continued

- had a history of unstable relationships with men
- functioned poorly under stress
- failed to comply with a child support order

Although the child has supervised visits with her mother every two weeks, the great-aunt has provided a stable and loving home for the child for virtually all her life and has done so with little support from either of the child's parents. In the event of her death or disability, she has arranged for two backup caretakers, aged forty-one and sixty-seven, who are family members well known to the child. She has also made financial arrangements to provide for the child. The mother opposes termination of her parental rights and granting of the petition.

SIDEBAR

Assuming that the father has consented to the adoption, what do you think the court should do given these facts? Explain your response. See if you agree with the appellate court's opinion in this case, *In re A.C.G.*, 894 A.2d 436 (D.C. App. Ct. 2006). The full opinion is available on the companion website.

Marital Status.   Technically, either single or married persons usually may adopt. However, as indicated earlier in this chapter, subtle, if not explicit, preferences for married couples still persist.

Race.   The pendulum has swung back and forth with respect to the role of race in adoption decisions. Prior to the 1950s, many states banned transracial adoptions by statute until such laws were struck down as unconstitutional. In the 1950s and 1960s, transracial adoptions became more common, given a decline in white infants available for adoption. However, by the 1970s, black advocacy groups took a strong stand against the adoption of black children by white families, even if it delayed placement, claiming that only black families could appropriately address the unique developmental needs of black children. Racial matching once again became the norm, motivated not by racial discrimination but rather by a concern for the best interests of minority children. The roller coaster finally stopped in 1994 when Congress passed the Multiethnic Placement Act (MEPA), which provides:

> A person or government that is involved in adoption or foster care placements may not (A) deny to any individual the opportunity to become an adoptive or a foster parent, on the basis of race, color, or national origin of the individual, or of the child involved; or (B) delay or deny the placement of a child for adoption or into foster care, on the basis of the race, color or national origin of the adoptive or foster parent, or the child, involved.[40]

As with custody decisions, race should not be used as the sole basis for adoption decisions, subject to limited exceptions. However, the court can consider race as a factor when determining if a particular placement will be in the best interests of the child. As a practical matter, courts and agencies often prefer to place a child with parents of the same race and ethnic background if possible. In the case of American Indian children, under federal law race MUST be considered, in an effort to address a Congressional finding that a high percentage of Indian families are broken up by the removal of their children by nontribal public and private agencies and placement in non-Indian foster and adoptive homes and institutions.[41] The Indian Child Welfare Act provides: "In any adoptive placement of an Indian child under state law, a preference shall be given, in the absence of good cause to the contrary, to a placement with (1) a member of the child's extended family; (2) other members of the Indian child's tribe; or (3) other Indian families."[42] The Act is intended to protect the best interests of Indian children and to promote the stability and security of Indian tribes and families. To that end, it established heightened standards that must be applied in child custody actions involving Indian children (including adoptions and actions to terminate parental rights). The Act defines an "Indian child" as "an unmarried person who is under eighteen and ... (b) is eligible for membership in an Indian tribe and is the biological child of a member of an Indian tribe."[43]

Religion. As a matter of practice, agencies customarily place children in homes practicing the same religion as their biological parents, especially when the child is older and has already begun practicing a particular religion. However, interfaith adoptions are not constitutionally prohibited.

Health. An individual with a disability should not be discriminated against as a potential adoptive parent, provided the disability does not unduly interfere with the capacity to parent such that an adoption would not be in the best interests of the child.

Sexual Preference. Increasing numbers of same-sex couples are seeking legal recognition not only of their relationships but also of their status as parents. Some have custody of children born to prior heterosexual marriages. Others have used reproductive technology to create the children they are parenting. Co-parents of the same sex seeking to adopt under these or other circumstances encounter distinctly different results depending on where they reside. When the decisions in such cases are not prescribed by statute or regulation, they are left to the court's discretion and are generally decided according to a best interests of the child standard. Lingering biases with respect to homosexuality may still influence these decisions in some cases.

- As of the summer of 2007, a handful of states such as Arkansas, Florida, Mississippi, and Utah expressly prohibit adoptions by same-sex partners by statute or administrative regulation.[44] The Mississippi statute states simply, "Adoption by couples of the same gender is prohibited."[45] The applicable Florida statute provides, "no person eligible to adopt under this statute may adopt if that person is a homosexual."[46] (See Case 14.2.) The constitutionality of these statutes is likely to continue to be challenged, given the U.S. Supreme Court's decision in *Lawrence v. Texas* holding unconstitutional a Texas statute banning private homosexual conduct between consenting adults.[47]
- Some states, such as California, Connecticut, and Vermont, have enacted legislation expressly allowing adoption by same-sex partners.[48] Vermont provides by statute that (1) any person may adopt or be adopted by another person for the purpose of creating the relationship of parent and child between them; (2) if a family unit consists of a parent and the parent's partner, and adoption is in the best interests of the child, the partner of a parent may adopt the child of the parent.[49] Prior to allowing same-sex marriage in June 2008, California had already provided by statute that domestic partners could adopt utilizing the same procedural rules as for step-parent adoption.[50]
- Appellate courts in several states such as Illinois, New Jersey, New York, Ohio, and Tennessee have interpreted their respective general adoption laws to allow same-sex partners or couples to adopt. A Delaware court described adoption by same-sex partners as a means to formalize the close emotional relationship of the two men involved in the case.[51]

PARALEGAL APPLICATION 14.8

WHERE DO YOU STAND?

In a case involving the Florida statute banning adoptions by homosexuals, the U.S. Court of Appeals for the Eleventh Circuit stated the following with respect to the state's rationale for the ban:

> Florida contends that the statute is only one aspect of its broader adoption policy, which is designed to create adoptive homes that resemble the nuclear family as closely as possible. Florida argues that the statute is rationally related to Florida's interest in furthering the best interests of adopted children by placing them in families with married mothers and fathers. Such homes, Florida asserts, provide the stability that marriage affords and the presence of both male and female authority figures, which it considers critical to optimal childhood development and socialization. In particular, Florida emphasizes a vital role that dual-gender parenting plays in shaping sexual and gender identity and in providing heterosexual role modeling. Florida argues that disallowing adoption into homosexual households, which are necessarily motherless or fatherless and lack the stability that comes with marriage, is a rational means of furthering Florida's interest in promoting adoption by marital families.[52]

> ...

> ...The State of Florida has made the determination that it is not in the best interests of its displaced children to be adopted by individuals who "engage in current, voluntary homosexual activity," Cox, 627 So. 2d at 1215, and we have found nothing in the Constitution that forbids this policy judgment. Thus any argument that the Florida legislature was misguided in its decision is one of legislative policy, not constitutional law. The legislature is the proper forum for this debate, and we do not sit as a superlegislature "to award by judicial decree what was not achievable by political consensus." Thomasson v. Perry, 80 F.3d 915, 923 (4th Cir. 1996).[53]

SIDEBAR

Despite Florida's stated public policy, Florida law permits adoption by unmarried individuals, and 25 percent of children coming out of the Florida foster care system are adopted by single parents.[54] Six plaintiffs brought this particular case. The most prominently featured was Steven Lofton, a gay foster father who had petitioned to adopt a boy born HIV-positive in 1991, whom he had raised for more than a decade since infancy. He had cared for several HIV-positive infants over the years, and the care he provided was described as "exemplary" by all accounts and was chronicled in news stories, editorials, and on national television.

Assume that you work for a legislator in a state that is considering restricting adoption to heterosexual married couples. She has solicited your opinion on the subject. How would you respond? What are the arguments in support of such legislation? Against it?[55]

Who May Be Adopted?

Although in the vast majority of cases the individual adopted (the adoptee) is a child, in most states both children and adults may be adopted, provided that all of the requirements for a valid adoption are satisfied. However, as indicated in

Chapter 5 on nonmarital families, adoptions of one partner by the other in a same-sex couple are not permitted in some states.

HOME STUDIES

Home study
assessments of prospective adoptive parents and home environments customarily conducted by state-licensed social workers

Home studies may occur at two points during the adoption process: pre- and post-temporary placement with the adoptive family. Although not usually required by the state in independent adoptions, in agency adoptions all states require that a home study be conducted to ensure the suitability of the adoptive home prior to placement. Virtually all states require post-placement studies, with limited exceptions such as step-parent adoptions. An example of the nature and focus of home studies is provided in Exhibit 14.2, which contains an excerpt from provisions of the Iowa Administrative Code for the Human Services Department governing adoption services.

Home studies customarily involve multiple visits. The first home study is designed to screen the adoptive parents and usually involves extensive interviews with the parents themselves regarding their goals and expectations with respect to the adoption as well as their attitudes and beliefs about childrearing. It may also include interviews with the parents' neighbors, school personnel, employers, extended family members, and other references in an effort to assess the adoptive parents' emotional and financial stability, character, work history, and relationships with others. The second home study is designed to assess the child's adjustment to the adoptive home before the adoption is finalized.

Home visits are usually conducted by state-licensed social workers who prepare reports and make recommendations to the court, much as GALs appointed by the courts do in contested custody cases. Although sometimes criticized by prospective adoptive parents as unwarranted, overly intrusive, and biased toward the middle-class concept of the ideal family, most social workers would agree that home visits serve to protect the safety and well-being of adopted children. Agencies and courts will not knowingly place adoptees in homes in which the parents have a documented history of substance abuse, violence, or criminal activity.

Courts recognize that there is no such thing as a perfect parent, but prospective adoptive parents need to be able to effectively care for children in a manner that supports and promotes the children's best interests. The prospective adoptive parents do not need to be wealthy, but they should at least be financially responsible and have sufficient resources to adequately provide for each individual child's unique needs. In some cases, those needs may be substantial. For example, a child may have a serious medical condition requiring around-the-clock care and major modifications to the physical structure of the adoptive home.

Jurisdiction and Venue

In order for a court to grant an adoption, the court must have subject matter jurisdiction over adoption. Subject matter jurisdiction is established by statute and may reside in a court of general jurisdiction such as a Superior Court, or in courts of limited jurisdiction such as a Family or Juvenile Court. Venue is commonly proper in the county where the child or the biological or the adoptive parent(s) reside.

EXHIBIT 14.2 Iowa Administrative Code/Human Services Department [441]/Chapter 108 Licensing and Regulation of Child-Placing Agencies/441-108.9(238)(4) Services to Adoptive Applicants (c) Adoptive Home Study and (d) Record checks

c. Adoptive home study. The home study consists of a family assessment which shall include at least two face-to-face interviews with the applicant and at least one face-to-face interview with each member of the household. At least one interview shall take place in the applicant's home. The assessment shall include, but need not be limited to, the following:

(1) Motivation for adoption and whether the family has biological, adopted or foster children.

(2) Family and extended family's attitude toward accepting an adopted child, and plans for discussing adoption with the child.

(3) The attitude toward adoption of the significant other people involved with the family.

(4) Emotional stability; marital history, including verification of marriages and divorces; assessment of marital relationship; and compatibility of the adoptive parents.

(5) Ability to cope with problems, stress, frustrations, crises, separation and loss.

(6) Medical, mental, or emotional conditions which may affect the applicant's ability to parent a child.

(7) Ability to provide for the child's physical and emotional needs and respect the child's cultural and religious identity.

(8) Adjustment of biological and previously adopted children, if any, including their attitudes toward adoption, relationship with others, and school performance.

(9) Capacity to give and receive affection.

(10) Statements from at least three references provided by the family and other unsolicited references that the agency may wish to contact.

(11) Attitudes of the adoptive applicants toward the birth parents and the reasons the child is available for adoption.

(12) Income information, ability to provide for a child, and a statement as to the need for adoption subsidy for a special needs child, or children.

(13) Disciplinary practices that will be used.

(14) History of abuse by family members and treatment.

(15) Assessment of, commitment to, and capacity to maintain other significant relationships.

(16) Substance use or abuse by members of the family and treatment.

(17) Recommendations for type of child, number, age, sex, characteristics, and special needs of children best parented by this family.

d. Record checks. The licensed child-placing agency shall submit record checks for each applicant and for anyone who is 14 years of age or older living in the home of the applicant to determine whether they have any founded child abuse reports or criminal convictions or have been placed on the sex offender registry....

Any adoption, other than one involving a step-parent, relative, or guardian that involves adoption of a child who is born or lives in one state (the "sending state") by someone who resides in another state (the "receiving state"), must comply with the requirements of the Interstate Compact on the Placement of Children (ICPC), adopted in all fifty states. Each state has a designated ICPC office charged with responsibility for coordinating interstate adoptions. When an adoption is proposed by a court in a sending state, the ICPC office in that state provides written notice of the proposed adoption to the ICPC office in the receiving state. The notice includes basic identifying information about the child, the child's parents or guardian, and the proposed placement along with the reason for the placement. The receiving state then conducts a home study and, if approved, notifies the sending state that approval for the child's entry to the receiving state to be placed has been granted. A failure to comply with ICPC requirements can result in a voiding of the adoption.

PETITION FOR ADOPTION

An adoption action is usually commenced when a Petition for Adoption is filed in the name of the child by the prospective adoptive parents or the agency (see Exhibit 14.3). In most jurisdictions, the Petition must be accompanied by the affidavits or consent forms from the biological parents surrendering their rights. The form and content of the petition varies state to state but usually includes the following at a minimum:

- The name(s) and address of the petitioners
- The nature of their relationship to each other (married, unmarried, partners)
- Data about the petitioners, such as their ages and occupations
- The name, sex, age (date of birth), and religion of the child
- The name by which the adoptive child will be known once adopted
- Documentation of any prior custodial actions involving the child
- Consents to the adoption attached or an indication of why there is no consent
- Type of adoption (agency, independent, etc.)
- Certification that there are no additional persons interested in the proceeding

NOTICE, PRELIMINARY HEARING, INTERLOCUTORY DECREE, PRE-ADOPTION PLACEMENT, AND FINAL DECREE

Paralegal Practice Tip
If the child is a nonmarital child and the biological father has neither consented to the adoption nor had his parental rights terminated, he should be served with notice of the petition for adoption—by personal service or by publication if necessary. Other interested parties who may be given notice include foster parents, relatives who may have been caring for the child.

Once the Petition is filed and served on all interested parties, the court schedules a preliminary hearing in which the pending adoption may or may not be contested. If it is uncontested or not successfully contested, the court customarily then issues an interlocutory decree granting temporary custody of the child to the adoptive parents. The adoption is generally not finalized until the final hearing is held six months to a year later. During that period, a follow-up home study is usually conducted.

Whatever their type, all adoptions must be approved by the court. The court makes a determination as to whether or not all statutory requirements have been met and the adoption will be in the best interests of the child. Most adoption final hearings are joyful events and may be conducted in the judge's chambers, depending on the circumstances. Even if held in the courtroom, the

EXHIBIT 14.3 Petition for Adoption

Courtesy of the State of Colorado

☐District Court ☐Denver Juvenile Court _____County, Colorado Court Address: **IN THE MATTER OF THE PETITION OF:** _____ (name of person(s) seeking to adopt) **FOR THE ADOPTION OF A CHILD**	
	▲ **COURT USE ONLY** ▲
Attorney or Party Without Attorney (Name and Address):	Case Number:
Phone Number: E-mail: FAX Number: Atty. Reg. #:	Division Courtroom

PETITION FOR ADOPTION

The Petitioner(s) being desirous of adopting a child so as to make said child for all intents and purposes the legal child of Petitioner(s) and to render him/her capable of inheriting their estate, state(s) the following facts:

Information about the Petitioner(s):

Petitioner #1: _____ (Full Name)

Date of Birth: _____ Race: _____ Place of Birth: _____

Current Mailing Address: _____

City & Zip: _____

Home Phone #: _____ Work Phone #: _____ Cell #: _____

Length of Residence in Colorado: _____ Occupation: _____

Place of residence at the time of birth of the child.

_____	_____	_____	_____
Street Address	City	State	Zip Code

Petitioner #2: _____ (Full Name)

Date of Birth: _____ Race: _____ Place of Birth: _____

Current Mailing Address: _____

City & Zip: _____

Home Phone #: _____ Work Phone #: _____ Cell #: _____

Length of Residence in Colorado: _____ Occupation: _____

Place of residence at the time of birth of the child.

_____	_____	_____	_____
Street Address	City	State	Zip Code

☐ If applicable, maiden name of adopting mother: _____ Date of Marriage: _____

☐ The Petitioner(s) has/have attached as "Attachment A" a current fingerprint-based criminal history records check as required by §19-5-207(2.5)(a)(I)-(IV), C.R.S.

☐ The Petitioner(s) has/have attached as "Attachment B" the TRAILS background check as required by §19-5-207, C.R.S.

continued

If the Petitioner(s) has/have been convicted of a felony or misdemeanor in any of the following areas, please check the appropriate box and identify for the Court the date of the conviction and if it was a felony or misdemeanor.

☐ child abuse or neglect on _____ (date). ☐Felony☐Misdemeanor

☐ spousal abuse on _____ (date). ☐Felony☐Misdemeanor

☐ any crime against a child on _____ (date). ☐Felony☐Misdemeanor

☐ any crime, the underlying factual basis of which has been found by the Court to include an act of domestic violence on _____ (date). ☐Felony☐Misdemeanor

☐ violation of a Protection/Restraining Order on _____ (date). ☐Felony☐Misdemeanor

☐ any crime involving violence, rape, sexual assault, or homicide on _____ (date). ☐Felony☐Misdemeanor

☐ any felony involving physical assault or battery on _____ (date). ☐Felony☐Misdemeanor

☐ any felony drug-related conviction within the past five years, at a minimum on _____(date). ☐Felony☐Misdemeanor

Identify all children of the Petitioner(s) (both natural and adopted and both living and deceased).

Full Name of Child	Full Name of Child

Facts concerning the child to be adopted. (Do not fill in if placement is by an agency or Department of Social Services.)

Full Name: _____ Date of Birth: _____

Place of Birth: _____ Relationship of child to Petitioner(s), if any _____

Place of Residence: _____

The child ☐is ☐is not a member or eligible to be a member of an Indian tribe as defined by the Indian Welfare Act. If applicable, name of tribe _____.

☐ Notice of this Petition has been provided to the parent or Indian custodian of the child and to the tribal agent of the tribe, as required by §19-1-126(1)(c), C.R.S.

☐ Reasonable efforts have been made to send notice to the identified persons as follows:

_____

_____

Attach the postal receipts to this petition, indicating that notice was properly sent. If the postal receipts have not been returned at the time of filing, the postal receipts or copies shall be filed with the Court within ten days of the filing of this petition.

☐ If applicable, inquiries have been made by the County Department of Social Services or child placement agency to determine whether the child is an Indian child as follows:

_____

_____

The child has been in the care and custody of Petitioner(s) since _____ (date).

The legal custody of the child is with _____ (name).

continued

Full description of the property of the child, if any: _____

_____
Name and address of the Guardian(s) of the child and estate of the child, if any, have been appointed:

_____

Name of agency, if any, to which custody of the child has been given by proper order of the Court:

_____

Information about the Birth Parents of the Child:

Full Name of Birth father: _____

_____
Street Address   City   State   Zip Code

Full Name of Birth Mother: _____

_____
Street Address   City   State   Zip Code

The written consent(s) of the birth parent(s) ❏is/are attached **or** ❏is/are not attached.

The child will not be the subject of a pending dependency and neglect action when the adoption is heard.

If parental rights are relinquished, are terminated, or are being terminated in this action pursuant to §§19-5-101-108, C.R.S., as amended, or parent is deceased, state details:

_____

_____

_____

_____

Wherefore, the Petitioner(s) pray(s) that a Decree of Adoption be entered herein declaring said child to be the child of Petitioner(s) and that the name of said child be changed to: _____ (full name) and that said child shall be entitled to all of the rights and privileges and be subject to all of the obligations now conferred and imposed by law.

VERIFICATION AND ACKNOWLEDGEMENT

I swear/affirm under oath that I have read the foregoing Petition and that the statements set forth herein are true and correct to the best of my knowledge and belief.

_____   _____
Petitioner Signature   Date   Petitioner Signature   Date

_____   _____
Petitioner's Attorney Signature, if any   Petitioner's Attorney Signature, if any

Subscribed and affirmed, or sworn to before me   Subscribed and affirmed, or sworn to before me
in the County of _____,   in the County of _____,
State of _____, this _____   State of _____, this _____
day of _____, 20 ____.   day of _____, 20 ____.
My Commission Expires: _____   My Commission Expires: _____

_____   _____
Notary Public/Deputy Clerk   Notary Public/Deputy Clerk

proceedings are closed to the public and the related records are sealed. Once the adoption is finalized, a Final Decree of Adoption is issued by the court, and a new birth certificate designating the adoptive parents as the child's legal parents is issued for the public record.

CHALLENGES TO THE ADOPTION

Adoption abrogation
an annulment, repeal, or undoing of an adoption

In general, adoptions are considered final, but challenges do arise. The three most common sources of challenges are unwed biological fathers who never received notice of their child's adoption (see Case 14.2), biological parents who seek to revoke their consents, and adoptive parents who seek to *abrogate* an adoption they believe was wrongfully procured by an agency or individual.

CASE **14.2** *In re Doe,* 159 Ill. 2d 347, 638 N.E.2d 181 (1994)

THE FACTS

Similar to the "Baby Jessica" case[56] in 1993, this high-profile case, popularly known as the "Baby Richard" case, caused a national media frenzy. Baby Richard was the biological child of Daniella Janikova and Otakar Kirchner. When he was born, his parents were not married. At the time of the birth, the father was out of the country taking care of his dying grandmother in Czechoslovakia. Four days after the child was born, Daniella consented to have the child adopted by John and Jane Doe after being told by a relative of the father that Otakar was involved with another woman. She subsequently told Otakar that the baby had died at birth. He was suspicious of her story and promptly began checking birth and death records and even checked the garbage at the mother's home to look for evidence that a baby was living there. Approximately two months after the birth, he learned the truth. Daniella and Otakar subsequently reconciled and were married about six months after the child's birth and sought the return of the child. They challenged the legality of the adoption and alleged that the father's consent was required, because he had not abandoned the child and there was no evidence that he was an unfit parent. He further argued that his lack of contact with the baby immediately after birth was solely due to the mother's fraudulent conduct.

The trial court held that the father was unfit because he had failed to demonstrate a reasonable degree of interest, concern, or responsibility for his son during the first thirty days of his life as required by statute and thus his consent was not required. The court determined it was in Richard's best interests to remain with his adoptive parents with whom he had lived since he was four days old. The trial court's decision was upheld by the appeals court, basing its decision on the best interests of the child. The appeals court stated:

> Fortunately, the time has long past when children in our society were considered the property of their parents. Slowly, but finally, when it comes to children even the law has rid itself of the Dred Scott mentality that a human being can be considered a piece of property "belonging" to another human being. To hold that a child is the property of his parents is to deny the humanity of the child. Thus, in the present case we start with the premise that Richard is not a piece of property with property rights belonging to either his biological or adoptive parents. Richard "belongs" to no one but himself.

continued

...

A child's best interest is not part of an equation. It is not to be balanced against any other interest.[57]

The Illinois Supreme Court disagreed, finding that the father had been wrongfully deprived of the opportunity to express his interest in the child. It focused in its analysis of the situation on the preemptive rights of a natural parent in his own children apart from the best interest of the child.

Multiple appeals by the adoptive parents eventually failed despite a national public outcry and efforts by both the governor and state legislature of Illinois to influence the outcome by enacting a Bill that provided for a hearing to consider a child's best interests when an adoption is denied or revoked on appeal as it was in this case. At the age of four, the crying child was taken from his adoptive mother's arms and handed over to his biological father in the bright media glare.

SIDEBAR

This case basically involved the weighing of the best interests of the child against the biological father's right to consent to the adoption of his child. What relative weight do you think should be given in such situations to the best interests of the child? The interests of the adoptive parents? The conduct of the mother? The interests of the nonmarital father? Should it matter whether the nonmarital father learns about the adoption before or after it is finalized? Do you agree with the outcome in this case? Explain your response. The opinion is available in its entirety on the companion website.

Adoptive parents are no different from biological parents in the sense that their adopted children do not always turn out as they might hope. However, neither biological nor adoptive parents get to trade in their children for models they like better! Much as the courts are resistant to allowing biological parents to revoke their consents to adoption, they are likewise reluctant to permit adoptive parents to abrogate (undo) an adoption. The majority view is that adoptions cannot be abrogated by an adoptive parent.

Whether a parent is a man or a woman, homosexual or heterosexual, or adoptive or biological, in assuming that role, a person also assumes certain responsibilities, obligations, and duties. That person may not simply choose to shed the parental mantle because it becomes inconvenient, seems ill-advised in retrospect, or becomes burdensome because of a deterioration in the relationship with the children's other parent. To the contrary, of key importance is the relationship between parent and children, not between parent and parent. What we must focus on is the duties owed by a parent to her children, and those duties do not evaporate along with the relationship between the parents—indeed, those duties do not evaporate even if the relationship between the parent and children deteriorates.[58]

However, a few states, by statute or case law, permit adoptive parents to abrogate an adoption in exceptional circumstances. In isolated cases, adoptive parents do not get what they believe they bargained for, because an adoption agency or biological parent failed to inform (or actively deceived) them with respect to a major issue relating to the adoptee. For example, an agency may have failed to

Wrongful adoption
a tort action that an adoptive parent can bring against an adoption agency for failure to provide prior to adoption accurate and sufficient information regarding an adoptive child.

disclose the existence of a serious or costly medical condition or a history of psychiatric and behavioral problems, including fire setting, animal abuse, or violent conduct. Adoption agencies cannot warranty the children they place, but they do have a duty to provide accurate information known to them on the basis of which adoptive parents can make informed decisions. When they fail to do so, the adoptive parents may seek to revoke the adoption and bring an action against the agency for the tort of *wrongful adoption.*

THE PARALEGAL'S ROLE IN ADOPTION CASES

The paralegal's role in adoption cases depends primarily on four factors:

1. the extent to which the firm where the paralegal is employed specializes in adoption
2. the type of adoption involved
3. the client's role in the litigation: Is he or she the petitioner? Is he or she seeking to block the adoption? Is the client an agency?
4. the nature and level of the paralegal's skills

Primary tasks performed may include the following:

- researching state and federal statutes, case law, and procedural rules and regulations governing adoption in the applicable jurisdiction(s)
- creating websites and marketing strategies to recruit prospective adoptive parents and locate potential adoptees
- interviewing prospective adoptive parents, parents considering relinquishing their rights, and parents facing involuntary termination of their rights, to gather information relevant to the client's case
- researching issues such as the rights of nonmarital fathers to object to an adoption, the right of a child to consent to his or her adoption, involuntary termination of parental rights, and adoption by single persons or same-sex partners
- conducting a thorough search for a biological father whose whereabouts are unknown
- drafting and filing necessary paperwork, including petitions, consents, surrenders, ICPC paperwork, etc.
- drafting open adoption agreements
- scheduling home studies
- providing support to clients as they progress through the often emotionally draining adoption process
- monitoring payments for medical expenses to a birth mother intending to give up her child for adoption

CHAPTER **SUMMARY**

This chapter opens by defining the nature and purposes of adoption. Various types of adoptions are classified and described according to who can adopt, who facilitates the adoption, and the extent of post-adoption contact between the biological parents and the adoptive parents and/or the child. The major steps required to effect an adoption are introduced. Special emphasis is given to the contrast between the rights of nonmarital fathers and the rights of nonmarital mothers in case law and practice, the nature and role of putative father

registries, and the importance of effective consents. Several additional topics related to adoption are discussed and illustrated in cases, paralegal applications, and practice tips, including termination of parental rights, characteristics of prospective adoptive parents (including co-parents), safe haven laws, home studies, and challenges to adoptions. Multistate variations in adoption law and procedure are highlighted. The chapter closes with a description of the roles a paralegal might be called upon to play in the context of adoption cases.

KEY **TERMS**

Adoptee
Adoption
Adoption abrogation
Adoption registry
Agency adoption
At-risk adoption
Biology-plus rule
Closed adoption
Co-parent

Cut-off rule
De facto adoption
Equitable adoption/adoption by estoppel
Foster parent
Home study
Illegal/black market adoption
Independent adoption
International adoption
Joint petition for adoption

Open adoption
Permanency planning
Putative father
Putative father registry
Safe haven law
Standing
Surrender (of parental rights)
Termination of parental rights
Wrongful adoption

REVIEW **QUESTIONS**

1. Define adoption.
2. Identify the categories of individuals who can adopt children.
3. Define and distinguish between an independent and an agency adoption.
4. Define and give an example of an equitable adoption.
5. Define and distinguish between an open and a closed adoption.
6. Identify the basic steps in the adoption process.
7. Describe the nature and significance of the "biology-plus rule."
8. Describe the tort of interference with parental relationships.
9. Describe the nature and purpose of putative father registries.

10. Identify the kinds of circumstances in which a parent's rights may be terminated.
11. Identify the nature and purpose of permanency planning.
12. Describe the nature and purpose of "safe haven laws." Is there any downside to such laws?
13. Describe the nature and potential significance of an at-risk adoption.
14. Identify who must consent to an adoption and under what circumstances a consent can be revoked.
15. Describe the role race plays in adoption determinations.
16. Describe the role sexual orientation plays in adoption determinations.
17. Describe the nature and purpose of a home study.
18. Identify three circumstances in which an adoption may be challenged.

FOCUS ON **THE JOB**

THE FACTS

Jessica and Scott met in 2003 at a local tavern, where Jessica was tending bar and dealing drugs on a small scale, essentially to support her own habit. They quickly became involved. Scott did not join Jessica in using drugs until after he was involved in an automobile accident and was initially prescribed oxycontin for pain. A year after they met, Jessica became pregnant. Although she did not entirely stop using drugs while pregnant, she did cut back and eventually gave birth on June 23, 2005, to a healthy baby boy they named Michael ("Mike") after Jessica's father. Scott formally acknowledged paternity, and his name appears on the child's birth certificate. The couple (along with the baby) lived with Jessica's parents until Scott lost his job and the parents found out about the couple's drug use. They blamed all of Jessica's problems on him and threw him out of the house but allowed her to continue living there.

Scott was unemployed and homeless for about two months before he entered detox for a week, a secure rehabilitation facility for a month, and then a halfway house for six months. He regularly visited Mike and sent whatever financial support he could to Jessica, although he feared it simply went toward her cocaine addiction. He eventually got a job in construction (earning approximately $48,000 a year) and met and married Hayley, a high school English teacher (earning $45,000 a year) who is a caring and supportive partner eager to make a good life with him and raise Mike. Jessica is relieved at the prospect of not being responsible for the boy and is willing to consent to a step-parent adoption by Hayley as long as they will allow her to visit with the child twice a year for an afternoon and send her pictures and letters on a monthly basis.

Jessica's last name is Olivio and Scott's is Martinelli. The baby was given the father's last name at birth. The mother's address is 33 Main Street in your city and state. Scott is living with Hayley in her home at 903 Hale Street in your city and state. Scott was born on October 21, 1976, and Hayley was born on November 17, 1978. They are members of a Unitarian church. Jessica was formerly a practicing Catholic but has left the church. She is presently unemployed. She was receiving public assistance for the benefit of Mike, but now Scott pays monthly child support through the state's IV-D agency.

THE ASSIGNMENT

Assume that you are employed by Attorney Juliana Wilson, whose office is located at 390 Main Street in your city and state, and that she represents Scott and Hayley in this matter.

Research the appropriate forms used in your state and draft the following:

1. A Petition for Adoption
2. A Surrender and Consent to the Adoption
3. A proposed open adoption agreement, assuming that such agreements are permitted in your jurisdiction.

FOCUS ON ETHICS

Assume that you are employed by Attorney Kelly Brantley, whose office is located at 220 High Street in your city and state. She has an established general practice and is well respected by her colleagues. The office has been retained to represent Jessica in the adoption action described in the above comprehensive fact pattern. In the initial interview you were assigned to conduct with Jessica, she asks if everything she tells you is "private," and you assure her that yes, all of her communications with the family law team working on her case are protected by the attorney-client privilege. She then tells you that Scott is not actually Mike's father, but that she convinced him he was so that he would acknowledge paternity and she would have no

problem applying for public assistance. It all worked out, she says, because Scott has gotten his life back together and has turned out to be a great father. She says everything is going well now and she doesn't want to upset the applecart by telling the truth. She just wants to give up her legal rights and get the adoption finalized as soon as possible. What are you going to do in response to this conversation? Personally, you would really like to see the adoption take place because it is clearly in the best interests of the child. Relate your response to the ethical canons for paralegals promulgated by the National Federation of Paralegal Associations (NFPA), which are contained in Appendix B of this text.

FOCUS ON CASE LAW

Locate and brief a case decided in your state within the past three years on one of the following topics:

1. Termination of parental rights
2. Revocation of parental consent to an adoption
3. Co-parent adoption
4. The state's putative father registry, if any
5. Access to adoption records

FOCUS ON STATE LAW AND PROCEDURE

Locate and review the laws and procedures governing adoption in your state of residence and then answer the following questions:

1. Under what circumstances, if any, may a parent have his or her parental rights terminated?
2. Is a parent permitted to revoke a consent to adoption and, if so, under what circumstances?
3. What kinds of adoptions are permitted?

4. Does your state have a safe haven law? If yes, describe its provisions.
5. Who may adopt and who may be adopted?
6. Does your state have a putative father registry? If yes, describe its provisions.
7. Are adult adoptees permitted to contact their biological parents? If yes, how do they go about doing so?

FOCUS ON TECHNOLOGY

WEBSITES OF INTEREST

http://www.abcadoptions.com

This site contains information about the adoption process and includes adoption postings. It serves as a support for both birth parents seeking adoptive parents and adoptive parents seeking children. It provides information for both populations and appears to act as a "meeting ground."

http://www.adoptioninstitute.org

This is the website for the Evan P. Donaldson Adoption Institute. It contains links to putative father registries, open records information, state registries, and confidentiality statutes. It states as its mission, "To provide leadership that improves adoption laws, policies, and practices—through sound research, education, and advocacy—in order to better the lives of everyone touched by adoption."

http://www.adoptionlawsite.org

This is the website of the National Center for Adoption Law and Policy, an organization of the Capital University Law School in Columbus, Ohio. It does not offer services to individuals, but rather operates to improve the laws and policies that govern adoption.

http://www.chask.org

"CHASK" is an acronym for Christian Homes and Special Kids. It is a Christian service organization that serves as a meeting place for adoptive parents who are willing to accept special needs children and birth mothers seeking adoptive homes for their special needs children.

http://www.childwelfare.gov

This is the website for the Child Welfare Information Gateway, an organization of the Department of Health and Human Services. This site contains links to a number of sites addressing topics such as open adoption, access to adoption records, single-parent adoption, and gay and lesbian adoptive parents. It provides links to federal and state laws, fact sheets, statistics, and publications.

http://www.law.cornell.edu

This site provides links to the adoption laws of all fifty states.

http://www.marecinc.org

This is the website for the Massachusetts Adoption Resource Exchange, a nonprofit organization that promotes placement of older and special needs children. It contains information on adoption, support groups, FAQs, and links to related websites.

http://www.ncfa-usa.org

This is the website of the National Council for Adoption. NCFA is a not-for-profit organization that engages in research, education, and advocacy for adoption.

Assignments

1. Locate websites for three adoption reunion registries and describe their content. Begin with the Georgia Adoption Reunion Registry, located at *http://www.adoptions.dhr.state.ga.us/reunion.htm.*

2. Locate websites for putative father registries in three states. Begin with the Illinois Registry at *http://www.state.il.us/dcfs/putative.htm.*

3. Locate three websites not listed above that offer information and support to gays and lesbians seeking to adopt.

chapter **fifteen**

FAMILY VIOLENCE

Joe has been served with a Complaint for Divorce, and he is furious. His rage is apparent to the paralegal in his attorney's office, who has suspected for some time that Joe abuses his wife. Fearful for the wife's safety, the paralegal speaks with the supervising attorney, and they both struggle with the question of what they should do.

After years of studying family and intimate violence, by the 1990s Richard Gelles wondered aloud how we had ever come to characterize the family as "warm, intimate, stress reducing, and the place that people flee for safety."[1] His research had shown that the family was one of society's most violent institutions, in that people were "more likely to be killed, physically assaulted, hit, beat up, slapped, or spanked in their own homes by other family members than anywhere else, or by anyone else."[2]

INTRODUCTION

The history of family violence in this country has long been colored by the old common law right of a husband to treat both his wife and his children as property and to maintain domestic order through the use of physical force. *Interspousal immunity* and the law of *couverture,* which gave men control over their wives' bodies and property, created a climate that essentially fostered and condoned violence in the home environment. Although there were isolated efforts to address this problem prior to the 1900s, it was not until the 1960s and 1970s that advocates for the rights of women and children galvanized public and legislative support for victims of family violence. Initially, the focus was on abuse as a mental health problem to be dealt with privately through treatment aimed primarily at maintenance of the family unit. In more recent years, the shift has been toward a focus on protection of victims and the treatment of abuse as a crime, a law enforcement issue calling for the allocation of substantial public attention and resources.

This chapter focuses on the deeply troubling topic of family violence, first with respect to adult intimate partners and then in the context of parent-child relationships. In each instance, we examine the nature and extent of the abuse, the federal government's recognition of the problem, and some of the remedies available to victims. We also consider how intimate partner violence and child abuse and neglect impact related issues, such as property division, spousal support, and custody determinations. Finally, we explore the duty of members of the family law team in cases involving family violence and the ethical challenges it presents.

DEFINING FAMILY VIOLENCE

Family violence goes by many names, most commonly domestic violence, domestic abuse, intimate partner abuse, and spousal and child abuse, among others. Generally, it involves a pattern of coercive behavior designed to exert power and control over a person in a familial relationship. It comes in no single form, but rather may involve any combination of behaviors such as threatening, intimidating, belittling, harassing, and outright physical attacks. Legal definitions of various kinds of abuse differ from state to state. Most focus on the infliction of physical abuse that causes bodily injury, compelled sexual activity, and fear of physical assault. Some definitions encompass abuse inflicted through neglect, *stalking* (including *cyberstalking*), and other psychological tactics and behaviors. A copy of the Missouri statute defining abuse is available on the companion website.

FAMILY VIOLENCE AGAINST ADULT VICTIMS
The Scope of the Problem

"Domestic violence crosses all geographic, socioeconomic, racial, cultural, religious, educational, and occupational boundaries. The overwhelming majority of domestic violence is committed by men against women, although some women are

Interspousal immunity
a doctrine preventing spouses from suing each other in civil actions

Couverture
the legal doctrine that upon marriage, a husband and wife become one person (the husband), and the wife loses many of the legal rights she possessed prior to marriage

Paralegal Practice Tip
Most family law textbooks treat family violence as two separate (and shorter) chapters, one focusing on "domestic" violence and one focusing on child abuse and neglect. To some extent, the two are treated separately in this chapter for purposes of organizational convenience. However, the reader should be aware that there is a significant overlap between the two. A majority of studies find that both forms of abuse occur in thirty to sixty percent of violent families.[3] From a family systems perspective, one form of violence in the family cannot be understood in isolation from the other.

Family violence
a pattern of coercive behavior designed to exert power and control over a person in a familial relationship

Stalking
a knowing and willful course of conduct intended to cause another substantial emotional distress or fear for his or her safety; includes behaviors such as following, telephoning, or watching a person's place of residence or employment

Cyberstalking
repeated use of the Internet, text messaging, e-mail, or other forms of electronic communication with the intent to harass, intimidate, torment, or embarrass another person

abusive to their male or female partners. It occurs with about the same statistical frequency in heterosexual and homosexual relationships, …"[4] (See Exhibit 15.1.) Although domestic violence appears disproportionately to impact minorities, immigrants, and individuals on welfare, the reader should not be misled by statistics into thinking that domestic violence is a problem solely in low-income families. Victims with financial resources have options that may allow them to conceal or escape abuse and avoid becoming public statistics. For example, the victim may be able to relocate to a new residence and/or file for divorce without ever having to seek public assistance. However, while having money increases options for some victims, it does not necessarily insulate them from abuse.

EXHIBIT 15.1 Family Violence—A Statistical Profile

- According to Bureau of Justice Statistics for 2005:
  - About 1 in 320 households was affected by intimate partner violence
  - Female victims were more likely to be victimized by intimates than were male victims[5]
- Averaged over the years 1993 through 2004:
  - drugs and/or alcohol were involved in 43% of the non-fatal intimate partner victimizations
  - the offender had a weapon in 15% of the offenses against female victims and 27% of the offenses against male victims
  - approximately 60% of the incidents of non-fatal intimate partner violence were unreported, and the primary reasons given for nonreporting included a preference for treating the incident as a private or family matter, a desire to protect the offender, a fear of reprisal, a belief that the crime was minor, and that, if contacted, the police would be biased, ineffective, or unresponsive.[6]
- Family violence accounted for 11% of all reported violent crimes between 1998 and 2002; approximately 49% of these offenses were committed against a spouse, 11% against a child by a parent, and 41% against another family member; 73% of victims were female and 76% of perpetrators were male.[7]
- Approximately 12% of persons murdered in 2005 were killed by a family member: approximately 5% involved the killing of a spouse, 3% a son or daughter, and 2% another family member.[8]
- In a study of adolescent mothers, approximately one of every eight pregnant adolescents reported having been physically assaulted by the father of her baby during the preceding twelve months.[9]
- Incidence of domestic violence varies considerably by race and ethnicity.[10] For example, Department of Justice statistics indicate that, averaged over the interval 1993 to 2004, African-American females were victims of intimate partner violence at a rate 30% higher than that of white females.[11] A survey of immigrant Korean women found that 60% had been battered by their husbands.[12]
- Domestic violence occurs in same-sex as well as in heterosexual relationships. Based on the National Violence Against Women Survey, 11% of lesbians and 15% of gay men who had lived with a same-sex partner reported being victimized.[13]

continued

- A 1997 review of research indicated that 50 to 60% of women receiving public assistance had experienced physical abuse by an intimate partner at some time in their lives.[14]
- A U.S. Department of Justice report has indicated that 37% of all women who sought care in hospital emergency rooms for violence-related injuries were injured by a current or former spouse, boyfriend, or girlfriend.[15]
- Although family violence remains a serious problem, Bureau of Justice Statistics data indicates that there has been a significant decline in intimate partner violence beginning in 1993.[16]

EXHIBIT 15.2 Elder Abuse

- Definitions of elder abuse vary. According to the National Center on Elder Abuse (NCEA), "elder abuse is a term referring to any knowing, intentional, or negligent act by a caregiver or any other person that causes harm or a serious risk of harm to a vulnerable adult."
- Despite persistent efforts of some legislative leaders, there still is no federal legislation that focuses exclusively on elder abuse, there is no official source of national data or uniform reporting system, and laws protecting elders vary from state to state.
- The 2004 National Center on Elder Abuse Survey of Adult Protective Services (APS) collected data from all fifty states, Guam, and the District of Columbia concerning elder and vulnerable adult abuse. Not all states collected and reported data on all elements of the survey. However, based on the data submitted:
  - In the thirty-two states that separated out reports of elder abuse from vulnerable adult abuse, there were 253,426 incidents of elder abuse, representing 8.3 reports of abuse for every 1,000 older Americans.
  - As baby boomers (born between 1946 and 1964) move into their senior years, the elderly population is increasing significantly and, with it, the likelihood of increases in elder abuse. Between 2000 and 2004, there was a 15.6% increase in substantiated cases of elder and vulnerable adult abuse.
  - Based on data from nineteen states, the types of substantiated maltreatment fell into the following categories: self-neglect (37.2%); caregiver neglect (20.4%); financial exploitation (14.7%); emotional/psychological/verbal abuse (14.8%); physical abuse (10.7%); sexual abuse (1%); and other (1.2%).
  - 89.3% of the incidents of alleged abuse were reported to have occurred in a domestic setting, clearly making elder abuse a family violence issue (thirteen states reporting).
  - In 2003, 65.7% of the elder abuse victims were women (data from fifteen states), and more than 40% were age eighty or older (twenty states reporting).

continued

- Slightly more than half of the alleged perpetrators were female (eleven states reporting).
- 32.6% of the perpetrators were adult children of the victims, 11.3% were spouses or intimate partners, and 21.5% were other family members (eleven states reporting).[18]
- The American Psychological Association reports that "every year 2.1 million older Americans are victims of physical, psychological, or other forms of abuse and neglect. ... For every case of elder abuse and neglect that is reported ... there may be as many as five cases that have not been reported."[19]
- "Research has uncovered several key perpetrator characteristics: (1) drug and/or alcohol abuse, (2) impairments such as mental illness and developmental disabilities, (3) financial dependence on the elder, and (4) a bad past relationship with the elder. When applied to family caregiving situations, these findings emphasize that, within the stressful context of caregiving, most people cope without resorting to violent or exploitive behavior. Family members who experience one or more of these risk factors are much more likely to develop an abusive relationship with an elder relative. Indeed, elder abuse resembles domestic violence with its cycle of violence and dynamic of power and control."[20]

FEDERAL RECOGNITION OF THE PROBLEM: THE VIOLENCE AGAINST WOMEN ACT

At the federal level the most dramatic illustration of the legislative attention brought to bear on the problem of family violence is the Violence Against Women Act, a comprehensive, landmark piece of legislation designed to improve criminal justice and community-based responses to domestic violence, dating violence, sexual assault, stalking, and trafficking. It was initially passed in 1994 (VAWA I) and reauthorized in 2000 (VAWA II), and the Violence Against Women and Department of Justice Reauthorization Act of 2005 was signed into law in January 2006, reauthorizing the Violence Against Women Act for fiscal years 2007 through 2011 (VAWA III).[21] It is administered by the Department of Health and Human Services and the Department of Justice. Since VAWA was signed into law, the following (among others) have become federal crimes: cyberstalking; crossing state or tribal boundary lines in order to injure, intimidate, or stalk an intimate partner or to violate a protective order; and stalking on Indian Reservations or military bases. From the outset, the Act also has provided crucial services by funding twenty-four-hour emergency hotlines, emergency shelters, and child advocacy centers. Selected highlights of VAWA III include the following:

- It provides funding for programs to train health care professionals to recognize the signs of domestic violence and refer victims to appropriate services.
- Past VAWA legislation addressed rape prevention and education, but VAWA III authorizes funding for rape crisis centers and service agencies to provide direct services to victims of sexual assault, including counseling, rape kits, legal assistance, and medical services.

- The Act includes provisions expanding transitional housing options for the homeless and ensures victims' confidentiality within the homeless services system. It also forbids domestic violence discrimination in public housing to prevent landlords from denying housing or evicting tenants based on their status of being victims of domestic violence.
- The reauthorization creates a resource center for employers that is designed to provide information on domestic violence and the workplace.
- VAWA III provides increased funding for victims with disabilities, the elderly, youth under the age of eighteen, and those who live in rural communities. Particular attention is given to the Native American population.
- It establishes a new grant program to enhance culturally and linguistically specific services designed to meet the needs of all women and not just those of one race, cultural background, or income level.
- The Act requires that states give full faith and credit to custody, visitation, and support provisions included in protective orders issued by courts in other states.

Successive versions of the Act have provided increased protections for immigrant victims of domestic violence. VAWA I provided immigrant spouses and children alternative procedures for obtaining visas without the cooperation of the abusive spouse by permitting them to self-petition for legal permanent resident status. VAWA II provided additional protections for immigrants who divorce their abusers or whose marriages are invalid because the citizen spouse was already married. VAWA III provides further assistance for immigrant victims. In recognition of the fact that immigrants often lack access to shelters, professionals, court interpreters, hotlines, and 911 services due to language barriers, the new legislation required the Secretary of Homeland Security to develop a pamphlet (translated into at least fourteen languages) containing information on the illegality of domestic violence and the rights of an abused immigrant.

REMEDIES AVAILABLE TO VICTIMS

In addition to the kinds of social services and assistance promoted by VAWA, other remedies available to victims of abuse include criminal prosecution, civil actions, protective orders, and guardianship.

Criminal Prosecution

Involvement of the criminal justice system most often begins when the police receive and respond to a 911 call reporting a "domestic incident." In general, when responding to such calls, an officer must use all reasonable means to prevent further abuse whenever there is reason to believe that a "family member" has been abused or is in danger of being abused. The officer usually is required by statute and/or department policy to do the following:

- provide protection for the victim at the scene
- assist the victim in obtaining medical treatment, if appropriate
- assist the victim in relocating to a safe location, if warranted
- provide oral and written instructions to the victim (preferably in the victim's native language) about how to apply for a protective order
- assist the victim in accessing emergency judicial help if the courts are closed (on a weekend or holiday, etc.)
- arrest the perpetrator of the abuse if the officer witnesses or has probable cause to believe that he or she has committed a felony, an assault and

Paralegal Practice Tip
States have in place procedures allowing plaintiffs to obtain emergency orders on weekends, holidays, and any other non-business days. This is generally accomplished by having local judges/magistrates serve twenty-four-hour on-call shifts on a rotating basis. Any orders issued on an emergency basis are usually effective only until the next business day, when a hearing can be held.

battery, or has violated a temporary or permanent restraining, vacate, or no-contact order (In some states or localities, arrest is mandatory regardless of the victim's wishes. In others it is discretionary.)

- advise the victim that if the abuser is arrested, he or she will likely be eligible for bail or release

The role of the police in investigation and documentation of abuse incidents is critically important because in many cases, the victim will refuse to participate as a complaining witness for a variety of reasons. (See Paralegal Application 15.1.) However, today many prosecutors have adopted "no-drop" policies and will proceed with **evidence-based prosecutions** using photographs, medical records, incident reports, and the testimony of police officers and other witnesses to establish a case. Supporters of mandatory arrest and "no-drop" policies assert that victims often are too helpless and/or too fearful to make appropriate decisions about arrest and prosecution. Opponents supportive of victims' rights argue that such policies disempower victims by depriving them of the opportunity to make decisions about how the abuser should be treated.[22] They view the chance to make such choices as opportunities for victims to realize strength and power.

Evidence-based prosecution prosecution of a defendant that relies on physical evidence and testimony of persons other than the victim, such as police officers; formerly called "victimless" prosecutions

PARALEGAL APPLICATION 15.1

"WHY DO THEY STAY? IF ANYONE EVER HIT ME, I WOULD BE OUT THE DOOR IN A MINUTE."

It is often difficult for people who have never been in such a situation to comprehend why a person would remain in an abusive relationship and/or not prosecute or testify against his or her abuser. As an unfortunate result, courts, juries, and members of the legal profession often do not find claims of abuse to be credible. Research indicates that victims (primarily women) protect their abuser and stay in such relationships for several reasons:

- Fear of retaliation against themselves and/or their children
- Isolation from friends and extended family, resulting in the lack of a social and emotional support system
- Fear of loss of social status and professional associations
- Economic dependence, lack of marketable skills, or lack of adequate public assistance
- Desire to keep the family together and fear of losing custody of children
- Cultural and religious beliefs about the permanence of marriage
- Sense of responsibility for or loyalty to the abuser
- Belief that they love their abuser and that he or she will change
- Fear that the abuser will reveal information pertaining to sexual preference, immigration, or HIV status, etc.[23]
- Chronic depression and exhaustion to the point of being unable to make decisions or major life changes
- Guilt and self-blame when the abuser convinces the victim the abuse is his or her fault
- Low self-esteem and feelings of failure as a spouse, partner, and/or person
- Conviction that no one other than the abuser would ever want or love them and that a bad relationship is better than no relationship at all

continued

- Learned helplessness, a condition in which the victim comes to believe that all avenues of escape are closed and that she or he is powerless to leave

- Traumatic bonding, a psychological adaptive response in which the victim actually becomes attached to or bonded with his or her abuser (as in "Stockholm Syndrome" when kidnapped victims bond with their kidnappers)

- Lack of information about options for escape and resources available such as shelters and hotlines

- Inability to make use of support services due to language or cultural barriers, disabilities, lifestyle issues, or substance abuse problems

- Lack of effective responses to prior efforts to seek assistance

Abusive conduct may be prosecuted under a variety of criminal statutes, ranging from murder and manslaughter in cases involving deaths, to assault, battery, aggravated assault, rape/sexual assault, stalking, and cyberstalking, among others. Many states have criminalized domestic battery specifically and provide for heightened penalties when other crimes are committed against family members.

Every state has enacted one or more anti-stalking measures that provide protection for victims of this specific form of abuse with or without the existence of a "special relationship." For example, a Georgia statute provides that:

> A person commits the offense of stalking when he or she follows, places under surveillance, or contacts another person at or about a place or places without the consent of the other person for the purpose of harassing and intimidating the other person. ... the term "harassing and intimidating" means a knowing and willful course of conduct directed at a specific person which causes emotional distress by placing such person in reasonable fear for such person's safety or the safety of a member of his or her immediate family, by establishing a pattern of harassing and intimidating behavior, and which serves no legitimate purpose....[24]

PARALEGAL APPLICATION 15.2

BATTERED WOMAN'S SYNDROME—A VIABLE DEFENSE?

Many states permit evidence of a history of abuse to be raised as a defense when a victim finally retaliates and causes injury or death to the abuser. What has come to be known as *battered woman's syndrome* is usually not a complete defense to a crime, but rather may serve to reduce the degree of the crime with which the defendant/victim is charged (from first-degree murder, for example, to second-degree murder or manslaughter) or to mitigate the sentence imposed.

This defense is by no means universally accepted. Many in the criminal justice system agree with commentators who contend it is just one of dozens of potential "abuse excuses" by means of which criminals fail to accept responsibility for their conduct. These critics assert that no prior acts of abuse justify taking affirmative steps to defend oneself absent an immediate act of provocation.

Battered woman's syndrome
a psychological condition of a woman who has been abused for a sustained period of time; sometimes used as a defense to justify or mitigate an attack on her abuser

SIDEBAR

Do you believe that evidence of a history of abuse should be admissible as a defense to the killing of one's abuser? Should it be a complete defense (resulting in a not guilty verdict) or only reduce the degree of the crime or the sentence? Are there circumstances in which the defense is more appropriate than others?

Additional examples of stalking behaviors include making repeated and unwelcome telephone calls, sending cards, leaving notes in various locations, impeding the victim's movement, appearing uninvited at the victim's residence or place of employment, and taking pictures of the victim, all with intent to cause fear and/or emotional distress. (See Exhibit 15.3.)

Most stalking statutes provide for enhanced penalties for aggravated stalking, such as when the stalking occurs in violation of a protective order or involves a repeated offense or the use of a weapon. Some states have enacted statutes that specifically address cyberstalking. The state of Washington's cyberstalking statute can be accessed on the companion website.

Civil Actions

Historically, the doctrine of interspousal immunity prevented spouses from suing each other in civil actions, such as tort actions that provide a remedy for civil wrongs that have caused harm to persons or property. The doctrine was designed to serve strong public policies favoring preservation of marriage and family harmony and prevention of fraudulent claims between spouses who had liability insurance. The doctrine has eroded to a considerable extent, such that several states now permit one spouse to sue the other spouse for intentional or negligent injury to property and for intentional (but not negligent) injury to

---

EXHIBIT 15.3 Stalking—A Statistical Profile

According to the Stalking Resource Center of the National Center for Victims of Crime, based on the results of a National Violence Against Women Survey (NVAW):

- 1 out of every 12 women and 1 out of 45 men will be stalked during their lifetime.
- More than a million women and more than 370,000 men are stalked annually.
- Overall, 87% of stalkers are men.
- 77% of female victims are stalked by someone they know (59% by an intimate partner), and 64% of male victims are stalked by someone they know (30% by an intimate partner).
- 81% of women stalked by a current or former spouse or cohabiting partner are also physically assaulted, and 31% are sexually assaulted by that partner.
- The top three reasons victims gave for why they were stalked were that the stalker wanted to control them, keep them in a relationship, and/or frighten them.
- 55% of female victims and 48% of male victims reported the stalking to the police.
- 28% of female victims and 10% of male victims obtained protection orders, and 69% of the orders granted to women and 81% of the orders granted to males were violated.
- The average length of stalking of intimate partners was 2.2 years.[25]

the person (e.g., assault, battery), especially if the parties are not living together. If a divorce is pending, the courts may require that such claims be raised in the context of that action. The premise is that, if a party receives a greater share of the marital property based on the other party's abusive conduct during the marriage, that party should not be permitted to file a post-divorce tort claim for battery or intentional infliction of emotional distress for injuries that occurred during the course of the marriage, thereby getting a "second bite of the apple."[26]

Protective Orders

Under civil domestic violence laws of all fifty states and the District of Columbia, a victim of family violence can seek an order of protection if he or she satisfies the threshold requirements regarding standing and qualifying conduct laid out in applicable statutes, which vary considerably from state to state.

Protective order
in the context of family violence cases, a court order directing a person to refrain from harming or harassing another person

Standing.   Standing to seek protective orders is generally available to individuals involved in spousal, intimate, or other "special" relationships. Depending on the state, this may include individuals who:

- are or were married to each other
- have a child in common or a child *in utero*
- are related by blood or marriage
- are or have been in a substantial dating relationship
- are or have lived together in the same household (this may include couples, parents and children, roommates, etc.)

A limited number of states expressly extend standing to individuals involved in same-sex as well as heterosexual intimate relationships. The decision with respect to who has standing often is ultimately a matter of judicial discretion. For example, under what circumstances will a couple be deemed to be in a "substantial" dating relationship? Will standing be extended to same-sex couples in states that have enacted statutes or constitutional amendments banning extension of the rights and benefits of marriage to same-sex couples?

Qualifying Conduct.   Some states require that the petitioner have suffered actual or attempted physical harm or have been caused to engage in sexual relations as a result of force or threat of force. In several states, a threat of serious physical harm is sufficient. A limited number of states extend standing when there is serious emotional or verbal abuse or malicious destruction of property, particularly when there is a history of violence on the perpetrator's part clearly evidencing a potential for harm. (See Case 15.1.) Typical examples of violent and controlling abusive behaviors considered by the courts include:

- slaps, punches, bites, or "head butts"
- grabbing, choking, pulling hair
- display or use of weapons in an intimidating manner
- intimidation by use of threatening gestures, shouting, driving recklessly, or refusing to allow entry or exit from a location
- destruction of furniture or other property
- ripping out phone lines, slashing tires, etc.
- threatening to harm the victim's children or take them away to another state or country
- injuring or threatening to injure pets

CASE **15.1** *Lefebre v. Lefebre,* 165 Ore. App. 297, 996 P.2d 518 (2000)

BACKGROUND

In this case, the defendant challenged the legal sufficiency of the allegations and evidence underlying a restraining order that had been entered against him. The petitioner had alleged that after their separation, her husband persistently harassed and frightened her, barricaded her out of her house, telephoned many of her friends telling them a "disparaging" story about her, and engaged in a number of other threatening acts. She said her fear was intensified because of an episode nine years earlier in which he was obsessed for six months with the idea of killing his former employer. She also indicated that he lived with his brother who was a police officer, and that he had easy access to guns. She did not allege that there had been any actual or overtly threatened harm. Her husband claimed that the restraining order should not be issued because there was no overt threat and only a "minimal level" of physical contact.

FROM THE OPINION

An overt threat is not required in order to authorize the issuance of an abuse prevention restraining order. Instead, FAPA requires that the respondent has "intentionally, knowingly or recklessly" placed the petitioner in fear of "imminent serious bodily injury." ORS 107.705(1); ORS 107.710(1). In addition, the petitioner must be in immediate danger of further abuse. Id. As to the latter requirement, respondent correctly points out that our previous reported decisions upholding FAPA orders have generally involved more overtly threatening conduct than that present here. ...

In Cottongim, we held that the respondent's behavior fulfilled the statutory definition of abuse because it "deviated considerably from that which a reasonable person would exhibit under similar circumstances [,] and a reasonable person faced with such behavior would be placed in fear of imminent serious bodily harm." Cottongim, 145 Ore. App. at 45. The same reasoning applies here as well. Respondent's conduct was erratic, intrusive, volatile, and persistent. He screamed obscenities in petitioner's face, unrestrained by the presence of their child, made numerous hang-up phone calls, and rummaged through her possessions. Notably, respondent's late night call describing the sleeping clothes petitioner was wearing put her on notice that he was lurking about her house, watching her, and that she was vulnerable. Moreover, petitioner knew that respondent had previously been obsessed with the idea of killing another person. Despite the lack of an explicit threat, the totality of the circumstances supports the petitioner's assertion that respondent at least recklessly placed her in fear of imminent serious bodily injury and in immediate danger of further abuse.

SIDEBAR

This opinion is available in its entirety on the companion website. Do you agree with the court's decision? Explain your response.

Procedure for Obtaining a Protective Order. The procedure for obtaining a protective order varies somewhat from state to state, but is invariably relatively simple:

- The plaintiff files a Complaint or Petition for a Protective Order requesting a variety of forms of relief. A copy of an Indiana Petition for an Order for Protection and Request for a Hearing is available on the companion website. The Complaint includes or is accompanied by an *affidavit* in which the plaintiff describes the nature of the abuse that has led to the filing. In some states, such as Indiana, if the petition is made on the basis of the petitioner's information and belief rather than on personal knowledge, the petitioner also must attach affidavits by one or more persons who have personal knowledge of the facts stated within the petition.

- The Complaint is filed in a court with jurisdiction over such matters. Usually several types of courts have *concurrent jurisdiction,* including courts that hear criminal, juvenile, and family matters. Most states do not require a filing fee, and those that do require one allow the fee to be waived upon proof of inability to pay.
- At the petitioner's request, the Complaint often is considered by the court initially on an **ex parte** basis (without notice to the defendant).
- A temporary order will be issued if the court believes there is reason to believe that abuse has occurred or is threatened. The extent of relief granted at this initial stage may be limited to *restraining, stay away,* or *no-contact orders.*
- The defendant is served with the Complaint and any *ex parte* orders in a manner consistent with local procedure.
- A second hearing is held within a statutorily prescribed period (commonly ten to twenty days), at which both the plaintiff and defendant have an opportunity to be heard, and the court decides whether to extend, modify, or vacate the initial order. In some states, this second hearing must be requested by the defendant, and a failure of the plaintiff to appear may result in automatic dismissal.
- An extended order will contain an expiration date. When that date approaches, if the plaintiff wants the order extended for an additional period, he or she must petition the court for an extension.

Because the procedure for obtaining a restraining order is relatively uncomplicated, it can be completed by the plaintiff on his or her own or with minimal technical assistance from court personnel. In some cases there is merit to proceeding *pro se,* as filing often represents the first time the victim has ever asserted his or her rights against the abuser. That psychological advantage aside, it may be helpful for the client to have assistance, particularly with completion of the affidavit, identification of potential forms of relief that may be available based on the parties' circumstances, and representation at court hearings when the defendant may be present.

Types of Relief Available in Protective Orders.   Courts may grant a variety of forms of relief tailored to the facts and circumstances of each case. For example, the court may order that the defendant:

- stay away from the plaintiff at home, work, school, or any other place he or she may be (The stay away order may also extend to locations where the plaintiff's child or children may be.)
- have no contact with the plaintiff by any means, including telephone, text messaging, e-mail, U.S. mail, notes on vehicle doors and windows, etc.
- refrain from abusing, injuring, or harassing the plaintiff either directly and/or with the assistance of third parties (This particular form of relief is usually referred to as a restraining order.)
- vacate the household (if the parties live together) regardless of who holds title to the property or is responsible for the lease (The court may permit the defendant to collect his or her personal belongings from the property—usually with police supervision.)

Affidavit
a written statement of facts based on firsthand knowledge, information, or belief and signed by the affiant under pain and penalty of perjury

Concurrent jurisdiction
when two or more courts have simultaneous jurisdiction over the same subject matter

Ex parte
made without advance notice to the opposing party; a matter considered and initially ruled on by the court without hearing from both parties

Restraining order
a court order, most commonly issued in domestic violence cases, restricting an individual from threatening and/or harassing another individual or individuals

Stay away order
a court order requiring a person to keep away from another individual wherever he or she may be (home, work, school, etc.)

No-contact order
a court order prohibiting an individual from having contact of any kind with a person he or she has threatened and/or abused in some manner

Paralegal Practice Tip
The victim may request in the Complaint that his or her address be impounded. The U.S. Postal Service will also keep an address confidential when the victim presents a copy of his or her protective order to the appropriate postal office employee, although the address will still be provided to agents of the state or federal government.

- surrender guns, license to carry a gun, and Firearm Identification Card (FID) (Exceptions may be available for individuals such as police officers and military personnel, who are required to carry a weapon as a condition of employment, but the exception applies only while the individual is on duty.)[27]
- pay compensation to the plaintiff for damages, losses, or expenses incurred as a direct result of the abuse (e.g., for repair of destroyed property, installation of new locks, uninsured medical and counseling expenses,[28] loss of time from work, relocation and moving expenses, costs of staying in a hotel, motel, or shelter, etc.)

In addition to other specific forms of relief, a majority of state statutes include a catchall provision authorizing courts to provide whatever relief is appropriate to stop the abuse and protect the victim in a given set of circumstances. For example, in a case in which a defendant is threatening to expose the plaintiff's HIV status, the court may order the defendant not to "directly or indirectly reveal any information about the Petitioner's health status to Petitioner's employer … with intent to cause emotional distress or harass the Petitioner, except pursuant to subpoena or court order."[29] Although on the surface such a provision may appear to restrain free speech, such orders have been granted.

Police usually play a major role in serving and enforcing protective orders. Although protective orders are initially civil in nature, violations constitute contempt of court as well as independent criminal offenses potentially punishable by jail sentences and/or fines. In order to prove a violation, a valid order must have issued (counsel should have a certified copy of the order); the defendant must have been served with the order; the order must have been in effect at the time of the violation; and the defendant must have violated the order. The extent to which a plaintiff has a legal "right" to enforcement of an order is not entirely clear. Critics often say that restraining orders are "not worth the paper they are printed on," that they create a false sense of security in victims, and that they often exacerbate rather than eliminate abuse. (See the *Town of Castle Rock v. Gonzales* case on the companion website (545 U.S. 748, 752, 125 S.Ct, 2796, 162 L. Ed. 2d 658 (2005).)

Occasionally a client will intentionally create a situation in which a violation of a protective order is inevitable. The potential for problems is especially great when the parties have a child in common. For example, assume both parents want to attend their child's basketball game, dance concert, or school play. Further assume that a protective order is in force requiring the defendant to stay at least five hundred feet away from the plaintiff. The defendant arrives at the event after the other parent, and the school auditorium is so small that it is impossible to be present without being within five hundred feet of the plaintiff. Technically there is a violation even if the defendant makes no effort whatsoever to approach, threaten, or otherwise communicate with the plaintiff, and the defendant may be subject to arrest in front of the child and others present if the plaintiff contacts the police. Absent a pattern of such behavior, there may be little that can be done other than to suggest to the client that such confrontations harm the innocent child most of all.

Most advocates argue that "mutual restraining orders" should be discouraged, particularly in cases where one of the parties strikes out only in self-defense. To issue a restraining order in such circumstances in effect relieves the abuser of responsibility. In addition, when mutual restraining orders are issued, they may create confusion for police trying to enforce them and for judges trying to make custody orders when prior history of abuse is a relevant factor to be considered. At least one state, Wisconsin, has addressed this issue to a limited extent in a requirement under its mandatory arrest statute. When the officer has reasonable grounds to believe that spouses, former spouses, or other persons who reside together or formerly resided together are committing or have committed domestic abuse against each other, the officer does not have to arrest both persons but should arrest the person whom the officer believes to be the primary aggressor.[31]

Most if not all states also provide for issuance of "domestic relations restraining orders" in the context of divorce and other family law proceedings. However, these orders are not technically protective orders, and the safety of victims is not their primary intended purpose. They may be included routinely in marital agreements or may issue at the discretion of the court. There is no requirement for abuse to have occurred to obtain a domestic relations restraining order. Essentially, they are designed to serve as reminders to parties that they are not to interfere in each other's lives.

Guardianship

Forms of relief such as protective orders reflect what has been termed an "empowerment model of domestic violence," which presumes that a victim of abuse is capable of deciding to leave an abusive relationship, hold the abuser accountable, and make use of available resources to move forward with life. This model fails to account for the fact that "a battered woman can become coercively controlled—so incapacitated by repeated abuse that she cannot protect herself or escape from her abuser."[32] "In extreme cases ... , the state-sanctioned intervention of guardianship is necessary because an abuser has brutally and systematically deprived a woman of her ability to exercise independent judgment. Existing resources available to a battered woman, such as restraining orders, shelters, and support groups, presuppose an ability to avail herself of assistance. However, when a battered woman is so controlled that she has lost her autonomy, these resources are not genuine options. A battered woman incapacitated by mental and physical abuse must be empowered by forcible removal from the control of an abuser."[33] Guardianship has the potential to bridge the gap between being totally subject to the control of the abuser and independence. The *guardian* is appointed by the court and is granted the authority to act on behalf of the "ward" for some or all purposes until such time as the court determines the ward has the capacity to act on his or her own behalf. The guardian can, for example, make housing arrangements for the ward, pay bills, make decisions regarding counseling and medical treatment, and represent the client in legal matters.

RECOGNIZING AND RESPONDING WHEN INTIMATE PARTNER VIOLENCE IS AN ISSUE IN A CASE

Many victims are afraid, ashamed, or embarrassed about the abuse they experience and have never reported it to the police or discussed it with counselors, physicians, family, friends, or attorneys. Perpetrators frequently are aware that their conduct is criminal but are unwilling to face the consequences of their

Guardian

an individual appointed by the court to have legal authority for another's person and/or property during a period of minority or incapacitation

actions by acknowledging it to others. As surprising as it may seem, some abusers do not recognize that they are perpetrators of family violence, especially when their conduct is culturally condoned, and many victims, particularly those who believe they are responsible for the abuse they suffer, do not perceive themselves as victims. Some clients will directly acknowledge that they are victims or perpetrators of abuse, particularly if the abuse is already a matter of public record, documented in police reports, and substantiated by medical records and other evidence such as photographs. More often, however, the abuse will not be revealed by the client at the outset of a case. Members of the family law team need to listen carefully to the client's language and also be sensitive to cues in behavior that suggest the existence of unacknowledged abuse.

Given the potential that a client is either a perpetrator or a victim of family violence, materials may be made available in law office lobbies regarding resources designed to assist both victims of abuse and perpetrators who might conceivably be motivated to change their behavior or be forced to accept the consequences. Such materials include, among others, hotline numbers, emergency shelter contacts, law enforcement agency numbers, names of victim advocates, instructions and forms for obtaining protective orders, and locations of resource centers, support groups, and batterers' programs. They may also include educational and consciousness-raising materials about what constitutes abuse and techniques for recognizing when someone is a victim or an abuser.

When the Client Is a Victim

The most important issue to address when the client is a victim of family violence is her safety. This is particularly the case if she has made the decision to leave the relationship and, if married, divorce the abusive spouse. She needs to have a plan of action and a supportive safety net in place when the departure occurs and/or the Complaint is served.

> When an abusive partner realizes that the victim truly has made affirmative efforts to leave him, he may feel emasculated. His threats, protestations of love, and domestic terrorism have all proved futile in his efforts to retain control over her. It is at this time that many batterers turn to other devices to exert domination over the fleeing partner. It is at this time that the risk of serious violence in intimate relationships is at its h[e]ight. After the victim has made efforts to escape, the batterer is most likely to seek to retaliate against her by sabotaging the independent life she tries to establish for herself. ... Victims constantly relay stories of the batterer's false reports to child protective services; false "anonymous" tip-offs to employers about the victim's disloyalty or dishonesty; and calls to employers or family members revealing damaging, truthful information about the victim.[34]

If the client is not yet committed to leaving the relationship, members of the family law team should listen to her patiently, allow her to freely express her feelings, and be sensitive to the many reasons why people remain in such relationships. Team members need to communicate the message that no one deserves to be threatened or beaten, but also be prepared to let the client make her own decision, even if it means not yet being ready to leave the relationship.

Paralegal Practice Tip
Because the victims of intimate partner violence are predominantly females, we will refer to them as females in the remainder of this section.

One of the reasons why the client may not be prepared to terminate the abusive relationship may be a sense of helplessness and inability to escape the situation. A common tool for helping victims develop a sense of control over their situation is a Safety Plan. Safety plans may be prepared by the victim independently or with the assistance of a family law team member. There are many models of such plans, one of which is available on the companion website.[35] Typically safety plans address topics such as the following:

- Contact numbers for resources such as the police, hotlines, and shelters
- Locations where the victim can go if forced to leave home
- Suggestions for increasing safety at home, work, and in the community
- Items and documents to take when leaving home
- Strategies for protecting children

When the Client Is a Perpetrator

Abusers rarely self-identify, and, therefore, members of the family law team may never learn of their conduct or, worse, may be taken by surprise by it! Abusers come in all forms and from all backgrounds, and there is no one mold into which they all fit. There are, however, some red flags to watch for, a cluster of characteristics that batterers in particular commonly share. (See Exhibit 15.4.) The team should be alert to these indicators.

EXHIBIT 15.4 Profile of an Abuser

Technically, there is no such thing as a profile of an abuser. However, there are certain common traits, attitudes, and behaviors that may be strong indicators. They typically include the following:

- He believes in traditional, rigid, hierarchical sex roles.
- He engages in jealous, possessive, and controlling behaviors.
- He has a two-sided personality—one mild and gentle, the other mean and abusive.
- He believes he is a victim.
- He is hypersensitive to criticism.
- He has a distorted self-image. (It may be in the form of low self-esteem and feelings of inadequacy or an inflated positive self-image.)
- He is self-centered.
- He is manipulative.
- He engages in minimization, denial, blame, and criticism.
- He is overly dependent on his partner and unable to see her as a separate person.
- He has an explosive temper and breaks or throws things when angry and hits, shoves, and kicks his partner and/or children.
- He is cruel to animals.
- He has difficulty expressing feelings.
- He has a history of bad relationships.
- He was abused as a child in his family of origin (physically, emotionally, and/or sexually).[36]

Impact of Intimate Partner Violence on Spousal Support and Property Division

Whatever the general rules may be, it is important to be aware of forms of relief that may be available in a particular jurisdiction to a client who has been abused. As indicated in Chapters 10 and 11, the states vary with respect to what role, if any, a history of abuse plays in the division of property and/or availability of spousal support upon divorce. Some equitable distribution jurisdictions, such as Massachusetts and Tennessee, include "conduct of the parties during the marriage" as a factor to be considered. Others do not, particularly in the context of a no-fault divorce. In an Iowa case, for example, a wife asked the court to consider alleged abuse under the statutory catchall provision allowing the court to consider "other factors the court may determine to be relevant in an individual case." The court declined to do so "because it would introduce the concept of fault into a dissolution-of-marriage action, a model rejected by our legislature in 1970."[37] However, possible options should always be explored even in community property jurisdictions. For example, in California, courts may consider domestic violence in certain circumstances:[38]

- A documented history of domestic violence is one of several factors a court may consider when ordering spousal support.[39]
- A criminal conviction for domestic violence gives rise to a rebuttable presumption that the abusive spouse is not entitled to a spousal support award.[40]
- The legislature has created a cause of action for the tort of domestic violence. The court may award general damages, special damages, punitive damages, and any other damages or equitable relief it deems appropriate.[41] When a dissolution action has commenced and a final judgment in a civil action for domestic violence damages is subsequently entered, the court can enforce the judgment by deducting the amount of the award from the abusive spouse's share of community property without first exhausting that spouse's separate property.[42]

If the client is an abuser, alleged or proven, the ethical challenges of representation are magnified. Members of the family law team need to remain as nonjudgmental and emotionally uninvolved as possible in order to serve as zealous advocates. The legal system in this country is based on the premise that everyone is entitled to competent representation, no matter how offensive or illegal his or her behavior may be. Perhaps the greatest challenge to the team is balancing the duty to maintain client confidentiality with a responsibility to prevent the commission of a crime that could cause serious physical injury or death to another individual. This sensitive question is discussed in greater depth at the end of this chapter.

CHILD VICTIMS OF FAMILY VIOLENCE

The Scope of the Problem

The most comprehensive and authoritative source of data on child abuse and neglect in the United States is generated through the National Child Abuse and Neglect Data System (NCANDS) by the Children's Bureau in the Administration for Children and Families of Health and Human Services (HHS). The Bureau collects and analyzes data submitted by the states, the District of Columbia, and Puerto Rico on an annual basis. The data is presented in an annual report, "Child Maltreatment," published each spring since 1990. Major findings of the 2006 report for fiscal year 2005 include the following:

- Approximately 3.3 million referrals involving about 6 million children were made to child protective service (CPS) agencies. Of this number, 62.1% were screened in for investigation or assessment and 25.2% were substantiated.
- More than half of the reports (55.8%) were made by professionals (police, teachers, medical and social services personnel, etc.) and the remainder by nonprofessionals (relatives, neighbors, friends, etc.).
- With respect to types of abuse experienced by confirmed victims, 62.8% suffered neglect; 16.6% physical abuse; 9.3% sexual abuse; and 7.1% emotional maltreatment. An estimated 1,460 children died as a result of child abuse or neglect, a rate of 1.96 deaths per 100,000 children.
- More than half of the victims (54.5%) were 7 years old or younger, and the highest rate of victimization (16.5 per 1,000 children) was of children younger than 3 years old.
- 50.7% of the child victims were female and 47.3% were male.
- 49.7% of the victims were white, 23.1% African-American, and 17.4% Hispanic.
- 79.4% of the 899,000 perpetrators of child maltreatment were parents, 6.8% were other relatives, and approximately 10% were unrelated caregivers (such as foster parents and day care providers). Unmarried partners of parents accounted for 3.8% of the total.
- 57.8% of the perpetrators were female and 42.2% were male.[43]

FEDERAL RECOGNITION OF THE PROBLEM

In 1974, Congress passed the first comprehensive federal legislation to address the problem of child abuse and neglect in the United States, the Child Abuse Prevention and Treatment Act (CAPTA).[44] The Act established the National Center of Child Abuse and Neglect (NCCAN) to serve as a clearinghouse for information on child protection programs and research. In addition to driving production of the NCANDS annual report described above, NCCAN provides grant money to states to study and prevent child abuse. Initially, only states with mandatory child abuse reporting laws were eligible for funding. All states now have such laws. Since 1974, reporting laws have been expanded to include mandatory disclosure by many professionals (including some who normally enjoy legally recognized privileged communications, such as physicians, psychologists, and licensed counselors) when the communications involve or pertain to child abuse or neglect. Largely in response to CAPTA, all states also now have in place comprehensive child protective systems vesting centralized responsibility in a single designated child protection agency.

TYPES OF CHILD ABUSE

As indicated in the summary "Child Maltreatment" report, children in the United States suffer a variety of forms of abuse in the family environment, ranging from, in the extreme, death at the hands of their parents, siblings, or caretakers, to emotional abuse and the potentially devastating effects of exposure to the abuse of other family members. Types of child abuse are defined by both federal and state law.[45] Under CAPTA, child abuse and neglect is defined as:

> … at a minimum, any recent act or failure to act on the part of a parent or caretaker, which results in death, serious physical or emotional harm, sexual abuse, or exploitation, or an act or failure to act which presents an imminent risk of serious harm;[46]

The forms of abuse most commonly specifically identified and further defined by the states are:

> Neglect
> Physical abuse
> Emotional abuse
> Sexual abuse
> Substance abuse

Abandonment
occurs when the whereabouts of a child's parent are unknown, the parent has left the child in unsafe circumstances, and/or has failed to maintain contact with or provide support for the child for an extended period of time

The states vary with respect to their treatment of ***abandonment*** as a category of child abuse and neglect. Several states (including Connecticut, Florida, Illinois, Kentucky, Louisiana, New Jersey, Texas, and Virginia) include abandonment in the definition of neglect. About a dozen states (including Indiana, Kansas, Maine, New Mexico, New York, Ohio, and South Carolina) establish a separate definition of abandonment. "In general, it is considered abandonment of the child when the parent's identity or whereabouts are unknown, the child has been left by the parent in circumstances where the child suffers serious harm, or the parent has failed to maintain contact with the child or to provide reasonable support for a specified period of time."[47]

Neglect

Neglect
failure by the caregiver to provide needed, age-appropriate care although financially able to do so, or offered financial or other means to do so

At the federal level, ***neglect*** is defined as "a type of maltreatment that refers to the failure by the caregiver to provide needed, age appropriate care although financially able to do so, or offered financial or other means to do so."[48] A distinction is made between an inability to provide for a child and a deliberate failure to provide with or without any apparent reason. Neglect usually involves an ongoing pattern of inadequate care falling into one or more categories: physical, emotional, medical, and educational.

Physical neglect
inadequate supervision and/or a failure to provide adequate food, shelter, and clothing such that the child's health, safety, growth, and development are endangered

- ***Physical neglect*** is the form most commonly reported. It generally involves inadequate supervision and/or a failure to provide adequate food, shelter, and clothing such that the child's health, safety, growth, and development are endangered.

Emotional neglect
a pattern of rejecting, isolating, and ignoring a child's needs for nurturance, stimulation and social contact

- ***Emotional neglect*** generally includes a pattern of rejecting, isolating, and ignoring the child's needs for nurturance, stimulation, and social contact.

Medical neglect
the failure of a parent or caretaker to provide appropriate health care for a child

- ***Medical neglect*** involves the failure of a parent or caretaker to provide appropriate health care for a child. Although medical neglect cases tend to be high profile, they commonly make up less than 5 percent of cases of child maltreatment. Medical neglect ranges from situations in which caretakers ignore medical advice in non-emergency situations to circumstances in which a parent refuses medical care for a seriously ill child due to religious beliefs, cultural traditions, or financial limitations. The state will usually intervene in an emergency or when the child has a life-threatening or chronic condition.

Educational neglect
a parent's failure to use his or her best efforts to ensure that a child of mandatory school age attends a legally recognized school or program of home schooling

- ***Educational neglect*** refers to a parent's failure to use his or her best efforts to ensure that a child of mandatory school age attends a legally recognized public or private school or participates in a state-monitored program of home schooling. A distinction is usually made when the child is a chronic truant through no apparent lack of supervision or effort on the parent's part.

Suspected neglect is usually reported by health care professionals, preschool and day care staff members, school personnel, and neighbors.[49]

Physical Abuse

In general at the federal level, physical abuse is defined as "non-accidental physical injury to the child"[52] that may be caused by behaviors such as punching, striking, kicking, biting, or burning. Although the most visible form of abuse, it is not as common as neglect. Physical abuse cases reflect varying degrees of culpability and involve:

- parents who deliberately and maliciously physically abuse their children
- parents who administer severe punishment to their children in the good-faith belief that they are acting in the children's best interests
- parents who have never developed effective parenting skills and who, as a result, are poor disciplinarians
- parents who accidentally injure their children

Investigations of physical abuse reports often reveal that alcohol and drug abuse as well as other forms of domestic violence are evident in a physically abused child's home environment.

Child Abuse or Discipline?   The common law recognized a parental privilege to use reasonable force in disciplining children. In describing the privilege, Blackstone commented that a parent "may lawfully correct his child, being under age, in a reasonable manner," and that "battery is, in some cases, justifiable or lawful; as where one who hath authority, a parent or a master, gives moderate correction to his child, his scholar, or his apprentice."[53] The U.S. Supreme Court has also held that parents have a constitutionally protected fundamental liberty interest in directing their children's upbringing.[54] However, the parental right to discipline is not unlimited, and the states have the right to restrict it to protect children from cruel and excessive punishment. (See Case 15.2.)

Although the Supreme Court has not set a fixed rule defining what constitutes unreasonable or excessive corporal punishment under all circumstances, a majority of states have adopted the common law standard of "reasonableness and moderation." For example, Ohio requires a parent's use of force to be "proper and reasonable under the circumstances."[55] In Washington State, "A parent has a right to use reasonable and timely punishment to discipline a minor child within the bounds of moderation and for the best interests of the child."[56] In Rhode Island, "[t]he test of unreasonableness is met at the point at which a parent ceases to act in good faith and with parental affection and acts immoderately, cruelly, or mercilessly with a malicious desire to inflict pain, rather than make a genuine effort to correct the child by proper means."[57] In Wisconsin, "the accepted degree of force must vary according to the age, sex, physical and mental condition and disposition of the child, the conduct of the child, the nature of the discipline, and all the surrounding circumstances."[58] Although it did not pass, in the winter of 2007 the Massachusetts legislature considered a bill to ban corporal punishment by parents with limited exceptions.

Emotional Abuse

All states and territories except Georgia and Washington include emotional maltreatment in their statutory definitions of types of abuse, sometimes referring to it as psychological abuse. More than twenty states presently specifically define emotional abuse. "Typical language used in these definitions is 'injury

Paralegal Practice Tip
The CAPTA Amendments of 1996 added a provision specifying that the Act does not establish a federal requirement that "a parent or legal guardian provide a child any medical service or treatment against the religious beliefs of the parent or legal guardian."[50] Approximately thirty states and the District of Columbia exempt from the definition of neglect those parents who do not seek medical care for their children on the basis of religious beliefs, and three states (Arizona, Connecticut, and Washington) specifically exempt Christian Scientists. About half of the thirty states authorize the court to intervene and order treatment when warranted by the circumstances.[51]

Paralegal Practice Tip

First identified in the early 1970s, **shaken baby syndrome** is a condition that results from repeated, vigorous shaking of a baby that causes brain damage and sometimes death. It can result from a single incident or a more prolonged pattern of abuse. "Violent shaking is especially dangerous to infants and young children because their neck muscles are not fully developed and their brain tissue is exceptionally fragile."[59] Caretakers who abuse very young children in this manner often claim that the babies fell but "The force of shaking a child in anger and frustration is five to 10 times greater than if the child were simply to trip and fall."[60] Initially, the condition can be difficult to diagnose because the resulting injuries are not always the same and are frequently not externally observable. They usually include brain damage and swelling, mental retardation or developmental delays, loss of sensory functions such as sight and hearing, and sometimes death. Because of its nature and the lack of a national database addressing this specific form of physical abuse, the number of children who are victims of shaken baby syndrome is unknown.

Shaken baby syndrome
a condition that results from repeated, vigorous shaking of a baby that causes brain damage and sometimes death and that can result from a single incident or a more prolonged pattern of abuse

CASE **15.2** *State of New Mexico v. Lefevre,* 138 N.M. 174, 2005 NMCA 101, 117 P.3d 980 (2005)

BACKGROUND

This case involved the father of a twelve-year-old daughter and her younger brother. The father had been divorced from his wife for several years, and their relationship was still contentious at the time of the incident addressed in this case. He visited regularly with their children (the daughter once a month and the son every other weekend and Wednesdays). He had become concerned that he was not receiving copies of "Wednesday Notes," which advised parents of school schedules and special activities. He had told his daughter that her brother had told him that she was removing the "Notes" from his backpack and that was why he was not seeing them. When the father went to school to pick up the children he approached them from the back, and it appeared that the daughter was removing something from her brother's backpack, which the father presumed was the notes he needed to see. He allegedly grabbed and squeezed her hand "really hard" and said, "That's not your backpack." When she said, "Dad, that's not fair," he replied, "I'm sick of you." The daughter continued on to a sports tryout and only later told her mother about the incident. The mother asked if she wanted to speak to the guardian *ad litem,* go to the hospital, or speak to the police about it. The guardian was unavailable and she declined to go see a doctor. She did, however, speak with the police. At the father's trial on a battery charge, a police officer testified that he saw a dime-sized bruise on the daughter's hand.

The father was convicted of battery and then appealed the conviction, arguing that the act of grabbing his daughter's hand was privileged under a parental control justification. He argued that: "(1) federal law recognizes a fundamental right of parents to make decisions concerning care, custody, and control of their children; (2) state law recognizes the common law parental control justification as an affirmative defense for offensive acts which would otherwise be punishable under the battery statute; (3) and the district court erred in finding that the touching was unlawful, …"

FROM THE OPINION

We hold that, in New Mexico, a parent has a privilege to use moderate or reasonable physical force, without criminal liability, when engaged in the discipline of his or her child. Discipline involves controlling behavior and correcting misbehavior for the betterment and welfare of the child. The physical force cannot be cruel or excessive if it is to be justified. …

2. Defendant's Act Fell Within The Parental Privilege

The battery offense of which the Defendant was convicted proscribes "the unlawful, intentional touching or application of force to the person of another, when done in a rude, insolent or angry manner." § 30–3–4. The State had the burden to prove beyond a reasonable doubt all elements of the offense, including unlawfulness. … When a parent's behavior falls within the parental privilege, the act is not unlawful. … Thus, when a question of parental privilege exists, the State must prove beyond a reasonable doubt that the parent's conduct did not come within the privilege. …

In considering whether the State has disproved the justification, the court or jury is entitled to consider such factors as "the age, physical condition, and

continued

other characteristics of a child as well as with the gravity of the misconduct." Arnold, 543 N.W.2d at 603; ... there must exist some threshold at which parental physical force in the discipline of children is justified even though, technically, the elements of the battery offense can be proven. ...

... there must exist for parents a harbor safe from prosecutorial interference in parental judgment. See Model Penal Code and Commentaries § 3.08, cmt. 2 (1985) ("So long as a parent uses moderate force for permissible purposes, the criminal law should not provide for review of the reasonableness of the parent's judgment."). In our view, an isolated instance of moderate or reasonable physical force as that in the present case that results in nothing more than transient pain or temporary marks or bruises is protected under the parental discipline privilege. ...

This protection for parents should exist even if the parent acts out of frustration or short temper. Parents do not always act with calmness of mind or considered judgment when upset with, or concerned about, their children's behavior. ... A reaction often occurs from behavior a parent deems inappropriate that irritates or angers the parent, causing a reactive, demonstrative act. Heat of the moment must not result in immoderate physical force and must be managed; however, an angry moment driving moderate or reasonable discipline is often part and parcel of the real world of parenting with which prosecutors and courts should not interfere. What parent among us can say he or she has not been angered to some degree from a child's defiant, impudent, or insolent conduct, sufficient to call for spontaneous, stern, and meaningful discipline?

In the present case, no reasonable minds could differ on the legal consequence of Defendant's acts. The district court did not find or determine that Defendant had no legitimate disciplinary purpose whatsoever in mind. Even were a disciplinary purpose questionable or obscure, Defendant's act was an isolated one. He reacted when he saw Daughter with her hand in Son's pack. His demonstrative act, even if an angry touching, resulted in only a temporary dime-sized bruise on Daughter's hand and transient pain. The force was relatively inconsequential; the injury was marginal. Defendant's conduct was not cruel or excessive, and considering the totality of the circumstances, it was moderate and reasonable. "If such acts, ... with no apparent evidence of any aggravating factors, are sufficient to support an assault charge, then any physical contact by a parent with a child that hurts the child may support an assault conviction if the State elects to prosecute." Wilder, 748 A.2d at 456.

We determine that Defendant's conduct did not reach beyond the point of departure from justified parental discipline and was privileged, and that, as a matter of law, the evidence in this case was insufficient to support a determination of guilt on the charge of battery beyond a reasonable doubt.

Conclusion

We reverse Defendant's conviction of battery and remand with instructions to enter a judgment of acquittal.

SIDEBAR

Do you agree with the decision of the appellate court in this case? Explain your response. The full opinion is available in its entirety on the companion website.

to the psychological capacity or emotional stability of the child as evidenced by an observable or substantial change in behavior, emotional response, or cognition,' or as evidenced by 'anxiety, depression, withdrawal, or aggressive behavior.'"[61]

Caretaker behavior that rises to the level of emotional abuse generally encompasses a persistent pattern of the behaviors described earlier under emotional neglect, along with more overt behaviors including verbally assaulting and belittling children, terrorizing them with threats of punishment and abandonment, humiliating and embarrassing them, and exploiting them by involving them in illegal behavior such as theft. It does not include occasional and unintentionally hurtful outbursts that can occur with even well-intentioned parents. It is more likely to occur among parents who were themselves abused as children, who have never had an opportunity to learn or develop effective parenting skills, and who have unrealistic expectations for their children. Whatever the cause, many researchers believe that emotional abuse is a stronger predictor of developmental problems than is physical abuse. "Although the visible signs of emotional abuse in children can be difficult to detect, the hidden scars of this type of abuse manifest in numerous behavioral ways, including insecurity, poor self-esteem, destructive behavior, angry acts (such as fire-setting and animal cruelty), withdrawal, poor development of basic skills, alcohol or drug abuse, suicide, difficulty forming relationships, and unstable job histories."[62]

Sexual Abuse

Under CAPTA's "minimum definition," sexual abuse includes:

- the employment, use, persuasion, inducement, enticement, or coercion of any child to engage in, or assist any other person to engage in, any sexually explicit conduct or simulation of such conduct for the purpose of producing a visual depiction of such conduct; or
- the rape, and in cases of caretaker or interfamilial relationships, statutory rape, molestation, prostitution, or other form of sexual exploitation of children, or incest with children.[63]

The states define sexual abuse in various ways, but they generally include both touching offenses (such as fondling the child's genitals, penetrating a child's vagina or anus to any extent directly or with an object, or having the child touch the caretaker's sex organs) and non-touching offenses such as exposing a child to sexual acts (masturbation, sexual relations, etc.) or to pornographic materials. They may also include sexual exploitation of children such as engaging them in acts of prostitution or using them as subjects of pornographic materials. (See Paralegal Application 15.3.)

Substance Abuse

CAPTA requires states to have policies and procedures to notify children's protective services of substance-exposed newborns (SENS) and to establish a plan of safe care for those affected by illegal substance abuse or withdrawal symptoms as a result of prenatal drug exposure. The states have chosen to address this requirement in a variety of ways. Some have placed priority on making drug treatment more accessible for pregnant women. For example, Illinois and Minnesota require mandated reporters to report pregnant women they suspect are abusing drugs so that they can be referred for treatment. California, Maryland, and Missouri, among other states, require that

PARALEGAL APPLICATION 15.3

CUTE LITTLE BABY PICTURE OR CHILD PORNOGRAPHY?

Many parents take pictures of their young children nude in a variety of settings such as bathtubs, beds, beaches, and backyards, pictures that come back to haunt at sixteenth and fiftieth birthday parties and other festive occasions. But at what point does a "cute little baby picture" become a "lewd exhibition of a child's genitals"? When does the photo cross the line between innocence and child pornography? The primary focus of the criminal law in this area is less on "obscenity" and more on protection of the child. "[T]he state can proscribe child pornography without requiring that the visual reproduction be obscene because the primary evil is not the visual reproduction's effect on the consumer, but its effect on the child."[64] The states have greater leeway regulating child pornography than adult pornography because "the use of children as subjects of pornographic materials is harmful to the physiological, emotional, and mental health of the child."[65]

Most states that have addressed this topic have applied the factors adopted by the Ninth Circuit in the *Dost* case (the "Dost" factors):[66]

1. whether the focal point of the visual depiction is on the child's genitalia or pubic area;

2. whether the setting of the visual depiction is sexually suggestive, i.e., in a place or pose generally associated with sexual activity;

3. whether the child is depicted in an unnatural pose, or in inappropriate attire, considering the age of the child;

4. whether the child is fully or partially clothed, or nude;

5. whether the visual depiction suggests sexual coyness or a willingness to engage in sexual activity;

6. whether the visual depiction is intended or designed to elicit a sexual response in the viewer.

When dealing with a case of this nature, the state's criminal statute must be read carefully to ensure that it covers the alleged offense and does not contain an exception for exposures "of a private, family nature not intended for distribution outside of the family; ..."[67]

when a substance-exposed newborn is identified, an assessment must be done of both the newborn and the child's family so that appropriate services can be arranged.[68]

Some states have attempted to criminalize prenatal substance abuse using a variety of existing statutes such as delivering drugs to a minor (through the umbilical cord), assault with a deadly weapon, corruption of a minor, criminal abuse and neglect of a child, and manslaughter. Still others treat it under civil child abuse laws and view it as a ground for terminating or suspending parental rights. The Wisconsin children's code as amended in 1998 grants that state's juvenile court exclusive jurisdiction over an unborn child when the pregnant mother "habitually lacks self-control" with regard to drugs or alcohol. The statute defines an unborn child as a "human being from the time of fertilization to the time of birth."[69] The Ohio Supreme Court delivered a similarly strong message in the case *In re Baby Boy Blackshear*,[70] when it held that if a newborn baby tests positive for drug exposure, it constitutes *per se* child abuse even though the civil child abuse law made no reference to prenatal child abuse. The court defined an "abused child" as one who suffers "physical or mental injury that harms or threatens to harm the child's health or welfare"[71] and did not specify when the harmful act must occur. The two dissenting judges would have remanded the case, because no evidence was presented directly linking the baby's symptoms to the mother's drug use. In addition, no injuries were identified that harmed or threatened to harm the baby, and the physician who noted a "positive drug scan" on a hospital record prescribed no need for follow-up medication or special care.[72]

Some states address by statute harm caused to a child of any age as a result of exposure to illegal drug activity. Approximately half the states do so in their criminal statutes and some (such as Alaska, Kansas, Minnesota, and Missouri) do so in their child endangerment statutes. Some states (California, Mississippi, Montana, North Carolina, and Washington, for example) impose enhanced penalties for the manufacturing of illegal drugs in the presence of a child. Idaho, Louisiana, and Ohio prosecute the manufacture or possession of any controlled substance in the presence of a child as a felony, and others (such as Illinois, Pennsylvania, and Virginia) specifically target the manufacture of methamphetamine in the presence of a child.

REPORTING OF CHILD ABUSE

Every state identifies individuals who are required to report suspected child abuse or neglect to a designated child protective services agency (sometimes called a social or human services agency). ***Mandatory reporters*** customarily include, at a minimum, law enforcement personnel, individuals in the health professions, social workers, teachers, and day care providers. Mandatory reporters are required to report suspected abuse and neglect or face civil and sometimes criminal penalties. ***Permissive reporters*** are individuals who may, but are not required to, report suspected abuse. These individuals include, among others, friends, family members, neighbors, storekeepers, and strangers who most commonly witness incidents of abuse in public areas, such as playgrounds, malls, and parking lots. Permissive reporters are not liable for reports filed in good faith. However, some states provide a penalty (usually a fine) for knowingly filing a false report. Some states require "all persons" to report child abuse, impliedly including attorneys and their employees. For example, the applicable New Jersey statute requires "Any person having reasonable cause to believe that a child has been subjected to child abuse or acts of child abuse shall report the same immediately to the Division of Youth and Family Services by telephone or otherwise."[73] The Act provides statutory immunity to those who file reports.[74] A failure to report constitutes a disorderly person's offense and may constitute evidence of negligence.[75] The ethical dilemma that reporting requirements impose on members of the family law team is discussed more fully at the conclusion of this chapter.

Reports are usually made to the state's designated child protection agency. The agency is responsible for:

- receiving reports of abuse or neglect
- promptly investigating reports, usually by making a home visit, interviewing relevant parties, and evaluating the child's living arrangements (An initial visit customarily must be made within twenty-four hours if a child is in imminent danger or, if not, within three to seven days.)
- developing plans for families in need of services
- providing a wide range of services directly or through third parties (e.g., counseling, parent education, educational assessments, homemaker services, etc.)
- removing children from homes where they are at risk of immediate serious harm with or without a court order or prior notice to the parent(s)
- scheduling court hearings before or immediately after removal so that parents are given an opportunity to challenge the agency's actions

- arranging for and monitoring appropriate foster care placements in homes or group facilities
- initiating proceedings to terminate parental rights where appropriate and facilitate adoptions or other long-term care
- referring cases involving serious physical injury or child rape to law enforcement authorities for investigation and possible criminal prosecution

When a report of abuse or neglect is received and processed by a child protection agency, the case customarily proceeds along one of four paths:

1. When the report is determined to be false or frivolous, it is deemed invalid.
2. When the agency determines that the report was made in good faith but finds no reasonable cause to believe the child is at risk, the case is designated unsubstantiated and is closed, although the record remains in the department's files.
3. When the report is substantiated, the agency develops a service plan with the parent(s)/caretaker(s). If the abuse is not serious and services are accepted and effectively implemented, the child may remain with the family. If the services are not accepted or successfully implemented, the agency may file a ***care and protection petition*** seeking temporary removal or removal and termination of parental rights, if appropriate.
4. When the agency has reasonable cause to believe that removal is necessary to ensure the child's safety, the agency may immediately remove the child and file a dependency action/care and protection petition for hearing usually within seventy-two hours. The court will determine whether a service plan should be developed and a reunification sought, or the agency should seek to terminate parental rights in anticipation of adoption or some other permanent placement in the best interests of the child.

Care and protection/dependency proceeding
a court proceeding in which the state seeks custody of a child

Parens patriae
the authority of a state to protect those within its boundaries who cannot protect themselves; Latin for "parent of the country"

The U.S. Supreme Court has long recognized the preservation of the family as a priority. It has also afforded constitutional protection to the right of parents to raise their children as they see fit. However, it has also recognized that parental rights must be balanced with the duty of the state to protect children. Removal of a child from his or her home is clearly an extreme measure, but the state has the authority to initiate such action under the legal doctrine of **parens patriae,** the Latin term for "parent of the country." However, it cannot do so arbitrarily, but rather only for good cause, and parents must be afforded due process to protect their parental rights.

The removal of a child from his or her home may be temporary or permanent. Temporary removal may be appropriate in situations where a report of abuse is substantiated and reasonable steps have been taken to keep the child at home, but the child remains at risk because the parents are "temporarily" unable to provide appropriate care. To remove the child on a temporary basis, the agency files a care and protection/dependency action in which it asks a court to find the child dependent or in need of care and protection. The court also must determine that remaining in the home is contrary to the child's best interests, and that the agency has made reasonable efforts to prevent removal. If successful, the agency is granted temporary custody, assumes primary responsibility for the child, and can make an appropriate placement in foster care while the parents complete the requirements of a service plan. If the removal will be permanent, the agency may convince the parents to voluntarily surrender their parental rights or, if that effort fails, may file a petition for involuntary ***termination of parental rights.***

Paralegal Practice Tip
In some cases, parents will voluntarily seek the assistance of the state with a child who, despite their best efforts, persistently runs away from home, willfully fails to attend school, and refuses to obey reasonable parental rules. When the parents believe they can no longer adequately care for or protect such a child, they may seek to have him or her designated by the court as a child in need of services, thereby triggering a host of alternative placement and treatment options under the supervision of the state.

Termination of parental rights
a judicial severing of the legal relationship between a parent and child

Reasonable efforts

the effort a child protective agency must make to prevent removal of a child from his or her home, or, if removed, to reunify the family within a specified period of time

Permanency planning

planning for the return home of a child following removal or for termination of parental rights within a legally specified period of time in an effort to promote stability for the child

---

Paralegal Practice Tip

After the U.S. Supreme Court's ruling in *DeShaney v. Winnebago County Department of Social Services*,[78] state agencies are unlikely to be subject to liability for returning children to abusive homes. In that case, five-year-old Joshua DeShaney's father beat him to the point that he became profoundly retarded. The child's guardian *ad litem* brought an action against the county department of social services and its employees, alleging that they had failed to intervene to protect the child from harm when they knew or should have known about the risk of violence posed by his father. Although the Supreme Court characterized the father's actions as "reprehensible," it held that the Fourteenth Amendment did not require the agency to protect the child from "private" violence not attributable to the conduct of its employees.[79]

Paralegal Practice Tip

Whenever abuse and neglect, removal, or termination of parental rights are at issue in a case, discovery should include a search of child protection agency records with respect to reports and service plans, etc.

A termination of parental rights severs the legal relationship between a parent and his or her biological or adopted child. Given that parental rights enjoy a high degree of constitutional protection, they cannot be terminated without clear and convincing evidence of parental unfitness.

Since the passage of the federal Adoption Assistance and Child Welfare Act of 1980 (CWA),[76] child protective agencies have had a duty to make "*reasonable efforts*" to keep families together before removing children, and, if removal is necessary, to make a reasonable effort to eventually reunite the family. This requirement sometimes has resulted in the premature return of children to high-risk family environments or, in the alternative, to lengthy stays in foster care. Partly to address these problems, in 1997 Congress passed the Adoption and Safe Families Act (ASFA), which retained the reasonable efforts requirement but gave considerable discretion to the states with respect to implementing it. The Act gave priority to the child's "health and safety" and also took steps to limit the time children spend in foster care.[77] ASFA requires that a *permanency planning* hearing be held no later than twelve months after a child has been placed in foster care (or sooner in cases in which reunification is an impossible or inappropriate goal, such as when the child has been abandoned, the parent has subjected the child to serious abuse, or the parent has murdered another family member).

Child protection litigation can be costly, dehumanizing, disempowering, and traumatic for the parties and particularly for children who have been removed from their homes and separated from their parents, siblings, and extended families for reasons usually not of their own making. An alternative to litigation is child protection mediation, which may be used at any stage of a child protection case. It is usually initiated by a child protection worker or an attorney. One commentator has described this procedure as follows:

> The purpose of this particular mediation process is to develop a case plan to reunify the family as soon as possible. If reunification is not possible, the goal of mediation becomes finding the most suitable permanent placement for the child within the time period established by law. Mediated issues often include the services the parents will use, conditions that must be satisfied before the child may return home, alternative options for child care, and parenting practices, including alternative nonviolent approaches.[80]

Statistics indicate that 60 to 85 percent of such mediations end in agreements and that they promote family progress and increased compliance with court orders.[81]

Custody Disputes

As discussed in Chapter 8, many states now have established presumptions favoring joint custody of children upon divorce. Even if a court is required to consider a history of domestic violence when making custody decisions, it is often only one of several factors the court considers. The Model Code of the National Council of Juvenile and Family Court Judges recommends that in every proceeding where there is a dispute as to the custody of a child, a determination by the court that domestic or family violence has occurred should raise a rebuttable presumption that "it is detrimental to the child and not in the best interests of the child, to be placed in sole custody, joint legal custody, or joint physical custody with the perpetrator of family violence."[82] A report to the American Bar Association has also recommended that, where there is proof of domestic violence, "batterers should be presumed by law to be unfit custodians for their children."[83] Many of the states have adopted such provisions in one form or another. Some statutes require the courts to consider a history of domestic violence before joint custody can be awarded; some require the court to factor domestic violence into the best interests test; and some mandate that the courts not award joint custody where abuse has been demonstrated.[84]

When the abuse has been interspousal and not actively directed at the parties' children, judges (and sometimes clients and attorneys as well) may fail to appreciate the impact that witnessing a parent's abusive behavior has on a child. A father who has abused a child's mother without treatment or legal consequences will not suddenly cease his behavior upon divorce. In fact, he is likely to intensify and repeat it in subsequent relationships. Even if the children have not been the direct recipients of his violence, they are victims as a result of exposure to it. "According to reports by battered mothers, 87% to 90% of their children witnessed the mothers' abuse."[87] They may actually see the physical, sexual, and emotional attacks; overhear them; experience the emotional tension in the residence; and/or be exposed to the aftermath, including both the mother's physical injuries and the destruction of property (phones ripped from the wall, dishes and chairs broken, etc.).

> Children who live in a battering relationship experience the most insidious form of child abuse. Whether or not they are physically abused by either parent is less important than the psychological scars they bear from watching their fathers beat their mothers. They learn to become part of a dishonest conspiracy of silence. ...

The effects of witnessing domestic violence are often severe and multifaceted. Certainly, not all children are affected by exposure to domestic violence in the same manner or to the same degree. Numerous factors influence the extent to which a child is affected. These factors include: age, gender, race, frequency and severity of the violence witnessed, and the degree of maternal impairment. Nonetheless, all children exposed to domestic violence are affected in some way. Witnessing domestic violence can affect children behaviorally, cognitively, emotionally, physically and socially.

The great extent to which children are affected by domestic violence justifies the state's interest in protecting children from domestic violence and expanding interventions to include child witnesses. If the state continues to ignore the reality that children are harmed by domestic violence, then society as a whole will suffer as violence increases and the health of these children declines.[88]

A mother who has been abused by her partner is "damned if she does and damned if she doesn't" fight for custody of her children. Her abuser may threaten to harm her and/or the children, take the children where she "will never find them," or, if the circumstances fit, expose her to some kind of criminal liability or embarrassment as a result of her drug use, immigration status, or HIV diagnosis. The court may not believe her allegations of abuse, particularly if they are undocumented, or if her chameleon spouse persuades the judge that her claims are unfounded or grossly exaggerated. In a state that criminalizes exposing a child to domestic violence, the mother may open herself to criminal liability if she fights back in self-defense against her abuser. In some states, permitting one's child to witness spousal abuse itself may constitute grounds for removing the child from the care and custody of both parents.[89]

Paralegal Practice Tip
Whenever a child who is or may be of American Indian heritage is the subject of a custody action (including adoption, foster care placement, termination of parental rights, or reunification proceedings), procedural safeguards of the Indian Child Welfare Act,[85] along with related state laws,[86] may be triggered. The Act is designed to promote the stability and security of Indian tribes and families by establishing minimum standards for removal of Indian children from their families and to promote placement in homes that reflect the values of Indian culture. Among other rights, the tribe has the right to obtain jurisdiction over the proceedings (by seeking transfer of the matter to a tribal court) or to intervene in a state court proceeding.

Paralegal Practice Tip
In addition to guardians *ad litem*, judges often make use of Court Appointed Special Advocates (CASA volunteers) in cases involving severely abused, abandoned, or neglected children. CASA is part of a national volunteer movement that began about three decades ago. It was initiated by a judge in Seattle, Washington, who sought a "voice in court" for abused and neglected children. There are now more than nine hundred CASA programs nationwide with at least one in every state. CASA volunteers serve as both mentors and advocates. They work with children who have been removed from their homes and placed in foster care. The one-on-one relationship formed with the child is often the only stable relationship he or she has in a world of social workers, attorneys, therapists, and caregivers. It positions the volunteer to provide the judge with information that will help safeguard the child's best interests and facilitate placement in a safe, permanent home.

PARALEGAL APPLICATION 15.4

MAKING THE CASE FOR CUSTODY OF A CHILD WHO HAS WITNESSED FAMILY VIOLENCE

Abusive parents frequently seek custody of their children, and they are often successful.[90] A client who has been abused and who makes a decision to pursue custody of her children usually faces an uphill battle, especially when those children have been exposed to her victimization. The family law team and client will need to work together to establish a solid case and to do so in a manner that does not expose the mother to liability and the children to further trauma. Depending on the judge's background and experience dealing with family violence issues, the paralegal may be asked to research the effects on children of exposure to domestic violence. The client will need to assist by suggesting witnesses, documents, and other evidence that will establish how the children have been, or are likely to be, affected by continued exposure to the abuser's violent conduct. Examples of demonstrated effects of children's exposure to domestic violence that may be evident include, but are not necessarily limited to, the following:[91]

- Aggressiveness, acting out, and antisocial conduct, including behaviors such as bullying, assaults, and destruction of property
- Generally lower levels of social competence
- Poor problem-solving skills
- Lower levels of empathy
- Depression, suicidal behaviors, anxieties, fears, and phobias
- Feelings that they are helpless and powerless
- Low self-esteem
- Guilt and self-blaming for the violence or their inability to prevent or stop it
- Anger at both the abuser and the victim
- A pervasive attitude that the use of violence is an appropriate means of expressing anger, solving problems, and intimidating and gaining control over others
- Greater likelihood of abusing a spouse or partner as an adult[92]
- Abuse of drugs and alcohol
- Running away
- Sexual acting out
- Fear for their lives and/or the lives of their parents and siblings
- Lower levels of cognitive and academic functioning
- Poor health, including colds, elevated blood pressure, insomnia, and bed-wetting
- Post-traumatic stress disorder[93]
- Injuries suffered as a result of trying to intervene and protect the abused parent

Children who have been exposed to domestic violence

> ... may have special needs that should be considered in connection with custody and parenting-time decisions. Bancroft and Silverman suggest six circumstances that promote healing. First, children need an environment that provides physical and emotional safety. Second, they require structure, appropriate limits, and a sense of predictability. Third, they benefit from a strong bond with the nonperpetrating parent. Fourth, they need to be relieved of the burden of caring for adults. Fifth, they may prefer to have some limited contact with the perpetrator if such contact is safe. Sixth, they benefit from the opportunity to reestablish relationships with siblings.[94]

"Relationships terminated by family abuse have different and unique characteristics that require the courts to implement different and unique resolutions. ... the father in a domestic violence case has not willingly accepted, nor will he ever accept, the idea that the relationship is over. He believes that he is the reigning king of the family and that only he can announce the end of the relationship. Therefore, the father's only goal is to depict the mother as unfit, immoral, and incapable of having his children."[95] Parents in abusive relationships do not come into court with equal power and ability to advocate for themselves and their children. The challenge is considerable for the client and counsel who try in such cases to raise the consciousness of the court regarding its "opportunity to assume a legitimate role in breaking the cycle of violence with every family that comes before it."[96] The court's custody order ideally should reflect a thoughtful assessment of the particular nature of the abuse experienced and its likely causes and effects. Based on the facts of the individual case, appropriate actions may range from termination of an abuser's parental rights to a plan in which visitation is permitted and a focus is placed on building the parties' skills in effective parenting, problem solving, and conflict management.

In general, when seeking custody on behalf of an abused mother, a proposed custody order needs to be carefully tailored to the facts of the case and designed to protect the safety and welfare of both the children and the mother. It may ask that the court order any one or more of the following conditions, which may be eased over time if the abusive parent remains in compliance and if it is in the best interests of the children.

- Sole legal and physical custody to the mother without visitation, because joint custody fosters continual conflict and gives the abuser an opportunity to continue his abuse, OR sole legal and physical custody to the mother with supervised visitation, preferably at a supervised visitation center that provides a safe location and trained personnel able to intervene if problems arise.
- A restraint on the abusive parent's communication with or proximity to the children except in the context of authorized visitation
- A requirement that the abuser not be granted, or permitted to continue, visitation unless he participates in and successfully completes a batterer's program or some other long-term treatment option that addresses anger, battering, and control issues in depth
- A requirement that the abusive parent not use alcohol or drugs during or within a specified time period prior to a visit
- Designation of a neutral location such as a social services agency, resource center, or police station for drop off and pickup of the children for visitation
- Impounding of any information revealing the address and phone numbers of the mother and children
- Denial of access to school and other records containing information regarding the residence of the mother and children
- Exemption for the mother from any required state-parenting program or, in the alternative, a requirement that the parents attend separate sessions where appropriate safety precautions can be arranged
- A requirement that the batterer be required to pay for counseling/therapy if needed for the mother and/or the children
- An appropriate recourse to address related disputes. Mediation should not be an option for dispute resolution, especially in cases where the dominant form of abuse is coercive control.

- Appointment of a parenting coordinator or master to manage recurring child custody disputes (an approach presently in place in several states)
- Exclusion of any "boilerplate" parental cooperation or "friendly parent" language in separation agreements

Parent coordinator

an individual, usually appointed by the court, who assists with creation and implementation of parenting agreements and enforcement of decrees in high-conflict cases involving minor children

In high-conflict child custody cases, ***parent coordinators*** can "assist parents in creating, implementing, and monitoring parenting plans.... typically parent coordinators make decisions or recommendations about day-to-day matters such as scheduling, activities, transportation, child care, discipline, education, and health care. They generally cannot modify custody, allow relocation, or make any other major changes to court orders."[97] "In those cases of domestic violence where one parent seeks to obtain and maintain power and control over the other, the role of the PC [parent coordinator] changes to an almost purely enforcement function. Here the PC is likely to be dealing with a court order, the more detailed the better, rather than a mutually agreed upon parenting plan; and the role is to ensure compliance with the details of the order and to test each request for variance from its terms with an eye to protecting the custodial parent's autonomy to make decisions based on the children's best interests and guarding against manipulation by the abusing parent."[98] The coordinator in some situations may also have an opportunity to model conflict resolution skills.

Criminal Actions Against Parents

Why are we so reluctant to prosecute parents when harm befalls their children as a result of parental negligence? One reason is that we persist in viewing wrongful acts committed against children as an intrafamily matter in which the state should intervene only reluctantly, and only when absolutely necessary. This general hesitance to intervene in family life, even to protect children, is a deeply ingrained historical tradition in this country.[99]

"Approximately fifteen children under the age of fourteen die every day in this country as a result of unintentional injuries, totaling more than 5600 children a year."[100] Some of these deaths inevitably have resulted from parental negligence. Some criminal laws place parents under a duty of care to protect their minor children based on the "special relationship" of parent and child, despite this country's long history of support for the principle of family autonomy and nonintervention by the state. In one researcher's study of prosecution of parents in such cases, she found that "... parents were in fact prosecuted in over fifty percent of the cases. Further, ... individuals not related to the victim fare even worse: nonrelatives were prosecuted in over eighty-eight percent of the cases. One particularly important ... finding was the disparate treatment of parents from different socioeconomic groups: parents in blue collar professions and parents who were unemployed were four times more likely to be prosecuted than parents from wealthier socioeconomic groups."[101] However, overall, parents generally receive more favorable treatment by the criminal justice system.

In the context of parenthood and the criminal justice system, family members are still far more likely to be excused for behavior that would be considered criminal if committed by third parties. Examples abound: the extraordinary difficulties prosecutors face in convicting parents on homicide charges in child abuse cases, the lighter sentences imposed on defendants who kill family members, the preferential treatment in some states given to sex offenders who victimize their own children rather than a stranger, and the outcry over prosecuting negligent parents.... This preferential treatment for parents persists even though young children in particular face far greater risk of danger from their relatives at home than they do from strangers in public places.[102]

Paralegal Practice Tip
Prosecutions for criminal offenses are subject to applicable statutes of limitations, which may vary from crime to crime and state to state. They may also vary in terms of when they begin to run. For example, statutes for crimes relating to sexual abuse of minors usually begin to run when the abuse is first discovered (or recalled) rather than when the injury first occurred.

When parents are prosecuted for abusive conduct toward their children, they may be prosecuted under a variety of criminal statutes:

- Statutes ranging from murder and manslaughter in cases involving deaths, to assault, battery, aggravated assault, rape/sexual assault, etc., with imposition of heightened penalties when the crime is committed against a child
- Statutes that address intentional crimes committed against children in particular, such as rape of a child, incest, child endangerment, or use of a child to commit a crime such as production of child pornography
- Statutes that criminalize parental/caretaker neglect

The same offense may be treated differently in different states. For example, some states treat the commission of an act of domestic violence in the presence of a child as a distinct criminal offense (as in the Utah statute accessible on the companion website) and others treat it as a more serious degree of assault, resulting in an enhanced penalty. (See the Oregon statute defining assault in the fourth degree, also on the companion website.)

Tort Actions

Between a Parent and a Child. Under early common law, parents were immune from liability for failure to prevent harm to their minor children resulting from the actions of third parties. Common sense and morality suggest that parents should have a legal duty to protect their children based on the "special relationship" between parent and child, and commentators often argue for the existence of such a duty.[103] However, there is little legislation or case law recognizing that parents who have not created the risk of harm have an affirmative duty to intervene to rescue a minor child from actual or potential harm caused by some other third party.

Tort
a civil wrong (other than breach of contract) for which a court provides a remedy, usually in the form of money damages; the wrong must involve harm resulting from breach of a legal duty owed to another

Between Parents and Third Parties. Although not technically abuse of a child, parents are sometimes sued by third parties, under a theory of negligent supervision, for damages caused by their children. "Under common law, parents can be liable for their children's acts 'where the parents' [own] negligence has made it possible for the child to cause the injury complained of and probable that the child would do so.'"[104] Section 316 of the Restatement (Second) of Torts provides that the duty of a parent to take reasonable measures to control a child arises when the parent knows or should know of the need to control the child and has both the ability and the opportunity to do so. The cause of action commonly known as **negligent supervision** is based on the premise that parents have a duty to society at large to exercise reasonable care in the supervision of their minor children in order to prevent them from intentionally causing injury to others.

Although parents will not necessarily be held liable for the intentional or malicious acts of their minor children, a majority of states have enacted statutes making

Negligent supervision
a cause of action based on a parent's duty to society to exercise reasonable care in the supervision of their minor children in order to prevent them from intentionally causing injury to others

parents liable in certain circumstances. Some states legislate parental responsibility laws in specific areas of conduct. For example, a Mississippi statute[105] provides that, subject to some exceptions, a parent may be found guilty of knowingly permitting a child under eighteen to have, own, or carry a concealed weapon, the carrying of which is prohibited by law. (See Paralegal Application 15.5.)

In Paralegal Application 15.5, Mavis Daniels appears to be a single mother, and the case makes no reference to the existence or identity of the youth's father. If there are two parents in the picture, each of whom plays a considerable role in the child's life, a question may arise as to whether both parents should be liable for negligent supervision or only the parent with primary custody. A Florida appellate court[106] considered this question as a matter of first impression

PARALEGAL APPLICATION 15.5

WAS MOM TO BLAME?

THE FACTS

At home one evening at 8.00 p.m., Mavis Daniels received a phone call from her employer. While she was on the phone, her fifteen-year-old son, Eddie Smith, left the house without her knowledge. At the time, he was subject to a 7:30 p.m. curfew Sunday through Thursday imposed by the youth court after he'd struck a boy at school. After Eddie left the house, he and two of his friends activated the alarm on a girl's car by hitting it with a ball. When the girl's boyfriend, Johnny Lee Williamson, Jr., came out to investigate, Eddie confronted him and, after a verbal exchange, pulled out a gun and shot the unarmed Williamson, leaving him paralyzed from the waist down. Williamson subsequently filed a complaint alleging Eddie's mother was negligent in her supervision of Eddie and that her negligence was the proximate cause of his injuries.

Eddie had been in trouble on several occasions prior to this particular incident: he wounded his uncle in a fight with a knife, knocked a boy unconscious at school, dropped out of school, and was accused of threatening a ten-year-old girl with a pellet gun and being the lookout for a robbery committed by some of his friends. Without his mother's knowledge, he obtained a handgun. Ms. Daniels testified that she had tried to enforce the curfew and attempted to discipline her son by grounding him, taking away his video games, and applying corporal punishment. When he dropped out of school, she took him to work with her at the Head Start agency and had him clean up around the school where she could keep an eye on him. She also took him to a mental health center for counseling.

In a negligent supervision action, the plaintiff, Williamson, must establish that the mother had a duty of care, that she breached that duty, that her breach was the proximate cause of his injuries, and that damages are warranted to compensate him for his loss. He must show not only that there was negligence and an injury, but also that the injury was reasonably foreseeable.

SIDEBAR

Do you think that Mavis Daniels should be held liable for the injury to Williamson? What are the arguments for both sides of the question? The case *Johnny Lee Williamson, Jr. v. Mavis C. Daniels*, 748 So.2d 754 (Miss. 1999), decided by the Mississippi Supreme Court, is available on the companion website. Read it and see if you agree with the court's decision.

in that state. The majority held that only the mother (who had primary residential custody) was liable to a school district for her son's malicious destruction of school property. A strong dissent argued that "On the one hand, the father in this case has successfully sought and procured an equal voice and equal participation in all of the major decision-making process involving the rearing of this minor child. . . ."[107] but on the other hand, was not being held accountable for his son's conduct.

TO KNOW OR NOT TO KNOW . . . TO TELL OR NOT TO TELL

Domestic violence often permeates many family law cases, whether or not it is revealed to or detected by counsel or other members of the family law team. If the issue does arise, it is often difficult, even frightening, for the family law team to address. What can be done when a battered spouse is being bullied into a poor property settlement to protect her children and herself or when counsel or the paralegal begins to suspect the client is abusing his or her children or partner and will very likely continue to do so? How can the attorney reconcile the ethical duties to maintain client confidentiality and advocate zealously for the client with the duties to prevent a fraud on the court and prevent the commission of a crime that could result in serious physical injury or death?

Clearly, family violence poses ethical issues of monumental dimensions for attorneys and their employees. The legal community itself is split between those who believe lawyers should disclose serious threats to third parties and those who believe they should not. For example, some argue that "in the context of domestic violence cases, lawyers have an affirmative duty to (1) screen battering clients who have indicated a likelihood of harming others, (2) attempt to dissuade them from carrying out planned violent crimes, and (3) warn identifiable abuse victims whom their clients have threatened."[108] On the other side, it is argued that mandatory child abuse reporting in the context of representing domestic violence victims interferes with confidentiality and open communication, exposes domestic violence victims and their children to harm, subjects victims to state intervention and potential criminal prosecution for abuse or neglect, and discourages victims from seeking legal assistance.[109]

CAPTA essentially leaves confidentiality and disclosure requirements to the discretion of the states. Little clear guidance is provided to attorneys in this area in state reporting requirements, statutes governing the attorney-client privilege, rules of professional responsibility, or occasional guidelines from bar associations and ethics opinions. Rule 1.6 of the American Bar Association (ABA) Model Rules of Professional Conduct (Model Rules) adopted in several states provides in part that a lawyer shall not reveal information relating to the representation of a client unless the client gives informed consent, the disclosure is impliedly authorized in order to carry out the representation, or the lawyer believes the disclosure is reasonably necessary to prevent death or substantial bodily harm or to comply with a law or court order.

The ABA Model Rules are not binding, however, and the states are not uniform in their disclosure requirements. "While some states' professional rules provide a general framework for warning third parties of impending harm, significant variation also occurs among jurisdictions. ... the laws of many states, such as Wyoming,[110] make explicit the voluntary nature of disclosure."[111]

- Some states (e.g., Delaware, Florida, Kentucky, Missouri, New Hampshire, and Rhode Island) specifically exclude attorneys from mandatory child abuse reporting requirements. The applicable Missouri statute provides: Any legally recognized privileged communication, except that between attorney and client or involving communications made to a minister or clergyperson, shall not apply to situations involving known or suspected child abuse or neglect and shall not constitute grounds for failure to report as required or permitted by sections 210.110 to 210.165, to cooperate with the division in any of its activities pursuant to sections 210.110 to 210.165, or to give or accept evidence in any judicial proceeding relating to child abuse or neglect.[112]
- The Model Rules for attorneys in Texas provide that "When a lawyer has confidential information clearly establishing that a client is likely to commit a criminal or fraudulent act that is likely to result in death or substantial bodily harm to a person, the lawyer shall reveal confidential information to the extent revelation reasonably appears necessary to prevent the client from committing the criminal or fraudulent act."[113]
- Although the relevant Georgia rule is permissive, Georgia Rule 1.6(b)(3) provides: "Before using or disclosing information pursuant to Subsection (1), if feasible, the lawyer must make a good faith effort to persuade the client either not to act or, if the client has already acted, to warn the victim."
- In one of the few ethics opinions on the subject of the attorney's role in reporting abuse, the Ethics Committee in New Jersey stated that an attorney is not required to report past child abuse in a custody action. However, in a supplement to the opinion, the Committee clarified that the privilege does not apply when the client demonstrates a "continued propensity" for abuse.[114]
- The state of Ohio requires attorneys to report suspected child abuse in limited circumstances,[115] but generally the client must waive "any testimonial privilege" prior to the attorney testifying as to the suspected neglect or abuse.[116]
- In Wisconsin, attorneys are permitted to use discretion with respect to reporting or not reporting child abuse.[117]

Rules that leave disclosure to the discretion of the attorney are perhaps the least helpful of all. "Discretionary disclosure may ... place lawyers in the untenable position of choosing preservation of their bar licenses over victim safety as well as expose them to liability in tort. None of the state professional rules protect the attorney from tort liability in the decision to disclose. Mandatory disclosure rules provide greater protection to practitioners, yet most state rules employ permissive language."[118]

PARALEGAL APPLICATION **15.6**

WHAT IS YOUR OPINION?

Do you believe members of the family law team should be mandated reporters? Explain your response. What is the attorney's duty in your state? What do you think the paralegal should do if his or her supervising attorney is a mandated reporter who fails to report?

CHAPTER **SUMMARY**

Family violence is a painful reality in our society, as the statistics provided in this chapter suggest. Members of the family law team need to recognize when it plays a role in the legal issues they address.

Domestic violence can have a far-reaching impact on almost any type of legal practice, community or family, whether located in a rural small town or a large urban area in any state. While criminal and family law practice are the most obvious, domestic violence issues can exist in almost every area of the law, including tort, health care, tax, property, immigration, international, housing, employment, corporate, public benefits and bankruptcy. For example, a wife might seek relief from federal tax liability because her abusive husband coerced her to sign the joint tax return. An employer must defend a wrongful death action alleging it failed to respond to an employee's risk of domestic violence on the job. An immigrant might ask whether she will be able to stay in the United States if she leaves her abusive husband and whether she can get the children back if he takes them to Mexico as he has threatened.[119]

Despite its significance, many members of family law teams have a very limited knowledge about family violence: its causes, manifestations, and effects. This chapter provides prospective paralegals with a very basic introduction to this multifaceted topic. It considers it in the contexts of both intimate partner and parent-child relationships. It introduces definitions and cold, hard statistics. It identifies a variety of legal remedies available to victims and their advocates. It reviews some of the subtle psychological and sociological dimensions of this complex topic. And finally, it raises troubling ethical questions confronting practitioners.

Child abuse and neglect cases clearly involve the balancing of critical and often competing public policies: a parent's right to raise his or her children free from governmental interference and the state's interest in protecting children. Everyone weighs in: parents, children, offenders, victims, judges, social workers, therapists, attorneys, and, of course, the general public. Paralegals may find themselves in the middle of wrenching situations, troubled deeply by what they see parents do to their children but also recognizing that the police and social service agencies may cross constitutional lines based on "good intentions" and insufficient information. Parents, even parents suspected of harming their children, are protected by constitutional rights. Family violence cases are minefields that challenge members of the family law team. They compel us to examine and control our personal biases and our cultural and religious beliefs about what constitutes appropriate behavior. They strain our emotions, our legal skills, and our ethics, and they remind many of us why we have chosen to specialize in family law.

KEY **TERMS**

Abandonment
Affidavit
Battered woman's syndrome
Care and protection/dependency
 proceeding
Concurrent jurisdiction
Couverture
Cyberstalking
Educational neglect
Emotional neglect
Evidence-based prosecution

Ex parte
Family violence
Guardian
Interspousal immunity
Mandatory reporter
Medical neglect
Neglect
Negligent supervision
No-contact order
Parens patriae
Parent coordinator

Permanency planning
Permissive reporter
Physical neglect
Protective order
Reasonable efforts
Restraining order
Shaken baby syndrome
Stalking
Stay away order
Termination of parental rights
Tort

REVIEW **QUESTIONS**

1. Define family violence.
2. Define elder abuse and indicate why it is considered a family violence problem.
3. Identify five benefits of the successive versions of the Violence Against Women Act.
4. Describe the nature of an evidence-based prosecution.
5. Identify a minimum of five reasons why victims stay in abusive relationships.

6. Define cyberstalking.
7. Describe battered woman's syndrome and indicate how it is sometimes used in criminal cases.
8. Describe the basic procedure for obtaining a protective order, including who can commonly seek one and the kinds of relief that can be sought.
9. Distinguish among restraining, no-contact, and stay away orders.

10. Explain when it may be appropriate to seek a guardianship in a family violence case.
11. Describe the nature and purpose of a personal safety plan.
12. Identify at least five common characteristics of abusers.
13. Identify and distinguish among the five forms of child abuse most commonly identified and defined by the states.
14. Identify the four most common forms of neglect.
15. Describe the nature of the parent's "right" to discipline his or her child.
16. Distinguish between mandatory and permissive reporters of child abuse.

17. Describe the nature and purpose of "reasonable efforts" and "permanency planning" in the context of child abuse and neglect actions.
18. Identify at least five conditions on visitation that may be appropriate in cases involving a history of child abuse and neglect.
19. Describe the tort of "negligent supervision" and give an example of circumstances in which it would be appropriate.
20. Explain whether or not members of the family law team have a duty to report suspected child abuse or other forms of family violence.

FOCUS ON **THE JOB**

The Facts

You are a paralegal working for Attorney Sabrina Cann, a private practitioner who specializes in family law. She has asked you to conduct a series of information-gathering meetings with a client, Sara Frazier, who is seeking a divorce from her husband, Joseph. During the course of your meetings, you have developed a suspicion that Sara is being abused by her husband. There have been several clues:

- She has insisted that she initiate all contact with the office and that no one contact her at home or leave e-mail or phone messages for her.
- As the date for filing has approached, she has become increasingly more anxious.
- She has told you that "everyone" says she must "get out of the marriage."
- She is insistent that she "must" have custody of the children and is fearful that she will lose them.
- She does not want to fight for a fair share of the marital property.
- She says she does not know what her husband will do when he is served with the Complaint for divorce and wants to be certain she knows exactly when that will take place.
- She has said that she thinks she must be responsible for the failure of the marriage because she is not a good

wife. She does not always have the meals prepared on time or have her husband's shirts ironed. Her husband says she is a bad mother as well because she "lets the kids get away with murder" and never disciplines them effectively.

- She says that her husband loves her so much that he worries about her every minute of the day. She and the children are so important to him that he wants them to spend all their time together, to the exclusion of other people.
- She always wears sunglasses and high-collared, long-sleeve shirts even when the weather is quite warm.

You have shared your concerns with your supervisor, and she has asked that you explore this issue with Sara in your next meeting.

The Assignment

Divide the class into groups of two. Each twosome should role-play the meeting in which the abuse issue is explored. One student will play the role of the paralegal, and the other student will play the role of Sara, the client. If necessary, one group can include three participants. The third member should play the role of Attorney Cann in an interview that includes the client, the attorney, and the paralegal.

FOCUS ON **ETHICS**

Assume that you are a female paralegal working for the attorney who represents Sara's husband, Joe, in the above fact pattern, and that Joe has recently been served with Sara's Complaint for Divorce on no-fault grounds. You are not comfortable working with Joe and have repeatedly expressed your discomfort to your supervisor, Attorney Jules Sanchez. Joe never misses an opportunity to make a sexist remark and

always tells you that you should be home, where women belong, making and raising babies. He never wants to meet with you and always says he wants to talk with the boss and get a few things straight. He has told you that up until now, he has kept his wife in line and that she will pay in more ways than one for thinking that she can do this to him. He comments that raising children is "woman's work" and that he isn't much of a parent. However, he says he will get the kids anyway. Besides, he says, "A bad father is better than no father at all." When encouraged, Joe admits that he has hit his wife on several occasions and that he believes he has a right to do whatever he wants in the privacy of his own home. He tells you not to worry, though, because there is no record of any abuse. He has "a friend on the force" who makes sure of that, and he never lets Sara seek medical attention for any injury she claims to have. He says she has gone too far challenging his authority this time. He is "the man of the house" and he intends to make her understand that fact or else. …

Based on what you have learned about family violence, you strongly believe that Joe is abusing Sara and that she is presently at greater risk than ever before of being seriously injured or perhaps worse. You have shared your concern with your supervisor, Attorney Sanchez, who finds it all hard to believe. He wants to approach the matter cautiously and asks you to research his legal and ethical duties in such situations. What ethical issues are raised in this situation? What is the attorney's duty in your state, given the facts of this case? Does the paralegal have a role to play? Do you find any guidance in the ethical canons for paralegals promulgated by the National Federation of Paralegal Associations (NFPA), contained in Appendix B of this text, or in any other code of ethics that may govern your conduct?

FOCUS ON **CASE LAW**

Locate the case *State of Hawaii v. Aiwohi,* 109 Haw. 115, 123 P.3d 1210 (2005), available on the companion website. Read the case and then respond to the following questions.

1. Describe the procedural history of the case.
2. Which issues have been raised on appeal and by whom?
3. What are the basic facts of the case?
4. What are the elements of the offense with which Tayshea was charged, each of which must be proved beyond a reasonable doubt?
5. How does the Hawaii Supreme Court define "recklessly" with respect to the offense charged in this case?
6. What does the Hawaii Supreme Court say the standard is for interpreting a statute?
7. How do the prosecution and the defense each define "person"?
8. What does the court say is the majority approach to prosecution of a mother for her own prenatal conduct that causes harm to her subsequently born child?
9. Which jurisdictions does the court indicate have adopted the majority position, and in each, what was the nature of the charge against the defendant?
10. How does the state of South Carolina define the word "child" in the context of its criminal statutes?
11. How do the majority of jurisdictions treat prosecutions of third parties who cause the death of a subsequently born child? Does the Hawaii Supreme Court agree with this position? Why?
12. What was the old English common law approach to the status of an unborn child in the criminal context?
13. What is the position of the Model Penal Code?
14. What is the majority's holding with respect to Aiwohi's conviction and why?
15. The majority does not reach the constitutional issues raised by the defendant. Why? After reading the concurring opinions, do you think the court would have upheld the constitutionality of the criminal statute at issue as applied by the trial court or not?

FOCUS ON **STATE LAW AND PROCEDURE**

Describe the procedure used in your jurisdiction to obtain a protective order against an abusive partner. Who is eligible to petition for an order? What forms of relief may be requested? Obtain copies of any documents that must be filed to obtain an order.

FOCUS ON **TECHNOLOGY**

Websites of Interest

http://www.aardvarc.org

Aardvarc stands for Abuse, Rape, and Domestic Violence Aid and Resource Collection. The site contains links to many resources by state, statistical data, and information about warning signs of abuse, safety plans, related immigration issues, etc.

http://www.abanet.org/domviol

This is the site for the American Bar Association's Commission on Domestic Violence. Among other services, it provides links to statistical reports on the prevalence of various forms of domestic violence, articles, and links to statutory summary charts on topics such as civil protection orders, advocate confidentiality laws, and prohibition of mutual protective orders, etc.

http://www.acf.hhs.gov

This is the website for the Children's Bureau of the Administration for Children and Families. It is a rich source of information about children and families in general. From its home page you can link (via drop-down menu) to the Administration's programs including the Children's Bureau. There you will find, among other resources, the full text of the most recent Child Maltreatment report.

http://www.afccnet.org

This is the website for the Association of Family and Conciliation Courts (AFCC). AFCC promotes collaborative approaches to dealing with family matters in general and those pertaining to the well-being of children in particular. The organization sponsors conferences, training, projects, task forces, and practice standards, all of which appear on the website. It provides resources for parents as well as professionals.

http://www.ama-assn.org

AMA is the American Medical Association. Its home page provides a search function. Searches on family violence, child abuse, and elder abuse each yield a number of resources—mostly journal articles relevant to the medical community's roles, responsibilities, practices, and liabilities in these areas.

http://www.avahealth.org

This is the website for the Academy on Violence and Abuse (AVA). AVA is an educational organization intended for health care professionals and dedicated to "making violence and abuse a core component of medical and related professional education." The website features online educational materials including video presentations, written articles, literature searches, and links to other sites with relevant information.

http://www.bwjp.org

This is the site for the Battered Women's Justice Project's Criminal and Civil Justice Office. The Project aims to promote change within community organizations and governmental agencies engaged in responding to domestic violence. It serves as a national clearinghouse for information about domestic violence and the policing, prosecuting, sentencing, and monitoring of domestic violence offenders.

http://www.cdc.gov

This site for the national Centers for Disease Control (CDC) provides links to a wide range of resources in response to a search for information on intimate partner violence.

http://www.childwelfare.gov

This is the site for the Child Information Gateway, a service of the Children's Bureau of the Administration for Children and Families. It provides a wealth of information on adoption, child abuse and neglect, and child welfare issues. Of particular value are links to statistical information and state laws on many related topics, such as definitions of abuse, grounds for termination of parental rights, infant safe haven laws, and parental drug use as child abuse.

http://www.findlaw.com

This site provides links to state laws that then can be searched by specific topic.

http://www.fvpf.org

This is the website for the Family Violence Prevention Fund. Its mission is to prevent violence in the home and in the community. It seeks to "transform" the way health care providers, police, judges, employers, and others address violence. A number of fact sheets are available on domestic violence and its relationship to topics such as children, teens, guns, housing, immigrants, and the military. Every month, its personal stories section showcases someone who has triumphed over violence in his or her life or who has made a significant contribution toward preventing violence against women and children.

http://www.gmdvp.org

This is the site of the Gay Men's Domestic Violence Project, a grassroots, nonprofit initiative supporting men in relationships with men who are victims and survivors of abuse. It offers education, advocacy, and direct services.

http://www.lrcvaw.org

This is the site for the Legal Resource Center on Violence Against Women, funded by a Violence Against Women grant. The primary focus of the Center is on improving legal representation for domestic violence survivors in interstate custody cases and providing technical assistance in such cases. It features links to other national and state resources on topics including crisis lines, abuse later in life, and assistance in battered immigrant cases. It also provides state-by-state links to child custody jurisdictional statutes (UCCJEA or UCCJA), long-arm statutes, and relocation statutes.

http://www.ncadv.org

The National Coalition Against Domestic Violence is accessed at this site. Among its other resources, it provides both topic- and state-specific fact sheets on domestic violence.

http://www.ncea.aoa.gov

This is the website for the National Center on Elder Abuse, a national center dedicated to preventing the mistreatment of elders. It is the major source of available statistics on elder abuse, neglect, and exploitation in the country, including abuse in domestic settings. It provides links to resources for locating state statutes, codes, Supreme Court opinions, and case law. It also provides a directory of state resources on elder abuse prevention.

http://www.ncvc.org/dvrc

This is the site for the National Center for Victims of Crime. A Stalking Resource Center is available at this site that provides information about federal stalking laws as well as links to state civil and criminal stalking laws. It also provides a wealth of statistical information and a digest of both federal and state stalking cases. A dating violence resource center is also accessible at this site.

http://www.ndvh.org

This is the website for the National Domestic Violence Hotline (1-800-799-7233 or 1-800-787-3224), which provides 24/7 access to calls from all states. Translation services are available in 140 languages. Advocates at the Hotline provide intervention, safety planning information, and referrals to agencies in all states.

http://www.neighborhoodlaw.org

A search of this site for materials relating to domestic violence yields a wealth of material including an online book from Western New England Legal Services called "Where Do We Go from Here: Self-Help Guide for Domestic Abuse Survivors and Their Advocates."

http://www.ojp.usdoj.gov/bjs

This is an excellent source for "official" crime data. Many reports on topics related to the content of this chapter are available at this site including, Shannon Catalano, PhD., *Intimate Partner Violence in the United States* (2006)

ASSIGNMENTS

1. Go to *http://www.childwelfare.gov/systemwide/laws_policies/statutes/defineall.pdf* and locate the definitions for various kinds of abuse in your state.

2. Using one or more of the websites of interest listed above, locate information about resources in your state for victims of elder abuse.

3. Using one or more of the sites listed above, learn what you can about civil protective orders in your state.

4. Using one or more of the above sites, locate the stalking laws of your state and at least one case addressing the issue of stalking.

5. Go to the site for the Indiana Judiciary *(http://www.in.gov/judiciary/forms/po)* and locate the Cover Sheet and Ex Parte Order for Protection that the court would complete and issue if a Petition for an Order for Protection is granted.

Endnotes

Chapter 1

1. In the New Hampshire Bar Association Ethics Committee Opinion #2005–06/3, the Ethics Committee opined that if the client wants to receive a copy of his or her file in electronic form, the firm must deliver it in digital format. See http://www.nhbar.org/legal-links/ethics-opinions. To reach this page, go to www.nhbar.org and then to the "Legal Links" drop-down menu and click on "Ethics Opinions and Practical Ethics Articles." Find article #2005–06/3.
2. This definition has been adopted in whole or in large part by other bodies. See, for example, the North Dakota Rules of Professional Conduct and South Dakota Supreme Court Rule 92–5.
3. NY CLS Dom Rel Appx §1400.1 (2007).
4. The revised Rules of Professional Conduct for New Hampshire Attorneys (effective January 1, 2008) permit lawyers from different firms to share fees if the fees are divided "in reasonable proportion to the services performed or responsibilities or risks assumed by each" or "based on an agreement with the referring lawyer" (sometimes called a naked referral). The client must agree to the fee division in writing, and the total fee cannot be increased as a consequence of the fee division.
5. *Missouri v. Jenkins*, 491 U.S. 274, 109 S. Ct. 2463, 105 L. Ed. 2d 229 (1989). See Footnote 10 in the opinion.
6. *Smith v. Lewis*, 530 P.2d 589 at 596 (Cal. 1975).
7. See *Hendrix v. Page*, 986 F.2d 195 (7th Cir. 1993). In this case, an appellant failed to cite the only case that was on point for the issue under appeal. The court stated that when an attorney knowingly conceals dispositive adverse authority, it constitutes professional misconduct.
8. New Hampshire Supreme Court Attorney Discipline System 2005 Annual Report, New Hampshire Bar News, May 19, 2006.
9. William D. Farber, J.D., L.L.M., *Legal Malpractice in Domestic Relations*, American Jurisprudence 44 Am. Jur. Proof of Facts 2d 377 (as of Aug. 2004).
10. *Hodges v. Carter*, 239 N.C. 517, 519–520, 80 S.E.2d 144, 145–146 (1954).
11. See Debra Levy Martinelli, *Are You Riding a Fine Line? Learn to Identify and Avoid Issues Involving the Unauthorized Practice of Law*, 15 Utah Bar J. 18 (2002).
12. 5 U.S.C.A. §555 (1967) allows a person appearing before a federal administrative agency to be represented by an attorney or a nonattorney deemed a "qualified representative" if the agency permits.
13. *United States v. Hardy*, 681 F. Supp. 1326, 1328–29 (N.D. Ill. 1988), as quoted in *Monroe v. Horwitch* et al, 820 F. Supp. 682 (D. Conn. 1993), a case involving a paralegal who advertised her availability to prepare uncontested divorce papers for clients.
14. National Federation of Paralegal Associations Model Code (Definitions).
15. For a good discussion of paralegal conflict of interest issues, see *Paralegals and Conflicts of Interest*, available on the website of the NFPA at http://www.paralegals.org/displaycommon.cfm?an=1&subarticlenbr=390.
16. *Bates v. State Bar of Arizona*, 433 U.S. 350, 97 S. Ct. 2691, 53 L. Ed. 2d 810 (1977), rehearing denied 434 U.S. 881, 98 S. Ct. 242, 54 L. Ed.2d 164 (1977).
17. Jennifer Baker, Forest Institute of Professional Psychology, Springfield, as quoted in http://www.DivorceStatistics.org.
18. The American Bar Association Model Rules of Professional Conduct (2007 edition), Rule 4.4 (b), states, "A lawyer who receives a document relating to the representation of the lawyer's client and knows or reasonably should know that the document was inadvertently sent shall promptly notify the sender." Each state Bar Association has its own rules, and many are based on the ABA Model Rules.

Chapter 2

1. See e.g. *Hastings v. Dickinson*, 7 Mass. 153 (1810).
2. The American Law Institute's Principles of the Law of Family Dissolution take the position that there is no difference between enforcement of premarital and postmarital agreements (the position adopted in New York, North Carolina, Wisconsin, and Utah, for example), but some states distinguish between them by case law or statute (e.g., Minnesota, New Jersey, and Louisiana). A leading case is that of *Casto v. Casto*, 508 So. 2d 330 (Fla. 1987), and another interesting and more recent case on point is *In re Marriage of Friedman*, 100 Cal. App. 4th 65 (2002).
3. Dubin, Arline, *Prenups for Lovers: A Romantic Guide to Prenuptial Agreements*, Random House, p. 15 (1999).
4. Erikson, Paula Burkes, *Prenuptial agreements would be a good idea for almost any couple*, Daily Oklahoman, July 10, 2005.
5. Grama, Joanna L., *The New Newlyweds: Marriage Among the Elderly. Suggestions to the Elder Law Practitioner*, 7 Elder L. J. 379 (1999).
6. Weaver, Donna Beck, CFLS, *The Collaborative Law Process for Premarital Agreements*, 4 Pepp. Disp. Resol. L.J. 337 (2004).
7. *Ibid.*
8. *Ex Parte Walters*, 580 So. 2d 1352 (Ala. 1991).
9. *Fletcher v. Fletcher*, 628 N.E.2d 1343 (Ohio 1994).
10. See e.g. *Spritz v. Lishner*, 355 Mass. 162, 243 N.E.2d 163 (1969) in which the court held that, absent fraud, the contract was binding regardless of whether its terms were understood.
11. *MacFarlane v. Rich*, 132 N.H. 608, 616–617 (1989).
12. See e.g. *Zummo v. Zummo*, 574 A.2d 1130 (Pa. Super. Ct. 1990) in which the court refused to enforce a verbal provision of a prenuptial agreement stipulating the religious upbringing of children from the marriage on the grounds that enforcement would involve excessive entanglement and encroachment by the state on a fundamental right of religious freedom protected by the First Amendment. But see *Ramon v. Ramon*, 34 N.Y.S.2d 100 (N.Y. Fam. CT. 1942).
13. An interesting decision on point is *Avitzur v. Avitzur*, 58 N.Y.2d 108, 459 N.Y.S.2d 572, 446 N.E.2d 136 (1983), cert. denied 464 U.S. 817, 104 S. Ct. 76, 78 L. Ed. 2d 88 (1983). In this case, the court enforced an agreement in which the husband agreed that if a civil divorce was obtained, he would appear before a rabbinical court, the Beth Din, so that the wife would be able to marry again under Jewish law.
14. *Favrot v. Barnes*, 332 So. 2d 873 (La. Ct. App. 1976), rev'd on other grounds; *Favrot v. Barnes*, 339 So. 2d 843 (La. 1976).
15. For a comprehensive treatment of this topic, see Sikaitis, Joline F., *Comment: A New Form of Family Planning? The Enforceability of No-Child Provisions in Prenuptial Agreements*, 54 Cath. U.L. Rev. 335 (Fall 2004).
16. ERISA requires private pension plans to offer spousal benefits for couples married for at least one full year before retirement or death, absent a written waiver. Waivers of ERISA and REA benefits must meet specific requirements:
    a. Effective waiver of a spouse's interest can be made only after the spouse is in fact married to the participant.
    b. Waiver must be in writing, witnessed by a plan administrator or notary public.
    c. Waiver must designate a different beneficiary or form of benefits, which may not be changed without spousal consent.
    d. The waiver must acknowledge the effect of the election.
    A good case on point is *Hagwood v. Newton*, 282 F.3d 285 (4th Circ. Ct. App. 2002).
17. See e.g. Massachusetts General Laws Chapter 209 Section 26, which requires that to be effective against third parties, a premarital agreement must be recorded at an appropriate Registry of Deeds within 90 days of execution.

18. Under California law, parties to a premarital agreement are not considered fiduciaries, and basic contract law will apply. In Maryland, parties to a premarital agreement are considered fiduciaries, and enforcement will be judged on a higher standard of fairness, full disclosure, and voluntary execution. See *Cannon v. Cannon*, 384 Md. 537, 865 A.2d 563 (2005). See also *DeLorean v. DeLorean*, 211 N.J. Super. 432, 511 A.2d 1257 (1986) for an analysis of the choice of law conflict between New Jersey and California (although the enforceability of the DeLorean agreement was held to have been determined in an arbitration proceeding).

19. See e.g. *MacFarlane v. Rich*, 132 N.H. 608 (1989). New Hampshire RSA 460:2-a invests prenuptial agreements with a presumption of validity that can be rebutted only if one or more of three standards of fairness have not been met:
   a. The agreement was not obtained through fraud, duress, or mistake, or through misrepresentation or nondisclosure of a material fact.
   b. The agreement is not unconscionable.
   c. The facts and circumstances have not changed since the agreement was executed so as to make the agreement unenforceable.

20. In some states, such as California, the general Statute of Frauds (§1624, subd. (a) of the Civil Code) provides that the requirement that a contract be in writing is subject to an implied exception for "part performance" of the contract's terms, but the Family Code provides that an interspousal transaction that changes the nature of community or separate property is not valid unless made in writing by an express declaration approved by the adversely affected spouse. See *In re Marriage of Benson*, 36 Cal. 4th 1096, 116 P.3d 1152, 32 Cal. Rptr. 3d 471 (2005). In Florida, the statute generally barring any action based on an agreement in consideration of marriage, unless in writing, has been interpreted as permitting oral premarital contracts if performed within one year or if there has been partial performance of the contract. See *O'Shea v. O'Shea*, 221 So. 2d 223 (Fla. 4th DCA 1969). In Massachusetts, the agreement must be in writing, but may consist of an exchange of letters.

Chapter 3

1. *Inhabitants of Milford v. Inhabitants of Worcester*, 7 Mass. 48 (1810).
2. *Goodridge v. Department of Public Health*, 440 Mass. 309, 343, 798 N.E.2d 941, 969 (2003) (Marshall, C.J.).
3. *Id.*
4. In 23 Pa, C.S. § 1103, the Pennsylvania legislature provides that "No common law marriage contracted after January 1, 2005 shall be valid." Any common law marriage entered prior to that date remains valid. A more complete break with common law marriage is sought in South Carolina. Bill (S 0137) (and similar H 3427) are before the S.C. legislature to amend that state's code by adding § 20-1-110 to provide that effective June 30, 2008, common law marriage will not be recognized in South Carolina, to provide that the license application fee will be waived for parties who are in a common law marriage, and to rescind § 20–1–360 relating to the validity of a marriage without the issuance of a license.
5. William Blackstone, *Commentaries on the Laws of England*, 441–442 (A. Strahan ed., 15th edition 1809).
6. *Orr v. Orr*, 440 U.S. 268, 279–280, 283, 99 S. Ct. 1102, 59 L. Ed. 2d 306 (1979), quoting *Stanton v. Stanton*, 421 U.S. 7, 10, 14–15, 95 S. Ct. 1373, 43 L. Ed. 2d 688 (1975).
7. See e.g. *Baehr v. Lewin*, 74 Haw. 530, 852 P.2d 44 (1993); *Baker v. State*, 744 A.2d 864, 81 A.L.R. 5th 627 (Vt. 1999); and *Lewis v. Harris*, 188 N.J. 415, 908 A.2d 196 (2006).
8. *Supra 2.*
9. *Griswold v. Connecticut*, 381 U.S. 479, 486, 85 S.Ct. 1678, 1682, 14 L. Ed. 2d 510 (1965) (Douglas, J.).
10. *People v. Liberta*, 64 N.Y.2d 152, 474 N.E.2d 567, 485 N.Y.S.2d 207 (1984).
11. *Barrett v. Vander-Muelen*, 264 Ky. 441, 94 S.W.2d 983 (1936).
12. *Loving v. Virginia.*, 388 U.S. 1, 87 S. Ct. 1817, 18 L. Ed. 2d 1010 (1967), citing *Skinner v. Oklahoma*, 316 U.S. 535, 542, 62 S. Ct. 1110, 86 L. Ed. 1655 (1942).

13. *Zablocki v. Redhail*, 434 U.S. 374, 98 S. Ct. 673, 54 L. Ed. 2d 618 (1978).
14. *Salisbury v. List*, 501 F. Supp. 105 (D. Nev. 1980).
15. *Turner v. Safley*, 482 U.S. 78, 107 S. Ct. 2254, 96 L. Ed. 64 (1987).
16. *Palmore v. Sidoti*, 466 U.S. 429, 104 S. Ct. 1879, 80 L. Ed. 2d 421 (1984), appeal after remand 472 So. 2d 843 (Fla. App. 1985).
17. *M.T. v. J.T.*, 140 N.J. Super. 7, 355 A.2d 204 (1976).
18. See e.g. *Littleton v. Prang*, 9 S.W.3d 223 (Tex. App. 1999).
19. The Mormon Church repudiated the practice of polygamy in 1890, but periodic, and high-profile, news stories, such as the removal of more than 450 children from the yeaming for Zion compound in Texas in the spring of 2008, indicate it is still practiced by a number of Mormon fundamentalists. On this topic, see Tom Green, *Common-Law Marriage and the Illegality of Putative Polygamy*, 17 BYU J. Pub. L. 141 (2002). See also Maura Strassberg, *The Crime of Polygamy*, 12 Temp. Pol. & Civ. Rts. L. Rev. 353 (2003).
20. A report of the National Society of Genetic Counselors indicates that the increased risk of significant birth defects in children born to first-cousin unions is only 1.7 to 2.8% above the risk level for the general population. See Robin L. Bennett et al., *Genetic Counseling and Screening of Consanguineous Couples and Their Offspring: Recommendations of the National Society of Genetic Counselors*, 11 Journal of Genetic Counseling 97 (2002).
21. *Johnson v. Johnson*, 104 N.W.2d 8, 14 (N.D. 1960).
22. See e.g. R.R.S. Neb. § 42–102 provides, "No person who is afflicted with a venereal disease shall marry in this state."
23. See e.g. M.G.L. c. 207 §42.
24. Massachusetts has a procedure by which an individual may apply for a special one-day designation to perform/solemnize marriages. M.G.L. 207 § 39 provides that the governor may "designate any other person to solemnize a particular marriage on a particular date and in a particular city or town...."
25. *Meister v. Moore*, 96 U.S. 76, 24 L. Ed. 826 (1877).
26. Cynthia Grant Bowman, *ARTICLE: A Feminist Proposal to Bring Back Common Law Marriage*, 75 Or. L. Rev. 709, 779 (Fall 1996).
27. The list of rights and duties identified in the GAO audit (GAO Report Number OGC-97–16 entitled Defense of Marriage Act) is available at www.gao.gov/archive/1977/og97016.pdf .
28. Immigration Marriage Fraud Amendments of 1986, § 2.
29. See e.g. *Dommer v. Dommer*, 829 N.E.2d 125 (Ind. App. 2005).
30. *Baehr v. Lewin*, 74 Haw. 530, 852 P.2d 44 (1993).
31. Hawaii Revised Statutes § 572–1. The state of Hawaii subsequently enacted "reciprocal beneficiaries" legislation affording some of the rights of marriage to same-sex couples, blood relatives, and housemates.
32. *Goodridge v. Department* of Public Health, 440 Mass. 309, 343, 798 N.E.2d 941, 969 (2003).
33. The Fourteenth Amendment of the U.S. Constitution provides that "[no] state shall...deny to any person within its jurisdiction the equal protection of the laws." The states have in place comparable equal protection provisions in their constitutions as well.
34. Lynn Wardle, *The End of Marriage*, 44 Fam. Ct. Rev. 45, 54 (January 2006).
35. *Lawrence v. Texas*, 123 S. Ct. 2472, 2490, 156 L. Ed. 2d 508 (2003).
36. Robert Wintemute, *Same-Sex Marriage: When Will It Reach Utah?*, 20 BYU J. Pub. L. 527 (2006).
37. Edward A. Zelinsky, *Deregulating Marriage: The Pro-Marriage Case for Abolishing Civil Marriage*, 27 Cardozo L. Rev. 1161, 1163 (January 2006).
38. 1 U.S.C.S. § 7.
39. 28 U.S.C.S. § 1738C.
40. *Griswold v. Connecticut*, 381 U.S. 479, 486, 85 S. Ct. 1678, 1682, 14 L. Ed. 2d 510 (1965) (Douglas, J.).
41. Census Bureau, Current Populaton Survey—Marital Status 1979–2000.
42. G. M. Felisko, *The Rites Wrangle*, 92 A.B.A.J. 44, November 2006.
43. Some of the states' constitutional amendments and statutes have already been challenged without success. See e.g. in Georgia, *Perdue v. O'Kelley*,

280 Ga.732, 632 S.E.2d 110 (2006), in which the Georgia Supreme Court unanimously upheld a state constitutional amendment barring same-sex couples from marriage and the benefits of civil unions; *Citizens for Equal Prot. v. Brunig,* 455 F.3d 859 (8th Cir. 2006), in which a three-judge panel of the 8th U.S. Circuit Court of Appeals reversed a federal district court ruling and upheld a Nebraska constitutional amendment banning same-sex marriage and civil unions; and *Andersen v. King County,* 158 Wn.2d 1, 138 P.3d 963 (2006), in which the Washington Supreme Court upheld that state's Defense of Marriage Act.

44. See Barbara A. Robb, *Constitutionality of the Defense of Marriage Act,* 32 New England Law Rev. 263 (1997).

Chapter 4

1. *Nerini v. Nerini,* 11 Conn. Sup. 361, 364–365 (1943).
2. Internal Revenue Service Publication 504, *Tax Information for Divorced or Separated Individuals,* p. 3. (2007 edition).
3. Tenn. Code Ann. §36–4–101(2) (2001).
4. For a Tennessee case addressing these issues, see *Janna Sheya Falk v. Geary Falk,* 2005 Tenn. App. LEXIS 34.
5. *Davis v. Davis,* 119 Conn. 194, 175 A. 574 (Conn. 1934).
6. *Irving v. Irving,* 134 P.3d 718 (Nev. 2006).
7. *Brown v. Watson,* 2005 Tenn. App. LEXIS 387. See also *Nave v. Nave,* 173 S.W.3d 766 (Tenn. App. 2005), in which a Conservator filed a petition to annul the marriage of her ward—her father—on the ground that he was mentally incapable of entering a marriage contract at the time of the ceremony. Before the court rendered its decision granting the annulment, the ward died. A Tennessee Court of Appeals held that the annulment action did not abate at the moment of death, and the Conservator was not deprived of standing to continue to pursue the annulment action. The judgment was entered *nunc pro tunc,* making the judgment effective prior to the death.
8. For an interesting unpublished case on this topic, see *Estate of Julia Dominguez, Deceased,* 2002 NY Slip Op 50481U, 2002 N.Y. Misc. LEXIS 1596. In this case, the "husband" in a "sham" marriage entered to assist him with his immigration status sought to be designated as Administrator of his wife's estate after she was killed in a plane accident. The deceased wife's daughter also sought to be named Administratrix of her mother's estate and to have the alleged husband disqualified as a surviving spouse based on the fact the marriage was a sham.
9. See e.g. N.C. Gen. Stat. § 51–3 (2006) The statute provides that no marriage followed by cohabitation and the birth of issue shall be declared void after the death of either of the parties for any cause except bigamy.
10. *In re the Marriage of Linda A. and Robert S. Owen,* 2002 Cal. App. Unpub. LEXIS 1500 at 6.
11. See e.g. Hawaii Revised Statutes §572–6 application; license; limitations.
12. See e.g. *Tagupa v. Tagupa,* 108 Haw. 459, 121 P.3d 924 (Haw. App. 2005).
13. See e.g. *Malik v. Malik,* 99 Md. App. 521, 638 A.2d 1184 (1994).
14. See e.g. *Spilke v. Spilke,* 2002 Conn. Super. LEXIS 811.
15. *M.T. v. J.T.,* 140 N.J. Super. 77, 355 A.2d 204 (1976).
16. *Kantaras v. Kantaras,* 884 So. 2d 155 (Fla. App. 2004).
17. See e.g. *Meagher v. Maleki,* 131 Cal. App. 4th 1, 31 Cal. Rptr. 3d 663 (2005).
18. See 4 Am. Jur. 2d. Annulment §11 (2002). However, the long-standing rule in most jurisdictions is that an annulment will not be granted on the basis of fraud if one partner conceals from the other partner a serious drinking problem for which he or she refuses to seek help even if it interferes with the parties' sexual relationship. See e.g. *Schaub v. Schaub,* 71 Cal. App.2d 467, 162 P.2d 966 (1945).
19. *V.J.S. v. M.J.B.,* 249 N.J. Super. 318, 592 A.2d 328 (1991).
20. *Robertson v. Roth,* 163 Minn. 501, 204 N.W. 329 (Minn. 1925).
21. *Tam v. Chen,* 2004 Cal. App. Unpub. LEXIS 6283.
22. See *Fryar v. Roberts,* 346 Ark. 432, 57 S.W.3d 727 (Ark. 2001). In this case, the Arkansas Supreme Court addresses this issue in considerable detail.
23. *Mayo v. Mayo,* 172 N.C. App. 844, 617 S.E.2d 672 (N.C. App. 2005).
24. *Adler v. Adler,* 805 So. 2d 952 (Fla. App. 2001).

25. *In re Marriage of Kramer,* 253 Ill. App. 3d 923, 625 N.E.2d 808 (Ill. App. 1993).
26. See e.g. *Guzman v. Guzman Alvares,* 205 S.W.3d 375 (Tenn. 2006).
27. *Mayo v. Mayo,* 172 N.C. App. 844, 617 S.E.2d 672 (2005), quoting *Weil v. Herring,* 207 N.C. 6, 175 S.E. 836 (N.C. 1934).
28. *Gibson's Suits in Chancery,* § 42 (4th ed.).
29. See e.g. the Connecticut annulment statute, General Statutes 46b-60.
30. *In re State ex rel. Dep't. of Econ. Sec. v. Demetz,* 212 Ariz. 287, 130 P.3d 986 (Ariz. App. 2006).

Chapter 5

1. Tavia Simmons and Martin O'Connell, *Married-Couple and Unmarried Partner Households: 2000,* U.S. Census Bureau, 2003.
2. Tavia Simmons and Grace O'Neill, *Households and Families: 2000,* U.S. Census Bureau, 2001.
3. U.S. Census Bureau, 2005 American Community Survey.
4. *Id.*
5. *Id.*
6. Joyce A. Martin et al., *Births: Final Data for 2004,* 55 National Vital Statistics Report, No. 1, Centers for Disease Control and Prevention, U.S. Dept. of Health and Human Services, 2006.
7. *Supra* n. 3.
8. Pamela Smock, *Cohabitation in the United States,* Annual Review of Sociology (2000).
9. For historical background, see www.JewishEncyclopedia.com. For current information and practice, see *Pilegesh.org.*
10. *Washington Post-ABC news survey,* July 2004. Results may be found at www.pollingreport.com/civil.htm. Last visited May 2007.
11. See Hillary Greene, *Note: Undead Laws: The Use of Historically Unenforced Criminal Statutes in Noncriminal Litigation,* 16 Yale L. & Pol'y Rev. 169 (1997) for an extensive discussion of the secondary enforcement of criminal laws that have essentially been abandoned by state criminal prosecutors.
12. In the spring of 2003, the North Dakota Senate rejected an effort to repeal its statute criminalizing cohabitation. See H.B. 1175, 58th Leg. Assem., Reg. Sess. (N.D. 2003), discussed in *North Dakota Senate Decides to Keep Cohabitation Illegal,* State Capitols Newsletters, Family Relations, Alexandria, VA, Apr. 7, 2003, at 9. The law provides that a person is guilty of a misdemeanor "if he or she lives openly and notoriously with a person of the opposite sex as a married couple without being married to the other person." N.D. Cent. Code 12.1–20–10 (1997). The maximum penalty if convicted was thirty days' incarceration and a fine of $1,000. N.D. Cent. Code 12.1–32–01 (1997). In 1999, the North Dakota Supreme Court thwarted the efforts of an angry spouse to compel the state to prosecute his unfaithful spouse for criminal cohabitation. See *Olsen v. Koppy,* 593 N.W.2d 762 (N.D. 1999).
13. Mich. Comp. Laws Ann. 750.335 (Supp 2003).
14. See *Ensminger v. Commissioner,* 610 F.2d 189, 191 (4th Cir. 1979). The court justified this inequality in taxation stating that "in the application of federal tax laws, taxpayers will be treated in their intimate and personal relationships as the state in which they reside treats them."
15. The definitions of alternative nonmarital partnerships provided in this chapter are generic. There are no fixed definitions that are consistent from state to state or country to country. It is also impossible to provide a set list of benefits and obligations that flow from any status as they, too, vary state to state and from time to time. See William N. Eskridge, Jr., *Equality Practice: Civil Unions and the Future of Gay Rights,* New York: Routledge (2002). Eskridge suggests a hierarchy of benefits conferred and relationships recognized from domestic partnerships, cohabitation, reciprocal beneficiaries, civil unions, and registered partnerships from least to greatest.
16. Hawaii Revised Statutes Chapter 572C.
17. California Family Code § 300 defines marriage as a relationship between a man and a woman, and § 308.5 restates that element of the definition. Family Code §§ 297 through 299.5 define, establish, and provide for domestic partnerships.

18. 2003 Me. Laws 672 (2004) codified at 22 M.R.S. § 2710.

19. The Health Care Benefits Act, which implements the Domestic Partnership Registration Rule of the District of Columbia, was passed in 1992 but went into effect only in 2002. The delay resulted from the fact that Congress prohibited the District from spending any local funds to implement the law until it lifted the prohibition in the appropriation for the District for 2002. Under the law, unmarried persons of the same or different sex or different genders and regardless of their place of residence may register as domestic partners. The benefits of a domestic partnership established under the initial law of the District of Columbia for government personnel first employed after October 1, 1987, have been significantly expanded in more recent legislation including but not limited to the Health Care Decisions Act of 2003, which gave domestic partners the right to make health care decisions for their partners, and the Domestic Partnership Equality Amendment Act of 2006, which extended many of the major rights and duties of spouses to domestic partners.

20. New Jersey also enacted a domestic partnership law, but it is now largely supplanted by the state's new civil union statute. New domestic partnerships are no longer formed, although there are some individuals still classified as domestic partners because they registered under the earlier legislation and have not changed that status.

21. Conn. Gen. Stat. §§ 46b-38aa. through 46b-38pp. and 46b-39.

22. RSA Chapter 457-A has been added to the New Hampshire code and deals in its entirety with civil unions. The enabling bill (HB437-FN-L) was signed into law on May 31, 2007, and became effective January 1, 2008. In its title the bill is described as "AN ACT permitting same gender couples to enter civil unions and have the same rights, responsibilities, and obligations as married couples."

23. Provisions of the NJ civil union law are woven into the corresponding provisions of the NJ marriage law (Title 37). Specific to civil unions are N.J. Stat. §§ 37:1–28 through 37:1- 36.

24. House Bill 2007 (HB 2007-A) §2 (3) can be found at http://www.leg.state.or.us/07reg/measures/hb2000.dir/hb2007.en.html.

25. Vt. Stat. Ann. Tit. 15 §§1201–1207 (2000).

26. *Goodridge v. Department of Public Health,* 440 Mass. 309, 798 N.E.2d 941 (Mass. 2003).

27. *Braschi v. Stahl Associates Co.,* 74 N.Y.2d 201, 543 N.E.2d at 55 (1989).

28. See *In the Matter of Adult Anonymous II,* 88 A.D.2d 30, 452 N.Y.S.2d 198 (N.Y. App. Div. 1982). But see *Matter of Robert Paul P.,* 63 N.Y.2d 233, 471 N.E.2d 424, 481 N.Y.S.2d 652 (1984).

29. *In re Marriage of Lindsay,* 101 Wash.2d 299 at 304–5; 678 P.2d 328 (1984). See also *Connell v. Francisco,* 127 Wash.2d 339, 898 P.2d 831 (Wash. 1995). For an excellent discussion of this concept, see Gavin M. Parr, *Notes and Comments: What Is a "Meretricious Relationship"?: An Analysis of Cohabitant Property Rights Under Connell v. Francisco,* 74 Wash. L. Rev. 1243 (1999).

30. See *Todd v. Workmen's Comp. Appeal Bd. (ncr Corp.),* 547 Pa. 687, 692 A.2d 1086 (1977).

31. Cynthia Grant Bowman, *Legal Treatment of Cohabitation in the United States,* 26 L. & POL'Y 119 (2004).

32. *Supra* n. 17 at § 308.5.

33. A comprehensive, current, and authoritative view of the status of same-sex marriage, civil unions, domestic partnerships, rights, and debates around the world is not available. The website of the International Lesbian and Gay Association, www.ilga-europe.org, publishes a country-by-country status of the European countries. A Pearson Education website, www.infoplease.com, provides broad summary information. The online encyclopedia wikipedia.com provides both historical and current information, which should be verified prior to use.

34. American Law Institute, *Principles of the Law of Family Dissolution: Analysis and Recommendations,* 6.03(1).

35. The city of Berkeley, CA, was the first municipality to extend domestic partnership benefits to its employees in 1984. Since then, many other cities across the country (such as Boston and Cambridge, MA, San Francisco, CA, and Seattle, WA) have extended employee benefits to domestic partners under a policy that recognizes them as spousal equivalents and/or because of a nondiscrimination policy encompassing sexual orientation. Most recognize both opposite-sex and same-sex partnerships broadly defined.

36. 22 M.R.S. § 2710 2.

37. For an authoritative but complex summary of these benefits, see a report entitled *Categories of Laws Involving Marital Status,* which was an enclosure to a letter found at www.gao.gov/archive/1997/og97016.pdf. A more straightforward, albeit less authoritative, list of these benefits is available on the Wikipedia website as *Rights and responsibilities of marriages in the United States.*

38. *Supra* n. 17 at § 297.5.

39. *Supra* at n. 24.

40. N.J. Stat. § 37:1–31 became effective on February 19, 2007, and New Jersey joined Vermont and Connecticut in granting same-sex civil unions. The legislation also applies to heterosexual couples in which at least one of the members is over the age of 62 and eligible for social security or supplemental social security income benefits because these couples are in a sense penalized if they marry, given that their benefits may be reduced or eliminated if they do so. The benefits extended are not as extensive as in Vermont and Connecticut. For example, they do not include rights to share property accumulated during the union, to seek financial support when the relationship terminates, or to be recognized as a family member for many public benefit programs. The precipitating case was *Lewis v. Harris,* 188 N.J. 415, 908 A.2d 196 (2006).

41. *Baker v. State,* 170 Vt. 194, 744 A.2d 864 (1999).

42. The New Jersey Lawyer, Inc. Vol. 15, No. 50, p. 5.

43. See e.g. *Dunphy v. Gregor,* 136 N.J. 99, 642 A.2d 372 (N.J. 1994).

44. *Lozoya v. Sanchez,* 133 N.M. 579, 2003 NMSC 9, 66 P.3d 948 (2003).

45. The Honorable J. Harvie Wilkinson, III, *Essay: Gay Rights and American Constitutionalism,* 56 Duke L. J.545 at 562, 563 (2006).

46. *Irizarry v. Bd. of Educ.,* 251 F.3d 604 (U.S. App. 2001). The court held that cost was a sufficiently rational basis for treating persons differently under the benefits rule.

47. For a discussion of this issue, see William C. Duncan, Symposium: Interjurisdictional Recognition of Civil Unions, Domestic Partnerships, and Benefits: *Article: Survey of Interstate Recognition of Quasi-Marital Statuses,* 3 Ave Maria L. Rev. 617 (Summer, 2005) p. 617.

48. For example, as of January 1, 2005, California's Domestic Partnership Law recognizes partnerships and unions created in other states, and New York City's 2002 Domestic Partnership Act recognizes civil unions formed in other jurisdictions.

49. *Lawrence v. Texas,* 539 U.S. 558, 123 S. Ct. 2472, 2490 156 L. Ed. 2d 508 (2003).

50. In its 2005 session, the Maryland legislature passed a bill establishing a limited form of domestic partnership, but the bill was vetoed by the Governor. New York State employees have been granted limited domestic partnership benefits under executive order of the Governor. Colorado's domestic partnership bill went before the voters in the November 2006 election as Referendum I and was defeated by only a 6% margin—47% in favor, 53% opposed.

51. Barbara J. Cox, *Essay: But Why Not Marriage: An Essay on Vermont's Civil Unions Law, Same-sex Marriage, and Separate but Unequal,* 25 Vt. L. Rev. 113 (2000).

52. *Supra* n. 48 at 635.

Chapter 6

1. Peter Y. Wolfe, *How a Mediator Enhances the Negotiation Process,* New Hampshire Bar Journal, Volume 46, Number 2 Summer 2005, p. 39.

2. Karen J. Borgstrom, *Mediated Divorce Agreements: Reconciling Equal Versus Equitable,* New Hampshire Bar Journal, Volume 46, Number 2 Summer 2005, p. 63.

3. *Id.* at 62.

4. Honey Hastings, *Dispute Resolution Options in Divorce and Custody Cases,* New Hampshire Bar Journal, Volume 46, Number 2 Summer 2005, p. 54. Although this article focuses specifically on the use of

alternative dispute resolution options in New Hampshire, it is an excellent, well-researched discussion of the basic nature of several ADR options.

5. *Id.* at p. 54, quoting Pauline H. Tesler, *Collaborative Law,* (2001) p. 8.
6. See e.g. *Kelm v. Kelm,* 623 N.E.2d 39 (Ohio 1993).
7. *McIntyre v. McIntyre,* 693 N.W.2d 822 (Mich. 2005).
8. MCL 600.5081(2).
9. *Williams v. North Carolina,* 317 U.S. 287, 298–299, 63 S. Ct. 207, 87 L. Ed. 279 (1942).
10. *Kulko v. Kulko,* 436 U.S. 84, 98 S. Ct. 1690, 56 L. Ed. 132 (1978).
11. *Burnham v. Superior Court,* 495 U.S. 604, 628, 110 S. Ct. 2105, 2119, 109 L. Ed. 2d 631, 650 (1990).
12. *Russo v. Russo,* 714 A.2d 466 (Pa. Sup. Ct. 1998).
13. Utah Code Ann. § 30–3–1. (3)(j).
14. See e.g. *Ricketts v. Ricketts,* 393 Md. 479, 903 A.2d 857 (Ct. App. 2006). In this case, a Maryland appellate court reversed a lower court's dismissal of a complaint for a limited divorce on the ground of constructive desertion based on an alleged denial of marital relations while the parties continued to live under the same roof in separate bedrooms.
15. *Shaffer v. Shaffer,* Not reported in S.E.2d, 2003 WL 21739039 (Va. App.).
16. § 750 ILCS 5/401 (1).
17. *Verplatse v. Verplatse,* 17 Ohio App. 3d 99, 477 N.E.2d 648 (1984). Also see e.g. *Hoppes v. Hoppes,* 5 Ohio Misc. 159, 214 N.E.2d 860 (cP 1964).
18. See e.g. *Routhier v. Routhier,* 128 N.H. 439, 514 A.2d 825 (1986).
19. M.G.L. c.208 §1.
20. O.C.G.A. § 19–5–3 (9) and (12).
21. 750 ILCS 5/401 (1).
22. Md. FAMILY LAW Code Ann. § 7–103 (a)(4).
23. O.C.G.A. § 19 -5-3 (8).
24. ORC Ann. 3105.01 (H).
25. Va. Code Ann. § 20–91 A. (3).
26. See e.g. 750 ILCS 5/401 (1).
27. See N.H. Rev. Stat. Ann. §458:7 VIII.
28. See e.g. Conn. Gen. Stat. § 46b-40 (c)(10).
29. Official Code of Georgia Annotated O.C.G.A. § 19–5–3 (5).
30. Md. FAMILY LAW Code Ann. § 7–103 (a)(8).
31. Utah Code Ann. § 30–3–1 (3)(d).
32. ORC Ann. 3105.01 (F).
33. In a Virginia case, the husband alleged four fault grounds (desertion, adultery, sodomy, and cruelty) and the wife cross-complained, alleging no-fault grounds, See *Jones v. Jones,* 2004 Va. App, LEXIS 455. The trial court's decree awarded the divorce to the wife, finding that the parties had lived separate and apart for more than the required one-year period.
34. In re Hightower, 830 N.E.2d 862 (Ill. App. Ct. 2005), quoting *Quagliano v. Quagliano,* 94 Ill. App. 2d 233, 237, 236 N.E.2d 748 (1968).
35. See *Vandevort v. Vandevort,* 134 P.3d 892 (Okla. Civ. App. 2005).
36. *In re Marriage of Cohee,* 994 P.2d 663 (Kan. Ct. App. 1999).
37. 50 U.S.C. § 521 (1982).
38. *Long v. Long,* 196 S.W.3d 460 (Tex. App. 2006).
39. See e.g. Mark Chinn, *The Exit Interview,* Family Advocate, Fall 2006, American Bar Association.

Chapter 7

1. *Hickman v. Taylor,* 329 U.S. 495, 67 S. Ct. 385, 91 L. Ed. 451 (1947). (Jackson, J., concurring).
2. Supp.Dom.Rel.P. Rule 410 Mandatory Self-Disclosure of Financial Documents.
3. *Electronic Evidence: The Essential Tools,* Family Advocate, American Bar Association, Vol. 29, No. 3, Winter 2007.
4. The content of this segment reflects, in part, observations made in a workshop handout prepared by Hon. Geoffrey A. Wilson, Franklin Probate and Family Court, titled "A Judge's Thoughts on Financial Statements (A Work in Progress)" and reprinted in several publications including Trying Divorce Cases, Volume I, Donald G. Tye et al, MCLE, Inc. (2005).

Chapter 8

1. *Troxel v. Granville,* 530 U.S. 57, 88–89, 120 S. Ct. 2054 (2000). (Stevens, J., dissenting).
2. *Garska v. McCoy,* 167 W.Va. 59, 278 S.E.2d at 360 (1981).
3. American Law Institute Principles of Marital Dissolution §2.03 (1). The ALI Principles refer to "allocation of parental responsibilities" rather than to "visitation" and "custody."
4. New Hampshire RSA 461-A.
5. The Uniform Child Custody Jurisdiction Act, 9(1A) U.L.A. 261 (1968).
6. The Uniform Child Custody Jurisdiction and Enforcement Act, 9(1A) U.L.A. 649 (1997).
7. Federal Parental Kidnapping Act, P.L. 96–611 § 6–10.
8. Convention on the Civil Aspects of International Child Abduction, held at The Hague on October 25, 1980. The language of the Convention can be found in Appendix 2 to the Department of State Notice, 51 FR 10498 March 26, 1986. The federal legislation that makes the terms of the Convention available as a judicial remedy in the United States is the International Child Abduction Remedies Act, Sec. 1 of P.L. 100–300, 42 U.S.C.A.11601 *et seq.* The Federal Regulations that define the State Department's role in implementing the Convention are found in 22 C.F.R. 94.4.
9. National Child Search Assistance Act, 42 USC §§ 5779 and 5780.
10. The International Child Abduction Remedies Act, 42 USC §11601 *et seq.*
11. The International Parental Kidnapping Crime Act (IPKCA) 18 USC §1204.
12. The Fugitive Felon Act, 18 USC §1073.
13. MCLS § 722.23.
14. Arizona Revised Statutes Annotated 25–403 Custody; Best interest of the child....
15. Wyo. Stat. Ann. §20–2–201(a).
16. Arizona Revised Statutes Annotated 25.403 Custody; Best interest of the child....
17. In Texas, custody cases may be heard by juries.
18. *In re Milovich,* 105 Ill. App.3d 596, 434 N.E.2d 811 (1982).
19. See e.g. *Burchard v. Garay,* 724 P.2d 486 (Cal. 1986.); *Maureen F.G. v. George W.G.,* 445 A.2d 934 (Del. 1982); *Agudo v. Agudo,* 411So. 2d 249 (Fla. Dist. Ct. App 1982); *Rolde v. Rolde,* 12 Mass. App. Ct. 398, 425 N.E.2d 388 (1981); *Maxfield v. Maxfield,* 452 N.W.2d 219 (Minn. 1990); *Riaz v. Riaz,* 789 S.W.2d 224 (Mo. App. Ct. 1990); *Burleigh v. Burleigh,* 650 P.2d 753 (Mont. 1982); *Crum v. Crum,* 505 N.Y.S.2d 656 (App. Div. 1986); *Moore v. Moore,* 574 A.2d 105 (Pa. Super. Ct. 1990); *Pusey v. Pusey,* 728 P.2d 117 (Utah 1986); *Harris v. Harris,* 546 A.2d 208 (Vt. 1988); *Garska v. McCoy,* 167 W.Va. 59, 278 S.E.2d at (360 1981).
20. See *Pascale v. Pascale,* 140 N.J. 583, 660 A.2d 485 (N.J. 1995).
21. American Law Institute, Principles of the Law of Family Dissolution: Analysis and Recommendations, §208.
22. *Kilsing v. Allison,* 343 S.C. 674, 541 S.E.2d 273 (S.C. App. 2001).
23. § 452.375 R.S. Mo.
24. *Source:* U.S. Census Bureau, Current Population Survey, April 1994–2002.
25. See e.g. *Linda R. v. Richard E.,* 162 A.D.2d 48, 561 N.Y.S.2d 29 (N.Y. App. Div. 1990).
26. MCLS § 722.23.
27. *Garrett v. Garrett,* 527 N.W.2d 213, 221–222 (Neb. Ct. App. 1995).
28. *Hicks v. Hicks,* 2005 PA Super. 58, 868 A.2d 1245 (2005). There are those who might argue that the court violates the Constitution by, in effect, preferring one religion over the other. Occasionally a dispute is about a particular religious practice between two parents who share the same faith. See *Sagar v. Sagar,* 57 Mass. App. Ct. 71, 781 N.E.2d 54 (2003).
29. *In re Stopher,* 328 Ill. App. 3d 1037, 263 Ill. Dec. 199, 767 N.E.2d 925 (2002). Other courts have reached a different result if, for example, the child had a serious medical problem that required complicated care and complex calculation and administration of medication.
30. *Matta v. Matta,* 44 Mass. App. Ct. 946, 693 N.E.2d 1063 (1998).
31. *Newton v. Riley,* 899 S.W.2d 509 (Ky. Ct. App. 1995).
32. *Taylor v. Taylor,* 345 Ark. 300, 47 S.W.3d 222 (2001).

33. See e.g. *Boyle v. Boyle,* 12 Neb. App. 681, 684 N.W. 2d 49 (2004).
34. *Resigno v. Annino,* 869 So. 2d 741 (Fla. 2004).
35. *In re Julie Anne,* 121 Ohio Misc. 2d 20, 2002 Ohio 4489, 780 N.E.2d 635 (Ohio Com. Pleas 2002).
36. MI. Rev. Stat. §25.312(3)(f).
37. Anderson v. Anderson, 278 Ga. 713, 606 S.E.2d 251 (2004).
38. Ill. Rev. Stat. § 750 ILCS 5/602.
39. Wyo. Stat. Ann. §20–2–201(a)(iii).
40. But in an Illinois case, the appeals court noted that "Neither the legislature or case law in Illinois has seen fit to set forth a rule of law that the killing of one parent by the other in the presence of the children, no matter what the circumstances, standing alone is sufficient to deprive that parent of his or her children on the basis of unfitness." *Tranel v. Lutgen,* 177 Ill. App. 3d 954, 127 Ill. Dec. 147, 532 N.E.2d 976 (2 Dist. 1988).
41. S.C. Code Ann. § 20–7–1515 (Supp. 2003)
42. *Bodne v. Bodne,* 277 Ga. 445, 588 S.E.2d 95 (Ga. App. 2002).
43. In Minnesota, a court-appointed task force has promulgated reasonable visitation schedules for consultation by parties and use by the courts when parents are unable to agree on their own terms. It is called "A Parental Guide to Making Child-Focused Parenting Time Decisions." An excellent manual has been produced in Massachusetts called "Planning for Shared Parenting: A Guide for Parents Living Apart." It combines research about children and the impact of divorce with strategies for addressing the practical needs of parents and children post-divorce. Sponsored by the Association of Family and Conciliation Courts and the Chief Justice of the Probate and Family Court, it is available through the Massachusetts Bar Association.
44. Sometimes innovative strategies are used, such as having parents who cannot talk reasonably with each other in person communicate by writing basic messages in a notebook. *Shenk v. Shenk,* 159 Md. App. 548, 860 A.2d 408 (2004).
45. See e.g. *Beck v. Beck,* 86 N.J. 480; 432 A.2d 63 (1981).
46. See e.g. *Cohen v. Cohen,* 162 Md. App. 599, 875 A.2d 814 (2005).
47. *Cleri v. Cleri,* No. 01D-0009-D1 (Conn. Prob. Ct. July 2, 2002), as cited in Gottfried, Sarah L., *Virtual Visitation: The New Wave of Communication between Children and Parents in Relocation Cases,* 9 Cardozo Women's L. J. 567, 582–583 Endnote 175. (2003).
48. *McCoy v. McCoy,* 336 N.J. Super. 172, 764 A. 2d 449 (N.J. Super. App. Div. 2001). See also *McCubbin v. Taylor,* 5 S.W.3d 202 (Mo. App. 1999); *Hartinger v. Hartinger,* 2000 WL 33418385 (Mich. App. 2000).
49. *Lazarevic v. Fogelquist,* 668 N.Y.S.2d 320 (1997).
50. For several years, Massachusetts judges, family service personnel, and family law practitioners have relied heavily on a set of age-appropriate time-sharing guidelines known as "The Cooperative Parenting Plan." The guidelines (incorporated in the Massachusetts document referenced in end note 43 above) resulted from the work of an interdisciplinary committee chaired by the Honorable Arline S. Rotman, a retired justice of the Massachusetts Probate and Family Court.
51. Rev. Code Wash. (ARCW) § 26.09.184.
52. The states that have adopted the UMDA as of September 2006 include: Arizona, Colorado (in part), Illinois, Kentucky, Minnesota, Missouri, Montana, and Washington.
53. See e.g. *Spahmer v. Gullette,* 113 P.3d 158 (Colo. 2005).
54. *Hawkes v. Spence,* 2005 VT 57, 178 Vt. 161, 878 A.2d 273 (2005).
55. Austin, William G., *Relocation Law and the Threshold of Harm: Integrating Legal and Behavioral Perspectives,* 34 Fam. L. Q. 63, 65 (Spring 2000) as quoted in *Fenwick v. Fenwick,* 114 S.W.3d 767 (Ky. 2003). See also *Tibor v. Tibor,* 598 N.W.2d 480, 485 (N.D. 1999), in which the court acknowledges that a "move which benefits the health and well-being of a custodial parent is certainly beneficial to the parent's child, and is consequently in the child's best interest."
56. Morgan v. Foretich, 546 A.2d 407 (D.C. App. 1988). See also *Morgan v. Foretich,* 564 A.2d1 (D.C. App. 1989), in which the contempt judgment was overturned.
57. Martinez, Sandra, *The Misinterpretation of Troxel v. Granville: Construing the New Standard for Third-Party Visitation,* 36 Fam. L. Q. No. 3, Fall 2002 at p. 495.
58. HAW. REV. STAT. § 571–46(2) (Supp. 2006). Given the decision in the *Troxel* case, this statute is likely unconstitutionally broad.
59. Mason, Mary Ann and Zayac, Nicole, *Rethinking Stepparent Rights: Has the ALI Found a Better Definition?* 36 Fam. L. Q. No. 2 (Summer 2002).
60. See e.g. *Michael H. v. Gerald D.,* 491 U.S. 110, 109 S. Ct. 2333, 105 L. Ed. 2d 91 (1989). In this case, the child had known both "fathers" in a paternal capacity. The Supreme Court upheld a California court's decision recognizing the mother's husband as the child's legal father rather than the biological father who sought to establish paternity.
61. *Supra* 59.
62. States imposing such obligations include Delaware, Hawaii, Iowa, Kentucky, Missouri, Montana, Nebraska, Nevada, New Hampshire, New York, North Carolina, North Dakota, Oregon, South Dakota, Vermont, and Washington.
63. In a Michigan case, for example, a court extended parental status to a step-parent, applying the concept of "equitable parenthood" under circumstances in which: (1) the husband and child mutually acknowledge a relationship as father and child, or the mother of the child has cooperated in the development of such a relationship over a time prior to the filing of the complaint for divorce, (2) the husband desires to have the rights afforded to a parent, and (3) the husband is willing to take on the responsibility of paying child support. *Atkinson v. Atkinson,* 160 Mich. App. 601, 408 N.W.2d 516 (1987). In the Minnesota case *Simmons v. Simmons,* 486 N.W.2d 788 (Minn. App. 1992), the court relied on the *in loco parentis* doctrine when it awarded visitation to a step-father over the mother's objection.
64. *In re Marriage of Rayman,* 273 Kan. 996, 47 P.3d 413 (Kan. 2002).
65. 50 USCS Appx. § 501 *et seq.*
66. 68 U.S. Department of Commerce, Census Bureau, *Children's Living Arrangements and Characteristics, March 2002* (June 2003).
67. Gregory, John DeWitt, *Family Privacy and the Custody and Visitation Rights of Adult Outsiders,* 36 FAM. L. Q. No. 1, Spring 2002 p. 163 at 168.
68. See e.g. *Blixt v. Blixt,* 437 Mass. 649, 774 N.E.2d 1052 (Mass. 2002).
69. *J.A.L. v. E.P.H.,* 453 Pa. Super. 78, 88–89; 682 A.2d 1314, 1319–1320 (1996).
70. See e.g. *V.C. v. M.L.B.,* 163 N.J. 200, 748 A.2d 539 (2000).
71. The U.S. Supreme Court has recognized the rights of a "mature" minor in some contexts, such as in the making of abortion decisions.
72. Woodhouse, Barbara Bennett, *Talking About Children's Rights in Judicial Custody and Visitation Decision-Making,* 36 FAM. L. Q. Number 1, Spring 2002, p. 105 at 129.
73. *Lawrence v. Lawrence,* 2004 WI App. 170; 276 Wis. 2d 403, 687 N.W.2d 748 (2004).
74. *Kendall v. Kendall,* 426 Mass. 238, 687 N.E.2d 1228 (1997).
75. Atkinson, Jeff, Modern Child Custody Practice, Vol. 1, § 4.1.
76. Gregory, John DeWitt, *Family Privacy and the Custody and Visitation Rights of Adult Outsiders,* 36 FAM. L. Q. No. 1, Spring 2002 p. 163 at 168.

Chapter 9

1. *Kirkpatrick v. O'Neal,* 197 S.W.3d 674 (Tenn. 2006).
2. Fam. Code, §7613, subd. (b) and see the case *K.M. v. E.G.,* 37 Cal. 4th 130, 117 P.3d 673, 33 Cal. Rptr. 3d 61 (Cal. 2005).
3. 42 U.S.C. § 666(a)(5)(D)(ii).
4. *Rodney P. v. Stacy B.,* 169 S.W.3d 834 (Ky. 2005). The Guidelines will usually be used to determine the level of each parent's obligation. The basic premise is that a parent who has the ability to pay should not be relieved of the duty to do so solely because the child is removed from his or her custody. However, the total payment from the parents to the government agency should not exceed the actual costs to the agency of caring for the child. See also *In re Katherine C.,* 390 Md. 554, 890 A.2d 295 (Md. 2006).
5. See e.g. *Columbus Bar Ass'n v. Albrecht,* 106 Ohio St. 3d 301, 2005 Ohio 4984, 834 N.E.2d 812 (2005).
6. 11 U.S.C. §§ 523(a)(5) and 507(a).
7. Pub. L. No. 93–647, 88 Stat. 2361 (codified as amended at 42 U.S.C. §§651–662).

8. Child Support Enforcement Amendments of 1984, Pub. L. No. 98–378, 98 Stat. 1321 (1984) (42 U.S.C. §667).

9. 42 U.S.C. § 666(a)(5).

10. Pub. L. No. 100–485, 102 Stat. 2343 (1988) as codified in U.S.C. 42 § 667(b).

11. Uniform Interstate Family Support Act. 9(1) U.L.A., 201 (Supp. 1996).

12. Pub. L. No. 100–485, 102 Stat. 2343 (1988) as codified in U.S.C. 42 § 666.

13. Pub. L. No. 104–193, 110 Stat. 2105 (42 U.S.C. § 601 *et seq.*).

14. 28 U.S.C. § 1738B. This Act is similar in structure and intent to UIFSA and the Acts are largely complementary and not contradictory. It was passed before UIFSA was adopted by all states in response to federal mandate.

15. 45 C.F.R. § 302.56 (g).

16. Beld, Jo Michelle and Biernat, Len, *Federal Intent for State Child Support Guidelines: Income Shares, Cost Shares, and the Realities of Shared Parenting,* 37 Fam. Law Q. No. 2 (Summer 2003).

17. See e.g. *In re Marriage of Rogers,* 213 Ill.2d 129, 820 N.E.2d 386 (2004).

18. See e.g. *In re State (Taylor),* 153 N.H. 700, 904 A.2d 619 (2006).

19. Kricken, Tori R.A., *Child Support and Social Security Dependent Benefits: A Comprehensive Analysis and Proposal for Wyoming,* 2 Wyo. L. Rev. 39 (2002) This article provides an in-depth review of how various states deal with SSDI benefits. The author concludes that Wyoming should adopt the majority position of including the benefit in the obligor's income and subsequently allowing a setoff of his or her support obligations.

20. See e.g. *Brown v. Brown,* 849 N.E.2d 610, (Ind. 2006); *Metz v. Metz,* 120 Nev. 786, 101 P.3d 779 (Nev. 2004); and *Groenstein v. Groenstein,* 2005 WY 6, 104 P. 3d 765, (Wyo. 2005) which are good examples of cases addressing this topic.

21. 42 U.S.C. §407(a).

22. 10 U.S.C.A. §1408 (c), (d), and (e) (1998 and Supp. 2004).

23. La.R.S. 9:315.

24. See e.g. *In re Bazemore,* 899 A.2d 225 (N.H. 2006).

25. An excellent case on this topic is *Caplan v. Caplan,* 182 N.J. 250, 864 A.2d 1108 (2005).

26. 45 C.F.R. §302.56 (c).

27. See *Wilkins v. Wilkins,* 269 Neb. 937, 697 N.W.2d 280 (2005). R.R.S. Neb. § 42-364.16 (2006) establishes that the Supreme Court of Nebraska shall provide child support guidelines by court rules. The language cited in the text is found in: Neb. Ct. R., Child Support Guideline T (2006).

28. *Emery v. Mofitt,* 269 Neb. 867, 697 N.W.2d 249 (2005).

29. *Busse v. Busse,* 141 Idaho 566, 113 P.3d 224 (2005).

30. RSA 461-A:14 (2006).

31. C.R.S. 14–10–115 §(1.5)(c), (1.6), (1.7) (1997).

32. M.G.L. c. 208 §28.

33. *In re Marriage of Vannausdle,* 668 N.W.2d 885 (Iowa 2003). See also *Gac v. Gac,* 186 N.J. 535, 897 A.2d 1018, (2006). This is a good case illustrating a court's consideration of factors related to coverage of the costs of higher education.

34. ARIZ. REV. STAT. §25.320 (2001).

35. COLO. REV. STAT. ANN. § 14–10–115 (West 1997 & Supp. 1998).

36. N.J. Court Rules, R., Appx. IX-A 2006 13.

37. Oklahoma Child Support Guidelines: 43 Ok. St. § 118 E 10a.

38. 19 A.M.R.S. § 2006 (5)(D-1). See *Jabar v. Jabar,* 2006 Me. 74, 899 A.2d 796 (2006).

39. N.D. Admin. Code, Section 75–02–04.1–08.2 (2003). Under North Dakota case law, the split custody offset will apply even when one parent assigns his or her right to receive child support to the state. See e.g. *Simon v. Simon,* 2006 ND 29, 709 N.W.2d 4 (N.D. 2006).

40. TEX. FAM. CODE §157.008. See e.g. *In the Interest of A.M.,* 192 S.W.3d 570 (Tex. 2006).

41. An excellent case on this topic is *Gladis v. Gladisova,* 382 Md. 654, 856 A.2d 703 (2004).

42. *Smith v. Freeman,* 149 Md. App. 1, 814 A.2d 65 (Md. Spec. App. 2002).

43. *Scott-Lasley v. Lasley,* 278 Ga. 671, 604 S.E.2d 761 (2004).

44. 42 U.S.C.A. §666(a)(10).

45. New York State Bar Association Committee on Professional Ethics, Op. 569 (Feb. 7, 1985).

46. See e.g. *Prisco v. Stroup,* 2004 D.C. Super. LEXIS 23 (2004).

47. Pub. L, No. 105–187, 112 Stat. 618 (1998) (codified at 18 U.S.C. § 228)—an amendment to the Child Support Recovery Act of 1992; Pub. L. No. 102–521, 106 Stat. 3403.

48. 18 U.S.C.A. § 228.

49. MCL 600.5809(4).

50. MCL 767.24(5). For a related case see e.g. *People v. Monaco,* 474 Mich. 48, 710 N.W.2d 46 (2005).

51. 42 U.S.C. § 666(a)(4).

52. 42 U.S.C. §666(a)(7).

53. *Zablocki v. Redhail,* 434 U.S. 374, 98 S. Ct. 673, 54 L. Ed. 2d 618 (1978).

54. *State v. Oakley,* 2001 WI 103, 245 Wis. 2d 447, 629 N.W.2d 200 (Wis. 2001).

55. I.C. §16–2005(1)(a).

56. There are three exceptions to the general rule: (1) The decree or parties' agreement provides that the noncustodial parent is entitled to the deduction 26 U.S.C. §152(e)(2)(A); (2) The noncustodial parent furnishes at least $600 in support, and a pre-1985 instrument provides that the noncustodial parent is entitled to the deduction 26 U.S.C. §152(e)(3)(A); and (3) a multiple-support agreement provides that the child is to be claimed as a dependent by a taxpayer other than the custodial parent 26 U.S.C. §152(e)(5). The exemption gets reduced or even eliminated in the case of taxpayers with higher incomes (I.R.C. §151(d)(3)).

57. I.R.C. §24(b). The Child Tax Credit phases out at a lower income level than does the dependency exemption.

Chapter 10

1. The Divorce Act of 1857 20&21 Vict. C. 85.

2. Chused, Richard, *Married Women's Property Law, 1800–1850,* 71 Georgetown Law Journal 1359 (1983). This article provides an overview of these laws along with passage dates.

3. *Orr v. Orr,* 440 U.S. 268, 279-280, 283, 99 S. Ct. 1102, 59 L. Ed. 2d 306 (1979).

4. See for example, *Austin v. Austin,* 445 Mass. 601, 839 N.E.2d 837 (2005).

5. *Chappelow v. Savastano,* 195 Misc. 2d 346, 758 N.Y.S.2d 782 (N.Y. Sup. 2003).

6. *Pendleton v. Pendleton,* 5 P.3d 839 (Cal. 2000).

7. Definitions based on Black's Law Dictionary, Abridged Eighth Edition, Bryan A. Garner, Editor in Chief, Thomson West (2005).

8. Uniform Marriage and Divorce Act (UMDA) 1970 as amended in 1971 and 1973 (U.L.A.). §308.

9. See Barbaruto, Patricia, *Standard of Living: what's it REALLY mean?* New Jersey Lawyer, Trends in Family Law, Volume 14, Number 36, p. A3. This is an interesting article on proving standard of living in New Jersey in particular.

10. See e.g. *Trs. of the AFTRA Health Fund v. Biondi,* 303 F.3d 765 (7th Cir. 2002).

11. *Miller v. Miller,* 356 Mass. 846, 314 N.E.2d 443 (1974).

12. The spousal support rules are located in the Internal Revenue Service Code, 26 U.S.C. §71 (1988).

13. On bankruptcy see Steinfeld, Shayna M. and Steinfeld, Bruce R., *Bankruptcy Strategies, Defensive Moves for Clients and Lawyers,* 25 Family Advoc. 43 (2003) and Steinfeld, Shayna M. and Steinfeld, Bruce R., *A Brief Overview of Bankruptcy and Alimony/Support Issues,* 38 FAM.L.Q. No. 1 (Spring 2004).

14. 11 U.S.C.A. §523(a)(5).

15. *In re Sarah,* 163 F.3d 397, 401 (6th Cir. 1998).

16. Va. Code Ann. § 20–107.1 (2006).

17. See Utah Code Ann. section 30–3–5 subsection 8 (b) (Supp. 1995).

18. *Riley v. Riley,* 2006 UT App 214, 138 P.3d 84 (Utah App. 2006).

19. As of 2007, the eight states that have adopted the Uniform Marriage and Divorce Act are Arizona, Colorado (in two parts), Illinois, Kentucky, Minnesota, Missouri, Montana, and Washington.

20. N.C. Gen. Stat. $31A-1 (2006).
21. See e.g. Ginsburg, Edward M., *The Place of Alimony in the Scheme of Things*, Massachusetts Family Law Journal, Volume 14, Number 5, January 1997. This article proposes guidelines that the author believes would be applicable in the great majority of cases. Now retired, Judge Ginsburg began applying "guidelines" in his alimony cases in western Massachusetts in the late 1970s in hopes of fostering predictability and limiting litigation regarding what constitutes reasonable need and ability to pay. His position was that need is a function of available income and that by making an equitable division of available income, the difficulties inherent in an open-ended, case-by-case approach can often be avoided.
22. On spousal support guidelines, see Ho, Victoria M. and Cohen, Jennifer J., *An Update on Florida Alimony Case Law: Alimony Guidelines a Part of Our Future*, 77 Fla. Bar J. 85 (2003); Gordon, Marie, *Spousal Support Guidelines and the American Experience: Moving Beyond Discretion*, 19 Can. J. Fam. L. 247 (2002); and Carbone, June, *The Futility of Coherence: The ALI's Principles of the Law of Family Dissolution, Compensatory and Spousal Support Payments*, 43 J. L. & Fam. Stud. 43 (2002).
23. *Bak v. Bak*, 24 Mass. App. Ct. 608 n.14, 511 N.E.2d 625 n.14 (1987).
24. IMDMA section 504.

Chapter 11

1. See *Solomon v. Solomon*, 383 Md. 176, 857 A.2d 1109 (2004), for an example of a case in which the court held that a non-equity club membership lacked the fundamental characteristics of property and was, therefore, not part of the marital estate.
2. See e.g. *In re Marriage of Keedy*, 249 Mont. 47, 813 P.2d 442 (1991). In this case, the Montana Supreme Court upheld a lower court's decision that a baseball card collection consisting of more than 100,000 cards was marital property worth $208,000, less the $5,000 portion the husband brought into the marriage.
3. See *Stageberg v. Stageberg*, 695 N.W.2d 609 (Minn. App. 2005). In this case involving contingent attorney's fees, a Minnesota appellate court upheld a lower court's conclusion that "the portion of a contingent fee for work in progress on the valuation date that is attributable to work done before the valuation date shall be treated as marital property for dissolution purposes."
4. See e.g. *In re Marriage of Anderson*, 811 P.2d 419 (Colo. App. 1990), finding that the portion of the husband's contract as a professional basketball player paid, but not expended, during the marriage was marital property subject to division.
5. See e.g. *Campbell v. Campbell*, 213 A.D.2d 1027, 624 N.Y.S.2d 493 (N.Y. App. Div. 1995). This case involves a determination that a spouse's share of lottery winnings on a ticket purchased with ten co-workers was marital property.
6. But see the New York case involving two roommates in which the court reached a decision based less on ownership of property and more on a sentimental, pet-centered best interests custody analysis. *Raymond v. Lachman*, 264 A.D.2d 340, 695 N.Y.S.2d 308 (N.Y. App. Div. 1999).
7. See *In re Marriage of Rogers*, 352 Ill. App.3d 896, 817 N.E.2d 562 (2004). In this case, an Illinois appellate court held that social security benefits may be considered in calculation of maintenance awards, although they are not subject to division upon dissolution of a marriage. The court noted: "Section 407(a) of the Social Security Act prohibits a beneficiary from transferring or assigning his or her benefits to another and imposes a broad bar against the use of any legal process to reach social security benefits.…however…Congress has carved out a narrow exception to this rule to allow the collection of past-due child support or alimony (maintenance).…A trial court dividing assets in a marital dissolution proceeding should simply not give any consideration to federal social security benefits; those benefits have already been divided by the Congress."
8. See *Brebaugh v. Deane*, 211 Ariz. 95, 118 P.3d 43 (Ariz. App. 2005), a case of first impression in Arizona addressing the issue of whether stock options that had not vested before the petition for dissolution was served can be divided as community property. The court examined approaches taken in other states before holding that unvested stock options received prior to service of the dissolution petition constitute community property based on the employer's intent, to the extent that they compensate the employee for past or present service and not as an incentive for future performance.
9. See *In re Marriage of Schriner*, 695 N.W.2d 493 (Iowa 2005), in which the Supreme Court of Iowa considered as a matter of first impression whether worker's compensation benefits awarded to one spouse during the marriage are divisible property at the time of divorce. After reviewing approaches taken in other jurisdictions, the Iowa Supreme Court held "that workers' compensation benefits received up to the time of the dissolution are property subject to an equitable division to the extent they have been retained and not spent. Benefits received after the divorce constitute separate property of the injured spouse." See also *Drake v. Drake*, 555 Pa. 481, 725 A.2d 717 (1999).
10. See *Landis & Landis*, 200 Ore. App. 107, 113 P.3d 456 (2005). In this case, an Oregon appeals court affirmed a lower court's decision to reopen a case based on the wife's discovery that, in listing his assets, the husband did not mention or account for a $16,687 lump-sum payment he had received as a Veteran's Disability Benefit.
11. *Buckl v. Buckl*, 373 Pa. Super. 521, 542 A.2d 65 (1988), quoting *White v. Rairdon*, 52 D. & C. 558, 559 (Delaware County 1944).
12. See e.g. *Baker v. Baker*, 2004 PA Super 413, 861 A.2d 298 (2004).
13. See Elizabeth Paek, *Fido Seeks Full Membership in the Family: Dismantling the Property Classification of Companion Animals by Statute*, 25 Hawaii L. Rev. 481 (2003). See also end note 6 above.
14. *Archer v. Archer*, 303 Md. 347, 357, 493 A.2d 1074, at 1079 (1985).
15. *Supra* n.1.
16. For convenience, the term *marital property* includes what would be called community property in community property states.
17. S.C. Code Ann. § 20 -7- 473 (2006).
18. See *Quinn v. Quinn*, 13 Neb. App. 155, 689 N.W.2d 605 (2004).
19. *Conrad v. Conrad*, 216 W. Va. 696, 612 S.E.2d 772 (2005). See also *Villasenor v. Villasenor*, 134 Ariz. 476, 657 P.2d 889 (Ariz. App. 1982), holding that the husband's disability compensation had both a disability component deemed separate property and a retirement component considered community property; *Gay v. Gay*, 573 So.2d 180 (Fla. App. 1991), holding that disability benefits are separate property because they replace future income; and *Allard v. Allard*, 708 A.2d 554 (R.I. 1998), holding that the disability pension at issue was separate property to the extent it compensated for lost earning capacity but marital property to the extent it constituted retirement pay earned by the disabled spouse during the marriage.
20. *Huber v. Huber*, 200 W. Va. 446, 490 S.E.2d 48 (W. Va. 1997).
21. See e.g. *Preiss v. Preiss*, 2000 WI App 185, 238 Wis.2d 368, 617 N.W.2d 514 (2000).
22. See e.g. *Bacon v. Bacon*, 26 Mass. App. Ct. 117, 524 N.E.2d 401 (1988), a case in which the assets derived from one spouse's family and the appreciation on it was due to inflation and sound investment advice received from that spouse's family. In such cases, courts will usually consider whether the parents intended a gift or a loan, as evidenced by appropriate documentation such as a letter and promissory note.
23. See e.g. *Wiese v. Wiese*, 46 Va. App. 399, 617 S.E.2d 427 (2005). This is a case of first impression in Virginia that addresses the question of whether refinancing precludes the possibility of tracing separate property or constitutes a transmutation of separate property into marital property. See also *Schmitz v. Schmitz*, 88 P.3d 1116 (Alas. 2004). This case addresses the complexities of appreciation, tracing, transmutation, and commingling issues in a determination of separate and marital property. See also Thomas J. Oldham, *Tracing, Commingling, and Transmutation*, 23 Fam. L. Q. 219 (1989), for a discussion of tracing.
24. Wisconsin adopted the Uniform Marital Property Act in 1986 (Wis. Stat. §766.31), which incorporates many community property principles. The IRS subsequently ruled that Wisconsin marital property is the equivalent of community property for income tax purposes. (Rev. Rul. 87–13,

1987–1 C.B. 20). The Wisconsin Act is different in several respects from other "community property" states, and property division upon divorce can be complex. In case law, the Wisconsin Supreme Court has held that the legislature did not intend, as a general rule, that the Marital Property Act change the state's statutory equitable distribution principles and that classification of property under the Marital Property Act is not necessarily determinative of property division on divorce. *Mausing v. Mausing,* 146 Wis. 2d 92, 429 N.W.2d 768 (1988). The Marital Property Act is concerned primarily with the spouses' ownership of property during the marriage and at their death, not on dissolution. *Kuhlman v. Kuhlman,* 146 Wis. 2d 588, 432 N.W.2d 295 (1988).

25. Alaska Statute § 34.77.030 (2007). Although not generally considered a community property state, the Alaska legislature enacted the Alaska Community Property Act, effective in 1998. The Act essentially adopts the Uniform Marital Property Act as Wisconsin had done in 1986. The Act is unique in that it allows, but does not require, a married couple who are both Alaska residents to elect to classify property as community property. In addition, under the Act, nonresident spouses may transfer property to an Alaska Community Property Trust (a form of Marital Property Agreement), and the property will be characterized as community property under Alaska law, provided at least one trustee is a "qualified" individual (essentially, a resident of Alaska).

26. See e.g. *Painter v. Painter,* 65 N.J. 196, 320 A.2d 484 (1974).

27. *Supra* n. 25.

28. Wis. Stat. § 766.55.

29. Internal Revenue Code §1041(b)(6). The one exception to this rule is that if separate property is converted to community property within a year of the decedent's death, it will pass back to the donor spouse and not receive a step-up in basis. Sec. 1014(e).

30. See e.g. RCW 26.16.030.

31. *In re Estate of Erikson,* 368 N.W.2d 525 (N.D. 1985).

32. Restatement (Second) of Conflicts of Laws, Introduction and §§ 258, 259.

33. *In re Marriage of Welchel,* 476 N.W.2d 104 (Iowa App. 1991).

34. See e.g. *Horner v. Horner,* 2004 ND 165, 686 N.W.2d 131 (2004).

35. See e.g. *Thompson v. Thompson,* 105 P.3d 346 (Okla. App. 2004).

36. *Bratcher v. Bratcher,* 26 S.W.3d 797 (Ky. App. 2000).

37. See Dylan A. Wilde, *Obtaining an Equitable Distribution of Retirement Plans in a Divorce Action,* 49 S.D. L. Rev. 141 (2003). See also Susan J. Prather, *Characterization, Valuation, and Distribution of Pensions at Divorce,* 15 J. Am. Acad. Matrimonial Law, 443 (1998).

38. See e.g. *Moore v. Moore,* 376 N.J. Super. 246, 870 A.2d 303 (2005). See also *Andrukiewicz v. Andrukiewicz,* 860 A.2d 235 (R.I. 2004), in which the Supreme Court of Rhode Island bound a husband who chose not to retire at "normal retirement age" to the terms of a written property settlement agreement between the parties incorporated in a Qualified Domestic Relations Order. The Agreement provided as follows: "The Husband agrees and acknowledges that the Wife will receive the first $583.00 of the monthly benefit that he will be entitled to receive at the time of his normal retirement date under the Husband's Pension Trust Benefit Plan that he has through the Town of Coventry...."

39. See *Fabich v. Fabich,* 144 N.H. 577, 744 A.2d 615 (1999). In this case of first impression in New Hampshire, the state Supreme Court adopted a functional approach to determining whether or not a retirement disability pension is divisible marital property after discussing the various approaches applied in other jurisdictions.

40. See e.g. *Kazel v. Kazel,* 3 N.Y.3d 331, 819 N.E.2d 1036, 786 N.Y.S.2d 420 (N.Y. 2004). In this case, a New York court of appeals held that "A judgment of divorce and qualified domestic relations order (QDRO) awarding an interest in the husband's pension plan do not automatically include pre-retirement death benefits available under the plan. If the intent is to distribute such benefits, that should be separately, and explicitly stated."

41. QDROs are not favored by plan administrators because they create additional "paperwork," or by parties who want their pensions to remain intact. Prior to 1984, companies were not permitted to distribute pension benefits to payees other than the employee participant.

42. *Hardy v. Hardy,* 311 S.C. 433, 429 S.E.2d 811 (S.C. App. 1992).

43. Internal Revenue Code §1041. See generally, Craig D. Bell, *Need-to-Know Divorce Tax Law for Legal Assistance Officers,* 177 Mil. L. Rev. (2003).

44. The *Solomon* case referenced in end notes 1 and 15 above includes a good discussion by the court regarding the issue of whether tax liabilities may be considered as "another factor" under the Maryland statute for purposes of distributing a marital property award.

45. See *Keff v. Keff,* 757 So. 2d 450 (Ala. Civ. App. 2000). In this case the court might have adopted the husband's position that his stock options should have been valued as of the date of the divorce, but the appellate court affirmed the lower court's decision, stating, "He cites no authority in support of this contention. An appellant's failure to cite supporting authority for his or her arguments leaves the court with no alternative but to affirm." In an Oregon case, *Timm & Timm,* 200 Ore. App. 621, 117 P.3d 301 (2005), the court remanded a case involving premarital contribution to marital assets, because the parties had relied on authority that was no longer controlling.

46. See e.g. *Rodrigue v. Rodrigue,* 55 F. Supp.2d 534 (E.D. La. 1999). This case involved a conflict between federal copyright law and the state of Louisiana's community property law concerning certain artworks produced by the husband, in which the wife claimed a copyright interest. See also *Coon v. Coon,* 364 S.C. 563, 614 S.E.2d 616 (2005), in which the South Carolina Supreme Court examined the relationship between federal and state law governing disposable military retirement pay. The court held that under federal law, states may treat disposable retired pay payable to a service member either as property solely of the member or as property of the member and his spouse, provided the award does not exceed 50 percent of the disposable retirement pay. The court held that South Carolina had elected to treat it as marital property.

Chapter 12

1. *Dominick v. Dominick,* 18 Mass. App. Ct. 85, 463 N.E.2d 564 (1984).

2. They may also ask that a constructive trust be imposed over the proceeds of the policy received by the new wife.

Chapter 13

1. Bruce Lord Wilder, *Current Status of Assisted Reproduction Technology: An Overview and Glance at the Future,* 39 FAM. L. Q. 573 (at 1) (No. 3 Fall 2005).

2. *Levy v. Louisiana,* 391 U.S. 68 (1968).

3. *Id.* at 72.

4. *Lehr v. Robertson,* 463 U.S. 248, 103 S. Ct. 2985, 77 L. Ed. 2d 614 (1983).

5. Id. at 262.

6. *Nguyen v. Immigration and Naturalization Services,* 533 U.S. 53, 121 S. Ct. 2053, 150 L. Ed. 2d 115 (2001).

7. 8 U.S.C.S. §1409.

8. *Id.* at §1409(c).

9. *Id.* at §1409(a).

10. *Supra* n. 6 at 63–65.

11. *Id.* at 94. (O'Connor, J., dissenting).

12. See Cynthia R. Mabry, *Who is the Baby's Daddy (And Why is it Important for the Child to Know)?* 34 U. Balt. L. Rev. 211 (Winter 2004). Based on the Census data cited, 48 percent of children not living with their fathers were African-American; 25 percent were Latino. Asian families reported the lowest number of children who lived with their single mothers, 13 percent.

13. The Court held that the biological father had no constitutionally protected relationship with his child. The Court also affirmed a summary judgment against the child. The plurality essentially reasoned that a natural father may have a protected right, but only if his rights do not conflict with the rights of the husband of the marriage into which the child was born.

14. Several courts across the country have held that both parents have a support obligation to a child who is the product of statutory rape. The

state's interest in obtaining economic support for minor children trumps its interest in protecting juveniles from statutory rape. See e.g. *State of Kansas* ex rel *Hermesmann v. Seyer*, 252 Kan. 646, 847 P.2d 1273 (1993).

15. E. Gary Spitko, *Sexual Orientation: Public Perceptions: From Queer to Paternity: How Primary Gay Fathers Are Changing Fatherhood and Gay Identity*, 24 St. Louis U. Pub. L. Rev. 195 at 216 (2005).

16. For a discussion of fathers as nurturers, see Nancy E. Dowd, *Essay: From Genes, Marriage and Money to Nurture: Redefining Fatherhood*, 10 Cardozo Women's L.J. 132 at 133–138 (Fall 2003).

17. See Katharine Baker, *Bargaining or Biology? The History and Future of Paternity Law and Parental Status*, 14 Cornell J. L. & Pub. Pol'y 1 at 6 (Fall 2004), for a comprehensive discussion of the rationale for and implementation of the duty of paternity support initially in the criminal context as "punishment for fornication and bastardy."

18. Dowd *supra*, n. 16 at 138.

19. *Supra* n. 6 at 62.

20. *Barnes v. Jeudevine*, 475 Mich. 696, at 715, 718 N.W.2d 311 (2006) (Markman, J., dissenting).

21. 41 U.S.C. 666(a)(5)(D)(iii).

22. 41 U.S.C. 666(a)(5)(D)(i).

23. Niccol D. Kording, *Little White Lies That Destroy Children's Lives—Recreating Paternity Fraud Laws to Protect Children's Interests*, 6 J.L. Fam. Stud. 237, 245 (2004).

24. Uniform Parentage Act of 2000 (as amended 2002), Article 2 §201.

25. Alaska Stat. § 25.27.166.

26. O.C.G.A. § 19–7–54.

27. Md. Code Ann., Fam. Law § 5–1038(a)(2)(i)2.

28. Ohio Revised Code Sections 3119.961 and 3119.962. Two Ohio courts of appeal have declared the statutes unconstitutional because the legislature, in effect, was dictating to the courts what to do with paternity judgments rendered years before, in violation of the separation of powers doctrine.

29. See e.g. *Doran v. Doran*, 2003 PA Super 129, 820 A.2d 1279 (2003), in which the court denied a request for an award in the amount of previously paid child support; but see *Denzik v. Denzik*, 197 S.W.3d 108 (Ky. 2006), in which the Kentucky Supreme Court reinstated a jury verdict in a husband's fraudulent misrepresentation action and allowed "restitution, albeit with considerations to limit the rate of payment in order to prevent detriment to the child(ren) supported."

30. *Langston v. Riffe*, 359 Md. 396 at 437, 754 A.2d 389 (Ct. App. 2000).

31. *Id.* at 416.

32. *Williams v. Williams*, 843 So. 2d 720 at 723 (Miss. 2003).

33. *Godin v. Godin*, 168 Vt. 514 at 523, 725 A.2d 904 (1998).

34. Mabry, *supra* n. 12 at 213, reflecting decisions of courts in New Jersey, Pennsylvania, Kansas, and Delaware.

35. *Betty L.W. v. William E.W.*, 212 W. Va. 1 at 12, 569 S.E.2d 77 (2002) (Maynard, J. dissenting).

36. http://www.paternityfraud.com.

37. Kording, *supra* n. 23, at 237.

38. Wilder, *supra* n. 1.

39. 750 ILCS 47.

40. N.H. Rev. Stat. §168-B: 19 and 14.

41. Mass. Gen. Laws Ch. 112 §12J.

42. 18 Pa. C. S. Ann. §3213(e).

43. Ark. Code Ann. § 23–85–137.

44. Md. Code Ann. §15–810(d) re limits and (b)(1) re mandates.

45. See Lars Noah, *Assisted Reproductive Technologies and the Pitfalls of Unregulated Biomedical Innovation*, 55 FLA. L. REV. 603 (2003).

46. For a symposium on this topic with a focus on the perspective of family law practitioners, see *Symposium on Assisted Reproduction Technology (ART)*, Family Law Quarterly Vol. 39, No. 3, Fall 2005.

47. Mich. Comp. Laws Ann. §722.855.

48. Mich. Comp. Laws Ann. §722.857.

49. 750 ILCS 47/50.

50. N.H. Rev. Stat. Ann. §168-B:16(I)(b).

51. Utah Code Ann. §78-45g-801(2) and (3).

52. Va. Code Ann. 20–165 (A)(B).

53. Wash. Rev. Code §26.26.240.

54. Nev. Rev. Stat. Ann. §126.045(1) and (3).

55. Ky. Rev. Stat. Ann. §199.590(4).

56. *Hodas v. Morin*, 442 Mass. 544, 814 N.E.2d 320 (Mass. 2004).

57. For an excellent resource on pre-birth parentage orders, see Steven H. Snyder and Mary Patricia Byrn, *The Use of Prebirth Parentage Orders in Surrogacy Proceedings*, 39 Fam. L. Q. 633–662 (No. 3 Fall 2005). The article includes as an appendix a state-by-state list of laws affecting surrogacy and pre-birth order proceedings.

58. *Doe v. Doe*, 710 A.2d 1297 (Conn. 1998).

59. *Johnson v. Calvert*, 5 Cal. 4th 84, 93, 851 P.2d 776, 19 Cal. Rptr. 2d 494(1993), cert. denied 510 U.S. 874, 114 S. Ct. 206, 126 L. Ed. 2d 163(1993).

60. *Id.*

61. *In the Matter of Baby M.*, 109 N.J. 396, 537 A.2d 1227 (1988).

62. *Id.* at 441, 442.

63. See Charles P. Kindregan and Maureen McBrien, *Embryo Donation: Unresolved Legal Issues in the Transfer of Surplus Cryopreserved Embryos*, 49 Vill. L. Rev. 169 at 170 (2004).

64. See Naomi D. Johnson, *Excess Embryos: Is Embryo Adoption a New Solution or a Temporary Fix*, 68 Brook. L. Rev. 853 (2003).

65. See N.H. Rev. Stat. Ann. § 168B:15 and La. Rev. Stat. Ann. § 9:129.

66. See generally La. Rev. Stat. Ann. §§9:121–9:135.

67. Fla. Stat. Ann. § 742.17.

68. 10 Okla. St. § 556.

69. *Davis v. Davis*, 842 S.W.2d 588 (Tenn. 1992).

70. *Id.* at 597.

71. *Id.* at 601.

72. *Id.* at 602.

73. *Id.* at 597.

74. *Kass v. Kass*, 91 N.Y.2d 554, 696 N.E.2d 174, 673 N.Y.S.2d 350 (N.Y. 1998).

75. *Id.* at 177.

76. *Id.*

77. *Id.* at 180.

78. *Supra* n. 24 Article 7 Section 707.

79. Fla. Stat. §742.17.

80. La. Civ. Code Ann. Art. 9:931.1.

81. See e.g. *Gillett-Netting v. Barnhart*, 371 F. 3d 593 (9th Cir, Ariz. 2004). See also 42 U.S.C. §402(d)(1) and 416(h)(2)(A).

82. See In re Estate of Kolacy, 753 A.2d 1257 (N.J. Super. Ct. Ch. Div. 2000), in which the court held that twins born eighteen months after their father's death were his legal heirs.

83. *Woodward v. Comm'r of Soc. Sec.*, 435 Mass. 536, 760 N.E.2d 257 (2002).

84. See *Kazmierazak v. Query*, 736 So. 2d 106 (Fla. Dist. Ct. App. 1999); *In re C.B.L.*, 723 N.E.2d 316 (Ill. App. Ct. 1999); *McGuffen v. Overton*, 542 N.W. 2d 288 (Mich. Ct. App. 1995); *Alison D. v. Virginia M.*, 572 N.E.2d 27 (N.Y. 1991); *In re Jones*, 2002 WL 940195 (Ohio Ct. App. 2002); and *In re Thompson*, 11 S.W.3d 913 (Tenn. Ct. App. 1999).

85. See e.g. *Nancy S. v. Michele G.*, 279 Cal. Rptr. 212 (Ct. App. 1991).

86. *Elisa B. v. Superior Court*, 117 P. 3d 660 (Cal. 2005).

87. *Principles of the Law of Family Dissolution: Analysis and Recommendations*, American Law Institute, Philadelphia, PA, www.ali.org.

88. *Supra* n. 24 Article 7 Section 703.

89. *Supra* n. 24 Article 7 Section 702.

90. *Jhordan C. v. Mary K.*, 179 Cal. App. 3d 386, 224 Cal. Rptr. 530 (Cal. App. 1986).

91. *Gleitman v. Cosgrove*, 227 A.2d 689, 695 (N.J. 1967). In this case, the plaintiff claimed that a physician's failure to inform or advise a pregnant mother of the dangers of birth defects when she contracted rubella deprived her of the opportunity to terminate the pregnancy and allowed the child to be born with birth defects.

92. *Harbeson v. Parke-Davis, Inc.*, 656 P.2d 483 (Wash. 1983).

93. See e.g. *Morgan v. Christman*, 1990 WL 137405 (D. Kan.), a case in which the use of the drug clomid resulted in the premature birth of four children who suffered from various impairments and deformities.

94. *Stiver v. Parker*, 975 F.2d 261 (6th Cir. 1992).

95. CAL. PENAL CODE §367g.

96. See Cyrene Grothaus-Day, *Criminal Conception: Behind the White Coat*, 39 FAM. L. Q, 707 (2005).

97. *Perry-Rogers v. Fasano*, 276 A.D. 67, 715 N.Y.S.2d 19 (2000).

98. See *Perry-Rogers v. Obasaju*, 282 A.D.2d 231 (N.Y. App. Div. 2001), in which the court denied the defendant's motion to dismiss and held it was foreseeable that implantation of the plaintiff's embryo in another woman would cause emotional distress.

99. *Fasano v. Nash*, 282 A.D.2d 277 (N.Y. App. Div. 2001). See also Raizil Liebler, *Are You My Parent? Are You My Child? The Role of Genetics and Race in Defining Relationships After Reproductive Technological Mistakes*, 5 DEPAUL J. HEALTH CARE L. 15, pp. 42–52 (2002).

100. See e.g. *Jeter v. Mayo Clinic of Arizona*, 121 P.3d 1256 (Ariz. App. Div. 1 2005).

101. See Charles P. Kindregan and Maureen McBrien, *Assisted Reproductive Technology: A Lawyer's Guide to Emerging Law and Science*, American Bar Association, 2005. Chapter 10 contains helpful pointers on the drafting of documents relating to assisted reproduction arrangements.

102. Melanie B. Jacobs, *When Daddy Doesn't Want to Be Daddy Anymore: An Argument Against Paternity Fraud Claims*, 16 Yale J.L. & Feminism 193, 208–209 (2004).

103. *Buzzanca v. Buzzanca*, 61 Cal. App. 4th 1410 at 1428–29, 72 Cal. Rptr. 2d 280 (1998).

Chapter 14

1. Barbara Bennett Woodhouse, *Waiting for Loving: The Child's Fundamental Right to Adoption*, 34 Cap. U. L. Rev. 297, 328 (Winter, 2005).

2. U.S. Census Bureau, *Adopted Children and Stepchildren: 2000* (2003) (www.census.gov/prod/2003pubs/censr-6.pdf).

3. M.G.L. Chapter 210 Section 1.

4. Utah Code Ann. 78–30–1.

5. Elizabeth J. Samuels, *Time to Decide? The Laws Governing Mothers' Consents to the Adoption of Their Newborn Infants*, 72 Tenn. L. Rev. 509, 518 (Winter 2005), referencing Sue Zeidler, "Internet Transforms U.S. Adoption Process," Reuters, May 21, 2004.

6. See e.g. Colo. Rev. Stat. §25–2–113.5.

7. See e.g. Massachusetts General Laws Chapter 210 Section 5D.

8. Ala. Code § 22–9A-12(c) 7 (d); Alaska Stat. § 18.50.5000(a); Kan. Stat. Ann. 65-§2423(a); and Or. Rev. Stat. § 432.240(1).

9. Erin Green, *Unwed Fathers' Rights in Adoption: The Virginia Code vs. The Uniform Adoption Act*, 11 Wm. & Mary J. of Women & L. 267, 273 (Winter 2005).

10. *Stanley v. Illinois*, 405 U.S. 645, 92 S. Ct. 1208, 31 L. Ed 2d 551 (1972).

11. *Lehr v. Robertson*, 463 U.S. 248 at 262, 103 S. Ct. 2985, 77 L. Ed. 2d 614 (1983).

12. For an interesting New Mexico case addressing whether or not a father's conduct prior to his child's birth can be used to terminate parental rights under a presumptive abandonment statute, see *Helen G. v. Mark J. H. (In re Adoption Petition of Romero)*, 2006 NMCA 136, 145 P.3d 98 (2006).

13. See e.g. *In re Adoption of Reeves*, 831 S.W.2d 607 (Ark. 1992). In this Arkansas case, an unwed father was not notified of a petition for adoption of his two children. The mother and stepfather, who adopted one of the children, swore that the father was "unknown." The Arkansas Supreme Court upheld the adoption despite the mother's and stepfather's deceit and the fact that the father had alleged he was the child's natural father, had established a substantial *de facto* relationship with him, and had received no notice of the paternity proceeding. The adoption was upheld because the father was not registered in the state's putative father registry.

14. See e.g. *Appeal of H.R.*, 581 A.2d 1141 (D.C. App. 1990).

15. *Kessel v. Leavitt*, 511 S.E.2d 720, 756 (W. Va. 1998).

16. Shirley Darby Howell, *Adoption: When Psychology and Law Collide*, 28 Hamline L. Rev. 29, 54 (Winter 2005). For a more extensive discussion

of this topic, see Robbin Potz Gonzalez, *The Rights of Putative Fathers to Their Infant Children in Contested Adoptions: Strengthening State Laws that Currently Deny Adequate Protection*, 13 Mich. J. Gender 7 L. 39 (2006).

17. Code of Ala. § 26–10C-1(f).

18. Code of Ala. § 26–10A-9(a)(5).

19. Minn. Stat. § 259.52(8). See also 750 Ill. Comp. Stat. § 50/12.1.

20. Ariz. Rev. Stat. §8–106.01(F).

21. Utah Code Ann. § 78–30–4.13(1)(a).

22. See Mo. Ann. Stat. § 192.016(9)(2,3).

23. Utah Code Ann. 78–30–4.12(4).

24. *G.P. v. State*, 842 So. 2d 1059 (Fla. Dist. Ct. App. 2003), invalidating Fla. Stat. Ann. §§ 63.087, 63.088, commonly known as the Scarlet Letter Provisions.

25. Kimberly Barton, *Who's Your Daddy?: State Adoption Statutes and the Unknown Biological Father*, 32 Cap. U.L. Rev. 113 (Fall 2003). See also Jeffrey A. Parness, *Adoption Notices to Genetic Fathers: No to Scarlet Letters, Yes to Good Faith Cooperation*, 36 Cumb. L. Rev. 63 (2005/2006).

26. Kan. Stat. Ann. § 59–2136(c) requires the court to order publication notice of the adoption hearing if no person is identified as the father or a possible father.

27. N.C. Gen. Stat. §§ 48–2–401(c)(3) and 48–2–402(b).

28. *Supra* n. 16 Howell at 46.

29. *Supra* n. 16 Howell at 47, describing *In re Valerie D.*, 223 Conn. 492, 613 A.2d 748 (1992).

30. Pub. L. No. 105–89, 11 Stat. 2115 (codified as amended in scattered sections of 2 U.S.C. and 42 U.S.C.).

31. *Supra* n. 1 at 303.

32. Fla. Stat. Ann. §383.50 (5). For a multistate review of the nature and complexity of safe haven laws, see Dayna R. Cooper, *Fathers Are Parents Too: Challenging Safe Haven Laws with Procedural Due Process*, 31 Hofstra L. Rev. 877 (2003), and Jeffrey A. Parness, *Deserting Mothers, Abandoned Babies, Lost Fathers: Dangers in Safe Havens*, 24 Quinnipiac L. Rev. 335 (2006).

33. Samuels *supra* n. 5 at 526, 527.

34. Samuels *supra* n. 5 at 528. For an example of a state statute regarding requirements for effective consents, see the following Vermont Statutes: 15A V.S.A. § 2–405 and 15A V.S.A. § 2–406. For an excellent resource, see Ann McLane Kuster and Marilyn T. Mahoney, *A Practitioner's Guide to Creating a Secure Adoption*, New Hampshire Bar Journal March 1996.

35. Massachusetts General Laws Chapter 210 Section 2.

36. Susan Calkins, *Ineffective Assistance of Counsel in Parental-Rights Termination Cases: The Challenge for Appellate Courts*, 6 J. App. Prac. 179 (Fall 2004). A problem sometimes arises when the adoption of a child is approved while termination of a parent's rights is under appeal. For a discussion of cases involving such situations, see Kate M. Heideman, *Avoiding the Need to "Unscramble the Egg": A Proposal for the Automatic Stay of Subsequent Adoption Proceedings When Parents Appeal a Judgment Terminating Their Parental Rights*, 24 St. Louis U. Pub. L. Rev. 445 (2005).

37. D.C. Code 16–2353(b).

38. 42 U.S.C.A §12101 *et seq.*

39. 42 U.S.C.A. §12132.

40. 42 U.S.C.A. § 1996b.

41. 25 U.S.C.A. § 1901.

42. 25 U.S.C.A. §1915(a) codifies this provision of the Indian Child Welfare Act. The Bureau of Indian Affairs has published Guidelines for state courts' implementation of the Act in 44 Fed. Reg. 67, 584. Guideline F.3 provides that good cause may be based on a request of the biological parents, established extraordinary physical or emotional needs of the child, or the unavailability of suitable families for placement after a diligent search. For a case applying this guideline, see *In re Adoption of B.G.J.*, 281 Kan. 552, 133 P.3d 1 (2006), decided by the Supreme Court of Kansas.

43. 25 U.S.C. §1903(4). For examples of recent cases addressing the requirements and application of the Indian Child Welfare Act, see *In re*

Dependency of T.L.G. et al., 126 Wn. App. 181, 108 P.3d 156 (2005), and *In the Matter of Baby Boy L.,* 2004 OK 93, 103 P.3d 1099 (2004).

44. Ala. Code 26–10A-5,6; Fla. Stat. Ann. 63.042(3); Miss. Code Ann. 93–17–3; and Utah Code Ann. 78–30–1.

45. Miss. Code Ann. 93–17–3.

46. Fla. Stat. Ann. 63.042(3).

47. *Lawrence v. Texas,* 539 U.S. 558, 123 S. Ct. 2472, 2490, 156 L. Ed. 2d 508 (2003). For opposing views on the likely impact of the *Lawrence* decision on adoption law, see Martin R. Gardner, *Adoption by Homosexuals in the Wake of Lawrence v. Texas,* 6 J.L. Fam. Stud. 19 (2004), and Mark Strasser, *The Legislative Backlash to Advances in Rights for Same-Sex Couples: Rebellion in the Eleventh Circuit: On Lawrence, Lofton and the Best Interests of Children,* 40 Tulsa L. Rev. 421 (Spring, 2005).

48. See Cal. Fam. Code 9000(b); Conn. Gen. Stat. Ann. 45a-724(a)(3); and Vt. Stat. Ann. Tit. 15A, 1–102(b).

49. VSA 1–102.

50. Cal. Fam. Code Section 9000(g).

51. *In re Adoption of Swanson,* 623A.2d 1095, 1096 (Del. 1993).

52. *Lofton v. Secretary of the Department of Children and Family Services,* 358 F.3d 804, 818–819 (11th Cir. 2005), reh'g en banc denied, 377 F.3d 1275 (11th Cir. 2004), cert. denied, 125 S. Ct. 869 (2005).

53. *Id.* at 827.

54. *Id.* at 820.

55. For an interesting, albeit clearly biased, perspective on the Florida ban and the *Lofton* case, see Mark Strasser, *The Legislative Backlash to Advances in Rights for Same Sex Couples: Rebellion in the Eleventh Circuit: On Lawrence, Lofton, and the Best Interests of Children,* 40 Tulsa L. Rev. 421 (Spring, 2005).

56. *DeBoer v. DeBoer,* 509 U.S. 1301, 114 S. Ct. 1, 125 L. Ed. 2d 755 (1993).

57. *In re Doe,* 254 Ill. App. 3d 405, 627 N.E.2d 648 at 651–652 (Ill.App. 1 Dist. 1993).

58. *Mariga v. Flint,* 822 N.E. 2d 620 (Ind. Ct. App. 2005).

Chapter 15

1. Gelles, R., *Intimate Violence in Families,* Third Edition, Thousand Oaks, CA, 1997, Sage, as quoted in Brownstein, Henry H., *The Social Reality of Violence and Violent Crime,* Allyn and Bacon, 2000, p. 77.

2. *Id.*

3. See Appel and Holden, *The Co-Occurrence of Spouse and Physical Child Abuse: A Review and Appraisal,* 12(4) Journal of Family Psychology. 578-599 (1998). See also S.M. Ross, *Risk of Physical Abuse to Children of Spouse Abusing Parents,* 20(7) Child Abuse & Neglect 589–598 (1996) (asserting that intimate partner violence increases the risk of child abuse from 5 percent after one abusive act to 100 percent after fifty acts of intimate partner violence).

4. Kathleen Finley Duthu, *Feature: Why Do [We] Need to Know [About] Domestic Violence? How Attorneys Can Recognize and Address the Problem,* 53 LA Bar Jnl. 20 (June, July 2005).

5. Bureau of Justice Statistics, 2005 Crime Characteristics

6. Shannon Catalano, PhD., Bureau of Justice Statistics, *Intimate Partner Violence in the United States,* December 2007.

7. Matthew R. Durose et al., U.S. Dep't of Justice., NCJ 207846, *Family Violence Statistics,* June 2005.

8. James Alan Fox and Marianne W. Zawitz, Bureau of Justice Statistics, *Homicide Trends in the United States,* January 1999; most recently updated July 11, 2007.

9. Constance M. Weimann et al., *Pregnant Adolescents: Experiences and Behaviors Associated with Physical Assault by an Intimate Partner,* 4 Maternal & Child Health J. 93 (2000).

10. The American Bar Association's Commission on Domestic Violence provides a comprehensive survey of recent statistics "as a service to legal practitioners and advocates who may find it useful to include current statistical data in their arguments to the court." The survey references a number of resources for data on domestic violence by race and ethnicity.

11. Catalano, *Supra* n. 6.

12. Patricia Tjaden and Nancy Thoennes, U.S. Dep't of Just. NCJ 181867, *Extent, Nature, and Consequences of Intimate Partner Violence: Findings from the National Violence Against Women Survey,* July 2000.

13. Patricia Tjaden, *Symposium on Integrating Responses to Domestic Violence: Extent and Nature of Intimate Partner Violence as Measured by the National Violence Against Women Survey,* 47 Loy. L. Rev. 41, 54 (2001).

14. Richard Tolman and Jody Raphael, *A Review of the Research on Welfare and Domestic Violence,* 56 J. of Soc. Iss. 655 (2000).

15. Michael R. Rand, U.S. Dep't of Just., NCJ 156921, *Violence-Related Injuries Treated in Hospital Emergency Departments,* August 1997.

16. Catalano, *Supra* n. 6.

17. Hilary Mayell, *Thousands of Women Killed for Family Honor,* National Geographic News, February 2, 2002.

18. Pamela B. Teaster et al., *2004 Survey of State Adult Protective Services: Abuse of Vulnerable Adults 18 Years of Age and Older,* National Adult Protective Services Association. A copy of the survey is available in PDF form on the National Center on Elder Abuse website at www.elderabusecenter.org.

19. American Psychological Association, *Elder Abuse and Neglect: In Search of Solutions,* APA Office on Aging,

20. Mary Twomey, M.S.W., Mary Joy Quinn, R.N., M.A., and Emily Dakin, M.S.S.A., PhD., *Courts Responding to Domestic Violence: From Behind Closed Doors: Shedding Light on Elder Abuse and Domestic Violence in Late Life,* 6 J. Center for Fam. Child. & Cts. 73 (2005) pp. 75, 76.

21. Violence Against Women Reauthorization Act of 2005, Pub. L. No. 109–162, 119 Stat. 2960 (2006). See Leila Abolfazli, *Violence Against Women Act,* 7 Geo. J. Gender and L. 863 (2006) for a description of the provisions of the successive VAWA acts.

22. See Erin L. Han, *Mandatory Arrest and No-Drop Policies: Victim Empowerment in Domestic Violence Cases,* 23 B.C. Third World L.J. 159, 176 (2003).

23. Laurie S. Kohn, *Why Doesn't She Leave? The Collision of First Amendment Rights and Effective Court Remedies for Victims of Domestic Violence,* 29 Hastings Const. L.Q. 1 at 5 ("Literature examining same-sex battering routinely refers to the fear of HIV 'outing' as being a primary cause of the secrecy that characterizes same-sex domestic violence.") ("Fearing homophobic responses, gay men and women often hide their sexual orientation from employers and family members. This fear gives batterers a manipulative tool to force victims to endure additional abuse. As long as a victim knows that a batterer intends to publicize this information and finds his threats credible, he may well stay in an abusive relationship rather than face the potential repercussions, which could include loss of child custody, employment, and family and personal relationships.")

24. G.A. § 16–5–90.

25. Tjaden, Patricia and Nancy Thoennes, *Stalking in America: Findings from the National Violence Against Women Survey,* U.S. Department of Justice, National Institute of Justice, Washington, D.C., as reported on the website of the National Center for Victims of Crime Stalking Resource Center in a fact sheet titled "Stalking in America—National Violence Against Women Survey (NVAW)." As of January 2008, the report can be accessed at www.ncvc.org.

26. See e.g. *Heacock v. Heacock,* 402 Mass. 21, 520 N. E. 2d 151 (1988), and *Heacock v. Heacock,* 30 Mass. App. Ct. 304, 568 N. E. 2d 621 (1991). (The Superior court dismissed a wife's tort action for unreasonable delay in serving process. In an effort to gain a tactical advantage in the parties' divorce action, the wife filed a tort action relating to an event that allegedly occurred during the marriage but did not attempt to serve it prior to the divorce, in order to avoid alerting her husband to the pending claim. The Appellate Court affirmed. The Supreme Court transferred the case from the Appellate Court and reversed on other grounds.)

27. See the Federal Gun Control Act of 1968 as amended codified at 18 U.S.C. §922 (g)(8).

28. In some states, such as Illinois, offenders convicted of domestic violence are liable by statute for the cost of counseling for children who witnessed their crimes. 720 ILCS 5/12–3.2.

29. Kohn *supra* n. 23 at page 10–11. This article provides an excellent discussion of the constitutionality of such speech restrictions. ("Although at least one court has granted such a restriction, none has resulted in an appellate decision. Because privacy invading speech in a domestic violence context does not fall into one of the predetermined categories of unprotected speech, the court would therefore engage in balancing, weighing the value of the speech against the countervailing interests to be protected by the injunction.")

30. *State v. Kidder,* 150 N.H. 600, 843 A.2d 312 (2004).

31. See Wis. Stat. 968.075(3)(a)1.b.

32. Ruth Jones, *Guardianship for Coercively Controlled Battered Women: Breaking the Control of the Abuser,* 88 Geo. L.J. 605, 612 (April 2000).

33. *Id.* at 609.

34. Kohn *supra* n. 23 at 59.

35. See *Domestic Violence: The Facts, An Information Handbook,* created by Peace at Home, Inc. www.peaceathome.org.

36. Much of this exhibit is based on a series of presentations by Douglas Gaudette, Director of the Family Violence Intervention Program at Holy Family Hospital in Methuen, Massachusetts.

37. *In re Marriage of Goodwin,* 606 N.W.2d 315 (Iowa 2000).

38. See Meredeth A. Felde, *Strengthening Protections for Domestic Violence Victims,* 36 McGeorge L. Rev. 922 (2005).

39. Cal. Fam. Code 4320 (i).

40. Cal. Fam. Code 4325(a).

41. Cal. Civ. Code 1708.6 (b)-(c).

42. Cal. Fam. Code 2603.5 (enacted by Chapter 299).

43. *Child Maltreatment 2005,* Administration for Children and Families, Report available online at http://www.acf.hhs.gov/programs/cb/pubs/cm05/index.htm.

44. The Child Abuse Prevention and Treatment Act of 1974 (CAPTA) codified at 42 U.S.C. 5101 through 5107 as most recently amended by the Keeping Children and Families Safe Act of 2003.

45. To assist in the search for statutory definitions in each state, go to www.childwelfare.gov/systemwide/laws_policies/statutes/defineall.pdf.

46. 42 U.S.C.A. §5106g (2).

47. *Definitions of Child Abuse and Neglect: Summary of State Laws,* p. 4, Child Information Gateway accessed September 2007 at www.childwelfare.gov.

48. Definition provided in the National Child Abuse and Neglect Data Collection System (NCANDS).

49. See the Child Neglect Fact Sheet accessed under the "protecting children" tab on the website of American Humane at www.americanhumane.org.

50. 42 U.S.C. § 5106i.

51. *Supra* n. 47 at p. 5.

52. *Supra* at n. 47 at p. 2.

53. *State v. Wilder,* 2000 ME 32, 748 A.2d 444, 449 n.6 (Me. 2000) (quoting William Blackstone, *Blackstone's Commentaries on the Laws of England 440* (Oxford reprint 1966), and William Blackstone, *Blackstone's Commentaries on the Law of England 120* (1768)).

54. *Wisconsin v. Yoder,* 406 U.S. 205, 213–215, 92 S.Ct. 1526, 32 L. Ed. 2d 15 (1972); *Pierce v. Society of Sisters,* 268 U.S. 510, 534–535, 45 S. Ct. 571, 69 L. Ed. 1070 (1925).

55. *State v. Adaranijo,* 153 Ohio App. 3d 266, 2003 Ohio 3822, 792 N.E.2d 1138, 1140 (2003).

56. *State v. Singleton,* 41 Wn. App. 721, 705 P.2d 825, 827 (Wash. App. 1985).

57. *State v. Thorpe,* 429 A.2d 785, 788, (R.I. 1981).

58. *State v. Kimberly B.,* 2005 WI App 115, 283 Wis. 2d 731, 699 N.W.2d 641 at 650 (Wis. App. 2005).

59. American Humane, *Shaken Baby Syndrome,* accessed September 2007 at www.americanhumane.org.

60. *Id.*

61. *Supra* n. 47 at p. 3.

62. American Humane, *Emotional Abuse,* accessed September 2007 at www.americanhumane.org.

63. 42 U.S.C.A. § 5106g(4).

64. *Purcell v. Commonwealth,* 149 S.W.3d 382 at 389 (Ky. 2004), referencing *New York v. Ferber,* 458 U.S. 747, 759–761, 102 S. Ct. 3348, 3355–3357, 73 L.Ed. 2d 1113 (1982).

65. *Id.* at 758.

66. *United States v. Dost,* 636 F. Supp. 828, 832 (S.D. Cal. 1986), aff'd, 812 F.2d 1239 (9th Cir. 1987).

67. See e.g. KRS 531.300 (4) (d).

68. *Parental Drug Abuse as Child Abuse: Summary of State Laws,* Child Welfare Information Gateway available online at www.childwelfare.gov/systemwide/laws_policies/statutes/drugexposed.cfm.

69. Wis. Stat. §§ 48.02 and 48.133.

70. *In re Baby Boy Blackshear,* 90 Ohio St. 3d 197, 2000 Ohio 173, 736 N.E.3d 462 (2000).

71. *Id.* at 199.

72. *Id.* at 202, 203.

73. N.J. Stat. Ann. §9:6–8.10.

74. *Id.* at Article 9:6–8.13.

75. *Id.* at Article 9:6–8.14. See Lauren E. Parsonage, *Note: Caught Between a Rock and a Hard Place: Harmonizing Victim Confidentiality Rights with Children's Best Interests,* 70 Mo. L. Rev. 863 (Summer 2005).

76. Pub. L. No. 96–272, 94 Stat. 500 (codified at 42 U.S.C. §§620-628 and 670–679).

77. See Kathleen Bean, *Reasonable Efforts: What State Courts Think,* 36 U. Tol. L. Rev. 321 (Winter 2005), for a comprehensive discussion of the federal reunification requirements and the states' interpretations and applications of those requirements.

78. *DeShaney v. Winnebago Department of Social Services,* 489 U.S. 189, 109 S. Ct. 998, 103 L. Ed.2d 249 (1989).

79. For an argument favoring imposition of liability on state actors for failure to protect victims of domestic violence and child abuse, see G. Kristian Miccio, *Notes From the Underground: Battered Women, the State, and Conceptions of Accountability,* 23 Harv. Women's L.J. 133 (Spring 2000).

80. Alicia Hehr, *A Child Shall Lead Them: Developing and Using Child Protection Mediation to Better Serve the Interests of the Child,* 22 Ohio St. J. on Disp. Resol. 443 at 455–456 (2007).

81. *Id.* at 457–458.

82. 25 U.S.C. § 1901 *et seq.*

83. See e.g. California Rules of Court, rule 1439(f); RCW 13.34.070 (Washington); and Title 10 O.S. 20 §40, the Oklahoma Indian Child Welfare Act, which essentially codifies the holding in *Mississippi Band of Choctaw Indians v. Holyfield,* 490 U.S. 30, 109 S. Ct. 1597, 104 L. Ed. 2d 29 (1989).

84. National Council of Juvenile & Family Court Judges, Family Violence: Model Code on Domestic and Family Violence, Chapter 4, Section 401 (1994). The Council has published a useful resource for judges entitled *Navigating Custody & Visitation Evaluations in Cases with Domestic Violence: A Judge's Guide.*

85. Nancy Ver Steegh, *Differentiating Types of Violence: Implications for Child Custody,* 65 La. L. Rev. 1379 at 1477 (Summer 2005), referencing Howard Davidson, *The Impact of Domestic Violence on Children, a Report to the President of the American Bar Association 13 (1994).*

86. Laurel Kent, *Comment: Addressing the Impact of Domestic Violence on Children: Alternatives to Laws Criminalizing the Commission of Domestic Violence in the Presence of a Child,* 2001 Wis. L. Rev. 1337 at 1363 (2001).

87. *Id.* at 1342, referencing K.J. Wilson, *When Violence Begins at Home: A Comprehensive Guide to Understanding and Ending Domestic Abuse,* p. 31 (1997), and Honore Hughes, *Impact of Spouse Abuse on Children of Battered Women: Implications for Practice,* Violence Update, Aug. 1992, at 1.

88. *Id.* at 1342.

89. This practice is not universally accepted. For example, in *Nicholson et al v. Scopetta,* 3 N.Y.3d 357, 820 N.E. 2d 840 (N.Y. 2004), New York's high court held that it is inappropriate to remove children from a parent based solely on the ground that they have been exposed to a parent's domestic violence. The victim's "failure to protect" the child must be understood in context before a determination of neglect can be reached. See Justine A. Dunlap, *Sometimes I Feel Like a Motherless*

Child: The Error of Pursuing Battered Mothers for Failure to Protect, 50 Loy. L. Rev. 565 (Fall 2004).

90. See American Judges Foundation, *Domestic Violence and the Court House: Understanding the Problem…Knowing the Victim,* available at http://aja.ncsc.dni.us/domviol/page5html (indicating that such abusive fathers are successful approximately 70 percent of the time).

91. The majority of the effects identified in this application are commonly accepted and well documented in Laurel A. Kent, *supra* n. 86. The content drew on additional sources including Dawn Bradley Berry, *The Domestic Violence Sourcebook* 8 (1998); Laura Crites & Donna Coker, *What Therapists See that Judges May Miss: A Unique Guide to Custody Decisions When Spouse Abuse Is Charged,* 27 Judges' J. (Spring 1988); John W. Fantuzzo & Wanda Mohr, *Prevalence and Effects of Child Exposure to Domestic Violence,* 9 Future of Children 21 (1999); K.J. Wilson, *When Violence Begins at Home: A Comprehensive Guide to Understanding and Ending Domestic Abuse* (1997). See also n. 96.

92. "Research indicates that children who witness or experience abuse are one thousand times more likely to abuse a spouse or partner than children from non-violent homes." Kent, *supra* n. 86 at 1345, referencing Dawn Bradley Berry, *The Domestic Violence Sourcebook* at 121 (1998).

93. "Studies assessing children living in domestic violence shelters for posttraumatic stress disorder have found incidence rates ranging from 13% to more than 50%." Hitchens and Van Horn *infra* n. 96 at 33.

94. Ver Steegh *supra* n. 85 p. 1385, referencing Lundy Bancroft and Jay G. Silverman, *The Batterer as Parent,* at 103–105. See also Ellen Marrus, *The Public and Private Faces of Family Law: Article: Fostering Family Ties: The State as Maker and Breaker of Kinship Relationships,* 2004 U. Chi. Legal F. 319, (2004). ("The loss of parents is a psychological devastating event. The tearing apart of other family relationships can enhance this trauma. Therefore, termination of sibling relationships should be treated as seriously as the termination of parental rights.")

95. Prentice L. White, *You May Never See Your Child Again: Adjusting the Batterer's Visitation Rights to Protect Children from Future Abuse,* 13 Am. U.J. Gender Soc. Pol'y & L. 327, 334 (2005).

96. Hon. Donna J. Hitchens and Patricia Van Horn, Ph.D., J.D., *Courts Responding to Domestic Violence: The Court's Role in Supporting and Protecting Children Exposed to Domestic Violence,* 6 J. Center for Fam. Child. & Cts. 31 (2005).

97. Ver Steegh *supra* note 85 at 1412. See Association of Family and Conciliation Courts (AFCC) Task Force on Parenting Coordination, *Parenting Coordination: Implementation Issues,* 41 Fam. Ct. Rev. 533 (2003).

98. *Id.* at 1413–1414 referencing Christine A. Coates et al., *Parenting Coordination for High Conflict Families,* 42 Fam. Ct. Rev. 246, 247 (2004).

99. Jennifer M. Collins, *Crime and Parenthood: The Uneasy Case for Prosecuting Negligent Parents,* 100 Nw. U.L. Rev. 807, 852 (Winter 2006).

100. *Id.* at 808. See Nat'l Safe Kids Campaign, *Report to the Nation: Trends in Unintentional Childhood Injury Mortality, 1987–2000* (2003), available at http://www.usa.safekids.org/content_documents/nskw03_report.pdf.

101. *Id.* at 809.

102. *Id.* at 810–811.

103. See e.g. Vincent R. Johnson and Clare G. Hargrove, *The Tort Duty of Parents to Protect Minor Children,* 51 Vill. L. Rev. 311 (2006).

104. *Dempsey v. Frazier,* 119 Miss. 1, 80 So. 341, 342 (1918).

105. Miss. Code. Ann. §§97–37–14 and 15.

106. *Canida v. Canida,* 751 So.2d 647 at 652 (Fla. App. 1999).

107. Id. at 652.

108. Sara Buel and Margeret Drew, *Do Ask and Do Tell: Rethinking the Lawyer's Duty to Ward in Domestic Violence Cases,* 75 U. Cin. L. Rev. 447 (Winter 2006). This article provides a detailed survey of disclosure rules in various states.

109. See Adrienne Jennings Lockie, *Salt in the Wounds: Why Attorneys Should Not Be Mandated Reporters of Child Abuse,* 36 N.M.L. Rev. 125 (Winter 2006).

110. Wyo. Prof. Conduct Rule 1.6(b)(1) (2006).

111. Buel and Drew *supra* n. 108 at 450.

112. Mo. Rev. Stat. § 210.140 (2000).

113. Tx. R. Prof. Conduct 1.05(e).

114. Lockie *supra* at n. 109, p. 139. Opinion 280, 97 N.J.L.T. 362 (1974).

115. ORC Ann. §2151.421(A)(1)(b).

116. ORC Ann. §2151.421(2).

117. Wis. Stat. 48.981(2)(c)

118. Buel and Drew *supra* at n. 108 at pages 450–451.

119. Duthu *supra* n. 4 at p. 20.

Appendix A

PARALEGAL AND LEGAL ASSISTANT ASSOCIATIONS

NATIONAL ASSOCIATION OF LEGAL ASSISTANTS (NALA)

1506 S. Boston; #200
Tulsa, Ok 74119
Phone: 918-587-6828
Website: *http://www.nala.org*
> This site provides links to NALA-affiliated paralegal/legal assistant associations in thirty-five states.

NATIONAL FEDERATION OF PARALEGAL ASSOCIATIONS, INC. (NFPA)

P.O. Box 2016
Edmonds, WA 98020
Phone: 425-967-0045
Fax: 425-771-9588
Website: *http://www.paralegals.org*
E-mail: *info@paralegals.org*
> The "membership" link on the NFPA home page provides links to Regional Associations and state and local associations in thirty-five states.

NATIONAL PARALEGAL ASSOCIATION (NPA)

P.O. Box 406
Solebury, PA 18963
Phone: 215-297-833
Fax: 215-297-8358
Website: *http://ww.nationalparalegal.org*
E-mail: *admin@nationalparalegal.org*
> The NPA membership focus is on pre-students, students, and school memberships.

Appendix B

NATIONAL FEDERATION OF PARALEGAL ASSOCIATIONS, INC.

MODEL CODE OF ETHICS AND PROFESSIONAL RESPONSIBILITY AND GUIDELINES FOR ENFORCEMENT

PREAMBLE

The National Federation of Paralegal Associations, Inc. ("NFPA") is a professional organization comprised of paralegal associations and individual paralegals throughout the United States and Canada. Members of NFPA have varying backgrounds, experiences, education and job responsibilities that reflect the diversity of the paralegal profession. NFPA promotes the growth, development and recognition of the paralegal profession as an integral partner in the delivery of legal services.

In May 1993 NFPA adopted its Model Code of Ethics and Professional Responsibility ("Model Code") to delineate the principles for ethics and conduct to which every paralegal should aspire.

Many paralegal associations throughout the United States have endorsed the concept and content of NFPA's Model Code through the adoption of their own ethical codes. In doing so, paralegals have confirmed the profession's commitment to increase the quality and efficiency of legal services, as well as recognized its responsibilities to the public, the legal community, and colleagues.

Paralegals have recognized, and will continue to recognize, that the profession must continue to evolve to enhance their roles in the delivery of legal services. With increased levels of responsibility comes the need to define and enforce mandatory rules of professional conduct. Enforcement of codes of paralegal conduct is a logical and necessary step to enhance and ensure the confidence of the legal community and the public in the integrity and professional responsibility of paralegals.

In April 1997 NFPA adopted the Model Disciplinary Rules ("Model Rules") to make possible the enforcement of the Canons and Ethical Considerations contained in the NFPA Model Code. A concurrent determination was made that the Model Code of Ethics and Professional Responsibility, formerly aspirational in nature, should be recognized as setting forth the enforceable obligations of all paralegals.

The Model Code and Model Rules offer a framework for professional discipline, either voluntarily or through formal regulatory programs.

§1. NFPA MODEL DISCIPLINARY RULES AND ETHICAL CONSIDERATIONS

1.1 A PARALEGAL SHALL ACHIEVE AND MAINTAIN A HIGH LEVEL OF COMPETENCE.

Ethical Considerations

EC-1.1 (a) A paralegal shall achieve competency through education, training, and work experience.

EC-1.1 (b) A paralegal shall aspire to participate in a minimum of twelve (12) hours of continuing legal education, to include at least one (1) hour of ethics education, every two (2) years in order to remain current on developments in the law.

EC-1.1 (c) A paralegal shall perform all assignments promptly and efficiently.

1.2 A PARALEGAL SHALL MAINTAIN A HIGH LEVEL OF PERSONAL AND PROFESSIONAL INTEGRITY.

Ethical Considerations

EC-1.2 (a) A paralegal shall not engage in any ex parte communications involving the courts or any other adjudicatory body in an attempt to exert undue influence or to obtain advantage or the benefit of only one party.

EC-1.2 (b) A paralegal shall not communicate, or cause another to communicate, with a party the paralegal knows to be represented by a lawyer in a pending matter without the prior consent of the lawyer representing such other party.

EC-1.2 (c) A paralegal shall ensure that all timekeeping and billing records prepared by the paralegal are thorough, accurate, honest, and complete.

EC-1.2 (d) A paralegal shall not knowingly engage in fraudulent billing practices. Such practices may include, but are not limited to: inflation of hours billed to a client or employer; misrepresentation of the nature of tasks performed; and/or submission of fraudulent expense and disbursement documentation.

EC-1.2 (e) A paralegal shall be scrupulous, thorough and honest in the identification and maintenance of all funds, securities, and other assets of a client and shall provide accurate accounting as appropriate.

EC-1.2 (f) A paralegal shall advise the proper authority of non-confidential knowledge of any dishonest or fraudulent acts by any person pertaining to the handling of the funds, securities or other assets of a client. The authority to whom the report is made shall depend on the nature and circumstances of the possible misconduct, (e.g., ethics committees of law firms, corporations and/or paralegal associations, local or state bar associations, local prosecutors, administrative agencies, etc.). Failure to report such knowledge is in itself misconduct and shall be treated as such under these rules.

1.3   **A PARALEGAL SHALL MAINTAIN A HIGH STANDARD OF PROFESSIONAL CONDUCT.**

Ethical Considerations

EC-1.3 (a)   A paralegal shall refrain from engaging in any conduct that offends the dignity and decorum of proceedings before a court or other adjudicatory body and shall be respectful of all rules and procedures.

EC-1.3 (b)   A paralegal shall avoid impropriety and the appearance of impropriety and shall not engage in any conduct that would adversely affect his/her fitness to practice. Such conduct may include, but is not limited to: violence, dishonesty, interference with the administration of justice, and/or abuse of a professional position or public office.

EC-1.3 (c)   Should a paralegal's fitness to practice be compromised by physical or mental illness, causing that paralegal to commit an act that is in direct violation of the Model Code/Model Rules and/or the rules and/or laws governing the jurisdiction in which the paralegal practices, that paralegal may be protected from sanction upon review of the nature and circumstances of that illness.

EC-1.3 (d)   A paralegal shall advise the proper authority of non-confidential knowledge of any action of another legal professional that clearly demonstrates fraud, deceit, dishonesty, or misrepresentation. The authority to whom the report is made shall depend on the nature and circumstances of the possible misconduct, (e.g., ethics committees of law firms, corporations and/or paralegal associations, local or state bar associations, local prosecutors, administrative agencies, etc.). Failure to report such knowledge is in itself misconduct and shall be treated as such under these rules.

EC-1.3 (e)   A paralegal shall not knowingly assist any individual with the commission of an act that is in direct violation of the Model Code/Model Rules and/or the rules and/or laws governing the jurisdiction in which the paralegal practices.

EC-1.3 (f)   If a paralegal possesses knowledge of future criminal activity, that knowledge must be reported to the appropriate authority immediately.

1.4   **A PARALEGAL SHALL SERVE THE PUBLIC INTEREST BY CONTRIBUTING TO THE IMPROVEMENT OF THE LEGAL SYSTEM AND DELIVERY OF QUALITY LEGAL SERVICES, INCLUDING PRO BONO PUBLICO SERVICES.**

Ethical Considerations

EC-1.4 (a)   A paralegal shall be sensitive to the legal needs of the public and shall promote the development and implementation of programs that address those needs.

EC-1.4 (b)   A paralegal shall support efforts to improve the legal system and access thereto and shall assist in making changes.

EC-1.4   A paralegal shall support and participate in the delivery of Pro Bono Publico

(c)   services directed toward implementing and improving access to justice, the law, the legal system or the paralegal and legal professions.

EC-1.4
(d)   A paralegal should aspire annually to contribute twenty-four (24) hours of Pro Bono Publico services under the supervision of an attorney or as authorized by administrative, statutory or court authority to:

1. persons of limited means; or
2. charitable, religious, civic, community, governmental and educational organizations in matters that are designed primarily to address the legal needs of persons with limited means; or
3. individuals, groups or organizations seeking to secure or protect civil rights, civil liberties or public rights.

The twenty-four (24) hours of Pro Bono Publico services contributed annually by a paralegal may consist of such services as detailed in this EC-1.4(d), and/or administrative matters designed to develop and implement the attainment of this aspiration as detailed above in EC-1.4(a) or (c), or any combination of the two.

1.5   A PARALEGAL SHALL PRESERVE ALL CONFIDENTIAL INFORMATION PROVIDED BY THE CLIENT OR ACQUIRED FROM OTHER SOURCES BEFORE, DURING, AND AFTER THE COURSE OF THE PROFESSIONAL RELATIONSHIP.

Ethical Considerations

EC-1.5
(a)   A paralegal shall be aware of and abide by all legal authority governing confidential information in the jurisdiction in which the paralegal practices.

EC-1.5
(b)   A paralegal shall not use confidential information to the disadvantage of the client.

EC-1.5
(c)   A paralegal shall not use confidential information to the advantage of the paralegal or of a third person.

EC-1.5
(d)   A paralegal may reveal confidential information only after full disclosure and with the client's written consent; or, when required by law or court order; or, when necessary to prevent the client from committing an act that could result in death or serious bodily harm.

EC-1.5
(e)   A paralegal shall keep those individuals responsible for the legal representation of a client fully informed of any confidential information the paralegal may have pertaining to that client.

EC-1.5
(f)   A paralegal shall not engage in any indiscreet communications concerning clients.

1.6   A PARALEGAL SHALL AVOID CONFLICTS OF INTEREST AND

SHALL DISCLOSE ANY POSSIBLE CONFLICT TO THE EMPLOYER OR CLIENT, AS WELL AS TO THE PROSPECTIVE EMPLOYERS OR CLIENTS.

Ethical Considerations

EC-1.6 (a)   A paralegal shall act within the bounds of the law, solely for the benefit of the client, and shall be free of compromising influences and loyalties. Neither the paralegal's personal or business interest, nor those of other clients or third persons, should compromise the paralegal's professional judgment and loyalty to the client.

EC-1.6 (b)   A paralegal shall avoid conflicts of interest that may arise from previous assignments, whether for a present or past employer or client.

EC-1.6 (c)   A paralegal shall avoid conflicts of interest that may arise from family relationships and from personal and business interests.

EC-1.6 (d)   In order to be able to determine whether an actual or potential conflict of interest exists a paralegal shall create and maintain an effective recordkeeping system that identifies clients, matters, and parties with which the paralegal has worked.

EC-1.6 (e)   A paralegal shall reveal sufficient non-confidential information about a client or former client to reasonably ascertain if an actual or potential conflict of interest exists.

EC-1.6 (f)   A paralegal shall not participate in or conduct work on any matter where a conflict of interest has been identified.

EC-1.6 (g)   In matters where a conflict of interest has been identified and the client consents to continued representation, a paralegal shall comply fully with the implementation and maintenance of an Ethical Wall.

1.7   A PARALEGAL'S TITLE SHALL BE FULLY DISCLOSED.

Ethical Considerations

EC-1.7 (a)   A paralegal's title shall clearly indicate the individual's status and shall be disclosed in all business and professional communications to avoid misunderstandings and misconceptions about the paralegal's role and responsibilities.

EC-1.7 (b)   A paralegal's title shall be included if the paralegal's name appears on business cards, letterhead, brochures, directories, and advertisements.

EC-1.7 (c)   A paralegal shall not use letterhead, business cards or other promotional materials to create a fraudulent impression of his/her status or ability to practice in the jurisdiction in which the paralegal practices.

EC-1.7 (d)   A paralegal shall not practice under color of any record, diploma, or certificate that has been illegally or fraudulently obtained or issued or which is misrepresentative in any way.

EC1.7   A paralegal shall not participate in the creation, issuance, or dissemination of

(e)   fraudulent records, diplomas, or certificates.

1.8   A PARALEGAL SHALL NOT ENGAGE IN THE UNAUTHORIZED PRACTICE OF LAW.

Ethical Considerations

EC-1.8
(a)   A paralegal shall comply with the applicable legal authority governing the unauthorized practice of law in the jurisdiction in which the paralegal practices.

§2.   NFPA GUIDELINES FOR THE ENFORCEMENT OF THE MODEL CODE OF ETHICS AND PROFESSIONAL RESPONSIBILITY

2.1   BASIS FOR DISCIPLINE

2.1(a)   Disciplinary investigations and proceedings brought under authority of the Rules shall be conducted in accord with obligations imposed on the paralegal professional by the Model Code of Ethics and Professional Responsibility.

2.2   STRUCTURE OF DISCIPLINARY COMMITTEE

2.2(a)   The Disciplinary Committee ("Committee") shall be made up of nine (9) members including the Chair.

2.2(b)   Each member of the Committee, including any temporary replacement members, shall have demonstrated working knowledge of ethics/professional responsibility-related issues and activities.

2.2(c)   The Committee shall represent a cross-section of practice areas and work experience. The following recommendations are made regarding the members of the Committee.

> 1) At least one paralegal with one to three years of law-related work experience.
> 2) At least one paralegal with five to seven years of law related work experience.
> 3) At least one paralegal with over ten years of law related work experience.
> 4) One paralegal educator with five to seven years of work experience; preferably in the area of ethics/professional responsibility.
> 5) One paralegal manager.
> 6) One lawyer with five to seven years of law-related work experience.
> 7) One lay member.

2.2(d) The Chair of the Committee shall be appointed within thirty (30) days of its members' induction. The Chair shall have no fewer than ten (10) years of law-related work experience.

2.2(e) The terms of all members of the Committee shall be staggered. Of those members initially appointed, a simple majority plus one shall be appointed to a term of one year, and the remaining members shall be appointed to a term of two years. Thereafter, all members of the Committee shall be appointed to terms of two years.

2.2(f) If for any reason the terms of a majority of the Committee will expire at the same time, members may be appointed to terms of one year to maintain continuity of the Committee.

2.2(g) The Committee shall organize from its members a three-tiered structure to investigate, prosecute and/or adjudicate charges of misconduct. The members shall be rotated among the tiers.

2.3   OPERATION OF COMMITTEE

2.3(a) The Committee shall meet on an as-needed basis to discuss, investigate, and/or adjudicate alleged violations of the Model Code/Model Rules.

2.3(b) A majority of the members of the Committee present at a meeting shall constitute a quorum.

2.3(c) A Recording Secretary shall be designated to maintain complete and accurate minutes of all Committee meetings. All such minutes shall be kept confidential until a decision has been made that the matter will be set for hearing as set forth in Section 6.1 below.

2.3(d) If any member of the Committee has a conflict of interest with the Charging Party, the Responding Party, or the allegations of misconduct, that member shall not take part in any hearing or deliberations concerning those allegations. If the absence of that member creates a lack of a quorum for the Committee, then a temporary replacement for the member shall be appointed.

2.3(e) Either the Charging Party or the Responding Party may request that, for good cause shown, any member of the Committee not participate in a hearing or deliberation. All such requests shall be honored. If the absence of a Committee member under those circumstances creates a lack of a quorum for the Committee, then a temporary replacement for that member shall be appointed.

2.3(f) All discussions and correspondence of the Committee shall be kept confidential until a decision has been made that the matter will be set for hearing as set forth in Section 6.1 below.

2.3(g) All correspondence from the Committee to the Responding Party regarding any charge of misconduct and any decisions made regarding the charge shall be mailed certified mail, return receipt requested, to the Responding Party's last known address and shall be clearly marked with a "Confidential" designation.

2.4   PROCEDURE FOR THE REPORTING OF ALLEGED VIOLATIONS OF THE MODEL CODE/DISCIPLINARY RULES

2.4(a)   An individual or entity in possession of non-confidential knowledge or information concerning possible instances of misconduct shall make a confidential written report to the Committee within thirty (30) days of obtaining same. This report shall include all details of the alleged misconduct.

2.4(b)   The Committee so notified shall inform the Responding Party of the allegation(s) of misconduct no later than ten (10) business days after receiving the confidential written report from the Charging Party.

2.4(c)   Notification to the Responding Party shall include the identity of the Charging Party, unless, for good cause shown, the Charging Party requests anonymity.

2.4(d)   The Responding Party shall reply to the allegations within ten (10) business days of notification.

2.5   PROCEDURE FOR THE INVESTIGATION OF A CHARGE OF MISCONDUCT

2.5(a)   Upon receipt of a Charge of Misconduct ("Charge"), or on its own initiative, the Committee shall initiate an investigation.

2.5(b)   If, upon initial or preliminary review, the Committee makes a determination that the charges are either without basis in fact or, if proven, would not constitute professional misconduct, the Committee shall dismiss the allegations of misconduct. If such determination of dismissal cannot be made, a formal investigation shall be initiated.

2.5(c)   Upon the decision to conduct a formal investigation, the Committee shall:

    1) mail to the Charging and Responding Parties within three (3) business days of that decision notice of the commencement of a formal investigation. That notification shall be in writing and shall contain a complete explanation of all Charge(s), as well as the reasons for a formal investigation and shall cite the applicable codes and rules;

    2) allow the Responding Party thirty (30) days to prepare and submit a confidential response to the Committee, which response shall address each charge specifically and shall be in writing; and

    3) upon receipt of the response to the notification, have thirty (30) days to investigate the Charge(s). If an extension of time is deemed necessary, that extension shall not exceed ninety (90) days.

2.5(d)   Upon conclusion of the investigation, the Committee may:

    1) dismiss the Charge upon the finding that it has no basis in fact;
    2) dismiss the Charge upon the finding that, if proven, the Charge would not constitute Misconduct;
    3) refer the matter for hearing by the Tribunal; or
    4) in the case of criminal activity, refer the Charge(s) and all

investigation results to the appropriate authority.

2.6   PROCEDURE FOR A MISCONDUCT HEARING BEFORE A TRIBUNAL

2.6(a)   Upon the decision by the Committee that a matter should be heard, all parties shall be notified and a hearing date shall be set. The hearing shall take place no more than thirty (30) days from the conclusion of the formal investigation.

2.6(b)   The Responding Party shall have the right to counsel. The parties and the Tribunal shall have the right to call any witnesses and introduce any documentation that they believe will lead to the fair and reasonable resolution of the matter.

2.6(c)   Upon completion of the hearing, the Tribunal shall deliberate and present a written decision to the parties in accordance with procedures as set forth by the Tribunal.

2.6(d)   Notice of the decision of the Tribunal shall be appropriately published.

2.7   SANCTIONS

2.7(a)   Upon a finding of the Tribunal that misconduct has occurred, any of the following sanctions, or others as may be deemed appropriate, may be imposed upon the Responding Party, either singularly or in combination:

      1) letter of reprimand to the Responding Party; counseling;
      2) attendance at an ethics course approved by the Tribunal; probation;
      3) suspension of license/authority to practice; revocation of license/authority to practice;
      4) imposition of a fine; assessment of costs; or
      5) in the instance of criminal activity, referral to the appropriate authority.

2.7(b)   Upon the expiration of any period of probation, suspension, or revocation, the Responding Party may make application for reinstatement. With the application for reinstatement, the Responding Party must show proof of having complied with all aspects of the sanctions imposed by the Tribunal.

2.8   APPELLATE PROCEDURES

2.8(a)   The parties shall have the right to appeal the decision of the Tribunal in accordance with the procedure as set forth by the Tribunal.

DEFINITIONS

"Appellate Body" means a body established to adjudicate an appeal to any decision made by a Tribunal or other decision-making body with respect to formally-heard Charges of Misconduct.

"Charge of Misconduct" means a written submission by any individual or entity to an ethics committee, paralegal association, bar association, law enforcement agency, judicial body, government agency, or other appropriate body or entity, that sets forth non-confidential information regarding any instance of alleged misconduct by an individual paralegal or paralegal entity.

"Charging Party" means any individual or entity who submits a Charge of Misconduct against an individual paralegal or paralegal entity.

"Competency" means the demonstration of: diligence, education, skill, and mental, emotional, and physical fitness reasonably necessary for the performance of paralegal services.

"Confidential Information" means information relating to a client, whatever its source, that is not public knowledge nor available to the public. ("Non-Confidential Information" would generally include the name of the client and the identity of the matter for which the paralegal provided services.)

"Disciplinary Hearing" means the confidential proceeding conducted by a committee or other designated body or entity concerning any instance of alleged misconduct by an individual paralegal or paralegal entity.

"Disciplinary Committee" means any committee that has been established by an entity such as a paralegal association, bar association, judicial body, or government agency to: (a) identify, define and investigate general ethical considerations and concerns with respect to paralegal practice; (b) administer and enforce the Model Code and Model Rules and; (c) discipline any individual paralegal or paralegal entity found to be in violation of same.

"Disclose" means communication of information reasonably sufficient to permit identification of the significance of the matter in question.

"Ethical Wall" means the screening method implemented in order to protect a client from a conflict of interest. An Ethical Wall generally includes, but is not limited to, the following elements: (1) prohibit the paralegal from having any connection with the matter; (2) ban discussions with or the transfer of documents to or from the paralegal; (3) restrict access to files; and (4) educate all members of the firm, corporation, or entity as to the separation of the paralegal (both organizationally and physically) from the pending matter. For more information regarding the Ethical Wall, see the NFPA publication entitled "The Ethical Wall—Its Application to Paralegals."

"Ex parte" means actions or communications conducted at the instance and for the benefit of one party only, and without notice to, or contestation by, any person adversely interested.

"Investigation" means the investigation of any charge(s) of misconduct filed against an individual paralegal or paralegal entity by a Committee.

"Letter of Reprimand" means a written notice of formal censure or severe reproof administered to an individual paralegal or paralegal entity for unethical or improper conduct.

"Misconduct" means the knowing or unknowing commission of an act that is in direct violation of those Canons and Ethical Considerations of any and all applicable codes and/or rules of conduct.

"Paralegal" is synonymous with "Legal Assistant" and is defined as a person qualified through education, training, or work experience to perform substantive legal work that requires knowledge of legal concepts and is customarily, but not exclusively performed by a lawyer. This person may be retained or employed by a lawyer, law office, governmental agency, or other entity or may be authorized by administrative, statutory, or court authority to perform this work.

"Pro Bono Publico" means providing or assisting to provide quality legal services in order to enhance access to justice for persons of limited means; charitable, religious, civic, community, governmental and educational organizations in matters that are designed primarily to address the legal needs of persons with limited means; or individuals, groups or organizations seeking to secure or protect civil rights, civil liberties or public rights.

"Proper Authority" means the local paralegal association, the local or state bar association, Committee(s) of the local paralegal or bar association(s), local prosecutor, administrative agency, or other tribunal empowered to investigate or act upon an instance of alleged misconduct.

"Responding Party" means an individual paralegal or paralegal entity against whom a Charge of Misconduct has been submitted.

"Revocation" means the recision of the license, certificate or other authority to practice of an individual paralegal or paralegal entity found in violation of those Canons and Ethical Considerations of any and all applicable codes and/or rules of conduct.

"Suspension" means the suspension of the license, certificate or other authority to practice of an individual paralegal or paralegal entity found in violation of those Canons and Ethical Considerations of any and all applicable codes and/or rules of conduct.

"Tribunal" means the body designated to adjudicate allegations of misconduct.

Appendix C

ORGANIZATIONS AND RESOURCES

Note: All of the following addresses, telephone numbers, and URLs were valid as of April 2008 but should be updated, if appropriate.

ACADEMY OF FAMILY MEDIATORS

P.O. Box 51090
Eugene, OR 97405
541-345-1629

http://www.igc.acp.org/afm

AMERICAN ACADEMY FOR ADOPTION ATTORNEYS

P.O. Box 33053
Washington, DC 20033
202-832-2222

http://www.adoptionattorneys.org

AMERICAN ACADEMY OF MATRIMONIAL LAWYERS

150 North Michigan Avenue
Chicago, IL 60601
312-263-7682

http://aaml.org

> Provides links to family law organizations, courts and cases, the IRS, relevant federal statutes, and sites addressing topics such as ADR, divorce, adoption, custody, parental kidnapping, etc.

AMERICAN BAR ASSOCIATION

321 N. Clark Street
Chicago, IL 60610
800-285-2221

http://www.abanet.org

> The ABA Model Code of Professional Responsibility is available at this site.
>
> *http://www.abanet.org/child/home.html*
>
> American Bar Association Center on Children and the Law

http://www.abanet.org/crimjust/juvjus/home.html
>American Bar Association Juvenile Justice Center

http://www.abanet.org/domviol/home.html
>American Bar Association Commission on Domestic Violence

http://www.abanet.org/family/home.html
>American Bar Association Family Law Section
>Tables summarizing various aspects of family law in the fifty states are available at this site.
>>Table 1 Alimony/Spousal Support
>>Table 2 Custody Criteria
>>Table 3 Child Support Guidelines
>>Table 4 Grounds for Divorce and Residency Requirements
>>Table 5 Property Division
>>Table 6 Third-Party Visitation
>>Table 7 Appointment Laws in Adoption, Guardianship, Unmarried Parent, and Divorce Cases

http://www.abanet.org/legalservices/clientdevelopment/adrules
>This is the ABA website link to state rules on legal advertising and solicitation.

AMERICAN COALITION FOR FATHERS AND CHILDREN

1718 M Street, NW #187
Washington, DC 20036
800-978-DADS (3237)

http://www.acfc.org

AMERICAN SOCIETY FOR REPRODUCTIVE MEDICINE

1209 Montgomery Highway
Birmingham, AL 35216-2809
205-978-5000

http://www.asrm.com
>Provides links to articles and websites on virtually every form of ART.

BATTERED WOMEN'S JUSTICE PROJECT CIVIL AND CRIMINAL JUSTICE OFFICE

1801 Nicollet Avenue South, Suite 102
Minneapolis, MN 55403
800-903-0111 ext. 1

http://www.bwjp.org
>This Project serves as a national clearinghouse for information about domestic violence and the policing, prosecuting, sentencing, and monitoring of domestic violence offenders. The website provides links to state domestic violence coalitions.

CHILDREN'S DEFENSE FUND

25 E Street, NW
Washington, DC 20001
800-CDF-1200

http://www.childrensdefense.org
>This site provides data links and state fact sheets on grandparents raising children.

CHILDREN'S RIGHTS COUNCIL

8181 Professional Place
Suite 240
Landover, MD 20785
301-459-1220

http://www.crckids.org

> Available at this site are links to state codes, contact numbers for legislators, information on pending legislation, etc.

CHILD WELFARE LEAGUE OF AMERICA

2345 Crystal Drive, Suite 250
Arlington, VA 22202
703-412-2400

http://www.cwla.org

EVAN P. DONALDSON ADOPTION INSTITUTE

128 E. 38th Street
New York, NY 10016
212-925-4089

http://www.adoptioninstitute.org

> This site contains links to state putative father registries, open records information, state registries, and confidentiality statutes. It also provides reports on the effectiveness of safe havens and the rights of all parties interested in the adoption process.

FEMINIST MAJORITY FOUNDATION

1600 Wilson Blvd. Suite 801
Arlington, VA 22209
866-444-3652

http://www.feminist.org

LAMBDA LEGAL (NATIONAL HEADQUARTERS)

120 Wall Street Suite 1500
New York, NY 10005-3904
212-809-8585

http://www.lambdalegal.org

> This site provides extensive information regarding states, municipalities, and other entities offering domestic partnership and civil union benefits. It also provides information on hot issues related to divorce, marriage, relationships, and family law.

NATIONAL ASSOCIATION OF SOCIAL WORKERS

750 First Street NE
Washington, DC 20002-4241
800-742-4089
202-408-8600

http://www.socialworkers.org

NATIONAL CENTER FOR MISSING AND EXPLOITED CHILDREN

Charles B. Wang International Children's Building
699 Prince Street
Alexandria, VA 22314-3175
703-274-3900
1-800-THE-LOST (843-5678) (24-hour hotline)

http://www.ncmec.org

http://www.missingkids.com

These sites provide resources in English and Spanish for parents, grandparents, childcare providers, law enforcement personnel, and attorneys.

NATIONAL CENTER FOR VICTIMS OF CRIME

2000 M Street NW Suite 480
Washington, DC 20036
202-467-8700

http://www.ncvc.org/dvrc

Available at this site is a stalking resource center that provides links to federal and state stalking laws and a digest of relevant cases. A dating violence resource center is also available at this site.

NATIONAL COUNCIL OF JUVENILE AND FAMILY COURT JUDGES

P.O. Box 8970
Reno, NV 89557
775-784-6012

http://www.ncjfcj.unr.org

NATIONAL COURT APPOINTED SPECIAL ADVOCATES FOR CHILDREN (CASA) ASSOCIATION

100 W. Harrison
North Tower Ste 500
Seattle, WA 98119
800-628-3233

http://www.casanet.org/

Provides links to state CASA programs.

NATIONAL GAY AND LESBIAN TASK FORCE

2320 17th Street, NW
Washington, DC 20009
202-332-6483

http://www.thetaskforce.org

NATIONAL ORGANIZATION FOR MEN

11 Park Place
New York, NY 10007
212-686-MALE

http://www.orgformen.com

NATIONAL ORGANIZATION FOR WOMEN

1000 16th Street, NW
Washington, DC 20036
202-331-0066

http://www.now.org

STEPFAMILY FOUNDATION

333 West End Avenue
New York, NY 10023
212-877-3244

http://www.stepfamily.org

Appendix D

WEBSITES OF GENERAL INTEREST

Note: The World Wide Web offers a wealth of freely accessible and rapidly changing information that may be immensely useful, but it should be verified when appropriate. The following URLs were all effective as of April 2008.

GOVERNMENT SITES

http://www.acf.hhs.gov

This is the site for the Administration for Children and Families (ACF). It provides links to a number of topics related to family law including adoption and foster care, child abuse and neglect, child support, etc.

http://www.acf.dhhs.gov/programs/cse

This is the website for the federal Office of Child Support Enforcement (OCSE). There is a wealth of material available on this website including the publication "Essentials for Attorneys in Child Support Enforcement." It also includes a list of, and links to, child support (IV-D) agencies in each state.

http://www.bioethics.gov/

Sponsored by the President's Council on Bioethics, this site offers a rich variety of sources including transcripts, reports, background materials, and books. The reports may either be downloaded or ordered in print form.

http://www.cdc.gov.nchs

This is the site for the Centers for Disease Control and Prevention—National Center for Health Statistics. It provides an alphabetical directory to offices of vital records in the individual states and territories. A variety of useful statistical reports on topics such as abuse and intimate partner violence are available at this site.

http://www.census.gov

A number of statistical supports relevant to family law topics are available on this government site.

http://www.childwelfare.gov

This is the website for the Child Information Gateway, an activity of the Department of Health and Human Services. This site contains links to federal and state laws, fact sheets, statistics, and publications on a variety of child-related topics including adoption, types of abuse, grounds for termination of parental rights, infant safe haven laws, and parental drug abuse. The text of the most recent "Child Maltreatment Report" is available at this site.

http://www.dol.gov/ebsa

> This is the Department of Labor's site for the Employee Benefits Security Administration. Available at this site is an informative forty-eight-page publication on QDROs produced by the U.S. Department of Labor. Extensive information is also available at the DOL site on occupational statistics and labor market trends.

http://www.irs.gov

> This is the home page of the Internal Revenue Service and provides access to general tax information, forms, and specific treasury regulations.

http://www.ncea.aoa.gov

> The National Center on Elder Abuse (NCEA) is the major source of available statistics on elder abuse, neglect, and exploitation in the United States, including abuse in family settings. The website provides links to resources for locating state statutes, codes, and case law.

http://www.ojp.usdoj.gov/bjs

> This is the foremost site for "official" crime statistics.

TOPICAL SITES

Adoption

http://www.adoptioncouncil.org

> This is the website for the National Council for Adoption, a not-for-profit organization that engages in research, education, and advocacy for adoption. The "2007 Fact Book" available at this site provides facts, statistics, and an analysis of state adoption laws.

Alternative Dispute Resolution

http://www.adrlawinfo.com

> This site provides a wealth of information about family and divorce mediation state to state. It also provides links to various model standards for mediation and arbitration.

Child Support

http://www.supportguidelines.com/main.html

> This is a comprehensive resource on child support guidelines in the United States. It provides a number of useful resources and links to state material. It also addresses additional topics relating to divorce and custody in particular.

Custody

http://www.ancpr.org/

> This is the site for the Alliance for Non-Custodial Parents' Rights, an organization that provides assistance to noncustodial parents on issues related to child support, custody, and visitation. It provides information about legal resources, UIFSA, recent cases, and obtaining school records. It also offers a "Winning Strategies Handbook" for sale.

http://www.coloradodivorcemediation.com.

> This is a court-sponsored site providing information about the psychological effects of divorce on children who are not physically close to their noncustodial parent. It offers age-specific suggestions on fostering the parent-child relationship through long-distance parenting.

http://www.deltabravo.net/custody/pplan3htm

> The stated goal of this site is to ensure that children of divorce have access to both parents regardless of their marital status. It offers links to a variety of resources including an online parenting plan generator.

Domestic Violence

http://www.childfindofamerica.org

> This site provides facts and statistics and offers free investigation and location services, kidnap prevention programs, and referral, media, and support services in parental abduction cases. 800-I-AM-LOST.

http://www.ncadv.org

> This is the site for the National Coalition Against Domestic Violence.

http://www.ndvh.org

> This is the site for the National Domestic Violence Hotline (800–799-SAFE; 800–787–3224). The line provides 24/7 help to callers from all states and has translation services available in 140 languages.

http://www.lrcvaw.org

> This is the site for the Legal Resource Center on Violence Against Women (funded by VAWA). The primary focus of the Center is on improving legal representation for domestic violence survivors, particularly in interstate custody cases. It features links to national and state resources on topics including crisis lines, abuse later in life, and immigration issues. It also provides state-by-state links to child custody jurisdictional statutes (UCCJEA and UCCJA), long-arm statutes, and relocation statutes.

Ethics

http://www.legalethics.com

> This site abstracts and provides links to recently published articles on a number of topics related to legal ethics. It also provides links to other ethics-related sites.

http://www.nala.org

> In addition to providing links to NALA-affiliated paralegal/legal assistant associations in thirty-five states, this site also contains the NALA Model Standards and Guidelines for Utilization of Legal Assistants. The Addendum to the Guidelines includes case references on a variety of ethical issues including Unauthorized Practice of Law (UPL).

Gender-Based Issues

http://www.mensdefense.org

> This site for the Men's Defense Organization provides Web assistance to men, particularly fathers.

http://www.ncfc.net/index.html

> This is the site for the National Congress for Fathers and Children.

Legislation

http://www.ncsl.org/programs/cyf

> This site for the National Conference of State Legislatures provides summaries of enacted and proposed legislation in the various states.

http://www.nccusl.org

> This is the site for the National Commission on Uniform State Laws. It provides copies of various iterations of uniform state laws and indicates which state(s) have adopted each act in whole or in part.

Nonmarital Families

http://www.unmarried.org

This is the site for the Alternatives to Marriage, a national nonprofit organization advocating equality and fairness for unmarried persons. It contains information and statistics on cohabitation, living single, domestic partner benefits, common law marriage, etc., as well as information on current news events, statistics, and advocacy efforts, particularly with respect to opposition to state constitutional amendments.

http://www.palimony.com

This is the site for Unmarried Partners and the Law.

Parental Rights

http://www.parentsrights.com

This is the site for the Coalition for the Restoration of Parents' Rights. It provides links to data sources, state statutes, and cases on third-party visitation (including grandparent visitation).

Reseach

http://www.alllaw.com

This site provides articles on many aspects of family law. It includes a generic child support guidelines calculator feature.

http://www.divorcelinks.com

This site features divorce and child custody laws with direct links to state and federal divorce laws by topic. As of January 2008, the site had a heavy emphasis on parenting plans.

http://www.divorcenet.com

This site contains information on a number of family law topics that can be searched by topic and/or by state. This site also offers links to state divorce laws and provides statutory references and brief narratives on topics such as residence, grounds for divorce, approaches to division of property, alimony, and child custody, visitation, and support.

http://www.divorceonline.com

This site provides a wide range of articles and information on various aspects of divorce along with links to state divorce laws.

http://www.findlaw.com

Users of this site can click on "Legal Professionals" and then "Family Law" under "Practice Areas" and then search by topic. The site also allows users to search specific areas and focus their research. It provides state-by-state links to laws relating to virtually every family law area along with generic articles and, in some cases, non-state specific forms. Some of the links it provides to divorce forms by state contain sample separation agreements and parenting plans. Findlaw's Legal Technology Center has an Electronic Discovery Rule Wizard, an online interactive tool to help legal professionals understand the amended Federal Rules of Civil Procedure and improve their use of e-discovery methods and procedures.

http://www.law.cornell.edu

This is the site for Cornell Law School. It provides a variety of links to federal and state codes. For example, see *http://www.law.cornell.edu/topics/TableMarriage.htm* on state marriage laws. The master topic list includes adoption, divorce, emancipation of children, and marriage.

http://lawcrawler.com

> This is a legal search engine provided by Findlaw. It links to federal, academic, commercial, and foreign law-related sources and other sites. Users can use keywords to find documents on their subject of interest.

http://www.law.emory.edu/library/

> This Law Library resource provides links to state codes and selected cases. It also provides an Internet legal research guide.

http://www.lectlaw.com

> Among other resources, this site provides articles on a range of topics related to marriage and divorce, custody and support, etc.

http://www.megalaw.com/top/family.php

> The Megalaw Family Law Center provides links to a range of family law resources including landmark and recent court cases, federal and state statutes, uniform acts, organizations, and forms. State-specific resources are provided for California, Colorado, Florida, Illinois, Michigan, New Jersey, New York, Ohio, and Texas.

SOURCES FOR DIVORCE FORMS (SOME FOR *PRO SE* LITIGANTS) IN SELECTED STATES

Note: These sites provide useful starting points, but care must always be taken to verify that the current version of an appropriate form is used.

> Alaska: *http://www.state.ak.us/courts/forms.htm*
> Arizona: *http://supreme.state.az.us/selfserv/ARFLP_forms.htm*
> Arkansas: *http://courts.state.ar.us/aoc/forms.efm*
> California: *http://www.courtinfo.ca.gov/forms/fillable/fl103.pdf*
> Colorado: *http://www.courts.state.co.us/*
> Connecticut: *http://www.jud2.ct.gov/webforms/*
> Delaware: *http://courts.delaware.gov/forms/*
> Florida: *http://www.flcourts.org/gen_public/family/familyforms*
> Georgia: *http://www.georgiacourts.org*
> Hawaii: *http://www.//courts.state.hi.us/*
> Idaho: *http://www.courtselfhelp.idaho.gov/*
> Illinois (Lake County): *http://www.19thcircuitcourt.state.il.us/forms/index.htm*
> Indiana: *http://www.in.gov/judiciary/forms/po*
> Iowa: *http://www.judicial.state.ia.us/court_Rules_and_Forms*
> Kansas: *http://www.ks.courts.org*
> Louisiana: *http://www.familycourt.org*
> Maine: *http://www.courts.state.me.us*
> Maryland: *http://www.courts.state.md.us/family/forms/*
> Massachusetts: *http://www.mass.gov/courtsandjudges/courts/probateandfamily court/documents/cjd106_000.pdf* (The Probate and Family Courts page is new.)
> Michigan: *http://courts.michigan.gov/scao/courtforms/domesticrelations*
> Missouri: *http://www.courts.mogov*
> Montana: *http://courts.mtgov/library/topics/end_marriage.asp*
> Nebraska: *http://www.supremecourt.ne.gov*
> Nevada: *http://lawlibrary.nvsupremecourt.us/forms*
> New Hampshire: *http://www.courts.state.nh.us*
> New Jersey: *http://www.judiciary.state.nj.us*
> New York: *http://www.nycourts.gov*
> North Dakota: *http://www.ndcourts.com*
> Oregon: *http://www.ojd.state.or.us*
> South Carolina: *http://www.judicial.state.sc.us/forms*

South Dakota: *http://www.sdjudicial.com*
Tennessee (Nashville Circuit Court): *http://www.nashville.gov/circuit/circuit/circuitforms.asp*
Utah: *http://www.utcourts.gov*
Vermont: *http://www.vermontjudiciary.org/eforms*
Virginia: *http://www.courts.state.va.us*
Washington: *http://www.courts.wa.gov/forms*
West Virginia: *http://www.state.wv.us*
Wisconsin: *http://www.wicourts.gov/*
Wyoming: *http://www.courts.state.wy.us*

Glossary

A

Abandonment (1) a fault ground for divorce in some states sometimes termed desertion; the plaintiff must show that the defendant deliberately and without consent or excuse left the marital relationship with no intention to return, and that the absence has continued for a specified continuous period of time (customarily a year or more); (2) a type of child neglect that occurs when the whereabouts of a child's parents are unknown, the parent has left the child in unsafe circumstances, and/or has failed to maintain contact with or provide support for the child for an extended period of time

Absolute divorce a total divorce of husband and wife, dissolving the marital bond and releasing the parties wholly from their matrimonial obligations; frees the parties to remarry

Abuse the causing of harm to another often in the family setting; may include physical, emotional, sexual, and other forms of abuse

Abuse of discretion the failure of a court to exercise sound, reasonable, impartial, and legal decision making

Acceptance of service acceptance and acknowledgment of receipt of a summons and complaint by a defendant

Acknowledgement of paternity a voluntary acknowledgment of paternity by the father of a child in a sworn (notarized) affidavit of parentage; sometimes a joint acknowledgment with the child's mother

Active appreciation increase in the value of an asset that results from effort rather than simply market forces or the passage of time

Actual service of process actual delivery of notice to the person for whom it is intended

Actuary a statistician who determines the present value of a future event; one who calculates insurance and pension values on the basis of empirically based tables

Adjudication of paternity a judicial decision declaring a man to be the legal father of a child

Adjusted gross income income after nonvoluntary deductions are taken out such as federal and state tax obligations, social security withholding, union dues, wage assignments related to prior support orders, etc.

Adoptee in an adoption, the individual who is adopted

Adoption the judicial process by which a new parent-child relationship is created and an adoptive parent assumes the legal rights and duties of a biological parent

Adoption abrogation an annulment, repeal, or undoing of an adoption

Adoption registry a vehicle available in some states that allows adoptees after a certain age (usually 18) to try to contact their biological parents and siblings

Adoptive parent a person who, by means of legal process, becomes a parent of a child to whom he or she is biologically unrelated

Adultery voluntary sexual intercourse between a married person and a person other than his or her spouse; a fault ground for divorce recognized in some states

Affidavit a written statement of facts based on first-hand knowledge, information or belief and signed by the affiant under pain and penalty of perjury

Affidavit of competency an affidavit from a physician that an individual is competent to perform a particular act

Affinity the relationship a spouse has to the blood relatives of the other spouse; relationship by marriage

Affirmative defense part of a defendant's answer to a complaint that sets forth new facts in support of the defendant's position that the plaintiff is not entitled to the relief sought

Age of consent the age at which a person becomes eligible to consent to his or her marriage without parental permission

Age of majority the age, usually eighteen, at which a person attains adulthood and associated legal rights

Agency adoption an adoption facilitated by an agency licensed by the state

Alimony See **Spousal support**

Alimony in gross sometimes called lump sum alimony; alimony ordered payable in the form of a definite sum usually in a single or limited number of installments; usually not subject to modification

Alimony *pendente lite* [Latin: while the action is pending] support awarded to a dependent spouse in order to maintain the status quo as to financial circumstances while a marital action is pending

Alimony recapture rule the IRS rule that the government can recover a tax benefit (such as the prior claiming of a deduction for payment of alimony) by taxing the income that no longer qualifies for the benefit

All property states states in which courts may distribute property at divorce without distinguishing between separate and marital property; all property, however acquired, may be reached if necessary to achieve an equitable division

Alternate payee a recipient of a pension payment other than the plan participant

Alternative dispute resolution (ADR) a procedure for settling a dispute by means other than litigation, such as mediation or arbitration

Annulment the legal procedure for declaring that a marriage is null and void because of an impediment existing at its inception

Answer a pleading filed by a defendant in response to a plaintiff's complaint setting forth the defendant's allegations, defenses and counterclaims

Antenuptial agreement See **Premarital agreement**

Anti-heartbalm statutes state laws that abolish the cause of action for breach of promise

Appearance (1) coming into court as a party in a lawsuit; (2) a document filed with the court by an attorney indicating that he or she will be representing one of the parties in a legal action

Appellant the party bringing an appeal of a lower court's judgment

Appellee the party against whom an appeal is brought

Appreciation an increase in value; active appreciation results from effort applied, and passive appreciation refers to an increase that would have occurred anyway, without any expenditure of effort.

Approximation rule the rule that the custodial responsibilities of the parents at dissolution should be allocated in a manner that approximates the proportion of time each parent spent caring for a child when the family was intact

Arbitration an alternative dispute resolution process in which one or more neutral third persons who are trained arbitrators, hear arguments, review evidence, and render a decision with respect to the issues identified for arbitration by the parties involved in a dispute

Arrearage a payment that is due but has not been made

Artificial insemination the process of inseminating a woman by means other than sexual intercourse

Assisted reproductive technology (ART) treatment or procedures designed to make parenthood possible for persons with fertility problems or individuals who are otherwise unable or personally unwilling to reproduce

At-risk adoption an adoption that is at risk of being challenged at a later date because the parental rights of one or both biological parents have not been terminated; an alternative to permanent or long term foster care

Attorney client privilege the client's right to refuse to disclose and to prevent the attorney from disclosing confidential communications between the client and his or her attorney unless the communication concerns future commission of a serious crime; The privilege is established by statute.

B

Bankruptcy a legal proceeding in which a party seeks to be relieved of responsibility for paying his or her debts

Basis the value assigned by the IRS to a taxpayer's investment in property

Battered woman's syndrome the psychological condition of a woman who has been abused for a sustained period of time sometimes used as a defense to justify or mitigate the penalty when the woman attacks her abuser

Beneficiary the person named in a document (such as a will, trust, or insurance policy) to receive property, money, or some other benefit

Best interest the legal standard for resolving custody disputes that focuses on the needs of the child over the rights or wishes of the parents

Bifurcated divorce a divorce in which the dissolution of marriage is resolved in one proceeding, and all other issues such as property division and child custody are resolved in one or more later separate proceedings in the same or another state

Bigamy the act of entering a subsequent marriage when a prior marriage of one or both of the parties is still in effect; a ground for annulment and for divorce in some states; in most states constitutes a criminal offense if committed knowingly

Binding arbitration arbitration in which the parties agree to abide by the arbitrator's decision as final and unappealable

Biological parent a blood-related parent who contributes half of a child's genetic material by means of a reproductive cell (egg or sperm); sometimes called a genetic or natural parent

Biology-plus rule the rule that an unwed father's parental rights are worthy of constitutional protection if the father grasps the opportunity to develop a relationship with and accept responsibility for the child

Black market adoption an adoption brokered by an individual who collects a substantial fee for locating a child who is transferred from one person or couple to another without proper legal process

Boilerplate standardized language that will fit in a variety of documents; contractual language that usually does not require negotiation

Bottom line the limit beyond which a party will not go in a negotiation

Breach of promise under common law, the breaking of an engagement without justification entitling the innocent party to damages

Burden of proof the requirement that a party or defendant prove a disputed assertion or charge

C

Canon law church law; a body of law developed within a particular religious tradition

Capacity the legal power to perform a particular act and to understand the nature and effect of that act

Capital gains tax a tax on income derived from the sale of a capital (long term) asset as defined by the Internal Revenue Code

Care and protection proceeding a court proceeding in which the state seeks custody of a child and termination of parental rights, if warranted

CASA program a national program that trains court appointed volunteer advocates to work one-on-one with abused and endangered children; CASA volunteers provide objective recommendations to the court concerning the environment that will best assure a particular child's safety and well being

Case law the body of law contained in court opinions

Case of first impression a case involving an issue being addressed for the first time in a given jurisdiction

Case registry a federally mandated compilation of information by each state regarding all child support orders issued by courts within the state; there exists a federal case registry as well.

Cause of action a legal theory on which a lawsuit can reasonably be based given a particular set of facts

Ceremonial marriage a marriage that complies with statutory requirements, such as obtaining a license and having the marriage performed by an authorized person

Child support the payments made by a parent to meet his or her legal obligation to contribute to the economic maintenance of a child until the age of majority or emancipation or some other time or circumstance set by a court

Child support guidelines guidelines that are presumed to generate an appropriate amount of child support given a particular set of assumptions and circumstances

Chose in action a pending right to recover something in a lawsuit such as an action for wrongful termination

Civil contempt a sanction for failure to obey a court order issued for another's benefit; a civil contempt proceeding is remedial in nature and its purpose is to promote compliance with the order

Civil law one of the two primary legal systems in the western world originating in the Roman Empire and influential in several parts of the world and a small number of states

Civil union a formal legal status that provides a same-sex couple with the rights, benefits, protections, and responsibilities that a married heterosexual couple has under state but not federal law

Clear and convincing evidence a standard of proof requiring that the evidence show it is highly probable or reasonably certain that an alleged fact is true or false as claimed; a greater burden than preponderance of the evidence, but less than evidence beyond a reasonable doubt, the standard for criminal trials

Cloning the genetic replication of a living organism

Closed adoption an adoption in which biological and adoptive parents essentially know nothing about each other, and adoptees have no access to their original birth certificates or identifying information about their parents

Cohabitation two unmarried people living together, commonly in an intimate relationship

Cohabitation agreement   an agreement between two unmarried individuals who live or intend to live together defining their intentions, rights, and obligations with respect to one another while living together and upon termination of their relationship

Collaborative law   an approach to reaching agreements and resolving differences that stresses cooperation, joint problem solving, and the avoidance of litigation

Collusion   an agreement by the parties to a divorce action to jointly deceive the court as to the true nature and purpose of the action; e.g., to claim the existence of marital fault when none exists

Comity, doctrine of   the practice of giving effect to the laws and judicial decisions of another jurisdiction (e.g. nation or state) out of mutual respect even if not legally obligated to do so

Commingling   mixing together a spouse's separate property with marital property, or mixing together the separate property of both spouses

Common law   judge-made law; the legal system that originated in England based on evolving case law and statutes

Common law marriage   a form of marriage created by the conduct of the parties rather than in a formal ceremony; usually requires capacity and intent to marry, cohabitation, and a holding out to the public as husband and wife; recognized in a limited number of states

Common law property   property acquired during the marriage and generally viewed as owned by the spouse who acquired or earned it; with limited exceptions, property acquired during the marriage is divided equitably upon divorce in common law property states

Community property   assets owned in common by a husband and wife as a result of having been acquired during the marriage by means other than an inheritance or gift to one of the spouses, each spouse generally holding a one-half interest in the property no matter in whose name it is held

Community property states   states in which a husband and wife hold property acquired during the marriage (exclusive of gifts and inheritances) in common with each spouse entitled to a one-half interest in the property upon divorce

Comparative rectitude, doctrine of   in the divorce context, the granting of a divorce to the party who is least at fault when both parties have committed marital wrongs

Compensatory damages   damages designed to compensate an injured person for a loss suffered

Complaint   the main pleading in a civil case that sets forth the nature of the action and the request for relief; called a petition in some states

Complaint for contempt   a complaint to obtain compliance with a court order or to punish a person for noncompliance.

Complaint for modification   a complaint seeking an alteration in an existing order based on a change of circumstances.

Conclusions of law   statements as to how governing law applies to a case

Concurrent jurisdiction   two or more courts have simultaneous jurisdiction over the same subject matter

Condonation   a defense to a divorce complaint claiming the forgiveness of an alleged matrimonial offense

Conflict of interest   a situation or circumstance that interferes with the attorney's or paralegal's duties of zealous advocacy and loyalty to the client

Conflict of law   a conflict arising out of a difference between the laws of two jurisdictions, such as two states or two nations

Connivance   a traditional defense in which the defendant alleges the plaintiff consented to, or participated in, the act complained of in the complaint

Consanguinity   a blood relationship between individuals

Consent   the approval, permission, or assent to some act or purpose, given voluntarily by a competent person, as in consent to an adoption

Consideration   a bargained for exchange or mutual promises underlying the formation of a contract

Consortium   companionship, affection, and, in the case of spouses, sexual relations, that one is entitled to receive from another based on existence of a legally recognized relationship (e.g. husband-wife, parent-child)

Constructive desertion   a situation in which a spouse's objectionable conduct is so abusive or otherwise intolerable that it renders continuation of the marital relationship impossible and forces the "innocent spouse" either to move out or into a separate area within the marital residence in order to maintain his or her health, safety, or self-respect

Constructive trust   a trust imposed by the court on an asset of a party who improperly or wrongfully acquired the property

Consummation   making a marriage complete by engaging in sexual intercourse

Contingent fee   the payment of a certain percentage of the amount recovered by the client in a settlement or court judgment (plus fees and costs) based on results obtained; common in personal injury cases but generally not permitted in divorce cases except in limited circumstances such as collection of past due child support

Continuing jurisdiction   when a court has acquired proper jurisdiction (as in a child custody case), the retention of that jurisdiction over the matter to the exclusion of other courts for purposes of modification, etc.

Contract   an agreement that establishes legally enforceable rights and obligations between two or more parties; elements of a valid contract include an offer, acceptance, and consideration; some contracts must be in writing

Co-parent   a person engaged in a non-marital relationship with the legal parent of a child, who regards him- or herself as a parent rather than as a legal stranger to the child; a person who shares childrearing responsibilities with a partner with or without benefit of a legally recognized relationship

Co-respondent   a person alleged to have had sexual intercourse with a defendant charged with adultery

Counterclaim   a defendant's claim against the plaintiff

Court of equity   a court that has authority to decide controversies in accordance with rules and principles of equity (principles of fairness)

Coverture (archaic couverture)   the legal doctrine that upon marriage, a husband and wife become one person (the husband), and that the wife loses many of the legal rights she possessed prior to marriage

Covenant marriage   a type of marriage that emphasizes the permanence of marriage and limits the availability of divorce to fault grounds

Criminal contempt   a punishment for failure to comply with a court order; a criminal contempt proceeding is punitive in nature and designed to punish an attack on the integrity of the court

Criminal conversation   a tort action for adultery brought against a third party who has sexual intercourse with another's spouse; abolished as a cause of action in most jurisdictions

Cruel and abusive treatment   a fault ground for divorce available in some states; conduct that is so physically or mentally damaging that it endangers the spouse's health, safety, or reason

Cryopreservation   freezing and storage of genetic material for later use in procreation or research

Curtesy   at common law, the right of a husband to lifetime use of land owned by his deceased wife during the marriage if children were born of the marriage

Custodial parent   the parent with whom the child primarily resides; the parent who has the right to have the child live with him or her

Cut-off rule   the rule requiring that a biological parent's rights to his or her child be terminated prior to adoption of the child by a third party; not applicable when a step- or co-parent is adopting the child

Cyberstalking   repeated use of the Internet, text messaging, email, or other forms of electronic communication with intent to harass, intimidate, torment, or embarrass another person

D

Decree *nisi*   [Latin: unless] a provisional judgment of divorce that ripens into a final decree after a certain period of time (usually 90 days) absent a challenge or request of the parties to vacate the judgment

Declaratory judgment   a binding adjudication that establishes the rights, status, or other legal relations between the parties

De facto adoption   [Latin: in point of fact] an adoption that does not meet formal statutory requirements but is considered an adoption based on the conduct of the parties and the surrounding circumstances; sometimes called an equitable adoption or adoption by estoppel

De facto parent   [Latin: in point of fact] an individual who performs a caretaking role without compensation for an extended period knowing he or she is not a child's legal parent; often with the consent of the legal parent(s)

Default judgment   a judgment entered against a defendant who fails to respond to a complaint or otherwise defend the action

Defense   a defendant's stated reason why a plaintiff has no valid claim or why the court should not grant the relief requested; usually expressed in statements of fact or legal theories

Defense of Marriage Act (DOMA) a federal law restricting the definition of marriage to the union of one man and one woman for purposes of federal law and allowing the states to deny full faith and credit to same-sex marriages valid in a sister state

Defined-benefit plan a retirement plan in which the amount of the benefit is usually determined according to a formula based on the participant's earnings, length of service, or a target monthly benefit

Defined-contribution plan a retirement plan funded by the employee's contributions and the employer's contributions (usually in a preset amount) in which the eventual benefit is based on the amount of contributions and investment earnings in the years during which the employee is covered by the plan

DNA (deoxyribonucleic acid) test a test used to determine inherited characteristics and establish parentage

Dependency exemption a deduction a taxpayer may take for a person principally dependent on him or her for support; in the custody context, usually taken by the parent with primary physical custody of a child although the parties may agree otherwise

Dependency proceeding See **Care and protection proceeding**

Deponent the individual who is asked to respond under oath to questions asked in a deposition

Deposition a method of pretrial discovery in which one party questions the other party or a third person (the deponent) under oath; responses to oral or written questions are reduced to writing for possible later use in a court proceeding

Desertion See **Abandonment**

Directory of new hires directories containing information from employers on new hires and applications for unemployment maintained by both the state and federal governments

Discharge a debt to relieve an obligor of the legal obligation to pay a debt

Discovery the process of gathering information relevant to a matter at issue; includes both formal and informal methods

Disestablishment of paternity a court order vacating an earlier paternity judgment or acknowledgment based on evidence the man is not the child's father, in effect disestablishing a previously existing father-child relationship

Dissipation the use of an asset for an illegal or inequitable purpose, such as when a spouse uses or expends marital property for personal benefit while a divorce is pending

Divisible divorce see **Bifurcated divorce**

Divorce a judicial determination that a marriage is legally terminated

Divorce *a mensa et thoro* [Latin: from board and hearth] a divorce from bed and board only; a legal separation

Divorce *a vinculo matrimonii* [Latin: from the chains of marriage] literally, a divorce from the chains or bonds of matrimony; an absolute divorce that frees the parties to remarry

Docket number the number assigned to a case by the court for organizational and reference purposes; the number appears on all papers filed in the case; sometimes called a calendar number

Domestic partnership a status granted to an unmarried couple who live together and receive a variety of economic and non-economic benefits customarily granted to spouses

Domestic violence See **Family violence**

Domicile a person's legal residence; the place a person considers his or her permanent home and to which he or she intends to return when away

Donee the one to whom a gift is made

Donor the one who gives a gift; in ART, a person who donates genetic material

Dower a widow's right to lifetime use of one-third of the land owned by her deceased husband during the marriage

Dual divorce a divorce granted to both parties

Dual property states states that distinguish between marital and separate property for distribution purposes and permit only marital property to be divided upon divorce

Due process the constitutional requirement that legal proceedings be conducted according to established rules and principles including notice and the right to a fair hearing

Durable power of attorney a document that grants someone authority to act in the grantor's stead for convenience and/or in the event of incapacity; the authority survives incapacity but terminates on the death of the grantor.

Duress a threat of harm made to compel a person to do something contrary to his or her free will or judgment

591

E

Ecclesiastical law   the law governing the doctrine and discipline of a particular church

Educational neglect   a parent's failure to use his or her best efforts to ensure that a child of mandatory school age attends a legally recognized school or program of home schooling

Electronic discovery   discovery of information in electronic form; refers to any information created, stored, or utilized with computerized technology of any sort

Emancipation   the point at which a child is considered an adult; usually occurs at the age of majority or upon the occurrence of certain acts or events, such as marriage or entering the armed services; usually frees the parent from a child support obligation

Emergency jurisdiction   jurisdiction based on a child's physical presence in a state and need for emergency protection

Emotional neglect   a pattern of rejecting, isolating, and ignoring a child's needs for nurturance, stimulation and social contact

Employee Retirement Income Security Act (ERISA)   a federal statute designed to protect qualified employee pensions in the event an employer goes out of business or declares bankruptcy; ERISA governs retirement plans that do not discriminate in favor of highly compensated employees.

Equal protection   constitutional protection provided by the 14th Amendment that prevents states from imposing arbitrary and discriminatory legislative classifications that treat citizens unfairly or unequally based on race, religion, disability, sex, age, or national origin

Equitable adoption   an adoption in which prospective adoptive parents accept a child into their home and raise the child as their own without ever formally finalizing the adoption; treated by some courts as an adoption to promote fairness and serve the ends of justice; sometimes called an adoption by estoppel

Equitable division   the legal concept that upon divorce property accumulated during a marriage should be divided between the parties equitably, but not necessarily equally, based upon principles of fairness

Equitable estoppel   preventing a party from asserting a claim or a defense because it would be unfair to an opposing party to do otherwise

Equitable parenthood   parenthood established on the basis of equitable principles of fairness rather than on biological connection; the equitable parent doctrine extends parental rights and responsibilities to an individual who is willing and able to assume parental rights and responsibilities and who has done so in the past

Equity   in real estate law, the fair market value of a property less any encumbrances (mortgage, loans, tax liens, etc.)

Equitable remedy   a remedy used by a court to achieve a just and fair result in situations not covered by existing laws

Error of law   a mistake made by a court in applying the law to the facts of a case

Estoppel   the doctrine that a person should be prevented by his or her prior conduct from claiming or denying the right of another person who has reasonably relied on that conduct

Escalation clause   a provision in an agreement that provides for an automatic increase in an amount owed such as in an alimony payment

Ethical wall   a screening mechanism designed to protect a client from a conflict of interest by preventing one or more lawyers (or paralegals) within a firm from participating in any legal matter involving that client

Ethics   the standards or rules of conduct to which members of a profession are expected to conform

Evidence-based prosecution   in abuse cases, prosecution of a defendant that relies on physical evidence and testimony of persons other than the victim, such as police officers; formerly called "victimless" prosecutions

Exhibit notebook   a notebook, prepared for the convenience of the court and counsel, containing all exhibits to be introduced at trial by either or both parties

Ex parte   without advance notice to or hearing argument from the opposing party based on the urgency of the matter or the harm that might otherwise result

Ex parte **motion**   [Latin: from the part] a motion made without advance notice to the opposing party; a motion considered and initially ruled on by the court without hearing from both parties

Expectation damages   compensation awarded for the loss of what a person reasonably anticipated from a contract or transaction that was not completed

Expert   a person who, through education or experience, has developed special skill or knowledge in a particular subject

Express contract a contract that is created by an actual articulated agreement of the parties as to certain terms of their relationship expressed orally or in writing

Extraordinary expense an unusual, unanticipated child-rearing expense that is substantial in cost and/or duration

F

Fair market value the price a willing buyer would pay a willing seller in an arm's length transaction when neither party is under any compulsion to buy or sell

Family law the body of the law that deals with marriage, divorce, custody, adoption, support, paternity, and other domestic relations issues including matters related to nonmarital family units

Family violence a pattern of coercive behavior designed to exert power and control over a person in a familial relationship; sometimes called domestic or intimate partner violence

Fault grounds grounds for divorce based on the fault of one of the parties

Federal Parent Locator Service (FPLS) a service operated by the OCSE for the purpose of locating parents delinquent in meeting their child support obligations when multiple states are involved

Fee agreement a contract between an attorney and a client regarding payment for the attorney's professional services

Fiduciary a person who owes another a duty of good faith, trust, loyalty, and candor

Fiduciary duty a duty of good faith, loyalty, and trust owed by one person to another based upon the existence of a special relationship

Filius nullius [Latin: the son of no one] the child of no one

Final judgment/judgment absolute the court's final decision determining the rights of the parties and issues in dispute

Financial statement a party's statement of his or her assets and liabilities signed under pain and penalty of perjury; sometimes called a financial affidavit or case information statement (CIS)

Flat fee a fixed dollar amount charged to handle a specific legal matter, such as the negotiating and drafting of a cohabitation agreement

Foreign divorce a divorce obtained in another state or country

Forensic accountant an accountant who applies accounting principles and analysis to gather and present evidence in a lawsuit

Formal discovery discovery methods that are subject to procedural and court rules

Forum non conveniens [Latin: an unsuitable court] a situation in which the forum where an action is filed is not convenient for the defendant; the court, in its discretion, may find that justice would be better served if the matter is heard in another court

Forum shopping seeking a court that will grant the most favorable ruling in a case

Foster parent a person or persons who provide a temporary home for a child when his or her parents are temporarily unwilling or unable to do so, usually through a child welfare agency for a modest payment

"Four corners" the face of a written instrument

IV-D Agency the state agency charged with responsibility for enforcing child support obligations

Fraud a false statement of a material fact with intent that another rely on the statement to his or her detriment

Front loading the making of substantial payments to a former spouse shortly after a divorce in an effort to disguise a property division as deductible alimony

Full faith and credit the recognition, acceptance, and enforcement of the laws, orders, and judgments of another jurisdiction

G

Genetic parent a biological parent who is genetically related to the child

Genetic test the position taken in parentage determinations that the individuals who contribute a child's genetic material should be considered his or her legal parents

Gestational mother a woman who carries and gives birth to a child; the woman may or may not be biologically related to the child

Gestational test the position taken in maternity determinations that the woman who carries and delivers a child should be deemed the child's legal mother

Get a "bill of divorce" in the Jewish religion

Green card a document (registration card) evidencing a resident alien's status as a permanent resident of the United States; a "green card marriage" is a sham marriage in which a United States citizen marries a foreign citizen for the sole purpose of allowing the foreign citizen to become a permanent United States resident

Gross income   total income from all sources before any deductions are made

Ground for divorce   the reason for filing the action, the basis on which relief is sought in a divorce action; may be a fault or no-fault ground

Guardian   an individual appointed by the court to have legal authority for another's person and/or property during a period of minority or incapacitation

Guardian *ad litem*   [Latin: for the suit] a person, usually a lawyer, appointed by the court to conduct an investigation or to represent a party who is a minor or otherwise unable to represent him- or herself in a legal proceeding; the guardian's role may be limited to a particular matter, such as custody

H

Health care proxy   a document granting another person the authority to make health care decisions for the grantor in the event of his or her incapacity

Hold harmless (indemnity) provision   a provision specifying that a particular spouse will be solely responsible for payment of certain debts and that the other spouse shall be free and clear of any obligation regarding those debts and will be indemnified by the debtor spouse if forced to pay the debt

Home state   jurisdiction in custody matters based on where a child has lived for a specified period of time; under UIFSA, the UCCJA and UCCJEA, the state where the child has lived for six consecutive months prior to the filing or since birth if the child is less than six months old

Home study   a means of assessing prospective adoptive parents and home environments; customarily conducted by social workers licensed by the state

I

Ignorantia legis non excusat   [Latin: ignorance of the law is not an excuse]

Illegal adoption   See Black market adoption.

Illegitimate child   a child born to unmarried parents; a term abandoned in most states

Impediment   a legal obstacle to formation of a valid marriage or contract

Implied-in-fact contract   a judicially created contract the existence of which is inferred from the conduct of the parties

Implied partnership/Joint venture   a judicially created partnership the existence of which is inferred from the conduct of the parties

Impotence   lack of capacity to procreate due to inability to have sexual intercourse or due to incompetent sperm or ova

Impounded   kept in the custody of the court and not available to the public, and, in some instances, to other parties

Imputed income   income that is attributed to a party based upon his or her earning capacity rather than on actual earnings

In camera   in the judge's chambers

Inception of title theory   a rule that fixes title/ownership at the time a property is acquired and holds that contributions are of no effect

Incest   sexual intercourse between two people who are too closely related for some purpose as defined by civil and criminal statutes; a term used in some states to describe prohibited degrees of consanguinity and affinity in the marriage context

Income withholding   an automatic deduction of child support from an obligor's paycheck

Incompatibility   a no-fault ground for divorce that exists when there is such discord in the marriage that the parties are unable to live together in a normal marital relationship

Incorporation (by reference)   adoption by reference; inclusion of the content of a document such as a separation agreement by referencing the agreement in a divorce judgment and indicating that the agreement should be treated as part of the divorce decree

Independent adoption   an adoption usually facilitated by a third party, such as a physician or attorney, rather than by a licensed state agency; sometimes called a private, designated, or identified adoption

Independent legal significance   a contract or other document that is legally binding in its own right

Informal discovery   information gathering not governed by specific procedural rules such as searches of public records and "Blue Book" values

In loco parentis   [Latin: in the place of the parent] taking on some or all of the responsibilities of a parent

Innocent spouse   a spouse who may be relieved of liability for taxes incurred if the other spouse prepared the tax forms, controlled the information that went into them, and is responsible for errors, omissions, and/or fraud that resulted in significant penalties; also generally refers to a spouse who did not engage in marital misconduct

In rem jurisdiction [Latin: against a thing] the court's authority over a property or thing rather than over persons located within its jurisdictional borders

Intangible property property that has no physical presence or form

Intent test the position taken in parentage determinations that the individual(s) who set the procreative process in motion with the intent of raising any resulting children should be deemed the legal parents of those children

Interlocutory order or decree an interim decree; a decree that is not final

International adoption an adoption in which a child residing in one country is adopted by a resident of another country

Interrogatories a method of discovery in which one party submits a series of written questions to an opposing party to be responded to in writing within a certain period of time under pain and penalty of perjury

Interspousal immunity a doctrine preventing spouses from suing each other in civil actions

Intestacy laws the laws governing distribution of property when a decedent dies without a valid will.

Intestate dying without leaving a valid will

In vitro fertilization [Latin] a technology that involves retrieval of eggs from a female to be fertilized in a laboratory by sperm from a male

Irreconcilable differences a no-fault ground for divorce the essence of which is that the marriage has irreparably broken down due to serious differences between the parties

Irremediable breakdown See **Irreconcilable differences**

J

Joint award an award made to both parties as in a joint custody award

Joint custody an arrangement in which both parents share in the responsibility for and authority over the child at all times, although one parent may exercise primary physical custody

Joint petition for adoption a petition to adopt a child that is brought by both parties to a marriage or by co-parents

Joint tenant with right of survivorship a form of ownership of property by two or more persons in which each tenant owns an identical interest in the property, and each joint tenant has a right of survivorship in the others' shares

Joint venture an express or implied agreement to conduct a common enterprise in which the parties have a mutual right of control

Judicial estoppel an equitable doctrine designed to prevent a party from gaining an unfair advantage over another party by making inconsistent statements on the same issue in different lawsuits

Judicial notice a court's acceptance of a well-known fact without requiring proof

Jurisdiction (1) a geographical area in which a certain law or procedure is governing; (2) the authority of a court to issue enforceable orders concerning a particular type of legal matter, person, or thing

L

Laches unreasonable delay in pursuing a right or claim that prejudices the other party's rights

Last resort jurisdiction jurisdiction based on the fact no other state is willing or able to exercise jurisdiction

Laws of descent and distribution the laws governing inheritance of property when a decedent dies without leaving a valid will

Lay witness a witness who is not an expert on a matter at issue in a legal proceeding who testifies as to opinions based on first hand knowledge

Legal custody custody relating to decision making authority with respect to major issues affecting a child; may be sole or joint

Legal parent a person who is recognized as a child's parent under state and/or federal law

Legal separation a judicial decree that allows spouses to live separate and apart without dissolving their legal relationship as husband and wife; sometimes called a limited divorce

Letter of engagement a letter from an attorney to a client confirming that the attorney agrees to represent the client in a particular legal matter

Letter of nonengagement/declination a letter from an attorney to an individual confirming that the attorney will NOT be representing that individual with respect to a particular legal matter

Letters rogatory   documents issued by a court in one state to a court in another state requesting that the "foreign" court serve process on an individual within the foreign jurisdiction

Liabilities   legal obligations, responsibilities, and debts

Lien   an encumbrance on the property of another that operates as a cloud against clear title to the property

Limited scope agreement   an agreement between an attorney and a client, which specifically limits the nature and extent of the professional representation to be provided

Liquidated damages   an amount agreed to in a contract as the measure of damages to be paid by the breaching party to the non-breaching party

Living separate and apart   a no-fault ground for divorce based on the fact that, due to a breakdown of the marriage, the parties have lived apart from each other for a requisite period of time

Long-arm statute   a statute setting forth the circumstances in which a state may exercise personal jurisdiction over a nonresident defendant; identifies the minimum contacts a defendant must have with the territory where the statute is in effect

Lord Mansfield's rule   the evidentiary rule that prohibited either spouse from testifying as to a husband's access to his wife at the time of conception if the testimony would tend to render the child illegitimate

Lump sum alimony   See **Alimony in gross**

M

Malpractice   intentional or negligent professional misconduct of an attorney that may occur in the form of a failure to properly supervise a paralegal

Mandatory reporter   an individual, who by virtue of his or her employment as a police officer, nurse, etc. is required by statute to report suspected child abuse and neglect

Mandatory self-disclosure   material specified by statute or court rule that each party in a particular legal action must provide to the other party within a certain period after filing and service of a summons and complaint

Marital communications privilege   the privilege that allows a spouse to refuse to testify, and to prevent others from testifying, about confidential communications between the spouses during their marriage; does not apply in certain contexts such as cases involving child custody and/or abuse

Marital debt   debt incurred during the marriage for the benefit of the marital enterprise regardless of which party incurred the obligation

Marital estate   See **Marital property**

Marital presumption   the presumption that when a woman gives birth to a child while married or within three hundred days of termination of the marriage, her husband is presumed to be the child's legal father

Marital property   the property acquired during the marriage other than by gift or inheritance that is subject to division at the time of marital dissolution

Marriage   a legal status that two people attain by entering a government approved and regulated contract with each other; a civil contract between a man and a woman or between two same-sex partners in a state that permits marriage of partners of the same sex

Marriage restriction laws   state laws that prevent certain persons from marrying each other, such as persons closely related by blood

Married Women's Property Acts   statutory reforms that helped improve the legal status of married women primarily by extending rights of property ownership and control denied them at common law

Material change in circumstances   a change in the physical, emotional, or financial condition of one or both of the parties (or their child) sufficient to warrant a change in a court order; a change that, if known at the time of the divorce decree, would have resulted in a different outcome

Maternal preference   the concept that custody should be awarded to a mother over a father provided she is fit

Mediation   an approach to resolving differences in which a neutral third person helps the parties clarify their differences, consider their options, and structure a mutually acceptable agreement

Medical neglect   the failure of a parent or caretaker to provide appropriate health care for a child

Meeting of the minds   a shared understanding with respect to the terms and conditions of a contract

Memorandum of *lis pendens*   [Latin: a pending lawsuit] a notice that ownership and disposition of certain real property is subject to a pending legal action and any interest acquired during the pendency of that action is subject to its outcome; usually filed in a registry of deeds where the property is located

Meretricious sex   unlawful or illicit sexual relations, such as prostitution or sex outside of marriage

Merger   the process by which a separation agreement is incorporated in a divorce judgment and does not survive but rather loses its separate identity as an independent contract

Military affidavit   an affidavit submitted by a party stating under pain and penalties of perjury that an absent party is currently not serving in the armed services

Minor child   a child who has not reached full legal age

Modification   a change in a court's order or judgment based on a change in circumstances; customarily sought by motion of one of the parties

Motion   a written or oral request that a court make a particular ruling or order

Motion to dismiss   a request that the court dismiss a case because of some procedural or other defect such as lack of jurisdiction or failure to state a claim on which relief can be based

Motion to vacate the judgment   a motion requesting the court to nullify or cancel a judgment before it becomes final

Motions *in Limine*   [Latin: at the outset] a motion asking the court to exclude or limit the use of certain evidence at trial

N

Natural parent   biological (genetic) parent of a child

Necessaries, doctrine of   under common law, a husband's duty to pay debts incurred by his wife or children for "necessaries" indispensable to living, such as food, shelter, and clothing

Neglect   failure by a caregiver to provide needed, age appropriate care although financially able to do so, or offered financial or other means to do so

Negligence   a failure to exercise reasonable care that results in harm to a person to whom one owes a duty of care

Negligent supervision   a cause of action based on a parent's duty to society to exercise reasonable care in the supervision of their minor children in order to prevent them from intentionally causing injury to others

Net income   total income from all sources minus voluntary and nonvoluntary deductions

Neutral case evaluation   a process in which a neutral third party, usually an experienced trial attorney or judge, listens to the parties' positions and offers an opinion about settlement potential and the likely outcome if the matter proceeds to trial

Nexus   a connection or link; in the custody context, a requirement that there be a connection between parental conduct and a detrimental effect on a child before the conduct will be considered by the court

No-contact order   a court order prohibiting an individual from having contact of any kind with a person he or she has threatened and/or abused in some manner

No-fault divorce   divorce based on an irremediable breakdown of the marital relationship rather than on the fault of one or both of the parties

No-fault ground   a ground for divorce based on the irremediable breakdown of the marital relationship rather than on the fault of one or both of the parties

Nonage   below the minimum age established by law to perform a particular act

Nonbinding arbitration   arbitration in which the parties are free to accept or reject the arbitrator's decision

Noncustodial parent   a parent who does not have sole or primary physical custody of a child but who is still a legal parent with enforceable rights and obligations

Notice of deposition   the notification sent to an opponent (or his or her attorney, if represented) of an intention to depose him or her at a certain date, place, and time

O

Obligee   a person to whom a duty is owed

Obligor   a person who owes a duty; in the child custody context, the parent who owes the duty of support

Open adoption   an adoption in which biological parents, adoptive parents, and the adoptee have varying degrees of contact with each other

Operation of law   a result that occurs automatically because the law mandates it regardless of whether or not a party agrees or intends that result; a party does not need to take any further action to bring about the result

P

Palimony   a term that originated in the media, palimony refers to a court-ordered allowance paid by one cohabitant to the other after their relationship terminates; recognized in case law in some states, but generally not by statute

Parens patriae doctrine [Latin: parent of the country] the doctrine holding that the government, as parent of the country, has standing to act on behalf of a citizen, particularly one who is a minor or under a disability

Parent locator service a federal or state government program that helps locate parents, particularly those who are delinquent in child support payments

Parental alienation syndrome a condition in which a child involved in a custody dispute comes to idealize one parent and demonize the other parent as a result of the former parent's pressure and manipulation

Parental responsibility law a statute that imposes vicarious liability on parents for the torts committed by their children

Parenthood by estoppel essentially provides that a man may be designated the legal father of a child if he has held himself out as the child's father and has supported the child emotionally and financially; a theory used to establish parenting rights that asserts a legal parent should not be permitted to deny a co-parent's parental status based on a prior agreement with the legal parent to raise a child together on which the co-parent relied

Parenting coordinator an individual, usually appointed by the court, who assists with creation and implementation of a parenting agreement and/or enforcement of a decree in a high conflict case involving minor children

Parenting plan a written agreement in which parents lay out plans for taking care of their children post separation or divorce

Parol evidence rule the rule that when a writing is intended to embody the entire agreement between the parties, its terms cannot later be varied or contradicted by evidence of earlier or contemporaneous agreements

Passive appreciation increase in the value of an asset that results without effort and as a result of market forces and/or the passage of time

Paternal preference the common law doctrine that fathers had an absolute right to the care and custody of their children

Paternity fraud fraud in which a mother has intentionally misled a man into believing he is the father of a child to whom he is genetically unrelated

Pendente lite [Latin] while the action is pending

Pension a job-related retirement benefit acquired by an employee and funded through contributions by the employer, the employee, or a combination of both

Permanency planning planning for the return home of a child following removal or for termination of parental rights within a legally specified period of time in an effort to promote stability for the child

Permanent alimony alimony usually payable in weekly or monthly installments either indefinitely or until a time or circumstance specified in a court order

Permissive reporter an individual who may, but is not required to, report suspected child abuse

Per se rule by itself without reference to additional facts; an agreement against the law or a strong public policy may be deemed *per se* invalid, invalid in and of itself, standing alone, without reference to any additional facts or circumstances

Personal jurisdiction the authority of a court to issue and enforce orders binding a particular individual; sometimes called *in personam* jurisdiction

Personal property any movable or intangible thing that is subject to ownership and not classified as real property

Physical custody custody relating to where and with whom the child resides; can be either sole or joint

Physical neglect inadequate supervision and/or a failure to provide adequate food, shelter, and clothing, such that the child's health, safety, growth, and development are endangered

Pleading a document in which a party to a legal proceeding sets forth or responds to a claim, allegation, defense, or denial

Polyandry the practice of a woman having more than one husband at the same time

Polygamy the practice of a man having more than one wife at the same time

Posthumous reproduction reproduction that occurs after the death of one or both of the gamete contributors

Postmarital agreement (postmarital contract, postnuptial agreement) an agreement made by two people already married to each other who want both to continue their marriage and also to define their respective rights upon separation, divorce, or death of one of them

Precedent a higher court's decision regarding a question of law that provides a basis for determining later cases that involve similar facts or issues in a given jurisdiction

Premarital agreement an agreement made by two persons about to be married defining for themselves their respective rights, duties, and responsibilities in the event their marriage terminates by death, annulment, separation, or divorce

Preponderance of the evidence   a standard of proof requiring that the evidence show that it is more likely than not that an alleged fact is true or false as claimed

Presumption   an assumption of fact that can reasonably be drawn based on other established facts

Presumptive child support guidelines   See **Child support guidelines**

Prima facie **showing**   a legally rebuttable showing

Primary authority   authority created by a governmental body such as a legislature or court—includes statutes, constitutions, and case law

Primary Caretaker   the individual who has performed most of the significant parenting tasks for the child since birth or in the years preceding the divorce

Privilege   a legal right or exemption granted to a person or a class of persons to not testify in a legal proceeding; generally based on the existence of a special relationship

Pro rata **theory**   [Latin] See **Source of funds theory**

Pro se   [Latin: for self] the condition under which a person represents himself or herself in a legal proceeding without the assistance of an attorney

Procedural Fairness   fairness in the negotiation and execution of an agreement

Procedural law   the technical rules for bringing and defending actions before a court or administrative agency, e.g. the steps to be followed in seeking child support

Property division   the distribution upon divorce of property accumulated during the marriage; if not agreed upon by the parties, the division will be based on community property or equitable distribution principles depending on the jurisdiction.

Proposed findings of fact   facts that a party asks a court to accept as true

Protective order   (1) a court order restricting or prohibiting a party from unduly burdening an opposing party or third party witness during the discovery process; (2) in the context of family violence cases, a court order directing a person to refrain from harming, intimidating, or harassing another person

Provocation   a traditional defense to divorce claiming that the plaintiff provoked the conduct alleged in the complaint and therefore should be denied relief

Proxy marriage   a marriage ceremony in which a designated agent stands in for and acts on behalf of one of the absent parties (prohibited in most states)

Psychological parent   the individual who has the strongest "parental" bond with the child, who has provided the most significant care in quality and quantity, and whom the child often regards as the "parent"

Public assistance programs   government programs providing financial and other forms of assistance to poor and low-income families

Public charge   a person dependent on public assistance programs for necessaries

Public policy   an idea or principle that is considered right and fair and is in the best interest of the general public

Putative father   a man reputed or believed to be the father of a child but who was not married to the mother when the child was born and whose paternity has not yet been established by legal process

Putative father registry   a vehicle available in several states that is designed to protect a putative father's parental rights by giving him notice of a pending adoption proceeding without his having to rely on the birth mother or prospective adoptive parents for information

Putative spouse   a person who believes in good faith that his or her invalid marriage is legally valid

Q

Qualified Domestic Relations Order (QDRO)   a court order directing the administrator of a pension plan to pay a specified portion of a current or former employee's pension to an alternate payee to satisfy a support or other marital obligation

Qualified Medical Child Support Order (QMCSO)   a court order requiring provision of medical support or health benefits for the child of a parent covered by a group insurance plan

Quantum meruit   [Latin: as much as he deserved] a basis for establishing damages based on the reasonable value of services one person has provided to another

Quasi-**community property**   [Latin: as if] property acquired during a marriage in a non-community property state that would be marital property if acquired in a community property state

Quasi-contract/Implied-in-law contract   [Latin: as if] a contract imposed by a court to prevent unjust enrichment of one party at the expense of the other

Quasi-marital property   [Latin: as if] property treated as if it was acquired by the parties during the marriage even though the marriage was never valid

Quid pro quo   an action or thing exchanged for another action or thing of relatively equal value

R

Ratification   acceptance or confirmation of a previous act thereby making it valid from the moment it was done

Real property   land and anything growing on, attached to, or erected on it, excluding anything that may be severed without injury to the land

Reasonable efforts   the level of effort a child protective agency must make to prevent removal of a child from his or her home, or, if removed, to reunify the family within a specified period of time

Rebuttable presumption   an inference drawn from certain facts that can be overcome by the introduction of additional or contradictory evidence

Recapture rule   the government's recovery of a tax benefit (such as a claimed deduction or credit) by taxing income or property that no longer qualifies for the benefit

Reciprocal beneficiaries   a nonmarital family status, available in a limited number of states, in which two adults residing together may register for certain benefits available to married persons

Recrimination   a defense to divorce raised when the defendant alleges the plaintiff has also committed a marital wrong and therefore should not be granted a divorce; sometimes addressed by application of the doctrine of comparative rectitude

Rehabilitative alimony   alimony designed to assist a divorced person in acquiring the education or training required to find employment outside the home or to reenter the labor force; sometimes called limited or transitional alimony

Reimbursement alimony   See Restitution alimony

Reliance damages   damages awarded to a plaintiff for losses incurred from having acted in reliance on a contract that was breached by the other party

Relocation   removal and establishment in a new place

Request for admissions   a discovery method in which a party makes written requests to an opposing party

calling for an admission or denial of specific facts at issue or verification or denial of the genuineness of documents relevant to a case

Request for physical or mental examination   a method of discovery in which one party requests that the court order the other party (or, in some instances, a third party) to submit to a physical or mental examination

Request for production of documents or things   a method of pretrial discovery in which a party makes a written request that the other party, or a third person, produce specified documents or other tangible things for inspection and/or copying

Res judicata   [Latin: a thing adjudicated] an issue that has been definitively settled by judicial decision; requires three essential elements: (1) an earlier decision on the issue, (2) a final judgment on the merits, and (3) the involvement of the original parties.

Rescission   the cancellation or unmaking of a contract for a legally sufficient reason

Respondeat superior, doctrine of   [Latin: let the superior make answer] the doctrine under which an attorney may be held vicariously liable for the acts of his or her employees performed within the scope of employment

Restitution alimony   alimony designed to repay a spouse who made financial contributions during the marriage that directly enhanced the future earning capacity of the other spouse; sometimes called reimbursement alimony

Restraining order   a court order, commonly issued in domestic violence cases, restricting an individual from threatening and/or harassing another individual or individuals; an order prohibiting a party from taking a certain action or actions such as selling a piece of property or removing the parties' children from the jurisdiction where the action is pending

Resulting trust   a trust created by the court when one party contributes funds or services towards the acquisition of property and title to that property is held in the name of another party

Retainer   used in general to describe the contract between the attorney and the client particularly with respect to fees; most commonly, the client advances a lump sum payment to an attorney for deposit in a client trust fund account, the attorney withdraws funds from the retainer as the client incurs fees and costs, and any unused portion of a retainer is returned to the client at the conclusion of the representation

Right of survivorship a joint tenant's right to succeed to the whole estate upon the death of the other joint tenant(s)

Rule of attorney-client confidentiality the duty of an attorney not to reveal any information relating to representation of a client; the rule is an ethical rule established in codes of professional conduct

S

Safe haven law a law that allows a parent, or an agent of a parent, of an unwanted newborn to anonymously leave the baby at a safe haven center, such as a hospital emergency room, without fear of legal charges of abandonment or child endangerment, etc., provided there is no evidence of abuse

Safety plan a plan to be prepared by a victim of family violence (sometimes with assistance) outlining actions to be taken in the event the victim needs to protect herself and/or escape from the presence of the abuser

Sanctions penalties imposed by a court when, for example, a party fails to comply with court rules or orders

Second look doctrine an approach to determining enforceability of premarital agreements adopted by some courts, which involves examining the terms of a premarital agreement for fairness at the time of performance as well as at the time of execution

Secondary authority publications that discuss but do not establish law including, for example, treatises, annotations, and law review articles

Separate maintenance court ordered spousal support while the parties are living separate and apart but not divorced

Separate property property that a spouse owned before marriage or acquired during marriage by inheritance or gift from a third party; may include property acquired during marriage in exchange for separate property

Separate support See **Separate maintenance**

Separation agreement an agreement made between spouses in anticipation of a divorce or legal separation concerning the terms of the divorce or separation and any continuing obligations of the parties to each other

Service of process the delivery of a summons and complaint to a defendant in a manner consistent with local procedural rules; usually accomplished by personal "in hand' service by an authorized individual such as a sheriff or by publication in a newspaper and mailing to the defendant's last known address

Service plan a plan developed by a child protection agency outlining services to be provided to parents to help them care for their children and identifying obligations the parents must perform in order for their children to remain in or be returned to the home

Shaken baby syndrome a condition that results from repeated, vigorous shaking of a baby that causes brain damage and sometimes death that can result from a single incident or a more prolonged pattern of abuse

Sham marriage a marriage in which one of the parties has no intention of fulfilling the responsibilities of marriage

Significant connection jurisdiction jurisdiction based on the existence in a state of substantial evidence concerning a child

Sole award an award made to one party only

Sole legal custody an arrangement by which one parent has full control and sole decision-making responsibility–to the exclusion of the other parent–on matters such as health, education, religion and living arrangements; sole custody can also apply to physical custody awards

Source of funds theory a rule that bases ownership of property on contribution; an asset may be characterized as both separate and marital in proportion to the respective contributions of the parties

Specific performance a court-ordered remedy requiring that the terms of a contract be fulfilled as fully as practicable when money damages are inappropriate or inadequate

Split custody a custodial arrangement in which each parent has sole legal and/or physical custody of one or more of the parties' children

Spousal support an allowance for support and maintenance that one spouse may be ordered by a court to pay to the other spouse while they are living apart or divorced; also called alimony, maintenance, and separate support depending on the circumstances and the jurisdiction

Stalking a knowing and willful course of conduct intended to cause another substantial emotional distress or fear for his or her safety; includes behaviors such as following, telephoning, or watching a person's place of residence or employment

Standing an individual's right to bring a matter before the court and seek relief based on a claim that he or she has a stake in the outcome of the case

Stare decisis [Latin: let the decision stand] the doctrine that requires a lower court to follow the precedent of a higher court in its jurisdiction (e.g. application of earlier case law to current cases)

State Case Registry See **Case registry**

State Directory of New Hires See **Directory of New Hires**

Statute of Frauds the requirement that certain types of contracts be in writing, such as a contract that by its terms cannot be completed within a year or a contract for the sale of land

Statute of limitations a statute that bars a certain type of claim after a specified period of time

Stay away order a court order requiring a person to keep away from another individual wherever they may be (home, work, school, etc.)

Step-parent a parent by virtue of marriage to a child's legal parent

Stipulation an agreement between the parties concerning some matter; may be filed with the court to be considered and entered as an order

Subject matter jurisdiction the authority of a court to hear and decide a particular type of claim or controversy

Subpoena a document ordering a witness to appear and provide testimony in a legal proceeding such as a deposition, court hearing, or trial

Subpoena *duces tecum* [Latin: bring with you] a subpoena ordering a witness to appear in a legal proceeding such as a deposition, court hearing, or trial, and to bring with him or her specified documents, records, or things

Substantive fairness fairness in the specific terms of an agreement

Substantive law laws that relate to rights and obligations/duties (e.g. the right to child support) rather than to technical procedures

Summons a formal notice from a court informing a defendant of an action filed against him or her and ordering the defendant to respond and answer the allegations of the plaintiff within a certain period or risk entry of a default judgment

Surrender in the context of parenthood, a formal document in which a legal (usually biological) parent gives up his or her parental rights to a specific child

Surrogate mother a woman who agrees to carry and deliver a baby with an understanding that she will surrender the child to the intended parents at birth or shortly thereafter; she may or may not be biologically related to the child

Surviving agreement an agreement of the parties incorporated in a court's divorce decree that also retains its existence as an independent contract enforceable under basic principles of contract law

T

Talak an Arabic word that means to release or divorce

Tangible property property that has a physical form capable of being touched and seen

Temporary alimony See **Alimony** *pendente lite*

Temporary orders orders designed to protect the parties and maintain the status quo while a matter is pending before the court

Tender years doctrine the doctrine holding that custody of very young children should be awarded to a mother rather than a father unless she is found to be unfit

Term alimony alimony payable in weekly or monthly installments that continues for a set period of time or until a condition specified in a court order or agreement

Termination of parental rights the judicial severing of the legal relationship between a parent and child; may be voluntary or involuntary based on clear and convincing evidence of parental unfitness

Third party beneficiary a person who, though not a party to a contract, benefits from performance of the contract

Tort a civil wrong (other than breach of contract) for which a court provides a remedy usually in the form of money damages; the wrong must involve harm resulting from breach of a duty owed to another

Tracing the process of tracking ownership of a property from the time of inception to the present usually in an effort to establish its character as separate or marital property

Transitional Assistance to Needy Families (TANF) the welfare system that replaced the former Aid to Families with Dependent Children Program (AFDC)

Transmutation a change in the classification of an asset from separate to marital or marital to separate

Trial notebook a term used loosely to describe the organizational system used by an attorney to assemble all of the material needed for a trial

Trust   a legal construct in which legal title to property is held by one or more persons (trustee(s)) for the benefit of another (the beneficiary)

Trustee process   a legal process by which a third party holds the property of a party in trust at the direction of a court

U

Unallocated support   support payments made to a former spouse that do not distinguish between alimony/spousal support and child support

Unauthorized practice of law (UPL)   engaging in the practice of law without a license

Unbundling of legal services   an alternative to full representation in which an attorney performs discrete tasks rather than comprehensive representation in a legal matter, usually at a substantial overall savings to the client

Unconscionable   so substantially unfair in terms or result as to shock the conscience

Unclean hands   the principle that a party should not be granted relief if he or she has acted unfairly, wrongfully, or illegally

Undue influence   the improper use of power or trust in a way that deprives a person of his or her free will and substitutes another's purposes in its place

Unearned income   income earned from investment rather than labor

Uniform Interstate Family Support Act (UIFSA)   adopted in all fifty states, a model act designed to facilitate establishment and enforcement of interstate child support orders

Uniform Law   an unofficial law proposed as legislation by the National Conference of Commissioners on Uniform State Laws for adoption by the states as written in the interest of promoting greater consistency among state laws such as the Uniform Marriage and Divorce Act (UMDA)

V

Valuation   the process of assessing the financial worth of property, real or personal

Venue   refers to the geographical location within which a particular action should be filed

Vest   gives a person an immediate, fixed right of ownership and present or future enjoyment; a vested interest is fixed or accrued and generally unable to be taken away by subsequent events or circumstances

Virtual visitation   communication between parents and children through the use of technology

Visitation   a noncustodial parent's period of access to a child

Void   invalid and of no legal effect

Void *ab initio*   [Latin: from the beginning] of no legal effect from the outset; A contract may be void *ab initio* if it seriously offends law or public policy; a marriage that is void *ab initio* usually does not require a decree of annulment to invalidate it

Voidable marriage   a marriage capable of being nullified because of a circumstance existing at the time it was established; the marriage remains valid unless and until it is declared invalid by a court of competent jurisdiction

W

Wage assignment/withholding   an order directing a support obligor's employer to take support payments directly out of that person's paycheck for the benefit of the obligee

Waiver   the giving up of a right or privilege

Work product   written or oral material prepared for or by an attorney in preparation for litigation either planned or in progress; not subject to discovery absent a court's finding of special need

Writ *ne exeat*   [Latin: that he not depart] a court order restraining a person from leaving the jurisdiction until the petitioner's claim has been satisfied

Wrongful adoption   a tort action that an adoptive parent can bring against an adoption agency for failure to provide accurate and sufficient information regarding an adoptive child prior to adoption

Wrongful birth   an action brought by parents claiming that the defendant's negligent conduct resulted in the birth of a child with serious defects or disabilities, thereby causing the parents serious emotional distress and expense

Wrongful life   an action brought by a plaintiff who claims he or she was brought into the world with a disability that was foreseeable and could have been prevented by a competent physician exercising due care

Table of Cases

Following each case citation is a brief reference in parentheses indicating in which chapter the case is found and in what form it appears. The format is n/x, where n is the number of the chapter in which the case is used and x will be one of three letters—c, d, or q. The letter c indicates that only the citation appears. The letter d indicates that the case is described in some way. The letter q indicates that the case is quoted to a limited extent. For each case that appears in multiple chapters, references are provided for each of those chapters.

U.S. Supreme Court

Bates v. State Bar of Arizona, 433 U.S. 350, 97 S. Ct. 2691, 53 L. Ed. 2d 810 (1977). (1/d) pp. 27,550

Burnham v. Superior Court, 495 U.S. 604, 628, 110 S. Ct. 2105, 2119, 109 L. Ed. 2d 631, 650 (1990). (6/d) pp. 163, 554

Caban v. Mohammed, 441 U.S. 380, 99 S. Ct. 1760, 60 L. Ed. 2d 297 (1979). (14/d) p. 483

DeBoer v. DeBoer, 509 U.S. 1301, 114 S. Ct. 1, 125 L. Ed. 2d 775 (1993). (14/c) pp. 504, 561

DeShaney v. Winnebago Department of Social Services, 489 U.S. 189, 109 S. Ct. 998, 103 L. Ed. 2d 249 (1989). (15/d) pp. 536, 562

Griswold v. Connecticut, 381 U.S. 479, 486, 85 S. Ct. 1678, 1682, 14 L. Ed. 2d 510 (1965) (Douglas, J.). (3/q) pp. 64, 85, 86, 551

Hickman v. Taylor, 329 U.S. 495, 67 S. Ct. 385, 91 L. Ed. 451 (1947). (7/q) pp. 203, 554

Kessel v. Leavitt, 511 S.E.2d 720 (W. Va. 1998). (14/q) pp. 484, 560

Kulko v. Kulko, 436 U.S. 84, 98 S. Ct. 1690, 56 L. Ed. 132 (1978). (1/d) (6/q) pp. 29, 163, 554

Lawrence v. Texas, 539 U.S. 558, 123 S. Ct. 2472, 156 L. Ed. 2d 508 (2003). (1/d) (3/q) (5/d)(14/d) pp. 84, 139, 496, 551

Lehr v. Robertson, 463 U.S. 248, 103 S. Ct. 2985, 77 L. Ed. 2d 614 (1983). (13/q)(14/q) pp. 430, 483, 558, 560

Levy v. Louisiana, 391 U.S. 68 (1968). (13/q) pp. 430, 558

Loving v. Va., 388 U.S. 1, 87 S. Ct. 1817, 18 L. Ed. 1010 (1967). (3/q) pp. 67–69, 81, 86, 551

Meister v. Moore, 96 U.S. 76, 24 L. Ed. 826 (1877). (3/d) pp. 77, 551

Michael H. v. Gerald D., 491 U.S. 110, 109 S. Ct. 2333, 105 L. Ed. 2d 91 (1989). (8/d)(13/d) pp. 433, 555, 558

Mississippi Band of Choctaw Indians v. Holyfield, 490 U.S. 30, 109 S. Ct. 1597, 104 L. Ed. 2d 29 (1989). (15/c) pp. 537, 562

Missouri v. Jenkins, 491 U.S. 274, 109 S. Ct. 2463, 105 L. Ed. 2d 229 (1989). (1/c) pp. 13, 550

New York v. Ferber, 458 U.S. 747, 102 S. Ct. 3348, 73 L. Ed. 2d 1113 (1982). (15/q) pp. 533, 562

Nguyen v. Immigration and Naturalization Services, 533 U.S. 53, 121 S. Ct. 2053, 150 L. Ed. 2d 115 (2001). (13/q) pp. 430, 558, 559,

Orr v. Orr, 440 U.S. 268, 279–280, 283, 99 S. Ct. 1102, 59 L. Ed. 2d 306 (1979). (3/q) (10/d) pp. 64, 314, 345, 551, 556

Palmore v. Sidoti, 466 U.S. 429, 104 S. Ct. 1879, 80 L. Ed. 2d 421 (1984). (3/d) (8/q) pp. 70, 244, 245, 551

Pierce v. Society of Sisters, 268 U.S. 510, 45 S. Ct. 571, 69 L. Ed. 1070 (1925). (15/c). p. 562

Quilloin v. Walcott, 434 U.S. 246, 98 S. Ct. 549, 54 L. Ed. 2d 511 (1978). (14/d) p. 483

Skinner v. Oklahoma, 316 U.S. 535, 542, 62 S. Ct. 1110, 86 L. Ed. 1655 (1942). (3/c) p. 551

Stanley v. Illinois, 405 U.S. 645, 92 S. Ct. 1208, 31 L. Ed. 2d 551 (1972). (14/q) pp. 482–483, 560

Stanton v. Stanton, 421 U.S. 7, 95 S. Ct. 1373, 43 L. Ed. 2d 688 (1975). (3/c) p. 551

Town of Castle Rock v. Gonzales, 545 U.S. 748, 125 S. Ct. 2796, 162 L. Ed. 2d 658 (2005). (15/d) pp. 522, 261

Troxel v. Granville, 530 U.S. 57, 120 S. Ct. 2054, 147 L. Ed. 2d 49 (2000). (8/d) pp. 232, 261–265, 274, 554

Turner v. Safley, 482 U.S. 78, 107 S. Ct. 2254, 96 L. Ed. 64 (1987). (3/d) pp. 67–68, 551

Williams v. North Carolina, 317 U.S. 287, 63 S. Ct. 207, 87 L. Ed. 279 (1942). (6/q) pp. 162, 554

Wisconsin v. Yoder, 406 U.S. 205, 92 S.Ct. 1526, 32 L. Ed. 2d 15 (1972). (15/c) p. 562

Zablocki v. Redhail, 434 U.S. 374, 98 S. Ct. 673, 54 L. Ed. 2d 618 (1978). (3/d) (9/c) pp. 67, 302, 551, 556

Other Federal Courts

Alma Society Inc v. Mellon, 601 F.2d 1225 (2d Cir. 1979). (14/q) pp. 478–480

Citizens for Equal Prot. v. Brunig, 455 F.3d 859 (8th Cir. 2006). (3/d) p. 552

Ensminger v. Commissioner, 610 F.2d 189, 191 (4th Cir. 1979). (5/d) pp. 130, 552

Gerber v. Hickman, 291 F.3d 617 (9th Circ. Ct. of Appeals 2002). (13/d) p.449

Gillett-Netting v. Barnhart, 371 F. 3d 593 (9th Cir. Ariz. 2004). (13/c) p. 559

Hagwood v. Newton, 282 F.3d 285 (4th Circ. Ct. App. 2002). (2/c) pp. 42, 550

Hendrix v. Page, 986 F.2d 195 (7th Cir. 1993). (1/c) pp. 17, 550

In re Sarah, 163 F.3d 397 (6th Cir. 1998). (10/q) pp. 342, 556

Irizarry v. Bd. of Educ., 251 F.3d 604 (U.S. App. 2001). (5/d) pp. 139, 553

Lofton v. Secretary of the Department of Children and Family Services, 358 F.3d 804 (11th Cir. 2005). (14/q) pp. 497, 561

Monroe v. Horwitch et al, 820 F. Supp. 682 (D. Conn. 1993). (1/q) pp. 24, 550

Rodrigue v. Rodrigue, 55 F. Supp.2d 534 (U.S. Dist. 1999). (11/d) p. 558

Salisbury v. List, 501 F. Supp. 105 (D. Nev. 1980). (3/d) pp. 67–68, 551

Stiver v. Parker, 975 F.2d 261 (6th Cir. 1992). (13/d) pp. 466, 560

Trs. of the AFTRA Health Fund v. Biondi, 303 F.3d 765 (7th Cir. 2002). (10/c) p. 556

United States v. Dost, 636 F. Supp. 828, 832 (S.D. Cal. 1986), aff'd, 812 F.2d 1239 (9th Cir. 1987). (15/d) pp. 533, 562

United States v. Hardy, 681 F. Supp. 1326 (N.D. Ill. 1988). (1/c) pp. 24, 550

Other State Courts

Index

Page numbers in boldface indicate the locations of marginal definitions of the corresponding terms. Each of these definitions is specific to the context to the chapter in which it appears. More general definitions of these terms appear in the glossary.

surrender, **490**
surviving agreement, **320**, 322
syndrome, parental alienation, **253**

T

talak, **148**
tax implications
    dependency exemption, 302–303
    innocent spouse, **382**
    of child support, 302–303
    of nonmarital families, 130, 139
    of property division, 381–382
temporary alimony, **320**
temporary orders, **181**
    child support, 277
tenants by the entirety, 80
tender years doctrine, **239**
Tennessee, 76, 91, 92, 96, 105, 110, 134, 162, 166, 167, 206, 287, 288, 296, 462, 463, 496, 526
termination of parental rights, **492**, 488–494, **535**
    involuntary, 492–494
Texas, 18, 36, 62, 63, 71, 76, 77, 84, 96, 98, 106, 134, 139, 154, 162, 191, 192, 284, 293, 367, 372, 377, 445, 462, 474, 486, 489, 496, 528, 544
third party beneficiary, **404**
tort, **80**, 138, **541**
    actions, 541–543
tracing, **359**
Transitional Assistance to Needy Families program (TANF), **281**
transmutation, **359**
trial notebook, **187**, 188–189
trust
    constructive, **127**, **193**

resulting, **127**
trustee process, **185**

U

unallocated support, 302
unauthorized practice of law, **9**, 21–22, 23, 24, 40
unbundling of legal services, **13**
unclean hands, doctrine of, **104**, **125**
unconscionable, **39**, 40
undue influence, 36, **100**
unearned income, **390**
uniform law, 3
Uniform Adoption Act, 441, 482
Uniform Child Custody Jurisdiction Act (UCCJA), 235–236
Uniform Child Custody Jurisdiction and Enforcement Act (UCCJEA), 3, 236–237, 445
Uniform Interstate Family Support Act (UISFA), 3, **280**, 282, 283, 340, 445
Uniform Marriage and Divorce Act (UMDA), 62, 258, 328, 342, 374
Uniform Parentage Act (UPA), 432, 445
Uniform Premarital Agreement Act (UPAA), 41, 317, 456, 462, 464
Uniform Putative and Unknown Fathers Act (UPUFA), 445
Uniform Reciprocal Enforcement of Support Act, 280
Uniform Status of Children of Assisted Conception Act (USCACA), 445
Utah, 62, 76, 96, 110, 134, 168, 476, 486, 496, 548

V

valuation, 363–365
value, fair market, **363**

venue, 166
Vermont, 76, 131, 133, 134, 137, 138, 237, 369, 447, 494, 496
vest, **321**
vested, **363**
Violence Against Women Act (VAWA), 514
Virginia, 67, 68–69, 76, 96, 134, 165, 171, 173, 453
visitation, 253–256
    defined v. flexible, 254–255
    supervised and unsupervised, 255
    virtual **255** -256
void **33**, **71**
void *ab initio*, **90**, **148**
voidable, **148**
voidable marriage, **90**

W

wage withholding. *See* income withholding
waiver, **39**, **317**, 401
Washington, 63, 76, 106, 131, 134, 257, 262, 372, 445, 453, 462, 494, 518, 529, 534, 537
West Virginia, 18, 76, 134, 243, 357, 358, 484
Wisconsin, 67, 76, 96, 134, 292, 302, 367, 372, 442, 444, 481, 494, 523, 529, 533, 544
work product, **222**
writ ne exeat, **340**
wrongful adoption, **506**
wrongful birth, **466**
wrongful life, **466**
Wyoming, 76, 134, 250, 250, 445, 462, 544